Third Edition

A First Book
of ANSI C

Gary J. Bronson

Fairleigh Dickenson University

BROOKS/COLE

THOMSON LEARNING

Australia ■ Canada ■ Mexico ■ Singapore ■ Spain ■ United Kingdom ■ United States

BROOKS/COLE

THOMSON LEARNING

Sponsoring Editor: *Kallie Swanson*
Marketing Team: *Chris Kelly, Samantha Cabaluna*
Editorial Assistant: *Grace Fujimoto*
Production Coordinator: *Kelsey McGee*
Production Service: *Forbes Mill Press/Robin Gold*
Manuscript Editor: *Philip Jochnowitz*
Permissions Editor: *Sue Ewing*
Interior Design: *John Edeen*

Cover Coordinator: *Roy R. Neuhaus*
Cover Design: *Denise Davidson*
Cover Photo: *PhotoDisc*
Print Buyer: *Jessica Reed*
Typesetting: *Wolf Creek Press/
   Linda Weidemann*
Cover Printing, Printing and
   Binding: *Webcom, Ltd.*

For more information about this or any other Brooks/Cole product, contact:
BROOKS/COLE
511 Forest Lodge Road
Pacific Grove, CA 93950 USA
www.brookscole.com
1-800-423-0563 (Thomson Learning Academic Resource Center)

Printed in Canada

10   9   8   7   6   5   4   3   2

Library of Congress Cataloging-in-Publication Data

Bronson, Gary (date)
   A first book of ANSI C / Gary Bronson—3rd. ed.
        p.   cm.
   Includes index.
      ISBN 0 534-37964-8 (text)
         1. C (Computer program language)   I . Title

QA76.73.C15 B74 2000   00-030402
005.13'3—dc21

To

Rochelle,

Matthew,

Jeremy,

David Bronson

Contents

Part 3

Part 4

Part **6**

Preface

A First Book of ANSI C is written for students who need to know the ANSI C language and how to write its syntax. The pedagogy helps students with common programming pitfalls, which makes this book more useful to a student than the typical reference-type book. It assumes no programming background, but can be used by someone who wants to learn this language. The primary purpose of the first two editions of this text was to make C more accessible as an applications programming language than was possible with texts that focused on C as an advanced operating systems language. The success of these editions and the many comments received from students and faculty stating that the book really did help them learn and teach C, respectively, have been extremely gratifying.

Based on suggestions and more in-depth responses from adopters, numerous new pedagogical features and material have been incorporated into this third edition. The most noticeable of these changes is that, in all program examples, `main`'s header line has been changed from `void main(void)` to `int main()`, and that the `main` function always returns a value to the operating system. This change was made to reflect current programming practice that the `main` function explicitly return a value. Additional changes to this edition include the following:

- New material on function templates has been added.
- Programming Notes, a single highlighted and informational reference, incorporates the previous Closer Look and Tips From the Pros boxes as well as new material.
- Information on creating C programs under both the Microsoft® Visual C⁺⁺ 6.0 and the Borland® C⁺⁺ Builder replaces previous information on outdated C compilers.
- All function prototypes are global.
- A chapter supplement on random number generation has been added.
- New material on C⁺⁺'s Standard Template Library has been included.

To facilitate using C as a basis for learning C⁺⁺, the two chapters introducing C⁺⁺ that were introduced in the second edition have been retained and updated to ANSI C⁺⁺ specifications. Thus, as with the second edition, this text can be used as an introduction to programming in general, as an introduction to the C language in particular, and as a basis for further study of the C⁺⁺ language.

The basic requirement of this third edition, however, remains the same as the first two editions: that is, that all topics be presented in a clear, unambiguous, and accessible manner to beginning students. Toward this end, the heart of the first two editions, which consisted of Chapters 1 through 11, remains essentially unchanged in the present edition. Thus, all of the topics, examples, explanations, and figures in the first 11 chapters of the previous editions remain in the third edition with the addition of the new material.

Distinctive Features of This Book

Writing Style.   I firmly believe that introductory texts do not teach students—professors teach students. An introductory textbook, if it is to be useful, must be the primary "supporting actor" to the "leading role" of the professor. Once the professor sets the stage, however, the textbook must encourage, nurture, and assist the student in acquiring and "owning" the material presented in class. To do this the text must be written in a manner that makes sense to the student. My primary concern, and one of the distinctive features of this book, is that it has been written for the student. As one of my reviewers has said of the first edition, "This book addresses the student and not the professional." Thus, first and foremost, I feel the writing style used to convey the concepts presented is the most important aspect of the text.

Modularity.   C, by its nature, is a modular language. Thus, the connection between C functions and modules is made early in the text, in Section 1.2, and continues throughout the book. To stress the modular nature of C, the first complete `main()` function illustrates calling four other functions. The first program that can be compiled, which calls the `printf()` function, is then presented.

The idea of argument passing into modules is also made early, in Section 1.3, with the use of the `printf()` function. In this manner, students are introduced to functions and argument passing as a natural technique of programming.

Software Engineering.   As with the first two editions, this revised edition introduces students to the fundamentals of software engineering right from the start. This introduction begins in Section 1.1, which introduces algorithms and the various ways that an algorithm can be described. The example illustrating three algorithms for summing the numbers from 1 to 100 (Figure 1.4) has been retained from the earlier editions.

The increased emphasis on software engineering is supported in the text, starting with Section 1.5, which introduces top-down program development. Here the importance of understanding the problem and selecting an appropriate algorithm is highlighted and the relationship between analysis, design, coding, and testing is introduced. Problem solving within this context is stressed throughout the text.

Introduction to Pointers.   One of the unique features of the first edition was the early introduction of pointer concepts. This was done by simply using the `printf()` function initially to display the addresses of variables, and then using variables to store addresses. This approach always seemed a more logical and intuitive method of understanding pointer variables than the indirection description in vogue at the time the first edition was released.

Since the first edition I have been pleased to see that the use of the `printf()` function to display addresses has become a standard way of introducing pointers. Although this approach, therefore, is no longer a unique feature of my book, I am very proud of its presentation and continue to use it in this new edition.

Program Testing.   Every C program in this text has been successfully compiled and run under the Microsoft Visual C++ 6.0 compiler. All programs have been written following the current ANSI C standard. Source code for all program examples used in the text is available online. This permits students both to experiment with and extend the existing programs and to modify them more easily as required by a number of end-of-section exercises.

Pedagogical Features

To facilitate my goal of making C accessible as a first-level course, the text includes the following pedagogical features.

End of Section Exercises.   Almost every section in the book contains numerous and diverse skill builder and programming exercises. Additionally, solutions to selected odd-numbered exercises are provided in an appendix.

Pseudocode and Flowchart Descriptions.   As in the first two editions, pseudocode is stressed throughout the text. Material on flowchart symbols and the use of flowcharts in visually presenting flow-of-control constructs is also presented.

Common Programming Errors and Chapter Review.   Each chapter ends with a section on common programming errors and a review of the main topics covered in the chapter.

Programming Notes.   A set of shaded boxes that highlight important concepts and useful technical points and programming techniques used by professional programmers is provided.

Enrichment Sections.   Given the many different emphases that can be applied in teaching C, a number of Enrichment Sections have been included as chapter supplements. These allow you to provide different emphasis with different students or different C class sections.

Appendices and Supplements.   As with the first two editions, an expanded set of appendices is provided in this third edition. These include appendices on operator precedence; ASCII codes; I/O and standard error redirection; the Standard C Library; the Standard Template Library (STL); program entry, compilation, and execution; using the Microsoft Visual C++ 6.0 compiler; and using the Borland C++ Builder compiler.

A final appendix offers solutions to selected odd-numbered problems. Source code for all program examples used in the text is available at

http://www.brookscole.com

An instructor's manual including chapter outlines and answers to selected even-numbered problems is also available.

Acknowledgments

The writing of this third edition is a direct result of the success (and limitations) of the first two editions. In this regard, my most heartfelt acknowledgment and appreciation is to the instructors and students who found these editions to be of service to them in their respective quests to teach and learn C.

Once a third edition was planned, its completion depended on the encouragement, skills, and efforts of many other people. For this I especially want to thank the staff of Brooks/Cole Publishing Company for their many contributions. First and foremost, this includes my project editor, Kallie Swanson. Additionally, I am very grateful to editorial assistants Grace Fujimoto and Meg Weist for handling numerous scheduling and review details that permitted me to concentrate on the actual writing of the text.

I also wish to express my gratitude to the individual reviewers:

Taret Alameldin, California State University at Fresno
John Avitabile, College of Saint Rose
Larry Booth, Highline Community College
Li-hsiang Cheo, William Paterson University
Yonina S. Cooper, University of Las Vegas
Ralph Ewton, University of Texas at El Paso
James Gips, Boston College
Richard A. Hatch, San Diego State University
Rick L. Homkes, Indiana University at Kokomo
Michael Milligan, Front Range Community College
Robert E. Norton, San Diego Mesa College
Robert Probasco, University of Idaho
Ashraf Saad, University of Cincinnati
Anthony Sako, Columbia Basin College
Robert Weaver, Mt. Holyoke College
Lee Westbrock, Trident Technical College
Bob Willis, Rogers State University

Each of them supplied extremely detailed and constructive reviews of both the original manuscript and a number of revisions. Their suggestions, attention to detail, and comments were extraordinarily helpful in the preparation of the various editions.

Finally, the task of turning the final manuscript into a textbook again required a dedicated production staff. For this I especially want to thank copy editor Philip Jochnowitz, production editor Robin Gold of Forbes Mill Press, manuscript keyer Sue Boshers, and compositor Linda Weidemann of Wolf Creek Press. Their dedication, attention to detail, and their high standards have helped immensely to improve the quality of this edition. Almost from the moment the book moved to the production stage they seemed to take personal ownership of the text, and I am very grateful to them.

Special thanks also go to Janie Schwark, Academic Product Manager of Developer Tools at Microsoft, for providing invaluable support and product information.

I also gratefully acknowledge the direct encouragement and support provided by my dean Dr. Paul Lerman, my associate dean, Dr. Ron Heim, and my chairperson, Dr. Youngboem Kim. Without their support, this text could not have been written.

Finally, I deeply appreciate the patience, understanding, and love provided by my wife, friend, and partner, Rochelle.

Gary Bronson

Part **1**

Fundamentals

Chapter 1

Getting Started

1.1 Introduction to Programming

A computer is a machine. Like other machines, such as an automobile or lawn mower, it must be turned on and then driven, or controlled, to do the task it was meant to do. In an automobile, for example, the driver provides control by sitting inside of and directing the car. In a computer, the driver is a set of instructions called a program. More formally, a *computer program* is a sequence of instructions used to operate a computer to produce a specific result. *Programming* is the process of writing these instructions in a language that the computer can respond to and that other programmers can understand. The set of instructions that can be used to construct a program is called a *programming language.*

Essentially, all computer programs do the same thing (Figure 1.1). They direct a computer to accept data (input), to manipulate the data (processing), and to produce reports (output). This means that all programming languages must provide similar capabilities for performing these operations. These capabilities are provided either as specific instruction types, or prepackaged groups of instructions that can be used to do specific tasks. In C, the prepackaged groups of instructions are called *library functions.* Table 1.1 lists the fundamental set of instructions and library functions provided by FORTRAN, BASIC, COBOL, Pascal, and C for performing input, processing, and output tasks.

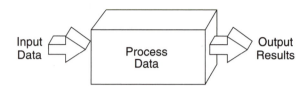

Figure 1.1   All programs perform the same operations

If all programming languages provide essentially the same features, why are there so many? The answer is that there are vast differences in the types of input data, calculations needed, and output reports required by applications. For example, scientific and engineering applications require precise numerical outputs, accurate to many decimal places. In addition, these applications typically use many mathematical equations to produce their results. For example, calculating the bacteria concentration level in a polluted pond, as illustrated in Figure 1.2, requires evaluation of an exponential equation. For such applications, the FORTRAN programming language, with its algebra-like instructions, was developed. FORTRAN, an acronym for FORmula TRANslation, was introduced in 1957 and specifically developed for translating formulas into a computer-readable form.

Business applications usually deal in whole numbers, representing inventory quantities, or dollar and cents data accurate to only two decimal places. These applications require simpler mathematical calculations than are needed for scientific applications. The outputs required from business programs frequently consist of reports containing extensive columns of formatted dollar and cents numbers and totals (see Figure 1.3). For these

Table 1.1   Programming language instruction summary

Operation	FORTRAN	BASIC	COBOL	Pascal	C
INPUT (Get the data)	READ	INPUT READ/DATA	READ ACCEPT	READ READLN	getchar() gets() scanf() sscanf() fscanf()
PROCESSING (Use the data)	= IF/ELSE DO	LET IF/ELSE FOR	COMPUTE IF/ELSE PERFORM	:= IF/ELSE FOR WHILE REPEAT	= if for while do
OUTPUT (Display the data)	WRITE PRINT	PRINT PRINT/ USING	WRITE DISPLAY	WRITE WRITELN	putchar() puts() printf() sprintf() fprintf()

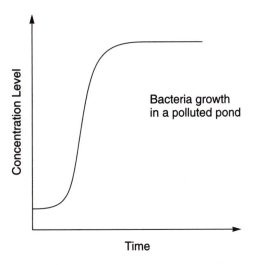

Figure 1.2   FORTRAN was developed for scientific and engineering applications

applications, the COBOL programming language, with its picture output formats, was introduced in the 1960s. COBOL is an acronym for COmmon Business Oriented Language.

Teaching introductory programming to students has its own set of requirements. Here, a straightforward, easy-to-understand computer language was needed that does not require detailed knowledge of a specific application. Both the BASIC and Pascal programming languages were developed for this purpose. BASIC stands for Beginners All-purpose Symbolic Instruction Code and was developed in the 1960s at Dartmouth College. Visual Basic, the updated object-based version of BASIC, is still ideal for creating small, easily developed, interactive programs.

Pascal was developed in the late 1970s to provide students with a firmer foundation in modular and structured programming than could be provided by BASIC. Modular programs

```
                    INVENTORY REPORT

    Item                          In     On    Unit
    No.        Description      Stock  Order   Cost

    10365   #4 Nails, Common      20      0    1.09
    10382   #6 Nails, Common      10     50    1.14
    10420   #8 Nails, Common       2     60    1.19
    10436  #10 Nails, Common       6
    10449  #12 Nails, Common
    10486  #16 Nails, Comm
```

Figure 1.3   COBOL is ideal for many business applications

consist of many small subprograms, each of which performs a clearly defined and specific task that can be tested and modified without disturbing other program sections. Pascal is not an acronym, like FORTRAN, COBOL, and BASIC, but is named after the seventeenth-century mathematician, Blaise Pascal. The Pascal language is so rigidly structured that there are no escapes from the structured modules. This is unacceptable for real-world projects and was one reason that Pascal did not gain wide acceptance in the scientific, engineering, and business fields. The design philosophy called *structured programming* that led to the development of Pascal is, however, relevant to C programmers. Using a structured programing approach results in readable, reliable, and maintainable programs. We will introduce the elements of this program design philosophy in the next section and continue expanding on it and using it throughout the text.

The C language was initially developed in the 1970s at AT&T Bell Laboratories. C evolved from a language called B, which was developed from the BCPL language. C has an extensive set of capabilities and is a true general-purpose programming language. It can be used for creating simple, interactive programs; for producing sophisticated applications, such as designing operating systems; and for both business and scientific programming applications. C's richness of library and instruction capabilities is clearly evident from Table 1.1. Besides providing many existing tools to build programs, C allows the programmer to easily create new tools. For this reason, C became known as the "professional programmer's language." The current standard for C is maintained by the American National Standards Institute (ANSI).

Algorithms

Before writing a program, a programmer must clearly understand the desired result and how the proposed program will produce it. In this regard, it is useful to realize that a computer program describes a computational procedure called an *algorithm*. An algorithm is a step-by-step sequence of instructions that describes how to perform a computation.

An algorithm answers the question, "What method will you use to solve this computational problem?" Only after we clearly understand the algorithm, and know the specific steps required to produce the desired result, can we write the program. Seen in this light, programming is the translation of the selected algorithm into a language that the computer can use.

To illustrate an algorithm, we will consider a simple requirement. Assume that a program must calculate the sum of all whole numbers from 1 through 100. Figure 1.4 illustrates three methods we could use to find the required sum. Each method constitutes an algorithm.

Clearly, most people do not bother listing the possible alternatives in a detailed step-by-step manner, as shown in Figure 1.4, and then selecting one of the algorithms to solve the problem. But then, most people do not think algorithmically; they tend to think intuitively. For example, if you had to change a flat tire on your car, you would not think of all the steps required—you would simply change the tire or call someone else to do the job. This is an example of intuitive thinking.

Unfortunately, computers do not respond to intuitive commands. A general statement such as "add the numbers from 1 to 100" means nothing to a computer, because the computer can only respond to algorithmic commands written in an acceptable language such

Method 1. *Columns:* Arrange the numbers from 1 to 100 in a column and add them:

$$
\begin{array}{c}
1 \\
2 \\
3 \\
4 \\
\cdot \\
\cdot \\
98 \\
99 \\
1100 \\
\hline
5050
\end{array}
$$

Method 2. *Groups:* Arrange the numbers in convenient groups that sum to 100. Multiply the number of groups by 100 and add in any unused numbers:

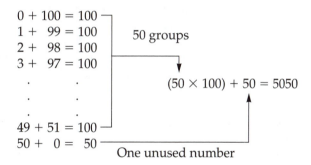

Method 3. *Formula:* Use the formula

$$\text{Sum} = \frac{n\,(a + b)}{2}$$

where

n = number of terms to be added (100)
a = first number to be added (1)
b = last number to be added (100)

$$\text{Sum 5}\ \frac{100\,(1 + 100)}{2} = 5050$$

Figure 1.4   Summing the numbers 1 through 100

as C. To program a computer successfully, you must clearly understand this difference between algorithmic and intuitive commands. A computer is an "algorithm-responding" machine; it is not an "intuitive-responding" machine. You cannot tell a computer to change a tire or to add the numbers from 1 through 100. Instead, you must give the computer a detailed, step-by-step set of instructions that, collectively, forms an algorithm. For example, the set of instructions

Set *n* equal to 100
Set *a* equal to 1
Set *b* equal to 100
Calculate sum $= \dfrac{n(a + b)}{2}$
Print the sum

forms a detailed method, or algorithm, for determining the sum of the numbers from 1 through 100. Notice that these instructions are not a computer program. Unlike a program, which must be written in a language the computer can understand, an algorithm can be written or described in various ways. When English phrases are used to describe the algorithm (the processing steps), as in this example, the description is called *pseudocode*. When mathematical equations are used, the description is called a *formula*. When pictures that employ specifically defined shapes are used, the description is called a *flowchart*. A flowchart provides a pictorial representation of the algorithm using the symbols shown in Figure 1.5. Figure 1.6 illustrates the use of these symbols in depicting an algorithm for determining the average of three numbers.

Because flowcharts are cumbersome to revise, using pseudocode to express an algorithm's logic has gained increased acceptance among programmers. Unlike flowcharts, where standard symbols are defined, there are no standard rules for constructing pseudocode. Any short English phrase may be used to describe an algorithm using pseudocode. For example, acceptable pseudocode to describe the steps needed to compute the average of three numbers is

Input the three numbers into the computer
Calculate the average by adding the numbers and dividing the sum by three
Display the average

Only after the programmer selects an algorithm and understands the required steps can he or she write the algorithm using computer-language statements. When computer-language statements are used to describe the algorithm, the description is called a *computer program*.

From Algorithms to Programs

Once selected, an algorithm must be converted into a form that can be used by a computer. Converting an algorithm into a computer program, using a language such as C, is called *coding* the algorithm (see Figure 1.7). The remainder of this text is devoted mostly to showing you how to develop algorithms and express these algorithms in C.

SYMBOL	NAME	DESCRIPTION

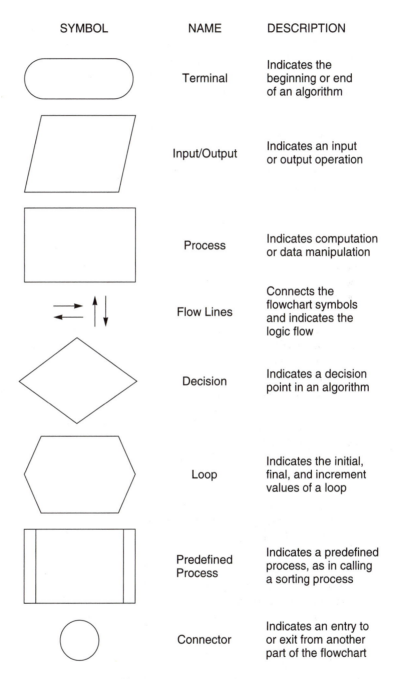

SYMBOL	NAME	DESCRIPTION
	Terminal	Indicates the beginning or end of an algorithm
	Input/Output	Indicates an input or output operation
	Process	Indicates computation or data manipulation
	Flow Lines	Connects the flowchart symbols and indicates the logic flow
	Decision	Indicates a decision point in an algorithm
	Loop	Indicates the initial, final, and increment values of a loop
	Predefined Process	Indicates a predefined process, as in calling a sorting process
	Connector	Indicates an entry to or exit from another part of the flowchart

Figure 1.5   Flowchart symbols

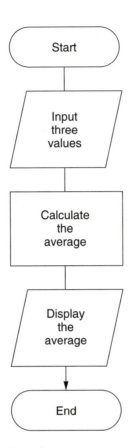

Figure 1.6   Flowchart for calculating the average of three numbers

Program Translation

Once a program is written in C, it cannot be executed without further translation on the computer. This is because the internal language of all computers consists of a series of 1s and 0s, called the computer's *machine language*. To generate a machine-language program that can be executed by a computer requires that the C program, which is referred to as the *source program,* be translated into the computer's machine language (see Figure 1.8).

A program can be translated into machine language in two ways. When each statement in the source program is translated individually and executed immediately, the programming language is called an *interpreted language,* and the program doing the translation is called an *interpreter.*

When all the statements in a source program are translated before any one statement is executed, the programming language is called a *compiled language.* In this case, the program doing the translation is called a *compiler.* C is a compiled language. Here, the source program is translated as a unit into machine language. The machine-language version of the original source program is a separate entity called the *object program.* (See Appendix F for a complete description of entering, compiling, and running a C program.)

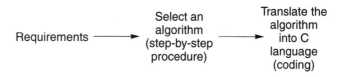

Figure 1.7 Coding an algorithm

Figure 1.8 Source programs must be translated

Exercises 1.1

1. Define the terms:
   a. computer program
   b. programming
   c. programming language
   d. algorithm
   e. pseudocode
   f. flowchart
   g. source program
   h. object program
   i. compiler
   j. interpreter

2. Determine and list a step-by-step procedure to complete the following tasks:

Note: There is no single correct answer for each of these tasks. This exercise is designed to give you practice in converting intuitive commands into equivalent algorithms and making the shift between the thought processes involved in the two types of thinking.

   a. Fix a flat tire.
   b. Make a telephone call.
   c. Go to the store and purchase a loaf of bread.
   d. Roast a turkey.

3. Determine and write an algorithm (list the steps) to interchange the contents of two cups of liquid. Assume that a third cup is available to temporarily hold the contents of either cup. Each cup should be rinsed before any new liquid is poured into it.

4. Write a detailed set of step-by-step instructions, in English, to calculate the dollar amount of money in a piggybank that contains h half-dollars, q quarters, n nickels, d dimes, and p pennies.

5. Write a detailed set of step-by-step instructions, in English, to find the smallest number in a group of three integer numbers.

6. a. Write a detailed set of step-by-step instructions, in English, to calculate the change remaining from a dollar after making a purchase. Assume that the cost of the goods purchased is less than a dollar. The change received should consist of the smallest number of coins possible.
   b. Repeat Exercise 6a, but assume the change is to be given only in pennies.

7. a. Write an algorithm to locate the first occurrence of the name "Jones" in a list of names arranged in random order.
   b. Discuss how to improve your algorithm for Exercise 7a if the list of names was arranged in alphabetical order.

8. Write an algorithm to determine the total occurrences of the letter *e* in any sentence.

9. Determine and write an algorithm to sort four numbers into ascending (from lowest to highest) order.

1.2   Introduction to Modularity

A well-designed program is constructed using a design philosophy similar to that used in constructing a well-designed building; it doesn't just happen, but depends on careful planning and execution for the final design to accomplish its intended purpose. Just as an integral part of a building design is its structure, the same is true for a program.

In programming, the term "structure" has two interrelated meanings. The first refers to the program's overall construction, which is discussed in this section. The second refers to the form used to carry out individual tasks within the program, which is discussed in Chapters 4 and 5. In relation to its first meaning, programs whose structure consists of interrelated segments, arranged in a logical and easily understandable order to form an integrated and complete unit, are referred to as *modular programs* (Figure 1.9). Modular programs are easier to develop, correct, and modify than programs constructed otherwise.

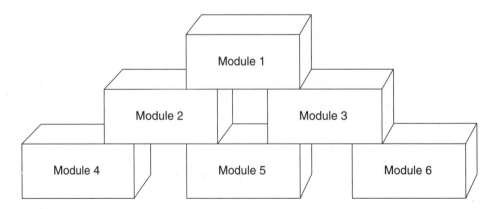

Figure 1.9   A well-designed program is built using modules

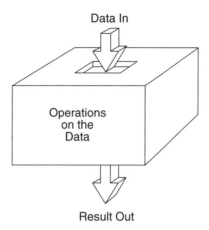

Data In

Operations
on the
Data

Result Out

Figure 1.10   A module must accept data, process the data, and produce a result

The smaller segments used to construct a modular program are called *modules.* Each module is designed and developed to perform a specific task and is really a small subprogram all by itself. A complete C program is constructed by combining as many modules as necessary to produce the desired result. The advantage of modular construction is that the overall program design can be developed before any single module is written. Once each module's requirements are finalized, it can be programmed and integrated within the overall program as the module is completed.

Since a module is really a small subprogram, each module must do what is required of all programs: receive and process data and produce a result (see Figure 1.10). Unlike a larger program, however, a module performs limited operations. Modules are meant to handle, at most, one or two functions required by the complete program. Since each module is designed to perform a specific function, the modules are called *functions* in C.[1]

Functions

It helps to think of a function as a small machine that transforms the data it receives into a finished product. Figure 1.11 illustrates a function that accepts two numbers as inputs and multiplies the two numbers to produce one output.

As illustrated in Figures 1.10 and 1.11, the interface to the function from the outside is its inputs and results. How the inputs are converted to results are both encapsulated and hidden within the function. In this regard the function can be thought of as a single unit providing a special-purpose operation.

One important requirement for designing a good function is to give it a name that conveys some idea about what the function does. The names permissible for functions are also used to name other elements of the C language and are collectively referred to as

---

[1] The terms *subprograms, procedures,* and *methods* are used in other languages to designate what in C are *functions.*

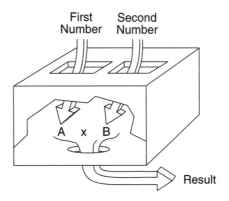

Figure 1.11   A multiplying function

identifiers. Identifiers are composed of any combination of letters, digits, and underscores (_) selected according to the following rules.

1. The first character of the name must be a letter or underscore (_).
2. Only letters, digits, or underscores may follow the initial letter. Blank spaces are not allowed. Distinguish words in a name consisting of multiple words by capitalizing the first letter of one or more of the words. (Although underscores may also be used for this purpose, they are increasingly being used only for compiler-dependent identifiers.)
3. An identifier cannot be one of the keywords listed in Table 1.2. (A *keyword* is a word that is set aside by the language for a special purpose and can only be used in a specified manner.[2])
4. An identifier may have no more than 31 characters (this is compiler dependent).

Examples of valid C identifiers are

```
grosspay    taxCalc     addNums     DegToRad
multTwo     salestax    netpay      bessel1
```

Examples of invalid identifiers are

```
1AB3      (begins with a number, which violates Rule 1)
E*6       (contains a special character, which violates Rule 2)
while     (is a keyword, which violates Rule 3)
```

---

[2] Keywords in C are also reserved words, which means they must be used only for their specified purpose. Attempting to use them for any other purpose generates an error message.

Programming Note

What Is Syntax?

A programming language's *syntax* is the set of rules for formulating grammatically correct language statements. This means that a C statement with correct syntax has the proper form specified for the compiler. As such, the compiler accepts the statement and does not generate an error message.

An individual statement or program can be syntactically correct and still be logically incorrect. Such a statement or program is correctly structured but produces an incorrect result. This is similar to an English statement that is grammatically correct but makes no sense. For example, although the sentence "The tree is a ragged cat" is grammatically correct, it makes no sense.

In addition to conforming to C's identifier rules, a C function name must always be followed by parentheses (the reason for these will be seen shortly). A good function name should also be *mnemonic,* that is, designed as a memory aid. For example, the function name DegToRad() (note that we have included the required parentheses after the identifier, which clearly marks this as a function name) is a mnemonic if it is the name of a function that converts degrees to radians. The name helps identify what the function does.

Examples of valid function names that are not mnemonics are

```
easy()      c3po()      r2d2()      theforce()      mike()
```

Nonmnemonic function names should not be used because they convey no information about the function.

Table 1.2 Keywords

auto	default	float	register	struct	volatile
break	do	for	return	switch	while
case	double	goto	short	typedef	
char	else	if	signed	union	
const	enum	int	sizeof	unsigned	
continue	extern	long	static	void	

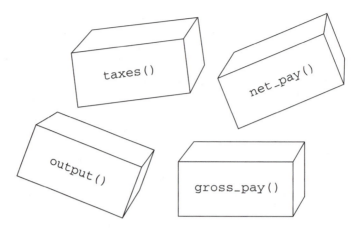

Figure 1.12   We need some order here!

Notice that all function names have been typed predominately in lowercase letters. This is traditional in C, although it is not required. All uppercase letters are usually used for named constants, a topic covered in Chapter 3. C is a *case-sensitive* language. This means that the compiler distinguishes between uppercase and lowercase letters. Thus, in C, the names TOTAL, total, and TotaL represent three distinct names.

The main() Function

Once functions have been named, we need a way to combine them into a complete program (see Figure 1.12). Notice that we have not yet described the actual writing of the functions. One of the nice features of C is that we can plan a program by first deciding what functions are needed and how they are to be linked. Then we can write each function to perform the task it is required to do.

To provide for the orderly placement and execution of functions, each C program must have one function called main(). The reserved word main tells the compiler where program execution is to begin. The main() function is sometimes referred to as a *driver function,* because it tells the other functions the sequence in which they are to operate (See Figure 1.13).[3]

Figure 1.14 illustrates a complete main() function. The first line of the function, in this case int main() is referred to as a *function header line.* A function header line, which is always the first line of a function, contains three pieces of information:

1. What type of data, if any, is returned from the function
2. The name of the function
3. What type of data, if any, is sent into the function

---

[3] Modules executed from main() may, in turn, execute other modules. Each module, however, always returns to the module that initiated its execution. This is true even for main, which returns control to the operating system in effect when main() was initiated.

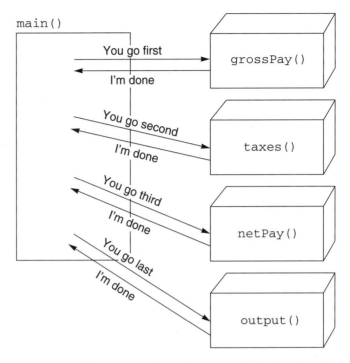

Figure 1.13   The `main()` function controls all other functions

The keyword before the function name defines the type of value the function returns when it has completed operating. When placed before the function's name the keyword `int` (see Table 1.2) designates that the function returns an integer value. Similarly, empty parentheses following the function name signify that no data are transmitted into the function when it is run. (Data transmitted into a function at run time are referred to as *arguments* of the function.) The braces, { and }, determine the beginning and end of the function body and enclose the statements that make up the function. The statements inside the braces determine what the function does. Each statement inside the function must end with a semicolon (;).

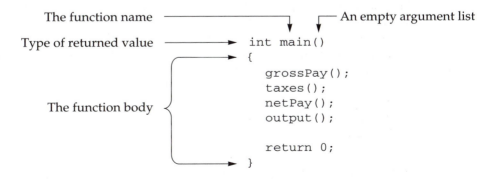

Figure 1.14   A sample `main()` function

The `main()` function illustrated in Figure 1.14 consists of five statements within the function's body. In this case, each of the first four statements is a command to execute another function. First the `grossPay()` function is called for execution. When `grossPay()` is finished, the `taxes()` function is called. After the `taxes()` function is completed, the `netPay()` function is called. Finally, the `output()` function is executed, and the `return` statement completes program execution. Although the functions `grossPay()`, `taxes()`, `netPay()`, and `output()` must still be written, the `main()` function is completed. After the four other functions are written, the program, consisting of `main()`, `grossPay()`, `taxes()`, `netPay()`, and `output()`, is complete.

You will be naming and writing many of your own C functions. In fact, the rest of this book is primarily about how to determine what functions are required and how to write the functions. Each program, however, must have one and only one `main()` function. Until we learn how to pass data into a function and return data from a function (the topics of Chapter 6), the header line illustrated in Figure 1.14 will serve us for all the programs we need to write. Using this construction, it is convenient to think of the first two lines

```
int main()
{
```

as designating that "the program begins here," and regard the last two lines

```
    return 0;
{
```

as simply designating the end of the program. Fortunately, many useful functions have already been written for us. We will now see how to use one of these functions to create our first working C program.

Exercises 1.2

1. State whether the following are valid function names. If they are valid, state whether they are mnemonic names. A mnemonic function name conveys some idea about what the function might do. If they are invalid names, state why.

m1234()	newBal()	abcd()	A12345()	1A2345()
power()	absVal()	invoices()	do()	while()
add5()	taxes()	netPay()	12345()	int()
newBalance()	a2b3c4d5()	salestax()	amount()	$taxes()

2. Assume that the following functions have been written:

```
oldBal(), sold(), newBal(), report()
```

a. Write a C program that calls these functions in the order they are listed.

b. From the functions' names, what do you think each function might do?

3. Assume that the following functions have been written:

```
input(), salestax(), balance(), calcbill()
```

   a. Write a C program that calls these functions in the order they are listed.
   b. From the functions' names, what do you think each function might do?

4. Assign names for functions that do the following:
   a. Find the maximum value in a set of numbers.
   b. Find the minimum value in a set of numbers.
   c. Convert a lowercase letter to an uppercase letter.
   d. Convert an uppercase letter to a lowercase letter.
   e. Sort a set of numbers from lowest to highest.
   f. Alphabetize a set of names.

Note for Exercises 5 through 10: Most programming and nonprogramming projects can be structured into smaller subtasks or units of activity. These smaller subtasks can often be delegated to different people so that when all the tasks are finished and integrated, the project or program is completed. For exercises 5 through 10, determine a set of subtasks that, taken together, complete the required task.

   The purpose of these exercises is to have you consider different ways that complex tasks can be structured. Although there is no single correct solution to these exercises, there are incorrect solutions and solutions that are better than others. An incorrect solution does not complete the task correctly. One solution is better than another if it more clearly or easily identifies what must be done.

5. You are given the job of planning a surprise birthday party. Determine a set of subtasks to accomplish this. (*Hint:* One such subtask would be to create a guest list.)

6. You are given the job of preparing a meal for five people next weekend. Determine the major tasks that must be handled to accomplish this. (*Hint:* One task, not necessarily the first one, is "Buy the food.")

7. You are a sophomore in college and plan to go to law school after graduation. List the major objectives that you must fulfill to meet this goal. (*Hint:* One objective is "Take the right courses.")

8. You wish to plant a vegetable garden. Determine the major tasks that must be handled to accomplish this. (*Hint:* One task is "Plan the garden.")

9. You are responsible for planning and arranging the family camping trip this summer. List the major tasks that must be accomplished to meet this objective successfully. (*Hint:* One task is "Select the camp site.")

10. a. A Wall Street investment firm desires a new computer system to track all stock trades made during the year. The system must be capable of accepting and storing all the trades. Additionally, the company wants to retrieve and output a printed report listing all trades that meet certain criteria. For example, all trades made in a particular month with a net value of more than a given dollar amount, all trades made in a year with a particular client, or all trades made with firms in a particular state. For this system, determine three or four major modules into which the system could be separated. (*Hint:* One module is "Input trades" to accept each day's trades.)

b. Suppose someone enters incorrect data about a trade, which is discovered after the trade has been entered and stored by the system. What module is needed to correct this problem? Discuss why such a module might or might not be required by most business systems.

c. Assume a module exists that allows a user to alter or change data that has been incorrectly entered and stored. Discuss the need for including an "audit trail" that would allow for a later reconstruction of the changes made, when they were made, and who made them.

1.3   The `printf()` Function

One of the most popular and useful prewritten functions in C is named `printf()`. This function, as its name suggests, is a print function that formats data given to it and sends it to the standard system display device. For most systems, this display device is a video screen. The function prints out whatever is given to it. For example, if the message `Hello there world!` is given to `printf()`, this message is printed (or displayed) on your terminal by the `printf()` function. Inputting data or messages to a function is called passing data to the function. The message `Hello there world!` is passed to the `printf()` function by simply enclosing the message in double quotes and placing it inside the parentheses in the function's name as follows:

```
printf("Hello there world!");
```

The purpose of the parentheses in all function names is to provide a funnel through which information can be passed to the function (see Figure 1.15). As noted earlier, the items that are passed to the function through the parentheses are referred to as the function's arguments.

Now let's put all this together into a working C program that can be run on your computer. Consider Program 1.1.

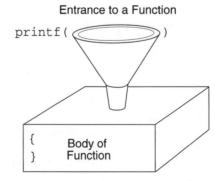

Figure 1.15   Passing a message to `printf()`

Program 1.1

```
/*
File: Pgm1-1.cpp
Description: Displays Hello there world!
Programmer: G. Bronson
Date: 6/15/00
*/
#include <stdio.h>

int main()
{
  printf("Hello there world!");

  return 0;
}
```

The first six lines of program code, starting with the slash and asterisk symbol pair on line one, /*, and ending with the matching asterisk slash pair, */, on line six, constitutes a comment block. This block of comment statements consists of all typed characters following the start of the comment, which begins with the /* symbols and ends when the closing */ symbol pair is encountered. We will have much more to say about comments in the next section, but for now it is important to understand that each source code program should begin with comments similar to those used here. These initial comment lines, at a minimum, should provide the file name under which the source code is saved, a short program description, the name of the programmer, and the date that the program was last modified. For all of the programs contained in this text, the file name refers to the name of the file as it exists on the source code provided with this text.

The seventh line of the program

```
#include <stdio.h>
```

is a preprocessor command. Preprocessor commands begin with a pound sign, #, and perform some action before the compiler translates the source program into machine code. Specifically, the #include preprocessor command causes the contents of the named file, in this case stdio.h, to be inserted where the #include command appears. The file stdio.h is referred to as a *header file* because it is placed at the top, or head, of a C program using the #include command. In particular, the stdio.h file provides a proper interface to the printf() function and should be included in all programs using printf(). As indicated in Program 1.1, preprocessor commands do not end with a semicolon.

Following the preprocessor command is the start of the program's main() function. The main() function has only two statements. Remember that statements end with a semicolon (;). The first statement in main() calls the function printf() and passes one argument to it. The argument is the message Hello there world!. The second statement returns control to the operating system.

Since printf() is a prewritten function, we do not have to write it; it is available for use just by calling it correctly. Like all C functions, printf() was written to do a specific task, which is to print results. It is versatile and can print results in many different forms. When a message is passed to printf(), the function sees to it that the message is correctly printed on your screen.

Messages are called *strings* in C, because they consist of a string of characters made up of letters, numbers, and special characters. The beginning and end of a string of characters is marked by double quotes ("message in here"). Thus, to pass a message to printf(), the string of characters making up the message must be enclosed in double quotes, as we have done in Program 1.1. The program output is

```
Hello there world!
```

Let's write another program to illustrate printf()'s versatility. Read Program 1.2 to determine what it does.

 Program 1.2

```
/*
File: Pgm1-2.cpp
Description: Test program
Programmer: G. Bronson
Date: 6/15/00
*/
#include <stdio.h>
int main()
{
  printf("Computers, computers everywhere");
  printf("\n   as far as I can C");

  return 0;
}
```

When Program 1.2 is run, the following is displayed:

```
Computers, computers everywhere
    as far as I can C
```

You might be wondering why the \n did not appear in the output. The two characters \ and n, when used together, are called a *newline escape sequence*. They tell printf() to start on a new line. In C, the backslash (\) character provides an "escape" from the normal interpretation of the character following it by altering the meaning of the next character. If the backslash was omitted from the second printf() call in Program 1.2, the n would be printed as the letter *n* and the program would print out:

```
Computers, computers everywheren   as far as I can C
```

Newline escape sequences can be placed anywhere within the message passed to printf(). See if you can determine what the next program prints.

```c
#include <stdio.h>
int main()
{
  printf("Computers everywhere\n as far as\n\nI can see");

  return 0;
}
```

The output for this program is

```
Computers everywhere
 as far as

I can see
```

Exercises 1.3

1. a. Use the printf() function to write a C program that prints your name on one line, your street address on a second line, and your city, state, and zip code on the third line.

   b. Run the program you have written for Exercise 1a on a computer. (*Note:* You must understand the procedures for entering and running a C program on the particular computer installation you are using.)

2. a. Write a C program to print out the following verse:

```
Computers, computers everywhere
   as far as I can see
I really, really like these things,
   Oh joy, Oh joy for me!
```

   b. Run the program you have written for Exercise 2a on a computer.

3. a. How many `printf()` statements would you use to print out the following:

```
Part No.      Price

T1267        $6.34
T1300        $8.92
T2401       $65.40
T4482       $36.99
```

   b. What is the minimum number of `printf()` statements that could be used to print the table in Exercise 3a? Why would you not write a program using the minimum number of `printf()` function calls?

   c. Write a complete C program to produce the output illustrated in Exercise 3a.

   d. Run the program you have written for Exercise 3c on a computer.

4. In response to a newline escape sequence, `printf()` positions the next displayed character at the beginning of a new line. This positioning of the next character actually represents two distinct operations. What are they?

5. a. Most computer operating systems provide the capability for redirecting the output produced by `printf()` either to a printer or directly to a floppy or hard disk file. Read the first part of Appendix C for a description of this redirection capability.

   b. If your computer supports output redirection, run the program written for Exercise 2a using this feature. Have your program's display redirected to a file named "poem".

   c. If your computer supports output redirection to a printer, run the program written for Exercise 2a using this feature.

1.4   Programming Style

The word `main` in a C program tells the computer where the program starts. Since a program can have only one starting point, every C language program must contain one and only one `main()` function. As we have seen, all statements that make up the `main()` function are included within the braces `{ }` following the function name. Although the `main()` function must be present in every C program, C does not require that the word `main`, the parentheses `()`, or the braces `{ }` be placed in any particular form. The form used in the last section

```
int main()
{
   program statements in here;

   return 0;
}
```

was chosen strictly for clarity and ease in reading.[4] For example, the following general form of a `main()` function also works:

---

[4] If one of the program statements was a call to `printf()`, the `#include <stdio.h>` preprocessor command would have to be used. If the `main()` function did not return any value before completing, the appropriate first line would be `void main()`.

```
int main
(
){ first statement;second statement;
third statement;fourth
statement;}
```

Note that more than one statement can be put on a line, or one statement can be written across lines. Except for messages contained within double quotes, function names, and reserved words, C ignores all *white space* (white space refers to any combination of one or more blank spaces, tabs, or new lines). For example, changing the white space in Program 1.1 while making sure not to split the message Hello there world! or the function names printf and main across two lines, and omitting all comments, results in the following valid program:

```
int
main
(
){printf
("Hello there world!"
);return 0;}
```

Although this version of main() does work, it is an example of extremely poor programming style. It is difficult to read and understand. For readability, the main() function should always be written in standard form as

```
int main()
{
  program statements in here;

  return 0;
}
```

In this standard form, the function name starts in column 1 and is placed with the required parentheses on a line by itself. The opening brace of the function body follows on the next line and is placed under the first letter of the function name. Similarly, the closing function brace is placed by itself in column 1 as the last line of the function. This structure serves to highlight the function as a single unit.

Within the function itself, all program statements are indented two spaces. Indentation is another sign of good programming practice, especially if the same indentation is used for similar groups of statements. Review Program 1.2 to see that the same indentation was used for both printf() function calls.

As you progress in your understanding and mastery of C, you will develop your own indentation standards. Just keep in mind that the final form of your programs should be consistent and should always serve as an aid to the reading and understanding of your programs.

Comments

Comments are explanatory remarks made within a program. When used carefully, comments help clarify what the complete program is about, what a specific group of statements is meant to accomplish, or what one line is intended to do.

The symbols /*, with no white space between them, designate the start of a comment, while the symbols */, as a single unit with no intervening white space, designate the end of a comment.[5] For example,

```
/* this is a comment */
/* this program prints out a message */
/* this program calculates a square root */
```

are all comment lines.

Comments can be placed anywhere within a program and have no effect on program execution. The computer ignores all comments—they are there strictly for the convenience of anyone reading the program.

A comment can be written either on a line by itself or on the same line containing a program statement. Program 1.3 illustrates the use of comments within a program.

 Program 1.3

```
/*
File: Pgm1-3.cpp
Description: Test program
Programmer: G. Bronson
Date: 6/15/00
*/
#include <stdio.h>
int main()   /* this program prints a message */
{
  printf("Hello there world!"); /* a call to printf() */

  return 0;
}
```

The second comment appears on the same line as the main function name and describes what the program does. This is generally a good location to include a short comment describing the program's purpose. If more comments are required, they can be

---

[5] Additionally, some compilers permit the start of a comment to be designated by double slashes (//). Such comments extend to the end of the line on which they are written.

placed, one per line, between the function name and the opening brace that encloses the function's statements. If a comment is too long to be contained on one line, it can be continued across two or more lines as illustrated below[6]:

```
/* this comment is used to illustrate a
comment that extends over two lines */
```

Under no circumstances may comments be nested—one comment containing another comment. For example,

```
/* this nested comment is /* always */ invalid */
```

In C, a program's structure is intended to make the program readable and understandable, making the use of extensive comments unnecessary. This is reinforced if function and variable names, described in the next chapter, are carefully selected to convey their meaning to anyone reading the program. However, if the purpose of a function or statement is still not clear from its structure, name, or context, include comments where clarification is needed. Obscure code with no comments is a sure sign of bad programing. Excessive comments are also a sign of bad programming because they imply that insufficient thought was given to making the code self-explanatory.

Typically, programs that you write should start with a set of initial program comments that include a short program description, your name, and the date that the program was last modified. For space considerations, and because all programs in this text were written by the author, initial comments will be used only for short program descriptions when they are not provided as part of the accompanying text.

Exercises 1.4

1. a. Will the following program work?

```
#include <stdio.h>
int main() {printf("Hello there world!"); return 0;}
```

b. Why is the program given in Exercise 1a not a good program?

2. Rewrite the following programs to conform to good programming practice.
a. ```
#include <stdio.h>
int main(
){
printf
(
```

---

[6] Additionally, some compilers permit C++ style comments that begin with a double slash (//) and extend to the end of the line they are written on. Such comments are called *line comments*.
```

```
"The time has come"
return 0;
);
```

b.
```
#include <stdio.h>
int main
(){printf("Newark is a city\n");printf(
"In New Jersey\n"); printf
(It is also a city\n"
); printf(In Delaware\n"
);return 0;}
```

c.
```
#include <stdio.h>
int main(){printf("Reading a program\n");printf(
"is much easier\n"
);printf("if a standard form for main is used\n")
;printf      ("and each statement is written\n");printf(
"on a line by itself\n")
);return 0;}
```

d.
```
#include <stdio.h>
int main
(){printf("Every C program"
);printf
("\nmust have one and only one"
);
printf("main function"
);
printf(
"\n the escape sequence of characters")
;printf(
"\nfor a new line can be placed anywhere"
);printf
("\n within the message passed to printf()"
);return 0;}
```

3. a. When used in a message, the backslash character alters the meaning of the character immediately following it. If we wanted to print the backslash character, we would have to tell `printf()` to escape from the way it normally interprets the backslash. What character do you think is used to alter the way a single backslash character is interpreted?

b. Using your answer to Exercise 3a, write the escape sequence for printing a backslash.

4. a. A *token* of a computer language is any sequence of characters that, as a unit, with no intervening characters or white space, has a unique meaning. Using this definition of a token, determine whether escape sequences, function names, and the keywords listed in Table 1.2 are tokens of the C language.

b. Discuss whether adding white space to a message alters the message. Discuss whether messages can be considered tokens of C.

c. Using the definition of a token given in Exercise 4a, determine whether the statement "Except for tokens of the language, C ignores all white space" is true.

1.5   Top-Down Program Development

Recall from Section 1.1 that writing a C program is essentially the last step in the programming process. The first step in the process is determining what is required and selecting the algorithm to be coded into C. In this section, we present a five-step program development procedure, called top-down development, for converting programming problems into working C programs. To make this development procedure more meaningful, we first apply it to a simple programming problem. As we will see, designing a program using a top-down approach results in a modular program design.

The five steps in the top-down development procedure are

1. Determine the desired output items that the program must produce.
2. Determine the input items.
3. Design the program as follows:
   a. Select an algorithm for transforming the input items into the desired outputs.
   b. Check the chosen algorithm, by hand, using specific input values.
4. Code the algorithm into C.
5. Test the program using selected test data.

Steps 1 and 2 in the development procedure are referred to as the *analysis phase,* Step 3 is called the *design phase,* Step 4 the *coding phase,* and Step 5 the *testing phase.*

In the analysis phase of program development (Steps 1 and 2) we are concerned with extracting the complete input and output information supplied by the problem, referred to as the problem's I/O, for short. Only after a problem's I/O has been determined is it possible to select an algorithm for transforming the inputs into the desired outputs. For example, consider the following simple programming problem:

The circumference, C, of a circle is given by the formula $C = 2\pi r$, where π is the constant 3.1416 (accurate to four decimal places), and r is the radius of the circle. Using this information, write a C program to calculate the circumference of a circle that has a 2-inch radius.

Step 1: Determine the Desired Output

The first step in developing a program for this problem statement is to determine the required outputs (Step 1 of the development procedure). Frequently, the statement of the problem will use such words as *calculate, print, determine, find,* or *compare,* which can be used to determine the desired outputs.

For our sample problem statement, the key phrase is "to calculate the circumference of a circle." This identifies an output item. Since there are no other such phrases in the problem, only one output item is required.

Step 2: Determine the Input Items

After we have clearly identified the desired output, Step 2 of the development process requires that we identify input items. It is essential, at this stage, to distinguish between input items and input values. An input *item* is the name of an input quantity, while an input *value* is a specific number or quantity that the input item can be. For example, in our sample problem statement, the input item is the radius of the circle (the known quantity). Although this input item has a specific numerical value in this problem (the value 2), actual input item values are generally not important in Step 2.

The reason that input values are not needed at this point is because the initial selection of an algorithm is typically independent of specific input values; the algorithm depends on knowing the output and input items and whether there are any special limits. Let's see why this is true as we determine a suitable algorithm for our sample problem statement.

Step 3a: Determine an Algorithm

From the problem statement, it is clear that the algorithm for transforming the input items to the desired output is given by the formula $C = 2\pi r$. Notice that this formula can be used regardless of the specific value assigned to r. Although we cannot produce an actual numerical value for the output item (circumference) unless we have an actual numerical value for the input item, the correct relationship between inputs and outputs is expressed by the formula. Recall that this is precisely what an algorithm provides: a description of how the inputs are to be transformed into outputs that work for all inputs. Thus, the complete algorithm, in pseudocode, for solving this problem is

> *Assign a value to r*
> *Calculate the circumference using the formula* $\mathbf{C = 2\pi r}$
> *Display the result*

Step 3b: Do a Hand Calculation
After we have selected an algorithm, the next step in the design procedure, Step 3b, is to check the algorithm manually using specific data. Performing a manual calculation, either by hand or by using a calculator, helps ensure that you really do understand the problem. An added feature of doing a manual calculation is that the results can be used later to verify the operation of your program in the testing phase. Then, when the final program is used with other data, you will have established a degree of confidence that a correct result is being calculated.

Doing a manual calculation requires that we have specific input values that can be applied to the algorithm to produce the desired output. For this problem, one input value is given: a radius of 2 inches. Substituting this value into the formula, we obtain a circumference of 2(3.1416)2 = 12.5664 inches for the circle.

Step 4: Write the Program
Having selected an algorithm for the problem, all that remains is to write the algorithm in C. Since all of the statements for converting this algorithm into C are not presented until the next chapter, there are parts of the program that will be unfamiliar to you. Nevertheless, we present the completed program for you to examine and see how it follows our previous pseudocode description.

Program 1.4

```
#include <stdio.h>
int main()
{
  float radius, circumference;

  radius = 2.0;
  circumference = 2.0 * 3.1416 * radius;
  printf("The circumference of the circle is %f",circumference);

  return 0;
}
```

When this program is executed, the following output is produced:

```
The circumference of the circle is 12.566400
```

Now that we have a working program that produces a result, the final step in the development process—testing the program—can begin.

Step 5: Test the Output

The purpose of testing is to verify that a program works correctly and fulfills its requirements. Once testing is complete, the program can be used to calculate outputs for differing input data without needing to retest. This is, of course, the real value in writing a program: the same program can be used over and over with new input data.

In theory, testing would reveal all existing program errors (in computer terminology, a program error is called a *bug*). In practice, this would require checking all possible combinations of statement execution. Because of the time and effort required, this is usually an impossible goal except for extremely simple programs such as Program 1.4. (In Section 4.7, we illustrate why this is generally an impossible goal.)

The inability to completely test most programs has led to various testing methodologies. The simplest of these methods is to verify the program's operation for carefully selected sets of input data. One set of input data that should always be used is the data that was selected for the hand calculation made previously in Step 3b of the development procedure. If testing reveals an error (a bug), the process of debugging, which includes locating, correcting, and verifying the correction, can be initiated. It is important to realize that although this type of verification testing may reveal the presence of an error, it does not necessarily indicate the absence of one. Thus, the fact that a test does not reveal an error does not indicate that another bug is not lurking somewhere else in the program.

In the case of Program 1.4, only a single calculation is performed and the result of the test run agrees with our hand calculation. Thus, the program has been completely tested and can now be used to calculate the circumference of other circles with confidence that the results being produced are accurate.

Modularity and Top-Down Design

The design of Program 1.4 was relatively simple because the algorithm was a simple formula that was given in the statement of the problem. For more complex problems the selection of an algorithm can be considerably more involved. In its more elaborate form, determining an algorithm is similar to receiving the pieces of a puzzle (the inputs) and deciding how to arrange them to form a completed structure (the desired output). Unlike a jigsaw puzzle, however, the pieces of a program design puzzle can be arranged in many different ways depending on the algorithm chosen for transforming the inputs into the desired outputs. In this regard, the program designer is similar to an architect who must draw up the plans for a house.

The general purpose of using a top-down development procedure to design programs is to create a modular program structure. To achieve this goal, the description of the algorithm starts from the highest-level requirement and proceeds to the parts that must be constructed to achieve this requirement. To make this more meaningful, consider that a computer program is required to track the number of parts in inventory. The required output for this program is a description of all parts carried in inventory and the number of units of each item in stock; the given inputs are the initial inventory quantity of each part, the gross number of items sold, the number of items returned, and the net number of items sold.

For these I/O specifications, a designer could initially organize the requirements for the program into the three sections illustrated in Figure 1.16. This is called a *first-level structure diagram* because it represents the first overall structure of the program selected by the designer.

In top-down algorithm design, the lower boxes in the structure diagram are refined until the tasks indicated in the boxes are small enough to be programmed as individual C functions. For example, both the data entry and report subsections shown in Figure 1.16 would be further refined into suitable modules. The data entry section certainly must include provisions for entering the data. Since it is the system designer's responsibility to

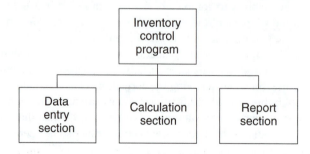

Figure 1.16   First-level structure diagram

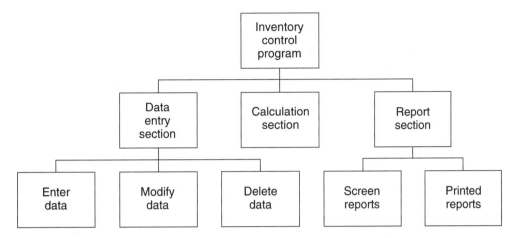

Figure 1.17   Second-level refinement structure diagram

plan for contingencies and human error, provisions must also be made for changing incorrect data after an entry has been made and for deleting a previously entered value. Similar subdivisions of the report section can also be made. Figure 1.17 illustrates a second-level structure diagram for an inventory tracking system that includes these further refinements.

The process of refinement continues until the last level of tasks can be coded using individual functions. Notice that the design produces a treelike structure where the levels branch out as we move from the top of the structure to the bottom. When the design is complete it specifies both how many functions are needed and the calling sequence of each unit (that is, lower-level modules in the diagram are called from higher-level modules). The individual tasks required for each box in the final structure diagram, which are coded as separate C functions, are frequently described using either flowcharts or pseudocode.

Exercises 1.5

Note: In each of these exercises, a programming problem is given. Read the problem statement first and then answer the questions pertaining to the problem.

1. Consider the following programming problem (*do not* program it): A C program is required that calculates the amount, in dollars, contained in a piggybank. The bank contains half-dollars, quarters, dimes, nickels, and pennies.
    a. For this programming problem, how many outputs are required?
    b. How many inputs does this problem have?
    c. Determine an algorithm for converting the input items into output items.
    d. Test the algorithm written for Exercise 1c using the following sample data: half dollars = 0, quarters = 17, dimes = 24, nickels = 16, pennies = 12.

2. Consider the following programming problem (*do not* program it): A C program is required to calculate the value of distance, in miles, given the relationship

$$\text{distance} = \text{rate} * \text{elapsed time}$$

   a. For this programming problem, how many outputs are required?
   b. How many inputs does this problem have?
   c. Determine an algorithm for converting the input items into output items.
   d. Test the algorithm written for Exercise 2c using the following sample data: rate = 55 miles per hour and elapsed time = 2.5 hours.
   e. How must the algorithm you determined in Exercise 2c be modified if the elapsed time is given in minutes instead of hours?

3. Consider the following programming problem (*do not* program it): A C program is required to determine the value of Ergies, given the relationship

$$\text{Ergies} = \text{Fergies} * \sqrt{\text{Lergies}}$$

   a. For this programming problem, how many outputs are required?
   b. How many inputs does this problem have?
   c. Determine an algorithm for converting the input items into output items.
   d. Test the algorithm written for Exercise 3c using the following sample data: Fergies = 14.65 and Lergies = 4.

4. Consider the following programming problem (*do not* program it): A C program is required to display the following name and address:

> Mr. J. Swanson
> 63 Seminole Way
> Dumont, NJ 07030

   a. For this programming problem, how many lines of output are required?
   b. How many inputs does this problem have?
   c. Determine an algorithm for converting the input items into output items.

5. Consider the following program problem (*do not* program it): A C program is required to determine how far a car has traveled after 10 seconds assuming the car is initially traveling at 60 miles per hour and the driver applies the brakes to uniformly decelerate at a rate of 12 miles/sec^2. Use the fact that distance $= st - (1/2)dt^2$, where s is the initial speed of the car, d is the deceleration, and t is the elapsed time.
   a. For this programming problem, how many outputs are required?
   b. How many inputs does this problem have?
   c. Determine an algorithm for converting the input items into output items.
   d. Test the algorithm written for Exercise 5c using the data given in the problem.

6. Consider the following programming problem (*do not* program it): In 1627, Manhattan Island was sold to Dutch settlers for approximately $24. If the proceeds of that sale had been deposited in a Dutch bank paying 5 percent interest, compounded annually, what would the principal balance be at the end of 1990? A display is required as follows: `Balance as of December 31, 1990, is xxxxxx` where xxxxxx is the amount calculated by your program.
   a. For this programming problem, how many outputs are required?
   b. How many inputs does this problem have?
   c. Determine an algorithm for converting the input items into output items.
   d. Test the algorithm written for Exercise 6c using the data given in the problem statement.

7. Consider the following programming problem (*do not* program it): A C program is required that calculates and displays the weekly gross pay and net pay of two individuals. The first individual is paid an hourly rate of $8.43, and the second individual is paid an hourly rate of $5.67. Both individuals have 20 percent of their gross pay withheld for income tax purposes, and both pay 2 percent of their gross pay, before taxes, for medical benefits.

a. For this programming problem, how many outputs are required?
b. How many inputs does this problem have?
c. Determine an algorithm for converting the input items into output items.
d. Test the algorithm written for Exercise 7c using the following sample data: The first person works 40 hours during the week and the second person works 35 hours.

8. Consider the following programming problem (*do not* program it): The formula for the standard normal deviate, *z*, used in statistical applications is

$$z = \frac{X - \mu}{\sigma}$$

where μ refers to a mean value and σ to a standard deviation. Using this formula, write a program that calculates and displays the value of the standard normal deviate when $X = 85.3$, $\mu = 80$, and $\sigma = 4$.

a. For this programming problem, how many outputs are required?
b. How many inputs does this problem have?
c. Determine an algorithm for converting the input items into output items.
d. Test the algorithm written for Exercise 8c using the data given in the problem.

9. Consider the following programming problem (*do not* program it): The equation describing exponential growth is:

$$y = e^x$$

Using this equation, a C program is required to calculate the value of *y*.
a. For this programing problem, how many outputs are required?
b. How many inputs does this problem have?
c. Determine an algorithm for converting the input items into output items.
d. Test the algorithm written for Exercise 9c assuming $e = 2.718$ and $x = 10$.

1.6 Common Programming Errors

Part of learning any programming language is making the elementary mistakes commonly encountered as you begin to use the language. These mistakes tend to be quite frustrating, since each language has its own set of common programming errors waiting for the unwary. The more common errors made when initially programming in C are

1. Omitting the parentheses after `main`.
2. Omitting or incorrectly typing the opening brace { that signifies the start of a function body.
3. Omitting or incorrectly typing the closing brace } that signifies the end of a function.
4. Misspelling the name of a function; for example, typing `print()` instead of `printf()`.

5. Forgetting to close the message to `printf()` with a double quote symbol.
6. Omitting the semicolon at the end of each statement.
7. Forgetting the `\n` to indicate a new line.

Our experience is that the third, fifth, sixth, and seventh errors in this list tend to be the most common. We suggest that you write a program and specifically introduce each of these errors, one at a time, to see what error messages are produced by your compiler. Then, when these error messages appear due to inadvertent errors, you will have had experience in understanding the message and correcting the errors.

On a more fundamental level, a major programming error made by all beginning programmers is rushing to code and run a program before fully understanding what is required and the algorithms and procedures that will be used to produce the desired result. A symptom of this haste to get a program entered into the computer is the lack of either an outline of the proposed program or a written program itself. Many problems can be caught just by checking a copy of the program, either handwritten or listed from the computer, before it is ever compiled.

1.7 Chapter Summary

1. A C program consists of one or more modules called functions. One of these functions must be called `main()`. The `main()` function identifies the starting point of a C program.

2. Many functions, like `printf()`, are supplied in a standard library of functions provided with each C compiler.

3. The simplest C program consists of the single function `main()`.

4. Following the function name, the body of a function has the general form:

```
{
   All program statements in here;
}
```

5. All C statements must be terminated by a semicolon.

6. The `printf()` function is used to display text or numerical results. The first argument to `printf()` can be a message, which is enclosed in double quotes. The text in the message is displayed directly on the screen and may include newline escape sequences for format control.

Data Types, Declarations, and Displays

We continue our introduction to the fundamentals of C in this chapter by presenting C's elementary data types, variables, declarations, and additional information on using the `printf()` function. These new concepts and tools enable us to both expand our programming abilities and gain insight into how data is stored in a computer.

Before reading this chapter, you should have an understanding of basic computer storage concepts and terms. If you are unfamiliar with the terms *bit, byte,* and *memory address,* read the supplement at the end of this chapter (Section 2.8) for an introduction to these terms.

2.1 Data Types

There are four basic data types used in C: integer, floating point, double precision, and character. The values associated with each data type are described below.

Integer Values

An *integer value,* which is called an *integer constant* in C, is any positive or negative number without a decimal point. Examples of valid integer constants are

5   –10   +25   1000   253   –26351   +36

As these examples show, integers may be signed (have a leading + or – sign) or unsigned (no leading + or – sign). No commas, decimal points, or special symbols, such as the dollar sign, are allowed. Examples of invalid integer constants are

$255.62   2,523   3.   6,243,892   1,492.89   +6.0

Compilers have internal limits on the largest (most positive) and smallest (most negative) integer values that can be used in a program. These limits are implementation dependent; they depend on how much storage each compiler sets aside for an integer. The more common storage allocations are listed in Table 2.1. By referring to your computer's reference manual or using the `sizeof` operator introduced in Section 2.5, you can determine the actual number of bytes allocated by your compiler for each integer value. (Review Section 2.8 if you are unfamiliar with the concept of a byte.)

Floating Point and Double Precision Numbers

Floating point and *double precision* numbers are any signed or unsigned numbers having a decimal point. Examples of floating point and double precision numbers are

+10.6255   5.   –6.2   3251.92   0.0 0.33   –6.67   +2.

As with integers, special symbols, such as the dollar sign and the comma, are not permitted in floating point or double precision numbers. Examples of invalid floating point and double precision constants are

5,326.25   24   123   6,459 $10.29

The difference between floating point and double precision numbers is how much storage a computer uses for each type. Most computers use twice the amount of storage

Table 2.1   Integer values and byte storage

Storage Area Reserved	Maximum Integer Value	Minimum Integer Value
1 byte	127	–128
2 bytes	32767	–32768
4 bytes	2147483647	–2147483648

for double precision numbers than for floating point numbers, which allows a double precision number to have approximately twice the precision of a floating point number (for this reason floating point numbers are sometimes called *single precision* numbers). The actual storage allocation for each data type, however, depends on the compiler. In compilers that allocate the same amount of storage for double precision and floating point numbers, the two data types become identical. The `sizeof` operator introduced in Section 2.5 will allow you to determine the amount of storage reserved by your compiler for each of these data types.

Exponential Notation

Floating point and double precision numbers can be written in exponential notation, which is commonly used to express either very large or very small numbers in a compact form. The following examples illustrate how numbers with decimal points can be expressed in exponential notation.

Decimal Notation	Exponential Notation
1625.	1.625e3
63421.	6.3421e4
.00731	7.31e–3
.000625	6.25e–4

In exponential notation the letter *e* stands for *exponent*. The number following the *e* represents a power of 10 and indicates the number of places the decimal point should be moved to obtain the standard decimal value. The decimal point is moved to the right if the number after the *e* is positive, or moved to the left if the number after the *e* is negative. For example, the *e*3 in the number 1.625*e*3 means move the decimal place three places to the right, so that the number becomes 1625. The *e*–3 in the number 7.31*e*–3 means move the decimal point three places to the left, so that 7.31*e*–3 becomes .00731.

Character Type

The fourth basic data type recognized by C is the *character type*. Characters are the letters of the alphabet (uppercase and lowercase), the ten digits 0 through 9, and special symbols such as + $. , – ! . A single character constant is any one letter, digit, or special symbol enclosed by single quotes. Examples of valid character constants are

```
'A' '$' 'b' '7' 'y' '!' 'M' 'q'
```

Character constants are typically stored in a computer using either the ASCII or ANSI codes. ASCII, pronounced ASS-KEE, is an acronym for American Standard Code for Information Interchange. ANSI, pronounced ANN-SEE, is an acronym for American National Standards Institute and is an extended set of 256 codes, the first 128 of which are the same as the ASCII codes. Each of these codes assigns individual characters to a specific pattern of

Table 2.2 The ASCII and ANSI letter codes

Letter	Code	Letter	Code	Letter	Code	Letter	Code
a	01100001	n	01101110	A	01000001	N	01001110
b	01100010	o	01101111	B	01000010	O	01001111
c	01100011	p	01110000	C	01000011	P	01010000
d	01100100	q	01110001	D	01000100	Q	01010001
e	01100101	r	01110010	E	01000101	R	01010010
f	01100110	s	01110011	F	01000110	S	01010011
g	01100111	t	01110100	G	01000111	T	01010100
h	01101000	u	01110101	H	01001000	U	01010101
i	01101001	v	01110110	I	01001001	V	01010110
j	01101010	w	01110111	J	01001010	W	01010111
k	01101011	x	01111000	K	01001011	X	01011000
l	01101100	y	01111001	L	01001100	Y	01011001
m	01101101	z	01111010	M	01001101	Z	01011010

0s and 1s. Table 2.2 lists the correspondence between bit patterns and the uppercase and lowercase letters of the alphabet used by both the ASCII and ANSI codes.

Using Table 2.2, we can determine how the character constants 'J', 'O', 'N', 'E', and 'S', for example, are stored inside a computer that uses the ASCII character code. Using the ASCII code, this sequence of characters requires five bytes of storage (one byte for each letter) and would be stored as illustrated in Figure 2.1.

Escape Sequences

When a backslash (\) is used in front of a select group of characters, the backslash tells the compiler to escape from the way these characters would normally be interpreted. For this reason, the combination of a backslash and these specific characters are called *escape sequences*. We have already encountered an example of this in the newline escape sequence, \n. Table 2.3 lists other common escape sequences.

Although each escape sequence listed in Table 2.3 is made up of two distinct characters, the combination of the two characters with no intervening white space causes the computer to store one character code. Table 2.4 lists the ASCII code byte patterns for the escape sequences listed in Table 2.3.

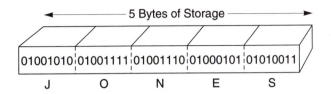

Figure 2.1   The letters "JONES" stored inside a computer

Table 2.3   Escape sequences in C

Escape Sequence	Meaning
\b	move back one space
\f	move to next page
\n	move to next line
\r	carriage return
\t	move to next tab setting
\\	backslash character
\'	single quote
\"	double quote
\nnn	treat nnn as an octal number

Table 2.4   The ASCII escape sequence codes

C Escape Sequence	Meaning	Computer Code
\b	backspace	00001000
\f	form feed	00001100
\n	new line	00001010
\r	carriage return	00001101
\t	tab	00010001
\\	backslash	01011100
\'	single quote	00100111
\"	double quote	00100010
\nnn	octal number	binary value of nnn

Exercises 2.1

1. Determine data types appropriate of the following data:
   a. the average of four grades
   b. the number of days in a month
   c. the length of the Golden Gate Bridge
   d. the numbers in a state lottery
   e. the distance from Brooklyn, N.Y., to Newark, N.J.

2. Convert the following numbers into standard decimal form:

$$6.34e5 \quad 1.95162e2 \quad 8.395e1 \quad 2.95e\text{--}3 \quad 4.623e\text{--}4$$

3. Convert the following decimal numbers into exponential notation:

$$1.26. \quad 656.23 \quad 3426.95 \quad 4893.2 \quad .321 \quad .0123 \quad .006789$$

4. Using the system reference manuals for your computer, determine the character code used by your computer.

5. Using the ASCII code listed in Table 2.2, show how the letters SWANSON would be stored in a computer's memory.

6. a. Using the ASCII code, determine the number of bytes required to store the letters KINGSLEY.
   b. Show how the letters KINGSLEY are stored inside a computer that uses the ASCII code. That is, draw a figure similar to Figure 2.1 for the letters KINGSLEY.

7. a. Repeat Exercise 6a using the letters of your own last name.
   b. Repeat Exercise 6b using the letters of your own last name.

8. Since most computers use different amounts of storage for integer, floating point, double precision, and character values, discuss how a program might alert the computer to the amount of storage needed for the various values in the program.

9. Although the total number of bytes varies from computer to computer, memory sizes of 65,536 to more than several million bytes are not uncommon. In computer language, the letter K is used to represent the number 1024, which is 2 raised to the tenth power, and the letter M is used to represent the number 1,048,576 which is 2 raised to the twentieth power. Thus, a memory size of 640K is really 640 times 1024, or 655,360 bytes, and a memory size of 4MB is 4 times 1,048,576 or 4,194,304 bytes. Using this information, calculate the actual number of bytes in:
   a. a memory containing 8MB
   b. a memory containing 116MB
   c. a memory containing 132MB
   d. a memory containing 196MB
   e. a memory consisting of 8MB words, where each word consists of 2 bytes
   f. a memory consisting of 16MB words, where each word consists of 4 bytes
   g. a floppy diskette that can store 1.44MB

2.2 Arithmetic Operators

Integers, floating point numbers, and double precision numbers may be added, subtracted, divided, and multiplied. Although it is better not to mix integers with the other two numerical data types when performing arithmetic operations, predictable results are obtained when different data types are used in the same arithmetic expression. Surprisingly, character data can also be added and subtracted with both character and integer data to produce useful results.

The operators used for these operations are called *arithmetic operators:*

Operation	Operator
Addition	+
Subtraction	−
Multiplication	*
Division	/

Each of these arithmetic operators is a binary operator that requires two operands.[1] A simple arithmetic expression consists of an arithmetic operator connecting two numerical operands. Examples of arithmetic expressions are

3 + 7
18 − 3
12.62 + 9.8
.08 * 12.2
12.6 / 2

The spaces around the arithmetic operators in these examples are inserted strictly for clarity and may be omitted without affecting the value of the expression.

An expression that contains only integer operands is called an *integer expression;* the result is an integer value. Similarly, an expression containing only floating point operands (single and double precision) is called a *floating point expression;* the result is a double precision value. An expression containing both integer and floating point operands is called a *mixed-mode expression.* Although it is usually better not to mix integer and floating point operands in an arithmetic operation, the data type of each operation is determined by the following rules:

---

[1] An operand can be a single constant, single variable (described in the next section), or valid combinations of constants and variables.

1. If all operands are integers, the result is an integer.
2. If any operand is a floating point or double precision value, the result is a double precision number.

Notice that the result of an arithmetic expression is never a floating point number because the computer temporarily converts all floating point numbers to double precision numbers when arithmetic is being done.

Integer Division

The division of two integers can produce rather strange results for the unwary. For example, dividing the integer 15 by the integer 2 yields an integer result. Since integers cannot contain a fractional part, the correct result, 7.5, is not obtained. In C, the fractional part of the result obtained when dividing two integers is dropped (*truncated*). Thus, the value of 15/2 is 7, the value of 9/4 is 2, and the value of 17/5 is 3.

There are times when we would like to retain the remainder of an integer division. To do this C provides an arithmetic operator that captures the remainder when two integers are divided. This operator, called the *modulus operator,* has the symbol %. The modulus operator can be used only with integers. For example,

9 % 4 is 1 (that is, the remainder is 1)

17 % 3 is 2 (that is, the remainder is 2)

14 % 2 is 0 (that is, there is no remainder)

A Unary Operator (Negation)

Besides the binary operators for addition, subtraction, multiplication, and division, C also provides *unary operators.* One of these unary operators uses the same symbol that is used for binary subtraction (–). The minus sign used in front of a single numerical operand negates (reverses the sign of) the number.

Table 2.5 summarizes the six arithmetic operations we have described so far and lists the data type of the result produced by each operator based on the data type of the operands involved.

Operator Precedence and Associativity

Besides such simple expressions as 5 + 12 and .08 * 26.2, we frequently need to create more complex arithmetic expressions. C, like most other programming languages, requires that certain rules be followed when writing expressions containing more than one arithmetic operator. These rules are

1. Two binary arithmetic operator symbols must never be placed side by side. For example, 5 * %6 is invalid because the two operators * and % are placed next to each other.

Table 2.5   Summary of arithmetic operators

Operation	Operator	Type	Operand	Result
Addition	+	Binary	Both integers One operand not an integer	Integer Double precision
Subtraction	–	Binary	Both integers One operand not an integer	Integer Double precision
Multiplication	*	Binary	Both integers One operand not an integer	Integer Double precision
Division	/	Binary	Both integers One operand not an integer	Integer Double precision
Remainder	%	Binary	Both integers	Integer
Negation	–	Unary	One integer One floating point or double precision operand	Integer Double precision

2. Parentheses may be used to form groupings, and all expressions enclosed within parentheses are evaluated first. For example, in the expression (6 + 4) / (2 + 3), the 6 + 4 and 2 + 3 are evaluated first, yielding 10 / 5. The 10 / 5 is then evaluated to yield 2. Sets of parentheses may also be enclosed by other parentheses. For example, the expression (2 * (3 + 7)) / 5 is valid. When parentheses are used within parentheses, the expressions in the innermost parentheses are always evaluated first. The evaluation continues from innermost to outermost parentheses until the expressions in all parentheses have been evaluated. The number of right-facing parentheses,), must always equal the number of left-facing parentheses, (, so that there are no unpaired sets.

3. Parentheses cannot be used to indicate multiplication. The multiplication operator, *, must be used. For example, the expression (3 + 4)(5 + 1) is invalid. The correct expression is (3 + 4) * (5 + 1).

As a general rule, parentheses should be used to specify logical groupings of operands and to indicate clearly to both the computer and programmers the intended order of arithmetic operations. In the absence of parentheses, expressions containing multiple operators are evaluated by the priority, or *precedence,* of each operator.

The precedence of an operator establishes its priority relative to all other operators. Operators at the top of Table 2.6 have a higher priority than operators at the bottom of the table. In expressions with multiple operators, the operator with the higher precedence is used before an operator with a lower precedence. For example, in the expression 6 + 4 / 2 + 3, the division is done before the addition, yielding an intermediate result of 6 + 2 + 3. The additions are then performed to yield a final result of 11.

Table 2.6   Operator precedence and associativity

Operator	Associativity
unary −	right to left
* / %	left to right
+ −	left to right

Expressions containing operators with the same precedence are evaluated according to their *associativity*. This means that evaluation is either from left to right or from right to left as each operator is encountered. For example, in the expression 8 + 5 * 7 % 2 * 4, the multiplication and modulus operator are of higher precedence than the addition operator and are evaluated first. Both of these operators, however, are of equal priority. Therefore, these operators are evaluated according to their left-to-right associativity, yielding

$$8\ +\ 5\ *\ 7\ \%\ 2\ *\ 4\ =$$
$$8\ +\ 35\ \%\ 2\ *\ 4\ =$$
$$8\ +\ 1\ *\ 4\ =$$
$$8\ +\ 4\ =\ 12$$

Table 2.6 lists both the precedence and associativity of the operators considered in this section.

Exercises 2.2

1. Listed here are algebraic expressions and incorrect C expressions corresponding to them. Find the errors and write corrected C expressions.

	Algebra	*C Expression*
a.	(2)(3) + (4)(5)	(2)(3) + (4)(5)
b.	$\dfrac{6 + 18}{2}$	6 + 18 / 2
c.	$\dfrac{4.5}{12.2 - 3.1}$	4.5 / 12.2 − 3.1
d.	4.6(3.0 + 14.9)	4.6(3.0 + 14.9)
e.	(12.1 + 18.9)(15.3 − 3.8)	(12.1 + 18.9)(15.3 − 3.8)

Note: Use C's rules of precedence and associativity to complete Exercises 2–6.

2. Assuming that amount = 1, $m = 50$, $n = 10$, and $p = 5$, evaluate the following expressions.
   a. $n / p + 3$
   b. $m / p + n - 10 *$ amount
   c. $m - 3 * n + 4 *$ amount
   d. amount / 5
   e. $18 / p$
   f. $18 \% p$
   g. $-p * n$
   h. $-m / 20$

i. $-m$ % 20   k. $m + n / p +$ amount

j. $(m + n) / (p +$ amount)

3. Repeat Exercise 2 assuming that amount = 1.0, m = 50.0, n = 10.0, and p = 5.0.

4. Determine the value of the following integer expressions:

a. $3 + 4 * 6$ e. $20 - 2 / 6 + 3$

b. $3 * 4 / 6 + 6$ f. $20 - 2 / (6 + 3)$

c. $2 * 3 / 12 * 8 / 4$ g. $(20 - 2) / 6 + 3$

d. $10 * (1 + 7 * 3)$ h. $(20 - 2) / (6 + 3)$

5. Determine the value of the following floating point expressions:

a. $3.0 + 4.0 * 6.0$ e. $20.0 - 2.0 / 6.0 + 3.0$

b. $3.0 * 4.0 / 6.0 + 6.0$ f. $20.0 - 2.0 / (6.0 + 3.0)$

c. $2.0 * 3.0 / 12.0 * 8.0 / 4.0$ g. $(20.0 - 2.0) / 6.0 + 3.0$

d. $10.0 * (1.0 + 7.0 * 3.0)$ h. $(20.0 - 2.0) / (6.0 + 3.0)$

6. Evaluate the following expressions and list the data type of the result. In evaluating the expressions be aware of the data types of all intermediate calculations.

a. $10.0 + 15 / 2 + 4.3$ f. $3 * 4.0 / 6 + 6$

b. $10.0 + 15$ % $2 + 4.3$ g. $20.0 - 2 / 6 + 3$

c. $10.0 + 15.0 / 2 + 4.3$ h. $10 + 17$ % $3 + 4$

d. $3.0 * 4 / 6 + 6$ i. $10 + 17$ % $3 + 4.$

e. $3.0 * 4$ % $6 + 6$ j. $10 + 17 / 3. + 4$

7. Although we have concentrated only on integer, floating point, and double precision numbers, C also allows characters and integers to be added or subtracted. This can be done because C always converts a character to an equivalent integer value whenever a character is used in an arithmetic expression. Thus, characters and integers can be freely mixed in such expressions. For example, if your computer uses the ASCII code, the expression 'a' + 1 is 'b', and 'z' - 1 is 'y'. Similarly, 'A' + 1 is 'B', and 'Z' - 1 is 'Y'. With this as background, determine the character results of the following expressions (assume that all characters are stored using the ASCII code).

a. 'm' - 5   e. 'b' - 'a'

b. 'm' + 5   f. 'g' - 'a' + 1

c. 'G' + 6   g. 'G' - 'A' + 1

d. 'G' - 6

8. a. The table in Appendix B lists the integer values corresponding to each letter stored using the ASCII code. Using this table, notice that the uppercase letters consist of contiguous codes starting with an integer value of 65 for the letter A and ending with 90 for the letter Z. Similarly, the lowercase letters begin with the integer value of 97 for the letter a and end with 122 for the letter z. With this as background, determine the character value of the expressions 'A' + 32 and 'Z' + 32.

b. Using Appendix B, determine the integer value of the expression 'a' - 'A'.

c. Using the results of Exercises 8a and 8b, determine the character value of the following expression, where *uppercase letter* can be any uppercase letter from A to Z:

```
uppercase letter + 'a' - 'A'
```

2.3   Displaying Numerical Results

In addition to displaying messages, the `printf()` function allows us to evaluate arithmetic expressions and display their results. To do this we must pass at least two items to `printf()`: a control string that tells the function where and in what form the result is to be displayed, and the value that we wish to be displayed. Recall that items passed to a function are always placed within the function name parentheses and are called arguments. Arguments must be separated from one another with commas, so that the function knows where one argument ends and the next begins. For example, in the statement

```
printf("The total of 6 and 15 is %d", 6 + 15);
```

the first argument is the message `The total of 6 and 15 is %d`, and the second argument is the expression `6 + 15`.

The first argument passed to `printf()` must always be a message. A message that also includes a *conversion control sequence,* such as `%d`, is termed a *control string.*[2] Conversion control sequences have a special meaning to the `printf()` function. They tell the function what type of value is to be displayed and where to display it. Conversion control sequences are also referred to as *conversion specifications* and *format specifiers.* A conversion control sequence always begins with a `%` symbol and ends with a conversion character (`c`, `d`, `f`, etc.). As we will see, additional formatting characters can be placed between the `%` symbol and the conversion character.

The percent sign `%` in a conversion control sequence tells `printf()` to print a value at the place in the message where the `%` is located. The `d`, placed immediately after the `%`, tells `printf()` that the value should be printed as an integer.

When `printf()` sees the conversion control sequence in its control string, it substitutes the value of the next argument in place of the conversion control sequence. Since this next argument is the expression 6 + 15, which has a value of 21, it is this value that is displayed. Thus, the statement

```
printf("The total of 6 and 15 is %d", 6 + 15);
```

causes the printout

```
The total of 6 and 15 is 21
```

Just as the `%d` conversion control sequence alerts `printf()` that an integer value is to be displayed, the conversion control sequence `%f` (The `f` stands for floating point) indicates that a number with a decimal point is to be displayed. For example, the statement

```
printf("The sum of %f and %f is %f.", 12.2, 15.754, 12.2 + 15.754);
```

---

[2] More formally, a control string is referred to as a *control specifier.* We will use the more descriptive term, control string, to emphasize that a string is being used.

causes the display

```
The sum of 12.200000 and 15.754000 is 27.954000.
```

As this display shows, the `%f` conversion control sequence causes `printf()` to display six digits to the right of the decimal place. If the number does not have six decimal digits, zeros are added to the number to fill the fractional part. If the number has more than six decimal digits, the fractional part is rounded to six decimal digits.

One caution should be mentioned here: The `printf()` function does *not* check the values it is given. If an integer conversion control sequence is used (`%d`, for example) but the value given the function is either a floating point or double precision number, the display will be machine dependent. Similarly, if a floating point conversion control sequence is used and the corresponding number is an integer, an unanticipated result will occur.

Character data is displayed using the `%c` conversion control sequence. For example, the statement

```
printf("The first letter of the alphabet is an %c.", 'a');
```

causes the display

```
The first letter of the alphabet is an a.
```

Program 2.1 illustrates using `printf()` to display the results of an expression within the statements of a complete program.

 Program 2.1

```
#include <stdio.h>
int main()
{
  printf("%f plus %f equals %f\n", 15.0, 2.0, 15.0 + 2.0);
  printf("%f minus %f equals %f\n", 15.0, 2.0, 15.0 - 2.0);
  printf("%f times %f equals %f\n", 15.0, 2.0, 15.0 * 2.0);
  printf("%f divided by %f equals %f", 15.0, 2.0, 15.0 / 2.0);

  return 0;
}
```

The output of Program 2.1 is

```
15.000000 plus 2.000000 equals 17.000000
15.000000 minus 2.000000 equals 13.000000
15.000000 times 2.000000 equals 30.000000
15.000000 divided by 2.000000 equals 7.500000
```

Each statement in Program 2.1 passes four arguments to the `printf()` function: one control string and three values. Within each control string are three `%f` conversion control sequences (one for each value that is to be displayed). The escape sequence `'\n'` within each `printf()` statement simply causes a new line to be started after each line is displayed.

Formatted Output

Besides displaying correct results, it is important that a program present its results attractively. Most programs are judged, in fact, on the perceived ease of data entry and the style and presentation of their output. For example, displaying a monetary result as 1.897000 is not in keeping with accepted report conventions. The display should be either $1.90 or $1.89, depending on whether rounding or truncation is used.

The format of numbers displayed by `printf()` can be controlled by *field width specifiers* included as part of each conversion control sequence. For example, the statement

```
printf("The sum of%3d and%4d is%5d.", 6, 15, 21);
```

causes the printout

```
The sum of  6 and  15 is   21.
```

The numbers 3, 4, and 5 in the control string are the field width specifiers. The 3 causes the first number to be printed in a total field width of three spaces, in this case two blank spaces followed by the number 6. The field width specifier for the second conversion control sequence, `%4d`, causes two blank spaces and the number 15 to be printed for a total field width of four spaces. The last field width specifier causes the 21 to be printed in a field of five spaces, which includes three blanks and the number 21. As illustrated, each integer is right-justified within the specified field.

Field width specifiers are useful in printing columns of numbers so that the numbers in each column align correctly. Program 2.2 illustrates how a column of integers would align in the absence of field width specifiers.

 Program 2.2

```c
#include <stdio.h>
int main()
{
  printf("\n%d", 6);
  printf("\n%d", 18);
  printf("\n%d", 124);
  printf("\n---");
  printf("\n%d", 6+18+124);

  return 0;
}
```

The output of Program 2.2 is

```
6
18
124
---
148
```

Since no field widths are given, the printf() function allocates enough space for each number as it is received. To force the numbers to align on the units digit requires a field width wide enough for the largest displayed number. For Program 2.2, a width of three suffices. The use of this field width is illustrated in Program 2.3.

 Program 2.3

```c
#include <stdio.h>
int main()
{
  printf("\n%3d", 6);
  printf("\n%3d", 18);
  printf("\n%3d", 124);
  printf("\n---");
  printf("\n%3d", 6+18+124);

  return 0;
}
```

The output of Program 2.3 is

```
  6
 18
124
---
148
```

Formatted floating point numbers require two field width specifiers. The first specifier determines the total display width, including the decimal point; the second determines how many digits are printed to the right of the decimal point. For example, the statement

```c
printf("|%10.3f|",25.67);
```

causes the printout

| 25.670|

The bar character, |, in the example is used to mark the beginning and end of the display field. The field width specifier 10.3 tells `printf()` to display the number in a total field of 10, which includes one decimal point and three digits to the right of the decimal point. Since the number contains only two digits to the right of the decimal point, the decimal part of the number is padded with a trailing zero.

For all numbers (integers, floating point, and double precision), `printf()` ignores the specified field width if the total field width is too small and allocates enough space for the integer part of the number to be printed. The fractional part of both floating point and double precision numbers is always displayed with the number of specified digits. If the fractional part contains fewer digits than specified, the number is padded with trailing zeros; if the fractional part contains more digits than called for in the specifier, the number is rounded to the indicated number of decimal places. Table 2.7 illustrates the effect of various field width specifiers.

Format Modifiers

In addition to the conversion control sequences (`%d`, `%f`, etc.) and the field width specifiers that may be used with them, C also provides a set of format modifiers that provide additional format control, such as left and right field justification. Format modifiers, if used, must always be placed immediately after the `%` symbol. The more commonly used format modifiers are discussed here.

Left Justification.   Numbers displayed using the `printf()` function are normally displayed right-justified with leading spaces inserted to fill the selected field width. To force

Table 2.7   Effect of field width specifiers

Specifier	Number	Display	Comments
`|%2d|`	3	`| 3|`	Number fits in field
`|%2d|`	43	`|43|`	Number fits in field
`|%2d|`	143	`|143|`	Field width ignored
`|%2d|`	2.3	Machine dependent	Floating point number in an integer field
`|%5.2f|`	2.366	`| 2.37|`	Field of 5 with 2 decimal digits
`|%5.2f|`	42.3	`|42.30|`	Number fits in field
`|%5.2f|`	142.364	`|142.36|`	Field width ignored but fractional specifier used
`|%5.2f|`	142	Machine dependent	Integer in a floating point field

the output to left-justify the display, a minus sign (−) format modifier can be used. For example, the statement

```
printf("|%-10d|",59);
```

causes the display

```
|59        |
```

Again, we have used the bar symbol, | to clearly identify the beginning and end of the designated display. Notice that the displayed number, 59, is printed at the beginning of the field (left-justification within the field) rather than at the end of the field, as would be obtained in the absence of the format modifier. Also notice that the format modifier within the `printf()` function is placed immediately after the % symbol.

Explicit Sign Display.   Normally, the sign of a number is only displayed for negative numbers. To force both positive and negative signs to be displayed, a plus (+) format modifier must be used. For example, the statement

```
printf("|%+10d|",59);
```

causes the display

```
|       +59|
```

In the absence of the plus sign immediately after the % symbol in the `printf()` function call, the output would not contain the sign of the positive number.

Format modifiers may be combined. For example, the conversion control sequence `%-+10d` would cause an integer number to both display its sign and be left-justified in a field width of 10 spaces. Because the order of the format modifiers is not critical, this conversion control sequence could have been written as `%+-10d`.

Other Number Bases[3]

When outputting integers, several display conversions are possible. As we have seen, the conversion control sequence `%d`, with or without a field width specifier, causes integers to be displayed in decimal (base 10) form. To have the value of an integer displayed in either a base 8 (octal) or base 16 (hexadecimal) form requires the use of the conversion control sequences `%o` and `%x`, respectively. Program 2.4 illustrates each of these conversion control sequences.

---

[3] This topic may be omitted on a first reading without loss of subject continuity.

Program 2.4

```
#include <stdio.h>
int main()    /* a program to illustrate output conversions */
{
  printf("The decimal (base 10) value of 15 is %d.", 15);
  printf("\nThe octal (base 8) value of 15 is %o.", 15);
  printf("\nThe hexadecimal (base 16) value of 15 is %x.", 15);

  return 0;
}
```

The output produced by Program 2.4 is

```
The decimal (base 10) value of 15 is 15.
The octal (base 8) value of 15 is 17.
The hexadecimal (base 16) value of 15 is f.
```

The display of integer values in one of the three possible number systems (decimal, octal, and hexadecimal) does not affect how the number is stored inside a computer. All numbers are stored using the computer's internal codes. The conversion control sequences used in printf() simply tell the function how to convert the internal code for output display purposes.

Besides displaying integers in octal or hexadecimal form, integer constants can also be written in a program in these forms. To designate an octal integer constant, the number must have a leading zero. The number 023, for example, is an octal number in C. Hexadecimal numbers are denoted using a leading 0x. The use of octal and hexadecimal integer constants is illustrated in Program 2.5.

 Program 2.5

```
#include <stdio.h>
int main()
{
  printf("The decimal value of 025 is %d.\n",025);
  printf("The decimal value of 0x37 is %d.\n",0x37);

  return 0;
}
```

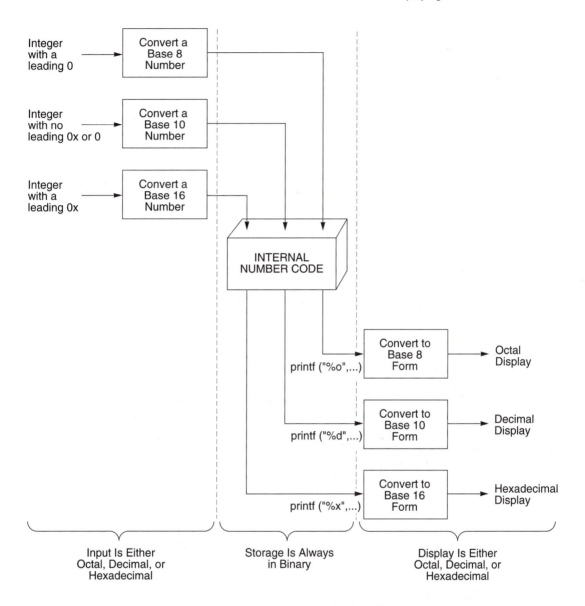

Figure 2.2   Input, storage, and display of integers

When Program 2.5 is run, the following output is obtained:

```
The decimal value of 025 is 21.
The decimal value of 0x37 is 55.
```

The relationship between the input, storage, and display of integers is illustrated in Figure 2.2.

To force both octal and hexadecimal numbers to be printed with a leading 0 and 0x, respectively, the # format modifier must be used. For example, the statement

```
printf("The octal value of decimal 21 is %#o",21);
```

produces the display

```
The octal value of decimal 21 is 025
```

Without the inclusion of the # format modifier within the conversion control sequence %o, the displayed octal value would be 25, with no leading 0. Similarly, the statement

```
printf("The hexadecimal value of decimal 55 is %#x",55);
```

produces the display

```
The hexadecimal value of decimal 55 is 0x37
```

Without the inclusion of the # format modifier within the conversion control sequence %x, the displayed hexadecimal value would be 37, with no leading 0x.

The same display conversions available for integers can also be used to display characters. In addition to the %c conversion control sequence, the %d conversion control sequence displays the value of the internal character code as a decimal number, and the %o and %x conversion control sequences cause the character code to be displayed in octal and hexadecimal form, respectively. These display conversions are illustrated in Program 2.6.

 Program 2.6

```
#include <stdio.h>
int main()
{
  printf("The decimal value of the letter %c is %d.", 'a', 'a');
  printf("\nThe octal value of the letter %c is %o.", 'a', 'a');
  printf("\nThe hex value of the letter %c is %x.", 'a', 'a');

  return 0;
}
```

When Program 2.6 is run, the following output is produced:

```
The decimal value of the letter a is 97.
The octal value of the letter a is 141.
The hex value of the letter a is 61.
```

The display conversions for character data are illustrated in Figure 2.3.

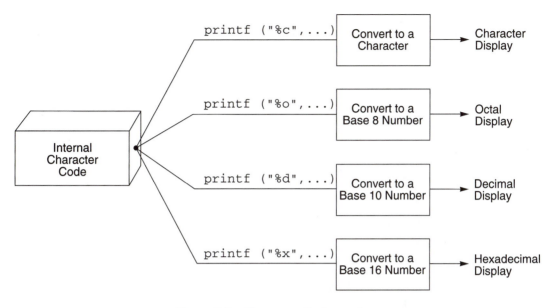

Figure 2.3 Character display options

Exercises 2.3

1. Determine the output of the following program:

```
#include <stdio.h>
int main()    /* a program illustrating integer truncation */
{

  printf("answer1 is the integer %d", 27/5);
  printf("\nanswer2 is the integer $d", 16/6)

  return 0;
}
```

2. Determine the output of the following program:

```
#include <stdio.h>
int main()    /* a program illustrating the % operator */
{

  printf("The remainder of 9 divided by 4 is %d", 9 % 4);
  printf("\nThe remainder of 17 divided by 3 is %d", 17 % 3);

  return 0;
}
```

3. Write a C program that displays the results of the expressions 3.0 * 5.0, 7.1 * 8.3 – 2.2, and 3.2 / (6.1 * 5). Calculate the value of these expressions manually to verify that the displayed values are correct.

4. Write a C program that displays the results of the expressions 15 / 4, 15 % 4, and 5 * 3 – (6 * 4). Calculate the value of these expressions manually to verify that the display produced by your program is correct.

5. Determine the errors in each of the following statements:
   a. `printf("%d," 15)`
   b. `printf("%f", 33);`
   c. `printf("%5d", 526.768);`
   d. `printf("a b c", 26, 15, 18);`
   e. `printf("%3.6f", 47);`
   f. `printf("%3.6", 526.768);`
   g. `printf(526.768, 33, "%f %d");`

6. Determine and write out the display produced by the following statements:
   a. `printf("|%d|",5);`
   b. `printf("|%4d|",5);`
   c. `printf("|%4d|",56829);`
   d. `printf("|%5.2f|",5.26);`
   e. `printf("|%5.2f|",5.267);`
   f. `printf("|%5.2f|",53,264);`
   g. `printf("|%5.2f|",534.264);`
   h. `printf("|%5.2f|",534.);`

7. Write out the display produced by the following statements:
   a. `printf("The number is %6.2f\n",26.27);`
      `printf("The number is %6.2f\n",682.3);`
      `printf("The number is %6.2f\n",1.968);`
   b. `printf("$%6.2f\n",26.27);`
      `printf(" %6.2f\n",682.3);`
      `printf(" %6.2f\n",1.968);`
      `printf("--------\n");`
      `printf("$%6.2f\n", 26.27 + 682.3 + 1.968);`
   c. `printf("$%5.2f\n",26.27);`
      `printf(" %5.2f\n",682.3);`
      `printf(" %5.2f\n",1.968);`
      `printf("--------\n");`
      `printf("$%5.2f\n", 26.27 + 682.3 + 1.968);`
   d. `printf("%5.2f\n",34.164);`
      `printf("%5.2f\n",10.003);`
      `printf("-----\n");`
      `printf("%5.2f\n", 34.164 + 10.003);`

8. a. Rewrite the `printf()` function calls in the following program

```
#include <stdio.h>
int main()
{
```

```
        printf("The sales tax is %f", .05 * 36);
        printf("The total bill is %f", 37.80);

        return 0;
}
```

to produce the display:

```
The sales tax is $ 1.80
The total bill is $37.80
```

b. Run the program written for Exercise 8a to verify the output display.

9. The following table lists the correspondence between the decimal numbers 1 through 15 and their octal and hexadecimal representation.

Decimal:	1	2	3	4	5	6	7	8	9	10	11	12	13	14	15
Octal:	1	2	3	4	5	6	7	10	11	12	13	14	15	16	17
Hexadecimal:	1	2	3	4	5	6	7	8	9	A	B	C	D	E	F

Using the above table, determine the output of the following program.

```
#include <stdio.h>
int main()
{

    printf("The value of 14 in octal is %o.\n",14);
    printf("The value of 14 in hexadecimal is %x.\n",14);
    printf("The value of 0xA in decimal is %d.\n",0xA);
    printf("The value of 0xA in octal is %o.\n",0xA);

    return 0;
}
```

10. a. Write a C program that uses the %d conversion control sequence to display the integer values of the lowercase letters *a, m,* and *n,* respectively. Do the displayed values for these letters match the values listed in Appendix B?

b. Expand the program written for Exercise 10a to display the integer value corresponding to the internal computer code for a newline escape sequence.

2.4 Variables and Declarations

All data used in a computer program must be stored and retrieved from the computer's memory. Consider the four bytes of memory storage illustrated in Figure 2.4. For purposes of illustration assume that the two bytes with addresses 1321 and 1322 are used to store one integer number and that the bytes with addresses 2649 and 2650 are used to store a second integer.

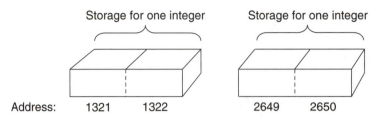

Figure 2.4   Enough storage for two integers

Before high-level languages such as C existed, actual memory addresses were used to store and retrieve data. For example, storing the number 62 in the first set of bytes illustrated in Figure 2.4 and 17 in the next set of bytes required instructions equivalent to

put a 62 in location 1321
put a 17 in location 2649

Notice that only the address of the first byte in each set of locations was given. The computer needed only this first address to locate the starting point for storage or retrieval. Adding the two numbers just stored and saving the result in another set of memory locations, for example at location 45, required a statement comparable to

add the contents of location 1321
to the contents of location 2649
and store the result into location 45

Clearly this method of storage and retrieval was cumbersome. In high-level languages such as C, symbolic names are used in place of actual memory addresses. These symbolic names are called *variables*. Variables are simply names given by programmers to computer storage locations. The term "variable" is used because the value stored in the variable can change, or vary. For each name that the programmer uses, the computer keeps track of the memory addresses corresponding to that name. Naming a variable is equivalent to putting a name on the door of a hotel room and referring to the room (or suite of rooms) by this name, such as the Blue Room, rather than using the actual room number.

The selection of variable names is left to the programmer, as long as the following rules are observed:

1. The variable name must begin with a letter or underscore (_) and may contain only letters, underscores, or digits. It cannot contain any blanks, commas, or special symbols, such as ( ) & , $ # . ! \ ? . Use capital letters to separate names consisting of multiple words.
2. A variable name cannot be a keyword (see Table 1.2).
3. A variable name can have no more than 31 characters (this is compiler dependent).

These rules are identical to those for selecting function names. As with function names, variable names should be mnemonics that give some indication of purpose. For

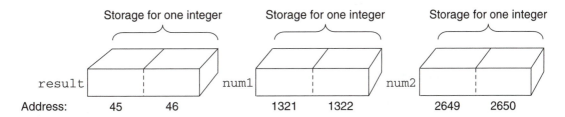

Figure 2.5   Giving storage locations names

example, a variable named total probably stores a value that is the total of some other values. As with function names, variable names are conventionally typed in lowercase letters. This again is traditional in C, although not required.

Now inspect Figure 2.5. Assume that the two bytes starting at address 1321 are given the variable name num1, that the two bytes starting at address 2649 are given the variable name num2, and that the two bytes starting at address 45 have been given the name result.

Using these variable names, the operations of storing 62 in location 1321, storing 17 in location 2649, and adding the contents of these two locations is accomplished by the C statements

```
num1 = 62;
num2 = 17;
result = num1 + num2;
```

These are called *assignment statements* because they tell the computer to assign (store) a value into a variable. Assignment statements always have an equal (=) sign and one variable name immediately to the left of this sign. The value on the right of the equal sign is determined first, and this value is assigned to the variable on the left of the equal sign. The blank spaces in the assignment statements are inserted for readability. We will have much more to say about assignment statements in the next chapter, but for now we can use them to store values in variables.

A variable name is useful because it frees the programmer from concern over where data are physically stored inside the computer. We simply use the variable names and let the computer worry about where in memory the data are actually stored. Before storing values into variables, however, C requires that we clearly define the type of data to be stored in each variable. We must tell the computer in advance the names of the variables used for characters, the names used for integers, and the names used to store the other data types supported by C. Then, when the variable name is used, the computer will know how many bytes of storage to access.

Declaration Statements

Naming and defining the data type that can be stored in each variable is accomplished by using *declaration statements*. Declaration statements within a function appear immediately after the opening brace of a function, and like all C statements must end with a semicolon. A C function containing declaration statements has the general form

Programming Note

Atomic Data

The variables we have declared have all been used to store atomic data values. An *atomic data value* is a value that is considered a complete entity in itself and is not decomposable into a smaller data type supported by the language. For example, although an integer can be decomposed into individual digits, C does not have a numerical digit data type. Rather, each integer is regarded as a complete value in itself and, as such, is considered atomic data. Similarly, since the integer data type only supports atomic data values, it is said to be an *atomic data type*. As you might expect, floats and chars are atomic data types also.

```
function name()
{
  declaration statements;

  other statements;
}
```

Declaration statements, in their simplest form, provide a data type and variable name, and have the syntax

```
dataType variableName;
```

where `dataType` designates a valid C data type and `variableName` is a user-selected variable name. For example, variables used to hold integer values are declared using the keyword `int` to specify the data type and have the form:

```
int variableName;
```

Thus, the declaration statement

```
int total;
```

declares `total` as the name of a variable capable of storing an integer value.

Variables used to hold floating point values are declared using the reserved word `float`, while variables that will be used to hold double precision values are declared using the reserved word `double`. For example, the statement

```
float firstnum;
```

declares `firstnum` as a variable that can be used to store a floating point number. Similarly, the statement

```
double secnum;
```

declares that the variable will be used to store a double precision number.

Program 2.7 illustrates the declaration and use of four floating point variables. The `printf()` function is then used to display the contents of one of these variables.

 Program 2.7

```c
#include <stdio.h>
int main()
{
  float grade1;   /* declare grade1 as a float variable */
  float grade2;   /* declare grade2 as a float variable */
  float total;    /* declare total as a float variable */
  float average;  /* declare average as a float variable */

  grade1 = 85.5;
  grade2 = 97.0;
  total = grade1 + grade2;
  average = total/2.0;   /* divide the total by 2.0 */

  printf("The average grade is %f\n",average);

  return 0;
}
```

The placement of the declaration statements in Program 2.7 is straightforward, although we will shortly see that the four individual declarations can be combined into a single declaration. When Program 2.7 is run, the following output is displayed:

```
The average grade is 91.250000
```

Two comments regarding the `printf()` function call made in Program 2.7 should be mentioned here. First, if a variable name is one of the arguments passed to a function, as it is to `printf()` in Program 2.7, the function receives only a copy of the value stored in the variable. It does not receive the variable's name. When the program sees a variable name in the function parentheses, it first goes to the variable and retrieves the value stored. This value is then passed to the function. Thus, when a variable is included in the `printf()` argument list, `printf()` receives the value stored in the variable and then displays this value. Internally, `printf()` does not know where the value it receives came from or the variable name under which the value was stored.

Although this procedure for passing data into a function may seem surprising, it is really a safety procedure for ensuring that a called function does not have access to the original variable. This guarantees that the called function cannot inadvertently change data in a variable declared outside itself. We will have more to say about this in Chapter 6, when we examine and begin writing our own functions.

The second comment concerns the `%f` conversion control sequence in Program 2.7. Although this conversion control sequence works for both floating point and double precision numbers, the conversion control sequence `%lf` may also be used for displaying the values of double precision variables. The letter `l` indicates that the number is a long floating point number, which is what a double precision number really is. Omitting the `l` conversion character has no effect on the `printf()` function when double precision values are displayed. As we shall see, however, it is essential in entering double precision values when the input function `scanf()` is used. This function is presented in the next chapter.

Just as integer, floating point, and double precision variables must be declared before they can be used, a variable used to store a character must also be declared. Character variables are declared using the reserved word `char`. For example, the declaration

```
char ch;
```

declares `ch` to be a character variable. Program 2.8 illustrates this declaration and the use of `printf()` to display the value stored in a character variable.

 Program 2.8

```
#include <stdio.h>
int main()
{
   char ch;      /* this declares a character variable */
   ch = 'a';     /* store the letter a into ch */
   printf("\nThe character stored in ch is %c.", ch);
   ch = 'm';     /* now store the letter m into ch */
   printf("\nThe character now stored in ch is %c.", ch);

   return 0;
}
```

When Program 2.8 is run, the output produced is

```
The character stored in ch is a.
The character now stored in ch is m.
```

Notice in Program 2.8 that the first letter stored in the variable `ch` is a and the second letter stored in `ch` is m. Because a variable can store only one value at a time, the assignment of m to the variable automatically causes the a to be overwritten.

Variables having the same data type can always be grouped together and declared using a single declaration statement. For example, the four separate declarations used in Program 2.7,

```
float grade1;
float grade2;
float total;
float average;
```

can be replaced by the single declaration statement

```
float grade1, grade2, total, average;
```

Similarly, the two character declarations,

```
char ch;
char key;
```

can be replaced with the single declaration statement

```
char ch, key;
```

Declaring multiple variables in a single declaration requires that the data type of the variables be given only once, that all the variables be separated by commas, and that only one semicolon be used to terminate the declaration. The space after each comma is inserted for readability and is not required.

Declaration statements can also be used to store an initial value into declared variables. For example, the declaration statement

```
int num1 = 15;
```

both declares the variable `num1` as an integer variable and sets the value of 15 into the variable. The first time a value is stored in a variable it is said to be *initialized*. Thus, in this example it is correct to say that `num1` has been initialized to 15. Similarly, the declaration statement

```
float grade1 = 87.0, grade2 = 93.5, total;
```

declares three floating point variables and initializes two of them. Constants, expressions using only constants (such as 87.0 + 12.2), and expressions using constants and previously initialized variables can all be used as initializers. For example, with initialization Program 2.8 would appear as:

```
#include <stdio.h>
int main()
{
  char ch = 'a'; /* declaration and initialization */

  printf("\nThe character stored in ch is %c.", ch);
  ch = 'm';       /* now store the letter m into ch */
  printf("\nThe character now stored in ch is %c.", ch);

  return 0;
}
```

Declaration Statements as Definition Statements

The declaration statements we have introduced have performed both software and hardware tasks. From a software perspective, declaration statements always provide a convenient, up-front list of all variables and their data types. In this software role, variable declarations also eliminate an otherwise common and troublesome error caused by the misspelling of a variable's name within a program. For example, assume that a variable named distance is declared and initialized using the statement

```
int distance = 26;
```

Now assume that this variable is inadvertently misspelled in the statement

```
mpg = distnce / gallons;
```

In languages that do not require variable declarations, the program would consider distnce as a new variable and either assign an initial value of zero to the variable or use whatever value happened to be in the variable's storage area. In either case, a value would be calculated and assigned to mpg, and finding the error or even knowing that an error occurred could be extremely troublesome. Such errors are impossible in C, because the compiler will flag distnce as an undeclared variable. The compiler cannot, of course, detect when one declared variable is typed in place of another declared variable.

In addition to their software role, declaration statements can also perform a distinct hardware task. Since each data type has its own storage requirements, the compiler can allocate sufficient storage for a variable only after knowing the variable's data type. Because variable declarations provide this information, they can be used to force the compiler to reserve sufficient physical memory storage for each variable. Declaration statements used for this hardware purpose are also called *definition statements,* because they define or tell the compiler how much memory is needed for data storage.

All the declaration statements we have encountered so far have also been definition statements. Later, we will see declaration statements that do not cause any new storage to be allocated and are used simply to declare or alert the program to the data types of previously created and existing variables.

Figure 2.6 illustrates the series of operations set in motion by declaration statements that also perform a definition role. The figure shows that definition statements (or, if you

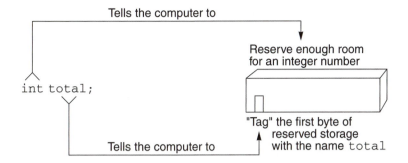

Figure 2.6a Defining the integer variable named `total`

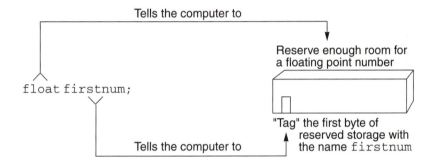

Figure 2.6b Defining the floating point variable named `firstnum`

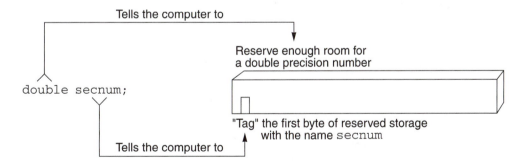

Figure 2.6c Defining the double precision variable named `secnum`

prefer, declaration statements that also cause memory to be allocated) "tag" the first byte of each set of reserved bytes with a name. This name is, of course, the variable's name and is used by the computer to correctly locate the starting byte of each variable's reserved memory area.

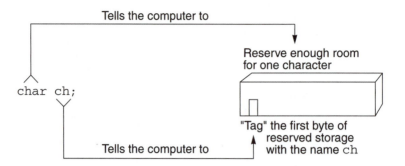

Figure 2.6d   Defining the character variable named ch

After a variable has been declared within a program, it is typically used by a programmer to refer to the contents of the variable (that is, the variable's value). Where in memory this value is stored is generally of little concern to the programmer. The computer, however, must know where each value is stored and be able to locate each variable. In this task, the computer uses the variable name to locate the first byte of storage previously allocated to the variable. Knowing the variable's data type allows the computer to store or retrieve the correct number of bytes.

Exercises 2.4

1. State whether the following variable names are valid or invalid. If they are invalid, state the reason.

```
proda       c1234       abcd        c3          12345
newbal      while       $total      new bal     a1b2c3d4
9ab6        sum.of      average     grade1      finGrad
```

2. State whether the following variable names are valid or invalid. If they are invalid, state the reason. Also indicate which of the valid variable names should not be used because they convey no information about the variable.

```
salestax    a243        r2d2        firstNum    ccA1
harry       sue         c3p0        average     sum
maximum     okay        a           awesome     goforit
3sum        for         tot.a1      c$five      netpay
```

3. a. Write a declaration statement to declare that the variable count will be used to store an integer.
   b. Write a declaration statement to declare that the variable grade will be used to store a floating point number.
   c. Write a declaration statement to declare that the variable yield will be used to store a double precision number.
   d. Write a declaration statement to declare that the variable initial will be used to store a character.

4. Write declaration statements for the following variables:
   a. num1, num2, and num3 used to store integer numbers
   b. grade1, grade2, grade3, and grade4 used to store floating point numbers
   c. tempa, tempb, and tempc used to store double precision numbers
   d. ch, let1, let2, let3, and let4 used to store character types

5. Write declaration statements for the following variables:
   a. firstnum and secnum used to store integers
   b. price, yield, and coupon used to store floating point numbers
   c. maturity used to store a double precision number

6. Rewrite each of these declaration statements as three individual declarations:
   a. int month, day = 30, year;
   b. double hours, rate, otime = 15.62;
   c. float price, amount, taxes;
   d. char in_key, ch, choice = 'f';

7. a. Determine what each statement causes to happen in the following program:

```
#include <stdio.h>
int main()
{
  int num1;
  int num2;
  int total;

  num1 = 25;
  num2 = 30;
  total = num1 + num2;
  printf("The total of %d and %d is %d\n.",num1,num2,total);

  return 0;
}
```

   b. What is the output that will be printed when the program listed in Exercise 7a is run?

8. Write a C program that stores the sum of the integer numbers 12 and 33 in a variable named sum. Have your program display the value stored in sum.

9. Write a C program that stores the integer value 16 in the variable length and the integer value 18 in the variable width. Have your program calculate the value assigned to the variable perimeter, using the assignment statement

```
perimeter = 2 * length + 2 * width;
```

and print out the value stored in the variable perimeter. Make sure to declare all the variables as integers at the beginning of the main() function.

10. Write a C program that stores the integer value 16 in the variable num1 and the integer value 18 in the variable num2. (Make sure to declare the variables as integers.) Have your program calculate the total of these numbers and their average. The total should be stored in the variable named total and the average in the variable named average. (Use the statement average = total/2.0; to calculate the average.) Use the printf() function to display the total and average.

11. Repeat Exercise 10, but store the integer value 15 in num1 instead of 16. With a pencil, write down the average of num1 and num2. What do you think your program will store in the integer variable that you used for the average of these two numbers? How can you ensure that the correct answer will be printed for the average?

12. Write a C program that stores the number 105.62 in the variable firstnum, 89.352 in the variable secnum, and 98.67 in the variable thirdnum. (Make sure to declare the variables first as either float or double.) Have your program calculate the total of the three numbers and their average. The total should be stored in the variable total and the average in the variable average. (Use the statement average = total /3.0; to calculate the average.) Use the printf() function to display the total and average.

13. Every variable has at least three items associated with it. What are these items?

14. a. A statement used to clarify the relationship between squares and rectangles is "All squares are rectangles but not all rectangles are squares." Write a similar statement that describes the relationship between definition and declaration statements.

b. Why must definition statements be placed before any other C statements using the defined variable?

Note for Exercises 15 through 17: Assume that a character requires one byte of storage, an integer two bytes, a floating point number four bytes, a double precision number eight bytes, and that variables are assigned storage in the order they are declared.

15. a. Using Figure 2.7 and assuming that the variable name rate is assigned to the byte having memory address 159, determine the addresses corresponding to each variable declared in the following statements. Also fill in the appropriate bytes with the initialization data included in the declaration statements (use letters for the characters, not the computer codes that would actually be stored).

```
float rate;
char ch1 = 'w', ch2 = 'o', ch3 = 'w', ch4 = '!';
double taxes;
int num, count = 0;
```

b. Repeat Exercise 15a, but substitute the actual byte patterns that a computer using the ASCII code would use to store the characters in the variables ch1, ch2, ch3, and ch4. (*Hint:* Use Table 2.2.)

16. a. Using Figure 2.7 and assuming that the variable named cn1 is assigned to the byte at memory address 159, determine the addresses corresponding to each variable declared in the following statements. Also fill in the appropriate bytes with the initialization data included in the declaration statements (use letters for the characters, not the computer codes that would actually be stored).

```
char cn1 = 'a', cn2 = ' ', cn3 = 'b', cn4 = 'u', cn5 = 'n';
char cn6 = 'c', cn7 = 'h', key = '\\', sch = '\'', inc = 'o';
char incl = 'f';
```

b. Repeat Exercise 16a, but substitute the actual byte patterns that a computer using the ASCII code would use to store the characters in each of the declared variables. (*Hint:* Use Table 2.2.)

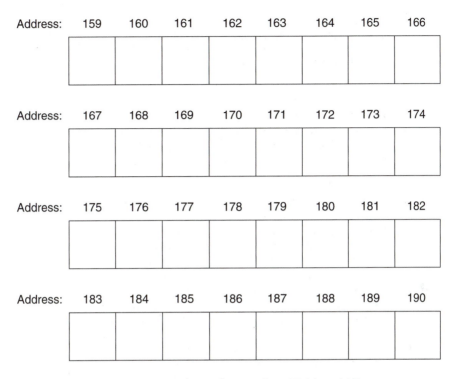

Figure 2.7   Memory bytes for exercises 15, 16, and 17

17. Using Figure 2.7 and assuming that the variable name `miles` is assigned to the byte at memory address 159, determine the addresses corresponding to each variable declared in the following statements:

```
float miles;
int count, num;
double dist, temp;
```

2.5 Integer Qualifiers

Integer numbers are generally used in programs as counters to keep track of the number of times that something has occurred. For most applications, the counts needed are less than 32,767, which is the maximum integer value that can be stored in two bytes. Since most compilers allocate at least two bytes for integers, there is usually no problem.

Sometimes, however, larger integer numbers are needed. In financial applications, for example, dates such as 7/12/2002 are typically converted to the number of days starting from a base date, such as 1/1/1900. This conversion makes it possible to store and sort dates using a single number for each date. Unfortunately, for dates after 1987, this number of days is larger than the maximum value of 32,767 allowed when only two bytes are allocated for each integer variable. For financial programs that are run on computers allocating only two bytes per integer, the limitation on the maximum integer value must be overcome.

To accommodate real application requirements such as this, C provides *long integer, short integer,* and *unsigned integer* data types. These three additional integer data types are obtained by adding the *qualifiers* long, short, or unsigned, respectively, to the normal integer declaration statements. For example, the declaration statement

```
long int days;
```

declares the variable days to be a long integer. The word int in a long integer declaration statement is optional, so the previous declaration statement can also be written as long days;. The amount of storage allocated for a long integer depends on the compiler being used. Although you would expect that a long integer variable would be allocated more space than a standard integer, this may not be the case, especially for compilers that reserve more than two bytes for normal integer variables. About all that can be said is that long integers will be provided no less space than regular integers. The actual amount of storage allocated by your compiler should be checked using the sizeof operator described at the end of this section.

Once a variable is declared as a long integer, integer values may be assigned as usual for standard integers, or an optional letter *L* (either uppercase or lowercase, with no space between the number and letter) may be appended to the integer. For example, the declaration statement

```
long days = 38276L;
```

declares days to be of type long integer and assigns the long integer constant 38276 to the variable days.

Printing long integer values using the printf() function requires the use of a lowercase *l*. Thus, to display a long integer, the conversion control sequence %ld must be used.

In addition to the long qualifier, C also provides for a short qualifier. Although you would expect a short integer to conserve computer storage by reserving fewer bytes than used for a standard integer, this is not always the case. Some compilers use the same amount of storage for both integers and short integers. Again, the amount of memory space allocated for a short integer data type depends on your compiler and can be checked using the sizeof operator (described at the end of this section). As with long integers, short integers may be declared using the terms short or short int in a declaration statement.

Once a variable is declared as a short integer, values are assigned as normally done with integers. Printing short integers using the printf() function requires no modifications to any of the conversion control sequences used for integers.

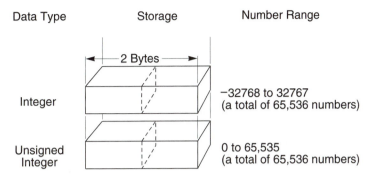

Figure 2.8   Unsigned integers can only be positive numbers

The final integer data type is the unsigned integer. This data type is obtained by prefixing the reserved word int with the qualifier unsigned. For example, the declaration statement

```
unsigned int days;
```

declares the variable days to be of type unsigned integer.

The unsigned integer data type is used to store positive integers only and effectively doubles the positive value that can be stored without increasing the number of bytes allocated to an integer. This is achieved by treating all unsigned integers as positive numbers, as illustrated in Figure 2.8.

Printing unsigned integers using the printf() function requires the use of the %u conversion control sequence in place of the %d normally used for integers.

Determining Storage Size

C provides an operator to determine how much storage your compiler allocates for each data type. The sizeof() operator returns the number of bytes of the object or data type included in the parentheses. Unlike a function, which is made up of C statements, the sizeof() operator is an integral part of the C language itself. Examples of the sizeof() operator are

```
sizeof(num1)    sizeof(int)    sizeof(char)
```

If the item in parentheses is a variable, as in the example sizeof(num1), sizeof() returns the number of bytes of storage that the compiler has reserved for the variable. If the item in parentheses is a data type, such as int or char, sizeof() will return the number of bytes of storage that the compiler allocates for the given data type. With either approach, we can use sizeof() to determine the amount of storage used by different data types. Consider Program 2.9.

Program 2.9

```c
#include <stdio.h>
int main()
{
   char ch;
   int num1;

   printf("Bytes of storage used by a character: %d",sizeof(ch));
   printf("\nBytes of storage used by an integer: %d",sizeof(num1));

   return 0;
}
```

Program 2.9 declares that the variable ch is used to store a character and that the variable num1 is used to store an integer. From our discussion in the last section, we know that each of these declaration statements is also a definition statement. As such, the first declaration statement instructs the computer to reserve enough storage for a character, and the second declaration statement instructs the computer to reserve enough storage for an integer. The sizeof() operator is then used to tell us how much room the compiler really set aside for these two variables. The sizeof() operator is used here as an argument to the printf() function. When Program 2.9 is run on an IBM personal computer, the following output is obtained:

```
Bytes of storage used by a character: 1
Bytes of storage used by an integer: 2
```

Note that the number of bytes given by the sizeof() operator is in terms of the storage reserved for one character. In ANSI C the specified storage allocation is one byte per character, so the value returned by sizeof() is a true byte count.

Exercises 2.5

1. a. Run Program 2.9 to determine how many bytes your computer uses to store character and integer data types.
   b. Expand Program 2.9 to determine how many bytes your computer uses for short integers, long integers, and unsigned integers.

2. After running the program written for Exercise 1, use Table 2.1 (see Section 2.1) to determine the maximum and minimum numbers that can be stored in integer, short integer, and long integer variables for your computer.

3. Program 2.9 did not actually store any values into the variables ch and num1. Why was this not necessary?

4. a. Expand Program 2.9 to determine how many bytes your computer uses to store floating point and double precision numbers.

b. Although there is no long float data class, double precision numbers are sometimes considered the equivalent long form for floating point numbers. Why is this so? Does the output of the program written for Exercise 4a support this statement?

2.6 Common Programming Errors

The common programming errors associated with the material presented in this chapter are

1. Forgetting to declare all the variables used in a program. This error is detected by the compiler, and an error message is generated for all undeclared variables.

2. Storing an incorrect data type in a declared variable. This error is not detected by the compiler. The assigned value is converted to the data type of the variable it is assigned to.

3. Using a variable in an expression before a value has been assigned to the variable. Whatever value happens to be in the variable will be used when the expression is evaluated, and the result will be meaningless.

4. Dividing integer values incorrectly. This error is usually disguised within a larger expression and can be very troublesome to detect. For example, the expression

$$3.425 + 2/3 + 7.9$$

yields the same result as the expression

$$3.425 + 7.9$$

because the integer division of 2/3 is 0.

5. Mixing data types in the same expression without clearly understanding the effect produced. Since C allows expressions with "mixed" data types, it is important to be clear about the order of evaluation and the data type of all intermediate calculations. As a general rule it is better never to mix data types in an expression unless a specific effect is desired.

6. Not including the correct conversion control sequence in `printf()` function calls for the data types of the remaining arguments.

7. Not closing the control string in `printf()` with a double quote symbol followed by a comma when additional arguments are passed to `printf()`.

8. Forgetting to separate all arguments passed to `printf()` with commas.

2.7 Chapter Summary

1. The four basic types of data recognized by C are integer, floating point, double precision, and character. Compilers typically assign different amounts of memory to store each of these types of data.

2. The `printf()` function can be used to display all of C's data types. The conversion control sequence for displaying integer, floating point, double precision, and character values are `%d`, `%f`, `%lf`, and `%c`, respectively. The `%f` conversion control sequence can be used in place of the `%lf` sequence for double precision values. Additionally, field width specifiers can be used to format displays.

3. Every variable in a C program must be declared as to the type of value it can store, and a variable can only be used after it is declared. Additionally, variables of the same type may be declared using a single declaration statement. Variable declaration statements have the general syntax:

   dataType variableName(s);

   Additionally, variables may be initialized when they are declared.

4. A simple C program containing declaration statements has the form:

   ```
   #include <stdio.h>
   int main()
   {
      declaration statements;

      other statements;

      return 0;
   }
   ```

5. Declaration statements always play the software role of informing the compiler of a function's valid variable names. When a variable declaration causes the computer to set aside memory locations for the variable, the declaration statement is also a definition statement. (All the declarations we have encountered so far have also been definition statements.)

6. The `sizeof` operator can be used to determine the amount of storage reserved for variables.

2.8   Chapter Supplement: Bits, Bytes, Addresses, and Number Codes

It would be convenient if computers stored numbers and letters the way that people do. The number 126, for example, would then be stored as 126, and the letter *A* stored as the letter *A*. Unfortunately, due to the physical components used in building a computer, this is not the case.

The smallest and most basic storage unit in a computer is called a *bit*. Physically, a bit is really a switch that can be either open or closed. By convention, the open and closed positions of each switch are represented as a 0 and a 1, respectively.

A single bit can represent only the values 0 and 1; by itself it has limited usefulness. All computers, therefore, group a set number of bits together. The grouping of eight bits to form a larger unit is an almost universal computer standard. Such groups are commonly referred to as *bytes*. A single byte consisting of eight bits, where each bit can be 0 or 1, can represent 256 different bit patterns. These consist of the pattern 00000000 (all eight switches open) to the pattern 11111111 (all eight switches closed), and all possible combinations of 0s and 1s in between. Each of these patterns can be used to represent either a letter of the alphabet, other single characters, such as a dollar sign or comma, a single digit, or numbers containing more than one digit. The patterns of 0s and 1s used to represent letters, single digits, and other single characters are called *character codes* (one such code, called the ASCII code, is presented in Section 2.1). The patterns used to store numbers are called *number codes* (one such code, called *two's complement,* is presented at the end of this section).

Words and Addresses

One or more bytes may be grouped into larger units called *words*. The advantage of combining bytes into words is that multiple bytes are stored or retrieved by the computer for each word access. For example, retrieving a word consisting of four bytes results in more information than that obtained by retrieving a word consisting of a single byte. Such a retrieval is also considerably faster than individual retrievals of four single bytes. The increase in speed, however, is achieved by an increase in the cost and complexity of the computer.

Early personal computers, such as the Apple IIe and Commodore machines, internally stored and transmitted words consisting of single bytes. The first IBM PCs used word sizes of two bytes, and current Pentium-based PCs store and process words consisting of four bytes each.

The arrangement of words in a computer's memory can be compared to the arrangement of suites in a very large hotel, where each suite is made up of rooms of the same size. Just as each suite has a unique room number to locate and identify it, each word has a unique numeric address. In computers that allow each byte to be individually accessed, each byte has its own address. Like room numbers, word and byte addresses are always positive, whole numbers that are used for location and identification purposes. Also, like

(-2^7)	(2^6)	(2^5)	(2^4)	(2^3)	(2^2)	(2^1)	(2^0)
-128	64	32	16	8	4	2	1

Figure 2.9   An eight-bit value box for two's complement conversion

hotel rooms with connecting doors for forming larger suites, words can be combined to form larger units to accommodate different-sized data types.

Two's Complement Numbers

The most common integer code using bit patterns is called the *two's complement* representation. Using this code, the integer equivalent of any bit pattern, such as 10001101, is easy to determine and can be found for either positive or negative numbers with no change in the conversion method. For convenience we will assume words consisting of a single byte, although the procedure also applies to larger-sized words.

The easiest way to determine the integer represented by a bit pattern is to first construct a simple device called a *value box*. Figure 2.9 illustrates such a box for a single byte.

Mathematically, each value in the box illustrated in Figure 2.9 represents an increasing power of two. Since two's complement numbers must be capable of representing both positive and negative integers, the leftmost position, in addition to having the largest absolute magnitude, also has a negative sign.

Conversion of any binary number, for example 10001101, simply requires inserting the bit pattern in the value box and adding the values having ones under them. Thus, as illustrated in Figure 2.10, the bit pattern 10001101 represents the integer number -115.

Reviewing the value box shows that any binary number with a leading 1 represents a negative number, and any bit pattern with a leading 0 represents a positive number. The value box can also be used in reverse, to convert a base 10 integer number into its equivalent binary bit pattern. Some conversions, in fact, can be made by inspection. For example, the base 10 number -125 is obtained by adding 3 to -128. Thus, the binary representation of -125 is 10000011, which equals $-128 + 2 + 1$. Similarly, the two's complement representation of the number 40 is 00101000, which is 32 plus 8.

Although the value box conversion method is deceptively simple, the method is directly related to the mathematical basis of two's complement binary numbers. The original name of the two's complement binary code was the *weighted-sign binary code,* which correlates directly to the value box. As the name "weighted sign" implies, each bit position has a weight, or value, of two raised to a power and a sign. The signs of all bits except the leftmost bit are positive and the sign of the leftmost or most significant bit is negative.

-128	64	32	16	8	4	2	1
1	0	0	0	1	1	0	1

$$-128 + 0 + 0 + 0 + 8 + 4 + 0 + 1 = -115$$

Figure 2.10   Converting 10001101 to a base 10 number

Chapter **3**

Assignments, Addresses, and Interactive Input

In Chapter 2 we explored how data is stored, introduced variables and their associated declaration statements, and became more comfortable using the `printf()` function. This chapter completes our introduction to C by discussing the proper use of both constants and variables in constructing expressions, presenting assignment expressions, and introducing addresses and the `scanf()` function for entering data interactively while a program is running.

Almost all of C's processing statements, except for function calls, use expressions, so it is important to have a clear understanding of what an expression is before proceeding. In its simplest form, an *expression* is any combination of variables and constants that can be evaluated to yield a result. The simplest expressions consist of a single constant or variable, such as

```
12.62  'a'  5  -10  rate  total
```

Here, each constant or variable yields a result; for individual constants, the result is the constant itself, while for individual variables, the result is the value stored in the variable.

Slightly more complex expressions involve combining both constants and variables using the arithmetic operators introduced in the last chapter. Examples of such expressions are

```
10 + amount
count + 1
16.3 + total
0.08 * purchase
rate * total
grade1 + grade2 + grade3 + grade4
```

If an expression used in a program contains one or more variables, as in these examples, the variables must first be declared and have values stored in them before the expression can be evaluated to yield a useful result. For example, if you are asked to multiply rate times total, you could not do it unless you first knew the values of rate and total. However, if you are told that rate is 5 and total is 10, you can multiply the two variables to yield 50. Expressions using both constants and variables are evaluated according to the rules presented in Chapter 2.

3.1 Assignment

We have already discussed simple assignment statements in Chapter 2. An assignment statement is simply an assignment expression that is terminated by a semicolon. In C, the equal sign, =, used in assignment statements is itself a binary operator. This differs from the way most other high-level languages process this symbol. The = symbol is called the *assignment operator* and is used in assignment expressions having the general form

variable = operand

The operand to the right of the assignment operator can be a constant, a variable, or another valid C expression. The assignment operator causes the value of the operand to the right of the equal sign to be stored in the variable to the left of the equal sign. Examples of valid assignment expressions are

```
    year = 1988
   value = 3000
     sum = 90.2 + 80.3 + 65.0
    rate = prime
  inches = 12 * feet
   total = total + newvalue
     tax = salestax * amount
interest = principal * interest
     sum = (grade1 + grade2 + grade3) * factor
```

The assignment operator has the lowest precedence of all binary and unary arithmetic operators (see Table A.1 in Appendix A). Thus, any other operators contained in an expression using an assignment operator are always evaluated first. For example, in the expression `tax = salestax * amount`, the expression `salestax * amount` is first evaluated to yield a value. This value is then stored in the variable `tax`.

Like all expressions, assignment expressions themselves have a value. The value of the complete assignment expression is the value assigned to the variable on the left of the assignment operator. For example, the expression `a = 5` both assigns a value of 5 to the variable `a` and results in the expression itself having a value of 5. The value of the expression can always be verified using a statement such as

```
printf("The value of the expression is %d", a = 5);
```

Here, the value of the expression itself is displayed and not the contents of the variable `a`. Although both the contents of the variable and the expression have the same value, it is worthwhile realizing that we are dealing with two distinct entities.

From a programming perspective, it is the actual assignment of a value to a variable that is significant in an assignment expression; the final value of the assignment expression itself is of little consequence. However, the fact that assignment expressions have a value has implications that must be considered when C's relational operators are presented.

When writing assignment expressions, you must be aware of two important considerations. Since the assignment operator has a lower precedence than any other arithmetic operator, the value of the operand to the right of the equal sign is always obtained first. For this value to have any meaning, all variables used in an expression to the right of the equal sign must have known values. For example, the expression `interest = principal * rate` will cause a valid number to be stored in `interest` only if the programmer first takes care to put valid numbers in `principal` and `rate`.

The second consideration to keep in mind is that because the value of an expression is stored in the variable to the left of the equal sign, there must be one variable listed immediately to the left of the equal sign. For example, the expression

```
amount + 1892 = 1000 + 10 * 5
```

is invalid. The expression on the right-hand side of the equal sign evaluates to the integer 1050, which can be stored only in a variable. Because `amount + 1892` is not a valid variable name, the computer does not know where to store the calculated value.

Any expression that is terminated by a semicolon becomes a C statement. The most common example of this is the assignment statement, which is simply an assignment expression terminated with a semicolon. For example, terminating the assignment expression `a = 33` with a semicolon results in the assignment statement `a = 33;`, which can be used in a program on a line by itself.

Since the equal sign is an operator in C, multiple assignments are possible in the same expression or its equivalent statement. For example, in the expression `a = b = c = 25` all the assignment operators have the same precedence. Since the assignment operator has a right-to-left associativity, the final evaluation proceeds in the sequence

```
c = 25
b = c
a = b
```

This has the effect of assigning the number 25 to each of the variables individually and can be represented as

```
a = (b = (c = 25))
```

Appending a semicolon to the original expression results in the multiple assignment statement

```
a = b = c = 25;
```

This latter statement is equivalent to the three individual statements

```
c = 25;
b = 25;
a = 25;
```

Program 3.1 illustrates the use of assignment statements in calculating the area of a rectangle.

 Program 3.1

```c
#include <stdio.h>
int main()
{
  float length, width, area;

  length = 27.2;
  width = 13.6;
  area = length * width;
  printf("The length of the rectangle is %f",length);
  printf("\nThe width of the rectangle is %f",width);
  printf("\nThe area of the rectangle is %f",area);

  return 0;
}
```

When Program 3.1 is run, the output obtained is

```
The length of the rectangle is 27.200000
The width of the rectangle is 13.600000
The area of the rectangle is 369.920000
```

Notice the flow of control that the computer uses in executing Program 3.1. The program begins with the keyword `main` and continues sequentially, statement by statement, until the closing brace. This flow of control is true for all programs. The computer works on one statement at a time, executing that statement with no knowledge of what the next statement will be. This explains why all operands used in an expression must have values assigned to them before the expression is evaluated.

When the computer executes the statement `area = length * width;` in Program 3.1, it uses whatever value is stored in the variables `length` and `width` at the time the assignment is executed. If no values have been specifically assigned to these variables before they are used in the expression `length * width`, the computer uses whatever values happen to occupy these variables when they are referenced. The computer does not "look ahead" to see that you might assign values to these variables later in the program.

As we saw in Section 2.4, when a value is assigned to a variable for the first time, the variable is said to be *initialized*. Subsequent assignments can, of course, be used to change the value assigned to a variable. For example, assume the following statements are executed one after another:

```
length = 3.7;
length = 6.28;
```

The first assignment statement causes the value 3.7 to be stored in the variable named `length`. If this is the first time a value is assigned to this variable, it is also correct to say that `length` is initialized to 3.7. (As noted in Section 2.4, variables can also be initialized when they are declared. For example, the declaration statement `float length = 3.7;` both declares and initializes the variable `length`.)

The second assignment statement causes the computer to assign a value of 6.28 to `length`. The 3.7 that was in `length` is overwritten with the new value of 6.28, because a variable can store only one value at a time. In this regard it is sometimes useful to think of the variable to the left of the equal operator as a temporary parking spot in a huge parking lot. Just as an individual parking spot can be used by only one car at a time, each variable can store only one value at a time. The "parking" of a new value in a variable automatically causes the computer to remove any value previously "parked" there.

Assignment Operators

Although only one variable is allowed immediately to the left of the equal sign in an assignment expression, the variable on the left of the equal sign can also be used on the right of the equal sign. For example, the assignment expression `sum = sum + 10` is valid. Clearly, in an algebra equation a variable could never be equal to itself plus 10. But in C, the expression `sum = sum + 10` is not an equation—it is an expression that is evaluated in two major steps. The first step is to calculate the value of `sum + 10`. The second step is to store the computed value in `sum`. See if you can determine the output of Program 3.2.

Program 3.2

```c
#include <stdio.h>
int main()
{
    int sum;

    sum = 25;
    printf("\nThe number stored in sum is %d.",sum);
    sum = sum + 10;
    printf("\nThe number now stored in sum is %d.",sum);

    return 0;
}
```

The assignment statement `sum = 25;` tells the computer to store the number 25 in `sum`, as shown in Figure 3.1. The first call to `printf()` in Program 3.2 causes the value stored in `sum` to be displayed by the message `The number stored in sum is 25`. The second assignment statement, `sum = sum + 10;` causes the computer to retrieve the 25 stored in `sum` and add 10 to this number, yielding the number 35. The number 35 is then stored in the variable on the left side of the equal sign, which is the variable `sum`. The 25 that was in `sum` is simply erased and replaced with the new value of 35, as shown in Figure 3.2.

Assignment expressions like `sum = sum + 25`, which use the same variable on both sides of the assignment operator, can be written using the following assignment operators:

```
+=   -=   *=   /=   %=
```

For example, the expression `sum = sum + 10` can be written as `sum += 10`. Similarly, the expression `price *= rate` is equivalent to the expression `price = price * rate`.

In using these new assignment operators it is important to note that the variable to the left of the assignment operator is applied to the complete expression on the right. For example, the expression `price *= rate + 1` is equivalent to the expression `price = price * (rate + 1)`, not `price = price * rate + 1`.

Figure 3.1 The integer 25 is stored in sum

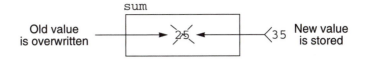

Figure 3.2 `sum = sum + 10;` causes a new value to be stored in `sum`

Accumulating

Assignment expressions like `sum += 10` or its equivalent, `sum = sum + 10`, are common in programming. These expressions are required in accumulating subtotals when data is entered one number at a time. For example, if we want to add the numbers 96, 70, 85, and 60 in calculator fashion, the following statements could be used:

Statement	Value in `sum`
`sum = 0;`	0
`sum = sum + 96;`	96
`sum = sum + 70;`	166
`sum = sum + 85;`	251
`sum = sum + 60;`	311

The first statement initializes `sum` to 0. This removes any number ("garbage" value) stored in `sum` that would invalidate the final total. As each number is added, the value stored in `sum` is increased accordingly. After completion of the last statement, `sum` contains the total of all the added numbers.

Program 3.3 illustrates the effect of these statements by displaying `sum`'s contents after each addition is made.

The output displayed by Program 3.3 is

```
The value of sum is initially set to 0.
  sum is now 96.
  sum is now 166.
  sum is now 251.
The final sum is 311.
```

Although Program 3.3 is not a practical program (it is easier to add the numbers by hand), it does illustrate the subtotaling effect of repeated use of statements having the form

variable = variable + newValue;

We will find many uses for this type of statement when we become more familiar with the repetition statements introduced in Chapter 5.

Program 3.3

```
#include <stdio.h>
int main()
{
  int sum;

  sum = 0;
  printf("\nThe value of sum is initially set to %d.", sum);
  sum = sum + 96;
  printf("\n sum is now %d.", sum);
  sum = sum + 70;
  printf("\n sum is now %d.", sum);
  sum = sum + 85;
  printf("\n sum is now %d.", sum);
  sum = sum + 60;
  printf("\n The final sum is %d.", sum);

  return 0;
}
```

Counting

A special type of assignment statement that is very similar to the accumulating statement is the counting statement. Counting statements have the form

$$variable = variable + fixedNumber;$$

Examples of counting statements are

```
i = i + 1;
n = n + 1;
count = count + 1;
j = j + 2;
m = m + 2;
kk = kk + 3;
```

In each of these examples, the same variable is used on both sides of the equal sign. After a statement is executed the value of the respective variable is increased by a fixed amount. In the first three examples the variables i, n, and count have all been increased by one. In the next two examples the respective variables have been increased by two, and in the final example the variable kk has been increased by three.

For the special case in which a variable is either increased or decreased by one, C provides two unary operators. Using the *increment operator*, ++, the expression *variable*

= *variable* + 1 can be replaced by the expression ++*variable*. Examples of the increment operator are

Expression	Alternative
i = i + 1	++i
n = n + 1	++n
count = count + 1	++count

Program 3.4 illustrates the use of the increment operator.

 Program 3.4

```c
#include <stdio.h>
int main()
{
  int count;

  count = 0;
  printf("\nThe initial value of count is %d.", count);
  ++count;
  printf("\n   count is now %d.", count);
  ++count;
  printf("\n   count is now %d.", count);
  ++count;
  printf("\n   count is now %d.", count);
  ++count;
  printf("\n   count is now %d.", count);

  return 0;
}
```

The output displayed by Program 3.4 is

```
The initial value of count is 0.
    count is now 1.
    count is now 2.
    count is now 3.
    count is now 4.
```

C also provides a *decrement operator*, --. As you might expect, the expression --*variable* is equivalent to the expression *variable* = *variable* - 1. Examples of the decrement operator are

Expression	Alternative
i = i - 1	--i
n = n - 1	--n
count = count - 1	--count

When ++ appears before a variable it is called a *prefix increment operator*. Besides appearing before (pre) a variable, the increment operator can also be applied after a variable; for example, in the expression n++. When the increment operator appears after a variable it is called a *postfix increment operator*. Both of these expressions, ++n and n++, correspond to the longer expression n = n + 1, but they have different effects when used in an assignment expression. For example, the expression k = ++n, which uses a prefix increment operator, does two things in one expression. Initially the value of n is incremented by one and then the new value of n is assigned to the variable k. Thus, the statement k = ++n; is equivalent to the two statements

```
n = n + 1;   /* increment n first       */
k = n;       /* then assign n's value to k  */
```

The assignment expression k = n++, which uses a postfix increment operator, reverses this procedure. A postfix increment operates after the assignment is completed. Thus, the statement k = n++; first assigns the current value of n to k and then increments the value of n by one. This is equivalent to the two statements

```
k = n;       /* assign n's value to k */
n = n + 1;   /* then increment n   */
```

Just as there are prefix and postfix increment operators, C also provides prefix and postfix *decrement* operators. For example, both of the expressions --n and n-- reduce the value of n by one. These expressions are equivalent to the longer expression n = n - 1. As with the increment operator, however, the prefix and postfix decrement operators produce different results when used in assignment expressions. For example, the expression k = --n first decrements the value of n by one before assigning the value of n to k. But the expression k = n-- first assigns the current value of n to k and then reduces the value of n by one.

The increment and decrement operators can often be used to reduce program storage requirements and increase execution speed. For example, consider the following three statements:

```
count = count + 1;
count += 1;
++count;
```

All perform the same function; however, when these instructions were compiled for execution on an IBM personal computer, the storage requirements for the executable instructions were 9, 4, and 3 bytes, respectively. Using the assignment operator, =, instead of the increment operator results in using three times the storage space for the instruction, with an accompanying decrease in execution speed.

Exercises 3.1

1. Determine and correct the errors in the following programs.

   a.
```
#include <stdio.h>
int main()
{

    width = 15
    area = length * width;
    printf("The area is %d",area
    return 0;
}
```

   b.
```
#include <stdio.h>
int main()
{
    int length, width, area;

    area = length * width;
    length = 20;
    width = 15;
    printf("The area is %d",area);
    return 0;
}
```

   c.
```
#include <stdio.h>
int main()
{
    int length = 20; width = 15, area;

    length * width = area;
    printf("The area is %d",area);
    return 0;
}
```

2. a. Write a C program to calculate and display the average of the numbers 32.6, 55.2, 67.9, and 48.6.
   b. Run the program written for Exercise 2a on a computer.

3. a. Write a C program to calculate the circumference of a circle. The equation for determining the circumference of a circle is *circumference = 2 * 3.1416 * radius*. Assume that the circle has a radius of 3.3 inches.
   b. Run the program written for Exercise 3a on a computer.

4. a. Write a C program to calculate the area of a circle. The equation for determining the area of a circle is *area = 3.1416 * radius * radius*. Assume that the circle has a radius of 5 inches.
   b. Run the program written for Exercise 4a on a computer.

5. a. Write a C program to calculate the volume of a pool. The equation for determining the volume is *volume = length * width * depth.* Assume that the pool has a length of 25 feet, a width of 10 feet, and a depth of 6 feet.

   b. Run the program written for Exercise 5a on a computer.

6. a. Write a C program to convert temperature in degrees Fahrenheit to degrees Celsius. The equation for this conversion is *Celsius = 5.0/9.0 * (Fahrenheit – 32.0).* Have your program convert and display the Celsius temperature corresponding to 98.6 degrees Fahrenheit.

   b. Run the program written for Exercise 6a on a computer.

7. a. Write a C program to calculate the dollar amount contained in a piggy bank. The bank currently contains 12 half-dollars, 20 quarters, 32 dimes, 45 nickels, and 27 pennies.

   b. Run the program written for Exercise 7a on a computer.

8. a. Write a C program to calculate the distance, in feet, of a trip that is 2.36 miles long. One mile is equal to 5,280 feet.

   b. Run the program written for Exercise 8a on a computer.

9. a. Write a C program to calculate the elapsed time it took to make a 183.67 mile trip. The equation for computing elapsed time is *elapsed time = total distance / average speed.* Assume that the average speed during the trip was 58 miles per hour.

   b. Run the program written for Exercise 9a on a computer.

10. a. Write a C program to calculate the sum of the numbers from 1 to 100. The formula for calculating this sum is *sum = (n/2) * (2*a + (n–1)*d),* where *n* = the number of terms to be added, *a* = the first number, and *d* = the difference between each number.

   b. Run the program written for Exercise 10a on a computer.

11. Determine why the expression a – b = 25 is invalid but the expression a – (b = 25) is valid.

3.2 Addresses

Three major items associated with every variable are the value stored in it, its address, and its data type. The value stored in a variable is referred to as the variable's contents, while the address of the first memory location used for the variable constitutes its address. The number of memory locations used by the variable depends on the variable's data type. The relationship between these items is illustrated in Figure 3.3.

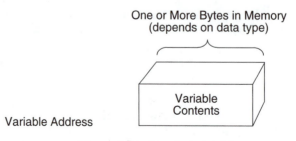

Figure 3.3   A typical variable

Programmers are usually concerned only with the value assigned to a variable (its contents) and give little attention to where the value is stored (its address). For example, consider Program 3.5.

 Program 3.5

```
#include <stdio.h>
int main()
{
  int num;

  num = 22;
  printf("The value stored in num is %d.",num);
  printf("\nThe computer uses %d bytes to store this value",sizeof(int));

  return 0;
}
```

The output displayed when Program 3.5 is run is

```
The value stored in num is 22.
The computer uses 2 bytes to store this value
```

Program 3.5 displays both the number 22, which is the value stored in the integer variable num (its contents), and the amount of storage used for an integer. The information provided by Program 3.5 is illustrated in Figure 3.4.

We can go further and obtain the address corresponding to the variable num. The address that is displayed corresponds to the address of the first byte set aside in the computer's memory for the variable.

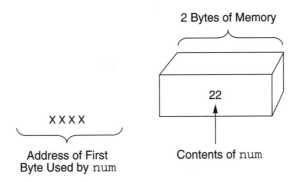

Figure 3.4 Somewhere in memory

To determine the address of num, we must use the address operator, &, which means *the address of,* directly in front of the variable name (no space between & and the variable). For example, &num means *the address of* num, &total means *the address of* total, and &price means *the address of* price. Program 3.6 uses the address operator to display the address of the variable num.

 Program 3.6

```
#include <stdio.h>
int main()
{
  int num;

  num = 22;
  printf("num = %d  The address of num is %p.", num, &num);

  return 0;
}
```

The output of Program 3.6 is

```
num = 22  The address of num is FFE0.
```

Figure 3.5 illustrates the additional address information provided by the output of Program 3.6.

Clearly, the address output by Program 3.6 depends on the computer used to run the program. Every time Program 3.6 is executed, however, it displays the address of the first byte used to store the variable num. Note also that the address is printed using the conversion control sequence %p. This conversion control sequence is provided in ANSI C to display addresses.[1] As illustrated by the output of Program 3.6, the address display is in

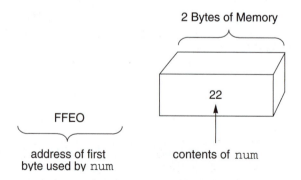

2 Bytes of Memory

22

FFE0

address of first
byte used by num

contents of num

Figure 3.5 A more complete picture of the variable num

Variable	Contents
numAddr	Address of num

Figure 3.6   Storing num's address into numAddr

hexadecimal notation. The display has no impact on how addresses are used internally to the program and merely provides us with a representation that is helpful in understanding what addresses are.

As we shall see, using addresses as opposed to only displaying them provides the C programmer with an extremely powerful programming tool. Addresses provide the ability to enter directly into the computer's inner workings and access its basic storage structure. This gives the C programmer capabilities and programming power that are not available in most other computer languages.

Storing Addresses

Besides displaying the address of a variable, as was done in Program 3.6, we can also store addresses in suitably declared variables. For example, the statement

```
numAddr = &num;
```

stores the address corresponding to the variable num in the variable numAddr, as illustrated in Figure 3.6. Similarly, the statements

```
d = &m;
tabPoint = &list;
chrPoint = &ch;
```

store the addresses of the variables m, list, and ch in the variables d, tabPoint, and chrPoint, respectively, as illustrated in Figure 3.7.

The variables numAddr, d, tabPoint, and chrPoint are all called *pointer variables,* or *pointers,* for short. Pointers are simply variables that are used to store the addresses of other variables.

---

[1] To obtain a decimal representation for the address the unsigned conversion control sequence %u may be used in place of %p. The %u conversion control sequence forces the address to be treated as an unsigned integer data type, and what is displayed is printf()'s representation of the address in a decimal format. An address, however, is not an unsigned integer data type—it is a unique data type that may or may not require the same amount of storage as an unsigned integer.

Variable   Contents

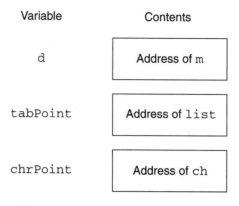

Figure 3.7   Storing more addresses

Using Addresses[2]

To use a stored address, C provides us with an *indirection operator,* *. The * symbol, when followed immediately by a pointer (no space allowed between the * and the pointer), means *the variable whose address is stored in.* Thus, if numAddr is a pointer (remember that a pointer is a variable that contains an address), *numAddr means *the variable whose address is stored in* numAddr. Similarly, *tabPoint means *the variable whose address is stored in* tabPoint, and *chrPoint means *the variable whose address is stored in* chrPoint. Figure 3.8 shows the relationship between the address contained in a pointer variable and the variable ultimately addressed.

Although *d literally means *the variable whose address is stored in* d, this is commonly shortened to *the variable pointed to by* d. Similarly, referring to Figure 3.8, *y can be read as *the variable pointed to by* y. The value ultimately obtained, as shown in Figure 3.8, is qqqq.

When using a pointer variable, the value that is obtained is always found by first going to the pointer variable (or pointer, for short) for an address. The address contained in the pointer is then used to get the desired contents. Certainly, this is a rather indirect way of getting to the final value, and not unexpectedly, the term *indirect addressing* is used to describe this procedure.

Since using a pointer requires the computer to do a double lookup (first the address is retrieved, then the address is used to retrieve the actual data), a worthwhile question is, why would you want to store an address in the first place? The answer to this question must be deferred until we get to real applications, when the use of pointers becomes invaluable. However, given what was previously presented for a variable's storage locations, the idea of storing an address should not seem overly strange.

---

[2] This topic may be omitted on first reading without loss of subject continuity.

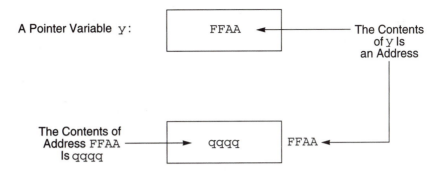

Figure 3.8   Using a pointer variable

Declaring Pointers[3]

Like all variables, pointers must be declared before they can be used. In declaring a pointer variable, C requires that we also specify the type of variable that is pointed to. For example, if the address in the pointer numAddr is the address of an integer, the correct declaration for the pointer is

```
int *numAddr;
```

This declaration is read as *the variable pointed to by* numAddr (from the *numAddr in the declaration) *is an integer.*

Notice that the declaration int *numAddr; specifies two things: first, that the variable pointed to by numAddr is an integer; second, that numAddr must be a pointer (because it is used with the indirection operator *). Similarly, if the pointer tabPoint points to (contains the address of) a floating point number and chrPoint points to a character variable, the required declarations are

```
float *tabPoint;
char *chrPoint;
```

These two declarations can be read as *the variable pointed to by* tabPoint *is a float* and *the variable pointed to by* chrPoint *is a character.* Consider Program 3.7.

The output of Program 3.7 is

```
The address stored in numAddr is FFDE
The value pointed to by numAddr is 22

The address now stored in numAddr is FFE0
The value now pointed to by numAddr is 158
```

---

[3] This topic may be omitted on first reading without loss of subject continuity.

Program 3.7

```c
#include <stdio.h>
int main()
{
    int *numAddr;       /* declare a pointer to an int     */
    int miles, dist;    /* declare two integer variables   */

    dist = 158;         /* store the number 158 into dist  */
    miles = 22;         /* store the number 22 into miles  */
    numAddr = &miles;   /* store the 'address of miles' in numAddr */

    printf("The address stored in numAddr is %p\n",numAddr);
    printf("The value pointed to by numAddr is %d\n\n",*numAddr);

    numAddr = &dist; /* now store the address of dist in numAddr */
    printf("The address now stored in numAddr is %p\n",numAddr);
    printf("The value now pointed to by numAddr is %d\n",*numAddr);

    return 0;
}
```

The only value of Program 3.7 is in helping us understand "what gets stored where." Let's review the program to see how the output was produced.

The declaration statement int *numAddr; declares numAddr to be a pointer variable used to store the address of an integer variable. The statement numAddr = &miles; stores the address of the variable miles into the pointer numAddr. The first call to printf() causes this address to be displayed. Note that we have again used the conversion control sequence %p to print out the address. The second call to printf() in Program 3.7 uses the indirection operator to retrieve and print out the *value pointed to by* numAddr, which is, of course, the value stored in miles.

Since numAddr has been declared as a pointer to an integer variable, we can use this pointer to store the address of any integer variable. The statement numAddr = &dist illustrates this by storing the address of the variable dist in numAddr. The last two printf() calls verify the change in numAddr's value and that the new stored address does point to the variable dist. As illustrated in Program 3.7, only addresses should be stored in pointers.

It certainly would have been much simpler if the pointer used in Program 3.7 could have been declared as point numAddr;. Such a declaration, however, conveys no information about the storage used by the variable whose address is stored in numAddr. This information is essential when the pointer is used with the indirection operator, as it is in the second printf() call in Program 3.7. For example, if the address of an integer is stored in numAddr, then only two bytes of storage are typically retrieved when the

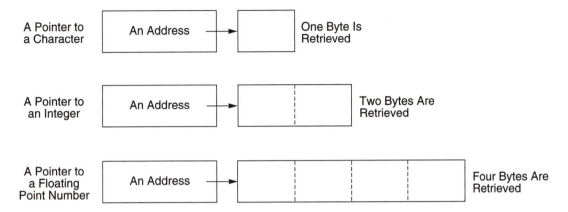

Figure 3.9 Addressing different data types using pointers

address is used. If the address of a character is stored in numAddr, only one byte of storage would be retrieved, and a float typically requires the retrieval of four bytes of storage. The declaration of a pointer must, therefore, include the type of variable being pointed to. Figure 3.9 illustrates this concept.

Exercises 3.2

1. If average is a variable, what does &average mean?

2. For the variables and addresses illustrated in Figure 3.10, determine &temp, &dist, &date, and &miles.

3. a. Write a C program that includes the following declaration statements:

```
char key, choice;
int num, count;
long date;
float yield;
double price;
```

Have the program use the address operator and the printf() function to display the addresses corresponding to each variable.

b. After running the program written for Exercise 3a, draw a diagram of how your computer has set aside storage for the variables in the program. On your diagram, fill in the addresses displayed by the program.

c. Modify the program written in Exercise 3a to display the amount of storage your computer reserves for each data type (use the sizeof() operator). With this information and the address information provided in Exercise 3b, determine if your computer set aside storage for the variables in the order they were declared.

4. If a variable is declared as a pointer, what must be stored in the variable?

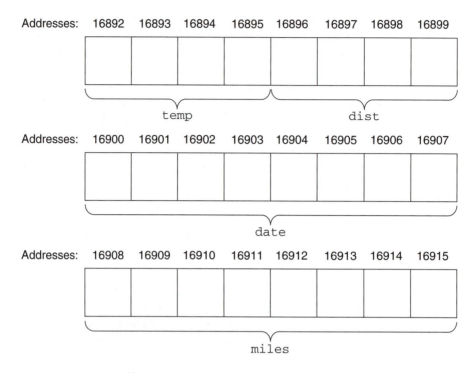

Figure 3.10   Memory bytes for Exercise 2

5. Using the indirection operator, write expressions for the following:
   a. The variable pointed to by xAddr
   b. The variable whose address is in yAddr
   c. The variable pointed to by ptYld
   d. The variable pointed to by ptMiles
   e. The variable pointed to by mptr
   f. The variable whose address is in pdate
   g. The variable pointed to by distPtr
   h. The variable pointed to by tabPt
   i. The variable whose address is in hoursPt

6. Write declaration statements for the following:
   a. The variable pointed to by yAddr is an integer.
   b. The variable pointed to by chAddr is a character.
   c. The variable pointed to by ptYr is a long integer.
   d. The variable pointed to by amt is a double precision variable.
   e. The variable pointed to by z is an integer.
   f. The variable pointed to by qp is a floating point variable.
   g. datePt is a pointer to an integer.
   h. yldAddr is a pointer to a double precision variable.
   i. amtPt is a pointer to a floating point variable.
   j. ptChr is a pointer to a character.

7. a. What are the variables `yAddr`, `chAddr`, `ptYr`, `amt`, `z`, `qp`, `datePtr`, `yldAddr`, `amtPt`, and `ptChr` used in Exercise 6 called?

b. Why are the variable names `amt`, `z`, and `qp` used in Exercise 6 not good choices for pointer variable names?

8. Write English sentence descriptions for the following declarations:

a. `char *keyAddr;`   d. `long *yPtr;`

b. `int *m;`   e. `float *pCou;`

c. `double *yldAddr;`   f. `int *ptDate;`

9. Which of the following are declarations for pointers:

a. `long a;`   f. `double w;`

b. `char b;`   g. `float *k;`

c. `char *c;`   h. `float l;`

d. `int x;`   i. `double *z;`

e. `int *p;`

10. For the following declarations,

```
int *xPt, *yAddr;
long *dtAddr, *ptAddr;
double *ptZ;
int a;
long b;
double c;
```

determine which of the following statements is valid.

a. `yAddr = &a;`   l. `dtAddr = c;`

b. `yAddr = &b;`   m. `ptZ = &a;`

c. `yAddr = &c;`   n. `ptAddr = &b;`

d. `yAddr = a;`   o. `ptAddr = &c`

e. `yAddr = b;`   p. `ptAddr = a;`

f. `yAddr = c;`   q. `ptAddr = b;`

g. `dtAddr = &a;`   r. `ptAddr = c;`

h. `dtAddr = &b;`   s. `yAddr = xPt;`

i. `dtAddr = &c;`   t. `yAddr = dtAddr;`

j. `dtAddr = a;`   u. `yAddr = ptAddr;`

k. `dtAddr = b;`

11. For the variables and addresses illustrated in Figure 3.11, fill in the appropriate data as determined by the following statements:

a. `ptNum = &m;`   e. `ptDay = zAddr;`

b. `amtAddr = &amt;`   f. `*ptYr = 1987;`

c. `*zAddr = 25;`   g. `*amtAddr = *numAddr;`

d. `k = *numAddr;`

12. Using the `sizeof()` operator, determine the number of bytes used by your computer to store the address of an integer, character, and double precision number. (*Hint:* `sizeof (int*)` can be used to determine the number of memory bytes used for a pointer to an integer.) Would you expect the size of each address to be the same? Why or why not?

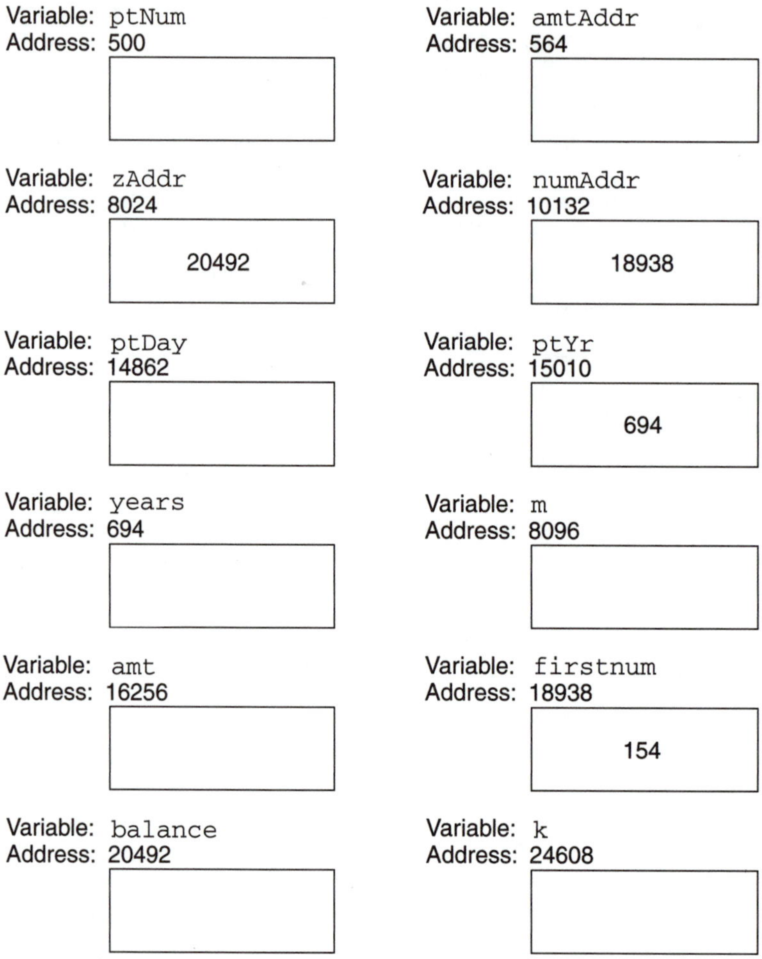

Variable: `ptNum`
Address: 500

Variable: `amtAddr`
Address: 564

Variable: `zAddr`
Address: 8024

20492

Variable: `numAddr`
Address: 10132

18938

Variable: `ptDay`
Address: 14862

Variable: `ptYr`
Address: 15010

694

Variable: `years`
Address: 694

Variable: `m`
Address: 8096

Variable: `amt`
Address: 16256

Variable: `firstnum`
Address: 18938

154

Variable: `balance`
Address: 20492

Variable: `k`
Address: 24608

Figure 3.11   Memory locations for Exercise 11

3.3   The `scanf()` Function

Data for programs that are only going to be executed once may be included directly in the program. For example, if we wanted to multiply the numbers 300.0 and .05, we could use Program 3.8.

The output displayed by Program 3.8 is

```
300.000000 times .050000 is 15.000000
```

Program 3.8 can be shortened, as illustrated in Program 3.9. Both programs, however suffer from the same problem: they must be rewritten to multiply different numbers. Both programs lack the facility for entering different numbers to be operated on.

Program 3.8

```
#include <stdio.h>
int main()
{
   float num1, num2, product;

   num1 = 300.0;
   num2 = .05;
   product = num1 * num2;
   printf("%f times %f is %f", num1, num2, product);

   return 0;
}
```

 Program 3.9

```
#include <stdio.h>
int main()
{
   printf("%f times %f is %f", 300.0, .05, 300.0*.05);

   return 0;
}
```

Except for the practice provided to the programmer of writing, entering, and running the program, programs that do a calculation only once, on one set of numbers, are clearly not very useful. After all, it is simpler to use a calculator to multiply two numbers than to enter and run either Program 3.8 or 3.9.

This section presents the scanf() function, which is used to enter data into a program while it is executing. Just as the printf() function displays a copy of the value stored inside a variable, the scanf() function allows the user to enter a value at the video screen (Figure 3.12). The value is then stored directly in a variable.

Like the printf() function, the scanf() function requires a control string as the first argument inside the function name parentheses. The control string tells the function the type of data being input and uses the same control sequences as the printf() function. Unlike the control string used in a printf() function, however, the control string passed to scanf() typically consists of conversion control sequences only. Also unlike printf(), where a list of variable names can follow the control string, scanf() requires that a list of variable addresses follow the control string. For example, the statement scanf("%d", &num1); is a call to the scanf() function. The conversion

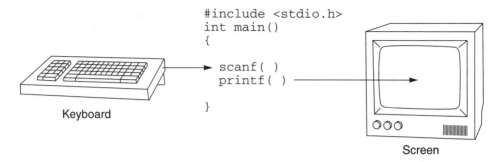

Figure 3.12   `scanf()` is used to enter data; `printf()` is used to display data

control sequence `%d` is identical to the conversion control sequence used in `printf()` in that it tells the `scanf()` function that it will be dealing with an integer number. The address operator `&` in front of the variable num1 is required for `scanf()`. Recall from Section 3.2 that &num1 is read *the address of* num1.

When a statement such as `scanf("%d",&num1);` is encountered, the computer stops program execution and continuously scans the keyboard for data (`scanf` is short for scan function). When a data item is typed, the `scanf()` function stores the item using the address it was given. The program then continues execution with the next statement after the call to `scanf()`. To see this, consider Program 3.10.

Program 3.10

```
#include <stdio.h>
int main()
{
  float num1, num2, product;

  printf("Please type in a number: ");
  scanf("%f",&num1);
  printf("Please type in another number: ");
  scanf("%f",&num2);
  product = num1 * num2;
  printf("%f times %f is %f",num1, num2, product);

  return 0;
}
```

The first call to `printf()` in Program 3.10 produces a *prompt*, which is a message that tells the person at the screen what should be typed. In this case the user is told to type a number. The computer then executes the next statement, which is a call to `scanf()`.

The scanf() function puts the computer into a temporary pause (or wait) state for as long as it takes the user to type a value. Then the user signals the scanf() function by pressing the ENTER key after the value has been typed. The entered value is stored in the variable, num1, whose address was passed to scanf(), and the computer is taken out of its paused state. Program execution then proceeds with the next statement, which in Program 3.10 is another call to printf(). This call causes the next message to be displayed. The second call to scanf() again puts the computer into a temporary wait state while the user types a second value. This second number is stored in the variable num2.

The following sample run was made using Program 3.10.

```
Please type in a number: 300.
Please type in another number:  .05
300.000000 times .050000 is 15.000000
```

In Program 3.10, each call to scanf() is used to store one value into a variable. The scanf() function, however, can be used to enter and store as many values as there are conversion control sequences in the control string. For example, the statement

```
scanf("%f %f",&num1,&num2);
```

results in two values being read from the terminal and assigned to the variables num1 and num2. If the data entered at the terminal was

```
0.052 245.79
```

the variables num1 and num2 would contain the values 0.052 and 245.79, respectively. The space in the control string between the two conversion control sequences, "%f %f", is strictly for readability. The control string "%f%f" would work equally well. When actually entering numbers such as 0.052 and 245.79, however, you must leave at least one space between the numbers, regardless of which control string, "%f %f" or "%f%f", is used. The space between the entered numbers clearly indicates where one number ends and the next begins. Inserting more than one space between numbers has no effect on scanf().

The only time that a space can affect the value being entered is when scanf() is expecting a character data type. For example, the statement scanf("%c%c%c",&ch1,&ch2,&ch3); causes scanf() to store the next three characters typed in the variables ch1, ch2, and ch3, respectively. If you type x y z, then x is stored in ch1, a blank is stored in ch2, and y is stored in ch3. If, however, the statement scanf("%c %c %c",&ch1,&ch2,&ch3); was used, scanf() looks for three characters, each character separated by exactly one space.

Any number of scanf() function calls may be made in a program, and any number of values may be input using a single scanf() function. Just be sure that a conversion control sequence is used for each value to be entered and that the address operator is used in front of the variable name where the value is to be stored. The conversion control sequences used in a scanf() control string are the same as those used in printf() calls, with one caution. In printing a double precision number using printf(), the conversion control sequence for a floating point variable, %f, can be used. This is not true when using scanf(). If a double precision number is to be entered, the conversion control sequence %lf must be used.

The scanf() function, like the printf() function, does not test the data type of the values being entered. It is up to the user to ensure that all variables are declared correctly and that any numbers entered are of the correct type. However, scanf() is "clever" enough to make a few data type conversions. For example, if an integer is entered in place of a floating point or double precision number, the scanf() function automatically supplies a decimal point at the end of the integer before storing the number. Similarly, if a floating point or double precision number is entered when an integer is expected, the scanf() function only uses the integer part of the number. For example, assume the following numbers are typed in response to the function call scanf("%f %d %f",&num1,&num2,&num3);:

        56   22.879   33.923

scanf() converts the 56 to 56.0 and stores this value in the variable num1. The function continues scanning the input, expecting an integer value. As far as scanf() is concerned, the decimal point after the 22 in the number 22.879 indicates the end of an integer and the start of a decimal number. Thus, the number 22 is stored in num2. Continuing to scan the typed input, scanf() takes the .879 as the next floating point number and stores this value in num3. As far as scanf() is concerned, 33.923 is extra input and therefore it is ignored until the next scanf(), if any, is encountered. However, if you do not initially type enough data, the scanf() function will continue to make the computer pause until sufficient data has been entered.

Exercises 3.3

1. For each of the following declaration statements, write a scanf() function call that will cause the computer to pause while the appropriate data is typed by the user.
   a. `int firstnum;`
   b. `float grade;`
   c. `double secnum;`
   d. `char keyval;`
   e. `int month, years;`
      `float average;`
   f. `char ch;`
      `int num1, num2;`
      `double grade1, grade2;`
   g. `float interest, principal, capital;`
      `double price, yield;`
   h. `char ch, letter1, letter2;`
      `int num1, num2, num3;`
   i. `float temp1, temp2, temp3;`
      `double volts1, volts2;`

2. For the following `scanf()` function calls, write appropriate declaration statements.
   a. `scanf("%d",&day);`
   b. `scanf("%c",&firChar);`
   c. `scanf("%f",&grade);`
   d. `scanf("%lf",&price);`
   e. `scanf("%d %d %c",&num1,&num2,&ch1);`
   f. `scanf("%f %f %d",&firstnum,&secnum,&count);`
   g. `scanf("%c %c %d %lf",&ch1,&ch2,&flag,&average);`

3. Given the following declaration statements,

```
int num1, num2;
float firstnum, secnum;
double price, yield;
```

   determine and correct the errors in the following `scanf()` function calls.
   a. `scanf("%d",num1);`
   b. `scanf("%f %f %f",&num1,firstnum,&price);`
   c. `scanf("%c %lf %f",&num1,&secnum,&price);`
   d. `scanf("%d %d %lf",num1,num2,yield);`
   e. `scanf(&num1,&num2);`
   f. `scanf(&num1,"%d");`

4. a. Write a C program that displays the following prompt:

```
Enter the radius of a circle:
```

   After accepting a value for the radius, your program should calculate and display the circumference of the circle. *Note: circumference = 2 * 3.1416 * radius.*

   b. Check the value displayed by the program written for Exercise 4a by calculating the result manually. After manually determining that the result produced by your program is correct, use your program to complete the following table:

Radius (in.)	Circumference (in.)
1.0	
1.5	
2.0	
2.5	
3.0	
3.5	

5. a. Write a C program that first displays the following prompt:

```
Enter the temperature in degrees Fahrenheit:
```

   Have your program accept a value entered from the keyboard and convert the temperature entered to degrees Celsius, using the equation *Celsius = (5.0 / 9.0) * (Fahrenheit – 32.0).* Your program should then display the temperature in degrees Celsius, using an appropriate output message.

   b. Compile and execute the program written for Exercise 5a. Verify your program by calculating, by hand, and then using your program, the Fahrenheit equivalent of the following test data:

```
Test data set 1: 0 degrees Celsius.
Test data set 2: 50 degrees Celsius
Test data set 3: 100 degrees Celsius
```

When you are sure your program is working correctly, use it to complete the following table:

Celsius	Fahrenheit
45	
50	
55	
60	
65	
70	

6. a. Write a C program that displays the following prompts:

```
Enter the length of the room:
Enter the width of the room:
```

After each prompt is displayed, your program should use a scanf() function call to accept data from the keyboard for the displayed prompt. After the width of the room is entered, your program should calculate and display the area of the room. The area displayed should be included in an appropriate message and calculated using the equation *area = length * width.*

b. Check the area displayed by the program written for Exercise 6a by calculating the result manually.

7. a. Write a C program that displays the following prompts:

```
Enter the miles driven:
Enter the gallons of gas used:
```

After each prompt is displayed, your program should use a scanf() function call to accept data from the keyboard for the displayed prompt. After the gallons of gas used has been entered, your program should calculate and display miles per gallon obtained. This value should be included in an appropriate message and calculated using the equation *miles per gallon = miles / gallons used.* Verify your program using the following test data:

```
Test data set 1: Miles = 276, Gas = 10 gallons.
Test data set 2: Miles = 200, Gas = 15.5 gallons
```

When you have completed your verification, use your program to complete the following table:

Miles driven	Gallons used	MPG
250	16.00	
275	18.00	
312	19.54	
296	17.39	

b. For the program written for Exercise 7a, determine how many verification runs are required to ensure the program is working correctly and give a reason supporting your answer.

8. a. Write a C program that displays the following prompts:

```
Enter the length of the swimming pool:
Enter the width of the swimming pool:
Enter the average depth of the swimming pool:
```

After each prompt is displayed, your program should use a scanf() function call to accept data from the keyboard for the displayed prompt. After the depth of the swimming pool is entered, your program should calculate and display the volume of the pool. The volume should be included in an appropriate message and calculated using the equation *volume = length * width * average depth.*

b. Check the volume displayed by the program written for Exercise 8a by calculating the result manually.

9. a. Write a C program that displays the following prompts:

```
Enter a number:
Enter a second number:
Enter a third number:
Enter a fourth number:
```

After the prompt is displayed, your program should use a scanf() function call to accept a number from the keyboard for the displayed prompt. After the fourth number has been entered, your program should calculate and display the average of the numbers. The average should be included in an appropriate message. Check the average displayed by your program using the following test data:

Test data set 1: 100, 100, 100, 100
Test data set 2: 100, 0, 100, 0

Then, use your program to complete the following table:

Numbers	Average
92, 98, 79, 85	
86, 84, 75, 86	
63, 85, 74, 82	

b. Repeat Exercise 9a, making sure that you use the same variable name, number, for each number input. Also use the variable sum for the sum of the numbers. (*Hint:* To do this, you must use the statement sum = sum + number; after each number is accepted. Review the material on accumulating presented in Section 3.1.)

10. Write a C program that prompts the user to type a number. Have your program accept the number as an integer and immediately display the integer using a printf() function call. Run your program three times. The first time you run the program enter a valid integer number, the second time enter a floating point number, and the third time enter a character. Using the output display, see what number your program actually accepted from the data you entered.

11. Repeat Exercise 10 but have your program declare the variable used to store the number as a floating point variable. Run the program four times. The first time enter an integer, the second time enter a decimal number with less than six decimal places, the third time enter a number with more than six decimal places, and the fourth time enter a character. Using the output display, keep track of what number your program actually accepted from the data you typed in. What happened, if anything, and why?

12. Repeat Exercise 10 but have your program declare the variable used to store the number as a double precision variable. Run the program four times. The first time enter an integer, the second time enter a decimal number with less than six decimal places, the third time enter a number with more than six decimal places, and the fourth time enter a character. Using the output display, keep track of what number your program actually accepted from the data you typed in. What happened, if anything, and why?

13. a. Why do you think that most successful commercial applications programs contain extensive data input validity checks? (*Hint:* Review Exercises 10, 11, and 12.)
    b. What do you think is the difference between a data type check and a data reasonableness check?
    c. Assume that a program requests that a month, day, and year be entered by the user. What are some checks that could be made on the data entered?

14. Write a C program that uses the declaration statement `double num;`. Then use the function call `scanf("%f", &num);` to input a value into num. (Notice that we have used the wrong control sequence for the variable num.) Run your program and enter a decimal number. Using a `printf()` function call, have your program display the number stored in num1. Determine what problem you can run into when an incorrect control sequence is used in `scanf()`.

15. Program 3.10 prompts the user to input two numbers, where the first value entered is stored in num1 and the second value is stored in num2. Using this program as a starting point, write a program that swaps the values stored in the two variables.

3.4 scanf() with Buffered Input[4]

Seemingly strange results are sometimes obtained when the `scanf()` function is used to accept characters. To see how this can occur consider Program 3.11, which uses `scanf()` to accept the next character entered at the keyboard, storing it in the variable fkey.

 Program 3.11

```
#include <stdio.h>
int main()
{
  char fkey;

  printf("Type in a character: ");
  scanf("%c", &fkey);
  printf("The keystroke just accepted is %d", fkey);

  return 0;
}
```

---

[4] This section contains supplementary material on the `scanf()` function and can be omitted on first reading without loss of subject continuity.

When Program 3.11 is run, the character entered in response to the prompt `Type in a character:` is stored in the character variable `fkey`. The decimal code for the character is displayed by the second `printf()` function call. The following sample run illustrates this:

```
Type in a character: m
The keystroke just accepted is 109
```

At this point, everything seems to be working just fine, although you might be wondering why we displayed the decimal value of m rather than the character itself. The reason for this will soon become apparent.

When you type m, you usually press two keys, the m key and the ENTER key. On most computer systems these two characters are stored in a temporary holding area called a *buffer* immediately after they are pressed, as illustrated in Figure 3.13.

The first key pressed, m in this case, is taken from the buffer and stored in `fkey`. This, however, still leaves the code for the ENTER key in the buffer. Any subsequent call to `scanf()` for a character input will automatically pick up the code for the ENTER key as the next character. For example, consider Program 3.12.

The following is a sample run for Program 3.12:

```
Type in a character: m
The keystroke just accepted is 109
Type in another character: The keystroke just accepted is 10
```

Let us review what has happened. When you enter m in response to the first prompt, you also press the ENTER key. From a character standpoint this represents the entry of two distinct characters. The first character is m, which is stored as `109`. The second character also gets stored in the buffer with the numerical code for the ENTER key. The second call to `scanf()` picks up this code immediately, without waiting for any additional key to be pressed. The last call to `printf()` displays the code for this key. The reason for displaying the numerical code rather than the character itself is because the ENTER key has no printable character associated with it that can be displayed.

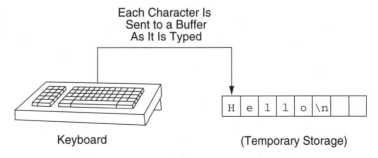

Figure 3.13   Typed keyboard characters are first stored in a buffer

Program 3.12

```
#include <stdio.h>
int main()
{
  char fkey, skey;

  printf("Type in a character: ");
  scanf("%c", &fkey);
  printf("The keystroke just accepted is %d"; fkey);
  printf("\nType in another character: ");
  scanf("%c", &skey);
  printf("The keystroke just accepted is %d", skey);

  return 0;
}
```

Remember that every key has a numerical code, including the ENTER, SPACE, ESCAPE, and CONTROL keys. These keys generally have no effect when entering numbers, because scanf() ignores them as leading or trailing whitespace input with numerical data. Nor do these keys affect the entry of a single character requested as the first user data to be input, as is the case in Program 3.11. Only when a character is requested after the user has already input some other data, as in Program 3.12, does the usually invisible ENTER key become noticeable.

There is a quick solution to the problem of having the ENTER key accepted as a legitimate character input. All we have to do is accept the ENTER key, store it as a character variable, and then just not use it. Program 3.13 illustrates this technique. The ENTER key is accepted along with the first character typed. This clears the computer's buffer and prepares the way for the character input.

In reviewing Program 3.13, observe that the first scanf() function call accepts two back-to-back characters. Now when the user types m and presses the ENTER key, the m is assigned to fkey and the code for the ENTER key is automatically assigned to skey. The next call to scanf() stores the code for the next key pressed in the variable skey also. This automatically erases the code for the ENTER key that was previously stored there. From the user's standpoint, the ENTER key has no effect except to signal the end of each character input. The following is a sample run for Program 3.13.

```
Type in a character: m
The keystroke just accepted is 109
Type in another character: b
The keystroke just accepted is 98
```

Program 3.13

```
#include <stdio.h>
int main()
{
  char fkey, skey;

  printf("Type in a character: ");
  scanf("%c%c", &fkey, &skey);     /* the enter code goes to skey */
  printf("The keystroke just accepted is %d", fkey);
  printf("\nType in another character: ");
  scanf("%c", &skey);    /* accept another code */
  printf("The keystroke just accepted is %d", skey);

  return 0;
}
```

The solution to the "phantom" ENTER key used in Program 3.13 is not the only solution possible (there is never just one way of doing something in C).[5] All solutions, however, center on the fact that the ENTER key is a legitimate character input and must be treated as such when using a buffered system.

3.5 Symbolic Constants

Literal data is any data within a program that explicitly identifies itself. For example, the constants 2 and 3.1416 in the assignment statement

```
circum = 2 * 3.1416 * radius;
```

are also called literals because they are literally included directly in the statement. Additional examples of literals are contained in the following C assignment statements. See if you can identify them.

```
perimeter = 2 * length * width;
y = (5 * p) / 7.2;
salestax = 0.05 * purchase;
```

---

[5] Two other solutions are to replace the last `scanf()` call in Program 3.12 with the statement `scanf("\n%c",&skey);`, or to place the statement `fflush(stdin);` after accepting a one character input. The `fflush()` function flushes the input buffer of any remaining characters.

The literals are the numbers 2, 5 and 7.2, and 0.05 in the first, second, and third statements, respectively.

The same literal often appears many times in the same program. For example, in a program used to determine bank interest charges, the interest rate would typically appear in different places throughout the program. Similarly, in a program used to calculate taxes, the tax rate might appear in many individual instructions. If either the interest rate or tax rate change, the programmer would have the cumbersome task of changing the literal value everywhere it appears in the program. Multiple changes, however, are subject to error—if just one rate value is overlooked and not changed, the result obtained when the program is run will be incorrect. Literal values that appear many times in the same program are referred to by programmers as *magic numbers*. By themselves the numbers are quite ordinary, but in the context of a particular application they have a special ("magical") meaning.

To avoid the problem of having a magic number spread throughout a program, C provides the programmer with the capability to define the value once by equating the number to a *symbolic name*. Then, instead of using the number throughout the program, the symbolic name is used instead. If the number ever has to be changed, the change need only be made once at the point where the symbolic name is equated to the actual number value. Equating numbers to symbolic names is accomplished using a #define statement. Two such statements are

```
#define SALESTAX 0.05  ← no semicolon
#define PI 3.1416  ←——— no semicolon
```

These two statements are called either #define or *equivalence* statements. The first #define statement equates the value 0.05 to the symbolic name SALESTAX, while the second #define statement equates the number 3.1416 to the symbolic name PI. Other terms for symbolic names are *named constants* and *symbolic constants*. We shall use these terms interchangeably.

It is common in C to use all uppercase letters for symbolic constants. Then, whenever a programmer sees all uppercase letters in a program, he or she will know the name is a symbolic constant defined in a #define statement, and not a variable name declared in a declaration statement.

The symbolic constants defined above can be used in any C statement in place of the numbers they represent. For example, the assignment statements

```
circum = 2 * PI * radius;
amount = SALESTAX * purchase;
```

are both valid. These statements must, of course, appear after the named constants are defined. Usually, all #define statements are placed at the top of a file, before any functions, including main(). #define and #include statements may be freely intermixed. Thus, in Program 3.14, the #include statement could have been placed above the #define statement.

Program 3.14

```c
#define SALESTAX 0.05
#include <stdio.h>
int main()
{
  float amount, taxes, total;

  printf("\nEnter the amount purchased: ");
  scanf("%f", &amount);
  taxes = SALESTAX * amount;
  total = amount + taxes;
  printf("The sales tax is $%4.2f",taxes);
  printf("\nThe total bill is $%5.2f",total);

  return 0;
}
```

The following sample run was made using Program 3.14.

```
Enter the amount purchased: 36.00
The sales tax is $1.80
The total bill is $37.80
```

Whenever a named constant appears in an instruction it has the same effect as if the literal value it represents was used. Thus, SALESTAX is simply another way of representing the value 0.05. Since SALESTAX and the number 0.05 are equivalent, the value of SALESTAX may not subsequently be changed by the program. An instruction such as SALESTAX = 0.06; is meaningless, because SALESTAX is not a variable. Since SALESTAX is only a stand-in for the value 0.05, this statement is equivalent to writing the invalid statement 0.05 = 0.06;.

Notice also that #define statements do not end with a semicolon. The reason for this is that #define statements are not processed by the regular C compiler used to translate C statements into machine language. The # sign is a signal to a C *preprocessor.* This preprocessor screens all program statements when a C program is compiled. When the preprocessor encounters a # sign, it recognizes an instruction to itself. The word define tells the preprocessor to equate the symbolic constant in the statement with the information or data following it. In the case of a statement like #define SALESTAX 0.05, the word SALESTAX is equated to the value 0.05. The preprocessor then replaces each subsequent occurrence of the word SALESTAX in the C program with the value 0.05.

This explains why a #define statement does not end with a semicolon. If a semicolon followed the literal value 0.05, the preprocessor would equate the word SALESTAX with 0.05;. Then, when it replaced SALESTAX in the assignment statement taxes = SALESTAX * amount;, the statement would become taxes = 0.05; * amount;, which is the valid statement taxes = 0.05; followed by the invalid statement * amount;.

Realizing that #define statements simply relate two items allows us to use them to create individualized programming languages. For example, the #define statements

```
#define BEGIN {
#define END }
```

equate the first brace { to the word BEGIN and the closing brace } to the word END. Once these symbols are equated the words BEGIN and END can be used in place of the respective braces. This is illustrated in Program 3.15.

 Program 3.15

```
#define SALESTAX 0.05
#define BEGIN {
#define END }
#include <stdio.h>
int main()
BEGIN
  float amount, taxes, total;

  printf("\nEnter in the amount purchased: ");
  scanf("%f", &amount);
  taxes = SALESTAX * amount;
  total = amount + taxes;
  printf("The sales tax is $%4.2f",taxes);
  printf("\nThe total bill is $%5.2f",total);

  return 0;
END
```

When Program 3.15 is compiled, the preprocessor faithfully replaces all occurrences of the words BEGIN and END with their equivalent symbols. Although using #define statements to create a new set of symbols equivalent to the standard C symbol set is usually not a good idea, Program 3.15 should give you an idea of the richness and diversity that C provides. Generally, the constructions that can be created in C are limited only by the imagination and good sense of the programmer.

Exercises 3.5

Determine the purpose of the programs given in Exercises 1 through 3. Then rewrite each program using #define statements for appropriate literals.

1.
```c
#include <stdio.h>
int main()
{
  float radius, circum;

  printf("\nEnter a radius: ");
  scanf("%f", &radius);
  circum = 2.0 * 3.1416 * radius;
  printf("\nThe circumference of the circle is %f", circum);

  return 0;
}
```

2.
```c
#include <stdio.h>
int main()
{
  float prime, amount, interest;

  prime = 0.08;        /* prime interest rate */
  printf("\nEnter the amount: ");
  scant("%f", &amount);
  interest = prime * amount;
  printf("\nThe interest earned is %f dollars", interest);

  return 0;
}
```

3.
```c
#include <stdio.h>
int main()
{
  float fahren, celsius;

  printf("\nEnter a temperature in degrees Fahrenheit: ");
  scanf("%f", &fahren);
  celsius = (5.0/9.0) * (fahren - 32.0);
  printf("\nThe equivalent Celsius temperature is %f", celsius);

  return 0;
}
```

3.6 Common Programming Errors

In using the material presented in this chapter, be aware of the following possible errors:

1. Forgetting to assign initial values to all variables before the variables are used in an expression. Initial values can be assigned when the variables are declared, by explicit assignment statements, or by interactively entering values using the `scanf()` function.

2. Applying the increment or decrement operators to an expression. For example, the expression

```
(count + n)++
```

is incorrect. The increment and decrement operators can only be applied to individual variables.

3. Attempting to store an address in a variable that has not been declared as a pointer.

4. Forgetting to pass addresses to `scanf()`. Since `scanf()` treats all arguments following the control string as addresses, it is up to the programmer to ensure that addresses are passed correctly.

5. Including a message within the control string passed to `scanf()`. Unlike `printf()`, `scanf()`'s control string typically contains only conversion control sequences.

6. Not including the correct control sequences in `scanf()` function calls for the data values that must be entered.

7. Not closing the control string passed to `scanf()` with a double quote symbol followed by a comma, and forgetting to separate all arguments passed to `scanf()` with commas.

8. Terminating a `#define` command to the preprocessor with a semicolon. By now you probably end every line in your C programs with a semicolon, almost automatically. But there are cases, such as preprocessor commands, where a semicolon should not end a line.

9. A more exotic error occurs when the increment and decrement operators are used with variables that appear more than once in the same expression. This error, explained in Chapter 13, occurs because C does not specify the order in which operands are accessed within an expression. For example, the value assigned to `result` in the statement

```
result = i + i++;
```

is compiler dependent. If your program accesses the first operand, `i`, first, the above statement is equivalent to

```
result = 2 * i;
i++;
```

However, if your program accesses the second operand, `i++`, first, the value of the first operand will be altered before it is used and a different value is assigned to `result`. As a general rule, therefore, do not use either the increment or decrement operators in expressions where the variables they operate on appear more than once in the expression.

3.7 Chapter Summary

1. An expression is a sequence of one or more operands separated by operators. An operand is a constant, a variable, or another expression. A value is associated with an expression.

2. Expressions are evaluated according to the precedence and associativity of the operators used in the expression.

3. The assignment symbol, =, is an operator. Expressions using this operator assign a value to a variable; additionally, the expression itself takes on a value. Since assignment is an operation in C, multiple uses of the assignment operator are possible in the same expression.

4. The increment operator, `++`, adds one to a variable, while the decrement operator, `--`, subtracts one from a variable. Both of these operators can be used as prefixes or postfixes. In prefix operation the variable is incremented (or decremented) before its value is used. In postfix operation the variable is incremented (or decremented) after its value is used.

5. Every variable has a data type, an address, and a value. In C, the address of a variable can be obtained by using the address operator, `&`. Programmers access a variable by using its name, while the compiler accesses the variable using its address.

6. A pointer is a variable that is used to store the address of another variable. Pointers, like all C variables, must be declared. The indirection operator, `*`, is used both to declare a pointer variable and to access the variable whose address is stored in a pointer.

7. The `scanf()` function is a standard library function used for data input. `scanf()` requires a control string and a list of addresses. The general form of this function call is

```
scanf("control string", &arg1, &arg2, . . . , &argn);
```

The control string typically contains only conversion control sequences, such as `%d`, and must contain the same number of conversion control sequences as argument addresses.

8. When a `scanf()` function is encountered the program temporarily suspends further statement execution until sufficient data has been entered for the number of variable addresses contained in the `scanf()` function call.

9. It is good programming practice to display a message, prior to a `scanf()` function call, that alerts the user as to the type and number of data items to be entered. Such a message is called a prompt.

10. Each compiled C program is automatically passed through a preprocessor. Lines beginning with # in the first column are recognized as commands to this preprocessor. Preprocessor commands are not terminated with a semicolon.

11. Expressions can be made equivalent to a single identifier using the preprocessor `#define` command. This command has the form

```
#define identifier expression
```

and allows the identifier to be used instead of the expression anywhere in the program after the command.

3.8   Chapter Supplement: Introduction to Abstraction

A very important programming concept, and one that you will increasingly encounter as you progress in your studies, is the idea of *abstraction*. This concept is fundamentally applied in three areas: data type abstraction, procedural abstraction, and abstract data types—all of which you now have the background to understand. In this section we first introduce the concept of abstraction and then use it to define these three types of abstractions.

In its most general usage, an abstraction is simply an idea or term that identifies general qualities or characteristics of a group of objects, independent of any one specific object in the group. For example, consider the term "car." As a term this is an abstraction: it refers to a group of objects that individually contain the characteristics associated with a car, such as a motor, passenger compartment, wheels, steering capabilities, brakes, etc. A particular instance of a car such as my car or your car are not abstractions—they are real objects that are classified as "type car" because they have attributes associated with a car.

Although we use abstract concepts all the time, we tend not to think of them as such. For example, the words "tree," "dog," "cat," "table," and "chair" are all abstractions, just as a car is. Each of these terms refers to a set of qualities that are met by a group of particular things. For each of these abstractions there are many individual trees, dogs, and cats, each instance of which conforms to the general characteristics associated with the abstract term.

In programming, especially more advanced work, we are much more careful to label appropriate terms as abstractions than we are in everyday life. The first such term that is really an abstraction is a *data type*. Let us see why this is so.

Just as "my car" is a particular instance or object of the more abstract "type car," a particular integer, say 5 for example, is a specific object or instance of the more abstract

Table 3.1　C's data types

Data Type	Minimum Acceptable Domain	Operations
integer (includes long, short, and unsigned	–32768 to +32767	+, –, *, /, %, =, ==, !=, <=, >=, and bit operations
floating point (includes double and long double)	–1E–37 to +1E+37	+, –, *, /, =, ==, !=, <=, >=
character	All characters with an ASCII value between 0 and 127	+, –, *, /, =, ==, !=, <=, >=

"type integer," where an integer is a signed or unsigned number having no decimal point. As such, each type—integer, character, and floating point—is considered an abstraction that defines a general type of which specific instances can be realized. Such types, then, simply identify common qualities of each group and make it reasonable to speak of integer types, character types, and floating point types.

Having defined what we mean by a type, we can now create the definition of a data type. In programming terminology a data type consists of *both* an acceptable range of values of a particular type *and* a set of operations that can be applied to those values. Thus, the integer data type not only defines a range of acceptable integer values, but also defines which operations can be applied to those values.

Although users of programming languages such as C ordinarily assume that mathematical operations such as addition, subtraction, multiplication, and division will be supplied for integers, the designers of C had to carefully consider which operations would be provided as part of the integer data type. For example, they did not include an exponentiation operator as part of the integer data type, while this operation is included in FORTRAN's data abstraction of integers (in C, exponentiation is supplied as a library function).

To summarize then, a data type is an abstraction that consists of:

1. A set of values of a particular type.
2. A set of operations that can be applied to those values.

The set of allowed values is more formally referred to as the data type's *domain*. Table 3.1 lists the domain and the most common operations defined for the data types int, float, and char.[6]

Built-in and Abstract Data Types

All of the data types listed in Table 3.1 are provided as part of the C language. As such, they are formally referred to as *built-in* or *primitive* data types (the two terms are synony-

---

[6] The actual domain for integers can be found in the <limits.h> header file supplied by your compiler. Similarly the domain for floating point numbers can be found in the header file <float.h>

mous). In contrast to built-in types, some programming languages permit programmers to create their own data types; that is, define a type of value with an associated domain and operations that can be performed on the acceptable values. Such user-defined data types are formally referred to as *abstract data types*. Although C does not provide the capability to create abstract data types, it is provided in C++. In C++ abstract data types are called *classes*, and the ability to create classes is the major enhancement provided to C by C++ (in fact, the original name for C++ was "C with Classes").

Procedural Abstraction

In addition to data abstraction, all programming languages permit assigning a name to a procedure or function. As a specific example, consider the `printf()` function. This function internally consists of a sequence of instructions that provides for the formatted display of data. The instructions, however, are invoked as a unit using the single name `printf`.

The assigning of a name to a function or procedure in such a way that the function is invoked by simply using a name with appropriate arguments is formally referred to as *procedural abstraction*. When you write your own user-named functions in Chapter 6, you will actually be creating procedural abstractions.

Procedural abstraction effectively hides the details of how a function performs its task. This hiding of the details is one of the hallmarks and strengths of abstraction. By thinking of tasks on an abstract, procedural level programmers can solve problems at a higher level without immediately being concerned with the nitty-gritty details of the actual solution implementation.

Flow of Control

Selection

The term *flow of control* refers to the order in which a program's statements are executed. Unless directed otherwise, the normal flow of control for all programs is *sequential*. This means that each statement is executed in sequence, one after another, in the order in which they are placed within the program.

Both selection and repetition statements allow the programmer to alter the normal sequential flow of control. As their names imply, *selection statements* provide the ability to select which statement will be executed next, while *repetition statements* provide the ability to go back and repeat a set of statements. In this chapter we present C's selection statements. Since selection requires choosing between alternatives, we begin this chapter with a description of C's selection criteria.

4.1 Relational Expressions

Besides providing addition, subtraction, multiplication, and division capabilities, all computers have the ability to compare numbers. Because many seemingly "intelligent"

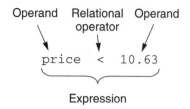

Operand   Relational   Operand
            operator

price   <   10.63

Expression

Figure 4.1   Anatomy of a simple relational expression

decision-making situations can be reduced to the level of choosing between two values, a computer's comparison capability can be used to create a remarkable facility much like intelligence.

The expressions used to compare operands are called *relational expressions.* A *simple relational expression* consists of a relational operator connecting two variable and/or constant operands, as shown in Figure 4.1. The relational operators available in C are given in Table 4.1. These relational operators may be used with integer, float, double, or character data, but must be typed exactly as given in Table 4.1. Thus, the following examples are all valid:

```
age > 40       length <= 50      temp > 98.6
3 < 4          flag == done      idNum == 682
day != 5       2.0 > 3.3         hours > 40
```

and the following are invalid:

```
length =< 50       /* operator out of order  */
2.0 >> 3.3         /* invalid operator        */
flag = = done      /* spaces are not allowed  */
```

Relational expressions are sometimes called *conditions,* and we will use both terms to refer to these expressions. Like all C expressions, relational expressions are evaluated to yield a numerical result.[1] In the case of relational expressions, the value of the expres-

Table 4.1   Relational operators in C

Relational operator	Meaning	Example
<	less than	age < 30
>	greater than	height > 6.2
<=	less than or equal to	taxable <= 20000
>=	greater than or equal to	temp >= 98.6
==	equal to	grade == 100
!=	not equal to	number != 250

---

[1] In this regard C differs from other high-level programming languages that yield a Boolean (true or false) result.

sion can only be an integer value of 1 or 0. *A condition that we would interpret as true evaluates to an integer value of 1, and a false condition results in an integer value of 0.* For example, because the relationship 3 < 4 is always true, the expression has a value of 1, and because the relationship 2.0 > 3.3 is always false, the expression has a value of 0. This can be verified using the statements

```
printf("The value of 3 < 4 is %d", 3 < 4);
printf("\nThe value of 2.0 > 3.3 is %d", 2.0 > 3.3);
```

which results in the display

```
The value of 3 < 4 is 1
The value of 2.0 > 3.3 is 0
```

The value of a relational expression such as `hours > 0` depends on the value stored in the variable `hours`.

In a C program, a relational expression's value is not as important as the interpretation C places on the value when the expression is used as part of a selection statement. In such statements, which are presented in the next section, we will see that a zero value is used by C to represent a false condition and any nonzero value is used to represent a true condition. The selection of which statement to execute next is then based on the value obtained.

In addition to numerical operands, character data can also be compared using relational operators. For example, in the ASCII code the letter *A* is stored using a code having a lower numerical value than the letter *B,* the code for a *B* is lower in value than the code for a *C,* and so on. For character sets coded in this manner, the following expressions are evaluated as listed.

Expression	Value	Interpretation
'A' > 'C'	0	False
'D' <= 'Z'	1	True
'E' == 'F'	0	False
'G' >= 'M'	0	False
'B' != 'C'	1	True

Comparing letters is essential in alphabetizing names or using characters to select a particular choice in decision-making situations.

Logical Operators

In addition to using simple relational expressions as conditions, more complex conditions can be created using the logical operations AND, OR, and NOT. These operations are represented by the symbols &&, | |, and !, respectively.

When the AND operator, &&, is used with two simple expressions, the condition is true only if both expressions are true by themselves. Thus, the compound condition

```
(age > 40) && (term < 10)
```

is true (has a value of 1) only if `age` is greater than 40 and `term` is less than 10. Because relational operators have a higher precedence than logical operators, the parentheses in this logical expression could have been omitted.

The logical OR operator, `||`, is also applied between two expressions. When using the OR operator, the condition is satisfied if either one or both of the two expressions are true. Thus, the compound condition

```
(age > 40) || (term < 10)
```

is true if either `age` is greater than 40, `term` is less than 10, or both conditions are true. Again, the parentheses surrounding the relational expressions are included to make the expression easier to read. Because of the higher precedence of relational operators with respect to logical operators, the same evaluation is made even if the parentheses are omitted.

For the declarations

```
int i, j;
float a, b, complete;
```

the following represent valid conditions:

```
a > b
i == j || a < b || complete
a/b > 5 && i <= 20
```

Before these conditions can be evaluated, the values of a, b, i, j, and `complete` must be known. Assuming

$$a = 12.0, \quad b = 2.0, \quad i = 15, \quad j = 30, \quad \text{and complete} = 0.0$$

the expressions yield the following results:

Expression	Value	Interpretation
`a > b`	1	True
`i == j || a < b || complete`	0	False
`a/b > 5 && i <= 20`	1	True

The NOT operator is used to change an expression to its opposite state; that is, if the expression has any nonzero value (true), *!expression* produces a zero value (false). If an expression is false to begin with (has a zero value), *!expression* is true and evaluates to 1. For example, assuming the number 26 is stored in the variable `age`, the expression `age`

Table 4.2 Precedence of operators in C

Operator	Associativity	Precedence
`!, unary -, ++, --`	right to left	highest
`*, /, %`	left to right	
`+, -`	left to right	
`<, <=, >, >=`	left to right	
`==, !=`	left to right	
`&&`	left to right	
`||`	left to right	
`+=, -=, *=, /=`	right to left	lowest

`> 40` has a value of zero (it is false), while the expression `!(age > 40)` has a value of 1. Since the NOT operator is used with only one expression, it is a unary operator.

The relational and logical operators have a hierarchy of execution similar to that of the arithmetic operators. Table 4.2 lists the precedence of these operators in relation to the other operators we have used.

The following example illustrates the use of precedence and associativity to evaluate relational expressions, assuming the following declarations:

```
char key = 'm';
int i = 5, j = 7, k = 12;
double x = 22.5;
```

Expression	Equivalent Expression	Value	Interpretation
`i + 2 == k - 1`	`(i + 2) == (k - 1)`	0	False
`3 * i - j < 22`	`((3 * i) - j) < 22`	1	True
`i + 2 * j > k`	`(i + (2 * j)) > k`	1	True
`k + 3 <= -j + 3 * i`	`(k + 3) <= ((-j) + (3*i))`	0	False
`'a' + 1 == 'b'`	`('a' + 1) == 'b'`	1	True
`key - 1 > 'p'`	`(key - 1) > 'p'`	0	False
`key + 1 == 'n'`	`(key + 1) == 'n'`	1	True
`25 >= x + 4.0`	`25 >= (x + 4.0)`	0	False

As with all expressions, parentheses can be used to alter the assigned operator priority and improve the readability of relational expressions. By evaluating the expressions within parentheses first, the following compound condition is evaluated as:

```
(6 * 3 == 36 / 2) || (13 < 3 * 3 + 4) && !(6 - 2 < 5)
        (18 == 18) ||    (13 < 9 + 4)  && !(4 < 5)
                1 ||    (13 < 13)      && !1
                1 ||        0          && 0
                1 ||        0
                1
```

A Numerical Accuracy Problem

A problem that can occur with C's relational expressions is a subtle numerical accuracy problem relating to floating point and double precision numbers. Because of the way computers store these numbers, tests for equality of floating point and double precision values and variables using the relational operator == should be avoided.

The reason for this is that many decimal numbers, such as 0.1, for example, cannot be represented exactly in binary using a finite number of bits. Thus, testing for exact equality for such numbers can fail. When equality of noninteger values is desired it is better to require that the absolute value of the difference between operands be less than some extremely small value. Thus, for floating point and double precision operands the general expression

```
operandA == operandB
```

should be replaced by the condition

```
fabs(operandA - operandB) < 0.000001
```

where the value 0.000001 can be altered to any other acceptably small value. Thus, if the absolute difference between the two operands is less than 0.000001 (or any other user-selected amount), the two operands are considered essentially equal.[2] For example, if x and y are floating point variables, a condition such as

```
x/y == 0.35
```

should be programmed as

```
fabs(x/y - 0.35) < EPSILON
```

where EPSILON is a named constant set to any acceptably small value, such as 0.000001. This latter condition ensures that slight inaccuracies in representing noninteger numbers in binary do not affect evaluation of the tested condition. Since all computers have an exact binary representation of zero, comparisons for exact equality to zero don't encounter this numerical accuracy problem.

---

[2] fabs() is a floating point absolute value function (described in more detail in Section 6.2) and requires inclusion of the math.h header file. This is done by placing the preprocessor statement #include <math.h> either immediately before or after the #include <stdio.h> preprocessor statement. For UNIX systems it also requires specific inclusion of the math library at compile time with a -lm command line argument.

Exercises 4.1

1. Determine the value of the following expressions. Assume a = 5, b = 2, c = 4, d = 6, and e =3.

   a. a > b   f. a * b

   b. a != b   g. a % b * c

   c. d % b == c % b   h. c % b * a

   d. a * c != d * b   i. b % c * a

   e. d * b == c * e

2. Using parentheses, rewrite the following expressions to correctly indicate their order of evaluation. Then evaluate each expression assuming a = 5, b = 2, and c = 4.

   a. a % b * c && c % b * a   c. b % c * a && a % c * b

   b. a % b * c || c % b * a   d. b % c * a || a % c * b

3. Write relational expressions to express the following conditions (use variable names of your own choosing):

   a. a person's age is equal to 30

   b. a person's temperature is greater than 98.6

   c. a person's height is less than 6 feet

   d. the current month is 12 (December)

   e. the letter input is *m*

   f. a person's age is equal to 30 and the person is taller than 6 feet

   g. the current day is the 15th day of the 1st month

   h. a person is older than 50 or has been employed at the company for at least 5 years

   i. a person's identification number is less than 500 and the person is older than 55

   j. a length is greater than 2 and less than 3 feet

4. Determine the value of the following expressions, assuming a = 5, b = 2, c = 4, and d = 5.

   a. a == 5

   b. b * d == c * c

   c. d % b * c > 5 || c % b * d < 7

4.2 The **if-else** Statement

The if-else statement directs the computer to select a sequence of one or more instructions based on the result of a comparison. For example, if a New Jersey resident's income is less than $20,000, the applicable state income tax rate is 2 percent. If the person's income is greater than $20,000, a different rate is applied to the amount over $20,000. The if-else statement can be used in this situation to determine the actual tax based on whether the gross income is less than or equal to $20,000. The general form of the if-else statement is

```
if (expression) statement1;
    else statement2;
```

The *expression* is evaluated first. If the value of the *expression* is nonzero, *statement1* is executed. If the value is zero, *statement2*, the statement after the reserved word else, is executed. Thus, one of the two statements (either *statement1* or *statement2*) is always executed depending on the value of the expression. Notice that the tested expression must be put in parentheses and a semicolon is placed after each statement.

For clarity, the if-else statement may also be written on four lines using the form

```
if (expression) ←──────────── no semicolon here
   statement1;
else ←──────────────────────── no semicolon here
   statement2;
```

The form of the if-else statement that is selected generally depends on the length of statements 1 and 2. However, when using the second form, do not put a semicolon after the parentheses or the reserved word else. The semicolons go only after the ends of the statements.

As an example, let us write an income tax computation program containing an if-else statement. As previously described, New Jersey state income tax is assessed at 2 percent of taxable income for incomes less than or equal to $20,000. For taxable income greater than $20,000, state taxes are 2.5 percent of the income that exceeds $20,000 plus a fixed amount of $400 (which is 2 percent of $20,000). The expression to be tested is whether taxable income is less than or equal to $20,000. An appropriate if-else statement for this situation is[3]

```
if (taxable <= 20000.0)
   taxes = 0.02 * taxable;
else
   taxes = 0.025 * (taxable - 20000.0) + 400.0;
```

Here we have used the relational operator <= to represent the relation "less than or equal to." If the value of taxable is less than or equal to 20,000, the condition is true (has a value of 1) and the statement taxes = 0.02 * taxable; is executed. If the condition is not true, the value of the expression is zero, and the statement after the reserved word else is executed. Program 4.1 illustrates the use of this statement in a complete program using named constants for the actual numerical values.

A blank line was inserted before and after the if-else statement to highlight it in the complete program. We will continue to do this throughout the text to emphasize the statement being presented.

To illustrate this selection in action, Program 4.1 was run twice with different input data. The results are

```
Please type in the taxable income: 10000.
Taxes are $ 200.00
```

and

---

[3] Note that in actual practice the numerical values in this statement would be defined as named constants.

```
Please type in the taxable income: 30000.
Taxes are $ 650.00
```

 Program 4.1

```c
#include <stdio.h>
#define LOWRATE 0.02    /* lower tax rate */
#define HIGHRATE 0.025 /* higher tax rate */
#define CUTOFF 20000.0 /* cut off for low rate */
#define FIXEDAMT 400    /* fixed dollar amount for higher rate amounts */

int main()
{
  float taxable, taxes;

  printf("Please type in the taxable income: ");
  scanf("%f",&taxable);

  if (taxable <= CUTOFF)
    taxes = LOWRATE * taxable;
  else
    taxes = HIGHRATE * (taxable - CUTOFF) + FIXEDAMT;

  printf("Taxes are $%7.2f",taxes);

  return 0;
}
```

Observe that the taxable income input in the first run of the program was less than $20,000, and the tax was correctly calculated as 2 percent of the number entered. In the second run, the taxable income was more than $20,000, and the else part of the if-else statement was used to yield a correct tax computation of

```
0.025 * ($30,000. - $20,000.) + $400. = $650.
```

Although any expression can be tested by an if-else statement, generally only relational expressions are used. However, statements such as

```
if (num)
  printf("Bingo!");
else
  printf("You lose!");
```

Programming Note

True and False

Many computer languages provide a logical or Boolean data type that consists of two values only, true and false, for evaluating relational expressions. In these languages relational and logical expressions are restricted to yielding one of these values, and selection statements are restricted to evaluating only relational and logical expressions. This is not the case in C.

In C any expression can be tested within a selection statement, be it a relational, arithmetic, or assignment expression, or even a function call. Within a selection statement, an expression that evaluates to zero or a function that returns a 0 is considered as false, while any nonzero value (negative or positive) is considered as true. If a relational or logical expression is tested, however, the expression itself will yield only 1 or 0; 1 if the relational or logical expression is true and 0 if it is false.

Sometimes it is convenient to create the following two symbolic constants:

```
#define TRUE 1;
#define FALSE 0;
```

These constants are convenient as values to clearly identify a true or false condition. For example, consider the algorithm

```
if (it is a leap year)
   set yearType to TRUE
else
   set yearType to FALSE
```

A C programmer will automatically understand this to mean "set year type to 1" and "set year type to 0", respectively.

are valid. Since num, by itself, is a valid expression, the message `Bingo!` is displayed if num has any nonzero value and the message `You lose!` is displayed if num has a value of zero.

Compound Statements

Although only a single statement is permitted in both the `if` and `else` parts of the `if-else` statement, this statement can be a single compound statement. A *compound statement* is any number of statements contained between braces as shown in Figure 4.2.

The use of braces to enclose a set of individual statements creates a single block of statements, which may be used anywhere in a C program in place of a single statement. The next example illustrates the use of a compound statement within the general form of an `if-else` statement.

```
          {
            statement1;
            statement2;
            statement3;
                    .
                    .
                    .
            last statement;
          }

          if (expression)
          {
            statement1;    /* as many statements as necessary */
            statement2;    /* can be put within the braces */
            statement3;    /* each statement must end with a ; */

          }
          else
          {
            statement4;
            statement5;
                    .
                    .
            statementn;
          }
```

Figure 4.2   A compound statement

Program 4.2 illustrates the use of a compound statement in an actual program.

Program 4.2

```
#include <stdio.h>
int main()
{
  char tempType;
  float temp, fahren, celsius;

  printf("Enter the temperature to be converted: ");
  scanf("%f",&temp);
  printf("Enter an f if the temperature is in Fahrenheit");
  printf("\n or a c if the temperature is in Celsius: ");
```

(Continued on next page)

(Continued from previous page)

```
scanf("\n%c",&tempType);          \* see footnote on page 111 *\

if (tempType == 'f')
{
   celsius = (5.0 / 9.0) * (temp - 32.0);
   printf("\nThe equivalent Celsius temperature is %6.2f", celsius);
}
else
{
   fahren = (9.0 / 5.0) * temp + 32.0;
   printf("\nThe equivalent Fahrenheit temperature is %6.2F", fahren);
}

return 0;
}
```

Program 4.2 checks whether the value in tempType is f. If the value is f, the compound statement corresponding to the if part of the if-else statement is executed. Any other letter results in execution of the compound statement corresponding to the else part. Following is a sample run of Program 4.2.

```
Enter the temperature to be converted: 212
Enter an f if the temperature is in Fahrenheit
  or a c if the temperature is in Celsius: f

The equivalent Celsius temperature is 100.00
```

One-Way Selection

A useful modification of the if-else statement involves omitting the else part of the statement altogether. In this case, the if statement takes the shortened and frequently useful form:

```
if (expression)
    statement;
```

The statement following the if (*expression*) is only executed if the *expression* has a nonzero value (a true condition). As before, the statement may be a compound statement.

This modified form of the if statement is called a *one-way* if *statement*. This kind of if statement is illustrated in Program 4.3, which checks a car's mileage and prints a message if the car has been driven more than 3000.0 miles.

Programming Note

Placement of Braces in a Compound Statement

A common practice for some programmers is to place the opening brace of a compound statement on the same line as the `if` and `else` statements. Using this convention the `if` statement in Program 4.2 would appear as shown below. This placement is a matter of style only—both styles are used and both are correct.

```
if (tempType == 'f') {
  celsius = (5.0 / 9.0) * (temp - 32.0);
  printf("\nThe equivalent Celsius temperature is %6.2f", celsius);
}
  else {
    fahren =  (9.0 / 5.0) * temp + 32.0;
    printf("\nThe equivalent Fahrenheit temperature is %6.2f", fahren);
}
```

 Program 4.3

```
#define LIMIT 3000.0
#include <stdio.h>
int main()
{
  int idNum;
  float miles;

  printf("Please type in car number and mileage: ");
  scanf("%d %f", &idNum, &miles);

  if(miles > LIMIT)
    printf("  Car %d is over the limit.\n",idNum);

  printf("End of program output.\n");

  return 0;
}
```

To illustrate the one-way selection criteria in action, Program 4.3 was run twice, each time with different input data. Only the input data for the first run causes the message `Car 256 is over the limit` to be displayed.

```
Please type in car number and mileage: 256 3562.8
   Car 256 is over the limit.
End of program output.
```

and

```
Please type in car number and mileage: 23 2562.3
End of program output.
```

Problems Associated with the `if-else` Statement

Two of the most common problems encountered in initially using C's `if-else` statement are

1. Misunderstanding the full implications of what an expression is.
2. Using the assignment operator, =, in place of the relational operator, ==.

Recall that an expression is any combination of operands and operators that yields a result. This definition is extremely broad and more encompassing than is initially apparent. For example, all of the following are valid C expressions:

```
age + 5
age = 30
age == 40
```

Assuming that the variable `age` is suitably declared, each of the above expressions yields a result. The following section of code uses the `printf()` function to display the value of these expressions when `age` is initially assigned the value 18.

```
age = 18;
printf("\nThe value of the first expression is %d", age + 5);
printf("\nThe value of the second expression is %d", age = 30);
printf("\nThe value of the third expression is %d", age == 40 );
```

The display produced by this section of code is

```
The value of the first expression is 23
The value of the second expression is 30
The value of the third expression is 0
```

As this output illustrates, each expression, by itself, has a value associated with it. The value of the first expression is the sum of the variable age plus 5, which is 23. The value of the second expression is 30, which is also assigned to the variable age. The value of the third expression is 0, since age is not equal to 40, and a false condition is represented in C with a value of 0. If the value in age had been 40, the relational expression a == 40 would be true and have a value of 1.

Now assume that the relational expression age == 40 was intended to be used in the if statement

```
if (age == 40)
   printf("Happy Birthday!");
```

but was mistyped as age = 40, resulting in

```
if (age = 40)
   printf("Happy Birthday!");
```

Since the mistake results in a valid C expression, and any C expression can be tested by an if statement, the resulting if statement is valid and causes the message Happy Birthday! to be printed regardless of what value was previously assigned to age. Can you see why?

The condition tested by the if statement does not compare the value in age to the number 40, but assigns the number 40 to age. That is, the expression age = 40 is not a relational expression at all, but an assignment expression. At the completion of the assignment the expression itself has a value of 40. Since C treats any nonzero value as true, the call to printf() is made. Another way of looking at this is to realize that the if statement is equivalent to the following two statements:

```
age = 40;        /* assign 40 to age */
if (age)         /* test the value of age */
   printf("Happy Birthday!");
```

Because a C compiler has no means of knowing that the expression being tested is not the desired one, you must be especially careful when writing conditions.

Exercises 4.2

1. Write appropriate if statements for each of the following conditions:
   a. If angle is equal to 90 degrees print the message "The angle is a right angle", else print the message that "The angle is not a right angle".
   b. If the temperature is above 100 degrees display the message "above the boiling point of water", else display the message "below the boiling point of water".
   c. If the number is positive add the number to positiveSum, else add the number to negativeSum.

d. If the slope is less than .5 set the variable `flag` to zero, else set `flag` to one.

e. If the difference between num1 and num2 is less than .001, set the variable `approx` to zero, else calculate `approx` as the quantity `(num1 - num2)/2.0`.

f. If the difference between `temp1` and `temp2` exceeds 2.3 degrees, calculate `error` as `(temp1 - temp2) * factor`.

g. If x is greater than y and z is less than 20, read in a value for the integer p.

h. If `distance` is greater than 20 and it is less than 35, read in a value for the integer `time`.

2. a. If money is left in a particular bank for more than 5 years, the interest rate given by the bank is 7.5 percent, else the interest rate is 5.4 percent. Write a C program that uses the `scanf()` function to accept the number of years into the variable `numYrs` and display the appropriate interest rate depending on the value input into `numYrs`.

   b. How many runs should you make for the program written in Exercise 2a to verify that it is operating correctly? What data should you input in each of the program runs?

3. a. In a pass/fail course, a student passes if the grade is greater than or equal to 70 and fails if the grade is lower. Write a C program that accepts a grade and prints the message `A passing grade` or `A failing grade`, as appropriate.

   b. How many runs should you make for the program written in Exercise 3a to verify that it is operating correctly? What data should you input in each of the program runs?

4. a. Write a C program to compute and display a person's weekly salary as determined by the following expressions:

   If the hours worked are less than or equal to 40, the person receives $8.00 per hour; else the person receives $320.00 plus $12.00 for each hour worked over 40 hours.

   The program should request the hours worked as input and should display the salary as output.

   b. How many runs should you make for the program written in Exercise 4a to verify that it is operating correctly? What data should you input in each of the program runs?

5. a. A senior salesperson is paid $400 a week and a junior salesperson $275 a week. Write a C program that accepts as input a salesperson's status in the character variable `status`. If `status` equals `'s'`, the senior person's salary should be displayed, else the junior person's salary should be output.

   b. How many runs should you make for the program written in Exercise 5a to verify that it is operating correctly? What data should you input in each of the program runs?

6. a. Write a C program that displays either the message `I feel great today!` or `I feel down today #$*!` depending on the input. If the character u is entered in the variable `ch`, the first message should be displayed, else the second message should be displayed.

   b. How many runs should you make for the program written in Exercise 6a to verify that it is operating correctly? What data should you input in each of the program runs?

7. a. Write a C program to display the following two prompts:

```
Enter a month (use a 1 for Jan, etc.):
Enter a day of the month:
```

   Have your program accept and store a number in the variable `month` in response to the first prompt, and accept and store a number in the variable `day` in response to the second prompt.

   If the month entered is not between 1 and 12 inclusive, print a message informing the user that an invalid month has been entered.

If the day entered is not between 1 and 31, print a message informing the user that an invalid day has been entered.

b. What will your program do if the user types a number with a decimal point for the month? How can you insure that your if statements check for an integer number?

8. Write a C program that accepts a character using the scanf() function and determines if the character is a lowercase letter. A lowercase letter is any character that is greater than or equal to 'a' and less than or equal to 'z'. If the entered character is a lowercase letter, display the message The character just entered is a lowercase letter. If the entered letter is not lowercase, display the message The character just entered is not a lowercase letter.

9. Write a C program that first determines if an entered character is a lowercase letter (see Exercise 8). If the letter is lowercase, determine and print out its position in the alphabet. For example, if the entered letter is c, the program should print out 3, since c is the third letter in the alphabet. (*Hint:* If the entered character is lowercase, its position can be determined by subtracting 'a' from the letter and adding 1.)

10. Repeat Exercise 8 to determine if the character entered is an uppercase letter. An uppercase letter is any character greater than or equal to 'A' and less than or equal to 'Z'.

11. Write a C program that first determines if an entered character is an uppercase letter (see Exercise 10). If the letter is uppercase, determine and print its position in the alphabet. For example, if the entered letter is G, the program should print out 7, since G is the seventh letter in the alphabet. (*Hint:* If the entered character is uppercase, its position can be determined by subtracting 'A' from the letter and adding 1.)

12. Write a C program that accepts a character using the scanf() function. If the character is a lowercase letter (see Exercise 8), convert the letter to uppercase and display the letter in its uppercase form. (*Hint:* Subtracting the integer value 32 from a lowercase letter yields the code for the equivalent uppercase letter. Thus, 'A' = 'a' - 32.)

13. The following program displays the message Hello there! regardless of the letter input. Determine where the error is and, if possible, why the program always causes the message to be displayed.

```
#include <stdio.h>
int main()
{
  char letter;

  printf("Enter a letter: ");
  scanf("%c",&letter);
  if (letter = 'm') printf("Hello there!");

  return 0;
}
```

14. Write a C program that asks the user to input two numbers. After your program accepts these numbers using one or more scanf() function calls, have your program check the numbers. If the first number entered is greater than the second number, print the message The first number is greater than the second, else print the message The first number is not greater than the second. Test your program by entering the numbers 5 and 8 and then using the numbers 2 and 11. What will your program display if the two numbers entered are equal?

4.3   Nested `if` Statements

As we have seen, an `if-else` statement can contain simple or compound statements. Any valid C statement can be used, including another `if-else` statement. Thus, one or more `if-else` statements can be included within either part of an `if-else` statement. For example, substituting the one-way `if` statement

```
if (hours > 6)
   printf("snap");
```

for *statement1* in the following `if` statement

```
if (hours < 9)
   statement1;
else
   printf("pop");
```

results in the nested `if` statement

```
if (hours < 9)
{
   if (hours > 6)
      printf("snap");
}
else
   printf("pop");
```

The braces around the inner one-way `if` are essential, because in their absence C associates an `else` with the closest unpaired `if`. Thus, without the braces, the above statement is equivalent to

```
if (hours < 9)
   if (hours > 6)
      printf("snap");
   else
      printf("pop");
```

Here the `else` is paired with the inner `if`, which destroys the meaning of the original `if-else` statement. Notice also that the indentation is irrelevant as far as the compiler is concerned. Whether the indentation exists or not, *the statement is compiled by associating the last `else` with the closest unpaired `if`, unless braces are used to alter this default pairing.*

The process of nesting if statements can be extended indefinitely, so that the printf("snap"); statement could itself be replaced by either a complete if-else statement or another one-way if statement.

The **if-else** Chain

Generally, the case in which the statement in the if part of an if-else statement is another if statement tends to be confusing and is best avoided. However, it can be extremely useful to place another if-else statement in the else part of an if statement. This takes the form:

```
if (expression1)
   statement1;
else
   if (expression2)
      statement2;
   else
      statement3;
```

As with all C programs, the indentation we have used is not required. In fact, the above construction is so common that it is typically written using the following arrangement:

```
if (expression1)
   statement1;
else if (expression2)
   statement2;
else
   statement3;
```

This construction is called an if-else *chain*. It is used extensively in applications programs. Each condition is evaluated in order, and if any condition is true the corresponding statement is executed and the remainder of the chain is terminated. The final else statement is only executed if none of the previous conditions are satisfied. This serves as a default or catch-all case that is useful for detecting an impossible or error condition.

The chain can be continued indefinitely by repeatedly making the last statement another if-else statement. Thus, the general form of an if-else chain is

```
if (expression1)
   statement1;
else if (expression2)
   statement2;
else if (expression3)
   statement3;
```

(Continued on next page)

(Continued from previous page)

```
        .
        .
        .
    else if (expressionn)
      statementn;
    else
      lastStatement;
```

As with all C statements, each individual statement can be a compound statement bounded by the braces { and }. To illustrate an if-else chain, Program 4.4 displays a person's marital status corresponding to a letter input. The following letter codes are used:

Marital Status	Input Code
Married	M
Single	S
Divorced	D
Widowed	W

Program 4.4

```
#include <stdio.h>
int main()
{
  char marcode;

  printf("Enter a marital code: ");
  scanf("%c", &marcode);

  if (marcode == 'M')
    printf("\nIndividual is married.");
  else if (marcode == 'S')
    printf("\nIndividual is single.");
  else if (marcode == 'D')
    printf("\nIndividual is divorced.\);
  else if (marcode == 'W')
    printf("\nIndividual is widowed.");
  else
    printf("An invalid code was entered.");

  return 0;
}
```

As a final example illustrating an if-else chain, let us calculate the monthly income of a salesperson using the following commission schedule:

Monthly Sales	Income
greater than or equal to $50,000	$375 plus 16% of sales
less than $50,000 but greater than or equal to $40,000	$350 plus 14% of sales
less than $40,000 but greater than or equal to $30,000	$325 plus 12% of sales
less than $30,000 but greater than or equal to $20,000	$300 plus 9% of sales
less than $20,000 but greater than or equal to $10,000	$250 plus 5% of sales
less than $10,000	$200 plus 3% of sales

The following if-else chain can be used to determine the correct monthly income, where the variable monthlySales is used to store the salesperson's current monthly sales:

```
if (monthlySales >= 50000.00)
   income = 375.00 + .16 * monthlySales;
else if (monthlySales >= 40000.00)
   income = 350.00 + .14 * monthlySales;
else if (monthlySales >= 30000.00)
   income = 325.00 + .12 * monthlySales;
else if (monthlySales >= 20000.00)
   income = 300.00 + .09 * monthlySales;
else if (monthlySales >= 10000.00)
   income = 250.00 + .05 * monthlySales;
else
   income = 200.000 + .03 * monthlySales;
```

Notice that this example makes use of the fact that the chain is stopped once a true condition is found. This is accomplished by checking for the highest monthly sales first. If the salesperson's monthly sales are less than $50,000, the if-else chain continues checking for the next highest sales amount until the correct category is obtained.

Program 4.5 uses this if-else chain to calculate and display the income corresponding to the value of monthly sales input in the scanf() function.

Program 4.5

```c
#include <stdio.h>
int main()
{
  float monthlySales, income;

  printf("Enter the value of monthly sales: ");
  scanf("%f", &monthlySales);

  if (monthlySales >= 50000.00)
     income = 375.00 + .16 * monthlySales;
  else if (monthlySales >= 40000.00)
     income = 350.00 + .14 * monthlySales;
  else if (monthlySales >= 30000.00)
     income = 325.00 + .12 * monthlySales;
  else if (monthlySales >= 20000.00)
     income = 300.00 + .09 * monthlySales;
  else if (monthlySales >= 10000.00)
     income = 250.00 + .05 * monthlySales;
  else
     income = 200.00 + .03 * monthlySales;
  printf("The income is $%7.2f",income);

  return 0;
}
```

A sample run using Program 4.5 is illustrated below.

```
Enter the value of monthly sales: 36243.89
Tthe income is $4674.27
```

Exercises 4.3

1. A student's letter grade is calculated according to the following schedule. Write a C program that accepts a student's numerical grade, converts the numerical grade to an equivalent letter grade, and displays the letter grade.

Numerical grade	Letter grade
greater than or equal to 90	A
less than 90 but greater than or equal to 80	B
less than 80 but greater than or equal to 70	C
less than 70 but greater than or equal to 60	D
less than 60	F

2. The interest rate used on funds deposited in a bank is determined by the amount of time the money is left on deposit. For a particular bank, the following schedule is used. Write a C program that accepts the time that funds are left on deposit and displays the interest rate corresponding to the time entered.

Time on deposit	Interest rate
greater than or equal to 5 years	.095
less than 5 years but greater than or equal to 4 years	.09
less than 4 years but greater than or equal to 3 years	.085
less than 3 years but greater than or equal to 2 years	.075
less than 2 years but greater than or equal to 1 year	.065
less than 1 year	.058

3. Write a C program that accepts a number followed by one space and then a letter. If the letter following the number is f, the program is to treat the number entered as a temperature in degrees Fahrenheit, convert the number to the equivalent degrees Celsius, and print a suitable display message. If the letter following the number is c, the program is to treat the number entered as a temperature in Celsius, convert the number to the equivalent degrees Fahrenheit, and print a suitable display message. If the letter is neither f nor c the program is to print a message that the data entered is incorrect and terminate. Use an if-else chain in your program and make use of the conversion formulas:

$$\text{Celsius} = (5.0 / 9.0) * (\text{Fahrenheit} - 32.0)$$
$$\text{Fahrenheit} = (9.0 / 5.0) * \text{Celsius} + 32.0$$

4. Using the commission schedule from Program 4.5, the following program calculates monthly income:

```c
#include <stdio.h>
int main()
{
  float monthlySales, income;

  printf("Enter the value of monthly sales: ");
  scanf("%f", &monthlySales);

  if (monthlySales >= 50000.00)
    income = 375.00 + .16 * monthlySales;
  if (monthlySales >= 40000.00 && monthlySales < 50000.00)
    income = 350.00 + .14 * monthlySales;
  if (monthlySales >= 30000.00 && monthlySales < 40000.00)
    income = 325.00 + .12 * monthlySales;
  if (monthlySales >= 20000.00 && monthlySales < 30000.00)
    income = 300.00 + .09 * monthlySales;
  if (monthlySales >= 10000.00 && monthlySales < 20000.00)
    income = 250.00 + .05 * monthlySales;
  if (monthlySales < 10000.00)
    income = 200.00 + .03 * monthlySales;

  printf("\n\nThe income is $%7.2f",income);

  return 0;
}
```

a. Will this program produce the same output as Program 4.5?

b. Which program is better and why?

5. The following program was written to produce the same result as Program 4.5:

```c
#include <stdio.h>
int main()
{
  float monthlySales, income;

  printf("Enter the value of monthly sales: ");
  scanf("%f", &monthlySales);

  if (monthlySales < 10000.00)
    income = 200.00 + .03 * monthlySales;
  else if (monthlySales >= 10000.00)
    income = 250.00 + .05 * monthlySales;
  else if (monthlySales >= 20000.00)
    income = 300.00 + .09 * monthlySales;
  else if (monthlySales >= 30000.00)
    income = 325.00 + .12 * monthlySales;
  else if (monthlySales >= 40000.00)
    income = 350.00 + .14 * monthlySales;
  else if (monthlySales >= 50000.00)
    income = 375.00 + .16 * monthlySales;

  printf("\n\nThe income is $%7.2f",income);

  return 0;
}
```

a. Will this program run?

b. What does this program do?

c. For what values of monthly sales does this program calculate the correct income?

4.4   The `switch` Statement

The `if-else` chain is used in programming applications where one set of instructions must be selected from many possible alternatives. The `switch` statement provides an alternative to the `if-else` chain for cases that compare the value of an integer expression to a specific value. The general form of a `switch` statement is

```
switch (expression)
{                     /* start of compound statement */
  case value1: ←——————————————— terminated with a colon
    statement1;
    statement2;
```
(Continued on next page)

(Continued from previous page)

```
          .
          .
          .
   break;
   case value2: ←─────────────── terminated with a colon
      statementm;
      statementn;

          .
          .
          .

   break;
          .
          .
          .
   case valuen: ←─────────────── terminated with a colon
      statementw;
      statementx;

          .
          .
          .

   break;
   default: ←─────────────── terminated with a colon
      statementaa;
      statementbb;
}                  /* end of switch and compound statement */
```

The switch statement uses four new keywords: switch, case, default, and break. Let's see what each of these words does.

The keyword switch identifies the start of the switch statement. The expression in parentheses following this word is evaluated, and the result of the expression is compared to various alternative values contained within the compound statement. The expression in the switch statement must evaluate to an integer result or a compilation error occurs.

Internal to the switch statement, the keyword case is used to identify or label individual values that are compared to the value of the switch expression. The switch expression's value is compared to each of these case values in the order that these values are listed until a match is found. When a match occurs, execution begins with the statement immediately following the match. Thus, as illustrated in Figure 4.3, the value of the expression determines where in the switch statement execution actually begins.

Any number of case labels may be contained within a switch statement, in any order. If the value of the expression does not match any of the case values, however, no statement is executed unless the keyword default is encountered. The word default is optional and operates the same as the last else in an if-else chain. If the value of the expression does not match any of the case values, program execution begins with the statement following the word default.

Once an entry point has been located by the switch statement, no further case evaluations are done; all statements that follow within the braces are executed unless a break statement is encountered. This is the reason for the break statement, which identifies the end of a particular case and causes an immediate exit from the switch statement. Thus, just as the word case identifies possible starting points in the compound

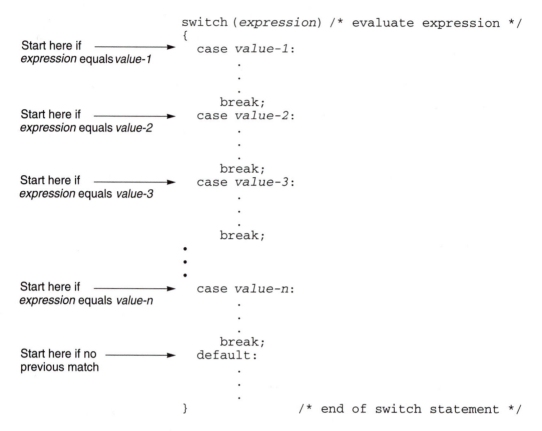

Figure 4.3   The expression determines entry point

statement, the `break` statement determines terminating points. If the `break` statements are omitted, all `case`s following the matching `case` value, including the `default` case, are executed.

When you write a `switch` statement, you can use multiple `case` values to refer to the same set of statements; the `default` label is optional. For example, consider the following:

```
switch (number)
{
  case 1:
    printf("Have a Good Morning\n");
    break;
  case 2:
    printf("Have a Happy Day\n");
    break;
  case 3: case 4: case 5:
    printf("Have a Nice Evening\n");
}
```

If the value stored in the variable number is 1, the message Have a Good Morning is displayed. Similarly, if the value of number is 2, the second message is displayed. Finally, if the value of number is 3 or 4 or 5, the last message is displayed. Since the statement to be executed for these last three cases is the same, the cases for these values can be "stacked together" as is done in the example. Also, since there is no default, no message is printed if the value of number is not one of the listed case values. Although it is good programming practice to list case values in increasing order, this is not required by the switch statement. A switch statement can have any number of case values, in any order; only the values being tested for need be listed.

Program 4.6 uses a switch statement to select the arithmetic operation (addition, multiplication, or division) to be performed on two numbers depending on the value of the variable opselect.

 Program 4.6

```c
#include <stdio.h>
int main()
{
  int opselect;
  double fnum, snum;

  printf("Please type in two numbers: ");
  scanf("%lf %lf", &fnum, &snum);
  printf("Enter a select code:");
  printf("\n        1 for addition");

  printf("\n        2 for multiplication");
  printf("\n        3 for division : ");
  scanf("%d", &opselect);

  switch (opselect)
  {
    case 1:
      printf("The sum of the numbers entered is %6.31f", fnum+snum);
      break;
    case 2:
      printf("The product of the numbers entered is %6.31f",fnum*snum);
      break;
    case 3:
      printf("The first number divided by the second is %6.31f",fnum/snum);
      break;          /* this break is optional */
  }     /* end of switch statement */

  return 0;
}   /* end of main() */
```

Program 4.6 was run twice. The resulting displays clearly identify the case selected. The results are

```
Please type in two numbers: 12 3
Enter a select code:
          1 for addition
          2 for multiplication
          3 for division : 2
The product of the numbers entered is 36.000
```

and

```
Please type in two numbers: 12 3
Enter a select code:
          1 for addition
          2 for multiplication
          3 for division : 3
The first number divided by the second is 4.000
```

In reviewing Program 4.6, notice the `break` statement in the last `case`. Although this `break` is not necessary, it is a good practice to terminate the last `case` in a `switch` statement with a `break`. This prevents a possible program error later, if an additional case is subsequently added to the `switch` statement. With the addition of a new `case`, the `break` between `cases` becomes necessary; having the `break` in place ensures you will not forget to include it at the time of the modification.

Since character data are always converted to their integer values in an expression, a `switch` statement can also be used to "switch" based on the value of a character expression. For example, assuming that `choice` is a character variable, the following `switch` statement is valid:

```
switch(choice)
{
  case 'a': case 'e': case 'i': case 'o': case 'u':
    printf("\nThe character in choice is a vowel");
    break;
  default:
    printf("\nThe character in choice is not a vowel");
}   /* end of switch statement */
```

Exercises 4.4

1. Rewrite the following `if-else` chain using a `switch` statement:

```
if (letterGrade == 'A')
  printf("The numerical grade is between 90 and 100");
else if (letterGrade == 'B')
  printf("The numerical grade is between 80 and 89.9");
else if (letterGrade == 'C')
  printf("The numerical grade is between 70 and 79.9");
else if (letterGrade == 'D');
  printf("How are you going to explain this one");
else
{
  printf("Of course I had nothing to do with my grade.");
  printf("\nThe professor was really off the wall.");
}
```

2. Rewrite the following `if-else` chain using a `switch` statement:

```
if (bondType == 1)
{
  inData();
  check();
}
else if (bondType == 2)
{
  dates();
  leapYr();
}
else if (bondType == 3)
{
  yield();
  maturity();
}
else if (bondType == 4)
{
  price();
  roi();
}
else if (bondType == 5)
{
  files();
  save();
}
else if (bondType == 6)
{
  retrieve();
  screen();
}
```

3. Each disk drive in a shipment of these devices is stamped with a code from 1 through 4, which indicates a drive manufacturer as follows:

Code	Disk Drive Manufacturer
1	3M Corporation
2	Maxell Corporation
3	Sony Corporation
4	Verbatim Corporation

Write a C program that accepts the code number as an input and, based on the value entered, displays the correct disk drive manufacturer.

4. Rewrite Program 4.4 in Section 4.3 using a switch statement.

5. Determine why the if-else chain in Program 4.5 cannot be replaced with a switch statement.

6. Repeat Exercise 3 in Section 4.3 using a switch statement instead of an if-else chain.

7. Rewrite Program 4.6 using a character variable for the select code. (*Hint:* Review Section 3.4 if your program does not operate as you think it should.)

4.5   Common Programming Errors

There are three programming errors common to C's selection statements.

1. Using the assignment operator, =, in place of the relational operator, ==. This can cause an enormous amount of frustration because any expression can be tested by an if-else statement. For example, the statement

```
if (opselect = 2)
  printf("Happy Birthday");
else
  printf("Good Day");
```

always results in the message Happy Birthday being printed, regardless of the initial value in the variable opselect. The reason for this is that the assignment expression opselect = 2 has a value of 2, which is considered a true value in C. The correct expression to determine the value in opselect is opselect == 2.

2. Letting the if-else statement appear to select an incorrect choice. In this typical debugging problem, the programmer mistakenly concentrates on the tested condition as the source of the problem. For example, assume that the following if-else statement is part of your program:

```
if (key == 'F')
{
  contemp = (5.0/9.0) * (intemp - 32.0);
```

(Continued on next page)

(Continued from previous page)

```
    printf("Conversion to Celsius was done");
}
else
{
    contemp = (9.0/5.0) * intemp + 32.0;
    printf("Conversion to Fahrenheit was done");
}
```

This statement always displays `Conversion to Celsius was done` when the variable `key` contains an `F`. Therefore, if this message is displayed when you believe `key` does not contain `F`, you need to investigate `key`'s value. As a general rule, whenever a selection statement does not act as you think it should, make sure to test your assumptions about the values assigned to the tested variables by displaying the values. If an unanticipated value is displayed, you have at least isolated the source of the problem to the variables themselves, rather than the structure of the `if-else` statement. From there, you need to determine where and how the incorrect value was obtained.

3. Using nested `if` statements without including braces to clearly indicate the desired structure. Without braces the compiler defaults to pairing `else`s with the closest unpaired `if`s, which sometimes destroys the original intent of the selection statement. To avoid this problem and to create code that is readily adaptable to change it is useful to write all `if-else` statements as compound statements in the form

```
if (expression)
{
    one or more statements in here
}
else
{
    one or more statements in here
}
```

By using this form, no matter how many statements are added later, the original integrity and intent of the `if` statement is maintained.

4.6   Chapter Summary

1. Relational expressions, which are also called simple conditions, are used to compare operands. If a relational expression is true, the value of the expression is the

integer 1. If the relational expression is false, it has an integer value of 0. Relational expressions are created using the following relational operators:

Relational operator	Meaning	Example
<	less than	`age < 30`
>	greater than	`height > 6.2`
<=	less than or equal to	`taxable <= 20000`
>=	greater than or equal to	`temp >= 98.6`
==	equal to	`grade == 100`
!=	not equal to	`number != 250`

2. More complex conditions can be constructed from relational expressions using C's logical operators, && (AND), || (OR), and ! (NOT).

3. `if-else` statements are used to select between two alternative statements based on the value of an expression. Although relational expressions are usually used for the tested expression, any valid expression can be used. In testing an expression, `if-else` statements interpret a nonzero value as true and a zero value as false. The general form of an `if-else` statement is

```
if (expression)
    statement1;
else
    statement2;
```

This is a two-way selection statement. If the expression has a nonzero value it is considered as true and `statement1` is executed; otherwise `statement2` is executed.

4. `if-else` statements can contain other `if-else` statements. In the absence of braces, each `else` is associated with the closest unpaired `if`.

5. The `if-else` chain is a multiway selection statement having the general form

```
if (expression1)
    statement1;
else if (expression2)
    statement2;
else if (expression3)
    statement3;

         .
         .
         .

else if (expressionm)
    statementm;
else
    statementn;
```

Each expression is evaluated in the order it appears in the chain. Once an expression is true (has a nonzero value), only the statement between that expression and the next else if or else is executed, and no further expressions are tested. The final else is optional, and the statement corresponding to the final else is only executed if none of the previous expressions are true.

6. A compound statement consists of any number of individual statements enclosed within the brace pair { and }. Compound statements are treated as a single unit and can be used anywhere a single statement is called for.

7. The switch statement is a multiway selection statement. The general form of a switch statement is

```
switch (expression)
{                               /* start of compound statement */
   case value1: ←───────────────── terminated with a colon
      statement1;
      statement2;
          .
          .
          .
      break;
   case value2: ←───────────────── terminated with a colon
      statementm;
      statementn;
          .
          .
          .
      break;
          .
          .
          .
   case valuen: ←───────────────── terminated with a colon
      statementw;
      statementx;
          .
          .
          .
      break;
   default: ←───────────────── terminated with a colon
      statementaa;
      statementbb;
          .
          .
          .
}                               /* end of switch and compound statement */
```

For this statement the value of an integer expression is compared to a number of integer or character constants or constant expressions. Program execution is transferred to the first matching case and continues through the end of the switch statement unless an optional break statement is encountered. cases in a switch statement can appear in any order, and an optional default case can be included. The default case is executed if none of the other cases is matched.

4.7   Chapter Supplement: Errors, Testing, and Debugging

The ideal in programming is to efficiently produce readable, error-free programs that work correctly and can be modified or changed with minimum testing required for reverification. In this regard, it is useful to know the different errors that can occur and how to detect and correct them.

Compile-Time and Run-Time Errors

A program error can be detected in a variety of ways:

1. Before a program is compiled
2. While the program is being compiled
3. While it is being run
4. After the program has been executed and the output is being examined
5. Not at all

Errors detected by the compiler are formally referred to as *compile-time* errors, and errors that occur while the program is being run are formally referred to as *run-time* errors.

Methods are available for detecting errors both before a program is compiled and after it has been executed. The method for detecting errors after a program has been executed is called *program verification and testing*. The method for detecting errors before a program is compiled is called *desk checking*, which consists of checking a program by hand at a desk or table for syntax and logic errors.

Syntax and Logic Errors

Computer literature distinguishes between two primary types of errors. A *syntax error* is an error in the structure or spelling of a statement. For example, the statement

```
if ( a lt b
{
  pintf("There are five syntax errors here\n")
  printf(" Can you find tem);
}
```

contains five syntax errors. These errors are

1. The relational operator in the first line is incorrect; it should be the symbol <
2. The closing parenthesis is missing in line one
3. The function name `printf` is misspelled in the third line
4. The third line is missing the terminating semicolon(;)
5. The string in the fourth line is not terminated with quotes

All these errors will be detected by the compiler when the program is compiled. This is true of all syntax errors—since they violate the basic rules of C, if they are not discovered by desk checking, the compiler detects them and displays an error message indicating that a syntax error exists.[4] In some cases, the error message is clear and the error is obvious; in other cases, it takes a little detective work to understand the error message displayed by the compiler. Since all syntax errors are detected at compile time, the terms "compile-time errors" and "syntax errors" are often used interchangeably. Strictly speaking, however, compile-time refers to *when* the error is detected and syntax refers to the *type* of error detected.

Note that the misspelling of the word `tem` in the second `printf()` function call is not a syntax error. Although this spelling error will result in an undesirable output line being displayed, it is not a violation of C's syntactical rules. This spelling error is simply a typographical error, commonly referred to as a "typo."

Logic errors are characterized by erroneous, unexcepted, or unintentional errors resulting from a flaw in the program's logic. These errors, which are never caught by the compiler, may be detected by desk checking, by program testing, by accident when a user obtains an obviously erroneous output, or while the program is executing. In this latter case, a run-time error occurs that results in an error message being generated and/or abnormal and premature program termination.

Since logic errors are not detected by the compiler and may go undetected at run-time, they are always more difficult to detect than syntax errors. If not detected by desk checking, a logic error can reveal itself in a number of ways. In one instance, the program executes to completion but produces incorrect results. Generally, logic errors of this type include

1. *No output.* This is caused by either the omission of a `printf()` statement or a sequence of statements that inadvertently bypasses a `printf()` function call.
2. *Unappealing or misaligned output.* This is always caused by an error in a `printf()` statement.
3. *Incorrect numerical results.* This is caused either by incorrect values assigned to the variables used in an expression, the use of an incorrect arithmetic expression, the omission of a statement, a roundoff error, or the use of an improper sequence of statements.

See if you can detect the logic error in Program 4.7.

---

[4] They may not, however, all be detected at the same time. Frequently, one syntax error "masks" another error, and the second error is only detected after the first error is corrected.

Program 4.7

```c
#include <stdio.h>
#include <math.h>
int main()       /* a compound interest program */
{
    int nyears;
    float capital, amount, rate;
    printf("This program calculates the amount of money\n");
    printf("in a bank account for an initial deposit\n");
    printf("invested for n years at an interest rate r.\n\n");
    printf("Enter the initial amount in the account: ");
    scanf("%f", &amount);
    printf("Enter the interest rate (ex. 5 for 5%): ");
    scanf("%f", &rate);
    capital = amount * pow( (1 + rate/100.), nyears);
    printf("\nThe final amount of money is $%8.2f", capital);

    return 0;
}
```

Following is a sample run of Program 4.7.

```
This program calculates the amount of money
in a bank account for an initial deposit
invested for n years at an interest rate r.

Enter the initial amount in the account: 1000.
Enter the interest rate (ex. 5 for 5%): 5

The final amount of money is $ 1000.00
```

As the output indicates, the final amount of money is the same as the initial amount input. Did you spot the error in Program 4.7 that produced this apparently erroneous output?

Unlike a misspelled output message, the error in Program 4.7 causes a computation mistake. Here, the error is that the program does not initialize the variable nyears before it is used in the calculation of capital. When the assignment statement that calculates capital is executed, the program uses whatever value is stored in nyears. On those systems that initialize all variables to zero, the value zero, will be used for nyears. However, on those systems that do not initialize all variables to zero, whatever "garbage" value that happens to occupy the storage locations corresponding to the variable nyears will be used (either use the manuals supplied with your compiler or run a quick test program with uninitialized variables to see which of these two actions your compiler takes). In either case, an error is produced.

The second type of logic error is one that may cause the program to prematurely terminate execution and that almost always results in a system error message being displayed. Examples of this type of error are attempts to divide by zero or take the square root of a negative number. When this type of logic error occurs, it becomes a run-time error.

Testing and Debugging

In theory, a comprehensive set of test runs will reveal all logic errors and ensure that a program will work correctly for any and all combinations of input and computed data. In practice, this requires checking all possible combinations of statement execution. Due to the time and effort required, this is impossible, except for extremely simple programs. Let us see why this is so. Consider Program 4.8.

 Program 4.8

```c
#include <stdio.h>
int main()
{
  int num;

  printf("Enter a number: ");
  scanf("%d", &num);
  if (num == 5) printf("Bingo!");
  else printf("Bongo!");

  return 0;
}
```

Program 4.8 has two paths that can be traversed from when the program is run to when the program reaches its closing brace. The first path, which is executed when the input number is 5, is in the sequence:

```c
printf("Enter a number: ");
scanf("%d", &num);
printf("Bingo!");
```

The second path, which is executed whenever any number except 5 is input, includes the sequence of instructions:

```
printf("Enter a number: ");
scanf("%d", &num);
printf("Bongo!");
```

To test each possible path through Program 4.8 requires two runs of the program, with a judicious selection of test input data to ensure that both paths of the `if` statement are exercised. Adding one more `if` statement in the program increases the number of possible execution paths by a factor of two and requires four (2^2) runs of the program for complete testing. Similarly, two additional `if` statements increase the number of paths by a factor of four, requiring eight (2^3) runs for complete testing, and three additional `if` statements would produce a program requiring sixteen (2^4) test runs.

Consider an application program consisting of ten modules, each containing five `if` statements. Assuming the modules are always called in the same sequence, there are 32 (2 raised to the fifth power) possible paths through each module and more than 1,000,000,000,000,000 (2 raised to the fiftieth power) possible paths through the complete program (all modules executed in sequence). The time needed to create individual test data to exercise each path and the actual computer run time required to check each path make the complete testing of such a program impossible.

The inability to fully test all combinations of statement execution sequences has led to the programming proverb that "There is no error-free program." It has also led to the realization that any testing that is done should be well thought out to maximize the possibility of locating errors. An important corollary to this is the realization that *although a single test can reveal the presence of an error, it does not verify the absence of one.* The fact that one error is revealed by testing does not indicate that another error is not lurking somewhere else in the program; *the fact that one test reveals no errors does not indicate that there are no errors.*

Once an error is discovered, however, the programmer must locate where the error occurs, and then fix it. In computer jargon, a program error is referred to as a *bug,* and the process of isolating, correcting, and verifying the correction is called *debugging.*

Although there are no hard and fast rules for isolating the cause of an error, there are some techniques that you can use. The first is a preventive technique. Errors are frequently introduced by the programmer in the rush to code and run a program before fully understanding what is required and how to achieve the result. A symptom of this is the lack of an outline of the proposed program (pseudocode or flowchart) or a handwritten program. You can eliminate many errors by desk checking a copy of the program before it is ever entered or compiled.

A second technique is to mimic the computer and execute each statement by hand. This means writing down each variable as it is encountered in the program and listing the value that should be stored in the variable as each input and assignment statement is encountered. Doing this also sharpens your programming skills, because it requires you to fully understand what each statement in your program causes to happen. This kind of checking is called *program tracing.*

A third and very powerful debugging technique is to use one or more diagnostic `printf()` function calls to display the values of selected variables. For example, since the program in Program 4.7 produced an incorrect value for `capital`, it is worthwhile placing a `printf()` statement immediately before the assignment statement for `capital` to display the value of all variables used in the computation. If the displayed values are correct, then the problem is the assignment statement. If the values are incorrect, we must determine where the incorrect values were actually obtained.

In this same manner, another use of `printf()` function calls in debugging is to immediately display all input data values. This technique is called *echo printing* and is useful in establishing that the computer is correctly receiving and interpreting the input data.

The most powerful debugging technique of all is to use a *debugger,* a program that allows you to single-step through a program, set breakpoints where execution is to be temporarily halted, and inspect the values stored in all (or selected) variables.

Finally, no discussion of debugging is complete without mentioning the primary ingredient in the successful isolation and correction of errors. This is the attitude and spirit you bring to the task. Since you wrote the program, your natural assumption is that it is correct or you would have changed it before it was compiled. It is extremely difficult to back away and honestly test and find errors in your own software. As a programmer, you must constantly remind yourself that just because you *think* your program is correct does not make it so. Finding errors in your own programs is a sobering experience, but one that will help you become a master programmer. It can also be exciting and fun if approached as a detection problem with you as the master detective.

Repetition

The programs examined so far have been useful in illustrating the correct structure of C programs and in introducing fundamental C input, output, assignment, and selection capabilities. By this time you should have gained enough experience to be comfortable with the concepts and mechanics of the C programming process. It is now time to move up a level in our knowledge and abilities.

The real power of most computer programs is their ability to repeat the same calculation or sequence of instructions many times, each time using different data, without rerunning the program for each new set of data values. In this chapter we explore the C statements that permit this. These statements are the `while`, `for`, and `do-while` statements.

5.1 The `while` Statement

The `while` statement is a general repetition statement that can be used in a variety of programming situations. The general form of the `while` statement is

```
while (expression) statement;
```

163

The expression contained within the parentheses is evaluated in exactly the same manner as an expression contained in an if-else statement; the difference is how the expression is used. As we have seen, when the expression is true (has a nonzero value) in an if-else statement, the statement following the expression is executed once. In a while statement the statement following the expression is executed repeatedly as long as the expression evaluates to a nonzero value. This naturally means that somewhere in the while statement there must be a statement that alters the value of the tested expression. As we will see, this is indeed the case. For now, however, considering just the expression and the statement following the parentheses, the process used by the computer in evaluating a while statement is

1. test the expression
2. if the expression has a nonzero (true) value
      a. execute the statement following the parentheses
      b. go back to step 1
   else
      exit the while statement

Notice that step 2b forces program control to be transferred back to step 1. The transfer of control back to the start of a while statement in order to reevaluate the expression is called a *program loop*. The while statement literally loops back on itself to recheck the expression until it evaluates to zero (becomes false).

This looping process is illustrated in Figure 5.1. A diamond shape is used to show the two entry and two exit points required in the decision part of the while statement.

To make this a little more tangible, consider the relational expression count <= 10 and the statement printf("%d ",count);. Using these, we can write the following valid while statement:

```
while (count <= 10)  printf("%d  ",count);
```

Although the above statement is valid, the alert reader will realize that we have created a situation in which the printf() function is either called forever (or until we stop the program) or is not called at all. Let us see why this happens.

If count has a value less than or equal to 10 when the expression is first evaluated, a call to printf() is made. The while statement then automatically loops back on itself and retests the expression. Since we have not changed the value stored in count, the expression is still true and another call to printf() is made. This process continues forever, or until the program containing this statement is prematurely stopped by the user. However, if count starts with a value greater than 10, the expression is false to begin with and the printf() function call is never made.

How do we set an initial value in count to control what the while statement does the first time the expression is evaluated? The answer, of course, is to assign values to each variable in the tested expression before the while statement is encountered. For example, the following sequence of instructions is valid:

```
count = 1;
while  (count <= 10)  printf("%d  ",count);
```

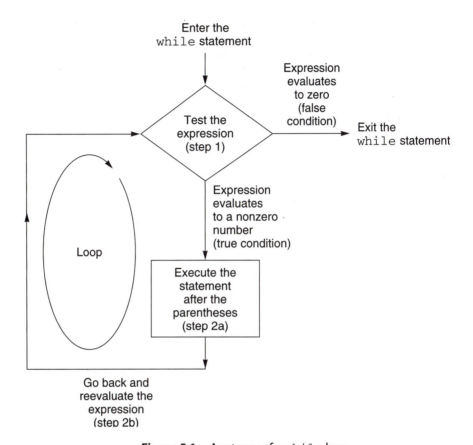

Enter the
while statement

Expression
evaluates
to zero
(false
condition)

Test the
expression
(step 1)

Exit the
while statement

Expression
evaluates
to a nonzero
number
(true condition)

Loop

Execute the
statement
after the
parentheses
(step 2a)

Go back and
reevaluate the
expression
(step 2b)

Figure 5.1   Anatomy of a while loop

Using this sequence of instructions, we have ensured that count starts with a value of 1. We could assign any value to count in the assignment statement—the important thing is to assign *some* value. In practice, the assigned value depends on the application.

We must still change the value of count so that we can finally exit the while statement. To do this requires an expression such as ++count to increment the value of count each time the while statement is executed. The fact that a while statement provides for the repetition of a single statement does not prevent us from including an additional statement to change the value of count. All we have to do is replace the single statement with a compound statement. For example:

```
count = 1;                 /* initialize count */
while (count <= 10)
{
   printf("%d  ",count);
   ++count;                /* increment count  */
}
```

For clarity, we have placed each statement in the compound statement on a different line. This is consistent with the convention adopted for compound statements in the last chapter. Let us now analyze the above sequence of instructions.

The first assignment statement sets `count` equal to 1. The `while` statement is then entered, and the expression is evaluated for the first time. Since the value of `count` is less than or equal to 10, the expression is true and the compound statement is executed. The first statement in the compound statement is a call to the `printf()` function to display the value of `count`. The next statement adds 1 to the value currently stored in `count`, making this value equal to 2. The `while` statement now loops back to retest the expression. Since `count` is still less than or equal to 10, the compound statement is again executed. This process continues until the value of `count` reaches 11. Program 5.1 illustrates these statements in an actual program.

 Program 5.1

```c
#include <stdio.h>
int main()
{
  int count;

  count = 1;                    /* initialize count */
  while (count <= 10)
  {
    printf("%d  ",count);
    ++count;                  /* add 1 to count      */
  }

  return 0;
}
```

The output for Program 5.1 is

1 2 3 4 5 6 7 8 9 10

There is nothing special about the name `count` used in Program 5.1. Any valid integer variable could have been used.

Before we consider other examples of the `while` statement, two comments concerning Program 5.1 are in order. First, the statement `++count` can be replaced with any statement that changes the value of `count`. A statement such as `count = count + 2`, for example, would cause every second integer to be displayed. Second, it is the programmer's responsibility to ensure that `count` is changed in a way that ultimately leads to a normal exit from the while. For example, if we replace the expression ++count with the expression --count, the value of count will never reach 11 and an infinite loop will be created. An *infinite loop* is a loop that never ends. The computer will not reach out, touch you, and say, "Excuse me, you have created an infinite loop." It just keeps displaying numbers until you realize that the program is not working as you expected.

Now that you have some familiarity with the while statement, see if you can read and determine the output of Program 5.2.

 Program 5.2

```c
#include <stdio.h>
int main()
{
   int i;

   i = 10;
   while (i >= 1)
   {
     printf("%d   ",i);
     --i;                  /* subtract 1 from i */
   }

   return 0;
}
```

The assignment statement in Program 5.2 initially sets the int variable i to 10. The while statement then checks to see if the value of i is greater than or equal to 1. While the expression is true, the value of i is displayed by the call to printf() and the value of i is decremented by 1. When i finally reaches zero, the expression is false and the program exits the while statement. Thus, the following display is obtained when Program 5.2 is run:

```
10 9 8 7 6 5 4 3 2 1
```

To illustrate the power of the while statement, consider the task of printing a table of numbers from 1 to 10 with their squares and cubes. This can be done with a simple while statement, as illustrated by Program 5.3.

Program 5.3

```
#include <stdio.h>
int main ()
{
  int num;

  printf("NUMBER     SQUARE      CUBE\n");
  printf("------     ------      ----\n");

  num = 1;
  while (num < 11)
  {
    printf("%3d      %3d       %4d\n", num, num*num, num*num*num);
    ++num;              /* add 1 to num */
  }

  return 0;
}
```

Program 5.3 produces the following display.

NUMBER	SQUARE	CUBE
1	1	1
2	4	8
3	9	27
4	16	64
5	25	125
6	36	216
7	49	343
8	64	512
9	81	729
10	100	1000

Note that the expression used in Program 5.3 is num < 11. For the integer variable num, this expression is exactly equivalent to the expression num <= 10. The choice of which to use is entirely up to you.

If you want to use Program 5.3 to produce a table of 1000 numbers, all you do is change the expression in the while statement from i < 11 to i < 1001. Changing the 11 to 1001 produces a table of 1000 lines—not bad for a simple five-line while statement.

All the program examples illustrating the while statement have checked for a fixed-count condition. Since any valid expression can be evaluated by a while statement, we are not restricted to constructing such loops. For example, consider the task of producing a Celsius-to-Fahrenheit temperature conversion table. Assume that Fahrenheit temperatures corresponding to Celsius temperatures ranging from 5 to 50 degrees are to be displayed in increments of five degrees. The desired display can be obtained with the series of statements:

```
celsius = 5;      /* starting Celsius value */
while (celsius <= 50)
{
   fahren = (9.0/5.0) * celsius + 32.0;
   printf("%5d%12.2f",celsius, fahren);
   celsius = celsius + 5;
}
```

As before, the while statement consists of everything from the word while through the closing brace of the compound statement. Prior to entering the while loop we have made sure to assign a value to the operand being evaluated, and there is a statement to alter the value of celsius to ensure an exit from the while loop. Program 5.4 illustrates the use of this code in a complete program.

 Program 5.4

```
#include <stdio.h>
int main()   /* program to convert Celsius to Fahrenheit */
{
  int celsius;
  float fahren;

  printf("DEGREES    DEGREES\n");
  printf("CELSIUS   FAHRENHEIT\n");
  printf("-------   ----------\n");
  celsius = 5;      /* starting Celsius value */
  while (celsius <= 50)
  {
     fahren = (9.0/5.0) * celsius + 32.0;
     printf("%5d%12.2f\n",celsius, fahren);
     celsius = celsius + 5;
  }

  return 0;
}
```

The display obtained when Program 5.4 is executed is

```
DEGREES    DEGREES
CELSIUS   FAHRENHEIT
-------   ----------
   5         41.00
  10         50.00
  15         59.00
  20         68.00
  25         77.00
  30         86.00
  35         95.00
  40        104.00
  45        113.00
  50        122.00
```

Exercises 5.1

1. Rewrite Program 5.1 to print the numbers 2 to 10 in increments of two. The output of your program should be

   ```
   2  4  6  8  10
   ```

2. Rewrite Program 5.4 to produce a table that starts at a Celsius value of –10 and ends with a Celsius value of 60, in increments of ten degrees.

3. a. For the following program determine the total number of items displayed. Also determine the first and last numbers printed.

   ```c
   #include <stdio.h>
   int main()
   {
     int num = 0;

     while (num <= 20)
     {
       ++num;
       printf("%d   ",num);
     }

     return 0;
   }
   ```

   b. Enter and run the program from Exercise 3a on a computer to verify your answers to the exercise.
   c. How would the output be affected if the two statements within the compound statement were reversed (that is, if the `printf()` call were made before the ++num statement)?

4. Write a C program that converts gallons to liters. The program should display gallons from 10 to 20 in one-gallon increments and the corresponding liter equivalents. Use the relationship that 1 gallon contains 3.785 liters.

5. Write a C program that converts feet to meters. The program should display feet from 3 to 30 in three-foot increments and the corresponding meter equivalents. Use the relationship that 1 meter is equivalent to 3.28 feet.

6. A machine purchased for $28,000 is depreciated at a rate of $4,000 a year for seven years. Write and run a C program that computes and displays a depreciation table for seven years. The table should have the form:

YEAR	DEPRECIATION	END-OF-YEAR VALUE	ACCUMULATED DEPRECIATION
1	4000	24000	4000
2	4000	20000	8000
3	4000	16000	12000
4	4000	12000	16000
5	4000	8000	20000
6	4000	4000	24000
7	4000	0	28000

7. An automobile travels at an average speed of 55 miles per hour for four hours. Write a C program that displays the distance driven, in miles, by the car every half hour until the end of the trip.

5.2 `scanf()` within a while Loop

Combining the `scanf()` function with the repetition capabilities of the `while` statement produces very adaptable and powerful programs. To understand the concept involved, consider Program 5.5, where a `while` statement is used to accept and then display four user-entered numbers, one at a time. Although it uses a very simple idea, the program highlights the flow-of-control concepts needed to produce more useful programs.

Following is a sample run of Program 5.5. The italicized numbers were input in response to the appropriate prompts.

```
This program will ask you to enter some numbers.

Enter a number: 26.2
The number entered is 26.200000
Enter a number: 5
The number entered is 5.000000
Enter a number: 103.456
The number entered is 103.456000
Enter a number: 1267.89
The number entered is 1267.890000
```

Let us review the program to clearly understand how the output was produced. The first message displayed is caused by execution of the first `printf()` function call. This call is outside and before the `while` statement, so it is executed once before any statement in the `while` loop.

Program 5.5

```c
#include <stdio.h>
int main()
{
  int count;
  float num;

  printf("\nThis program will ask you to enter some numbers.\n");
  count = 1;

  while (count <= 4)
  {
    printf("\nEnter a number: ");
    scanf("%f", &num);
    printf("The number entered is %f", num);
    ++count;
  }

  return 0;
}
```

Once the `while` loop is entered, the statements within the compound statement are executed while the tested condition is true. The first time through the compound statement, the message `Enter a number:` is displayed. The program then calls `scanf()`, which forces the computer to wait for a number to be entered at the keyboard. Once a number is typed and the ENTER key is pressed, the call to `printf()` displaying the number is executed. The variable `count` is then incremented by one. This process continues until four passes through the loop have been made and the value of `count` is 5. Each pass causes the message `Enter a number:` to be displayed, causes one call to `scanf()` to be made, and causes the message `The number entered is` to be displayed. Figure 5.2 illustrates this flow of control.

Rather than simply displaying the entered numbers, Program 5.5 can be modified to use the entered data. For example, we can add the numbers entered and display the total. To do this, we must be very careful in how we add the numbers, since the same variable, num, is used for each number entered. Because of this the entry of a new number in Program 5.5 automatically causes the previous number stored in num to be lost. Thus, each number entered must be added to the total before another number is entered. The required sequence is

> ***Enter a number***
> ***Add the number to the total***

How do we add a single number to a total? A statement such as `total = total + num;` does the job perfectly. This is the accumulating statement introduced in Section

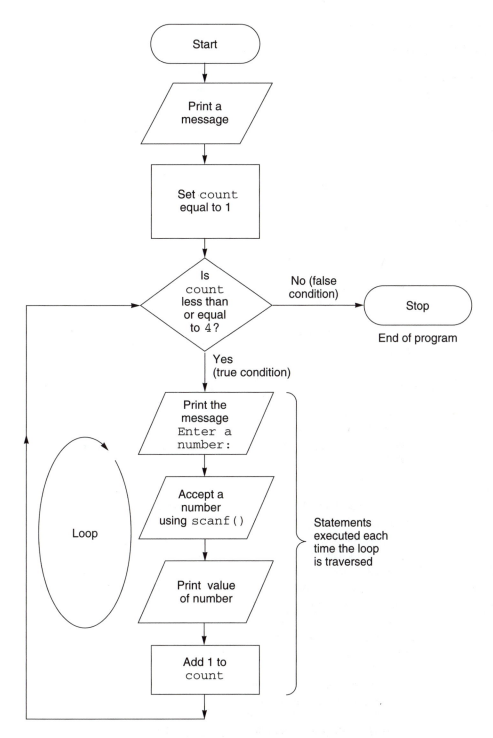

Figure 5.2   Flow-of-control diagram for Program 5.5

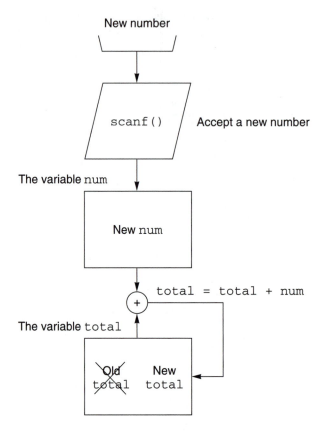

Figure 5.3 Accepting and adding a number to a total

3.1. After each number is entered, the accumulating statement adds the number into the total, as illustrated in Figure 5.3. The complete flow of control required for adding the numbers is illustrated in Figure 5.4.

In reviewing Figure 5.4, observe that we have made a provision for initially setting the total to zero before the while loop is entered. If we were to clear the total inside the while loop, it would be set to zero each time the loop was executed and any value previously stored would be erased.

Program 5.6 incorporates the necessary modifications to Program 5.5 to total the numbers entered. As indicated in the flow diagram shown in Figure 5.4, the statement total = total + num; is placed immediately after the scanf() function call. Putting the accumulating statement at this point in the program ensures that the entered number is immediately "captured" into the total.

Let us review Program 5.6. The variable total was created to store the total of the numbers entered. Prior to entering the while statement the value of total is set to zero. This ensures that any previous value present in the storage location(s) assigned to

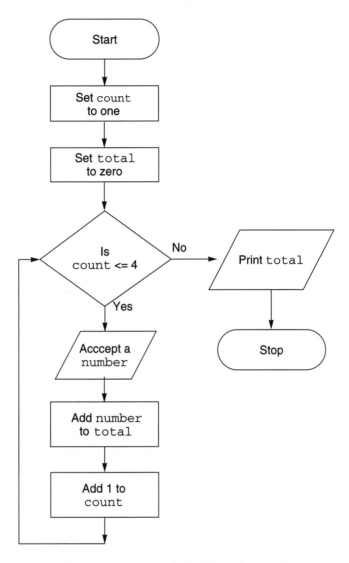

Figure 5.4   Accumulation flow of control

the variable `total` is overwritten. When the `while` loop is entered, the statement `total = total + num;` is used to add the value of the entered number into `total`. As each value is entered, it is added into the existing `total` to create a new total. Thus, `total` becomes a running subtotal of all the values entered. Only when all numbers are entered does `total` contain the final sum of all the numbers. After the `while` loop is finished, the last `printf()` function call is used to display the sum.

Program 5.6

```c
#include <stdio.h>
int main()
{
  int count;
  float num, total;

  printf("\nThis program will ask you to enter some numbers.\n");
  count = 1;
  total = 0;

  while (count <= 4)
  {
    printf("\nEnter a number: ");
    scanf("%f", &num);
    total = total + num;
    printf("The total is now %f", total);
    ++count;
  }
  printf("\n\nThe final total is $f",total);

  return 0;
}
```

Using the same data that was entered in the sample run for Program 5.5, the following sample run of Program 5.6 was made.

```
This program will ask you to enter some numbers.

Enter a number: 26.2
The total is now 26.200000
Enter a number: 5
The total is now 31.200000
Enter a number: 103.456
The total is now 134.656000
Enter a number: 1267.89
The total is now 1402.546000

The final total is 1402.546000
```

Having used an accumulating assignment statement to add the numbers entered, we can now go further and calculate the average of the numbers. Where do we calculate the average—within the while loop or outside it?

In the case at hand, calculating an average requires that both a final sum and the number of items in that sum be available. The average is then computed by dividing the final sum by the number of items. At this point, we must ask, "At what point in the program is the correct sum available, and at what point is the number of items available?" In reviewing Program 5.6 we see that the correct sum needed for calculating the average is available after the `while` loop is finished. In fact, the whole purpose of the `while` loop is to ensure that the numbers are entered and added correctly to produce a correct sum. After the loop is finished, we also have a count of the number of items used in the sum. However, due to the way the `while` loop was constructed, the number in `count` (5) when the loop is finished is one more than the number of items (4) used to obtain the total. Knowing this, we simply subtract 1 from `count` before using it to determine the average. With this as background, see if you can read and understand Program 5.7.

 Program 5.7

```c
#include <stdio.h>
int main()
{
  int count;
  float num, total,average;

  printf("\nThis program will ask you to enter some numbers.\n");
  count = 1;
  total = 0;

  while (count <= 4)
  {
    printf("Enter a number: ");
    scanf("%f", &num);
    total = total + num;
    ++count;
  }
  --count;
  average = total / count;
  printf("\nThe average of the numbers is %f",average);

  return 0;
}
```

Program 5.7 is almost identical to Program 5.6, except for the calculation of the average. We have also removed the constant display of the total within and after the `while` loop. The loop in Program 5.7 is used to enter and add four numbers. Immediately after the loop is exited, the average is computed and displayed. Following is a sample run using Program 5.7:

```
This program will ask you to enter some numbers.
Enter a number: 26.2
Enter a number: 5
Enter a number: 103.456
Enter a number: 1267.89

The average of the numbers is 350.636500
```

Sentinels

In many situations the exact number of items to be entered is not known in advance or the items are too numerous to count beforehand. For example, when entering a large amount of market research data we might not want to take the time to count the number of actual data items that are to be entered. In cases like this we want to be able to enter data continuously and, at the end, type in a special data value to signal the end of data input.

In computer programming, data values used to signal either the start or end of a data series are called *sentinels*. The sentinel values must, of course, be selected so as not to conflict with legitimate data values. For example, if we were constructing a program that accepts a student's grades, and assuming that no extra credit is given that could produce a grade higher than 100, we could use any grade higher than 100 as a sentinel value. Program 5.8 illustrates this concept. In Program 5.8 data is continuously requested and accepted until a number larger than 100 is entered. Entry of a number higher than 100 alerts the program to exit the `while` loop and display the sum of the numbers entered.

Program 5.8

```c
#include <stdio.h>
int main()
{
  float grade, total;

  grade = 0;
  total = 0;
  printf("\nTo stop entering grades, type in any number")
  printf("\n greater than 100.\n\n");
  while (grade <= 100)
  {
    printf("Enter a grade: ");
    scanf("%f", &grade);
    total = total + grade;
  }
  printf("\nThe total of the grades is %f",total-grade);

  return 0;
}
```

Following is a sample run using Program 5.8. As long as grades less than or equal to 100 are entered, the program continues to request and accept additional data. When a number greater than 100 is entered, the program adds this number to the total and exits the while loop. Outside of the loop and within the printf() function call, the value of the sentinel that was added to the total is subtracted and the sum of the legitimate grades that were entered is displayed.

```
To stop entering grades, type in any number
  greater than 100.

Enter a grade: 95
Enter a grade: 100
Enter a grade: 82
Enter a grade: 101

The total of the grades is 277.000000
```

One useful sentinel provided in C is the named constant EOF, which stands for End Of File. The actual value of EOF is compiler-dependent, but it is always assigned a code that is not used by any other character. The way that EOF works is as follows:

Each computer operating system has its own code for an End Of File mark. In the UNIX operating systems this mark is generated whenever the ctrl and D keys are pressed simultaneously, while in the IBM-DOS operating system the mark is generated whenever the ctrl and Z keys are pressed simultaneously. When a C program detects this combination of keys as an input value, it converts the input value into its own EOF code, as illustrated in Figure 5.5.

The actual definition of the EOF constant, using the #define statement described in Section 3.5, is available in the compiler source file stdio.h. Thus, the EOF named constant can be used in all programs that have included stdio.h. For example, consider Program 5.9.

Notice that the first line in Program 5.9 is the #include <stdio.h> statement. Since the stdio.h file contains the definition of EOF, this constant may now be referenced in the program.

EOF is used in Program 5.9 to control the while loop. The expression scanf("%f", &grades) != EOF makes use of the fact that the scanf() function returns an EOF value if an attempt is made to read an End Of File mark. From a user's viewpoint, assuming an IBM computer is being used, pressing both the ctrl and Z keys simultaneously generates an End Of File mark, which is converted to the EOF constant by scanf(). Following is a sample run using Program 5.9.

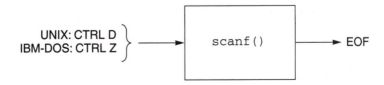

Figure 5.5 Generation of the EOF constant by the scanf() function

Program 5.9

```c
#include <stdio.h>
int main()
{
  float grade, total = 0;        /* note the initialization here */

  printf("\nTo stop entering grades, press either the F6 key");
  printf("\n or the ctrl and Z keys simultaneously on IBM computers");
  printf("\n or the ctrl and D keys for UNIX operating systems.\n\n");
  printf("Enter a grade: ");
  while (scanf("%f", &grade) != EOF)
  {
    total = total + grade;
    printf("Enter a grade: ");
  }

  printf("\nThe total of the grades is %f",total);

  return 0;
}
```

```
            To stop entering grades, press either the F6 key
             or the ctrl and Z keys simultaneously on IBM computers
             or the ctrl and D keys for UNIX operating systems.

            Enter a grade: 100
            Enter a grade: 200
            Enter a grade: 300
            Enter a grade: ^Z

            The total of the grades is 600.000000
```

One distinct advantage of Program 5.9 over Program 5.8 is that the sentinel value is never added into the total, so it does not have to be subtracted later.[1] One disadvantage of Program 5.9, however, is that it requires the user to type in an unfamiliar combination of keys to terminate data input.

---

[1] This method of input will be very useful when reading data from files rather than the keyboard. (File input is presented in Chapter 11.)

`break` and `continue` Statements

Two useful statements in connection with repetition statements are the `break` and `continue` statements. We have previously encountered the `break` statement in relation to the `switch` statement. The general form of this statement is

```
break;
```

A `break` statement, as its name implies, forces an immediate break, or exit, from `switch`, `while`, `for`, and `do-while` statements only.

For example, execution of the following `while` loop is immediately terminated if a number greater than 76 is entered.

```
while(count <= 10)
{
  printf("Enter a number: ");
  scanf("%f", &num);
  if (num > 76)
  {
    printf("You lose!");
    break;          /* break out of the loop */
  }
  else
  printf("Keep on truckin!");
}
/* break jumps to here */
```

The `break` statement violates pure structured programming principles because it provides a second, nonstandard exit from a loop. Nevertheless, the `break` statement is extremely useful for breaking out of loops when an unusual condition is detected. The `break` statement is also used to exit from a `switch` statement, but this is because the desired case has been detected and processed.

The `continue` statement is similar to the `break` statement but applies only to loops created with `while`, `do-while`, and `for` statements. The general format of a `continue` statement is

```
continue;
```

When a `continue` is encountered in a loop, the next iteration of the loop begins immediately. For `while` loops this means that execution is automatically transferred to the top of the loop and reevaluation of the tested expression is initiated. Although the `continue` statement has no direct effect on a `switch` statement, it can be included within a `switch` statement that itself is contained in a loop. Here the effect of `continue` is the same: the next loop iteration begins.

As a general rule the `continue` statement is used less than the `break` statement, but it is convenient for skipping over data that should not be processed while remaining in a loop. For example, invalid grades are simply ignored in the following section of code, and only valid grades are added into the total[2]:

```
while (count < 30)
{
  printf("Enter a grade: ");
  scanf("%f", &grade);
  if(grade < 0 || grade > 100)
    continue;
  total = total + grade;
  count = count + 1;
}
```

The Null Statement

Statements are always terminated by a semicolon. A semicolon with nothing preceding it is also a valid statement, called the *null statement.* Thus, the statement

```
;
```

is a null statement. This is a do-nothing statement that is used where a statement is syntactically required, but no action is called for. Null statements typically are used either with while or for statements. An example of a for statement using a null statement is found in Program 5.10c.

Exercises 5.2

1. Rewrite Program 5.6 to compute the total of eight numbers.

2. Rewrite Program 5.6 to display the prompt:

   ```
   Please type in the total number of data values to be added:
   ```

   In response to this prompt, the program should accept a user-entered number and then use this number to control the number of times the while loop is executed. Thus, if the user enters 5 in response to the prompt, the program should request the input of five numbers and display the total after five numbers have been entered.

3. a. Write a C program to convert Celsius degrees to Fahrenheit. The program should request the starting Celsius value, the number of conversions to be made, and the increment between Cel-

---

[2] The continue is not essential, however, and the selection can be written as:

```
If (grade >= 0 && grade <= 100)
{
  total = total + grade
  count = count + 1
}
```

sius values. The display should have appropriate headings and list the Celsius value and the corresponding Fahrenheit value. Use the relationship: Fahrenheit = (9.0 / 5.0) * Celsius + 32.0.

   b. Run the program written in Exercise 3a on a computer. Verify that your program begins at the correct starting Celsius value and contains the exact number of conversions specified in your input data.

4. a. Modify the program written in Exercise 3 to request the starting Celsius value, the ending Celsius value, and the increment. Thus, instead of the condition checking for a fixed count, the condition checks for the ending Celsius value.

   b. Run the program written in Exercise 4a on a computer. Verify that your output starts at the correct beginning value and ends at the correct ending value.

5. Rewrite Program 5.7 to compute the average of ten numbers.

6. Rewrite Program 5.7 to display the prompt:

   ```
   Please type in the total number of data values to be averaged:
   ```

   In response to this prompt, the program should accept a user-entered number and then use this number to control the number of times the `while` loop is executed. Thus, if the user enters 6 in response to the prompt, the program should request the input of six numbers and display the average of the next six numbers entered.

7. By mistake, a programmer put the statement `average = total / count;` within the `while` loop immediately after the statement `total = total + num;` in Program 5.7. Thus, the `while` loop becomes

   ```
   while (count <= 4)
   {
     printf("\nEnter a number: ");
     scanf("%f", &num);
     total = total + num;
     average = total / count;
     ++count;
   }
   ```

   Will the program yield the correct result with this `while` loop? From a programming perspective, which `while` loop is better to use, and why?

8. a. Modify Program 5.8 to compute the average of the grades entered.

   b. Run the program written in Exercise 8a on a computer and verify the results.

9. a. A bookstore summarizes its monthly transactions by keeping the following information for each book in stock:

   Book identification number
   Inventory balance at the beginning of the month
   Number of copies received during the month
   Number of copies sold during the month

   Write a C program that accepts this data for each book and then displays the book identification number and an updated book inventory balance using the relationship:

> New Balance = Inventory balance at the beginning of the month
> + Number of copies received during the month
> − Number of copies sold during the month

Your program should use a `while` statement with a fixed count condition so that information on only three books is requested.

b. Run the program written in Exercise 9a on a computer. Review the display produced by your program and verify that the output produced is correct.

10. Modify the program you write for Exercise 9 to keep requesting and displaying results until a sentinel identification value of 999 is entered. Run the program on a computer.

11. a. The following data were collected on a recent automobile trip.

	Mileage	**Gallons**
Start of trip:	22495	Full tank
	22841	12.2
	23185	11.3
	23400	10.5
	23772	11.0
	24055	12.2
	24434	14.7
	24804	14.3
	25276	15.2

Write a C program that accepts a mileage and gallons value and calculates the miles-per-gallon (mpg) achieved for that segment of the trip. The miles-per-gallon is obtained as the difference in mileage between fill-ups divided by the number of gallons of gasoline received in the fill-up.

b. Modify the program written for Exercise 11a to additionally compute and display the cumulative mpg achieved after each fill-up. The cumulative mpg is calculated as the difference between each fill-up mileage and the mileage at the start of the trip divided by the sum of the gallons used to that point in the trip.

5.3   The `for` Statement

The `for` statement performs the same functions as the `while` statement, but uses a different form. In many situations, especially those that use a fixed count condition, the `for` statement format is easier to use than its `while` equivalent.

The general form of the `for` statement is

```
for (initializing list; expression; altering list)
    statement;
```

Although the `for` statement looks a little complicated, it is really quite simple if we consider each of its parts separately.

Within the parentheses of the `for` statement are three items, separated by semicolons. Each of these items is optional and can be described individually, but the semicolons must be present. As we shall see, the items in parentheses correspond to the initialization, expression evaluation, and altering of expression values that we have already used with the while statement.

The middle item in the parentheses, the expression, is any valid C expression, and there is no difference in the way for and while statements use this expression. In both statements, as long as the expression has a nonzero (true) value, the statement following the parentheses is executed. This means that prior to the first check of the expression, initial values for the tested expression's variables must be assigned. It also means that before the expression is reevaluated, there must be one or more statements that alter these values. Recall that the general placement of these statements using a while statement follows the pattern:

```
initializing statements;
while (expression)
{
  loop statements;
          .
          .
          .

  expression-altering statements;
}
```

The need to initialize variables or make some other evaluations prior to entering a repetition loop is so common that the for statement allows all the initializing statements to be grouped together as the first set of items within the for's parentheses. The items in this initializing list are executed only once, before the expression is evaluated for the first time.

The for statement also provides a single place for all expression-altering statements. These items can be placed in the altering list, which is the last list contained within the for's parentheses. All items in the altering list are executed by the for statement at the end of the loop, just before the expression is reevaluated. Figure 5.6 illustrates the for statement's flow-of-control diagram.

The following section of code illustrates the correspondence between the for and while statements:

```
count = 1;
while (count <= 10)
{
  printf("%d", count);
  ++count:
}
```

The for statement corresponding to this section of code is

```
for (count = 1; count <= 10; ++count)
  printf("%d", count);
```

As seen in this example, the only difference between the for statement and the while statement is the placement of equivalent expressions. The grouping together of

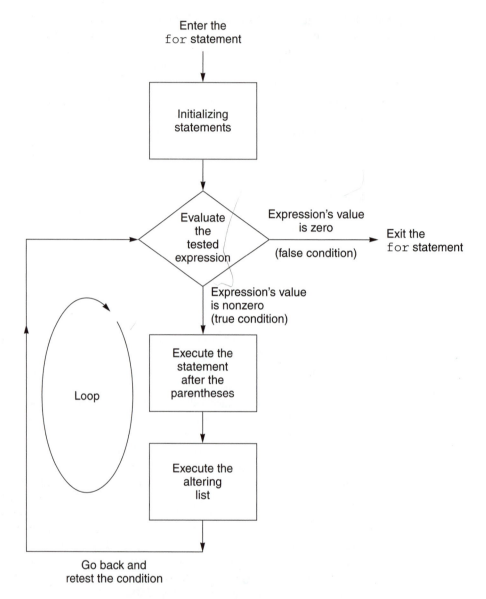

Figure 5.6   `for` statement flow of control

the initialization, expression test, and altering list in the `for` statement is very convenient, especially when they are used to create fixed-count loops. Consider the following `for` statement:

```
for (count = 2; count <= 20; count = count + 2)
    printf("%d  ",count);
```

All the loop control information is contained within the parentheses. The loop starts with a count of 2, stops when the count exceeds 20, and increments the loop counter in steps of 2. Program 5.10 illustrates this for statement in an actual program.

 Program 5.10

```
#include <stdio.h>
int main()
{
   int count;

   for (count = 2; count <= 20; count = count + 2)
     printf("%d  ",count);

   return 0;
}
```

The output of Program 5.10 is

2   4   6   8   10   12   14   16   18   20

The for statement does not require that any of the items in parentheses be present or that they be used for initializing or altering the values in the expression statements. However, the two semicolons must be present within the for's parentheses. For example, the construction for (; count <= 20;) is valid.

If the initializing list is missing, the initialization step is omitted when the for statement is executed. This, of course, means that the programmer must provide the required initializations before the for statement is encountered. Similarly, if the altering list is missing, any expressions needed to alter the evaluation of the tested expression must be included directly within the statement part of the loop. The for statement only ensures that all expressions in the initializing list are executed once, before evaluation of the tested expression, and that all expressions in the altering list are executed at the end of the loop before the tested expression is rechecked. Thus, Program 5.10 can be rewritten in any of the three ways shown in Programs 5.10a, 5.10b, and 5.10c.

Program 5.10a

```c
#include <stdio.h>
int main()
{
  int count;
  count = 2;     /* initializer outside for statement */
  for ( ; count <= 20; count = count + 2)
    printf("%d  ",count);

  return 0;
}
```

Program 5.10b

```c
#include <stdio.h>
int main()
{
  int count;

  count = 2;     /* initializer outside for statement    */
  for( ; count <= 20; )
  {
    printf("%d  ",count);
    count = count + 2;     /* alteration statement */

  return 0;
  }
}
```

Program 5.10c

```c
#include <stdio.h>
int main()  /* all expressions within the for's parentheses */
{
  int count;

  for (count = 2; count <= 20; printf("%d  ",count), count = count + 2);

  return 0;
}
```

Programming Note

Where Do the Opening Braces Go?

There are two styles of writing `for` loops that are used by professional C programmers. These styles come into play only when the `for` loop contains a compound statement. The style illustrated and used in the text takes the form:

```
for (expression)
{
  compound statement
}
```

An equally acceptable style that is used by many programmers places the initial brace of the compound statement on the first line. Using this style a `for` loop appears as:

```
for (expression) {
  compound statement
{
```

The advantage of the first style is that the braces line up under one another, making it easier to locate brace pairs. The advantage of the second style is that it makes the code more compact and saves a display line, permitting more code to be viewed in the same display area. Both styles are used, but are almost never intermixed. Select whichever style appeals to you or is specified by your professor or place of work, and be consistent in its use. As always, the indentation you use within the compound statement (two or four spaces, or a tab) should also be consistent throughout all of your programs. The combination of styles that you select becomes a "signature" for your programming work.

In Program 5.10a `count` is initialized outside the `for` statement and the first list inside the parentheses is left blank. In Program 5.10b, both the initializing list and the altering list are removed from within the parentheses. Program 5.10b also uses a compound statement within the `for` loop, with the expression-altering statement included in the compound statement. Program 5.10c includes all items within the parentheses, so there is no need for any useful statement following the parentheses. Here the null statement satisfies the syntactical requirement that one statement follow the `for`'s parentheses. Observe also in Program 5.10c that the altering list (the last set of items in parentheses) consists of two items and that a comma separates these items. The use of commas to separate items in both the initializing and altering lists is required if either of these two lists contains more than one item. Finally note the fact that Programs 5.10a, 5.10b, and 5.10c are all inferior to Program 5.10. The `for` statement in Program 5.10 is much clearer since all the expressions pertaining to the tested expression are grouped together within the parentheses.

Although the initializing and altering lists can be omitted from a `for` statement, omitting the tested expression results in an infinite loop. For example, such a loop is created by the statement

```
for (count = 2; ; ++count)
   printf("%d",count);
```

As with the `while` statement, both `break` and `continue` statements can be used within a `for` loop. The `break` forces an immediate exit from the `for` loop, as it does in the `while` loop. The `continue`, however, forces control to be passed to the altering list in a `for` statement, after which the tested expression is reevaluated. This differs from the action of a `continue` in a `while` statement, where control is passed directly to the reevaluation of the tested expression.

To understand the enormous power of the `for` statement, consider the task of printing a table of numbers from 1 to 10, including their squares and cubes, using this statement. Such a table was previously produced using a `while` statement in Program 5.3. You may wish to review Program 5.3 and compare it to Program 5.11 to get a further sense of the equivalence between the `for` and `while` statements.

 Program 5.11

```
#include <stdio.h>
int main()
{
  int num;

  printf("NUMBER      SQUARE       CUBE\n");
  printf("------      ------       ----\n");

  for (num = 1; num <= 10; ++num)
    printf("%3d       %3d        %4d\n", num, num*num, num*num*num);

  return 0;
}
```

Program 5.11 produces the following display:

NUMBER	SQUARE	CUBE
------	------	----
1	1	1
2	4	8
3	9	27
4	16	64
5	25	125
6	36	216
7	49	343
8	64	512
9	81	729
10	100	1000

Simply changing 10 in the `for` statement of Program 5.11 to 1000 creates a loop that is executed 1000 times and produces a table of numbers from 1 to 1000. As with the `while` statement, this small change produces an immense increase in the processing and output provided by the program.

`scanf()` within a `for` Loop

Using a `scanf()` function call inside a `for` loop produces the same effect as when this function is called inside a `while` loop. For example, in Program 5.12 a `scanf()` function call is used to input a set of numbers. As each number is input, it is added to a total. When the `for` loop is exited, the average is calculated and displayed.

The `for` statement in Program 5.12 creates a loop that is executed five times. The user is prompted to enter a number each time through the loop. After each number is entered, it is immediately added to the total. Although, for clarity, `total` was initialized to zero before the `for` statement, this initialization could have been included with the initialization of `count`, as follows:

```
for (total = 0.0, count = 0; count < 5; ++count)
```

Nested Loops

There are many situations in which it is very convenient to have a loop contained within another loop. Such loops are called *nested loops*. A simple example of a nested loop is

```
for(i = 1; i <= 5; ++i)                   /* start of outer loop  <------+ */
{                                         /*                             | */
   printf("\ni is now %d\n",i)            /*                             | */
   for(j = 1; j <= 4; ++j)                /* start of inner loop         | */
     printf("  j = %d", j);               /* end of inner loop           | */
}                                         /* end of outer loop    <------+ */
```

Program 5.12

```c
#include <stdio.h>
int main()
/* This program calculates the average */
/* of five user-entered numbers.       */
{
  int count;
  float num, total, average;

  total = 0.0;

  for (count = 0; count < 5; ++count)
  {
    printf("\nEnter a number: ");
    scanf("%f", &num);
    total = total + num;
  }

  average = total / count;
  printf("\n\nThe average of the data entered is %f", average);

  return 0;
}
```

The first loop, controlled by the value of i, is called the *outer loop*. The second loop, controlled by the value of j, is called the *inner loop*. Notice that all statements in the inner loop are contained within the boundaries of the outer loop and that we have used a different variable to control each loop. For each single trip through the outer loop, the inner loop runs through its entire sequence. Thus, each time the i counter increases by 1, the inner for loop executes completely. This situation is illustrated in Figure 5.7.

Program 5.13 includes the above code in a working program.

 Program 5.13

```c
#include <stdio.h>
int main()
{
  int i,j;
```

(Continued on next page)

(Continued from previous page)

```
for(i = 1; i <= 5; ++i)       /* start of outer loop <------+ */
{                             /*                            | */
  printf("\ni is now %d\n",i)/*                            | */
  for(j = 1; j <=4; ++j)      /* start of inner loop        | */
    printf("  j = %d", j);    /* end of inner loop          | */
}                             /* end of outer loop   <------+ */

  return 0;
}
```

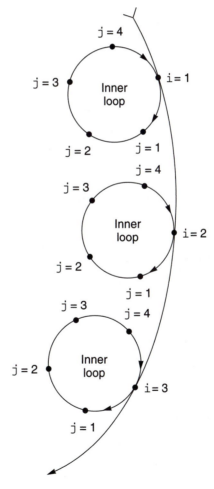

Figure 5.7   j loops once for each i

Programming Note

Do You Use a `for` or `while` Loop?

A question commonly asked by beginning programmers is which loop structure they should use—a `for` or `while` loop? This is a good question because both of these loop structures in C can be used to construct both fixed-count and variable-condition loops.

In almost all other computer languages the answer is relatively straightforward, because the `for` statement can be used only to construct fixed-count loops. Thus, in most other languages `for` statements are used to construct fixed-count loops, and `while` statements are generally used only when constructing variable-condition loops.

In C, this easy distinction does not hold, since each statement can be used to create each type of loop. The answer in C, then, is really a matter of style. Since `for` and `while` loops are interchangeable in C, either loop is appropriate. Some professional programmers always use a `for` statement for every loop they create and almost never use a `while` statement. Others always use a `while` statement and rarely use a `for` statement. Still a third group tends to retain the convention used in other languages—a `for` loop is generally used to create fixed-count loops and a `while` loop is used to create variable-condition loops. In C it is all a matter of style, and you will encounter all three styles in your programming career.

Following is the output of a sample run of Program 5.13.

```
i is now 1
  j = 1  j = 2  j = 3  j = 4
i is now 2
  j = 1  j = 2  j = 3  j = 4
i is now 3
  j = 1  j = 2  j = 3  j = 4
i is now 4
  j = 1  j = 2  j = 3  j = 4
i is now 5
  j = 1  j = 2  j = 3  j = 4
```

Let us use a nested loop to compute the average grade for each student in a class of 20. Each student has taken four exams during the course of the semester. The final grade is calculated as the average of these examination grades.

The outer loop in our program will consist of 20 passes. Each pass through the outer loop is used to compute the average for one student. The inner loop will consist of 4 passes. One examination grade is entered in each inner loop pass. As each grade is entered it is added to the total for the student, and at the end of the loop the average is calculated and displayed. Program 5.14 uses a nested loop to make the required calculations.

Program 5.14

```c
#include <stdio.h>
int main()
{
  int i,j;
  float grade, total, average;
  for (i = 1; i <= 20; ++i)      /* start of outer loop */
  {
    total = 0;                        /* clear the total for this student */
    for (j = 1; j <= 4; ++j)      /* start of inner loop */
    {
      printf("Enter an examination grade for this student: ");
      scanf("%f", &grade);
      total = total + grade;     /* add the grade into the total  */
    }                            /* end of the inner for loop     */
    average = total / 4;         /* calculate the average         */
    printf("\nThe average for student %d is %f\n\n",i,average);
  }                              /* end of the outer for loop     */

  return 0;
}
```

In reviewing Program 5.14, pay particular attention to the initialization of `total` within the outer loop before the inner loop is entered. The variable `total` is initialized 20 times, once for each student. Also notice that the average is calculated and displayed immediately after the inner loop is finished. Since the statements that compute and print the average are also contained within the outer loop, 20 averages are calculated and displayed. The entry and addition of each grade within the inner loop use techniques we have seen before, which should now be familiar to you.

Exercises 5.3

1. Determine the output of the following program.

```c
#include <stdio.h>
int main()
{
  int i;

  for (i = 20; i >= 0; i -= 4)
```

(Continued on next page)

(Continued from previous page)

```
        printf("%d ",i);

    return 0;
}
```

2. Modify Program 5.11 to produce a table of the numbers 0 through 20 in increments of 2, with their squares and cubes.

3. Modify Program 5.11 to produce a table of numbers from 10 to 1, instead of 1 to 10, as it currently does.

4. Write and run a C program that displays a table of 20 temperature conversions from Fahrenheit to Celsius. The table should start with a Fahrenheit value of 20 degrees and be incremented in values of 4 degrees. Recall that Celsius = (5.0/9.0) * (Fahrenheit − 32.0).

5. Modify the program written for Exercise 4 to initially request the number of conversions to be displayed.

6. Write a C program that converts Fahrenheit temperature to Celsius in increments of 5 degrees. The initial value of the Fahrenheit temperature and the total conversion to be made are to be requested as user input during program execution. Recall that Celsius = (5.0/9.0) * (Fahrenheit − 32.0).

7. Write and run a C program that accepts six Fahrenheit temperatures, one at a time, and converts each value entered to its Celsius equivalent before the next value is requested. Use a for loop in your program. The conversion required is Celsius = (5.0/9.0) * (Fahrenheit − 32.0).

8. Write and run a C program that accepts ten individual values of gallons, one at a time, and converts each value entered to its liter equivalent before the next value is requested. Use a for loop in your program. There are 3.785 liters in 1 gallon.

9. Modify the program written for Exercise 8 to initially request the number of data items that will be entered and converted.

10. Write and run a C program that calculates and displays the amount of money available in a bank account that initially has $1,000 deposited in it and that earns 8 percent interest a year. Your program should display the amount available at the end of each year for a period of ten years. Use the relationship that the money available at the end of each year equals the amount of money in the account at the start of the year plus .08 times the amount available at the start of the year.

11. A machine purchased for $28,000 is depreciated at a rate of $4,000 a year for seven years. Write and run a program that computes and displays a depreciation table for seven years. The table should have the form:

```
DEPRECIATION SCHEDULE
----------------------
```

YEAR	DEPRECIATION	END-OF-YEAR VALUE	ACCUMULATED DEPRECIATION
1	4000	24000	4000
2	4000	20000	8000
3	4000	16000	12000
4	4000	12000	16000
5	4000	8000	20000

6	4000	4000	24000
7	4000	0	28000

12. a. Modify the program written for Exercise 10 to initially prompt the user for the amount of money initially deposited in the account.

  b. Modify the program written for Exercise 10 to initially prompt the user for both the amount of money initially deposited and the number of years that should be displayed.

  c. Modify the program written for Exercise 10 to initially prompt for the amount of money initially deposited, the interest rate to be used, and the number of years to be displayed.

13. A well-regarded manufacturer of widgets has been losing 4 percent of its sales each year. The annual profit for the firm is 10 percent of sales. This year the firm has had $10 million in sales and a profit of $1 million. Determine the expected sales and profit for the next 10 years. Your program should complete and produce a display as follows:

```
SALES AND PROFIT PROJECTION
---------------------------

YEAR            EXPECTED SALES          PROJECTED PROFIT
----            --------------          ----------------
  1             $10000000.00             $1000000.00
  2             $ 9600000.00             $ 960000.00
  3                   .                        .
  .                   .                        .
  .                   .                        .
  .                   .                        .
 10                   .                        .
-----------------------------------------------------------
Totals:         $      .                 $      .
```

14. Four experiments are performed, each consisting of six test results. The results for each experiment are given below. Write a C program using a nested loop to compute and display the average of the test results for each experiment.

1st experiment results:	23.2	31.5	16.9	27.5	25.4	28.6
2nd experiment results:	34.8	45.2	27.9	36.8	33.4	39.4
3rd experiment results:	19.4	16.8	10.2	20.8	18.9	13.4
4th experiment results:	36.9	39.5	49.2	45.1	42.7	50.6

15. Modify the program written for Exercise 14 so that the number of test results for each experiment is entered by the user. Write your program so that a different number of test results can be entered for each experiment.

16. a. A bowling team consists of five players. Each player bowls three games. Write a C program that uses a nested loop to enter each player's individual scores and then computes and displays the average score for each bowler. Assume that each bowler has the following scores:

1st bowler:	286	252	265
2nd bowler:	212	186	215
3rd bowler:	252	232	216
4th bowler:	192	201	235
5th bowler:	186	236	272

  b. Modify the program written for Exercise 16a to calculate and display the average team score. (*Hint:* Use a second variable to store the total of all the players' scores.)

17. Rewrite the program written for Exercise 16a to eliminate the inner loop. To do this, you have to input three scores for each bowler rather than one at a time. Each score must be stored in its own variable name before the average is calculated.

18. Write a C program that calculates and displays the yearly amount available if $1,000 is invested in a bank account for 10 years. Your program should display the amounts available for interest rates from 6 percent to 12 percent inclusively, at 1 percent increments. Use a nested loop, with the outer loop having a fixed count of 7 and the inner loop a fixed count of 10. The first iteration of the outer loop should use an interest rate of 6 percent and display the amount of money available at the end of the first 10 years. In each subsequent pass through the outer loop, the interest rate should be increased by 1 percent. Use the relationship that the money available at the end of each year equals the amount of money in the account at the start of the year plus the interest rate times the amount available at the start of the year.

5.4 The do Statement

Both the `while` and `for` statements evaluate an expression at the start of the repetition loop. There are cases, however, where it is more convenient to test the expression at the end of the loop. For example, suppose we have constructed the following `while` loop to calculate sales taxes:

```
printf("Enter a price:");
scanf("%f", &price);
while (price != SENTINEL)
{
    salestax = RATE * price;
    printf("The sales tax is $%5.2f",salestax);
    printf("\nEnter a price: ");
    scanf("%f", &price);
}
```

Using this `while` statement requires either duplicating the prompt and `scanf()` function calls before the loop and then within the loop, as we have done, or resorting to some other artifice to force initial execution of the statements within the `while` loop.

The do statement, as its name implies, allows us to do some statements before an expression is evaluated. In many situations this can be used to eliminate the duplication illustrated in the previous example. The general form of the do statement is

```
do
    statement;
while (expression);  ←——————— don't forget the final ;
```

As with all C programs, the single statement in the do may be replaced with a compound statement. A flow-control diagram illustrating the operation of the do statement is shown in Figure 5.8.

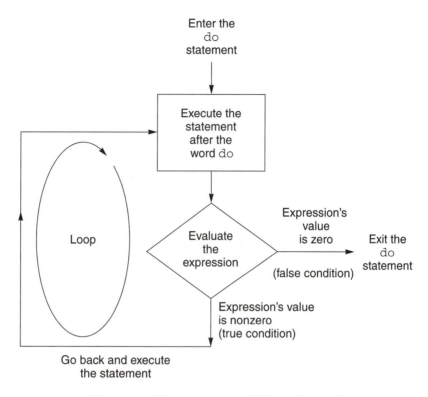

Figure 5.8   The do statement's flow of control

As illustrated in Figure 5.8, all statements within the do statement are executed at least once before the expression is evaluated. Then, if the expression has a nonzero value, the statements are executed again. This process continues until the expression evaluates to zero. For example, consider the following do statement:

```
do
{
  printf("\nEnter a price: ");
  scanf("%f", &price);
  if (fabs(price - SENTINEL) < 0.0001)
    break;
  salestax = RATE * price;
  printf("The sales tax is $%5.2f", salestax);

}
while (price != SENTINEL);
```

Here the compound statement within the loop will always be executed at least once, regardless of the value of the tested condition. They will then be repeatedly executed as long as the condition remains true. Notice that in this section of code the loop is also stopped when the sentinel value is encountered.

As with all repetition statements, the do statement can always replace or be replaced by an equivalent while or for statement. The choice of which statement to use depends on the application and the style preferred by the programmer. In general, the while and for statements are preferred because they clearly let anyone reading the program know what is being tested "right up front" at the top of the program loop.

Validity Checks

The do statement is particularly useful in filtering user-entered input and providing data validity checks. For example, assume that an operator is required to enter a valid customer identification number between the numbers 1000 and 1999. A number outside this range is to be rejected, and a new request for a valid number made. The following section of code provides the necessary data filter to verify the entry of a valid identification number:

```
do
{
  printf("\nEnter an identification number: ");
  scanf("%f", &idNum);
}
while (idNum < 1000 || idNum > 1999);
```

Here, a request for an identification number is repeated until a valid number is entered. This section of code is "bare bones" in that it neither alerts the operator to the cause of the new request for data nor allows premature exit from the loop if a valid identification number cannot be found. An alternative for removing the first drawback is

```
do
{
  printf("\nEnter an identification number: ");
  scanf("%f", &idNum);
  if (idNum < 1000 || idNum > 1999)
  {
    printf("\n An invalid number was just entered");
    printf("\nPlease check the ID number and re-enter");
  }
  else
    break;     /* break if a valid id num was entered */
} while(1);    /* this expression is always true */
```

Here we have used a break statement to exit the loop. Because the expression being evaluated by the do statement is always 1 (true), an infinite loop has been created that is exited only when the break statement is encountered.

Exercises 5.4

1. a. Using a do statement, write a C program to accept a grade. The program should request a grade continuously as long as an invalid grade is entered. An invalid grade is any grade less than 0 or greater than 100. After a valid grade has been entered, your program should display its value.

b. Modify the program written for Exercise 1a so that the user is alerted when an invalid grade has been entered.

c. Modify the program written for Exercise 1b so that it allows the user to exit the program by entering the number 999.

d. Modify the program written for Exercise 1b so that it automatically terminates after five invalid grades are entered.

2. a. Write a C program that continuously requests a grade to be entered. If the grade is less than 0 or greater than 100, your program should print an appropriate message informing the user that an invalid grade has been entered, else the grade should be added to a total. When a grade of 999 is entered the program should exit the repetition loop and compute and display the average of the valid grades entered.

b. Run the program written in Exercise 2a on a computer, and verify the program using appropriate test data.

3. a. Write a C program to reverse the digits of a positive integer number. For example, if the number 8735 is entered, the number displayed should be 5378. (*Hint:* Use a do statement and continuously strip off and display the units digit of the number. If the variable num initially contains the number entered, the units digit is obtained as (num % 10). After a units digit is displayed, dividing the number by 10 sets up the number for the next iteration. Thus, (8735 % 10) is 5 and (8735 / 10) is 873. The do statement should continue as long as the remaining number is not zero).

b. Run the program written in Exercise 3a on a computer, and verify the program using appropriate text data.

4. Print the decimal, octal, and hexadecimal values of all characters between the start and stop characters entered by a user. For example, if the user enters an a and z, the program should print all the characters between a and z and their respective numerical values. Make sure that the second character entered by the user occurs later in the alphabet than the first character. If it does not, write a loop that repeatedly asks the user for a valid second character until one is entered.

5. Repeat any of the exercises in Section 5.3 using a do statement rather than a for statement.

5.5 Common Programming Errors

Five errors are commonly made by beginning C programmers when using repetition statements. Two of these pertain to the tested expression and have already been encountered with the if and switch statements.

1. Inadvertently using the assignment operator, =, instead of the equality operator, ==, in the tested expression. An example of this error is typing the assignment expression a = 5 instead of the desired relational expression a == 5. Since the tested expression can be any valid C expression, including arithmetic and assignment expressions, this error is not detected by the compiler.

2. As with the if statement, repetition statements should not use the equality operator, ==, when testing floating point or double precision operands. For example, the expression fnum == .01 should be replaced by an equivalent test requiring that the absolute value of fnum - .01 be less than an acceptable amount. The reason is that all numbers are stored in binary form. Using a finite number of bits, decimal numbers such as .01 have no exact binary equivalent, so that tests requiring equality with such numbers can fail.

3. Placing a semicolon at the end of the for's parentheses, which frequently produces a do-nothing loop. For example, consider the statements

```
for(count = 0; count < 10; ++count);
   total = total + num;
```

Here, the semicolon at the end of the first line of code is a null statement. This has the effect of creating a loop that is traversed 10 times with nothing done except the incrementing and testing of count. This error tends to occur because C programmers are used to ending most lines with a semicolon.

4. Using commas to separate the items in a for statement instead of the required semicolons. An example of this is the statement

```
for (count = 1, count < 10, ++count)
```

Commas must be used to separate items within the initializing and altering lists, and semicolons must be used to separate these lists from the tested expression.

5. Omitting the final semicolon from the do statement. This error is usually made by programmers who have learned to omit the semicolon after the parentheses of a while statement and continue this habit when the reserved word while is encountered at the end of a do statement.

5.6 Chapter Summary

1. The while, for, and do repetition statements create program loops. These statements evaluate an expression and, based on the resulting expression value, either terminate the loop or continue with it. Each pass through the loop is referred to as a repetition or iteration.

2. The while statement checks its expression before any other statement in the loop. This requires that any variables in the tested expression have values assigned before the while is encountered. Within a while loop there must be a statement

that alters the tested expression's value. The most commonly used form of this loop is

```
while (expression)
{
   statements;
}
```

An example of a `while` loop is

```
count = 1;              /* initialize count */
while (count <= 10)
{
  printf("%d ",count);
  ++count;                /* increment count */
}
```

The `while` statement always checks its expression at the top of the loop. This requires that any variables in the tested expression must have values assigned before the `while` is encountered. Within the `while` loop there must be a statement that alters the tested expression's value.

3. The `for` statement is extremely useful in creating loops that must be executed a fixed number of times. Initializing expressions, the tested expression, and expressions affecting the tested expression can all be included in parentheses at the top of a `for` loop. Additionally, any other loop statement can be included within the `for`'s parentheses as part of its altering list. The most commonly used form of this loop is

```
for (initializing list; expression; altering list)
{
   statements;
}
```

An example of a `for` loop is

```
for (total = 0, count = 1; count < 10; ++count)
{
  printf("Enter a grade: ");
  scanf("%f", &grade);
  total = total + grade;
}
```

In this `for` statement, the initializing list is used to initialize both `total` and `count`. The expression determines that the loop will execute as long as the value in `count` is less than 10, and the value of `count` is incremented by one each time through the loop.

4. The do statement checks its expression at the end of the loop. This ensures that the body of a do loop is executed at least once. Within a do loop there must be at least one statement that alters the tested expression's value. The most commonly used form of this loop is

```
do
{
    statements;
}
while (expression);
```

5.7   Chapter Supplement: Character-Oriented Graphics

Traditionally, there have been two approaches to producing graphical images in C. The first approach is to use the alphanumeric characters that C recognizes to produce a desired figure. The "trick" in producing such character-based figures is to determine an appropriate algorithm for producing the desired image, which can range from the simple to the sophisticated. Graphical library functions are often provided with C compilers to help in the production of the desired image, or a graphical function library can be purchased. The second approach has been to purchase special high-resolution graphics hardware and an associated software package.

More recently, a third approach has emerged: to include the capability to easily construct and use graphical objects, such as circles and windows, within the context of an existing, character-based language. Examples of this approach are Visual Basic, which provides the ability to manipulate a set of presupplied graphical objects, and C++, which adds an object creation and manipulation capability to C.

In this section we explore the basics of the first approach. We present a commonly used character-oriented graphical algorithm that can be used to construct relatively simple geometric shapes and that also illustrates the importance of algorithm development in graphics programming.

Character-at-a-time Display

In this method of graphical output the desired character, which is usually either an *, -, +, or blank space symbol, is placed, character-by-character, in the desired position on the output medium (paper or screen) to produce a desired geometric display. For example, the graphical image shown in Figure 5.9 is made up entirely of the asterisk symbol, *, placed to form a triangular shape.

Images such as that shown in Figure 5.9 are typically produced making repeated calls to a single function that is capable of displaying one or more of the selected symbol across a screen or paper medium. To see how this is accomplished, we first construct the simpler shape illustrated in Figure 5.10. This figure consists of five blank spaces followed by nine consecutive asterisks.

Figure 5.9   A graphical figure

Left-hand page margin

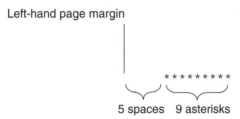

5 spaces   9 asterisks

Figure 5.10   A simple graphical figure

For now, assume that we have constructed a function named display() that is capable of printing consecutive repetitions of the same character. Using this function, the two function calls

```
display(5,' ');
display(9,'*')
```

would produce the display shown on Figure 5.10. The actual construction of display() is rather trivial. The pseudocode for this function is

> ***Function display( )***
>   ***Accept the number of repetitions and a character symbol as arguments***
>   ***For the number of repetitions***
>   ***print the character***
>   ***End For***

In C, this algorithm can be written as:

```c
/* this function prints n occurrences of a character */
void display(int howmany, char symbol)
{
  int i;

  for (i = 1; i <= howmany; ++i)
    printf("%c", symbol);
}
```

Having constructed the `display()` function, we can now use it to produce the shape shown in Figure 5.9, which is produced by repeated calls to `display()`.

Notice that each line shown in Figure 5.9 consists of a series of blank spaces followed by one or more asterisks. As such, each line in the figure is really a specific instance of the line shown in Figure 5.10, with differing values for the blank and asterisk repetition values. Thus, each line in Figure 5.9 can be produced by two calls to display— one to display the spaces and one to display the asterisks. The "trick" in producing figures such as the triangle shown in Figure 5.9 is to determine an algorithm for finding the repetitions required for each line.

The required spaces and asterisks needed to produce each line of Figure 5.9 are listed in Table 5.1.

Table 5.1 Required elements for Figure 5.9

Line No.	Spaces	Asterisks
1	5	1
2	4	3
3	3	5
4	2	7
5	1	9
6	0	11

From Table 5.1 it can be seen that the number of spaces preceding the asterisk in the figure can be calculated as $6 - i$, where i is the line number. Similarly, it can be determined that the number of asterisks displayed on each line is $2 * i - 1$, where i is again the line number.

Thus, producing Figure 5.9 requires six calls to `display()` for printing the leading spaces and six calls to `display()` for printing the asterisks. For each line in the figure the number of space repetitions passed to `display()` is $6 - i$, and the number of asterisk repetitions is $2 * i - 1$. In pseudocode the algorithm is described by:

> *For line number equal 1 to 6*
> *   display(6 – line number,' ')*
> *   display(2 * line number – 1,'*')*
> *EndFor*

Program 5.15 provides the C code for producing Figure 5.9.

Program 5.15

```c
#include <stdio.h>
#define NUMLINES 6
int main()
{
  int i, indent, howmany;
  void display(int, char);

  for(i = 1; i <= NUMLINES; ++i)
  {
    display((NUMLINES + 1 - i), ' ');
    display((2 * i - 1), '*');
    printf("\n");
  }
}
/* this function prints n occurrences of a character */
void display(int howmany, char symbol)
{
  int i;

  for (i = 1; i <= howmany; ++i)
    printf("%c", symbol);

  return 0;
}
```

A sample run using Program 5.15 yields the single required output figure:

```
     *
    ***
   *****
  *******
 *********
***********
```

Exercises 5.7

1. Write a C program to create the following figures:

   a.
   ```
   -----*
   ----***
   ---*****
   --*******
   -*********
   **********
   ```
   b.
   ```
   *
    *
     *
      *
       *
        *
   ```

2. Write a C program to create the following figures:

   a.
   ```
          *
         *
        *
       *
      *
     *
   ```
   b.
   ```
            *
           **
          ***
         ****
        *****
       ******
   ```

3. Write a C program to create the following figures:

   a.
   ```
   ***********
    **********
     *********
      ********
       *******
        ******
   ```
   b.
   ```
   **********
    **********
     **********
      **********
       **********
        **********
   ```

4. Write a C program to create the following figures:

   a.
   ```
        *
       ***
      *****
     *******
    *********
   ***********
    *********
     *******
      *****
       ***
        *
   ```
   b.
   ```
        *
       * *
      *   *
     *     *
    *       *
   ***********
   ```

Functions

Chapter **6**

Writing Your Own Functions

In the programs we have written so far, the only two functions we have called have been `printf()` and `scanf()`. Although these two functions have been enormously helpful to us, it is now time to create our own useful functions, in addition to the `main()` function that is required in all programs.

In this chapter we learn how to write these functions, pass data to them, process the passed data and return a result to the calling function.

6.1 Function Definitions and Declarations

The purpose of a C function, whether library or user-written, is to receive data, operate on the data, and directly return at most a single value.[1] In creating our own functions we must be concerned with both the function itself and how it interfaces with other functions.

---

[1] In Section 6.5 we will see how a function can indirectly return more than one value.

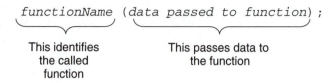

This identifies
the called
function

This passes data to
the function

Figure 6.1 Calling and passing data to a function

Before describing how user-written functions are defined and declared, however, let us briefly review what we already know about calling and using ANSI C provided functions.

As we have already seen with the `printf()` and `scanf()` functions, a function is called, or used, by giving the function's name and passing any data to it in the parentheses following the function's name (see Figure 6.1). The called function must be able to accept the data passed to it by the function doing the calling. Only after the called function successfully receives the data can the data be manipulated to produce a useful result.

To clarify the process of sending and receiving data, consider Program 6.1, which calls a function named `findMax()`. The program, as shown, is not yet complete. Once the function `findMax()` is written and included in Program 6.1, the completed program, consisting of the functions `main()` and `findMax()`, can be run.

Program 6.1

```
#include <stdio.h>

float findMax(float, float);   /* the function declaration (prototype)   */

int main()
{
  float firstnum, secnum, maxnum;

  printf("Enter a number: ");
  scanf("%f", &firstnum);
  printf("\nGreat! Please enter a second number: ");
  scanf("%f", & secnum);

  maxnum = findMax(firstnum,secnum);   /* the function is called here */
  printf("\nThe maximum of the two numbers entered is %f", maxnum);

  return 0;
}
```

Let us examine declaring and calling the function `findMax()` from the `main()` function. We will then write `findMax()` to accept the data passed to it and determine the largest or maximum value of the two passed values.

The function `findMax()` is referred to as the *called function,* since it is called or summoned into action by its reference in the `main()` function. The function that does the calling, in this case `main()`, is referred to as the *calling function.* The terms "called" and "calling" come from standard telephone usage, where one party calls the other on the telephone. The party initiating the call is referred to as the calling party, and the party receiving the call is referred to as the called party. The same terms describe function calls. The called function, in this case `findMax()`, is declared as expecting to receive two floating point values and as returning one floating point value. This declaration is formally referred to as a *function prototype,* and is described in detail later in this section. Let us now see how to write the function `findMax()`.

Defining a Function

A function is defined when it is written. Each function is defined once (that is, written once) in a program and can then be used by any other function in the program for which it is suitably declared. In keeping with C's convention, a function is restricted to directly returning at most a single value (see Figure 6.2).

Like the `main()` function, every C function consists of two parts, a function header and a function body, as illustrated in Figure 6.3. The purpose of the *function header* is to identify the data type of the value returned by the function, provide the function with a name, and specify the number, order, and type of values expected by the function. The purpose of the *function body* is to operate on the passed data and return, at most, one value directly back to the calling function. (We will see in Section 6.5 how a function can be made to return multiple values, indirectly, using pointers.)

In ANSI C, a function header consists of a single line that contains the function's returned value type, its name, and the name and data types of its arguments. If the returned value type is omitted, the function, by default, is defined to return an integer value. For example, the function header

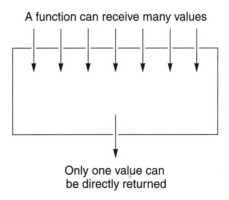

A function can receive many values

Only one value can
be directly returned

Figure 6.2   A function returns at most a single value

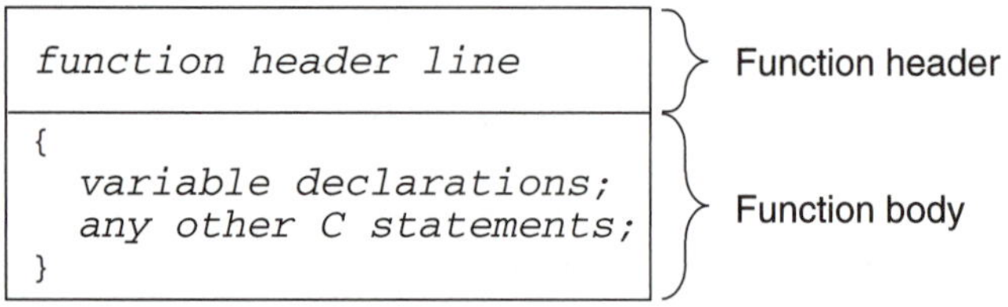

```
function header line          } Function header
{
    variable declarations;    } Function body
    any other C statements;
}
```

Figure 6.3 General format of a function

```
float findMax(float x, float y)  ←──────  no semicolon
```

declares the returned data type and name of the function as well as declaring the names and data types of all arguments.[2] The argument names in the header line are formally referred to as *parameters* or *formal arguments,* and we shall use these terms inter-changeably.[3]

The function name and all parameter names in the header line, in this case findMax, x, and y, are chosen by the programmer. Any names selected according to the rules used to choose variable names can be used. All parameters listed in the function header line must be separated by commas and must have their individual data types specified separately. If a data type is omitted, the parameter, by default, is of type integer. For example, the declarator findMax(float x, y) *does not* declare both of the parameters, x and y, to be of type float; rather, it declares x to be of type float and y to be of type integer. Similarly, omitting the data type of the function immediately preceding the function's name, by default, defines the function's return value to be of type integer. Thus both function headers

```
int maxIt(float x, float y
```

and

```
maxIt(float x, float y)
```

define the function maxIt() as returning an integer value.

Within a function header the keyword void is used to declare either that the function returns no value or has no arguments. For example, the function header

```
void display(int x, double y)
```

declares that the function display() returns no value, while the function header

```
double printMessage(void)
```

---

[2] Recall that an *argument* is a value that is passed into a function when the function is actually called.

[3] The portion of the function header that contains the function name and parameters is formally referred to as a *function declarator,* which should not be confused with a function declaration (prototype).

```
{
    variable declarations (if any)
    other C statements
}
```

Figure 6.4   Structure of a function body

declares that the function `printMessage()` has no parameters but returns a value of type double. As illustrated, a function header line is never terminated with a semicolon.

Now that we have written the function header for the `findMax()` function, we can construct the body of this function. Let us assume that the `findMax()` function selects the larger of two numbers passed to it and returns this number to the calling routine.

As illustrated in Figure 6.4, a function body begins with an opening brace, {, contains any necessary variable declarations followed by any valid C statements, and ends with a closing brace, }. This structure should be familiar to you because it is the same structure used in all the `main()` functions we have written. This fact should not be a surprise because `main()` is itself a function and must adhere to the rules required for constructing all legitimate functions.

In the body of the function `findMax()` we will declare one variable to store the maximum of the two numbers passed to it. We will then use an `if-else` statement to find the maximum of the two numbers. Once the maximum value is determined, all that remains is to include a statement within the function to cause the return of this value to the calling function. To return a value, a function must use a `return` statement, which has the form[4]:

```
return(expression);
```

When the `return` statement is encountered, the expression inside the parentheses is evaluated first. The value of the expression is then automatically converted to the data type declared in the function header line before being sent back to the calling function. After the value is returned, program control reverts back to the calling function. Thus, the complete function definition for the `findMax()` function is

```
float findMax(float x, float y)  /* function header            */
{                                /* start of function body     */
    float maxnum;                /* variable declaration       */

    if (x >= y)                  /* find the maximum number    */
        maxnum = x;
    else
        maxnum = y;

    return (maxnum);             /* return the value           */
}                                /* end of function definition */
```

---

[4] The parentheses in a `return` statement are optional. Thus, the statements `return(expression);` and `return expression;` can be used interchangeably.

When this function is called, the parameter x will be used to store the first value passed to it, and the parameter y will be used to store the second value passed at the time of the function call. The function itself will not know where the values come from when the call is made.

Note that within the `return` statement the data type of the returned variable correctly matches the data type in the function's header line. It is up to the programmer to ensure that this is so for every function returning a value. Failure to match the `return` value with the function's defined data type will not result in an error when your program is compiled, but it may lead to undesirable results, since the returned value is always converted to the data type specified in the function's header line. Usually this is only a problem when the fractional part of a returned floating point or double precision number is truncated because the function was defined to return an integer value.

Having completely defined (written) the `findMax()` function, let us now see how this function can be called.

Function Prototypes

Before a function can be called, it must be declared by the function that will do the calling. The declaration statement for a function is formally referred to as a *function prototype*. The function prototype tells the calling function the type of value that will be returned, if any, and the data type of the values that the calling function should transmit to the called function. For example, the function prototype previously used in Program 6.1:

```
float findMax(float, float);
```

declares that the function `findMax()` expects two floating point values to be sent to it, and that this particular function returns a floating point value. Function prototypes may be placed with the variable declaration statements within the calling function, above the calling function name as in Program 6.1, or in a separate header file that is included using a `#include` preprocessor directive. Thus, the function prototype for `findMax()` could have been placed either before or after the statement `#include <stdio.h>`, which contains the function prototypes for the `printf()` and `scanf()` functions, or within `main()`'s variable declaration statements.

Placing the prototype before `main()` makes this declaration available to *all* functions in the file, thus permitting all functions to call `findMax()`.[5] Placing the prototype within `main()` makes the declaration available only to `main()`, which only gives `main()` the right to call it. Similarly, any other function that needs to use `findMax()` can also include the prototype within itself. In this text we will always list a prototype at the top of a file so that the single declaration serves for all functions in the file. (Reasons for the choice of placement are presented in Section 6.3.) The syntax of function prototype statements is

```
returnDataType  functionName(list of argument data types);
```

---

[5] An alternate procedure is to place the `findMax()` functions itself at the top of the file.

Programming Note

Function Definitions and Function Prototypes

A *function definition* defines a function. Thus, when you write a function, you are really writing a function definition. Each definition begins with a header line that includes a parameter list, if any, enclosed in parentheses and ends with the closing brace that terminates the function's body. The parentheses are required whether or not the function uses any parameters. The syntax for a function definition is

```
returnDataType functionName(parameter list)
{
    variable declarations;

    other C statements;

    return (expression)
}
```

A *function prototype* declares a function. The syntax for a function prototype, which provides the return data type of the function, the function's name, and a list of parameter data types (argument names are optional), is

```
returnDataType functionName(list of parameter data types);
```

Thus, the prototype along with pre- and postcondition comments (see Programming Note on p. 223) should provide a user with all the programming information needed to successfully call the function.

Generally, all function prototypes are placed at the top of the program, and all definitions are placed after the `main()` function. However, this placement can be changed. The only requirement in C is that a function cannot be called before it has been either declared or defined.

The `returnDataType` refers to the data type that will be returned by the function and must match the data type used in the function's header line. Similarly, the list of argument data types must match the parameter data types (in number, order, and type) used in the function's definition.

Examples of function prototypes are

```
int fmax(float, float);
float roi(int, char, char, double);
void display(double, double);
```

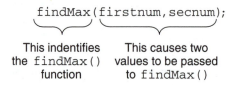

Figure 6.5 Calling and passing two values to `findMax()`

In the first example, the function prototype for `fmax()` declares that this function expects to receive two floating point arguments and will return an integer value. The function prototype for `roi()` declares that this function requires four arguments consisting of an integer, two characters, and a double precision argument, in this order, and will return a floating point number. Finally, the function prototype for `display()` declares that this function requires two double precision arguments and does not return any value. Such a function might be used to display the results of a computation directly, without returning any value to the called function.

The use of function prototypes permits error checking of data types by the compiler. If the function prototype does not agree with the return and parameter data types contained in the function's header line, an error message (typically `Undefined symbol`) occurs. The prototype also serves another task: It ensures conversion of all arguments passed to the function to the declared data type when the function is called.

Calling a Function

Calling a function is a rather easy operation. The only requirements are that the name of the function be used and that any data passed to the function be enclosed within the parentheses following the function name using the same order, number, and type as declared in the function prototype. The items enclosed within the parentheses in the call statement, as we have seen, are called *arguments* of the function (see Figure 6.5). Other terms used as synonyms for arguments are *actual argument* and *actual parameters*. All of these terms refer to the data values supplied to a function within the calling statement when the call is made.

If a variable is one of the arguments in a function call, the called function receives a copy of the value stored in the variable. For example, the statement

```
maxnum = findMax(firstnum,secnum);
```

calls the function `findMax()`, causes the values currently residing in the variables `firstnuma` and `secnum` to be passed to `findMax()`, and assigns the function's returned value to `maxnum`. The variable names in parentheses are actual arguments that provide values to the called function. After the values are passed, control is transferred to the called function.

As illustrated in Figure 6.6, *the function* `findMax()` *does not receive the variables named* `firstnum` *and* `secnum` *and has no knowledge of these variable names.*[6] The function simply receives copies of the values in these variables and must itself determine

---

[6] This is significantly different from computer languages such as FORTRAN, in which functions and subroutines automatically receive access to the variables and can pass data back through them.

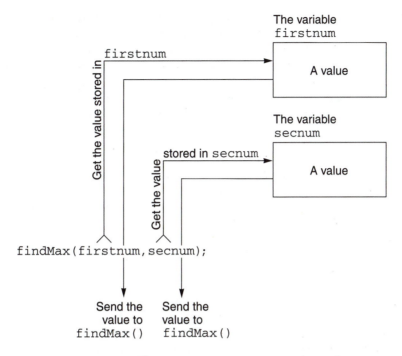

Figure 6.6   `findMax()` receives values

where to store these values before it does anything else. Although this procedure for passing data to a function may seem surprising, it is really a safety procedure for ensuring that a called function does not inadvertently change data stored in a variable. The function gets a copy of the data to use. It may change its copy and, of course, change any variables declared inside itself. However, unless specific steps are taken to do so, a function is not allowed to change the contents of variables declared in other functions.

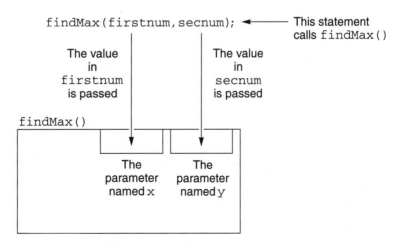

Figure 6.7   Storing values into parameters

The parameters in the function definition are used to store the values passed to the function when it is called. As illustrated in Figure 6.7, the parameter x is used to store the first value passed to findMax(), and the parameter y is used to store the second value passed at the time of the function call. The findMax() function does not know where the values come from when the call is made from main(). The first part of the call procedure executed by the program involves going to the variables firstnum and secnum and retrieving the stored values. These values are then passed to findMax() and ultimately stored in the parameters x and y. The parameters x and y within the findMax() function are treated like variables by findMax(), where the initialization of the values for these parameters occurs from outside the function.

Program 6.2 includes the findMax() function within the program code previously listed in Program 6.1.

 Program 6.2

```c
#include <stdio.h>

float findMax(float, float);   /* the function prototype */

int main()
{
  float firstnum, secnum, maxnum;

  printf("Enter a number: ");
  scanf("%f", &firstnum);
  printf("\nGreat! Please enter a second number: ");
  scanf("%f", &secnum);

  maxnum = findMax(firstnum,secnum);   /* the function is called here */
  printf("\nThe maximum of the two numbers entered is %f", maxnum);
return0;
}

/* the following is the function findMax          */
float findMax(float x, float y) /* function header             */
{                               /* start of function body      */
  float maxnum;                 /* variable declaration        */

  if (x >= y)                   /* find the maximum number     */
    maxnum = x;
  else
    maxnum = y;

  return(maxnum);               /* return the value            */
}                               /* end of function definition */
```

Program 6.2 can be used to select and print the maximum of any two real numbers entered by the user. The following is a sample run using Program 6.2:

```
Enter a number: 25.0
Great! Please enter a second number: 5.0
The maximum of the two numbers is 25.000000
```

In reviewing Program 6.2 it is important to note the four items we have introduced in this section. The first item is the function prototype (declaration) for findMax(). This statement, which ends with a semicolon as all statements do, alerts main() to the data type that findMax() will be returning and the number and type of arguments that must be supplied to findMax(). The second item to notice in main() is the use of an assignment statement to call findMax() and to store the returned value in the variable maxnum. We have also made sure to correctly declare maxnum as a floating point variable within main()'s variable declarations so that it matches the data type of the returned value.

The last two items to note concern the coding of the findMax() function. The header line of findMax() defines the function as returning a floating point value and declares the order, names, and data types of the arguments required by the function. Finally, the expression in the return statement evaluates to the correct return value data type defined in the function's header line. Thus, findMax() is internally consistent in sending a floating point value back to any function that might be used to call it, and from the calling side, main() has been correctly alerted to receive and use the returned value.

In writing your own functions you must always keep these four items in mind. For another example, see if you can identify these four items in Program 6.3.

In reviewing Program 6.3 let us first analyze the function tempvert(). The complete definition of the function begins with the function's header line and ends with the closing brace after the return statement. The function is declared as a double, which means the expression in the function's return statement must evaluate to a double precision number. Since a function header line is not a statement but the start of the code defining the function, the header line does not end with a semicolon.

Within tempvert(), inTemp is declared as a double precision parameter. Because an expression with a double precision number yields a double precision value, the correct data type, a double precision number, is returned by the function.

For the receiving side, there is a function prototype statement for the function tempvert() that agrees with tempvert()'s function definition. No variable is declared in main() to store the returned value from tempvert() because the returned value is immediately passed to printf() for display.

Placing user-written functions after the main() function, as is done in both Program 6.2 and Program 6.3, is a matter of choice. Some programmers prefer to put all called functions at the top of a program and make main() the last function listed. We prefer to list main() first because it is the driver function that should give anyone reading the program an idea of what the complete program is about before encountering the details of each function. Either placement approach is acceptable, and you will encounter both styles in your programming work. In no case, however, can a user-written function be placed inside another function. This is true for all C functions: *Each function must be defined by itself outside any other function.* Each C function is a separate and independent entity with its own parameters and variables; nesting of functions is never permitted.

Program 6.3

```c
#include <stdio.h>

double tempvert(double);         /* function prototype    */

int main()
{
  int count;                        /* start of declarations */
  double fahren;

  for(count = 1; count <= 4; ++count)
  {
    printf("Enter a Fahrenheit temperature: ");
    scanf("%lf", &fahren);
    printf("The Celsius equivalent is %6.2f\n\n", tempvert(fahren) );
  }

  return 0;
}

double tempvert(double inTemp)    /* function header */
{
  return ( (5.0/9.0) * (inTemp - 32.0) );
}
```

Placement of Statements

C does not impose a rigid statement ordering structure on the programmer. The general rule for placing statements in a program is simply that all preprocessor directives, variables, named constants, and functions (except main()) must be either declared or defined *before* they can be used. As we have noted previously, although this rule permits both preprocessor directives and declaration statements to be placed throughout a program, doing so results in a very poor program structure.

As a matter of good programming form, the following statement ordering should form the basic structure around which all of your C programs are constructed:

```c
preprocessor directives
named constants
function prototypes

int main()
{
```

(Continued on next page)

Programming Note   *Veed to know: Quiz.*

Preconditions and Postconditions

Preconditions are any set of conditions required by a function to be true if it is to operate correctly. For example, if a function uses the named constant MAXCHARS, which must have a positive value, a precondition is that MAXCHARS be declared with a positive value before the function is called.

Similarly, a postcondition is a condition that is true after the function is executed, assuming that the preconditions are met.

Pre- and postconditions are typically documented as user comments. For example, consider the following function header line and comments:

```
int leapyr(int year)
/* Precondition: the parameter year must be a year as a four-digit integer, such as 2001
   Postcondition: a 1 is returned if the year is a leap year; otherwise
      a 0 will be returned
*/
```

Pre- and postcondition comments should be included with both function prototypes and function definitions whenever clarification is needed.

(Continued from previous page)

```
    variable declarations;

    other executable statements;

    return value;
}

function definitions
```

As always, comment statements can be freely intermixed anywhere within this basic structure.

Function Stubs

An alternative to completing each function required in a complete program is to write the main() function first, and add the functions later, as they are developed. The problem that arises with this approach, however, is that the complete program cannot be run until all of the functions are included. For example, reconsider Program 6.2, before the findMax() function has been written:

```c
#include <stdio.h>

float findMax(float, float); /* the function declaration */

int main()
{
  float firstnum, secnum, maxnum;

  printf("Enter a number: ");
  scanf("%f", &firstnum);
  printf("\nGreat! Please enter a second number: ");
  scanf("%f", &secnum);

  maxnum = findMax(firstnum,secnum); /* the function is called here */
  printf("\nThe maximum of the two numbers entered is %f", maxnum);

  return 0;
}
```

This program would be complete if there were a function definition for findMax(). But we really don't need a *correct* findMax() function to test and run what has been written; we just need a function that *acts* like it is correct: a "fake" findMax() that accepts the proper number and types of parameters and returns a value of the proper type for the function call is all we need to allow initial testing. This fake function is called a stub. A *stub* is the beginning of a final function that can be used as a placeholder for the final unit until the unit is completed. A stub for findMax() is as follows:

```c
float findMax(float x, float y)
{
  printf("In findMax()\n");
  printf("The value of x is %f\n", x);
  printf("the value of x is %f\n ", y);

  return 1.0;
}
```

This stub function can now be compiled and linked with the previously completed code to obtain an executable program. The code for the function can then be further developed, and when it is completed, it replaces this stub portion. As illustrated, a stub should always display the name of the function that it represents.

The minimum requirement of a stub function is that it compile and link with its calling module. In practice, it is a good idea to have a stub display both a message that it has been entered successfully and the value(s) of its received arguments, as in the stub for findMax().

As the function is refined, you let it do more and more, perhaps allowing it to return intermediate or incomplete results. This incremental, or stepwise, refinement is an important concept in efficient program development that provides you with the means to run a program that does not yet meet all of its final requirements.

Programming Note

Isolation Testing

One of the most successful software testing methods known is always to embed the code being tested within an environment of working code. For example, assume you have two untested functions that are called in the order shown below, and the result returned by the second function is incorrect.

Function 1 ——— calls ⟶ Function 2 ————⟶ Returned value is incorrect

From the information shown in this figure, one or possibly both of the functions could be operating incorrectly. The first order of business is to isolate the problem to a specific function.

One of the most powerful methods of performing this code isolation is to decouple the functions. This is done either by testing each function individually or by testing one function first and, only when you know it is operating correctly, reconnecting it to the second function. Then, if an error occurs you have isolated the error to either the transfer of data between functions or the internal operation of the second function.

This specific procedure is an example of the basic rule of testing, which states that *each function should only be tested in a program in which all other functions are known to be correct.* This means that one function must first be tested by itself, using stubs if necessary for any called functions, then a second tested function should be tested either by itself or with a previously tested function, and so on. This ensures that each new function is isolated within a test bed of correct functions, with the final program effectively built-up of tested function code.

Functions with Empty Parameter Lists

Although useful functions having an empty parameter list are extremely limited (one such function is provided in Exercise 14), they can occur. The function prototype for such a function requires either writing the keyword `void` or nothing at all between the parentheses following the function's name. For example, both prototypes

```
int display(void);
```

and

```
int display();
```

indicate that the `display()` function takes no arguments and returns an integer. A function with an empty parameter list is called by its name with nothing written within the required parentheses following the function's name. For example, the statement `display();` correctly calls the `display()` function whose prototype is given above.

Exercises 6.1

1. For the following function headers, determine the number, type, and order (sequence) of values that should be passed to the function when it is called and the data type of the value returned by the function.

   a. `int factorial(int n)`
   b. `doubleprice(int type, doubleyield, doublematurity)`
   c. `doubleyield(int type, doubleprice, doublematurity)`
   d. `char interest(char flag, float price, float time)`
   e. `int total(float amount, float rate)`
   f. `float roi(int a, int b, char c, char d, float e, float f)`
   g. `void getVal(int item, int iter, char decflag)`

2. Write function headers for the following:

   a. A function named `check()`, which has three parameters. The first parameter should accept an integer number, the second parameter a floating point number, and the third parameter a double precision number. The function returns no value.

   b. A function named `findAbs()` that accepts a double precision number passed to it and displays its absolute value.

   c. A function named `mult()` that accepts two floating point numbers as parameters, multiplies these two numbers, and returns the result.

   d. A function named `sqrIt()` that computes and returns the square of the integer value passed to it.

   e. A function named `powFun()` that raises an integer number passed to it to a positive integer power (also passed as an argument) and returns the result.

   f. A function that produces a table of the numbers from 1 to 10, their squares, and their cubes. No arguments are to be passed to the function, and the function returns no value.

3. Write C function prototypes corresponding to each of the function header lines given in Exercise 1.

4. a. Write a C function named `check()`, which has three parameters. The first parameter should accept an integer number, the second parameter a floating point number, and the third parameter a double precision number. The body of the function should just display the values of the data passed to the function when it is called.

   Note: When tracing errors in functions, it is very helpful to have the function display the values it has been passed. Quite frequently, the error is not in what the body of the function does with the data, but in the data received and stored. This type of error occurs when a different data type is passed to the function than the data type declared for the parameters.

   b. Include the function written in Exercise 4a in a working program. Make sure your function is called from `main()`. Test the function by passing various data to it that are of a different data type than that specified for each parameter.

5. a. Write a C function named `findAbs()` that accepts a double precision number passed to it, computes its absolute value, and returns the absolute value to the calling function. The absolute value of a number is the number itself if the number is positive and the negative of the number if the number is negative.

   b. Include the function written in Exercise 5a in a working program. Make sure your function is called from `main()` and correctly returns a value to `main()`. Have `main()` use a function prototype to declare the `findAbs()` function and use `printf()` to display the value returned. Test the function by passing various data to it.

6. a. Write a C function called `mult()` that accepts two double precision numbers as parameters, multiplies these two numbers, and returns the result to the calling function.

   b. Include the function written in Exercise 6a in a working program. Make sure your function is called from `main()` and correctly returns a value to `main()`. Have `main()` use a function prototype to declare the `mult()` function and use `printf()` to display the value returned. Test the function by passing various data to it.

7. a. Write a C function named `sqrIt()` that computes the square of the value passed to it and displays the result. The function should be capable of squaring numbers with decimal points.

   b. Include the function written in Exercise 7a in a working program. Make sure your function is called from `main()`. Test the function by passing various data to it.

8. a. Write a C function named `powFun()` that raises an integer number passed to it to a positive integer power (also passed as an argument) and displays the result. The positive integer should be the second value passed to the function. Declare the variable used to store the result as a long integer data type to ensure sufficient storage for the result.

   b. Include the function written in Exercise 8a in a working program. Make sure your function is called from `main()`. Test the function by passing various data to it.

9. a. Write a C function that produces a table of numbers from 1 to 10, their squares, and their cubes. The function should produce the same display as that produced by Program 5.11.

   b. Include the function written in Exercise 9a in a working program. Make sure your function is called from `main()`. Test the function by passing various data to it.

10. a. Modify the function written for Exercise 9 to accept the starting value of the table, the number of values to be displayed, and the increment between values. Name your function `selTab()`. A call to `selTab(6,5,2);` should produce a table of 5 lines, the first line starting with the number 6 and each succeeding number increasing by 2.

    b. Include the function written in Exercise 10a in a working C program. Make sure your function is called from `main()`. Test the function by passing various data to it.

11. a. Rewrite the function `tempvert()` in Program 6.3 to accept a temperature and a character as parameters. If the character passed to the function is the letter `f`, the function should convert the passed temperature from Fahrenheit to Celsius, else the function should convert the passed temperature from Celsius to Fahrenheit.

    b. Modify the `main()` function in Program 6.3 to call the function written for Exercise 11a. Your `main()` function should ask the user for the type of temperature being entered and pass the type (`f` or `c`) into `tempvert()`.

12. a. Write a C function that accepts an integer argument and determines whether the passed integer is even or odd. (*Hint:* Use the `%` operator.)

    b. Include the function written for Exercise 12a in a working C program. Make sure your function is called from `main()` and correctly returns a value to `main()`. Have `main()` display the value returned and test the function by passing various data to it and verifying the returned value.

13. a. Write a function named `hypotenuse()` that accepts the lengths of two sides of a right triangle as the parameters a, and b, respectively. The function should determine and return the hypotenuse, c, of the triangle (*Hint:* Use Pythagoras' theorem that $c^2 = a^2 + b^2$).

    b. Include the function written for Exercise 13a in a working C program. Make sure your function is called from `main()` and correctly returns a value to `main()`. Have `main()` display the value returned and test the function by passing various data to it and verifying the returned value.

14. a. A useful function with an empty parameter list can be constructed to return a value for π that is accurate to the maximum number of decimal places allowed by your computer. This value

is obtained by taking the arcsine of 1.0, which is $\pi/2$, and multiplying the result by 2. In C, the required expression is *2.0 * asin(1.0)*, where the `asin()` function is provided in the standard C mathematics library (make sure to include the `math.h` header file). Using this expression, write a C function named `Pi()` that calculates and displays the value of π.

b. Include the function written for Exercise 14a in a working C program. Make sure your function is called from `main()` and correctly returns a value to `main()`. Have `main()` display the value returned and test the function by passing various data to it and verifying the returned value.

15. a. Write a function named `distance()` that accepts the rectangular coordinates of two points x_1, y_1 and x_2, y_2 and calculates and returns the distance between the two points. The distance, d, between two points is given by the formula

$$d = \sqrt{(x_2 - x_1)^2 + (y_2 - y_1)^2}$$

b. Include the function written for Exercise 15a in a working C program. Make sure your function is called from `main()` and correctly returns a value to `main()`. Have `main()` display the value returned and test the function by passing various data to it and verifying the returned value. In particular, make sure your function returns a value of zero when both points are the same; for example, $(x_1, y_1) = (5,2)$ and $(x_1, y_1) = (5,2)$.

16. a. The volume of a right circular cylinder is given by its radius squared times its height times π. Write a function that accepts two floating point arguments corresponding to the cylinder's radius and height, respectively, and returns the cylinder's volume.

b. Include the function written for Exercise 16a in a working C program. Make sure your function is called from `main()` and correctly returns a value to `main()`. Have `main()` display the value returned and test the function by passing various data to it and verifying the returned value.

17. Write the function named `payment()` that has three parameters named principal, which is the amount financed, int, which is the monthly interest rate, and months, which is the number of months the loan is for. The function should return the monthly payment according to the following formula:

$$payment = \frac{principal}{\left[\dfrac{1-(1 + interest^{-months}}{interest}\right]}$$

Note that the interest value used in this formula is a monthly rate, as a decimal. Thus, if the yearly rate were 10%, the monthly rate is (0.10/12). Test your function. What argument values cause it to malfunction (and should not be input)?.

18. a. A second-degree polynomial in x is given by the expression $ax^2 + bx + c$, where a, b, and c are known numbers and a is not equal to zero. Write a function named `polyTwo(a,b,c,x)` that computes and returns the value of a second-degree polynomial for any passed values of a, b, c, and x.

b. Include the function written in Exercise 18a in a working program. Make sure your function is called from `main()` and correctly returns a value to `main()`. Have `main()` display the value returned. Test the function by passing various data to it.

19. a. An extremely useful programming algorithm for rounding a real number to n decimal places is

Step 1   multiply the number by 10^n
Step 2   add .5
Step 3   delete the fractional part of the result
Step 4   divide by 10^n

For example, using this algorithm to round the number 78.374625 to three decimal places yields

Step 1 $78.374625 \times 10^3 = 78374.625$
Step 2 $78374.625 + .5 = 78375.125$
Step 3   retaining the integer part = 78375
Step 4   78375 divided by $10^3 = 78.375$

Use this information to write a C function named `round()` that rounds the value of its first parameter to the number of decimal places specified by its second parameter.

b. Incorporate the `round()` function written for Exercise 19a into a program that accepts a user-entered amount of money, multiplies the entered amount by an 8.675% interest rate, and displays the result rounded to two decimal places. Enter, compile, and execute this program, and verify the result for the following test data:

Amount: $1000, $0, $100, $10

20. a. Write a C function named `whole()` that returns the integer part of any number passed to the function. (*Hint:* Assign the passed argument to an integer variable.)

b. Include the function written in Exercise 20a in a working program. Make sure your function is called from `main()` and correctly returns a value to `main()`. Have `main()` use `printf()` to display the value returned. Test the function by passing various data to it.

21. a. Write a C function named `fracpart()` that returns the fractional part of any number passed to the function. For example, if the number 256.879 is passed to `fracpart()`, the number .879 should be returned. Have the function `fracpart()` call the function `whole()` that you wrote in Exercise 20. The number returned can then be determined as the number passed to `fracpart()` less the returned value when the same argument is passed to `whole()`. The completed program should consist of `main()` followed by `fracpart()` followed by `whole()`.

b. Include the function written in Exercise 21a in a working program. Make sure your function is called from `main()` and correctly returns a value to `main()`. Have `main()` use `printf()` to display the value returned. Test the function by passing various data to it.

6.2   Standard Library Functions

All C programs have access to a standard, preprogrammed set of functions for handling input and output of data, computing mathematical quantities, and manipulating strings of characters. These preprogrammed functions are stored in a system library that contains the collection of standard and tested functions available on your system.

Before using the functions available in the system library, you must know

- the name of each available function
- the arguments required by each function
- the data type of the result (if any) returned by each function
- a description of what each function does
- how to include the library containing the desired function

The first three items are provided by the function header. For example, consider the function named `sqrt()`, which calculates the square root of its argument. The function header for this function is

```
double sqrt(double num)
```

This header lists all the information required to call the `sqrt()` function. `sqrt()` expects a double precision argument and returns a double precision value.

Many library functions require a standard set of common declarations and other information for proper operation. This information is always contained in a standard header file. To include the information in this file in your program, the following statement must be included as the first statement of your program:

```
#include <header-file-name>   ⟵——— no semicolon
```

If you intend to use a library function in your program, placing the appropriate `#include` statement at the top of the program ensures proper access to the library function to all subsequent functions in your program.

Input/Output Library Functions

We have already made extensive use of two input/output (I/O) library functions, `printf()` and `scanf()`. In this section we present two additional I/O library routines. These two routines are written and contained within the header file `stdio.h`, thus they require inclusion of the `stdio.h` header file in any program that uses them.[7]

The `getchar()` routine can be used for single character input. The header for `getchar()` is

```
int getchar()
```

`getchar()` expects no arguments to be passed to it and returns an integer data type. The reason for returning characters in integer format is to allow the End-Of-File (EOF) sentinel, previously described in Section 5.2, to be returned. The EOF sentinel has an integer code, and if this sentinel is to be correctly recognized when input, `getchar()` must return integer values. The `getchar()` routine is used to return the next single character entered at the terminal. For example, a statement such as,

```
inChar = getchar();
```

causes the next character entered at the terminal to be stored in the variable `inChar`. This is equivalent to the longer statement `scanf("%c",&inChar);`. The `getchar()` routine is extremely useful when continuously inputting strings of characters from data files, which is the topic of Chapter 11.

---

[7] Formally, these two routines are created as macros within the `stdio.h` header file. The writing of macros is presented in Section 12.3.

Table 6.1   Commonly available mathematical functions (requires the `math.h` header file)

Function Header	Description
`int abs(int num)`	Returns the absolute value of an integer argument.
`long labs(long num)`	Returns the absolute value of a long integer argument.
`double fabs(double num)`	Returns the absolute value of a double precision argument.
`double pow(double x, double y)`	Returns *x* raised to the *y* power.
`int rand(void)`	Returns a pseudorandom number.
`double sin(double angle)`	Returns the sine of an angle. The angle must be in radians.
`double cos(double angle)`	Returns the cosine of an angle. The angle must be in radians.
`double sqrt(double num)`	Returns the square root of its argument. Returns a zero for negative arguments.

The output library routine corresponding to `getchar()` is the `putchar()` routine. `putchar()` expects a single character argument and displays the character passed to it on the terminal. For example, the statement `putchar('a')` causes the letter a to be displayed on the standard output device—it is equivalent to the longer statement `printf("%c",'a')`.

Mathematical Library Functions

Although addition, subtraction, multiplication, and division are easily accomplished using C's arithmetic operators, no such operators exist for raising a number to a power, finding the square root of a number, or determining absolute values. To facilitate these and other mathematical calculations each C compiler provides a standard set of preprogrammed mathematical functions. The most commonly used of these functions are listed in Table 6.1.

To access the mathematical functions listed in the table requires that programs using them include the header file named `math.h`. This header file contains appropriate prototypes for each mathematical function and, in some cases, includes the function itself. Thus, you must include the following preprocessor statement at the top of any program using a mathematical function[8]:

    #include <math.h> ←——— *no semicolon*

As with all C functions, the arguments passed to a mathematical library function do not have to be numbers. Expressions can also be arguments provided that the expression

---

[8] Additionally, if you are using a Unix operating system, you must include the `-lm` option when compiling your program.

Table 6.2   Selected function examples

Original Expression	Evaluated Expression	Returned Value
sqrt(4.0 + 7.0 * 3.0)	sqrt(25.0)	5.0
sqrt(25.0 * 3.0 - 1.04)	sqrt(73.96)	8.6
square(-32.0/8.0 - 6.0)	square(-10.0)	100
abs(-24/3 + 6)	abs(-2)	2

can be evaluated to yield an argument of the required data type. For example, the following arguments are valid for the given functions:

```
sqrt(4.0 + 7 * 3)        abs(-24 % 3 + 6)
sqrt(25.0 * 3 - 1.04)    abs(a * b - m * n)
sqrt(a * b - c/6.0)      pow(p*q,5.0)
sqrt(32.0/8.0)           pow(2.,n+3.)
```

The expressions in parentheses are evaluated first to yield a specific value. Thus, before the variables a, b, c, m, n, p, and q are used in the above expressions, actual values would have to be assigned to these variables. The value of the expression is then passed to the function. Table 6.2 lists the final value of selected expressions and the value returned by the listed function.

Like user-written functions, library functions can be included as part of a larger expression. The value returned by the function is computed before any other operation is performed. For example:

```
5 * square(2.0 * 7.0 - 4.0) - 200 = 5 * 100.0 - 200 + 300.0
3.0 * pow(2,10) / 5.0 = 3 * 1024.0 / 5.0 = 614.4
36 / sqrt(3.0 * 4.0 - 3.0) = 36 / 3.0 = 12.0
```

The step-by-step evaluation of the expression

```
4 * sqrt(5.0*20.0-3.96) / 7.0
```

is

Step	Result
1. Perform multiplication in argument	4*sqrt(100.0-3.96)/7.0
2. Complete argument computation	4*sqrt(96.04)/7.0
3. Call the function	4*9.8/7.0
4. Perform the multiplication	29.2/7
5. Perform the division	5.6

Program 6.4 illustrates the use of the `sqrt()` function to determine the time it will take a ball to hit the ground after it has been dropped from a building. The mathematical formula used to calculate the time in seconds that it takes to fall a given distance in feet is

$$time = sqrt(2 * distance / g)$$

where g is the gravitational constant equal to 32.2 ft/sec^2.

 Program 6.4

```
#include <stdio.h> /* this line may be placed second instead of first */
#include <math.h> /* this line may be placed first instead of second */
#define GRAV 32.2
int main()
{
  double time, distance;

  printf("Enter the distance (in feet): ");
  scanf("%lf", &distance);
  time = sqrt(2 * distance / GRAV);

  printf("\nIt will take %4.2lf seconds", time);
  printf("\nto fall %6.2lf feet.", distance);

  return 0;
}
```

Notice that Program 6.4 contains `#include` statements for both the `stdio.h` and `math.h` header files and a `#define` statement that equates the value of the gravitational constant 32.2 to the symbolic name GRAV. A sample output of Program 6.4 is

```
Enter the distance (in feet): 600

It will take 6.10 seconds
to fall 600.00 feet.
```

As used in Program 6.4, the value returned by the `sqrt()` function is assigned to the variable `time`. In addition to assigning a function's returned value to a variable, the returned value may be included within a larger expression, or even used as an argument to another function. For example, the expression

```
sqrt( abs(theta) )
```

is valid. The computation proceeds from the inner to the outer pairs of parentheses. Thus, the absolute value of theta is computed first and is then used as an argument to the sqrt() function.

Casts

We have already seen the conversion of an operand's data type within mixed-mode arithmetic expressions (Section 2.3) and across assignment operators (Section 3.1). In addition to these implicit data type conversions that are automatically made within mixed-mode arithmetic and assignment expressions, C also provides for explicit user-specified type conversions. The operators used to force the conversion of a value to another type are the cast operators. These are unary operators having the syntax:

(data-type) expression

where *data-type* is the desired data type of the *expression* following the cast. For example, the expression

```
(int) (a * b)
```

ensures that the value of the expression a * b is converted to an integer value (both a and b's stored values remain unchanged). Because the cast operator has a higher precedence than the multiplication operator, the parentheses around the expression a * b are required if it is the complete expression's value that are to be cast into an integer. Thus, for example, if a has the value of 3.2 and b the value 5.3, the value of the expression (int) (a * b) is evaluated as:

```
(int) (3.2 * 5.3)
= (int) 16.96
= 16
```

As a last example, consider the expression (int) a * b, where a again has the value of 3.2 and b the value 5.3. Here, only a's value is cast into an integer before multiplication by b (a's stored value remains unchanged). The value of this expression is evaluated as:

```
(int) 3.2 * 5.3
= 3 * 5.3
= 15.9
```

String Library Functions

Almost all C compilers have an extensive set of library functions for the input, comparison, manipulation, and output of strings of characters. A list and brief description of these functions is given in Table 6.3. A full presentation of these functions is provided in Chapter 9.

Table 6.3 String library functions (Requires the header file `string.h`)

Name	Description
`strcat(string1,string2)`	Concatenate `string2` to `string1`.
`strchr(string,character)`	Locate the position of the first occurrence of the character within the string.
`strcmp(string1,string2)`	Compare `string2` to `string1`.
`strcpy(string1,string2)`	Make `string1` equal to `string2`.
`strlen(string)`	Determine the length of the string.

Table 6.4 Miscellaneous routines (Requires the header file `ctype.h`)

Name	Description
`isalpha(character)`	Returns a nonzero number if the character is a letter; otherwise it returns a zero.
`isupper(character)`	Returns a nonzero number if the character is uppercase; otherwise it returns a zero.
`islower(character)`	Returns a nonzero number if the character is lowercase; otherwise it returns a zero.
`isdigit(character)`	Returns a nonzero number if the character is a digit (0 through 9); otherwise it returns a zero.
`toupper(character)`	Returns the uppercase equivalent if the character is lowercase; otherwise it returns the character unchanged.
`tolower(character)`	Returns the lowercase equivalent if the character is uppercase; otherwise it returns the character unchanged.

Miscellaneous Routines

In addition to the input/output, mathematical, and string functions, all system libraries have an extensive collection of miscellaneous functions and other routines. Some of the more useful of these are listed in Table 6.4.

These routines are included in a standard file named `ctype.h`. To access and use them in a program requires the following statement before `main()`:

> `#include <ctype.h>` ⟵——— *no semicolon*

The routines listed in Table 6.4 are particularly useful in checking characters input by a user. For example, Program 6.5 continuously requests that a user enter a character and determines if the character is a letter or a digit. The program exits the `while` loop when an f is typed. So that the user won't have to decide whether a lowercase or uppercase f must be entered to stop the program, the program converts all input to lowercase and just checks for a lowercase f.

Program 6.5

```
#include <stdio.h>
#include <ctype.h>
int main()
{
  char inChar;

  do
  {
    printf("\nPush any key (type an f to stop) ");
    inChar = getchar();        /* get the next character typed */
    inChar = tolower(inChar);          /* convert to lowercase */
    getchar();                 /* get and ignore the ENTER key */
    if ( isalpha(inChar) )    /* a nonzero value is true in C */
      printf("\nThe character entered is a letter.");
    else if ( isdigit(inChar) )
    printf("\nThe character entered is a digit.");
  } while (inChar != 'f');
}
```

A few remarks are in order in reviewing Program 6.5. First, the condition being tested in the if-else statement makes use of the fact that a condition is considered true if it evaluates to a nonzero value. Thus, the condition (isalpha(inChar)) could have been written as (isalpha(inChar) != 0), and the condition (isdigit(inChar)) could have been written (isdigit(inChar) != 0). The second call to getchar() in the do-while loop is used to remove the ENTER key.

Since functions return values, a function may itself be an argument to a function (including itself). For example, the two statements in Program 6.5

```
inChar = getchar();        /* get the next character typed */
inChar = tolower(inChar);          /* convert to lowercase */
```

may be combined into the single statement:

```
inChar = tolower(getchar());
```

Exercises 6.2

1. Write a C program that calculates the square root of a user-entered number. The program should keep prompting the user for a number until the number 999 is entered.

2. Write a C program that calculates the absolute value of a user-entered integer number. The program should keep prompting the user for an integer number until the number 999 is entered. Determine what happens if a user types in a number with a decimal point rather than an integer.

3. Write a C program that raises the first number input by a user to the power of the second number entered. The program should contain a `for` statement that causes four repetitions of the input prompts and calls to the `pow()` function.

4. Write a C function named `root4()` that returns the fourth root of the argument passed to it. In writing `root4()` use the `sqrt()` library function.

5. Write a C program using the `getchar()`, `toupper()`, and `putchar()` functions that echo back all letters entered in their uppercase form. The program should terminate when either an f or F is entered. (*Hint:* Convert all letters to uppercase and test only for an F.)

6. Rewrite Program 6.5 using a `while` statement in place of the `do-while` statement used in the program.

7. Write a C program that uses the `getchar()` function to input a character from the terminal into the variable `inChar`. Include the function call within a `do-while` loop that continues to prompt the user for an additional character until the + key is pressed. After each character is entered, print the decimal value used to store the character using the `printf()` function call `printf("%d",inChar);`. From the output of your program, create a table by hand, listing all the characters on your keyboard and the internal code used by your computer to store them.

6.3   Variable Scope

Now that we have begun to write programs containing more than one function, we can look more closely at the variables declared within each function and their relationship to variables in other functions.

By their very nature, C functions are constructed to be independent modules. As we have seen, values are passed to a function using the function's argument list and a value is returned from a function using a return statement. Seen in this light, a function can be thought of as a closed box, with slots at the top to receive values and a single slot at the bottom to return a value (see Figure 6.8).

The metaphor of a closed box is useful because it emphasizes the fact that what goes on inside the function, including all variable declarations within the function's body, is hidden from the view of all other functions. Since the variables created inside a function are available only to the function itself, they are said to be local to the function, or *local variables*. This term refers to the *scope* of a variable, where scope is defined as the section of the program where the variable is valid or "known." A variable can have either a local scope or a global scope. A variable with a *local scope* is simply one that has had storage locations set aside for it by a declaration statement made within a function body.

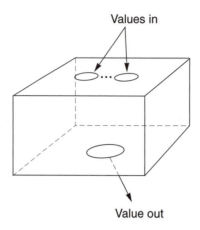

Values in

Value out

Figure 6.8   A function can be considered a closed box

Local variables are only meaningful when used in expressions or statements inside the function that declares them. This means that the same variable name can be declared and used in more than one function. For each function that declares the variable, a distinct variable is created.

All the variables we have used until now have been local variables. This is a direct result of placing our declaration statements inside functions and using them as definition statements that cause the compiler to reserve storage for the declared variable. As we shall see, declaration statements can be placed outside functions and need not act as definitions that cause new storage areas to be reserved for the declared variable.

A variable with *global scope*, more commonly termed a *global variable*, is one whose storage has been created for it by a declaration statement located outside any function. These variables can be used by all functions in a program that are physically placed after the global variable declaration. This is shown in Program 6.6 where we have purposely used the same variable name inside both functions contained in the program.

The variable `firstnum` in Program 6.6 is a global variable because its storage is created by a declaration statement located outside a function. Since both functions, `main()` and `valfun()`, follow the declaration of `firstnum`, both of these functions can use this global variable with no further declaration needed.

Program 6.6 also contains two separate local variables, both named `secnum`. Storage for the `secnum` variable named in `main()` is created by the declaration statement located in `main()`. A different storage area for the `secnum` variable in `valfun()` is created by the declaration statement located in the `valfun()` function. Figure 6.9 illustrates the three distinct storage areas reserved by the three declaration statements found in Program 6.6.

Program 6.6

```c
#include <stdio.h>

int firstnum;     /* create a global variable named firstnum */

void valfun();  /* function prototype (declaration) */

int main()
{
  int secnum;           /* create a local variable named secnum */

  firstnum = 10;      /* store a value into the global variable */
  secnum = 20;        /* store a value into the local variable  */

  printf("\nFrom main(): firstnum = %d",firstnum);
  printf("\nFrom main(): secnum = %d\n",secnum);
  valfun();           /* call the function valfun */
  printf("\nFrom main() again: firstnum = %d",firstnum);
  printf("\nFrom main() again: secnum = %d",secnum);

  return 0;
}
void valfun()             /* no values are passed to this function */
{
  int secnum;   /* create a second local variable named secnum    */
  secnum = 30;  /* this only affects this local variable's value */
  printf("\nFrom valfun(): firstnum = %d",firstnum);
  printf("\nFrom valfun(): secnum = %d\n",secnum);
  firstnum = 40; /* this changes firstnum for both functions      */
  return;
}
```

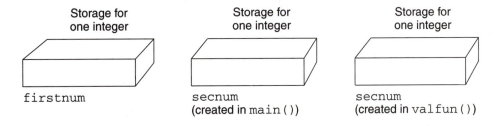

Figure 6.9   The three storage areas created by Program 6.6

Each of the variables named `secnum` are local to the function in which their storage is created, and each of these variables can only be used from within the appropriate function. Thus, when `secnum` is used in `main()`, the storage area reserved by `main()` for its `secnum` variable is accessed, and when `secnum` is used in `valfun()`, the storage area reserved by `valfun()` for its `secnum` variable is accessed. Program 6.6 produces the following output.

```
From main(): firstnum = 10
From main(): secnum = 20

From valfun(): firstnum = 10
From valfun(): secnum = 30

From main() again: firstnum = 40
From main() again: secnum = 20
```

Let us analyze the output produced by Program 6.6. Because `firstnum` is a global variable, both the `main()` and `valfun()` functions can use and change its value. Initially, both functions print the value 10 that `main()` stored in `firstnum`. Before returning, `valfun()` changes the value of `firstnum` to 40, which is the value displayed when the variable `firstnum` is next displayed from within `main()`.

Since each function only "knows" its own local variables, `main()` can only send the value of its `secnum` to the `printf()` function, and `valfun()` can only send the value of its `secnum` to the `printf()` function. Thus, whenever `secnum` is obtained from `main()` the value 20 is displayed, and whenever `secnum` is obtained from `valfun()` the value 30 is displayed.

C does not confuse the two `secnum` variables because only one function can execute at a given moment. While a function is executing, only the storage area for the variables and parameters created by this function are automatically accessed. If a variable that is not local to the function is used by the function, the program searches the global storage areas for the correct name.

The scope of a variable in no way influences or restricts the data type of the variable. Just as a local variable can be a character, integer, float, double, or any of the other data types (long/short) we have introduced, so can global variables be of these data types, as illustrated in Figure 6.10. The scope of a variable is determined solely by the placement of the declaration statement that reserves storage for it, while the data type of the variable is determined by using the appropriate keyword (`char`, `int`, `float`, `double`, etc.) before the variable's name in a declaration statement.

Misuse of Global Variables

One caution should be mentioned here. Global variables allow the programmer to "jump around" the normal safeguards provided by functions. Rather than passing variables to a function, it is possible to make all variables global. *Do not do this.* By indiscriminately making all variables global you instantly destroy the safeguards C provides to make functions independent and insulated from each other, including the necessity of carefully

Scope

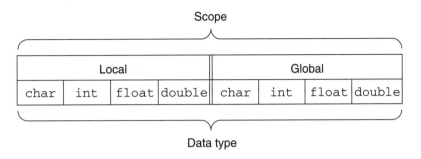

Figure 6.10   Relating the scope and type of a variable

designating the type of parameters needed by a function, the variables used in the function, and the value returned.

Using only global variables can be especially disastrous in larger programs that have many user-created functions. Because all variables in a function must be declared, creating functions that use global variables requires that you remember to write the appropriate global declarations at the top of each program using the function—they no longer come along with the function. Even more devastating is the horror of trying to track down an error in a large program using global variables. Because a global variable can be accessed and changed by any function following the global declaration, it is a time-consuming and frustrating task to locate the origin of an erroneous value.

Global variables, however, are sometimes useful in creating variables that must be shared among many functions. Rather than passing the same value to each function, it is easier to define a variable once as a global. Doing so also alerts anyone reading the program that many functions use the variable. Most large programs almost always make use of a few global variables. Smaller programs containing a few functions, however, should almost never contain global variables. The same scoping rules apply to named constants and function prototypes. Although named constants are typically defined globally because of their more general nature (for example, the value of π, they can also be declared locally, within a function. The same is true for function prototypes.

Exercises 6.3

1. a. For the following section of code, determine the data type and scope of all declared variables. To do this use a separate sheet of paper and list the three column headings that follow (we have filled in the entries for the first variable):

Variable name	Data type	Scope
price	integer	global to `main()`, `roi()`, and `step()`

```
int price;
long int years;
double yield;
```

```
int main()
{
  int bondtype;
  double interest, coupon
        .
        .
        .
  return 0;
}

double roi(int mat1, int mat2)
{
  int count;
  double effectiveInt;
        .
        .
        .
  return(effectiveInt);
}
int step(float first,float last)
{
  int numofyrs;
  float fracpart;
        .
        .
        .
  return(10*numofyrs);
}
```

b. Draw boxes around the appropriate section of the above code to enclose the scope of each variable.

c. Determine the data type of the parameters for the functions `roi()` and `step()` and the data type of the value returned by these functions.

2. a. For the following section of code, determine the data type and scope of all declared variables. To do this use a separate sheet of paper and list the three column headings that follow (we have filled in the entries for the first variable):

Variable name	Data type	Scope
key	character	global to `main()`, `func1()`, and `func2()`

```
char key;
long int number;
int main()
{
  int a,b,c;
  double x,y;
        .
        .
        .
  return 0;
}
double secnum;
int func1(int num1, int num2)
{
```

```
        int o,p;
        float q;
              .
              .
              .
        return(p);
    }
    double func2(float first, float last)
    {
        int a,b,c,o,p;
        float r;
        double s,t,x;
              .
              .
              .
        return(s*t);
    }
```

b. Draw a box around the appropriate section of the above code to enclose the scope of the variables key, secnum, y, and r.

c. Determine the data type of the parameters for the functions func1() and func2() and the data type of the value returned by these functions.

3. Besides speaking about the scope of a variable, we can also apply the term to the parameters declared a function header. What do you think is the scope of all function parameters?

4. Determine the values displayed by each call to printf() in the following program:

```
int firstnum = 10;   /* declare and initialize a global variable */
#include <stdio.h>
int main()
{
   int firstnum = 20; /* declare and initialize a local variable   */
   void display(); /* function prototype (declaration) */

   printf("\nThe value of firstnum is %d",firstnum);
   display();

   return 0;
}

void display()
{
   printf("\nThe value of firstnum is now %d",firstnum);
}
```

6.4 Variable Storage Class

The scope of a variable defines the location within a program where that variable can be used. Given a program, you could take a pencil and draw a box around the section of the program where each variable is valid. The space inside the box represents the scope of a variable. From this viewpoint, the scope of a variable can be thought of as the space within the program where the variable is valid.

In addition to the space dimension represented by its scope, variables also have a time dimension. The time dimension refers to the length of time that storage locations are reserved for a variable. This time dimension is referred to as the variable's "lifetime." For example, all variable storage locations are released back to the operating system when a program is finished running. However, while a program is still executing, interim variable storage areas are also reserved and subsequently released back to the operating system. Where and how long a variable's storage locations are kept before they are released can be determined by the *storage class* of the variable.

The four available storage classes are called `auto`, `static`, `extern`, and `register`. If one of these class names is used, it must be placed before the variable's data type in a declaration statement. Examples of declaration statements that include a storage class designation are

```
auto int num;       /* auto storage class and int data type   */
static int miles;   /* static storage class and int data type    */
register int dist;  /* register storage class and int data type */
extern int price;   /* extern storage class and int data type    */
auto float coupon;  /* auto storage class and float data type    */
static double yrs;  /* static storage class and double data type */
extern float yld;   /* extern storage class and float data type  */
auto char inKey;    /* auto storage class and char data type     */
```

To understand what the storage class of a variable means, we will first consider local variables (those variables created inside a function) and then global variables (those variables created outside a function).

Local Variable Storage Classes

Local variables can only be members of the `auto`, `static`, or `register` storage classes. If no class description is included in the declaration statement, the variable is automatically assigned to the `auto` class. Thus, `auto` is the default class used by C. All the local variables we have used, since the storage class designation was omitted, have been `auto` variables.

The term `auto` is short for *automatic*. Storage for automatic local variables is automatically reserved (that is, created) each time a function declaring automatic variables is called. As long as the function has not returned control to its calling function, all automatic variables local to the function are "alive"—that is, storage for the variables is available. When the function returns control to its calling function, its local automatic variables "die"—that is, the storage of the variables is released back to the operating system. This process repeats itself each time a function is called. For example, consider Program 6.7, where the function `testauto()` is called three times from `main()`.

Program 6.7

```c
#include <stdio.h>

void testauto();   /* function prototype */

int main()
{
  int count;   /* create the auto variable count */

  for(count = 1; count <= 3; ++count)
    testauto();

  return 0;
}
void testauto()
{
  int num = 0;   /* create the auto variable num */
                 /* and initialize to zero       */
  printf("\nThe value of the automatic variable num is %d", num);
  ++num;
  return;
}
```

Program 6.7 produces the following:

```
The value of the automatic variable num is 0
The value of the automatic variable num is 0
The value of the automatic variable num is 0
```

Each time `testauto()` is called, the automatic variable num is created and initialized to zero. When the function returns control to `main()` the variable num is destroyed along with any value stored in num. Thus, the effect of incrementing num in `testauto()`, before the function's return statement, is lost when control is returned to `main()`.

For most applications, the use of automatic variables works just fine. There are cases, however, where we want a function to remember values between function calls. This is the purpose of the `static` storage class. A local variable that is declared as `static` causes the program to keep the variable and its latest value even when the function that declared it is through executing. Examples of static variable declarations are

```c
static int rate;
static float taxes;
static double amount;
static char inKey;
static long years;
```

A local static variable is not created and destroyed each time the function declaring the static variable is called. Once created, local static variables remain in existence for the life of the program. This means that the last value stored in the variable when the function is finished executing is available to the function the next time it is called.

Because local static variables retain their values, they are not initialized within a declaration statement in the same way as automatic variables. To see why, consider the automatic declaration int num = 0;, which causes the automatic variable num to be created and set to zero each time the declaration is encountered. This is called a *run-time initialization* because initialization occurs each time the declaration statement is encountered. This type of initialization is disastrous for a static variable, because resetting the variable's value to zero each time the function is called destroys the very value we are trying to save.

The initialization of static variables (both local and global) is done only once, when the program is first compiled. At compilation time, the variable is created and any initialization value is placed in it.[9] Thereafter, the value in the variable is kept without further initialization each time the function is called. To see how this works, consider Program 6.8.

 Program 6.8

```
#include <stdio.h>

void teststat();      /* function prototype */

int main()
{
  int count;                    /* count is a local auto variable */

  for(count = 1; count <= 3; ++count)
    teststat();

  return 0;
}
void teststat()
{
  static int num = 0;      /* num is a local static variable */

  printf("\nThe value of the static variable num is now %d", num);
  ++num;
  return;
}
```

[9] Some compilers initialize local static variables the first time the definition statement is executed rather than when the program is compiled.

The output produced by Program 6.8 is

```
The value of the static variable num is now 0
The value of the static variable num is now 1
The value of the static variable num is now 2
```

As illustrated by the output of Program 6.8, the static variable num is set to zero only once. The function teststat() then increments this variable just before returning control to main(). The value that num has when leaving the function teststat() is retained and displayed when the function is next called.

Unlike automatic variables that can be initialized by either constants or expressions using both constants and previously initialized variables, static variables can only be initialized using constants or constant expressions, such as 3.2 + 8.0. Also unlike automatic variables, all static variables are set to zero when no explicit initialization is given. Thus, the specific initialization of num to zero in Program 6.8 is not required.

The remaining storage class available to local variables, the register class, is not used as extensively as either the automatic or static variable classes. Examples of register variable declarations are

```
register int time;
register double diffren;
register float coupon;
```

Register variables have the same time duration as automatic variables; that is, a local register variable is created when the function declaring it is entered and is destroyed when the function completes execution. The only difference between register and automatic variables is where the storage for the variable is located.

Storage for all variables (local and global), except register variables, is reserved in the computer's memory area. Most computers have a few additional high-speed storage areas located directly in the computer's processing unit that can also be used for variable storage. These special high-speed storage areas are called *registers*. Since registers are physically located in the computer's processing unit, they can be accessed faster than the normal memory storage areas located in the computer's memory unit. Computer instructions that access registers typically require less space than instructions that access memory locations because there are fewer registers that can be accessed than there are memory locations.

For example, although the AT&T WE® 32100 Central Processing Unit has nine registers that can be used for local C program variables, it can be connected to memories that have more than four billion bytes. Most other computers have a similar set of user-accessible registers but millions of memory locations. When the compiler substitutes the location of a register for a variable during program compilation, less space in the instruction is needed than is required to address a memory having millions of locations.

Besides decreasing the size of a compiled C program, using register variables can also increase the execution speed of a C program, if the compiler you are using supports this data type. Variables declared with the register storage class are automatically switched to the auto storage class if the compiler does not support register variables or if the declared register variables exceed the computer's register capacity.

Programming Note

Storage Classes Rules

1. Variables of the type `auto` and `register` are always local variables.
2. Only nonstatic global variables may be `extern`ed. Doing so either extends the variable's scope
   a. into another file, which makes the variable global in the new file, or
   b. into a function within another file, which makes the variable local to the function
3. Because global `static` variables cannot be `extern`ed, these variables are private to the file in which they are declared.
4. Except for `static` variables (global and local), all variables are initialized each time they come into scope.

The only restriction in using the `register` storage class is that the address of a register variable, using the address operator &, cannot be taken. This is easily understood when you realize that registers do not have standard memory addresses.

Global Variable Storage Classes

Global variables are created by declaration statements external to a function. By their nature, these externally defined variables do not come and go with the calling of any function. Once an external (global) variable is created, it exists until the program in which it is declared is finished executing. Thus, global variables cannot be declared as members of either the `auto` or `register` storage classes, which are created and destroyed as the program is executing. Global variables may, however, be declared as members of the `static` or `extern` storage classes (but not both). Examples of declaration statements including these two class descriptions are

```
extern int sum;
extern double price;
static double yield;
```

The global `static` and `extern` classes affect both the scope and time duration of these variables. As with static local variables, all static global variables are initialized to zero at compile time if no explicit initialization is present.

The purpose of the `extern` storage class is to extend the scope of a global variable beyond its normal boundaries. To understand this, we must first note that all of the programs we have written so far have always been contained together in one file. Thus, when

```
file1                                 file2

int price;                            double interest;
float yield;                          int func3()
static double coupon;                 {
int main()                               .
{                                        .
   func1();                              .
   func2();                           }
   func3();                           int func4()
   func4();                           {
   return 0                              .
}                                        .
int func1()                              .
{                                     }
   .
   .
   .

}
int func2()
{
   .
   .
   .

}
```

Figure 6.11   A program may extend beyond one file

you saved or retrieved programs you needed only to give the computer a single name for your program. This is not required by C.

Larger programs typically consist of many functions that are stored in multiple files. An example of this is shown in Figure 6.11, where the three functions main(), func1(), and func2() are stored in one file and the two functions func3() and func4() are stored in a second file.

For the files illustrated in Figure 6.11, the global variables price, yield, and coupon declared in file1 can only be used by the functions main(), func1(), and func2() in this file. The single global variable, interest, declared in file2 can only be used by the functions func3() and func4() in file2.

Although the variable price has been created in file1, we may want to use it in file2. Placing the declaration statement extern int price; in file2, as shown in Figure 6.12, allows us to do this. Putting this statement at the top of file2 extends the scope of the variable price into file2 so that it may be used by both func3() and func4().

Similarly, placing the statement extern float yield; in func4() extends the scope of this global variable, created in file1, into func4(). The scope of the global variable interest, created in file2, is extended into func1() and func2() by the declaration statement extern double interest; placed before func1(). Notice interest is not available to main().

file1

```
int price;
float yield;
static double coupon;
int main()
{
  func1();
  func2();
  func3();
  func4();
}
extern double interest;
int func1()
{

    .

    .

    .

}
int func2()
{

    .

    .

    .

}
```

file2

```
double interest;
extern int price;
int func3()
{

    .

    .

    .

}
int func4()
{

  extern float yield;

    .

    .

    .

}
```

Figure 6.12   Extending the scope of a global variable

A declaration statement that specifically contains the word extern is different from every other declaration statement in that it does not cause the creation of a new variable by reserving new storage for the variable. An extern declaration statement simply informs the compiler that the variable already exists and can now be used. The actual storage for the variable must be created somewhere else in the program using one, and only one, global declaration statement in which the word extern has not been used. Initialization of the global variable can, of course, be made with the original declaration of the global variable. Initialization within an extern declaration statement is not allowed and causes a compilation error.

The existence of the extern storage class is the reason we have been so careful to distinguish between the creation and declaration of a variable. Declaration statements containing the word extern do not create new storage areas; they only extend the scope of existing global variables.

The last global class, static, is used to prevent the extension of a global variable into a second file. Global static variables are declared in the same way as local static variables, except that the declaration statement is placed outside any function.

The scope of a global static variable cannot be extended beyond the file in which it is declared. This provides a degree of privacy for static global variables. Since they are only "known" and can only be used in the file in which they are declared, other files cannot access or change their values. Static global variables cannot be subsequently extended to a second file using an extern declaration statement. Trying to do so results in a compilation error.

Exercises 6.4

1. a. List the storage classes available to local variables.

b. List the storage classes available to global variables.

2. Describe the difference between a local automatic variable and a local static variable.

3. What is the difference between the following functions:

```
int init1()
{
  static int yrs = 1;
  printf("\nThe value of yrs is %d", yrs);
  yrs = yrs + 2;
}

void init2()
{
  static int yrs;

  yrs = 1;
  printf("\nThe value of yrs is %d", yrs);
  yrs = yrs + 2;
}
```

file1

```
char choice;
int flag;
long date, time;
int main()
{

    .
    .
    .

}
double coupon;
void price()
{

    .
    .
    .

}
void yield()
{

    .
    .
    .

}
```

file2

```
char band Type;
double maturity;
void roi()
{

    .
    .
    .

}
void pduction()
{

    .
    .
    .

}
void bid()
{

    .
    .
    .

}
```

Figure 6.13   Files for Exercise 6

4. a. Describe the difference between a static global variable and an external global variable.

   b. If a variable is declared with an `extern` storage class, what other declaration statement must be present somewhere in the program?

5. The declaration statement `static double years;` can be used to create either a local or global static variable. What determines the scope of the variable `years`?

6. For the function and variable declarations illustrated in Figure 6.13, place an `extern` declaration to individually accomplish the following:

   a. Extend the scope of the global variable `choice` into all of `file2`.

   b. Extend the scope of the global variable `flag` into function `pduction()` only.

   c. Extend the scope of the global variable `date` into `pduction()` and `bid()`

   d. Extend the scope of the global variable `date` into `roi()` only.

   e. Extend the scope of the global variable `coupon` into `roi()` only.

   f. Extend the scope of the global variable `bondType` into all of `file1`.

   g. Extend the scope of the global variable `maturity` into both `price()` and `yield()`.

6.5   Passing Addresses

In the normal course of operation, a called function receives values from its calling function, stores the passed values in its own local parameters, manipulates these parameters appropriately, and possibly returns a single value. This method of calling a function and passing values to it is referred to as a function *pass by value,* and the parameters receiving the values are referred to as *value parameters.*

This pass by value procedure is a distinct advantage of C. It allows functions to be written as independent entities that can use any variable and parameter names without concern that other functions may also be using the same names. It also alleviates any concern that altering a value parameter or a local variable in one function may inadvertently alter the value of a variable in another function. In writing a function, value parameters can conveniently be thought of as either initialized variables or variables that are assigned values when the function is executed. At no time, however, does the called function have direct access to any local variable contained in the calling function.

There are times when it is convenient to give a function access to local variables of its calling function. This allows the called function to use and change the value in the variable without the knowledge of the calling function, where the local variable is declared. To do this requires that the address of the variable be passed to the called function. Once the called function has the variable's address, it "knows where the variable lives," so to speak, and can access the variable using the address and the indirection operator.

Passing addresses is referred to as a function *pass by reference,*[10] since the called function can reference, or access, the variable using the passed address. In this section we describe the techniques required to pass addresses to a function and have the function accept and use the passed addresses.

---

[10] It can also be referred to as a *call by reference* when it is clearly understood that the term applies only to those parameters whose addresses have been passed.

Passing, Storing, and Using Addresses

To pass, store, and use addresses requires the use of the address operator (`&`), pointers, and the indirection operator (`*`). Let us review these topics before applying them to writing a function.

The address operator is the ampersand symbol, `&`. Recall that the ampersand followed immediately by a variable means "the address of" the variable. Examples of this are

```
&firstnum  means "the address of firstnum"
&secnum  means "the address of secnum"
```

Addresses themselves are values that can be stored in variables. The variables that store addresses are called *pointers*. Again, recall that pointers, like all variables, must be declared. In declaring pointers, the data type corresponding to the contents of the address being stored must be included in the declaration. Since all addresses appear the same, this additional information is needed by the computer to know how many storage locations to access when it uses the address stored in the pointer. Examples of pointer declarations are

```
char *inAddr;
int *numPtr;
float *destAddr:
double *nm1Addr;
```

To understand pointer declarations, read them "backwards," starting with the indirection operator, the asterisk, `*`. Again, recall that an asterisk followed immediately by a variable or argument can be translated as either "the variable (or argument) whose address is stored in" or "the variable (or argument) pointed to by." Thus, `*inAddr` can be read as either "the variable whose address is stored in `inAddr`" or "the variable pointed to by `inAddr`." Applying this to pointer declarations, the declaration `chr *inKey;`, for example, can be read as either "the variable whose address is stored in `inKey` is a character" or "the variable pointed to by `inKey` is a character." Both of these statements are frequently shortened to the simpler statement that "`inKey` points to a character." As all three interpretations of the declaration statement are correct, select and use whichever description makes a pointer declaration meaningful to you.

We now put all this together to pass two addresses to a function named `sortnum()`. The function will be written to compare the values contained in the passed addresses and swap the values, if necessary, so that the smaller value is stored in the first address.

Passing addresses to a function should be familiar to you, because we have been using addresses each time we called the `scanf()` function. Consider Program 6.9.

Observe in Program 6.9 that addresses are passed to both `scanf()` and `sortnum()` (see also Figure 6.14). Had just the values of `firstnum` and `secnum` been passed to `sortnum()`, the function could not swap values in the variables because it would not have access to `firstnum` and `secnum`.

🖥️ **Program 6.9**

```
#include <stdio.h>

void sortnum(double *, double *); /* function prototype */

int main()
{
  double firstnum, secnum;

  printf("Enter two numbers: ");
  scanf("%lf %lf", &firstnum, &secnum);

  sortnum(&firstnum, &secnum);

  printf("\nThe smaller number is %lf", firstnum);
  printf("\nThe larger number is %lf",secnum);

  return 0;
}
```

The function prototype for `sortnum()` declares that the function does not directly return a value and uses two pointer parameters (two addresses), each of which points to (is the address of) a double precision value.

One of the first requirements in writing `sortnum()` is to declare two parameters that can store the passed addresses. Parameters used to store addresses are formally referred to as *reference paramteters*. The following declarations can be used:

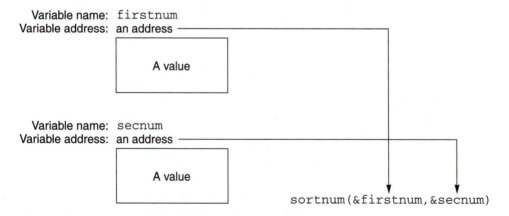

Figure 6.14   Passing addresses to `sortnum()`

```
double *nm1Addr; /* nm1Addr points to a double precision variable*/
double *nm2Addr; /* nm2Addr points to a double precision variable*/
```

The choice of the parameter names nm1Addr and nm2Addr is, as with all parameter names, up to the programmer.

Putting what we have together, the function header for sortnum() is

```
sortnum(double *num1Addr, double *num2Addr) /* function header */
```

Before writing the body of sortnum() to actually compare and swap values, let's first check that the values accessed using the addresses in nm1Addr and nm2Addr are correct. This is done in Program 6.10.

 Program 6.10

```
#include <stdio.h>

void sortnum(double *, double *);   /* function prototype */

int main()
{
  double firstnum = 20.0, secnum = 5.0;

  sortnum(&firstnum, &secnum);

  return 0;
}
void sortnum(double *num1Addr, double *num2Addr)
{
  printf("The number whose address is in nm1Addr is %lf", *nm1Addr);
  printf("\nThe number whose address is in nm2Addr is %lf", *nm2Addr);

  return;
}
```

The display produced by Program 6.10 is

```
The number whose address is in nm1Addr is 20.000000
The number whose address is in nm2Addr is 5.000000
```

In reviewing Program 6.10, note two things. First, the function prototype void sortnum(double *, double *) declares that sortnum() returns no value directly and that its parameters are two pointers that "point to" double precision values.

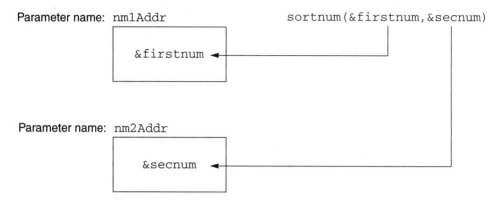

Parameter name: `nm1Addr`   `sortnum(&firstnum,&secnum)`

`&firstnum`

Parameter name: `nm2Addr`

`&secnum`

Figure 6.15   Storing addresses in parameters

As such, when the function is called it will require that two addresses be passed, and that each address is the address of a double precision value. Second, within `sortnum()`, the indirection operator is used to access the values stored in `firstnum` and `secnum`. `sortnum()` itself has no knowledge of these variable names, but it does have the address of `firstnum` stored in `nm1Addr` and the address of `secnum` stored in `nm2Addr`. The expression `*nm1Addr` used in the first `printf()` call means "the variable whose address is in `nm1Addr`." This is of course the variable `firstnum`. Similarly, the second `printf()` call obtains the value stored in `secnum` as "the variable whose address is in `nm2Addr`." Thus, we have successfully used pointers to allow `sortnum()` to access variables in `main()`. Figure 6.15 illustrates the concept of storing addresses in reference parameters.

Having verified that `sortnum()` can access `main()`'s local variables `firstnum` and `secnum`, we can now expand `sortnum()` to compare the values in these variables with an `if` statement to see if they are in the desired order. Using pointers, the `if` statement takes the form

```
if (*nm1Addr > *nm2Addr)
```

This statement should be read as "if the variable whose address is in `nm1Addr` is larger than the variable whose address is in `nm2Addr`." If the condition is true, the values in `main()`'s variables `firstnum` and `secnum` can be interchanged from within `sortnum()` using this three-step interchange algorithm:

1. Store `firstnum`'s value in a temporary location.
2. Store `secnum`'s value in `firstnum`.
3. Store the temporary value in `secnum`.

Using pointers from within `sortnum()`, this takes the form:

1. Store the value held by the variable pointed to by `nm1Addr` in a temporary location. The statement `temp = *nm1Addr;` does this (see Figure 6.16).
2. Store the value held by the variable whose address is in `nm2Addr` in the variable whose address is in `nm1Addr`. The statement `*nm1Addr = *nm2Addr;` does this (see Figure 6.17).
3. Store the value in the temporary location into the variable whose address is in `nm2Addr`. The statement `*nm2Addr = temp;` does this (see Figure 6.18).

Program 6.11 contains the final form of `sortnum()`, written according to our description.

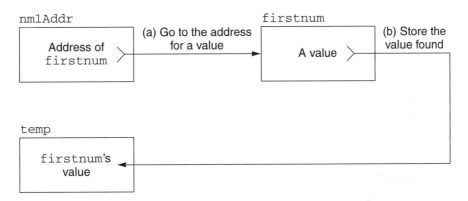

Figure 6.16 Indirectly storing `firstnum`'s value

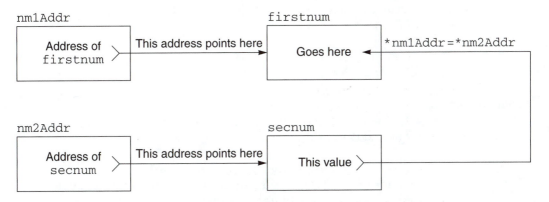

Figure 6.17 Indirectly changing `firstnum`'s value

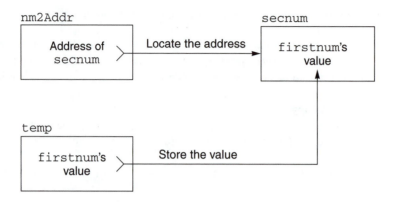

Figure 6.18 Indirectly changing secnum's value

Program 6.11

```
#include <stdio.h>

void sortnum(double *, double *); /* function prototype */

int main()
{
  double firstnum, secnum;

  printf("Enter two numbers: ");
  scanf("%lf %lf", &firstnum, &secnum);
  sortnum(&firstnum, &secnum);                /* call sortnum() */
  printf("The smaller number is %6.2lf", firstnum);
  printf("\nThe larger number is %6.2lf",secnum);

  return 0;
}
void sortnum(double *num1Addr, double *num2Addr)
{
  double temp;

  if (*nm1Addr > *nm2Addr)
  {
    temp = *nm1Addr;            /* save firstnum's value */
    *nm1Addr = *nm2Addr;        /* move secnum's value into firstnum */
    *nm2Addr = temp;            /* change secnum's value */
  }
  return;
}
```

The following sample run was obtained using Program 6.11:

```
Enter two numbers:  20.6 3.9
The smaller number is   3.90
The larger number is   20.60
```

In reviewing Program 6.11, note that the sole reason for using pointers is to allow us to swap `firstnum`'s value if the values are not in the desired order.

Exercises 6.5

1. Write declaration statements for
   a. a parameter named `price` that will be used to accept the address of a double precision number
   b. a parameter named `minutes` that will be used to accept the address of an integer number
   c. a parameter named `key` that will be used to accept the address of a character
   d. a parameter named `yield` that will be used to store the address of a double precision number

2. The addresses of the integer variables `sec`, `min`, and `hours` are to be passed to a function named `time(a,b,c)`. Write a suitable function header for `time()`.

3. Rewrite the `findMax()` function in Program 6.2 so that the variable `max` is declared in `main()` and the maximum value of the two passed numbers is written directly to `max`. (*Hint:* The address of `max` will also have to be passed to `findMax()`.)

4. Write a C function named `change()` that accepts a floating point number and the addresses of the integer variables named `quarters`, `dimes`, `nickels`, and `pennies`. The function should determine the number of quarters, dimes, nickels, and pennies in the number passed to it and write these values directly into the respective variables declared in its calling function.

5. a. The time in hours, minutes, and seconds is to be passed to a function named `secs()`. Write `secs()` to accept these values and determine the total number of seconds in the passed data. Write this function so that the total number of seconds is returned by the function as an integer number.
   b. Repeat Exercise 5a but also pass the address of the variable `totSec` to the function `secs()`. Using this passed address, have `secs()` directly alter the value of `totSec`.

6. Write a C function named `time()` that accepts an integer number of seconds and the addresses of three variables named `hours`, `min`, and `sec`. The function is to convert the passed number of seconds into an equivalent number of hours, minutes, and seconds and directly alter the value of the respective variables using their passed addresses.

7. Write a C function named `yrCalc()` that accepts a longer integer representing the total number of days from the date 1/1/1900 and the addresses of the variables `year`, `month`, and `day`. The function is to calculate the current year, month, and day for the given number of days and write these values directly in the respective variables using the passed addresses. For this problem assume that each year has 365 days and each month has 30 days.

8. Write a C function named `liquid()` that is to accept an integer number and the addresses of the variables `gallons`, `quarts`, `pints`, and `cups`. The passed integer represents the total number of cups, and the function is to determine the number of gallons, quarts, pints, and cups in the passed value. Using the passed addresses, the function should directly alter the respective

variables in the calling function. Use the relationships of 2 cups to a pint, 4 cups to a quart, and 16 cups to a gallon.

9. The following program uses the same variable names in both the calling and called functions. Determine if this causes any problem for the computer. What problems might this code pose to a programmer? Also determine the type of data stored in each variable.

```c
#include <stdio.h>

void time(int *, int *);

int main()
{
   int min, hour;

   printf("Enter two numbers :");
   scanf("%d %d", &min, &hour);
   time(&min,&hour);

   return 0;
}
void time(int *min, int *hour)
{
   int sec;

   sec = ( (*hour) *60 + *min ) * 60;
   printf("The total number of seconds is %d", sec);

   return;
}
```

10. Assume that the following declaration has been made:

```c
int *pt1, *pt2;
```

Since the asterisk, *, is used for both multiplication and indirection, how is the expression

```c
* pt1 * * pt2
```

evaluated by the computer? Why does the computer evaluate the expression in the order you have indicated? Rewrite this expression to make its meaning clearer to anyone reading it.

6.6 Common Programming Errors

An extremely common programming error related to functions is passing incorrect data types. The values passed to a function must correspond to the data types of the parameters declared for the function. The simplest way to verify that correct values have been received is to display all passed values within a function's body before any calculations are made. Once this verification has taken place, the display can be removed.

Another common error occurs when the same variable is declared locally within both the calling and called functions. Even though the variable name is the same, a change to one local variable does not alter the value in the other local variable.

Related to this error is the error caused when a local variable has the same name as a global variable. Within the function declaring it, the use of the local variable name affects only the local variable's contents. Thus, the value of the global variable can never be altered by the function.

Another common error is omitting a called function's prototype. The called function must be alerted to the data types of the return value and any parameters; this information is provided by the function prototype. This declaration can only be omitted if the called function is physically placed in a program before its calling function or the called function returns an integer or void data type. The actual value returned by a function can be verified by displaying it both before and after it is returned.

The last two common errors are terminating a function's header line with a semicolon and forgetting to include the data type of a function's parameters.

6.7   Chapter Summary

1. A function is called by giving its name and passing any data to it in the parentheses following the name. If a variable is one of the arguments in a function call, the called function receives a copy of the variable's value.

2. The commonly used form of a user-written function is

```
returnType functionName(parameter list)
{
  declarations;

  statements;
  return (expression);
}
```

The first line of the function is called the *function header.* The opening and closing braces of the function and all statements in between these braces constitute the function's *body.*

The function's storage class may also, optionally, be specified in the header and can be either `static` or `extern`. If no storage class is specified it defaults to `extern`. The returned data type is, by default, an integer when no returned data type is specified. The function declarator must be included for each function and is of the form:

```
functionName(parameter list)
```

The parameter list must include the names of all parameters and their data types.

3. A function's return type is the data type of the value returned by the function. If no type is declared the function is assumed to return an integer value. If the function does not return a value it should be declared as a void type.

4. Functions can directly return at most a single value to their calling functions. This value is the value of the expression in the return statement.

5. Functions can be declared to all calling functions by means of a *function prototype.* The prototype provides a declaration for a function that specifies the data type returned by the function, its name, and the data types of the parameters expected by the function. As with all declarations, a function prototype is terminated with a semicolon and may be specified as a global declaration or included within a function's local variable declarations. The most common form of a function prototype is

```
returnDataType functionName(parameter data types);
```

If the called function is placed physically above the calling function no further declaration is required since the function's definition serves as a global declaration to all following functions.

6. A set of preprogrammed functions for input, output, mathematical procedures, and string handling are included in the standard library provided with each C compiler. To use one of these functions you must obtain the name of the function, the arguments expected by the function, the data type of the returned value (if any), and a description of what the function does.

7. Every variable used in a program has *scope,* which determines where in the program the variable can be used. The scope of a variable is either local or global and is determined by where the variable's definition statement is placed. A local variable is defined within a function and can only be used within its defining function or block. A global variable is defined outside a function and can be used in any function following the variable's definition. All nonstatic global variables are initialized to zero and can be shared between files using the keyword `extern`.

8. Every variable has a class. The *class* of a variable determines how long the value in the variable will be retained. Automatic (`auto`) variables are local variables that exist only while their defining function is executing. `register` variables are similar to automatic variables but are stored in a computer's internal registers rather than in memory. `static` variables can be either global or local and retain their values for the duration of a program's execution. `static` variables are also set to zero or blanks when they are defined.

9. A function can also be passed the address of a variable. By passing addresses, a function has the capability of effectively returning many values.

6.8   Chapter Supplement: Generating Random Numbers

There are many problems in which probability must be considered or statistical sampling techniques must be used. For example, applications such as simple computer games and more involved gaming scenarios can only be described statistically. All of these statistical models require the generation of *random numbers;* that is, a series of numbers whose order cannot be predicted.

In practice, there are no truly random numbers. Dice never are perfect; cards are never shuffled completely randomly; the supposedly random motions of molecules are influenced by the environment; and digital computers can handle numbers only within a finite range and with limited precision. The best one can do is generate *pseudorandom* numbers, which are sufficiently random for the task at hand.

Some computer languages contain a library function that produces random numbers; other do not. All C compilers provide two functions for creating random numbers; `rand()` and `srand()`. The `rand()` function produces a series of random numbers in the range $0 \leq rand() \leq RAND\_MAX$, where the constant RAND_MAX is defined in the `stdlib.h` header file. The `srand()` function provides a starting "seed" value for `rand()`. If `srand()` or some other equivalent "seeding" technique is not used, `rand()` will always produce the same series of random numbers.

The general procedure for creating a series of N random numbers using C's library functions is illustrated by the following code:

```
srand(time(NULL));   /* this generates the first "seed" value */
for (int i = 1; i <= N; ++i)   /* this generates N random numbers */
{
   randvalue = rand();
   printf("%f\n", randvalue);
}
```

Here, the argument to the `srand()` function is a call to the `time()` function with a NULL argument. With this argument the `time()` function reads the computer's internal clock time, in seconds. The `srand()` function then uses this time, converted to an unsigned int, to the random number generator function `rand()`.[11] Program 6.12 uses this code to generate a series of 10 random numbers:

The following output is produced by one run of Program 6.12:

```
13947
 7783
 8639
```

---

[11] Alternatively, many C compilers have a `randomize()` routine that is defined using the `srand()` function. If this routine is available, the call `randomize()` can be used in place of the call `srand(time(NULL))`. In either case, the initializing "seed" routine is only called once, after which the `rand()` function is used to generate a series of numbers.

```
    721
   2298
  31313
  23303
   6697
  31397
  31353
```

 Program 6.12

```c
#include <stdio.h>
#include <stdlib.h>
#include <time.h>

/* this program generates ten pseudo-random numbers
   using C's rand() function
*/
int main()
{
  float ranvalue;
  int i;

  srand(time(NULL));
  for (i = 1; i <= 10; ++i)
  {
    randvalue = rand();
    printf("%6.0f\n", randvalue);
  }

  return 0;
}
```

Because of the `srand()` function call in Program 6.12 the series of ten random numbers will differ each time the program is executed. Without the randomizing "seeding" effect of this function the same series of random numbers would always be produced. Note also the inclusion of the `stdlib.h` and `time.h` header files. The `stdlib.h` file contains the function prototypes for the `srand()` and `rand()` functions, while the `time.h` header file contains the function prototype for the `time()` function.

Scaling

One modification to the random numbers produced by the `rand()` function typically must be made in practice. In most applications either the random numbers are required as floating point values within the range 0.0 to 1.0 or as integers within a specified range, such as 1 to 100. The method for adjusting the random numbers produced by a random number generator to reside within such ranges is called *scaling.*

Scaling random numbers to reside within the range 0.0 to 1.0 is easily accomplished by dividing the returned value of `rand()` by RAND_MAX. Thus, the expression `float(rand())/RAND_MAX` produces a floating point random number between 0.0 and 1.0.

Scaling a random number as an integer value between 0 and N is accomplished using either of the expressions `rand() % (N+1)` or `int((rand()/RAND_MAX) * N)`. For example, the expression `int(rand()/RAND_MAX * 100)` produces a random integer between 0 and 100.[12]

To produce an integer random number between 1 and N the expression `1 + rand() % N` can be used. For example, in simulating the roll of a die, the expression `1 + rand() % 6` produces a random integer between 1 and 6. The more general scaling expression `a + rand() % (b + 1 - a)` can also be used to produce a random integer between the numbers a and b.

---

[12] Many C compilers have a routine named `random()` that can be used to produce the same result. For example, if your compiler has the `random()` function, the call `random(100)` will produce a random integer between 0 and 100.

Complex Data Types

Arrays

The variables used so far have all had a common characteristic: each variable can only be used to store a single value at a time. For example, although the variables `inKey`, `counter`, and `price` declared in the statements

```
char inKey;
int counter;
float price;
```

are of different data types, each variable can only store one value of the declared data type. These types of variables are called *scalar variables*. A scalar variable is a single variable whose stored value is an atomic type. This means that the value cannot be further subdivided or separated into a legitimate data type.

Frequently we may have a set of values, all of the same data type, that form a logical group. For example, Figure 7.1 illustrates three groups of items. The first group is a list of five integer grades, the second group is a list of four character codes, and the last group is a list of six floating point prices.

A simple list consisting of individual items of the same scalar data type is called a single-dimensional array. In this chapter we describe how single-dimensional arrays

Grades	Codes	Prices
98	x	10.96
87	a	6.43
92	m	2.58
79	n	.86
85		12.27
		6.39

Figure 7.1   Three lists of items

are declared, initialized, stored inside a computer, and used. We will explore the use of single-dimensional arrays with example programs and present the procedures for declaring and using multidimensional arrays.

7.1   Single-Dimensional Arrays

A *single-dimensional array,* which is also referred to as a *one-dimensional array,* is a list of values of the same data type. For example, consider the list of grades illustrated in Figure 7.2. All the grades in the list are integer numbers and must be declared as such. However, the individual items in the list do not have to be declared separately. The items in the list can be declared as a single unit and stored under a common variable name called the *array name.* For convenience, we will choose grades as the name for the list shown in Figure 7.2. To declare that grades is to be used to store five individual integer values requires the declaration statement int grades[5];. Notice that this declaration statement gives the data type of the items in the array, the array (or list) name, and the number of items in the array. A common, and good, programming practice is to define the number of array items as a symbolic constant before declaring the array. Using this convention, the previous declaration would be written using two statements, such as:

```
#define NUMELS 5      /* this creates the symbolic constant */
int grades[NUMELS]; /* this is the actual array declaration */
```

Here, the symbolic constant name, NUMELS, can be replaced with any valid identifier of your choice. For simplicity, we will continue to use only one declaration statement for each array, but will point out a distinct advantage of using a symbolic constant when we consider processing array elements later in this section.

Further examples of array declarations are

```
char code[4];       /* an array of four character codes */
double prices[6];   /* an array of six double precision prices */
float amount[100];  /* an array of 100 floating point amounts */
```

Each array has sufficient memory reserved for it to hold the number of data items given in the declaration statement. Thus, the array named code has storage reserved for four

Grade

98
87
92
79
85

Figure 7.2   A list of grades

characters, the `prices` array has storage reserved for six double precision numbers, and the array named `amount` has storage reserved for 100 floating point numbers, Figure 7.3 illustrates the storage reserved for the `code` and `grades` arrays. For illustrative purposes, we have assumed that each character is stored using one byte and that each integer requires two bytes of storage.

Each item in a list is officially called an *element* or *component* of the array. The individual elements stored in the arrays illustrated in Figure 7.3 are stored sequentially, with the first array element stored in the first reserved location, the second element stored in the second reserved location, and so on until the last element is stored in the last reserved location.

To access individual elements in a one-dimensional array requires some unique means of identifying each element. Because each item in the list is stored sequentially, any single item can be accessed by giving the name of the array and the position of the item in the array. The element's position is called its *subscript* or *index value*. The first element has a subscript of 0, the second element has a subscript of 1, and so on. The subscript gives the number of elements to move over, starting from the beginning of the array, to locate the desired element. In C, the array name and subscript are combined by listing the subscript in square brackets after the array name. For example:

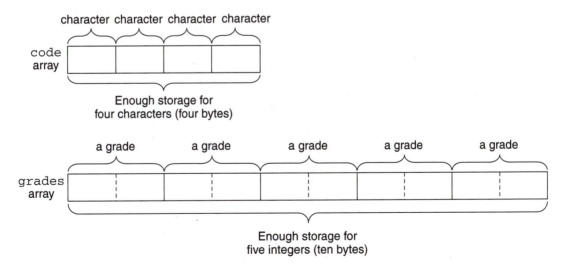

Figure 7.3   The `code` and `grades` arrays in memory

> *Programming Note*
>
> ## Aggregate Data Types
>
> In contrast to atomic types, such as integer, floating point, and double precision data, there are aggregate types. An aggregate type, which is referred to as both a *structured type* and a *data structure,* is any type whose values can be decomposed and are related by some defined structure. Additionally, operations must be available for retrieving and updating individual values in the data structure.
>
> Single-dimensional arrays are examples of a structured type. In a single-dimensional array, such as an array of integers, the array is composed of individual integer values where integers are related by their position in the list. Indexed variables provide the means of accessing and modifying values in the array.

`grades[0]`   refers to the first grade stored in the `grades` array
`grades[1]`   refers to the second grade stored in the `grades` array
`grades[2]`   refers to the third grade stored in the `grades` array
`grades[3]`   refers to the fourth grade stored in the `grades` array
`grades[4]`   refers to the fifth grade stored in the `grades` array

Figure 7.4 illustrates the `grades` array in memory with the correct designation for each array element. Each individual element is called an *indexed variable* or a *subscripted variable,* since both a variable name and an index or subscript value must be used to reference the element. Remember that the index or subscript value gives the position of the element in the array. When we read a subscripted variable such as *grades[0],* we read the variable as "grades sub zero." This is a shortened way of saying "the grades array subscripted by zero" and distinguishes the first element in an array from a scalar variable that could be declared as `grades0`. Similarly, `grades[1]` is read as "grades sub one" and `grades[4]` is read as "grades sub four."

Although it may seem unusual to refer to the first element with an index of zero, doing so increases the computer's speed of accessing array elements. Internally, unseen by the programmer, the computer uses the index as an offset from the array's starting

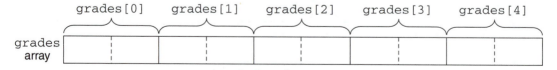

Figure 7.4   Identifying individual array elements

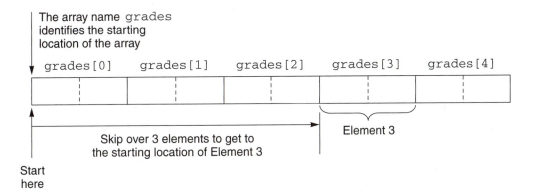

Figure 7.5   Accessing Element 3

position. As illustrated in Figure 7.5, the index tells the computer how many elements to skip over, starting from the beginning of the array, to get to the desired element.

Subscripted variables can be used anywhere that scalar variables are valid. Examples using the elements of the `grades` array are

```
grades[0] = 98;
grades[1] = grades[0] - 11
grades[2] = 2 * (grades[0] - 6);
grades[3] = 79;
grades[4] = (grades[2] + grades[3] - 3)/2;
total = grades[0] + grades[1] + grades[2] + grades[3] + grades[4];
```

The subscript contained within square brackets need not be an integer. Any expression that evaluates to an integer may be used as a subscript.[1] For example, assuming that i and j are integer variables, the following subscripted variables are valid:

```
grades[i]
grades[2*i]
grades[j-i]
```

One extremely important advantage of using integer expressions as subscripts is that it allows sequencing through an array using a `for` loop. This makes statements such as

```
total = grades[1] + grades[2] + grades[3] + grades[4] + grades[5];
```

---

[1] Some compilers permit floating point variables as subscripts; in these cases the floating point value is truncated to an integer value.

unnecessary. The subscript value in each of the subscripted variables in this statement can be replaced by the counter in a `for` loop to access each element in the array sequentially. For example, the code

```
total = 0;                       /* initialize total to zero */
for (i = 0; i <= 4; ++i)
   total = total + grades[i]; /* add in a grade */
```

sequentially retrieves each array element and adds the element to the total. Here the variable `i` is used both as the counter in the `for` loop and as a subscript. As `i` increases by one each time through the `for` loop, the next element in the array is referenced. The procedure for adding the array elements within the `for` loop is the same procedure we have used many times before.

The advantage of using a `for` loop to sequence through an array becomes apparent when you work with larger arrays. For example, if the `grades` array contains 100 values rather than just 5, simply changing the number 4 to 99 in the `for` statement is sufficient to sequence through the 100 grades and add each grade to the total. A change, of course, would also have to be made to the array's declaration statement.

It is in situations such as this that using a symbolic constant to declare the array has a distinct advantage. For example, using a symbolic constant, the following is equivalent to the previous code:

```
#define NUMELS 5     /* this creates the symbolic constant */
int grades[NUMELS]; /* this is the actual array declaration */

total = 0;
for(i = 0; i < NUMELS; ++i)
   total = total + grades[i];
```

Notice that the same symbolic constant is used both to declare the array and in the `for` loop statement that processes each array element. Now, if the array size needs to be altered, only one change, rather than two, is required. This change is to the preprocessor directive that creates the symbolic constant. This single change automatically alters both the array's size and the `for` loop used to process each array element.

As another example of using a `for` loop to sequence through an array, assume that we want to locate the maximum value in an array of 1000 elements named `price`. The procedure we will use to locate the maximum value is to assume initially that the first element in the array is the largest number. Then, as we sequence through the array, the maximum is compared to each element. When an element with a higher value is located, that element becomes the new maximum.

```
maximum = price[0];         /* set the maximum to element zero    */
for(i = 1; i <= 999; ++i) /* cycle through the rest of the array */
   if (price[i] > maximum) /* compare each element to the maximum */
      maximum = price[i];   /* capture the new high value          */
```

In this code, the `for` statement consists of one `if` statement. The search for a new maximum value starts with element 1 of the array and continues through the last element. In a thousand-element array, the last element is element 999.

Input and Output of Array Values

Individual array elements can be assigned values using individual assignment statements or, interactively, using the `scanf()` function. Examples of individual data entry statements are

```
price[5] = 10.69;
scanf("%d %lf", &grades[0], &price[2])
scanf("%c", &code[0]);
scanf("%d %d %d", &grades[0], &grades[1], &grades[2]);
```

In the first statement, the value 10.69 is assigned to the variable named `price[5]`. The second statement causes two values to be read and stored in the variables `grades[0]` and `price[2]`. The third statement causes a single character to be read and stored in the variable named `code[0]`. Finally, the last statement causes three values to be read and stored in the variables `grades[0]`, `grades[1]`, and `grades[2]`, respectively.

Alternatively, a `for` statement can be used to cycle through the array for interactive data input. For example, the code

```
for(i = 0; i <= 4; ++i)
{
  printf("Enter a grade: ");
  scanf("%d", &grades[i]);
}
```

prompts the user for five grades.[2] The first grade entered is stored in `grades[0]`, the second in `grades[1]`, and so on until all five grades are entered.

One caution should be mentioned about storing data in an array. C does not check the value of the index being used (called a *bounds check*). If an array has been declared as consisting of 10 elements, for example, and you use an index of 12, which is outside the bounds of the array, C will not notify you of the error when the program is compiled. The program will attempt to access element 12 by skipping over the appropriate number of bytes from the start of the array. Usually this results in a program crash—but not always. If the accessed location itself contains a data value, the program will attempt to use the value in the accessed memory locations. This can lead to more errors, which are particularly troublesome to locate, especially if the value has been changed and the variable legitimately assigned to the storage location is used at a different point in the program.

---

[2] An equivalent statement is `for(i = 0; i < 5; ++i)`. Which statement you use is a matter of choice.

During output, individual array elements can be displayed using the `printf()` function or complete sections of the array can be displayed by including a `printf()` function call within a `for` loop. Examples of this are

```
printf("%lf," price[6]);
printf("The value of element %d is %d", i, grades[i]);
for(n = 5; n <= 20; ++n)
  printf("%d %lf", n, price[n]);
```

The first call to `printf()` displays the value of the double precision subscripted variable `price[6]`. The second call to `printf()` displays the value of i and the value of `grades[i]`. Before this statement can be executed, i needs to have an assigned value. Finally, the last example includes `printf()` within a `for` loop. Both the value of the index and the value of the elements from 5 to 20 are displayed.

Program 7.1 illustrates these input and output techniques using an array named `grades` that is defined to store five integer numbers. Included in the program are two `for` loops. The first `for` loop is used to cycle through each array element and allows the user to input individual array values. After five values have been entered, the second `for` loop is used to display the stored values.

 Program 7.1

```
#include <stdio.h>
int main()
{
  int i, grades[5];

  for (i = 0; i <= 4; ++i)          /* Enter five grades */
  {
    printf("Enter a grade: ");
    scanf("%d", &grades[i]);
  }
  for (i = 0; i <= 4; ++i)          /* Print five grades */
    printf("\ngrades %d is %d", i, grades[i]);

  return 0;
}
```

Following is a sample run using Program 7.1:

```
Enter a grade: 85
Enter a grade: 90
```
(Continued on next page)

(Continued from previous page)

```
Enter a grade: 78
Enter a grade: 75
Enter a grade: 92

grades 0 is 85
grades 1 is 90
grades 2 is 78
grades 3 is 75
grades 4 is 92
```

In reviewing the output produced by Program 7.1, pay particular attention to the difference between the subscript value displayed and the numerical value stored in the corresponding array element. The subscript value refers to the location of the element in the array, whereas the subscripted variable refers to the value stored in the designated location.

In addition to simply displaying the values stored in each array element, the elements can also be processed by appropriately referencing the desired element. For example, in Program 7.2, each element's value is accumulated in a total, which is displayed upon completion of the individual display of each array element.

Program 7.2

```c
#include <stdio.h>
int main()
{
  int i, grades[5], total = 0;

  for (i = 0; i <= 4; ++i)        /* Enter five grades */
  {
    printf("Enter a grade: ");
    scanf("%d", &grades[i]);
  }

  printf("\nThe total of the grades ");
  for (i = 0; i <= 4; ++i)        /* Display and total the grades */
  {
    printf("%d   ", grades[i]);
    total += grades[i];
  }
  printf("is   %d", total);

  return 0;
}
```

Following is a sample run using Program 7.2:

```
Enter a grade: 85
Enter a grade: 90
Enter a grade: 78
Enter a grade: 75
Enter a grade: 92


The total of the grades 85   90   78   75   92   is   420
```

Notice that in Program 7.2, unlike Program 7.1, only the numerical value stored in each array element is displayed and not their subscript values. Although the second `for` loop was used to accumulate the total of each element, the accumulation could also have been accomplished in the first loop by placing the statement `total += grades[i];` after the `scanf()` call used to enter a value. Also notice that the `printf()` call used to display the total made outside of the second `for` loop so that the total is displayed only once, after all values have been added to the total. If this `printf()` call is placed inside the `for` loop five totals are displayed, with only the last displayed total containing the sum of all of the array values.

Exercises 7.1

1. Write array declarations for the following:
   a. a list of 60 double precision interest rates
   b. a list of 30 floating point temperatures
   c. a list of 25 characters, each representing a code
   d. a list of 100 integer years
   e. a list of 26 double precision coupon rates
   f. a list of 1000 floating point distances
   g. a list of 20 integer code numbers

2. Write appropriate notation for the first, third, and seventh elements of the following arrays:
   a. `int grade[20];`
   b. `float grade[10];`
   c. `float amps[16];`
   d. `double dist[15];`
   e. `double velocity[25];`
   vf. `double time[100];`

3. a. Write individual `scanf()` function calls that can be used to enter values into the first, third, and seventh elements of each of the arrays declared in Exercises 2a through 2f.
   b. Write a `for` loop that can be used to enter values for the complete array declared in Exercise 2a.

4. a. Write individual `printf()` function calls that can be used to print the values from the first, third, and seventh elements of each of the arrays declared in Exercises 2a through 2f.
   b. Write a `for` loop that can be used to display values for the complete array declared in Exercise 2a.

5. List the elements that will be displayed by the following sections of code:
   a. `for (m = 1; m <= 5; ++m)`
      `printf("%d ",a[m]);`
   b. `for (k = 1; k <= 5; k = k + 2)`
      `printf("%d ",a[k]);`
   c. `for (j = 3; j <= 10; ++j)`
      `printf("%f ",b[j]);`
   d. `for (k = 3; k <= 12; k = k + 3)`
      `printf("%f ",b[k]);`
   e. `for (i = 2; i < 11; i = i + 2)`
      `printf("%lf ",c[i]);`

6. a. Write a C program to input the following values into an array named `prices`: 10.95, 16.32, 12.15, 8.22, 15.98, 26.22, 13.54, 6.45, 17.59. After the data are entered, have your program output the values.
   b. Repeat Exercise 6a, but after the data are entered, have your program display them in the following form:

   ```
   10.95      16.32      12.15
    8.22      15.98      26.22
   13.54       6.45      17.59
   ```

7. a. Write a C program to input 15 integer numbers into an array named `temp`. As each number is input, add the number into the total. After all numbers are input, display the numbers and their average.
   b. Repeat Exercise 7a, but locate the maximum number in the array (do not add the numbers) as the values are being input. (*Hint:* Set the maximum equal to zero before the `for` loop used to input the numbers.)
   c. Repeat Exercise 7b, keeping track of both the maximum element in the array and the index number for the maximum. After displaying the numbers, print the two messages:

   ```
   The maximum value is: _____
   This is element number _____ in the list of numbers
   ```

   Have your program display the correct values in place of the underlines in the messages.
   d. Repeat Exercise 7c, but have your program locate the minimum value of the data entered.

8. a. Write a C program to input the following integer numbers into an array named `grades`: 89, 95, 72, 83, 99, 54, 86, 75, 92, 73, 79, 75, 82, 73. As each number is input, add the numbers to the total. After all numbers are input and the total is obtained, calculate the average of the numbers and use the average to determine the deviation of each value from the average. Store each deviation in an array named `deviation`. Each deviation is obtained as the element value less the average of all the data. Have your program display each deviation alongside its corresponding element from the grades array.
   b. Calculate the variance of the data used in Exercise 8a. The variance is obtained by squaring each individual deviation and dividing the sum of the squared deviations by the number of deviations.

9. Write a C program that declares three single-dimensional arrays named `price`, `quantity`, and `amount`. Each array should be capable of holding ten elements. Using a `for` loop, input values for the `price` and `quantity` arrays. The entries in the `amount` array should be the product of the corresponding values in the `price` and `quantity` arrays (thus, `amount[i]` = `quantity[i]` * `price[i];`). After all of the data has been entered, display the following output:

```
Quantity              Price              Amount
--------              -----              ------
```

Under each column heading display the appropriate value.

10. a. Write a program that inputs ten double precision numbers into an array named `raw`. After ten user-input numbers are entered into the array, your program should cycle through `raw` ten times. During each pass through the array, your program should select the lowest value in `raw` and place the selected value in the next available slot in an array named `sorted`. Thus, when your program is complete, the `sorted` array should contain the numbers in `raw` in sorted order from lowest to highest. (*Hint:* Make sure to reset the lowest value selected during each pass to a very high number so that it is not selected again. You will need a second `for` loop within the first `for` loop to locate the minimum value for each pass.)

b. The method used in Exercise 10a to sort the values in the array is very inefficient. Can you determine why? What might be a better method of sorting the numbers in an array?

7.2   Array Initialization

Arrays, like scalar variables, can be declared either inside or outside a function. Arrays declared inside a function are *local arrays,* and arrays declared outside a function are *global arrays.* For example, consider the following section of code:

```
int gallons[20];              /* a global array */
static double dist[25];       /* a static global array */
void mpg(int);                /* function prototype */
int main()
{
  int i;

  for (i = 1; i <= 10; ++i)
    mpg(i);                   /* call mpg() ten times */
         .
  return 0;
}
void mpg(int carNum)
{
  int miles[15];              /* an automatic local array */
  static double course[15];   /* a static local array     */
         .
         .
         .
  return;
}
```

As indicated in the code, both the `dist` and `gallons` arrays are globally declared arrays, `miles` is an automatic local array, and `course` is a `static` local array. As with scalar variables, all global arrays and local `static` arrays are created once, at compilation time, and retain their values until `main()` finishes executing. `auto` arrays are created and destroyed each time the function they are local to is called. Thus, the `dist`, `gallons`, and `course` arrays are created once, and the `miles` array is created and destroyed ten times.

Array elements can be initialized within their declaration statements in the same manner as scalar variables, except that the initializing elements must be included in braces. Examples of such initializations for automatic, static, and global arrays are[3]

```
int grades[5] = {98, 87, 92, 79, 85};
char codes[6] = {'s', 'a', 'm', 'p', 'l', 'e'};
double width[7] = {10.96, 6.43, 2.58, .86, 5.89, 7.56, 8.22};
static int temp[4] = {10, 20, 30, 40};
static float temp[4] = {98.6, 97.2, 99.0, 101.5};
```

Initializers are applied in the order they are written, with the first value used to initialize element 0, the second value used to initialize element 1, and so on, until all values have been used. Thus, in the declaration

```
int grades[5] = {98, 87, 92, 79, 85};
```

`grades[0]` is initialized to 98, `grades[1]` is initialized to 87, `grades[2]` is initialized to 92, `grades[3]` is initialized to 79, and `grades[4]` is initialized to 85.

Because white space is ignored in C, initializations may be continued across multiple lines. For example, the declaration

```
int gallons[20] = {19, 16, 14, 19, 20, 18,   /* initializing values */
                   12, 10, 22, 15, 18, 17,   /* may extend across   */
                   16, 14, 23, 19, 15, 18,   /* multiple lines       */
                   21, 5 };
```

uses four lines to initialize all of the array elements.

If the number of initializers is less than the declared number of elements listed in square brackets the initializers are applied starting with array element 0. Thus, in the declaration

```
float length[7] = {7.8, 6.4, 4.9, 11.2};
```

only `length[0]`, `length[1]`, `length[2]`, and `length[3]` are initialized with the listed values. The other array elements will be initialized to zero. Unfortunately, there is no method to either indicate repetition of an initialization value or initialize later array elements without first specifying values for earlier elements.

---

[3] Note that in older versions of C (non-ANSI) only global (static or nonstatic) and local static arrays could be initialized within their declaration statements. Local automatic arrays could not be initialized within their declaration statements.

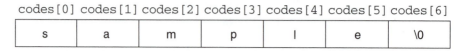

Figure 7.6   A string is terminated with a special sentinel

If no specific initializers are given in the declaration statement, all numerical array elements are set to zero. For example, the declaration int dist[100]; sets all elements of the dist array equal to zero at compilation time. Similarly, since length[4] through length[7] were not specifically initialized when the length array was declared, these elements are also set to zero.

A unique feature of initializers is that the size of an array may be omitted when initializing values are included in the declaration statement. For example, the declaration

```
int gallons[] = {16, 12, 10, 14, 11};
```

reserves enough storage room for five elements. Similarly, the following two declarations are equivalent:

```
char codes[6] = {'s', 'a', 'm', 'p', 'l', 'e'};
char codes[] = {'s', 'a', 'm', 'p', 'l', 'e'};
```

Both of these declarations set aside six character locations for an array named codes. An interesting and useful simplification can also be used when initializing character arrays. For example, the declaration

```
char codes[] = "sample";    /* no braces or commas */
```

uses the string "sample" to initialize the codes array. Recall that a string is any sequence of characters enclosed in double quotes. This last declaration creates an array named codes having seven elements and fills the array with the seven characters illustrated in Figure 7.6. The first six characters, as expected, consist of the letters s, a, m, p, l, and e. The last character, which is the escape sequence \0, is called the *null character.* The null character is automatically appended to all strings by the C compiler. This character has an internal storage code that is numerically equal to zero (the storage code of the zero character has a numerical value of 48, so the two cannot be confused by the computer) and is used as a marker, or sentinel, to mark the end of a string. As we shall see in Chapter 9, this marker is invaluable when manipulating strings of characters.

Exercises 7.2

1. Write array declarations, including initializers, for the following:
   a. a list of ten integer grades; 89, 75, 82, 93, 78, 95, 81, 88, 77, 82
   b. a list of five double precision amounts: 10.62, 13.98, 18.45, 12.68, 14.76
   c. a list of 100 double precision interest rates; the first six rates are 6.29, 6.95, 7.25, 7.35, 7.40, 7.42
   d. a list of 64 floating point temperatures; the first ten temperatures are 78.2, 69.6, 68.5, 83.9, 55.4, 67.0, 49.8, 58.3, 62.5, 71.6
   e. a list of 15 character codes; the first seven codes are f, j, m, q, t, w, z

2. The string of characters "Good Morning" is to be stored in a character array named `good-str1`. Write the declaration for this array in three different ways.

3. a. Write declaration statements to store the string of characters "Input the Following Data" in a character array named `messag1`, the string "----------------" in the array named `messag2`, the string "Enter the Date:" in the array named `messag3`, and the string "Enter the Account Number:" in the array named `messag4`.
   b. Include the array declarations written in Exercise 3a in a program that uses the `printf()` function to display the messages. For example, the statement `printf("%s", messag1);` causes the string stored in the `messag1` array to be displayed. Your program will require four such statements to display the four individual messages. Using the `printf()` function with the `%s` control sequence to display a string requires that the end-of-string marker `\0` is present in the character array used to store the string.

4. a. Write a declaration to store the string "This is a test" into an array named `strtest`. Include the declaration in a program to display the message using the following loop:

   ```
   for (i = 0; i <= 14; ++i) printf("%c", strtest[i]);
   ```

   b. Modify the `for` statement in Exercise 4a to display only the array characters t, e, s, and t.
   c. Include the array declaration written in Exercise 4a in a program that uses the `printf()` function to display characters in the array. For example, the statement `printf("%s", strtest);` will cause the string stored in the `strtest` array to be displayed. Using this statement requires that the last character in the array be the end-of-string marker `\0`.
   d. Repeat Exercise 4a using a `while` loop. (*Hint:* Stop the loop when the `\0` escape sequence is detected. The expression `while (strtest[i] != '\0')` can be used.)

5. a. Write a declaration to store the following values in an array named `prices`: 16.24, 18.98, 23.75, 16.29, 19.54, 14.22, 11.13, 15.39. Include the declaration in a program that displays the values in the array.
   b. Repeat Exercise 5a, but make the array a nonstatic global array.

6. Write a C program that uses a declaration statement to store the following numbers in an array named `rates`: 17.24, 25.63, 5.94, 33.92, 3.71, 32.84, 35.93, 18.24, 6.92. Your program should then locate and display both the maximum and minimum values in the array.

7. Write a C program that stores the following prices in a global array: 9.92, 6.32, 12.63, 5.95, 10.29. Your program should also create two automatic arrays named `units` and `amounts`, each capable of storing five double precision numbers. Using a `for` loop and a `scanf()`

function call, have your program accept five user-input numbers into the `units` array when the program is run. Your program should store the product of the corresponding values in the `prices` and `units` arrays in the `amounts` array (for example, `amounts[1] = prices[1] * units[1]`) and display the following output (fill in the table appropriately):

```
Price           Units           Amount
-----           -----           ------
 9.92             .                .
 6.32             .                .
12.63             .                .
 5.95             .                .
10.29             .                .
                                ------
Total:                            .
```

7.3 Passing Arrays

Individual array elements are passed to a function by simply including them as sub-scripted variables in the function call argument list. For example, the function call `findMin(grades[2], grades[6]);` passes the values of the elements `grades[2]` and `grades[6]` to the function `findMin()`.

Passing a complete array to a function is in many respects an easier operation than passing individual elements. The called function receives access to the actual array, rather than a copy of the values in the array. For example, if `grades` is an array, the function call `findMax(grades);` makes the complete `grades` array available to the `findMax()` function. This is different from passing a single variable to a function.

Recall that when a single scalar argument is passed to a function, the called function receives only a *copy* of the passed value, which is stored in one of the function's value parameters. If arrays were passed in this manner, a copy of the complete array would have to be created. For large arrays, making duplicate copies of the array for each function call would waste computer storage, consume execution time, and frustrate the effort to return multiple element changes made by the called program. To avoid these problems, the called function is given direct access to the original array. Thus, any changes made by the called function are made directly to the array itself. For the following specific examples of function calls, assume that the arrays `nums`, `keys`, `units`, and `prices` are declared as:

```
int nums[5];                       /* an array of five integers    */
char keys[256];                    /* an array of 256 characters   */
double units[500], prices[500];    /* two arrays of 500 doubles    */
```

For these arrays, the following function calls can be made:

```
findMax(nums);
findCh(keys);
calcTot(nums, units, prices);
```

In each case, the called function receives direct access to the named array.

On the receiving side, the called function must be alerted that an array is being made available. For example, suitable function headers for the previous functions are

```
int findMax(int vals[5])
char findCh(chr inKeys[256])
void calcTot(int arr1[5], double arr2[500], double arr3[500])
```

In each of these function declarations, the names in the parameter list are chosen by the programmer and are local to the function. However, the internal local names used by the functions still refer to the original array created outside the function. This is made clear in Program 7.3.

  Program 7.3

```
#include <stdio.h>

void findMax(int [5]);     /* function prototype */

int main()
{
  int nums[5] = {2, 18, 1, 27, 16};

  findMax(nums);

  return 0;
}

void findMax(int vals[5]) /* find the maximum value */
{
  int i, max = vals[0];

  for (i = 1; i <= 4; ++i)
    if (max < vals[i])
      max = vals[i];
  printf("The maximum value is %d", max);

  return;
}
```

Notice that the function prototype for findMax() declares that findMax() returns no value. Only one array is created in Program 7.3. In main(), this array is known as nums, and in findMax(), the array is known as vals. As illustrated in Figure 7.7, both names refer to the same array. Thus, in Figure 7.7 vals[3] is the same element as nums[3].

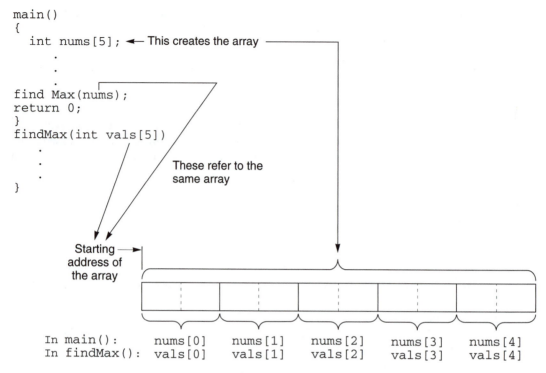

Figure 7.7 Only one array is created

The argument and parameter declarations in the findMax() prototype and the function header line, respectively, in Program 7.3 actually contain extra information that is not required by the function. All that findMax() must know is that the parameter vals refers to an array of integers. Since the array has been created in main() and no additional storage space is needed in findMax(), the declaration for vals can omit the size of the array. Thus, an alternative function header is

```
findMax(int vals[])
```

This form of the function header makes more sense when you realize that only one item is actually passed to findMax() when the function is called. As you might have suspected, the item passed is the starting address of the nums array, as illustrated in Figure 7.8.

Since only one item is passed to findMax, the number of elements in the array need not be included in the declaration for vals.[4] In fact, it is generally advisable to omit the

---

[4] An important consequence of this is that findMax() has direct access to the passed array. This means that any change to an element of the vals array actually is a change to the nums array. This is significantly different from the situation with scalar variables, where the called function does not receive direct access to the passed variable.

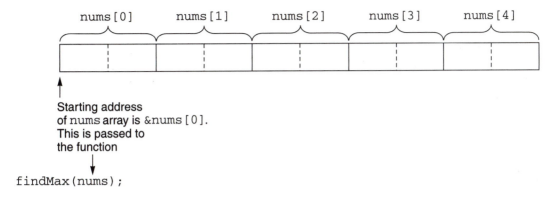

Figure 7.8   The starting address of the array is passed

size of the array in the function header line. For example, consider the more general form of findMax(), which can be used to find the maximum value of an integer array of arbitrary size.

```
int findMax(int vals[], int numEls)   /* find the maximum value */
{
  int i, max = vals[0];

  for (i = 1; i < numEls; ++i)
   if (max < vals[i])
     max = vals[i];

  return(max);
}
```

The more general form of findMax() declares that the function returns an integer value. The function expects the starting address of an integer array and the number of elements in the array as arguments. Then, using the number of elements as the boundary for its search, the function's for loop causes each array element to be examined in sequential order to locate the maximum value. Program 7.4 illustrates the use of findMax() in a complete program.

Program 7.4

```c
#include <stdio.h>

int findMax(int [], int);   /* function prototype */

int main()
{
  int nums[5] = {2, 18, 1, 27, 16};
  int findMax();

  printf("The maximum value is %d", findMax(nums,5));

  return 0;
}
int findMax(int vals[], int numEls)
{
  int i, max = vals[0];

  for (i = 1; i < numEls; ++i)
   if (max < vals[i])
     max = vals[i];

  return(max);
}
```

The output displayed when Program 7.4 is executed is

```
The maximum value is 27
```

Exercises 7.3

1. The following declaration was used to create the `prices` array:

   ```c
   double prices[500];
   ```

   Write two different function header lines for a function named `sortArray()` that accepts the `prices` array as a parameter named `inArray` and returns no value.

2. The following declaration was used to create the `keys` array:

   ```c
   char keys[256];
   ```

Write two different function header lines for a function named findKey() that accepts the keys array as a parameter named select and returns no value.

3. The following declaration was used to create the rates array:

```
float rates[256];
```

Write two different function header lines for a function named prime() that accepts the rates array as a parameter named rates and returns a float.

4. a. Modify the findMax() function in Program 7.3 to locate the minimum value of the passed array. Rename the function findMin().
   b. Include the function written in Exercise 4a in a complete program and run the program on a computer.

5. Write a program that has a declaration in main() to store the following numbers into an array named rates: 6.5, 7.2, 7.5, 8.3, 8.6, 9.4, 9.6, 9.8, 10.0. There should be a function call to show() that accepts the rates array as a parameter named rates and then displays the numbers in the array.

6. a. Write a program that has a declaration in main() to store the string "Vacation is near" into an array named message. There should be a function call to display() that accepts message in a parameter named strng and then displays the contents of the message.
   b. Modify the display() function written in Exercise 6a to display the first eight elements of the message array.

7. Write a program that declares three single-dimensional arrays named price, quantity, and amount. Each array should be declared in main() and should be capable of holding ten double precision numbers. The numbers that should be stored in price are 10.62, 14.89, 13.21, 16.55, 18.62, 9.47, 6.58, 18.32, 12.15, 3.98. The numbers that should be stored in quantity are 4, 8.5, 6, 7.35, 9, 15.3, 3, 5.4, 2.9, 4.8. Your program should pass these three arrays to a function called extend(), which should calculate the elements in the amount array as the product of the equivalent elements in the price and quantity arrays (for example, amount[1] = price[1] * quantity[1]). After extend() has put values into the amount array, the values in the array should be displayed from within main().

8. Write a C program that includes two functions named calcAvg() and variance(). The calcAvg() function should calculate and return the average of the values stored in an array named testvals. The array should be declared in main() and include the values 89, 95, 72, 83, 99, 54, 86, 75, 92, 73, 79, 75, 82, 73. The variance() function should calculate and return the variance of the data. The variance is obtained by subtracting the average from each value in testvals, squaring the differences obtained, adding their squares, and dividing by the number of elements in testvals. The values returned from calcAvg() and variance() should be displayed using printf() function calls in main().

7.4 Two-Dimensional Arrays

A *two-dimensional array,* which is sometimes referred to as a *table,* consists of both rows and columns of elements. For example, the array of numbers

8	16	9	52
3	15	27	6
14	25	2	10

is a two-dimensional array of integers. This array consists of three rows and four columns. To reserve storage for this array, both the number of rows and the number of columns must be included in the array's declaration. Calling the array `val`, the appropriate declaration for this two-dimensional array is[5]

```
int val[3][4];
```

Similarly, the declarations

```
double prices[10][5];
char code[6][26];
```

declare that the array `prices` consists of 10 rows and 5 columns of double precision numbers and that the array `code` consists of 6 rows and 26 columns of characters.

Each element in a two-dimensional array is located by identifying its position in the array. As illustrated in Figure 7.9, the term `val[1][3]` uniquely identifies the element in row 1, column 3. As with single-dimensional array variables, double-dimensional array variables can be used anywhere that scalar variables are valid. Examples that use elements of the `val` array are

```
num = val[2][3];
val[0][0] = 62;
newnum = 4 * (val[1][0] - 5);
sumrow0 = val[0][0] + val[0][1] + val[0][2] + val[0][3];
```

The last statement causes the values of the four elements in row 0 to be added and the sum to be stored in the scalar variable `sumrow0`.

---

[5] This declaration can also be made by using symbolic constants such as

```
#define ROWS 3
#define COLS 4
int val[ROWS][COLS];
```

As always, the symbolic constant names are programmer selectable.

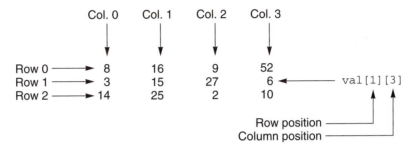

Figure 7.9   Each array element is identified by its row and column

As with single-dimensional arrays, two-dimensional arrays can be declared either inside or outside a function. Arrays declared inside a function are local arrays; arrays declared outside a function are global arrays. For example, consider the following section of code:

```
int bingo[2][3];
int main()
{
   double pickSix[52][6];
               .
               .
               .
   return 0;
}
```

The `bingo` array is a globally declared two-dimensional array consisting of 2 rows and 3 columns, and the `pickSix` array is a local array of 52 rows and 6 columns.

As with single-dimensional arrays, double-dimensional arrays can be initialized from within their declaration statements. This is done by listing the initial values within braces and separating them by commas. Additionally, braces can be used to separate individual rows. For example, the declaration

```
int val[3][4] = { {8,16,9,52},
                  {3,15,27,6},
                  {14,25,2,10} };
```

declares `val` to be an array of integers with three rows and four columns, with the initial values given in the declaration. The first set of internal braces contains the values for row 0 of the array, the second set of internal braces contains the values for row 1, and the third set of braces the values for row 2.

Although the commas in the initialization braces are always required, the inner braces can be omitted. Thus, the initialization for `val` may be written as

```
int val[3][4] = {8,16,9,52,
                 3,15,27,6,
                 14,25,2,10};
```

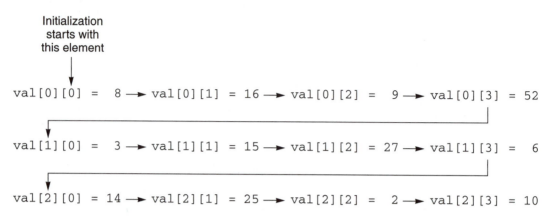

Figure 7.10   Storage and initialization of the `val[]` array

The separation of initial values into rows in the declaration statement is not necessary since the compiler assigns values beginning with the [0][0] element and proceeds row by row to fill in the remaining values. Thus, the initialization

```
int val[3][4] = {8,16,9,52,3,15,27,6,14,25,2,10};
```

is equally valid but does not clearly illustrate to another programmer where one row ends and another begins.

As illustrated in Figure 7.10, the initialization of a two-dimensional array is done in row order. First the elements in the first row are initialized, then the elements in the second row are initialized, and so on until the initializations are completed. This row ordering is also the same ordering used to store two-dimensional arrays. That is, array `element[0][0]` is stored first, followed by `element[0][1]`, followed by `element[0][2]`, and so on. Following the first row's elements are the second row's element, and so on for all the rows in the array.

As with single-dimensional arrays, double-dimensional arrays may be displayed by individual element notation or by using loops (either `while` or `for`). This is illustrated by Program 7.5, which displays all the elements of a three-by-four two-dimensional array using two different techniques.

The display produced by Program 7.5 is

```
Display of val array by explicit element
 8   16    9   52
 3   15   27    6
14   25    2   10

Display of val array using a nested for loop
 8   16    9   52
 3   15   27    6
14   25    2   10
```

Program 7.5

```c
#include <stdio.h>
int main()
{
  int i, j, val[3][4] = {8,16,9,52,3,15,27,6,14,25,2,10};

  printf("\nDisplay of val array by explicit element");
  printf("\n%2d  %2d  %2d  %2d",val[0][0],val[0][1],val[0][2],val[0][3]);
  printf("\n%2d  %2d  %2d  %2d",val[1][0],val[1][1],val[1][2],val[1][3]);
  printf("\n%2d  %2d  %2d  %2d",val[2][0],val[2][1],val[2][2],val[2][3]);
  printf("\n\nDisplay of val array using a nested for loop");
  for (i = 0; i < 3; ++i)
  {
    printf("\n");       /* start a new line for each row */
    for (j = 0; j < 4; ++j)
      printf("%2d  ", val[i][j]);
  }

  return 0;
}
```

The first display of the `val` array produced by Program 7.5 is constructed by explicitly designating each array element. The second display of array element values, which is identical to the first, is produced using a nested `for` loop. Nested loops are especially useful when dealing with two-dimensional arrays because they allow the programmer to easily designate and cycle through each element. In Program 7.5, the variable `i` controls the outer loop and the variable `j` controls the inner loop. Each pass through the outer loop corresponds to a single row, with the inner loop supplying the appropriate column elements. After a complete row is printed a new line is started for the next row. The effect is a display of the array in a row-by-row fashion.

Once two-dimensional array elements have been assigned, array processing can begin. Typically, `for` loops are used to process two-dimensional arrays because, as previously noted, they allow the programmer to easily designate and cycle through each array element. For example, the nested `for` loop in Program 7.6 is used to multiply each element in the `val` array by the scalar number 10 and display the resulting value.

The output produced by Program 7.6 is

```
Display of multiplied elements

 80  160   90  520
 30  150  270   60
140  250   20  100
```

Program 7.6

```c
#include <stdio.h>
int main()
{
int i, j, val[3][4] = {8,16,9,52,
                       3,15,27,6,
                       14,25,2,10};

  /* multiply each element by 10 and display it */
  printf("\nDisplay of multiplied elements\n");
  for (i = 0; i < 3; ++i)
  {
    printf("\n");          /* start a new line */
    for (j = 0; j < 4; ++j)
    {
      val[i][j] = val[i][j] * 10;
      printf("%3d  ", val[i][j]);
    }  /* end of inner loop */
  }    /* end of outer loop */

  return 0;
}
```

Passing two-dimensional arrays into functions is a process identical to passing one-dimensional arrays. The called function receives access to the entire array. For example, the function call `display(val);` makes the complete `val` array available to the function named `display()`. Thus, any changes made by `display()` are made directly to the `val` array. Assuming that the following two-dimensional arrays named `test`, `code`, and `stocks` are declared as:

```c
int test[7][9];
char code[26][10];
float stocks[256][52];
```

the following function calls are valid:

```c
findMax(test);
obtain(code);
price(stocks);
```

On the receiving side, the called function must be alerted that a two-dimensional array is being made available. For example, suitable function header lines for the previous functions are

```
int findMax(int nums[7][9])
char obtain(char key[26][10])
void price(float names[256][52])
```

In each of these function headers, the parameter names chosen are local to the function. However, the internal parameter names used by the function still refer to the original array created outside the function. If the array is a global one, there is no need to pass the array because the function could access the array by its global name. Program 7.7 illustrates passing a local, two-dimensional array into a function that displays the array's values.

  Program 7.7

```
#include <stdio.h>

void display(int [3][4]);   /* function prototype */

int main()
{
   int val[3][4] = {8,16,9,52,
                    3,15,27,6,
                    14,25,2,10};

   display(val);

   return 0;
}

void display(int nums[3][4])
{
   int rowNum, colNum;

   for (rowNum = 0; rowNum < 3; ++rowNum)
   {
     for(colNum = 0; colNum < 4; ++colNum)
       printf("%4d",nums[rowNum][colNum]);
     printf("\n");
   }

   return;
}
```

Only one array is created in Program 7.7. This array is known as val in main() and as nums in display(). Thus, val[0][2] refers to the same element as nums[0][2].

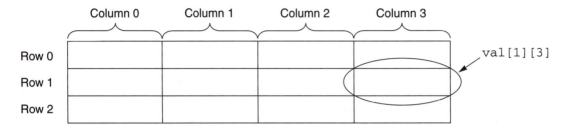

Figure 7.11 Storage of the `val` array

Notice the use of the nested `for` loop in Program 7.7. Nested `for` statements are especially useful when dealing with multidimensional arrays because they allow the programmer to cycle through each element. In Program 7.7, the variable `rowNum` controls the outer loop and the variable `colNum` controls the inner loop. For each pass through the outer loop, which corresponds to a row, the inner loop makes one pass through the column elements. After a complete row is printed, the `\n` escape sequence causes a new line to be started for the next row. The effect is a display of the array in a row-by-row fashion:

```
 8    16    9    52
 3    15   27     6
14    25    2    10
```

The parameter declaration for `nums` in `display()` contains extra information not required by the function. The declaration for `nums` can omit the row size of the array. Thus, an alternative function prototype is

```
void display(int[][4]);
```

and an alternative function header line is

```
void display(int nums[][4])
```

The reason the column size must be included whereas the row size is optional becomes obvious when you consider how the array elements are stored in memory. Starting with element `val[0][0]`, each succeeding element is stored consecutively, row by row, as `val[0][0]`, `val[0][1]`, `val[0][2]`, `val[0][3]`, `val[1][0]`, `val[1][1]`, etc., as illustrated in Figure 7.11.

As with all array accesses, an individual element of the `val` array is obtained by adding an offset to the starting location of the array. For example, assuming an integer requires 2 bytes of storage, the element `val[1][3]` is located at an offset of 14 bytes from the start of the array. Internally, the computer uses the row subscript, columns subscript, and column size to determine this offset using the following calculation:

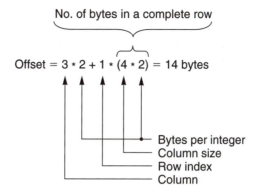

No. of bytes in a complete row

Offset $= 3 * 2 + 1 * (4 * 2) = 14$ bytes

Bytes per integer
Column size
Row index
Column

The number of columns is necessary in the offset calculation so that the computer can determine the number of positions to skip over to get to the desired row.

Larger Dimensional Arrays

Although arrays with more than two dimensions are not commonly used, C does allow any number of dimensions to be declared. This is done by listing the maximum size of all dimensions for the array. For example, the declaration `int response[4][10][6];` declares a three-dimensional array. The first element in the array is designated as `response[0][0][0]` and the last element as `response[3][9][5]`.

Conceptually, as illustrated in Figure 7.12, a three-dimensional array can be viewed as a book of data tables. Using this visualization, the first subscript can be thought of as the location of the desired row in a table, the second subscript value as the desired column, and the third subscript value, which is often called the *rank,* as the page number of the selected table.

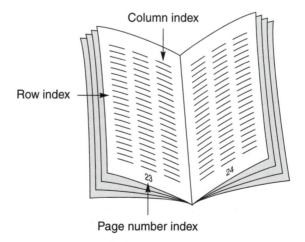

Figure 7.12   Representation of a three-dimensional array

Similarly, arrays of any dimension can be declared. Conceptually, a four-dimensional array can be represented as a shelf of books where the fourth dimension is used to declare a desired book on the shelf. A five-dimensional array can be viewed as a bookcase filled with books where the fifth dimension refers to a selected shelf in the bookcase. A six-dimensional array can be considered a row of bookcases, where the sixth dimension references the desired bookcase in the row. A seven-dimensional array can be considered multiple rows of bookcases, where the seventh dimension references the desired row, and so on. Alternatively, arrays of three, four, five, six, or more dimensions can be viewed as mathematical n-tuples of order three, four, five, six, and so on, respectively.

Exercises 7.4

1. Write appropriate declaration statements for
   a. an array of integers with 6 rows and 10 columns
   b. an array of integers with 2 rows and 5 columns
   c. an array of characters with 7 rows and 12 columns
   d. an array of characters with 15 rows and 7 columns
   e. an array of double precision numbers with 10 rows and 25 columns
   f. an array of double precision numbers with 16 rows and 8 columns

2. Write a function that multiplies each element of a 7-by-10 array of integers by a scalar number. Both the array name and the number by which each element is to be multiplied are to be passed into the function as arguments. Assume the array is an array of integers.

3. Write a C function that adds the values of all elements in a two-dimensional array that is passed to the function, Assume that the array is an array of double precision numbers having 4 rows and 5 columns.

4. Write a C function that adds respective values of two double-dimensional arrays named `first` and `second`. Both arrays have 2 rows and 3 columns. For example, element `[1][2]` of the resulting array should be the sum of `first[1][2]` and `second[1][2]`. Assume the arrays are arrays of integers. The first and second arrays should be initialized as follows:

First				Second		
16	18	23		24	52	77
54	91	11		16	19	59

5. a. Write a C function that finds and displays the maximum value in a two-dimensional array of integers. The array should be declared as a 10-row-by-20-column array of integers in `main()`, and the starting address of the array should be passed to the function.
   b. Modify the function written in Exercise 5a so that it also displays the row and column number of the element with the maximum value.
   c. Can the function you wrote for Exercise 5a be generalized to handle any size two-dimensional array?

6. Write a C function that can be used to sort the elements of a 10-by-20 two-dimensional array of integers. (*Hint:* Use the `sortnum()` function in Program 6.12 to swap array elements.)

7. a. A professor has constructed a two-dimensional array of floating point numbers having 35 rows and 4 columns. This array currently contains the numerical grades of the students in the

professor's four classes. Write a C program that determines the total number of grades in the ranges less than 60, greater than or equal to 60 and less than 70, greater than or equal to 70 and less than 80, greater than or equal to 80 and less than 90, and greater than or equal to 90.

b. How might the function you wrote for Exercise 7a be modified to include the case where no grade is present? That is, what grade could be used to indicate an invalid grade, and how does your function have to be modified to exclude counting such a grade?

8. a. Write a function that finds and displays the maximum value in a two-dimensional array of integers. The array should be declared as a 10-by-20 array of integers in `main()`.

b. Modify the function written in Exercise 8a so that it also displays the row and column number of the element with the maximum value.

c. Can the function you wrote for Exercise 8a be generalized to handle any size two-dimensional array?

9. Write a C function that can be used to sort the elements of a 10-by-20 two-dimensional array of integers. (*Hint:* Read Section 7.7 before doing this exercise.)

7.5 Common Programming Errors

Four common errors are associated with using arrays.

1. Forgetting to declare the array. This error results in a compiler error message equivalent to "invalid indirection" each time a subscripted variable is encountered within a program.

2. Using a subscript that references a nonexistent array element. For example, declaring the array to be of size 20 and using a subscript value of 25. This error is not detected by most C compilers. However, it causes a run-time error that results either in a program "crash" or a value that has no relation to the intended element being accessed from memory. In either case it is usually an extremely troublesome error to locate. The only solution to this problem is to make sure, either by specific programming statements or by careful coding, that each subscript references a valid array element.

3. Not using a large enough conditional value in a `for` loop counter to cycle through all the array elements. This error usually occurs when an array is initially specified to be of size n and there is a `for` loop within the program of the form `for (i = 0; i < n; ++i)`. The array size is then expanded but the programmer forgets to change the interior `for` loop parameters. Using a symbolic constant both to declare an array's size and for the maximum subscript value in the `for` statement eliminates this error.

4. Forgetting to initialize the array. Although many compilers automatically set all elements of integer and real valued arrays to zero and all elements of character arrays to blanks, it is up to the programmer to ensure that each array is correctly initialized before the processing of array elements begins.

7.6 Chapter Summary

1. A single-dimensional array is a data structure that can be used to store a list of values of the same data type. Such arrays must be declared by giving the data type of the values that are stored in the array and the array size. For example, the declaration

```
int num[100];
```

creates an array of 100 integers.

2. Array elements are stored in contiguous locations in memory and referenced using the array name and a subscript, for example, num[22]. Any nonnegative integer-value expression can be used as a subscript, and the subscript 0 always refers to the first element in the array.

3. Two-dimensional arrays are declared by specifying both a row and a column size. For example, the declaration

```
float rates[12][20];
```

reserves memory space for a table of 12 by 20 floating point values. Individual elements in a two-dimensional array are identified by providing both a row and a column subscript. The element in the first row and first column has row and column subscripts of 0.

4. Arrays are passed to a function by passing the name of the array as an argument. The value actually passed is the address of the first array storage location. Thus, the called function receives direct access to the original array, not a copy of the array elements. Within the called function, a parameter must be declared to receive the passed array name. The declaration of the parameter can omit the row size of the array.

7.7 Chapter Supplement: Searching and Sorting Methods

Most programmers encounter the need both to sort and search a list of data items at some time in their programming careers. For example, experimental results might have to be arranged in either increasing (ascending) or decreasing (descending) order for statistical analysis, lists of names may have to be sorted in alphabetical order, or a list of dates may have to be rearranged in ascending date order. Similarly, a list of names may have to be searched to find a particular name, or a list of dates may have to be searched to locate a particular date. In this section, we introduce the fundamentals of both searching and sorting lists. It should be noted that it is not necessary to sort a list before searching it, although, as we shall see, much faster searches are possible if the list is in sorted order.

Search Algorithms

A common requirement of many programs is to search a list for a given element. For example, in a list of names and telephone numbers, we might search for a specific name so that the corresponding telephone number can be printed, or we might wish to search the list simply to determine if a name is there. The two most common methods of performing such searches are the linear and binary search algorithms.

Linear Search

In a *linear search,* which is also known as a *sequential search,* each item in the list is examined in the order it occurs in the list until the desired item is found or the end of the list is reached. This is analogous to looking at every name in the phone directory, beginning with Aardvark, Aaron, until you find the one you want or until you reach Zzxgy, Zora.

Obviously, this is not the most efficient way to search a long alphabetized list. However, the advantages of the linear search are that:

1. The algorithm is simple, and
2. The list need not be in any particular order

In a linear search, the search begins at the first item and continues sequentially, item by item, through the list. The pseudocode for a function performing a linear search is

> *Set a "found" flag to FALSE*
> *Set an index value to –1*
> *Begin with the first item in the list*
> *While there are still items in the list AND the "found" flag is FALSE*
>   *compare the item with the desired item*
>   *If the item was found*
>   *Set the index value to the item's position in the list*
>   *Set the "found" flag to TRUE*
>   *EndIf*
> *EndWhile*
> *Return the index value*

Notice that the function's return value indicates whether the item was found or not. If the return value is –1, the item was not in the list; otherwise, the return value provides the index of where the item is located within the list.

The function `linearSearch()` illustrates this procedure as a C function:

```
linearSearch(int list[], int size, int key)
/* this function returns the location of key in the list */
/* a -1 is returned if the value is not found            */
{
  int index, found, i;
```
(Continued on next page)

(Continued from previous page)

```
index = -1;
found = FALSE;
i = 0;
while (i < size && !found)
{
  if (list[i] == key)
  {
    found = TRUE;
    index = i;
  }
  ++i;        /* move to next item in the list */
}
return (index);
}
```

In reviewing `linearSearch()` notice that the while loop is simply used to access each element in the list, from first element to last, until a match is found with the desired item. If the desired item is located, the logical variable `found` is set to `true`, which causes the loop to terminate; otherwise, the search continues until the end of the list is encountered.

To test this function we have written a `main()` driver function to call it and display the results returned by `linearSearch()`. The complete test program is illustrated in Program 7.8.

The following are sample runs using Program 7.8.

```
Enter the item you are searching for: 101
The item was found at index location 9
```

and

```
Enter the item you are searching for: 65
The item was not found in the list
```

As has already been pointed out, an advantage of linear searches is that the list does not have to be in sorted order to perform the search. Another advantage is that if the desired item is located toward the front of the list, only a small number of comparisons are done. The worst case, of course, occurs when the desired item is at the end of the list. On average, however, and assuming that the desired item is equally likely to be anywhere within the list, the number of required comparisons are N/2, where N is the number of items in the list. Thus, for a ten-element list, the average number of comparisons needed for a linear search is five, and for a 10,000-element list, the average number of comparisons is 5,000. As we show next, this number can be significantly reduced using a binary search algorithm.

Program 7.8

```c
#include <stdio.h>
#define TRUE 1
#define FALSE 0
#define NUMEL 10

int linearSearch (int [], int, int);

int main()
{
  int nums[NUMEL] = {5,10,22,32,45,67,73,98,99,101};
  int item, location;

  printf("Enter the item you are searching for: ");
  scanf("%d", &item);

  location = linearSearch(nums, NUMEL, item);

  if (location > -1)
    printf("The item was found at index location %d\n", location);
  else
    printf("The item was not found in the list\n");

  return 0;
}

linearSearch(int list[], int size, int key)
/* this function returns the location of key in the list */
/* a -1 is returned if the value is not found            */
{
  int index, found, i;
  index = -1;
  found = FALSE;
  i = 0;
  while (i < size && !found)
  {
    if (list[i] == key)
    {
      found = TRUE;
      index = i;
    }
    ++i;      /* move to next item in the list */
  }
  return (index);
}
```

Binary Search

In a *binary search* the list must be in sorted order to begin with. Starting with an ordered list, the desired item is first compared to the element in the middle of the list (for lists with an even number of elements, either of the two middle elements can be used). Three possibilities present themselves once the comparison is made: (1) the desired item may be equal to the middle element, (2) it may be greater than the middle element, or (3) it may be less than the middle element.

In the first case the search has been successful, and no further searches are required. In the second case, because the desired item is greater than the middle element, if it is found at all, it must be in the upper part of the list. This means that the lower part of the list, consisting of all elements from the first to the midpoint element, can be discarded from any further search. In the third case, because the desired item is less than the middle element, if it is found at all, it must be found in the lower part of the list. For this case the upper part of the list, consisting of all elements from the midpoint element to the last element, can be discarded from any further search.

The algorithm for implementing this search strategy is illustrated in Figure 7.13 and defined by the following pseudocode:

> *Set a "found" flag to FALSE*
> *Set an index value to –1*
> *Set the lower index to 0*
> *Set the upper index to one less than the size of the list*
> *Begin with the first item in the list*
> *While the lower index is less than or equal to the upper index and a match is not yet found*
>   *Set the midpoint index to the integer average of the lower and upper index values*
>   *Compare the desired item to the midpoint element*
>   *If the desired element equals the midpoint element*
>   *the item has been found*
>   *Else if the desired element is greater than the midpoint element*
>   *set the lower index value to the midpoint value plus 1*
>   *Else if the desired element is less than the midpoint element*
>   *set the upper index value to the midpoint value less 1*
>   *EndIf*
> *EndWhile*
> *Return the index value*

As illustrated by both the pseudocode and the flowchart, a `while` loop is used to control the search. The initial list is defined by setting the lower index value to 0 and the upper index value to one less than the number of elements in the list. The midpoint element is then taken as the integerized average of the lower and upper values. Once the comparison to the midpoint element is made, the search is subsequently restricted by moving either the lower index to one integer value above the midpoint, or by moving the upper index one integer value below the midpoint. This process is continued until the desired element is found or the lower and upper index values become equal. The function `binarySearch()` presents the

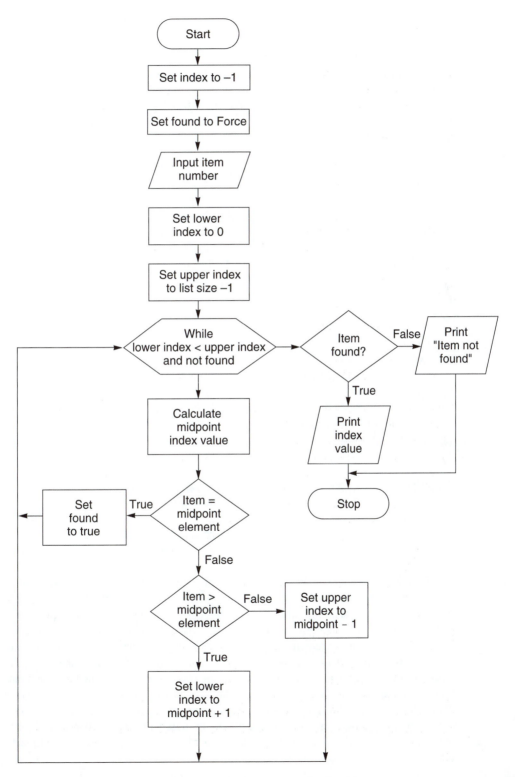

Figure 7.13   The binary search algorithm

C version of this algorithm. In this function the variables named `left` and `right` correspond to the lower and upper indices, respectively.

```
binarySearch(int list[], int size, int key)
/* this function returns the location of key in the list   */
/* a -1 is returned if the value is not found              */
{
  int index, found, left, right, midpt;

  index = -1;
  found = FALSE;
  left = 0;
  right = size -1;
  while (left <= right && !found)
  {
    midpt = (int) ((left + right) / 2);
    if (key == list[midpt])
    {
      found = TRUE;
      index = midpt;
    }
    else if (key > list[midpt])
      left = midpt + 1;
    else
      right = midpt - 1;
  }
  return (index);
}
```

For purposes of testing this function, we use Program 7.9.

A sample run using Program 7.9 yielded the following:

```
Enter the item you are searching for: 101
The item was found at index location 9
```

The value in using a binary search algorithm is that the number of elements that must be considered is cut in half each time through the `while` loop. Thus, the first time through the loop, N elements must be considered; the second time through the loop, N/2 of the elements have been eliminated and only N/2 remain. The third time through the loop, another half of the remaining elements have been eliminated and so on. In general, after p passes through the loop, the number of values remaining to be searched is $N/(2^p)$. In the worst case the search can continue until there are less than or equal to 1 element remaining to be searched. Mathematically, this can be expressed as $N/(2^p) \leq 1$. Alternatively, this may be rephrased as p is the smallest integer such that $2^p \geq N$. For example, for a 1000-element array, N is 1000 and the maximum number of passes, p, required for a binary search is 10. Table 7.1 compares the number of loop passes needed for a linear and binary search for various list sizes.

Program 7.9

```c
#include <stdio.h>
#define TRUE 1
#define FALSE 0
#define NUMEL 10

int binarySearch(int [], int, int);

int main()
{
  int nums[NUMEL] = {5,10,22,32,45,67,73,98,99,101};
  int item, location;

  printf("Enter the item you are searching for: ");
  scanf("%d", &item);
  location = binarySearch(nums, NUMEL, item);
  if (location > -1)
    printf("The item was found at index location %d\n", location);
  else
    printf("The item was not found in the array\n");

  return 0;
}

binarySearch(int list[], int size, int key)
/* this function returns the location of key in the list */
/* a -1 is returned if the value is not found            */
{
  int index, found, left, right, midpt;
  index = -1;
  found = FALSE;
  left = 0;
  right = size -1;
  while (left <= right && !found)
  {
    midpt = (int) ((left + right) / 2);
    if (key == list[midpt])
    {
      found = TRUE;
      index = midpt;
    }
    else if (key > list[midpt])
      left = midpt + 1;
    else
      right = midpt - 1;
  }
  return (index);
}
```

Table 7.1 A comparison of `while` loop passes for linear and binary searches

Array Size	10	50	500	5,000	50,000	500,000	5,000,000	50,000,000
Average Linear Search Passes	5	25	250	2,500	25,000	250,000	2,500,000	25,000,000
Maximum Linear Search Passes	10	50	500	5,000	50,000	500,000	5,000,000	50,000,000
Maximum Binary Search Passes	4	6	9	13	16	19	23	26

As illustrated in Table 7.1, the maximum number of loop passes for a fifty-item list is almost ten times more for a linear search than for binary search, and even more spectacular for larger lists. As a rule of thumb, fifty elements are usually taken as the switch-over point; for lists smaller than fifty elements linear searches are acceptable, while for larger lists a binary search algorithm should be used.

Big O Notation

On average, over a large number of linear searches with N items in a list, we expect to examine half (N/2) of the items before locating the desired item. In a binary search the maximum number of passes, p, occurs when $N/2^p = 1$. This relationship can be algebraically manipulated to $2^p = N$, which yields $p = \log_2 N$, which approximately equals $3.33 \log_{10} N$.

For example, finding a particular name in an alphabetical directory with N = 1000 names would require an average of 500 = (N/2) comparisons using a linear search. With a binary search, only about 10 ($\approx 3.33 * \log_{10} 1000$) comparisons are required.

A common way to express the number of comparisons required in any search algorithm using a list of N items is to give the order of magnitude of the number of comparisons required, on average, to locate a desired item. Thus, the linear search is said to be of order N and the binary search of order $\log_2 N$. Notationally, this is expressed as O(N) and O($\log_2 N$), where the O is read as "the order of" and the notation is called Big O notation.

Sort Algorithms

For sorting data, two major categories of sorting techniques exist, called internal and external sorts, respectively. *Internal sorts* are used when the data list is not too large and the complete list can be stored within the computer's memory, usually in an array. *External sorts* are used for much larger data sets that are stored in large external disk or tape files, and cannot be accommodated within the computer's memory as a complete unit. Here we present two internal sort algorithms. The algorithms presented are commonly used when sorting lists with less than approximately fifty elements. For larger lists more sophisticated sorting algorithms, such as the Quicksort algorithm, are typically employed.

The Selection Sort

One of the simplest sorting techniques is the selection sort. In a *selection sort,* the smallest value is initially selected from the complete list of data and exchanged with the first element in the list. After this first selection and exchange, the next smallest element in the revised list is selected and exchanged with the second element in the list. The smallest element is thus already in the first position in the list, so the second pass need consider only the second through last elements. For a list consisting of N elements, this process is repeated $N–1$ times, with each pass through the list requiring one less comparison than the previous pass.

For example, consider the list of numbers in Figure 7.14. The first pass through the initial list results in the 32 being selected and exchanged with the first element in the list. The second pass, made on the reordered list, results in the 155 being selected from the second through fifth elements. This value is then exchanged with the second element in the list. The third pass selects 307 from the third through fifth elements in the list and exchanges this value with the third element. Finally, the fourth and last pass through the list selects the remaining minimum value and exchanges it with the fourth list element. Although each pass in this example resulted in an exchange, no exchange is made in a pass if the smallest value is already in the correct location.

In pseudocode, the selection sort is described as:

Set interchange count to zero (not required; done just to keep track of the interchanges)
For each element in the list from first to next-to-last
   Find the smallest element from the current element being referenced to the last element by:
     Setting the minimum value equal to the current element
     Saving (storing) the index of the current element
     For each element in the list from the current element + 1 to the last element in the list
       If element[inner loop index] < minimum value
         Set the minimum value = element[inner loop index]
         Save the index of the new found minimum value
       EndIf
     EndFor
     Swap the current value with the new minimum value
     Increment the interchange count
EndFor
Return the interchange count

Initial List	Pass 1	Pass 2	Pass 3	Pass 4
690	32	32	32	32
307	307	155	155	155
32	690	690	307	307
155	155	307	690	426
426	426	426	426	690

Figure 7.14   A sample selection sort

The function `selectionSort()` incorporates this procedure into a C function.

```c
int selectionSort(int num[], int numel)
{
  int i, j, min, minidx, temp, moves = 0;

  for ( i = 0; i < (numel - 1); i++)
  {
    min = num[i];   /* assume minimum is first element in sublist */
    minidx = i;       /* index of minimum element */
    for(j = i + 1; j < numel; j++)
    {
      if (num[j] < min)    /* if we've located a lower value */
      {                    /* capture it */
        min = num[j];
        minidx = j;
      }
    }
    if (min < num[i])    /* check if we have a new minimum */
    {                    /* and if we do, swap values */
      temp = num[i];
      num[i] = min;
      num[minidx] = temp;
      moves++;
    }
  }
  return (moves);
}
```

The `selectionSort()` function expects two parameters, the list to be sorted and the number of elements in the list. As specified by the pseudocode, a nested set of `for` loops performs the sort. The outer `for` loop causes one less pass through the list than the total number of data items in the list. For each pass, the variable `min` is initially assigned the value `num[i]`, where `i` is the outer `for` loop's counter variable. Because `i` begins at 0 and ends at one less than `numel`, each element in the list, except the last, is successively designated as the current element.

The inner loop cycles through the elements below the current element and is used to select the next smallest value. Thus, this loop begins at the index value `i+1` and continues through the end of the list. When a new minimum is found, its value and position in the list are stored in the variables named `min` and `minidx`, respectively. Upon completion of the inner loop, an exchange is made only if a value less than that in the current position was found.

Program 7.10 was constructed for purposes of testing `selectionSort()`. This program implements a selection sort for the same list of ten numbers that was previously used to test our search algorithms. For later comparison to the other sorting algorithm that is presented, the number of actual moves made by the program to get the data into sorted order is counted and displayed.

Program 7.10

```c
#include <stdio.h>
#define NUMEL 10

int selectionSort(int [], int);

int main()
{
  int nums[NUMEL] = {22,5,67,98,45,32,101,99,73,10};
  int i, moves;

  moves = selectionSort(nums, NUMEL);

  printf("The sorted list, in ascending order, is:\n");
  for (i = 0; i < NUMEL; ++i)
    printf("%d  ",nums[i]);
  printf("\n %d moves were made to sort this list\n", moves);

  return 0;
}

int selectionSort(int num[], int numel)
{
  int i, j, min, minidx, temp, moves = 0;

  for ( i = 0; i < (numel - 1); i++)
  {
    min = num[i];   /* assume minimum is first element in sublist */
    minidx = i;      /* index of minimum element */
    for(j = i + 1; j < numel; j++)
    {
      if (num[j] < min)    /* if we've located a lower value */
      {                    /* capture it */
        min = num[j];
        minidx = j;
      }
    }
    if (min < num[i])   /* check if we have a new minimum */
    {                   /* and if we do, swap values */
      temp = num[i];
      num[i] = min;
      num[minidx] = temp;
      moves++;
    }
  }
  return (moves);
}
```

Following is the output produced by Program 7.10:

```
The sorted list, in ascending order, is:
5   10   22   32   45   67   73   98   99   101
  8 moves were made to sort this list
```

Clearly, the number of moves displayed depends on the initial order of the values in the list. An advantage of the selection sort is that the maximum number of moves that must be made is N−1, where N is the number of items in the list. Further, each one is a final move that results in an element residing in its final location in the sorted list.

A disadvantage of the selection sort is that N(N−1)/2 comparisons are always required, regardless of the initial arrangement of the data. This number of comparisons is obtained as follows: the last pass always requires one comparison, the next-to-last pass requires two comparisons, and so on, to the first pass, which requires N−1 comparisons. Thus, the total number of comparisons is

$$1 + 2 + 3 + \dots N{-}1 = N(N{-}1)/2 = N^2/2 - N/2.$$

For large values of N the N^2 dominates, and the order of the selection sort is $O(N^2)$.

An Exchange ("Bubble") Sort

In an *exchange sort,* adjacent elements of the list are exchanged with one another in such a manner that the list becomes sorted. One example of such a sequence of exchanges is provided by the bubble sort, where successive values in the list are compared, beginning with the first two elements. If the list is to be sorted in ascending (from smallest to largest) order, the smaller value of the two being compared is always placed before the larger value. For lists sorted in descending (from largest to smallest) order, the smaller of the two values being compared is always placed after the larger value.

For example, assuming that a list of values is to be sorted in ascending order, if the first element in the list is larger than the second, the two elements are interchanged. Then the second and third elements are compared. Again, if the second element is larger than the third, these two elements are interchanged. This process continues until the last two elements have been compared and exchanged, if necessary. If no exchanges were made during this initial pass through the data, the data are in the correct order and the process is finished; otherwise, a second pass is made through the data, starting from the first element and stopping at the next-to-last element. The reason for stopping at the next-to-last element on the second pass is that the first pass always results in the most positive value "sinking" to the bottom of the list.

As a specific example of this process, consider the list of numbers in Figure 7.15. The first comparison results in the interchange of the first two element values, 690 and 307. The next comparison, between elements two and three in the revised list, results in the interchange of values between the second and third elements, 690 and 32. This comparison and possible switching of adjacent values are continued until the last two elements have been compared and possibly switched. This process completes the first pass through the data and results in the largest number moving to the bottom of the list. As the

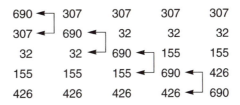

Figure 7.15   First pass of an exchange sort

largest value sinks to its resting place at the bottom of the list, the smaller elements slowly rise, or "bubble," to the top of the list. As a result, the exchange sort is also sometimes called a *bubble sort.*

Because the first pass through the list ensures that the largest value always moves to the bottom of the list, the second pass stops at the next-to-last element. This process continues with each pass stopping at one higher element than the previous pass, until either N–1 passes through the list have been completed or no exchanges are necessary in any single pass. In both cases the resulting list is in sorted order. The pseudocode describing this sort is

Set interchange count to zero (not required; done just to keep track of the interchanges)
For the first element in the list to one less than the last element (i index)
    For the second element in the list to the last element (j index)
    If num[j] < num[j – 1]
    {
        Swap num[j] with num[j – 1]
        Increment interchange count
    }
    EndFor
EndFor
Return interchange count

This sort algorithm is coded in C as the function `bubbleSort()`, and is tested in Program 7.11. This program tests `bubbleSort()` with the same list of ten numbers used in Program 7.10 to test `selectionSort()`. For comparison to the earlier selection sort, the number of adjacent moves (exchanges) made by `bubbleSort()` is also counted and displayed.

Following is the output produced by Program 7.11.

```
The sorted list, in ascending order, is:
5  10  22  32  45  67  73  98  99  101
 18 moves were made to sort this list
```

As with the selection sort, the number of comparisons using a bubble sort is O(N²), and the number of required moves depends on the initial order of the values in the list. In the worst case, when the data are in reverse sorted order, the selection sort performs better

Program 7.11

```c
#include <stdio.h>
#define NUMEL 10

int bubbleSort(int [], int);

int main()
{
  int nums[NUMEL] = {22,5,67,98,45,32,101,99,73,10};
  int i, moves;

  moves = bubbleSort(nums, NUMEL);

  printf("The sorted list, in ascending order, is:\n");
  for (i = 0; i < NUMEL; ++i)
    printf("%d  ",nums[i]);
  printf("\n %d moves were made to sort this list\n", moves);

  return 0;
}

int bubbleSort(int num[],int numel)
{
  int i, j, temp, moves = 0;

  for ( i = 0; i < (numel - 1); i++)
  {
    for(j = 1; j < numel; j++)
    {
      if (num[j] < num[j-1])
      {
       temp = num[j];
       num[j] = num[j-1];
       num[j-1] = temp;
       moves++;
      }
    }
  }
  return (moves);
}
```

than the bubble sort. Here, both sorts require N(N–1)/2 comparisons, but the selection sort needs only N–1 moves while the exchange sort needs N(N–1)/2 moves. The additional moves required by the exchange sort result from the intermediate exchanges between adjacent elements to "settle" each element into its final position. In this regard, the selection sort is superior because no intermediate moves are necessary. For random data, such as those used in Programs 7.10 and 7.11, the selection sort generally performs as well as or better than the bubble sort.

A modification to the bubble sort that causes the sort to terminate whenever no exchanges have been made in a pass, which indicates that the list is in order, can make the bubble sort operate as an O(N) sort in specialized cases.

Arrays, Addresses, and Pointers

There is a direct and intimate relationship among arrays, addresses, and pointers. In fact, generally unknown to programmers of other high-level languages, addresses run rampant throughout the executable versions of their programs. These addresses are used by the program to keep track of where data and instructions are kept.

One of C's advantages is that it allows the programmer access to the addresses used by a program. Although we have already used addresses in calling the scanf() function and in passing arguments by reference, the real power of pointers is in dealing with arrays, strings, and other data structure elements. In this chapter we explore the exceptionally strong connection that exists among arrays, addresses, and pointers. The programming techniques learned in this chapter are then extended in the following chapters on strings and data structures.

8.1 Array Names as Pointers

Although pointers are simply, by definition, variables and parameters used to store addresses, they are closely associated with array names. In this section we describe this association in detail.

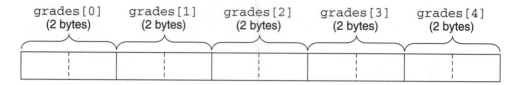

Figure 8.1   The grades array in storage

Figure 8.1 illustrates the storage of a single-dimensional array named grades, which contains five integers. Assume that each integer requires two bytes of storage.

Using subscripts, the fourth integer stored in the grades array is referred to as grades[3]. The use of a subscript, however, conceals the extensive use of addresses by the computer. Internally, the computer immediately uses the subscript to calculate the address of the desired element based on both the starting address of the array and the amount of storage used by each element of the array. Calling the fourth stored integer grades[3] forces the computer, internally, into the address computation (assuming 2 bytes for each integer)

&grades[3] = &grades[0] + (3 * 2)

Remembering that the address operator, &, means "the address of," this last statement is read "the address of grades[3] equals the address of grades[0] plus 6." Figure 8.2 illustrates the address computation used to locate grades[3], assuming two bytes of storage for each integer element in the array.

Recall that a pointer is a variable used to store addresses. If we create a pointer to store the address of the first integer stored in the grades array, we can mimic the operation used by the computer to access the array elements. Before we do this, let us first consider Program 8.1.

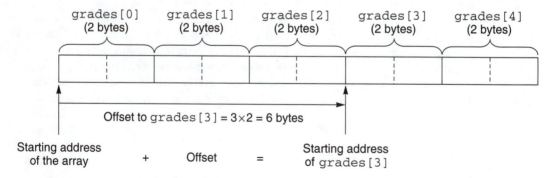

Figure 8.2   Using a subscript to obtain an address

Program 8.1

```
#include <stdio.h>
int main()
{
  int i;
  int grades[] = {98, 87, 92, 79, 85};

  for (i = 0; i <= 4; ++i)
    printf("\nElement %d is %d", i, grades [i]);

  return 0;
}
```

When Program 8.1 is run, the following display is obtained:

```
Element 0 is 98
Element 1 is 87
Element 2 is 92
Element 3 is 79
Element 4 is 85
```

Program 8.1 displays the values of the array `grades` using standard subscript nota-tion. Now, let us store the address of array element 0 in a pointer. Then, using the indirection operator, `*`, we can use the address in the pointer to access each array element. For example, if we store the address of `grades[0]` into a pointer named `gPtr` (using the assignment statement `gPtr = &grades[0];`), then, as illustrated in Figure 8.3, the expression `*gPtr`, which means "the variable pointed to by `gPtr`," references `grades[0]`.

One unique feature of pointers is that *offsets* may be included in expressions using pointers. For example, the 1 in the expression `*(gPtr + 1)` is an offset. The complete

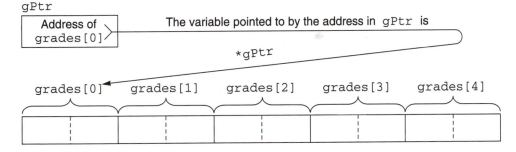

Figure 8.3 The variable pointed to by `*gPtr` is `grades[0]`

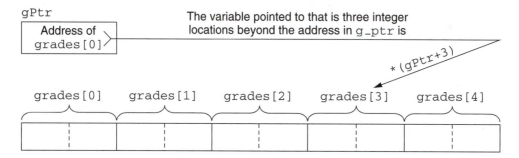

Figure 8.4 An offset of three from the address in `gPtr`

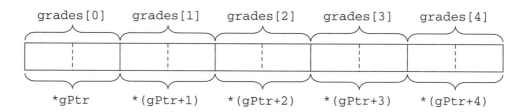

Figure 8.5 The relationship between array elements and pointers

expression accesses the integer variable that is one beyond the integer pointed to by `gPtr`.[1] Similarly, as illustrated in Figure 8.4, the expression `* (gPtr + 3)` references the variable that is three integers beyond the variable pointed to by `gPtr`. This is the variable `grades[3]`.

Table 8.1 lists the complete correspondence between elements referenced by subscripts and by pointers and offsets. The relationships listed in Table 8.1 are illustrated in Figure 8.5.

Using the correspondence between pointers and subscripts illustrated in Figure 8.5, the array elements previously accessed in Program 8.1 using subscripts can now be accessed using pointers. This is done in Program 8.2.

---

[1] The offset tells the number of variables that are to be skipped over. The correspondence between the number of bytes and number of variables is handled by the compiler.

Table 8.1 Array elements may be accessed in two ways

Array Element	Subscript Notation	Pointer Notation
Element 0	grades[0]	*gPtr
Element 1	grades[1]	*(gPtr + 1)
Element 2	grades[2]	*(gPtr + 2)
Element 3	grades[3]	*(gPtr + 3)
Element 4	grades[4]	*(gPtr + 4)

Program 8.2

```
#include <stdio.h>
int main()
{
  int *gPtr;              /* declare a pointer to an int */
  int i;
  int grades[] = {98, 87, 92, 79, 85};

  gPtr = &grades[0];      /* store the starting array address */
  for (i = 0; i <= 4; ++i)
    printf("\nElement %d is %d", i, *(gPtr + i) );

  return 0;
}
```

The following display is obtained when Program 8.2 is run:

```
Element 0 is 98
Element 1 is 87
Element 2 is 92
Element 3 is 79
Element 4 is 85
```

Notice that this is the same display produced by Program 8.1.

The method used in Program 8.2 to access *individual* array elements simulates how the computer internally accesses *all* array elements. Any subscript used by a programmer is automatically converted to an equivalent pointer expression by the computer. In our case, because the declaration of gPtr included the information that integers are pointed to, any offset added to the address in gPtr is automatically scaled by the size of an integer. Thus,

`* (gPtr + 3)`, for example, refers to the address of `grades[0]` plus an offset of six bytes (`3 * 2`). This is the address of `grades[3]` illustrated in Figure 8.2.

The parentheses in the expression `* (gPtr + 3)` are necessary to access the desired array element correctly. Omitting the parentheses results in the expression `*gPtr + 3`. This expression adds 3 to "the variable pointed to by `gPtr`." Since `gPtr` points to `grades[0]`, this expression adds the value of `grades[0]` and 3 together. Note also that the expression `* (gPtr + 3)` does not change the address stored in `gPtr`. Once the computer uses the offset to locate the correct variable from the starting address in `gPtr`, the offset is discarded and the address in `gPtr` remains unchanged.

Although the pointer `gPtr` used in Program 8.2 was specifically created to store the starting address of the `grades` array, this was, in fact, unnecessary. When an array is created, the compiler automatically creates an internal *pointer constant* for it and stores the starting address of the array in this pointer. In almost all respects, a pointer constant is identical to a pointer variable created by a programmer; but as we shall see, there are some differences.

For each array created, the name of the array becomes the name of the pointer constant created by the compiler for the array, and the starting address of the first location reserved for the array is stored in this pointer. Thus, declaring the `grades` array in Programs 8.1 and 8.2 actually reserved enough storage for five integers, created an internal pointer named `grades`, and stored the address of `grades[0]` in the pointer. This is illustrated in Figure 8.6.

The implication is that every access to `grades` using a subscript can be replaced by an equivalent access using `grades` as a pointer. Thus, wherever the expression `grades[i]` is used, the expression `* (grades + i)` can also be used. This is illustrated in Program 8.3, where `grades` is used as a pointer to access all of its elements.

Program 8.3 produces the same output as Program 8.1 and Program 8.2. However, using `grades` as a pointer made it unnecessary to declare and initialize the pointer `gPtr` used in Program 8.2.

```
grades
```
```
&grades[0]
```

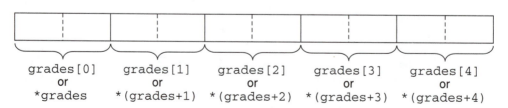

| grades[0] or *grades | grades[1] or * (grades+1) | grades[2] or * (grades+2) | grades[3] or * (grades+3) | grades[4] or * (grades+4) |

Figure 8.6 Creating an array also creates a pointer

Program 8.3

```
#include <stdio.h>
int main()
{
  int i;
  int grades[] = {98, 87, 92, 79, 85};

  for (i = 0; i <= 4; ++i)
    printf("\nElement %d is %d", i, *(grades + i) );

  return 0;
}
```

In most respects an array name and pointer can be used interchangeably. *A true pointer, however, is a variable, and the address stored in it can be changed. An array name is a pointer constant, and the address stored in the pointer cannot be changed by an assignment statement.* Thus, a statement such as grades = &grades[2]; is invalid. This should come as no surprise. Since the whole purpose of an array name is to correctly locate the beginning of the array, allowing a programmer to change the address stored in the array name would defeat this purpose and lead to havoc whenever array elements were referenced. Also, expressions taking the address of an array name are invalid because the pointer created by the compiler is internal to the computer, not stored in memory, as are pointer variables. Thus, trying to store the address of grades using the expression &grades results in a compiler error.

An interesting sidelight to the observation that elements of an array can be accessed using pointers is that a pointer access can always be replaced using subscript notation. For example, if numPtr is declared as a pointer variable, the expression *(numPtr + i) can also be written as numPtr[i]. This is true even though numPtr is not created as an array. As before, when the compiler encounters the subscript notation, it replaces it internally with the pointer notation.

Exercises 8.1

1. Replace each of the following references to a subscripted variable with a pointer reference.

a. prices[5]
b. grades[2]
c. yield[10]
d. dist[9]
e. mile[0]
f. temp[20]
g. celsius[16]
h. num[50]
i. time[12]

2. Replace each of the following references using a pointer with a subscript reference.

message[6]

a. *(message + 6)
b. *amount
c. *(yrs + 10)
d. *(stocks + 2)
e. *(rates + 15)
f. *(codes + 19)

3. a. List the three things that the declaration statement `doubleprices[5];` causes the compiler to do.

    b. If each double precision number uses four bytes of storage, how much storage is set aside for the `prices` array?

    c. Draw a diagram similar to Figure 8.6 for the `prices` array.

    d. Determine the byte offset relative to the start of the `prices` array corresponding to the offset in the expression `*(prices + 3)`.

4. a. Write a declaration to store the string `"This is a sample"` into an array named `samtest`. Include the declaration in a program that displays the values in `samtest` in a `for` loop that uses a pointer to access each element in the array.

    b. Modify the program written in Exercise 4a to display only array elements 10 through 15 (these are the letters *s, a, m, p, l,* and *e*).

5. Write a declaration to store the following values into a static array named `rates`: 12.9, 18.6, 11.4, 13.7, 9.5, 15.2, 17.6. Include the declaration in a program that displays the values in the array using pointer notation.

6. Repeat Exercise 6 in Section 7.2, but use pointer references to access all array elements.

7. Repeat Exercise 7 in Section 7.2, but use pointer references to access all array elements.

8.2 Pointer Arithmetic

Pointer variables, like all variables, contain values. The value stored in a pointer is, of course, an address. Thus, by adding and subtracting numbers to pointers we can obtain different addresses. Additionally, the addresses in pointers can be compared using any of the relational operators (`==`, `!=`, `<`, `>`, etc.) that are valid for comparing other variables. In performing arithmetic on pointers we must be careful to produce addresses that point to something meaningful. In comparing pointers, we must also make comparisons that make sense. Consider the declarations:

```
int nums[100];
int *nPtr;
```

To set the address of `nums[0]` into `nPtr`, either of the following two assignment statements can be used:

```
nPtr = &nums[0];
nPtr = nums;
```

The two assignment statements produce the same result because `nums` is a pointer constant that itself contains the address of the first location in the array. This is, of course, the address of `nums[0]`. Figure 8.7 illustrates the allocation of memory resulting from the previous declaration and assignment statements, assuming that each integer requires two bytes of memory and that the location of the beginning of the `nums` array is at address 18934.

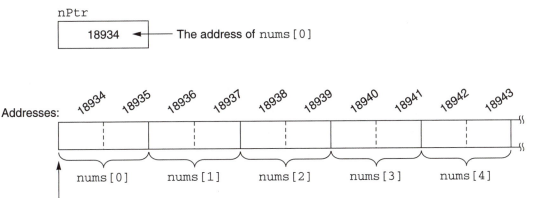

Figure 8.7   The nums array in memory

Once nPtr contains a valid address, values can be added to and subtracted from the address to produce new addresses. When adding or subtracting numbers to pointers, the computer automatically adjusts the number to ensure that the result still "points to" a value of the correct type. For example, the statement nPtr = nPtr + 4; forces the computer to scale the 4 by the correct number to ensure that the resulting address is the address of an integer. Assuming that each integer requires two bytes of storage, as illustrated in Figure 8.7, the computer multiplies 4 by two and then adds the calculated value of eight to the address in nPtr. The resulting address is 18942, which is the correct address of nums [4].

This automatic scaling by the computer ensures that the expression nPtr + i, where i is any positive integer, correctly points to the *i*th element beyond the one currently being pointed to by nPtr. Thus, if nPtr initially contains the address of nums [0], nPtr + 4 is the address of nums [4], nPtr + 50 is the address of nums [50], and nPtr + i is the address of nums [i]. Although we have used actual addresses in Figure 8.7 to illustrate the scaling process, the programmer need never know or care about the actual addresses used by the computer. The manipulation of addresses using pointers generally does not require knowledge of the actual address.

Addresses can also be incremented or decremented using both prefix and postfix increment and decrement operators. Adding 1 to a pointer causes the pointer to point to the next element of the type being pointed to. Decrementing a pointer causes the pointer to point to the previous element. For example, if the pointer variable p is a pointer to an integer, the expression p++ causes the address in the pointer to be incremented to point to the next integer. This is illustrated in Figure 8.8.

In reviewing Figure 8.8, notice that the increment added to the pointer is correctly scaled to account for the fact that the pointer is used to point to integers. It is, of course, up to the programmer to ensure that the correct type of data is stored in the new address contained in the pointer.

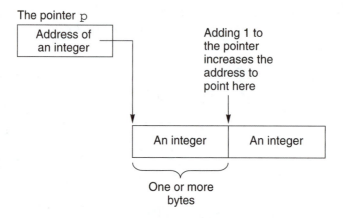

Figure 8.8 Increments are scaled when used with pointers

The increment and decrement operators can be applied as both prefix and postfix pointer operators. All of the following combinations using pointers are valid:

```
*ptNum**       /* use the pointer and then increment it */
*++ptNum       /* increment the pointer before using it */
*ptNum--       /* use the pointer and then decrement it */
*--ptNum       /* decrement the pointer before using it */
```

Of the four possible forms, the most commonly used is the *ptNum++. This is because such an expression allows each element in an array to be accessed as the address is "marched along" from the starting address of the array to the address of the last array element. To see the use of the increment operator, consider Program 8.4. In this program each element in the nums array is retrieved by successively incrementing the address in nPtr.

Program 8.4

```c
#include <stdio.h>
int main()
{
  int nums[5] = {16, 54, 7, 43, -5};
  int i, total = 0, *nPtr;

  nPtr = nums;     /* store address of nums[0] in nPtr */
  for (i = 0; i <= 4; ++i)
    total = total + *nPtr++;
  printf("The total of the array elements is %d", total);

  return 0;
}
```

The output produced by Program 8.4 is

```
The total of the array elements is 115
```

The expression `total = total + *nPtr++` used in Program 8.4 is a standard accumulating expression. Within this expression, the term `*nPtr++` first causes the program to retrieve the integer pointed to by `nPtr`. This is done by the `*nPtr` part of the term. The postfix increment, `++`, then adds one to the address in `nPtr` so that `nPtr` now contains the address of the next array element. The increment is, of course, scaled by the compiler so that the actual address in `nPtr` is the correct address of the next element.

Pointers may also be compared. This is particularly useful when dealing with pointers used to access elements in the same array. For example, rather than using a counter in a `for` loop to correctly access each element in an array, the address in a pointer can be compared to the starting and ending address of the array itself. The expression

```
nPtr <= &nums[4]
```

is true (nonzero) as long as the address in `nPtr` is less than or equal to the address of `nums[4]`. Because `nums` is a pointer constant that contains the address of `nums[0]`, the term `&nums[4]` can be replaced by the equivalent term `nums + 4`. Using either of these forms, Program 8.4 can be rewritten as Program 8.5 to continue adding array elements while the address in `nPtr` is less than or equal to the address of the last array element.

 Program 8.5

```c
#include <stdio.h>
int main()
{
  int nums[5] = {16, 54, 7, 43, -5};
  int total = 0, *nPtr;

  nPtr = nums;     /* store address of nums[0] in nPtr */

  while (nPtr <= nums + 4)
    total += *nPtr++;

  printf("The total of the array elements is %d", total);

  return 0;
}
```

Notice that in Program 8.5 the compact form of the accumulating expression, `total += *nPtr++`, was used in place of the longer form, `total = total + *nPtr++`. Also, the expression `nums + 4` does not change the address in `nums`. Because `nums` is an array name and not a pointer variable, its value cannot be changed. The expression nums + 4 first retrieves the address in nums, adds 4 to this address (appropriately scaled) and uses the result for comparison purposes. Expressions such as *nums++, which attempt to change the address, are invalid. Expressions such as *nums or *(nums + i), which use the address without attempting to alter it, are valid.

Pointer Initialization

Like all variables, pointers can be initialized when they are declared. When initializing pointers, however, you must be careful to set an address in the pointer. For example, an initialization such as

```
int *ptNum = &miles;
```

is only valid if miles itself is declared as an integer variable before ptNum is declared. Here we are creating a pointer to an integer and setting the address in the pointer to the address of an integer variable. If the variable miles is declared after ptNum is declared, as follows,

```
int *ptNum = &miles;
int miles;
```

an error occurs. This is because the address of miles is used before miles has even been defined. Since the storage area reserved for miles has not been allocated when ptNum is declared, the address of miles does not yet exist.

Pointers to arrays can be initialized within their declaration statements. For example, if prices has been declared as an array of floating point numbers, either of the following two declarations can be used to initialize the pointer named zing to the address of the first element in prices:

```
float *zing = &prices[0];
float *zing = prices;
```

The last initialization is correct because prices is itself a pointer constant containing an address of the proper type. (The variable name zing was selected in this example to reinforce the idea that any variable name can be selected for a pointer.)

Exercises 8.2

1. Replace the while statement in Program 8.5 with a for statement.

2. a. Write a C program that stores the following numbers in an array named rates: 6.25, 6.50, 6.8, 7.2, 7.35, 7.5, 7.65, 7.8, 8.2, 8.4, 8.6, 8.8, 9.0. Display the values in the array by changing the address in a pointer called dispPt. Use a for statement in your program.
   b. Modify the program written in Exercise 2a to use a while statement.

3. a. Write a program that stores the string `Hooray for All of Us` into an array named `strng`. Use the declaration `char strng[] = "Hooray for All of Us";`, which ensures that the end-of-string escape sequence `\0` is included in the array. Display the characters in the array by changing the address in a pointer called `messPtr`. Use a `for` statement in your program.

  b. Modify the program written in Exercise 3a to use the `while` statement `while (*messPtr++ != '\0')`.

  c. Modify the program written in Exercise 3a to start the display with the word `All`.

4. Write a C program that stores the following numbers in the array named `miles`: 15, 22, 16, 18, 27, 23, 20. Have your program copy the data stored in `miles` to another array named `dist` and then display the values in the `dist` array.

5. Write a program that stores the following letters in the array named `message`: `This is a test`. Have your program copy the data stored in `message` to another array named `mess2` and then display the letters in the `mess2` array.

6. Write a program that declares three single-dimensional arrays named `miles`, `gallons`, and `mpg`. Each array should be capable of holding ten elements. In the `miles` array store the numbers 240.5, 300.0, 189.6, 310.6, 280.7, 216.9, 199.4, 160.3, 177.4, 192.3. In the `gallons` array store the numbers 10.3, 15.6, 8.7, 14, 16.3, 15.7, 14.9, 10.7, 8.3, 8.4. Each element of the `mpg` array should be calculated as the corresponding element to the `miles` array divided by the equivalent element of the `gallons` array; for example, `mpg[0] = miles[0]/gallons[0]`. Use pointers when calculating and displaying the elements of the `mpg` array.

8.3 Passing and Using Array Addresses

When an array is passed to a function, this address is the only item actually passed. By this we mean the address of the first location used to store the array, as illustrated in Figure 8.9. Since the first location reserved for an array corresponds to element 0 of the array, the "address of the array" is also the address of element 0.

For a specific example in which an array is passed to a function, let us consider Program 8.6. In this program, the `nums` array is passed to the `findMax()` function using conventional array notation.

The output displayed when Program 8.6 is executed is

```
The maximum value is 27
```

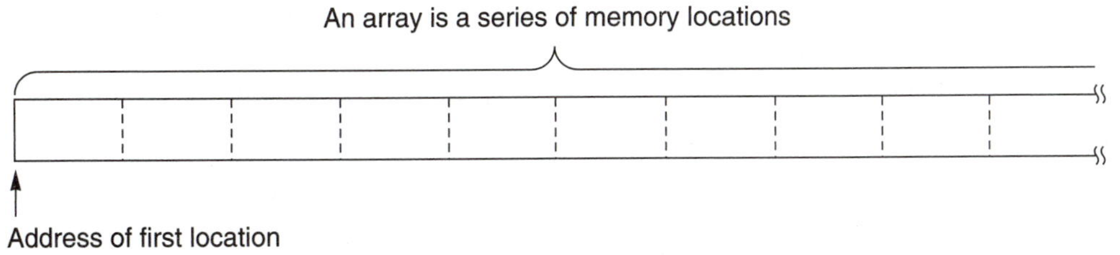

An array is a series of memory locations

Address of first location

Figure 8.9   The address of an array is the address of the first location reserved for the array

Program 8.6

```c
#include <stdio.h>

int findMax(int[], int);   /* prototype */

int main()
{
  int nums[5] = {2, 18, 1, 27, 16};

  printf("The maximum value is %d", findMax(nums,5));

  return 0;
}

int findMax(int vals[], int numEls)   /* find the maximum value */
{
  int i, max = vals[0];

  for (i = 1; i < numEls; ++i)
   if (max < vals[i])
     max = vals[i];

  return (max);
}
```

The parameter named `vals` in the header line for `findMax()` actually receives the address of the array `nums`. Hence, `vals` is really a pointer, because pointers are variables (or parameters) used to store addresses. Because the address passed into `findMax()` is the address of an integer, another suitable header line for `findMax()` is:

```c
findMax(int *vals, int numEls) /* vals declared as a pointer to an integer */
```

The declaration `int *vals` in the header line declares that `vals` is used to store an address of an integer. The address stored is, of course, the location of the beginning of an array. The following is a rewritten version of the `findMax()` function that uses the new pointer declaration for `vals` but retains the use of subscripts to refer to individual array elements:

```c
int findMax(int *vals, int numEls)     /* find the maximum value */
                      /* vals declared as a pointer to an integer */
  {
    int i, max = vals[0];
```

(Continued on next page)

(Continued from previous page)

```
  for (i = 1; i < numEls; ++i)
    if (max < vals[i])
      max = vals[i];

  return(max);
}
```

One further observation needs to be made. Regardless of how `vals` is declared in the function header or how it is used within the function body, it is truly a pointer parameter. Thus, the address in `vals` may be modified. This is not true for the name `nums`. Since `nums` is the name of the originally created array, it is a pointer constant. As described in Section 8.1, this means that the address in `nums` cannot be changed and that the expression `&nums` is invalid. No such restrictions, however, apply to the pointer parameter named `vals`. All the address arithmetic that we learned in the previous section can be legitimately applied to `vals`.

We shall write two additional versions of `findMax()`, both using pointers instead of subscripts. In the first version we simply substitute pointer notation for subscript notation. In the second version we use address arithmetic to change the address in the pointer.

As previously stated, a reference to an array element using the subscript notation `arrayName[i]` can always be replaced by the pointer notation `*(arrayName + i)`. In our first modification to `findMax()`, we make use of this correspondence by simply replacing all notations of the form `vals[i]` with the equivalent notation `*(vals + i)`.

```
int findMax(int *vals, int numEls)     /* find the maximum value */
                    /* vals declared as a pointer to an integer */
{
  int i, max = *vals;

  for (i = 1; i < numEls; ++i)
    if (max < *(vals + i) )
      max = *(vals + i);

  return(max);
}
```

Our second version of `findMax()` makes use of the fact that the address stored in `vals` can be changed. After each array element is retrieved using the address in `vals`, the address itself is incremented by 1 in the altering list of the `for` statement. The expression `*vals++` used initially to set `max` to the value of `vals[0]` also adjusts the address in `vals` to point to the second integer stored in the array. The element obtained from this expression is the array element pointed to by `vals` before `vals` is incremented. The postfix increment, `++`, does not change the address in `vals` until after the address has been used to retrieve the first integer in the array.

```
int findMax(int *vals, int numEls)    /* find the maximum value */
                                       /* vals declared as a pointer */
{
    int i, max = *vals++;    /* get the first element and increment */

    for (i = 1; i < numEls; ++i, ++vals)
        if (max < *vals)
            max = *vals;
    return(max);
}
```

Let us review this version of findMax(). Initially the maximum value is set to "the thing pointed to by vals." Since vals initially contains the address of the zeroth element in the array passed to findMax(), the value of this initial element is stored in max.

The address in vals is then incremented by 1. The 1 that is added to vals is automatically scaled by the number of bytes used to store integers. Thus, after the increment, the address stored in vals is the address of the next array element. This is illustrated in Figure 8.10. The value of this next element is compared to the maximum, and the address is again incremented, this time from within the altering list of the for statement. This process continues until all the array elements have been examined.

The version of findMax() that appeals to you is a matter of personal style and taste. Generally, beginning programmers feel more at ease using subscripts than using pointers. Also, if the program uses an array as the natural storage structure for the application and data at hand, an array access using subscripts is more appropriate to clearly indicate the intent of the program. However, as we learn about strings and data structures, the use of pointers becomes an increasingly useful and powerful tool in its own right. In other situations, such as the dynamic allocation of memory (see Section 10.5), there is no simple or easy equivalence using subscripts.

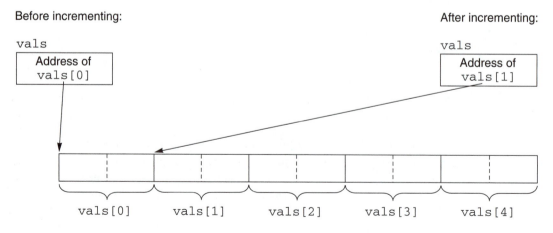

Figure 8.10   Pointing to different elements

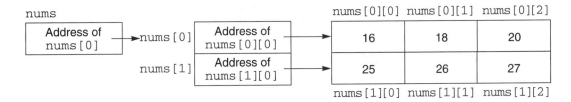

Figure 8.11   Storage of the nums array and associated pointer constants

One further "neat trick" can be gleaned from our discussion. Because passing an array to a function really involves passing an address, we can just as well pass any valid address. For example, the function call

```
findMax(&nums[2],3)
```

passes the address of nums [2] to findMax (). Within findMax () the pointer vals stores the address and the function starts the search for a maximum at the element corresponding to this address. Thus, from findMax ()'s perspective, it has received an address and proceeds appropriately.

Advanced Pointer Notation[2]

Access to multidimensional arrays can also be made using pointer notation, although the notation becomes more and more cryptic as the array dimensions increase. An extremely useful application of this notation occurs with two-dimensional character arrays, one of the topics in the next chapter. Here we consider pointer notation for two-dimensional numeric arrays. For example, consider the declaration

```
int nums[2][3] = { {16,18,20},
                   {25,26,27} };
```

This declaration creates an array of elements and a set of pointer constants named nums, nums [0], and nums [1]. The relationship between these pointer constants and the elements of the nums array is illustrated in Figure 8.11.

The availability of the pointer constants associated with a two-dimensional array allows us to access array elements in a variety of ways. One way is to consider the two-dimensional array as an array of rows, where each row is itself an array of three elements. Considered in this light, the address of the first element in the first row is provided by nums [0] and the address of the first element in the second row is provided by nums [1]. Thus, the variable pointed to by nums [0] is nums [0] [0] and the variable pointed to by nums [1] is nums [1] [0]. Once the nature of these

---

[2] This topic may be omitted with no loss of subject continuity.

constants is understood, each element in the array can be accessed by applying an appropriate offset to the appropriate pointer. Thus, the following notations are equivalent:

Pointer Notation	Subscript Notation	Value
`*nums[0]`	`nums[0][0]`	16
`*(nums[0] + 1)`	`nums[0][1]`	18
`*(nums[0] + 2)`	`nums[0][2]`	20
`*nums[1]`	`nums[1][0]`	25
`*(nums[1] + 1)`	`nums[1][1]`	26
`*(nums[1] + 2)`	`nums[1][2]`	27

We can now go even further and replace `nums[0]` and `nums[1]` with their respective pointer notations, using the address of `nums` itself. As illustrated in Figure 8.11, the variable pointed to by `nums` is `nums[0]`. That is, `*nums` is `nums[0]`. Similarly, `*(nums + 1)` is `nums[1]`. Using these relationships leads to the following equivalences:

Pointer Notation	Subscript Notation	Value
`*(*nums)`	`nums[0][0]`	16
`*(*nums + 1)`	`nums[0][1]`	18
`*(*nums + 2)`	`nums[0][2]`	20
`*(*(nums + 1))`	`nums[1][0]`	25
`*(*(nums + 1) + 1)`	`nums[1][1]`	26
`*(*(nums + 1) + 2)`	`nums[1][2]`	27

The same notation applies when a two-dimensional array is passed to a function. For example, assume that the two-dimensional array `nums` is passed to the function `calc()` using the call `calc(nums);`. Here, as with all array arguments, an address is passed. A suitable function header for the function `calc()` is

```
calc(int pt[2][3])
```

As we have already seen, the parameter declaration for `pt` can also be

```
int pt[][3]
```

Using pointer notation, another suitable declaration is

```
int (*pt)[3]
```

In this last declaration, the parentheses are required to create a single pointer to objects of three integers. Each object is, of course, equivalent to a single row of the nums array. By suitably offsetting the pointer, each element in the array can be accessed. Notice that without the parentheses the parameter declaration becomes

```
int *pt[3]
```

which creates an array of three pointers, each one pointing to a single integer.

Once the correct declaration for pt is made (any of the three valid declarations), the following notations within the function calc() are all equivalent:

Pointer Notation	Subscript Notation	Value
*(*pt)	pt[0][0]	16
*(*pt+1)	pt[0][1]	18
*(*pt+2)	pt[0][2]	20
((pt+1))	pt[1][0]	25
((pt+1)+1)	pt[1][1]	26
((pt+1)+2)	pt[1][2]	27

The last two notations using pointers are encountered in more advanced C programs. The first of these occurs because functions can return any valid C scalar data type, including pointers to any of these data types. If a function returns a pointer, the data type being pointed to must be declared in the function's header header line and prototype. For example, the header line

```
int *calc()
```

declares that calc() returns a pointer to an integer value. This means that *an address* of an integer variable is returned. Similarly, the header line

```
float *taxes()
```

declares that taxes() returns a pointer to a floating point value. This means that *an address* of a floating point variable is returned.

In addition to declaring pointers to integers, floating point numbers, and C's other data types, pointers can also be declared that point to (contain the address of) a function. Pointers to functions are possible because function names, like array names, are themselves pointer constants. For example, the header line

```
int (*calc)()
```

declares calc to be a pointer to a function that returns an integer. This means that calc contains the address of a function, and the function whose address is in the variable calc returns an integer value. If, for example, the function `sum()` returns an integer, the assignment `calc = sum;` is valid.

Exercises 8.3

1. The following declaration was used to create the `prices` array:

```
double prices[500];
```

Write three different header lines for a function named `sortArray()` that accepts the `prices` array as a parameter named `inArray` and returns no value.

2. The following declaration was used to create the `keys` array:

```
char keys[256];
```

Write three different header lines for a function named `findKey()` that accepts the `keys` array as a parameter named `select` and returns no value.

3. The following declaration was used to create the `rates` array:

```
float rates[256];
```

Write three different header lines for a function named `prime()` that accepts the `rates` array as a parameter named `rates` and returns a `float`.

4. Modify the `findMax()` function to locate the minimum value of the passed array. Write the function using only pointers and rename the function `findMin()`.

5. In the last version of `findMax()` presented, `vals` was incremented inside the altering list of the `for` statement. Instead, suppose that the incrementing was done within the condition expression of the `if` statement as follows:

```
int findMax(int *vals, int numEls)      /* incorrect version      */
                                        /* vals declared as a pointer */
{
  int i, max = *vals++;    /* get the first element and increment */

  for (i = 1; i < numEls; ++i)
    if (max < *vals++)
      max = *vals;
  return (max);
}
```

This version produces an incorrect result. Determine why.

6. a. Write a C program that has a declaration in `main()` to store the following numbers into an array named `rates`: 6.5, 7.2, 7.5, 8.3, 8.6, 9.4, 9.6, 9.8, 10.0. There should be a function

call to show() that accepts rates in a parameter named rates and then displays the numbers using the pointer notation * (rates + i).

   b. Modify the show() function written in Exercise 6a to alter the address in rates. Use the expression *rates rather than * (rates + i) to retrieve the correct element.

7. a. Write a C program that has a declaration in main() to store the string "Vacation is near" into an array named message. There should be a function call to display() that accepts message in a parameter named strng and then displays the message using the pointer notation * (strng + i).

   b. Modify the display() function written in Exercise 7a to alter the address in message. Use the expression *strng rather than * (strng + i) to retrieve the correct element.

8. Write a C program that declares three single-dimensional arrays named price, quantity, and amount. Each array should be declared in main() and be capable of holding ten double precision numbers. The numbers to be stored in price are 10.62, 14.89, 13.21, 16.55, 18.62, 9.47, 6.58, 18.32, 12.15, 3.98. The numbers to be stored in quantity are 4, 8.5, 6, 7.35, 9, 15.3, 3, 5.4, 2.9, 4.8. Have your program pass these three arrays to a function called extend(), which calculates the elements in the amount array as the product of the equivalent elements in the price and quantity arrays (for example, amount[1] = price[1] * quantity[1]). After extend() has put values into the amount array, display the values in the array from within main(). Write the extend() function using pointers.

9. a. Determine the output of the following program:

```
#include <stdio.h>

void arr(int[][3]);

int main()
{
  int nums[2][3] + { {33,16,29},
                     {54,67,99}};

   arr(nums);
return 0;
}

void arr(int (*val)[3])
{
    printf("\n %d",*(*val) );
    printf("\n %d",*(*val + 1) );
    printf("\n %d",*(*(val + 1) + 2) );
    printf("\n %d",*(*val) + 1 );

   return;
}
```

   b. Given the declaration for val in the arr() function, would the notation val[1][2] be valid within the function?

8.4   Common Programming Errors

A common programming error occurs when pointers are used to reference nonexistent array elements. For example, if nums is an array of ten integers, the expression * (nums + 15) points to a location six integer locations beyond the last element of the array. As C does not do any bounds checking on array references, this type of error is not caught by the compiler. This is the same error as using a subscript to access an out-of-bounds array element disguised in its pointer notation form.

The remaining errors are not specific to pointers used for array accesses, but are common whenever pointer notation is used. These errors result from incorrect use of the address and indirection operators. For example, if pt is a pointer variable, the expressions

```
pt + &45
pt + &(miles + 10)
```

are both invalid because they attempt to take the address of a value. Notice that the expression pt = &miles + 10, however, is valid. Here, 10 is added to the address of miles. Again, it is the programmer's responsibility to ensure that the final address "points to" a valid data element.

Addresses of pointer constants cannot be taken. For example, given the declarations

```
int nums[25];
int *pt;
```

the assignment

```
pt = &nums;
```

is invalid. nums is a pointer constant that is itself equivalent to an address. The correct assignment is pt = nums.

Another common mistake made by beginner programmers is to initialize pointer variables incorrectly. For example, the initialization

```
int *pt = 5;
```

is invalid. Because pt is a pointer to an integer, it must be initialized with a valid address.

A more confusing error results from using the same name as both a pointer and a nonpointer variable. For example, assume that minutes is declared as an integer variable in main() and that main() passes the address of minutes to the function time() using the function call time(&minutes);. Due to the scope of local variables, the same names used in main() can also be used in time() without causing the compiler any confusion. Thus, a valid function header for time() could be

```
time(int *minutes)
```

With these declarations, the value stored in `minutes` within `main()` is accessed using the variable's name, while the same value is accessed in `time()` using the notation `*minutes`. This can be very confusing to a beginning programmer. To avoid this, most programmers usually develop their own systems for naming pointer parameters and variables. For example, prefixing pointer names by `ptr` or suffixing them with the characters `Addr` helps to indicate clearly that the parameters or variable are pointers.

The final error that occurs is one common to pointer usage in general. The situation always arises when the beginning C programmer becomes confused about whether a variable *contains* an address or *is* an address. Pointer variables and pointer parameters contain addresses. Although a pointer constant is synonymous with an address, it is useful to treat pointer constants as pointer variables with two restrictions:

1. The address of a pointer constant cannot be taken.
2. The address "contained in" the pointer constant cannot be altered.

Except for these two restrictions, pointer constants and pointer variables can be used almost interchangeably. Therefore, when an address is required, any of the following can be used:

a pointer variable name
a pointer parameter name
a pointer constant name
a nonpointer variable name preceded by the address operator (e.g., `&variable`)
a nonpointer argument name preceded by the address operator (e.g., `&argument`)

Some of the confusion surrounding pointers is caused by the cavalier use of the word *pointer.* For example, the phrase "a function requires a pointer parameter" is more clearly understood when it is realized that the phrase really means "a function requires an address as a parameter." Similarly, the phrase "a function returns a pointer" really means "a function returns an address."

If you are ever in doubt as to what is really contained in a variable or parameter, or how it should be treated, use the `printf()` function to display the contents of the variable or parameter, the "thing pointed to," or "the address of the variable or parameter." Seeing what is displayed frequently helps sort out what is really in the variable or parameter.

8.5 Chapter Summary

1. An array name is a pointer constant. The value of the pointer constant is the address of the zeroth element in the array. Thus, if `val` is the name of an array, `val` and `&val[0]` can be used interchangeably.

2. Any access to an array element using subscript notation can always be replaced using pointer notation. That is, the notation `a[i]` can always be replaced by the notation `*(a + i)`. This is true whether `a` was initially declared explicitly as an array or as a pointer.

3. Arrays are passed to functions by reference. The called function always receives direct access to the originally declared array elements.

4. When a single-dimensional array is passed to a function, the parameter declaration for the array can be either an array declaration or a pointer declaration. Thus, the following parameter declarations are equivalent:

```
float a[]
float *a
```

5. Pointers can be incremented, decremented, and compared. Numbers added to or subtracted from a pointer are automatically scaled. The scale factor used is the number of bytes required to store the data type originally pointed to.

Chapter **9**

Character Strings

9.1 String Fundamentals

9.2 Pointers and Library Functions

9.3 String Definitions and Pointer Arrays

9.4 Formatting Strings

9.5 Common Programming Errors

9.6 Chapter Summary

On a fundamental level, strings are simply arrays of characters that can be manipulated using standard element-by-element array-processing techniques. On a higher level, string library functions are available for treating strings as complete entities. This chapter explores the input, manipulation, and output of strings using both approaches. We will also examine the particularly close connection between string-handling functions and pointers.

9.1 String Fundamentals

A *string literal* is any sequence of characters enclosed in double quotes. A string literal is also referred to as a *string constant* and *string value,* and more conventionally as a *string.* For example, "This is a string", "Hello World!", and "xyz 123 *!#@&" are all strings.

A string is stored as an array of characters terminated by a special end-of-string symbolic constant named Null. The value assigned to the Null constant is the escape sequence '\0' and is the sentinel marking the end of the string. For example, Figure 9.1 illustrates how the string "Good Morning!" is stored in memory. The string uses

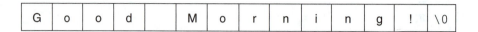

Figure 9.1 Storing a string in memory

fourteen storage locations, with the last character in the string being the end-of-string marker \0. The double quotes are not stored as part of the string.

Because a string is stored as an array of characters, the individual characters in the array can be input, manipulated, or output using standard array-handling techniques utilizing either subscript or pointer notations. The end-of-string null character is useful for detecting the end of the string when handling strings in this fashion.

String Input and Output

Although the programmer has the choice of using either a library or a user-written function for processing a string already in memory, inputting a string from a keyboard or displaying a string always requires some reliance on standard library functions. Table 9.1 lists the commonly available library functions for both character-by-character and complete string input and output.

The gets() and puts() functions deal with strings as complete units. Both are written using the more elemental routines getchar() and putchar(). The getchar() and putchar() routines provide for the input and output of individual characters. Programs that access any of these four routines must contain an #include instruction of the form #include <stdio.h>. The stdio.h file contains definitions required by the accessed library functions.

Program 9.1 illustrates the use of gets() and puts() to input and output a string entered at the user's terminal.

The following is a sample run of Program 9.1:

```
Enter a string:
This is a test input of a string of characters.
The string just entered is:
This is a test input of a string of characters.
```

Table 9.1   Standard string and
Character library functions

Input	Output
gets()	puts()
scanf()	printf()
getchar()	putchar()

Program 9.1

```c
#include <stdio.h>
int main()
{
   char message[81];    /* enough storage for a complete line */

   printf("Enter a string:\n");
   gets(message);
   printf("The string just entered is:\n");
   puts(message);

   return 0;
}
```

The gets() function used in Program 9.1 continuously accepts and stores the characters typed at the terminal into the character array named message. Pressing the Enter key at the terminal generates a newline character, \n, which is interpreted by gets() as the end-of-character entry. All the characters encountered by gets(), except the newline character, are stored in the message array. Before returning, the gets() function appends the null character to the stored set of characters, as illustrated in Figure 9.2a. The puts() function is then used to display the string. As illustrated in Figure 9.2b, the puts() function automatically sends a newline escape sequence to the display terminal after the string has been printed.

In general, a printf() function call can always be used in place of a puts() function call. For example, the statement printf("%s\n", message); is a direct replacement for the statement puts(message); used in Program 9.1. The newline escape sequence in the printf() function call substitutes for the automatic newline generated by puts() after the string is displayed.

The one-to-one correspondence between the output functions printf() and puts() is not duplicated by the input functions scanf() and gets(). For example,

characters \n ⟶ gets() ⟶ *characters* \0

Figure 9.2a   gets() substitutes \0 for the entered \n

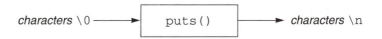

characters \0 ⟶ puts() ⟶ *characters* \n

Figure 9.2b   puts() substitutes \n when \0 is encountered

`scanf("%s",message)` and `gets(message)` are not equivalent. The `scanf()` function reads a set of characters up to either a blank space or a newline character, whereas `gets()` stops accepting characters only when a newline is detected. Trying to enter the characters This is a string using the statement `scanf("%s",message);` results in the word This being assigned to the `message` array. Entering the complete line using a `scanf()` function call would require a statement such as

```
scanf("%s %s %s %s", message1, message2, message3, message4);
```

Here, the word This would be assigned to the string `message1`, the word is assigned to the string `message2`, and so on. The fact that a blank is used as a delimiter by `scanf()` makes it less useful for entering string data than it is for entering numerical data.

Note that if the `scanf()` function *is* used for inputting string data, the & is not used before the array name. Since an array name is a pointer constant equivalent to the address of the first storage location reserved for the array, `message` is the same as `&message[0]`. Thus, the function call `scanf("%s",&message[0])` can be replaced by `scanf("%s",message)`.

String Processing

Strings can be manipulated using either standard library functions or standard array-processing techniques. The library functions typically available for use are presented in the next section. For now, we concentrate on processing a string in a character-by-character fashion. This allows us to understand how the standard library functions are constructed and to create our own library functions. For a specific example, consider the function `strcopy()`, which copies the contents of `string2` to `string1`.

```c
/* copy string2 to string1 */
void strcopy(char string1[], char string2[])    /* two arrays are passed */
{
  int i = 0;                    /* i will be used as a subscript   */

  while (string2[i] != '\0')    /* check for the end-of-string     */
  {
    string1[i] = string2[i];    /* copy the element to string1 */
    ++i;
  }
  string1[i] = '\0';            /* terminate the first string */
  return;
}
```

Although this string copy function can be shortened considerably and written more compactly, the function illustrates the main features of string manipulation. The two strings are passed to `strcopy()` as arrays. Each element of `string2` is then assigned to the equivalent element of `string1` until the end-of-string marker is encountered. The detection of the Null character forces the termination of the `while` loop controlling the copying of elements. Because the `Null` character is not copied from `string2` to `string1`, the last statement in `strcopy()` appends an end-of-string character to `string1`. Prior to calling `strcopy()`, the programmer must ensure that sufficient space has been allocated for the `string1` array to store the elements of the `string2` array.

Program 9.2 includes the `strcopy()` function in a complete program. Notice the function prototype declares that the function expects to receive two character arrays.

 Program 9.2

```c
#include <stdio.h>

void strcopy(char [], char []); /* expects two arrays of chars */

int main()
{
  char message[81];      /* enough storage for a complete line   */
  char newMessage[81];   /* enough storage for a copy of message */
  int i;

  printf("Enter a sentence: ");
  gets(message);
  strcopy(newMessage, message);    /* pass two array addresses */
  puts(newMessage);

  return 0;
}
/* copy string2 to string 1 */
void strcopy (char string1[], char string2[])  /* two arrays are passed */
{
  int i = 0;.                   /* i will be used as a subscript */

  while ( string2[i] != '\0')   /* check for the end-of-string   */
  {
    string1[i] = string2[i];    /* copy the element to string1   */
    ++i;
  } string1
  string[i] = '\0';             /* terminate the first string   */
  return;
}
```

The following is a sample run of Program 9.2:

```
Enter a sentence: How much wood could a woodchuck chuck.
How much wood could a woodchuck chuck.
```

Character-by-Character Input

Just as strings can be processed using character-by-character techniques, they can also be entered and displayed in this manner. For example, consider Program 9.3, which uses the character-input function `getchar()` to enter a string one character at a time. The shaded portion of Program 9.3 essentially replaces the `gets()` function previously used in Program 9.1.

 Program 9.3

```
#include <stdio.h>
int main()
{
  char message[81],c;    /* enough storage for a complete line */
  int i;

  printf("Enter a string:\n");

  i = 0;
  while( i < 80 && (c = getchar()) != '\n')
  {
    message[i] = c;       /* store the character entered */
    ++i;
  }
  message[i] = '\0';      /* terminate the string */

  printf("The string just entered is: \n");
  puts(message);

  return 0;
}
```

The following is a sample run of Program 9.3:

```
Enter a string;
This is a test input of a string of characters.
The string just entered is:
This is a test input of a string of characters.
```

The `while` statement in Program 9.3 causes characters to be read providing the number of characters entered is less than 81 and the character returned by `getchar()` is not the newline character. The parentheses around the expression `c = getchar()` are necessary to assign the character returned by `getchar()` to the variable `c` prior to comparing it to the newline escape sequence. Otherwise, the comparison operator, `!=`, which takes precedence over the assignment operator, causes the entire expression to be equivalent to

```
c = (getchar() != '\n')
```

This has the effect of first comparing the character returned by `getchar` to `'\n'`. The value of the relational expression `getchar() != '\n'` is either 0 or 1, depending on whether or not `getchar()` received the newline character. The value assigned to `c` then would also be either 0 or 1, as determined by the comparison.

Program 9.3 also illustrates a very useful technique for developing functions. The shaded statements constitute a self-contained unit for entering a complete line of characters from a terminal. As such, these statements can be removed from `main()` and placed together as a new function. Program 9.4 illustrates placing these statements in a new function called `getline()`.

 Program 9.4

```c
#include <stdio.h>

void getline(char []);   /* function prototype */

int main()
{
  char message[81];    /* enough storage for a complete line */
  int i;

  printf("Enter a string: \n");
  getline(message);
  printf("The string just entered is:\n");
  puts(message);

  return 0;
}

void getline(char strng[])
{
  int i = 0;
  char c;

  while( i < 80 && (c = getchar()) != '\n')
  {
    strng[i] = c;        /* store the character entered */
    ++i;
  }
  strng[i] = '\0';     /* terminate the string          */
  return;
}
```

We can go further with `getline()` and write it more compactly by having the character returned by `getchar()` assigned directly to the `strng` array. This eliminates the need for the local variable `c` and results in the following version:

```
void getline (char strng[])
{
  int i = 0;

  while( i < 80 && (strng[i++] = getchar()) != '\n')
    ;
  strng[i] = '\0';         /* terminate the string  */
  return;
}
```

Notice that in addition to assigning the returned character from `getchar()` directly to the `strng` array, the assignment statement

```
strng[i++] = getchar()
```

additionally increments the subscript `i` using the postfix operator, `++`. The null statement, `;`, then fulfills the requirement that a `while` loop contain at least one statement. Both versions of `getline()` are suitable replacements for `gets()` and show the interchangeability of user-written and library functions.

C's enormous flexibility is shown by this ability to replace a library function with a user-written version and its ability to have functions written in various ways. Neither version of `getline()` is "more correct" from a programming standpoint. Each version presented (and more versions can be created) has its advantage and disadvantages. While the second version is more compact, the first version is clearer to beginning programmers. In creating your own C programs, select a style that is comfortable and remain with it until your growing programming expertise dictates modifications to your style.

Exercises 9.1

1. a. The following function can be used to select and display all vowels contained within a user-input string:

```
void vowels(char strng[])
{
  int i = 0;
  char c;

  while ((c = strng[i++]) != '\0')
    switch(c)
    {
        case 'a':
        case 'e':
```

```
        case 'i':
        case 'o':
        case 'u':
           putchar(c);
     } /* end of switch */
   putchar('\n');

   return;
}
```

Notice that the `switch` statement in `vowels()` uses the fact that selected cases "drop through" in the absence of `break` statements. Thus, all selected cases result in a `putchar()` function call. Include `vowels()` in a working program that accepts a user-input string and then displays all vowels in the string. In response to the input `How much is the little worth worth?`, your program should display `ouieieoo`.

b. Modify the `vowels()` function to count and display the total number of vowels contained in the string passed to it.

2. Modify the `vowels()` function given in Exercise 1a to count and display the individual numbers of each vowel contained in the string.

3. a. Write a C function to count the total number of characters, including blanks, contained in a string. Do not include the end-of-string `Null` marker in the count.

   b. Include the function written for Exercise 3a in a complete working program.

4. Write a C program that accepts a string of characters from a terminal and displays the hexadecimal equivalent of each character.

5. Write a C program that accepts a string of characters from a terminal and displays the string one word per line.

6. Write a C function that reverses the characters in a string. (*Hint:* This can be considered as a string copy starting from the back end of the first string.)

7. Write a C function named `delChar()` that can be used to delete characters from a string. The function should accept three arguments: the string name, the number of characters to delete, and the starting position in the string where characters should be deleted. For example, the function call `delChar(strng,13,5)`, when applied to the string `all enthusiastic people`, should result in the string `all people`.

8. Write a C function named `addChar()` to insert one string of characters into another string. The function should accept three arguments: the string to be inserted, the original string, and the position in the original string where the insertion should begin. For example, the call `add_Char("for  all",message,6)` should insert the characters `for  all` in `message` starting at `message[5]`.

9. a. Write a C function named `toUpper()` that converts individual lowercase letters into uppercase letters. The expression `ch - 'a' + 'A'` can be used to make the conversion for any lowercase character stored in `ch`.

   b. Add a data input check to the function written in Exercise 9a to verify that a valid lowercase letter is passed to the function. A character is lowercase if it is greater than or equal to `a` and less than or equal to `z`. If the character is not a valid lowercase letter, have the function `toUpper()` return the passed character unaltered.

   c. Write a C program that accepts a string from a terminal and converts all lowercase letters in the string to uppercase letters.

10. Write a C program that accepts a string from a terminal and converts all uppercase letters in the string to lowercase letters.

11. Write a C program that counts the number of words in a string. A word is encountered whenever a transition from a blank space to a nonblank character is encountered. Assume the string contains only words separated by blank spaces.

9.2   Pointers and Library Functions

Pointers are exceptionally useful in constructing string-handling functions. When pointer notation is used in place of subscripts to access individual characters in a string, the resulting statements are both more compact and more efficient. In this section, we describe the equivalence between subscripts and pointers when accessing individual characters in a string.

Consider the strcopy() function introduced in the previous section. This function was used to copy the characters of one string to a second string. For convenience, this function is repeated here.

```
/* copy string2 to string1 */
void strcopy(char string1[], char string2[])
{
  int i = 0;

  while ( string2[i] != '\0')  /* check for the end-of-string */
  {
    string1[i] = string2[i];   /* copy the element to string1 */
    ++i;
  }
  string1[i] = '\0'            /* terminate the first string  */
  return,
}
```

The function strcopy() is used to copy the characters from one array to another array, one character at a time. As currently written, the subscript i in the function is used successively to access each character in the array named string2 by "marching along" the string one character at a time. Before we write a pointer version of strcopy(), we will make two modifications to the function to make it more efficient.

The while statement in strcopy() tests each character to ensure that the end of the string has not been reached. As with all relational expressions, the tested expression, string2[i] != '\0', is either true or false. Using the string this is a string illustrated in Figure 9.3 as an example, as long as string[i] does not access the end-of-string Null character the value of the expression is nonzero and is considered to be true. The expression is false only when the value of the expression is zero. This occurs when the last element in the string is accessed.

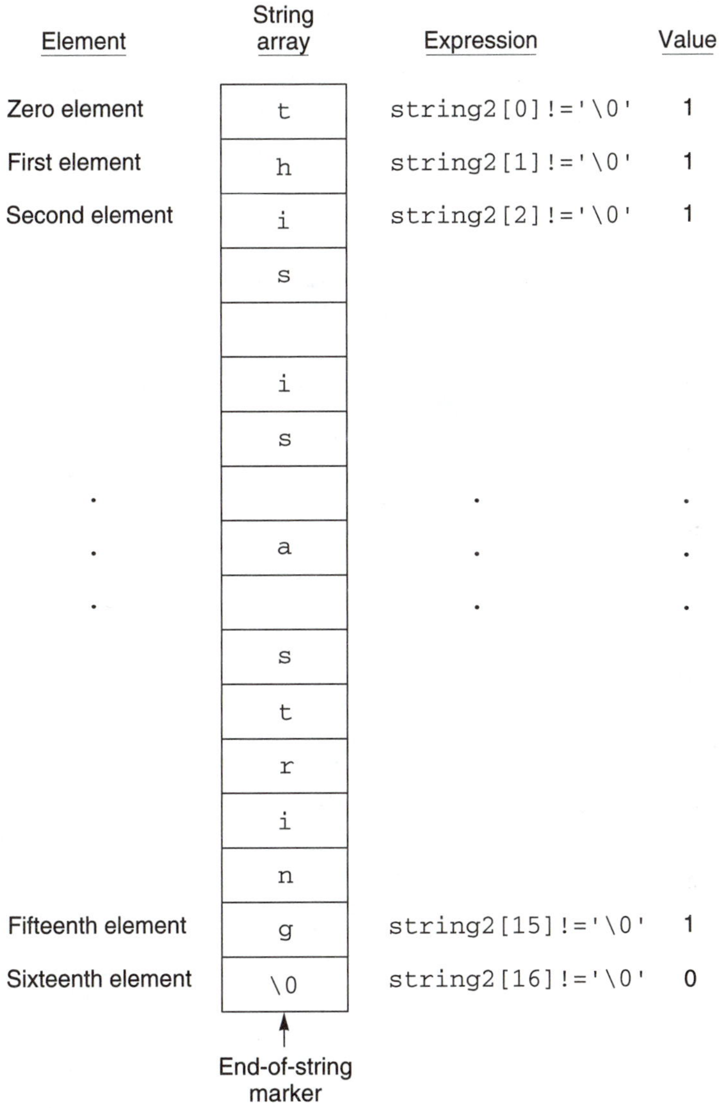

Element	String array	Expression	Value
Zero element	t	`string2[0]!='\0'`	1
First element	h	`string2[1]!='\0'`	1
Second element	i	`string2[2]!='\0'`	1
	s		
	i		
	s		
·	·	·	·
·	a	·	·
·		·	·
	s		
	t		
	r		
	i		
	n		
Fifteenth element	g	`string2[15]!='\0'`	1
Sixteenth element	\0	`string2[16]!='\0'`	0

End-of-string
marker

Figure 9.3   The `while` test becomes false at the end of the string

Recall that C defines false as zero and true as anything else. Thus, the expression `string2[i] != '\0'` becomes zero, or false, when the end of the string is reached. It is nonzero, or true, everywhere else. Because the Null character has an internal value of zero by itself, the comparison to `'\0'` is not necessary. When `string2[i]` accesses the end-of-string character, the value of `string2[i]` is zero. When `string2[i]` accesses any other character, the value of `string[i]` is the value of the code used to store the character and is nonzero. Figure 9.4 lists the ASCII codes for the string `this is a string`. As seen in the figure, each element has a nonzero value except for the Null character.

String array	Stored codes	Expression	Value
t	116	string2[0]	116
h	104	string2[1]	104
i	105	string2[2]	105
s	115		
	32		
i	105		
s	115		
	32	.	.
a	97	.	.
	32	.	.
s	115		
t	116		
r	114		
i	105		
n	110		
g	103	string2[15]	103
\0	0	string2[16]	0

Figure 9.4   The ASCII codes used to store `this is a string`

Because the expression `string[i]` is only zero at the end of a string and nonzero for every other character, the expression `while (string2[i] != '\0')` can be replaced by the simpler expression `while (string2[i])`. Although this may appear confusing at first, the revised test expression is certainly more compact than the longer version. End-of-string tests are frequently written by professional C programmers in this shorter form, so it is worthwhile to become familiar with it. Including the shorter form in `strcopy()` results in the following version of `strcopy()` shown.

```
/* copy string2 to string1 */
void strcopy(char string1[], char string2[])
{
  int i = 0;

  while (string2[i])
  {
    string1[i] = string2[i];    /* copy the element to string1 */
    ++i;
  }
  string1[i] = '\0';            /* terminate the first string  */
  return,
}
```

The second modification that would be made to this string copy function by an experienced C programmer is to include the assignment inside the test portion of the `while` statement. Our new version of the string copy function is

```
void strcopy(char string1[], char string2[])    /* copy string2 to string1 */
{
  int i = 0;

  while (string1[i] = string2[i])
    ++i;
  return;
}
```

Notice that including the assignment statement within the test part of the `while` statement eliminates the necessity of separately terminating the first string with the `Null` character. The assignment within the parentheses ensures that the `Null` character is copied from the second string to the first string. The value of the assignment expression becomes zero only after the `Null` character is assigned to `string1`, at which point the `while` loop is terminated.

The conversion of `strcopy()` from subscript notation to pointer notation is now straightforward. Although each subscript version of `strcopy` can be rewritten using pointer notation, the following is the equivalent of our last subscript version:

```
void strcopy(char *string1, char *string2) /* copy string2 to string1 */
{
  while (*string1 = *string2)
  {
    string1++;
    string2++;
  }
  return;
}
```

Programming Note

Initializing and Processing Strings

Each of the following declarations produces the same result.

```
char test[5] = "abcd";
char test[] = "abcd";
char test[5] = {'a', 'b', 'c', 'd', '\0'};
char test[] = {'a', 'b', 'c', 'd', '\0'};
```

Each declaration creates storage for exactly five characters and initializes this storage with the characters 'a', 'b', 'c', 'd', and '\0'. Since a string literal is used for initialization in the first two declarations, the compiler automatically supplies the end-of-string NULL character.

String variables declared in either of these ways preclude the use of any subsequent assignments, such as `test = "efgh";`, to the character array. In place of an assignment, you can use the `strcpy()` function, such as `strcpy(test,"efgh")`. The only restriction on using `strcpy()` is the size of the declared array, which in this case is five elements. Attempting to copy a larger string value into `test` causes the copy to overflow the destination array beginning with the memory area immediately following the last array element. This overwrites whatever was in these memory locations and typically causes a runtime crash when the overwritten areas are accessed via their legitimate identifier name(s).

The same problem can arise when using the `strcat()` function. It is your responsibility to ensure that the concatenated string will fit into the original string.

An interesting situation arises when string variables are defined using pointers (see Section 9.3). In these situations assignments can subsequently be made.

In both subscript and pointer versions of `strcopy()`, the function receives the name of the array being passed. Recall that passing an array name to a function actually passes the address of the first location of the array. In our pointer version of `strcopy()` the two passed addresses are stored in the pointer parameters `string1` and `string2`, respectively.

The declarations `char *string2;` and `char *string1;` used in the pointer version of `strcopy()` indicate that `string2` and `string1` are both pointers containing the address of a character and stress the treatment of the passed addresses as pointer values rather than array names. These declarations are equivalent to the declarations `char string2[]` and `char string1[]`, respectively.

Internal to `strcopy()`, the pointer expression `*string2`, which refers to *the element whose address is in* `string2`, replaces the equivalent subscript expression string2[i]. Similarly, the pointer expression *string1 replaces the equivalent subscript expression string1[i]. The expression *string1 = *string2 causes the element pointed to by string2 to be assigned to the element pointed to by string1. Because the starting addresses of both strings are passed to strcopy() and stored in string2 and string1, respectively, the expression *string2 initially refers to string2[0] and the expression *string1 initially refers to string1[0].

Consecutively incrementing both pointers in strcopy() with the expressions string2++ and string1++ simply causes each pointer to "point to" the next consecutive character in the respective string. As with the subscript version, the pointer version of strcopy steps along, copying element by element, until the end of the string is copied.

One final change to the string copy function can be made by including the pointer increments as postfix operators within the test part of the while statement. The final form of the string copy function is

```
void strcopy(char *string1, char *string2) /* copy string2 to string1 */
{

   while (*string1++ = *string2++)
      ;
   return;
}
```

There is no ambiguity in the expression *string1++ = *string2++, even though the indirection operator, *, and increment operator, ++, have the same precedence. Here, the character pointed to is accessed before the pointer is incremented. Only after completion of the assignment *string1 = *string2 are the pointers incremented to correctly point to the next characters in the respective strings.

The string copy function included in the standard library supplied with C compilers is typically written exactly like our pointer version of strcopy().

Library Functions

Extensive collections of string- and character-handling functions and routines are included with most C compilers. These were previously listed in Section 6.3, and for convenience are repeated in Table 9.2.

Library functions and routines are called in the same manner that all C functions are called. This means that if a library function returns a value the function must be declared within your program before it is called. For example, if a library function named strngfoo() returns a pointer to a character, the calling function must be alerted that an address is being returned. Thus, the function prototype char *strngfoo();, which declares that strngfoo() returns the address of a character (a pointer to char), must be placed either as a global declaration or directly within the calling function's variable declarations.

The most commonly used functions listed in Table 9.2 are the first four. The strcpy() function copies a source string expression, which consists of either a string literal or the contents of a string variable, into a destination string variable. For example,

Table 9.2 String and character library functions and routines

Name	Description
strcat(string1,string2)	Concatenates string2 to string1.
strcpy(string1,string2)	Copies string2 to string1.
strlen(string)	Returns the length of the string.
strchr(string,character)	Locates the position of the first occurrence of the character within the string. Returns the address of the character.
strcmp(string1,string2)	Compares string2 to string1.
isalpha(character)	Returns a nonzero number if the character is a letter; otherwise it returns a zero.
isupper(character)	Returns a nonzero number if the character is uppercase; otherwise it returns a zero.
islower(character)	Returns a nonzero number if the character is lowercase; otherwise it returns a zero.
isdigit(character)	Returns a nonzero number if the character is a digit (0 through 9); otherwise it returns a zero.
toupper(character)	Returns the uppercase equivalent if the character is lowercase; otherwise it returns the character unchanged.
tolower(character)	Returns the lowercase equivalent if the character is uppercase; otherwise it returns the character unchanged.

in the function call strcpy(string1, "Hello World!") the source string literal "Hello World!" is copied into the destination string variable string1. Similarly, if the source string is a string variable named srcString the function call strcpy(string1, srcString) copies the contents of srcString into string1. In both cases it is the programmer's responsibility to ensure that string1 is large enough to contain the source string.

The strcat() function appends a string expression onto the end of a string variable. For example, if the contents of a string variable named destString is "Hello", then the function call strcat(destString, " there World!") results in the string value "Hello there World!" being assigned to destString. As with the strcpy() function, it is the programmer's responsibility to ensure that the destination string has been defined large enough to hold the additional concatenated characters.

The strlen() function returns the number of characters in its string argument but does not include the terminating Null character in the count. For example, the value returned by the function called strlen("Hello World!") is 12.

Finally, two string expressions may be compared for equality using the `strcmp()` function. Each character in a string is stored in binary using either the ASCII or ANSI code. The first 128 characters of the extended 8-bit ANSI code are identical to the complete 128 characters ASCII code. In both of them, a blank precedes (is less than) all letters and numbers, the letters of the alphabet are stored in order from A to Z, and the digits are stored in order from 0 to 9. Additionally, in both codes the digits come before (that is, are less than) the uppercase letters, which, in turn come before the lowercase letters.

When two strings are compared their individual characters are compared a pair at a time (both first characters, then both second characters, and so on). If no differences are found, the strings are equal; if a difference is found, the string with the first lower character is considered the smaller string. Thus,

`"Good Bye"` is less than `"Hello"` because the first `'G'` in `Good Bye'` is less than the first `'H'` in `Hello`

`"Hello"` is less than `"hello"` because the first `'H'` in `Hello` is less than the first `'h'` in `hello`

`"Hello"` is less than `"Hello "` because the `'\0'` terminating the first string is less than the `' '` in the second string

`"SMITH"` is greater than `"JONES"` because the first `'S'` in `SMITH` is greater than the first `'J'` in `JONES`

`"123"` is greater than `"1227"` because the third character, `'3'`, in `123` is greater than the third character, `'2'`, in `1227`

`"1237"` is greater than `"123"` because the fourth character, `'7'`, in `1237` is greater than the fourth character, `'\0'`, in `123`

`"Behop"` is greater than `"Beehive"` because the third character, `'h'`, in `Behop` is greater than the third character, `'e'`, in `Beehive`.

Before attempting to use any standard library functions, check that they are included in the C compiler available on your computer system. Be careful to check the type of parameters expected by the function, the data type of any returned value, and the standard header file, such as `ctype.h`, that must be included in your program to access these routines.

Exercises 9.2

1. Determine the value of `*text,* (text + 3)`, and `* (text + 10)`, assuming that `text` is an array of characters and the following has been stored in the array:
   a. `now is the time`
   b. `rocky raccoon welcomes you`
   c. `Happy Holidays`
   d. `The good ship`

2. a. The following function, `convert()`, "marches along" the string passed to it and sends each character in the string one at a time to the `toUpper()` function until the `Null` character is encountered.

```
char toUpper(char);   /* function prototype */

void convert(char strng[])     /* convert a string to uppercase letters*/
{
  int i = o;

  while (strng[i] != '\0');
  {
    strng[i] = toUpper(strng[i]);
    ++i;
  }
  return;
}

char toUpper(char letter)     /* convert a character to uppercase */
{
  if( letter >= 'a' && letter <= 'z')
    return (letter - 'a' + 'A');
  else
    return (letter);
}
```

The `toUpper()` function takes each character passed to it and first examines it to determine if the character is a lowercase letter (a lowercase letter is any character between *a* and *z*, inclusive). Assuming that characters are stored using the standard ASCII character codes, the expression `letter - 'a' + 'A'` converts a lowercase letter to its uppercase equivalent. Rewrite the `convert()` function using pointers.

b. Include the `convert()` and `toUpper()` functions in a working program. The program should prompt the user for a string and echo the string back to the user in uppercase letters. Use `gets()` and `puts()` for string input and display.

3. Using pointers, repeat Exercise 1 from Section 9.1.

4. Using pointers, repeat Exercise 2 from Section 9.1.

5. Using pointers, repeat Exercise 3 from Section 9.1.

6. Write a function named `remove()` that deletes all occurrences of a character from a string. The function should take two arguments: the string name and the character to be removed. For example, if `message` contains the string `HappyHolidays`, the function call `remove(message, 'H')` should place the string `appyolidays` into `message`.

7. Using pointers, repeat Exercise 6 from Section 9.1.

8. Write a program using the `getchar()`, `toupper()`, and `putchar()` library functions that echo back each letter entered in its uppercase form. The program should terminate when the digit 1 key is pressed.

9. Write a function that uses pointers to add a single character at the end of an existing string. The function should replace the existing `\0` character with the new character and append a new `\0` at the end of the string.

10. Write a C function that uses pointers to delete a single character from the end of a string. This is effectively achieved by moving the `\0` character one position closer to the start of the string.

11. Determine the string-handling functions that are available with your C compiler. For each available function list the data types of the parameters expected by the function and the data type of any returned value.

12. Write a C function named `trimfrnt()` that deletes all leading blanks from a string. Write the function using pointers.

13. Write a C function named `trimrear()` that deletes all trailing blanks from a string. Write the function using pointers.

14. Write a C function named `strlen()` that returns the number of characters in a string. Do not include the `\0` character in the returned count.

9.3 String Definitions and Pointer Arrays

The definition of a string automatically involves a pointer. For example, the definition `static char message1[81];` both reserves storage for 81 characters and automatically creates a pointer constant, `message1`, that contains the address of `message1[0]`. As a pointer constant, the address associated with the pointer cannot be changed—it must always "point to" the beginning of the created array.

Instead of initially creating a string as an array, however, it is also possible to create a string using a pointer. This is similar in concept to declaring a passed array as either an array or a pointer parameter internal to the receiving function. For example, the definition `char *message2;` creates a pointer to a character. In this case, `message2` is a true pointer variable. Once a pointer to a character is defined, assignment statements, such as `message2 = "this is a string";`, can be made. In this assignment, `message2` receives the address of the first location used by the computer to store the string.

The main difference in the definitions of `message1` as an array and `message2` as a pointer is the way the pointer is created. Defining `message1` using the declaration `static char message1[81]` explicitly calls for a fixed amount of storage for the array. This causes the compiler to create a pointer constant. Defining `message2` using the declaration `char *message2` explicitly creates a pointer variable first. This pointer is then used to hold the address of a string when the string is actually specified. This difference in definitions has both storage and programming consequences.

From a programming perspective, defining `message2` as a pointer to a character allows string assignments, such as `message2 = "this is a string";`, to be made. Similar assignments are not allowed for strings defined as arrays. Thus, the statement `message1 = "this is a string";` is not valid. Both definitions, however, allow initializations to be made using a string assignment. For example, both of the following initializations are valid:

```
char message1[81] = "this is a string";
char *message2 = "this is a string";
```

The initialization of the `message1` array is straightforward and follows the pattern previously presented at the end of Section 7.2. The same is not true for `message2`. The initialization of `message2` consists of setting an initial address into a pointer variable.

Programming Note

Pointers, Array Declarations, and lvalues

Although the two declarations

```
char test[5] = "abcd";
```

and

```
char *test = "abcd";
```

both create storage for the characters `'a'`, `'b'`, `'c'`, `'d'`, and `'\0'`, there is a subtle difference between the two declarations and how values can be assigned to `test`.

Except within the declaration, an array declaration, such as `char test[5];`, precludes the use of any subsequent assignment expression, such as `test = "efgh"`, to assign values to the array. The use of a `strcpy()`, such as `strcpy()test, "efgh")`, however, is subsequently valid. The only restriction on the `strcpy()` is the size of the array, which in this case is 5 elements. This situation is reversed when a pointer is created.

A pointer declaration, such as `char *test;`, precludes the use of a `strcpy()` to initialize the memory locations pointed to by the pointer, but it does allow assignments. For example, the following sequence of statements is valid:

```
char *test;
test = "abcd";
test = "here is a longer string";
```

Once a string of characters has been assigned to `test`, a `strcpy()` can be used provided the copy uses no more elements than are currently contained in the string.

The difference in usage is explained by the fact that the compiler automatically allocates sufficient new memory space for any string pointed to by a pointer variable, but does not do so for an array of characters. The array size is fixed by the definition statement.

Formally, any expression that yields a value that can be used on the left side of an assignment expression is said to be an *lvalue*. Thus, a pointer variable can be an `lvalue` but an array name cannot.

From a storage perspective, the allocation of space for `message1` and `message2` is different, as illustrated in Figure 9.5. As shown in the figure, both initializations cause the computer to store the same string internally. In the case of `message1`, a specific set of 81 storage locations is reserved and the first 17 locations are initialized. For `message1`, different strings can be stored, but each string will overwrite the previously stored characters. The same is not true for `message2`.

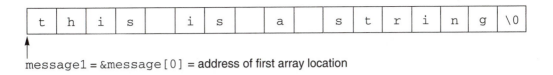

message1 = &message[0] = address of first array location

a. Storage allocation for a string defined as an array

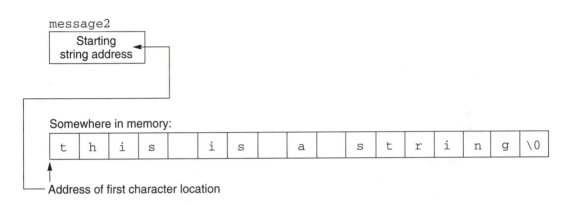

b. Storage of a string using a pointer

Figure 9.5 String storage allocation

The definition of message2 reserves enough storage for one pointer. The initialization then causes the string to be stored and the address of the string's first character, in this case, the address of the t, to be loaded into the pointer. If a later assignment is made to message2, the initial string remains in memory and new storage locations are allocated to the new string. Program 9.5 uses the message2 character pointer to successively "point to" two different strings.

A sample output for Program 9.5 is[1]

```
The string is: this is a string
 The first address of this string is 00420094
The string is now: A new message
 The first address of this string is 00420038
```

In Program 9.5 the variable message2 is initially created as a pointer variable and loaded with the starting storage address of the first string. The printf() function is then used to display this string. When the %s conversion control sequence is encountered by

_____

[1] The actual addresses used by this program for the storage of the messages are machine dependent.

Program 9.5

```
#include <stdio.h>
int main()
{
   char *message2 = "this is a string";

   printf("\nThe string is %s", message2);
   printf("\n The first address of this string is %p", message2);

   message2 = "A new message";
   printf("\nThe string is now: %s", message2);
   printf("\n The first address of this string is %p", message2);

   return 0;
}
```

printf(), it alerts the function that a string is being referenced. The printf() function then expects either a string constant or a pointer containing the address of the first character in the string. This pointer can be either an array name or a pointer variable. The printf() function uses the address provided to correctly locate the string, and then continues accessing and displaying characters until it encounters a null character. As illustrated by the output, the hexadecimal address of the first character in the first string is 00420094.

After the first string and its starting address are displayed, the next assignment statement in Program 9.5 causes the computer to store a second string and change the address in message2 to point to the starting location of this new string. The printf() function then displays this string and its starting storage address.

It is important to realize that the second string assigned to message2 does not overwrite the first string but simply changes the address in message2 to point to the new string. As illustrated in Figure 9.6, both strings are stored inside the computer. Any additional string assignment to message2 results in the additional storage of the new string and a corresponding change in the address stored in message2.

Pointer Arrays

The declaration of an array of character pointers is an extremely useful extension to single-string pointer declarations. For example, the declaration

```
char *seasons[4];
```

creates an array of four elements, where each element is a pointer to a character. As individual pointers, each pointer can be assigned to point to a string using string assignment statements. Thus, the statements

message2 is a pointer variable

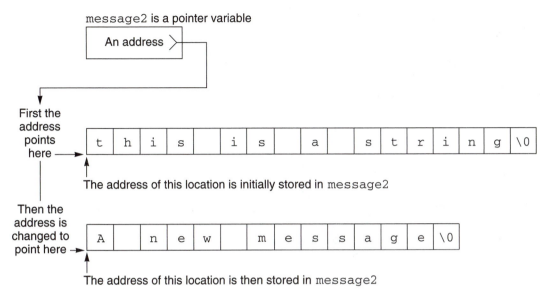

Figure 9.6   Storage allocation for Program 9.5

```
seasons[0] = "Winter";
seasons[1] = "Spring";
seasons[2] = "Summer";
seasons[3] = "Fall";
```

set appropriate addresses into the respective pointers. Figure 9.7 illustrates the addresses loaded into the pointers for these assignments.

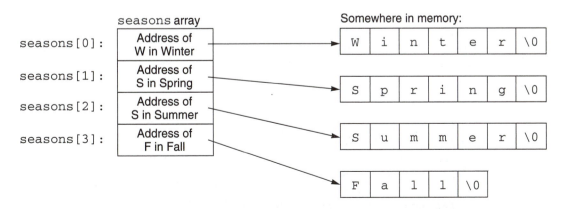

Figure 9.7   The addresses contained in the seasons[] pointers

As illustrated in Figure 9.7, the `seasons` array does not contain the actual strings assigned to the pointers. These strings are stored elsewhere in the computer, in the normal data area allocated to the program. The array of pointers contains only the address of the starting location for each string.

The initializations of the `seasons` array can also be incorporated directly within the definition of the array as follows:

```
char *seasons[4] = { "Winter",
                     "Spring",
                     "Summer",
                     "Fall"};
```

This declaration both creates an array of pointers and initializes the pointers with appropriate addresses. Once addresses have been assigned to the pointers, each pointer can be used to access its corresponding string. Program 9.6 uses the `seasons` array to display each season using a `for` loop.

   Program 9.6

```c
#include <stdio.h>
int main()
{
  int n;
  char *seasons[] = { "Winter",
                      "Spring",
                      "Summer",
                      "Fall"};

  for(n = 0; n < 4; ++n)
    printf("\nThe season is %s.",seasons[n]);

  return 0;
}
```

The output obtained from Program 9.6 is

```
The season is Winter.
The season is Spring.
The season is Summer.
The season is Fall.
```

The advantage of using a list of pointers is that logical groups of data headings can be collected together and accessed with one array name. For example, the months in a year can be collectively grouped in one array called `months`, and the days in a week collectively grouped together in an array called `days`. The grouping of like headings allows the programmer to access and print an appropriate heading by simply specifying the correct position of the heading in the array. Program 9.7 uses the `seasons` array to correctly identify and display the season corresponding to a user-input month.

 Program 9.7

```c
#include <stdio.h>
int main()
{
  int n;
  char *seasons[] = {"Winter",
                     "Spring",
                     "Summer",
                     "Fall"};

  printf("\nEnter a month (use 1 for Jan., 2 for Feb., etc.): ");
  scanf("%d", &n);
  n = (n % 12) / 3;    /* create the correct subscript */
  printf("The month entered is a %s month.",seasons[n]);

  return 0;
}
```

Except for the expression `n = (n % 12) / 3`, Program 9.7 is rather straightforward. The program requests the user to input a month and accepts the number corresponding to the month using a `scanf()` function call.

The expression `n = (n % 12) / 3` uses a common programming "trick" to scale a set of numbers into a more useful set. In this case, the first set is the numbers 1 through 12 and the second set is the numbers 0 through 3. The months of the year, which correspond to the numbers 1 through 12, are thus adjusted to correspond to the correct season subscript using this expression. First the expression `n % 12` adjusts the month entered to lie within the range 0 through 11, with 0 corresponding to December, 1 corresponding to January, etc. Dividing by 3 then causes the resulting number to range between 0 and 3, corresponding to the possible `seasons` elements. The result of the division by 3 is assigned to the integer variable n. The months 0, 1, and 2, when divided by 3, are set to 0; the months 3, 4, and 5 are set to 1; the months 6, 7, and 8 are set to 2; and the months 9, 10, and 11 are set to 3. This is equivalent to the following assignments:

Months	Season
December, January, February	Winter
March, April, May	Spring
June, July, August	Summer
September, October, November	Fall

The following is a sample output obtained for Program 9.7:

```
Enter a month (use 1 for Jan., 2 for Feb., etc.): 12
The month entered is a Winter month.
```

Exercises 9.3

1. Write two declaration statements that can be used in place of the declaration `char text[]` `= "Hooray!";`.

2. Determine the value of `*text`, `*(text + 3)`, and `*(text + 7)` for each of the following sections of code:

   a. `char *text;`
      `char message[] = "the check is in the mail";`
      `text = message;`

   b. `char *text;`
   `char formal[] = {'t', 'h', 'i', 's', ' ', 'i', 's', ' ', 'a', 'n', ' ',`
   `                 'i', 'n', 'v', 'i', 't', 'a', 't', 'i', 'o', 'n', '\0'};`
      `text = &formal[0];`

   c. `char *test;`
      `char more[] = "Happy Holidays";`
      `text = &more[4];`

   d. `char *text, *second;`
      `char blip[] = "The good ship";`
      `second = blip;`
      `text = ++second;`

3. Determine the error in the following program:

```
#include <stdio.h>
int main()
{
  int i = 0;
  char message[] = {'H', 'e', 'l', 'l', 'o', '\0'};

  for( ; i < 5; ++i)
    {putchar(*message); ++message;}

  return 0;
}
```

4. a. Write a C function that displays the day of the week corresponding to a user-entered input number between 1 and 7. That is, in response to an input of 2, the program displays the name Monday. Use an array of pointers in the function.

   b. Include the function written for Exercise 4a in a complete working program.

5. Modify the function written in Exercise 4a so that the function returns the address of the character string containing the proper day to be displayed.

6. Write a C function that will accept ten lines of user-input text and store the entered lines as ten individual strings. Use a pointer array in your function.

9.4 Formatting Strings

Besides the special string-handling functions in the standard library provided with your C compiler, both the printf() and scanf() functions have string-formatting capabilities. Additionally, two related functions, sprintf() and sscanf(), provide further string-processing features. In this section we present the additional features that these functions provide when used with strings.

Field-width specifiers can be included in a printf() control sequence to control the spacing of integers and decimal numbers. These specifiers can also be used with the %s control sequence to control the display of a string. For example, the statement

```
printf("|%25s|","Have a Happy Day");
```

displays the message Have a Happy Day, right justified, in a field of 25 characters, as follows

```
|          Have a Happy Day|
```

We have placed a bar (|) at the beginning and end of the string field to clearly delineate the field being printed. Placing a minus sign (-) in front of the field-width specifier forces the string to be left justified in the field. For example, the statement

```
printf("|%-25s|","Have a Happy Day");
```

causes the display:

```
|Have a Happy Day          |
```

If the field-width specifier is too small for the string, the specifier is ignored and the string is displayed using sufficient space to accommodate the complete string.

The precision specifier used for determining the number of digits displayed to the right of a decimal number can also be used as a string specifier. When used with strings, the precision specifier determines the maximum number of characters that will be displayed. For example, the statement

Programming Note

Data Type Conversions

Converting from character data to numerical data, in all languages, requires some thought. One neat "trick" that can be applied in C is to use the sscanf() function to make the conversions for you. For example, assume you need to extract the month, day, and year from the string 07/01/94, which is stored in a character array named date. The simple statement

```
sscanf(date,"%d/%d/%d", &month, &day, &year);
```

extracts the data and converts it into integer form. Such ASCII-to-number conversions really become simple in C! Of course, like other languages, C also provides library functions for simple conversions. The function atoi() converts a string to a single integer value, and the function atof() converts a string to a double precision value. Some compilers provide itoa() and ftoa() functions, for converting a single integer and floating point number, respectively, to their ASCII representations. But if these functions are not available, a call to sprint() can be used for these numeric-to-string conversions.

```
printf("|%25.12s|","Have a Happy Day");
```

causes the first twelve characters in the string to be displayed, right justified, in a field of 25 characters. This produces the display:

```
|            Have a Happy|
```

Similarly, the statement

```
printf("|%-25.12s|","Have a Happy Day");
```

causes twelve characters to be left justified in a field of 25 characters. This produces the display:

```
|Have a Happy            |
```

When a precision specifier is used with no field-width specifier, the indicated number of characters is displayed in a field sufficiently large to hold the designated number of characters. Thus, the statement

```
printf("|%.12s|","Have a Happy Day");
```

causes the first twelve characters in the string to be displayed in a field of 12 characters. If the string has less than the number of characters designated by the precision specifier, the display is terminated when the end-of-string is encountered.

In-Memory String Conversions

While `printf()` displays data to the standard device used by your computer for output and `scanf()` scans the standard device used for input, the `sprintf()` and `sscanf()` functions provide similar capabilities for writing and scanning strings to and from memory variables. For example, the statement

```
sprintf(disStrn,"%d %d", num1, num2);
```

writes the numerical values of `num1` and `num2` into `disStrn` rather than displaying the values on the standard output terminal. Here, `disStrn` is a programmer-selected variable name that must be declared as either an array of characters, sufficiently large to hold the resulting string, or as a pointer to a string.

Typically, the `sprintf()` function is used to "assemble" a string from smaller pieces until a complete line of characters is ready to be written, either to the standard output device or to a file (writing data to a file is described in Chapter 11). For example, another string could be concatenated to `disStrn` using the `strcat()` function and the complete string displayed using the `printf()` function.

In contrast to `sprintf()`, the string scan function `sscanf()` may be used to "disassemble" a string into smaller pieces. For example, if the string `"$23.45   10"` were stored in a character array named `data`, the statement

```
sscanf(data,"%c%lf %d",&dol,&price,&units);
```

would scan the string stored in the data array and "strip off" three data items. The dollar sign would be stored in the variable named `dol`, the `23.45` would be converted to a double precision number and stored in the variable named `price`, and the `10` would be converted to an integer value and stored in the variable named `units`. For a useful result, the variables `dol`, `price`, and `units` would have to be declared as the appropriate data types. In this way `sscanf()` provides a useful means of converting parts of a string into other data types. Typically, the string being scanned by `sscanf()` is used as a working storage area, or buffer, for storing a complete line from either a file or the standard input. Once the string has been filed, `sscanf()` disassembles the string into component parts and suitably converts each data item into the designated data type. For programmers familiar with COBOL, this is equivalent to first reading data into a working storage area before moving the data into smaller fields.

Format Strings

When you use any of the four functions, `printf()`, `scanf()`, `sprintf()`, or `sscanf()`, the control string containing the conversion control sequences need not be explicitly contained within the function. For example, the control string `"$%5.2d %d"` contained within the function call

```
printf("$%5.2f %d",num1,num2);
```

can itself be stored as a string and the address of the string can be used in the call to printf(). If either of the following declarations for fmat are made:

```
char *fmat = "$%5.2f %d";
```

or

```
char fmat[] = "$%5.2f %d";
```

the function call, printf(fmat,num1,num2); can be made in place of the previous call to printf(). Here, fmat is a pointer that contains the address of the control string used to determine the output display.

The technique of storing and using control strings in this manner is very useful for clearly listing format strings with other variable declarations at the beginning of a function. If a change to a format must be made, it is easy to find the desired control string without the necessity of searching through the complete function to locate the appropriate printf() or scanf() function call. Restricting the definition of a control string to one place is also advantageous when the same format control is used in multiple function calls.

Exercises 9.4

1. Determine the display produced by each of the following statements:
   a. printf("!%10s!","four score and ten");
   b. printf("!%15s!","Home!");
   c. printf("!%-15s!","Home!");
   d. printf("!%15.2s!","Home!");
   e. printf("!%-15.2s!","Home!");

2. a. Assuming that the following declaration has been made

   ```
   char *text = "Have a nice day!";
   ```

   determine the display produced by the statements

   ```
   printf("%s", text);
   printf("%c", *text);
   ```

   b. Since both printf() function calls in Exercise 2a display characters, determine why the indirection operator is required in the second call but not in the first.

3. Write a C program that accepts three user-entered numbers as one string. Once the string has been accepted, have the program pass the string and the addresses of three floating point variables to a function called separate(). The separate() function should extract the three floating point values from the passed string and store them using the passed variable addresses.

4. Modify the program written for Exercise 3 to display the input string using the format `"%6.2f %6.2f %6.2f"`.

5. Write a C program that accepts a string and two integer numbers from a user. Each of these inputs should be preceded by a prompt and stored using individual variable names. Have your program call a function that assembles the input data into a single string. Display the assembled string using a `puts()` call.

9.5   Common Programming Errors

Three errors are frequently made when pointers to strings are used. The most common is using the pointer to "point to" a nonexistent data element. This error is, of course, the same error we have already seen using subscripts. Because C compilers do not perform bounds checking on arrays, it is the programmer's responsibility to ensure that the address in the pointer is the address of a valid data element.

The second common error lies in not providing sufficient space for the end-of-string `Null` character when a string is defined as an array of characters and not including the `\0 Null` character when the array is initialized.

The last error relates to a misunderstanding of terminology. For example, if `text` is defined as

```
char *text;
```

the variable `text` is sometimes referred to as a string. Thus, the terminology "store the characters `Hooray for the Hoosiers` into the `text` string" may be encountered. Strictly speaking, calling `text` a string or a string variable is incorrect. The variable `text` is a pointer that contains the address of the first character in the string. Nevertheless, referring to a character pointer as a string occurs frequently enough that you should be aware of it.

9.6   Chapter Summary

1. A string is an array of characters that is terminated by the `Null ('\0')` character.

2. Strings can always be processed using standard array-processing techniques. The input and display of a string, however, always require reliance on a standard library function.

3. The `gets()`, `scanf()`, and `getchar()` library functions can be used to input a string. The `scanf()` function tends to be of limited usefulness for string input because it terminates input when a blank is encountered.

4. The `puts()`, `printf()`, and `putchar()` functions can be used to display strings.

5. In place of subscripts, pointer notation and pointer arithmetic are especially useful for manipulating string elements.

6. Many standard library functions exist for processing strings as a complete unit. Internally, these functions manipulate strings in a character-by-character manner, usually using pointers.

7. String storage can be created by declaring an array of characters or a pointer to be a character. A pointer to a character can be assigned a string directly. String assignment to an array of characters is invalid except when done in a declaration statement.

8. Arrays can be initialized using a string assignment of the form

   ```
   char *arrayName[] = "text";
   ```

   This initialization is equivalent to

   ```
   char *arrayName[] = {'t','e','x','t','\0'};
   ```

Chapter **10**

Structures

In the broadest sense, *structure* refers to how individual elements of a group are arranged or organized. For example, a corporation's structure refers to the organization of the people and departments in the company, and a government's structure refers to its form or arrangement. In programming, a structure refers to the way individual data items are arranged to form a cohesive and related unit.

To make the discussion more tangible, consider data items that might be stored for a video game character, as illustrated in Figure 10.1.

```
Name:
Type:
Location in Dungeon:
Strength Factor:
Intelligence Factor:
Type of Armor:
```

Figure 10.1 Typical components of a video game character

```
Name: Golgar
Type: Monster
Location in Dungeon: G7
Strength Factor: 78
Intelligence Factor: 15
Type of Armor: Chain Mail
```

Figure 10.2   The form and contents of a record

Each of the individual data items listed in Figure 10.1 is an entity by itself that is referred to as a *data field.* Taken together, all the data fields form a single unit that is referred to as a *record.* In C, a record is referred to as a *structure,* and we use these terms interchangeably.

Although there could be hundreds of characters in a video game, the form of each character's record is identical. In dealing with records, it is important to distinguish between a record's form and its contents.

A record's *form* consists of the symbolic names, data types, and arrangement of individual data fields in the record. The record's *contents* refer to the actual data stored in the symbolic names. Figure 10.2 shows acceptable contents for the record form in Figure 10.1.

In this chapter, we describe the C statements required to create, fill, use, and pass structures between functions.

10.1   Single Structures

Using structures requires the same two steps needed for using any C variable. First the structure must be declared. Then specific values can be assigned to the individual structure elements. Declaring a structure requires listing the data types, data names, and arrangement of data items. For example, the definition

```
struct
{
   int month;
   int day;
   int year;
}   birth;
```

gives the form of a structure named `birth` and reserves storage for the individual data items listed in the structure. The `birth` structure consists of three data items, which are called *members of the structure.*

Assigning actual data values to the data items of a structure is called *populating the structure* and is a relatively straightforward procedure. Each member of a structure is accessed by giving both the structure name and individual data item name, separated by a period. Thus, `birth.month` refers to the first member of the `birth` structure, `birth.day` refers to the second member of the structure, and `birth.year` refers to the third member. Program 10.1 illustrates assigning values to the individual members of the `birth` structure (observe that the `printf()` statement call has been continued across two lines).

 Program 10.1

```c
#include <stdio.h>
int main()
{
  struct
  {
    int month;
    int day;
    int year;
  } birth;

  birth.month = 12;
  birth.day = 28;
  birth.year = 1982;

  printf("My birth date is %d/%d/%d",
          birth.month,birth.day,birth.year % 100);

  return 0;
}
```

The output produced by Program 10.1 is

```
My birth date is 12/28/82
```

Notice that although we have stored the year as a 4-digit number, the output displays the year in conventional 2-digit form.

As in most C statements, the spacing of a structure definition is not rigid. For example, the `birth` structure could just as well have been defined

```c
struct {int month; int day; int year;} birth;
```

Also, as with all C definition statements, multiple variables can be defined in the same statement. For example, the definition statement

```c
struct {int month; int day; int year;} birth, current;
```

creates two structures having the same form. The members of the first structure are accessed by the individual names `birth.month`, `birth.day`, and `birth.year`,

---

Programming Note

Homogeneous and Heterogeneous Data Structures

Both arrays and structures are structured data types (see Programming Note on page 272). The difference between these two data structures are the types of elements they contain. An array is a *homogeneous* data structure, which means that each of its components must be of the same type. A record is a *heterogeneous* data structure, which means that each of its components can be of different data types. Thus, an array of records is a homogeneous data structure whose elements are of the same heterogeneous type.

---

whereas the members of the second structure are accessed by the names `current.month`, `current.day`, and `current.year`. Notice that the form of this particular structure definition statement is identical to the form used in defining any program variable: the data type is followed by a list of variable names.

The most commonly used modification for defining structures is listing the form of the structure with no following variable names. In this case, however, the list of structure members must be preceded by a user-selected *structure type name*. For example, in the declaration

```
struct Date
{
   int month;
   int day;
   int year;
};
```

the term `Date` is a structure type name: It creates a new structure type that is of the declared form. By convention the first letter of user-selected structure type names is uppercase, as in the name `Date`, which helps to identify them when they are used in subsequent definition statements. Here, the declaration for the `Date` structure creates a new data type without actually reserving any storage locations. As such, it is not a definition statement. It simply declares a `Date` structure type and describes how individual data items are arranged within the structure. Actual storage for the members of the structure is reserved only when specific variable names are assigned. For example, the definition statement

```
struct Date birth, current;
```

reserves storage for two `Date` structure variables named `birth` and `current`, respectively. Each of these individual structures has the form previously declared for the `Date` structure.

Like all variable declarations, a structure may be declared globally or locally. Program 10.2 illustrates the global declaration of a Date structure. Internal to main(), the variable birth is defined as a local variable of Date type.

Program 10.2

```c
#include <stdio.h>
struct Date
{
  int month;
  int day;
  int year;
};
int main()
{
  struct Date birth;

  birth.month = 12;
  birth.day = 28;
  birth.year = 1982;

  printf("My birth date is %d/%d/%d",
         birth.month,birth.day,birth.year % 100);

  return 0;
}
```

The output produced by Program 10.2 is identical to the output produced by Program 10.1.

The initialization of structures follows the same rules as for the initialization of arrays: Structures may be initialized by following the definition with a list of initializers.[1] For example, the definition statement

```c
struct Date birth = {12, 28, 1982};
```

can be used to replace the first four statements internal to main() in Program 10.2. Notice that the initializers are separated by commas, not semicolons.

The individual members of a structure are not restricted to integer data types, as they are in the Date structure. Any valid C data type can be used. For example, consider an employee record consisting of the following data items:

---

[1] This is true for ANSI C compilers. For non-ANSI C compilers the keyword static must be placed before the keyword struct for initialization within the declaration statement. This is because static local structures may be initialized, whereas automatic local structures cannot be initialized in non-ANSI C compilers.

Name:
Identification Number:
Regular Pay Rate:
Overtime Pay Rate:

A suitable declaration for these data items is

```
struct PayRecord
{
  char name[20];
  int idNum;
  float regRate:
  float otRate;
};
```

Once the `payRecord` structure type is declared, a specific structure variable using this type can be defined and initialized. For example, the definition

```
struct PayRecord employee = {"H. Price",12387,15.89,25.50};
```

creates a structure named `employee` of the `PayRecord` type. The individual members of `employee` are initialized with the respective data listed between braces in the definition statement.

Notice that a single structure is simply a convenient method for combining and storing related items under a common name. Although a single structure is useful in explicitly identifying the relationship among its members, the individual members could be defined as separate variables. The real advantage to using structures is realized only when the same structure type is used in a list many times over. Creating lists with the same structure type is the topic of the next section.

Before leaving the topic of single structures, it is worth noting that because individual members of a structure can be any valid C data type, they can also be arrays and structures. An array of characters was used as a member of the `employee` structure defined previously. Accessing an element of a member array requires giving the structure's name, followed by a period, followed by the array designation. For example, `employee.name[4]` refers to the fifth character in the `employee` structure's `name` array.

Including a structure within a structure follows the same rules for including any data type in a structure. For example, assume that a structure is to consist of a name and a date of birth, where a `Date` structure has been declared as

```
struct Date
{
  int month;
  int date;
  int year;
};
```

A suitable definition of a structure that includes a name and a `Date` structure is

```
struct
{
  char name[20];
  struct Date birth;
} person;
```

Notice that in declaring this structure, the term `Date` is a structure type name. In defining the `person` variable, `person` is the name of a specific structure. The same is true of the variable named `birth`. This is the name of a specific structure having the form of `Date`. Individual members in the `person` structure are accessed by preceding the desired member with the structure name followed by a period. For example, `person.birth.month` refers to the `month` variable in the `birth` structure contained in the `person` structure.

Exercises 10.1

1. Declare a structure type named `Stemp` for each of the following records:
   a. a student record consisting of a student identification number, number of credits completed, and cumulative grade point average
   b. a student record consisting of a student's name, date of birth, number of credits completed, and cumulative grade point average
   c. a mailing list consisting of a person's name and address (street, city, state, and zip)
   d. a stock record consisting of the stock's name, the price of the stock, and the date of purchase
   e. an inventory record consisting of an integer part number, part description, number of parts in inventory, and an integer reorder number

2. For the individual structure types declared in Exercise 1, define a suitable structure variable name and initialize each structure with the appropriate following data:
   a. `Identification Number: 4672`
      `Number of Credits Completed: 68`
      `Grade Point Average: 3.01`
   b. `Name: Rhona Karp`
      `Date of Birth: 8/4/1980`
      `Number of Credits Completed: 96`
      `Grade Point Average: 3.89`
   c. `Name: Kay Kingsley`
      `Street Address: 614 Freeman Street`
      `City: Indianapolis`
      `State: IN`
      `Zip Code: 47030`
   d. `Stock:IBM`
      `Price: 115.375`
      `Date Purchased: 12/7/1999`

e. Part Number: 16879
   Description: Battery
   Number in Stock: 10
   Reorder Number: 3

3. a. Write a C program that prompts a user to input the current month, day, and year. Store the data entered in a suitably defined array and display the date in an appropriate manner.

b. Modify the program written in Exercise 3a to accept the current time in hours, minutes, and seconds.

4. Write a program that uses a structure for storing the name of a stock, its estimated earnings per share, and its estimated price-to-earnings ratio. Have the program prompt the user to enter these items for five different stocks, each time using the same structure to store the entered data. When the data have been entered for a particular stock, have the program compute and display the anticipated stock price based on the entered earnings and price-per-earnings values. For example, if a user entered the data XYZ 1.56 12, the anticipated price for a share of XYZ stock is (1.56)*(12) = $18.72.

5. Write a C program that accepts a user-entered time in hours and minutes. Have the program calculate and display the time one minute later.

6. a. Write a C program that accepts a user-entered date. Have the program calculate and display the date of the next day. For purposes of this exercise, assume that all months consist of thirty days.

b. Modify the program written in Exercise 6a to account for the actual number of days in each month.

10.2   Arrays of Structures

The real power of structures is realized when the same structure is used for lists of data. For example, assume that the data shown in Figure 10.3 must be processed.

Clearly, the employee numbers can be stored together in an array of long integers, the names in an array of pointers, and the pay rates in an array of either floating point or double precision numbers. In organizing the data in this fashion, each column in Figure 10.3

Employee number	Employee name	Employee pay rate
32479	Abrams, B.	6.72
33623	Bohm, P.	7.54
34145	Donaldson, S.	5.56
35987	Ernst, T.	5.43
36203	Gwodz, K.	8.72
36417	Hanson, H.	7.64
37634	Monroe, G.	5.29
38321	Price, S.	9.67
39435	Robbins, L.	8.50
39567	Williams, B.	7.20

Figure 10.3   A list of employee data

	Employee number	Employee name	Employee pay rate
1st record ⟶	32479	Abrams, B.	6.72
2nd record ⟶	33623	Bohm, P.	7.54
3rd record ⟶	34145	Donaldson, S.	5.56
4th record ⟶	35987	Ernst, T.	5.43
5th record ⟶	36203	Gwodz, K.	8.72
6th record ⟶	36417	Hanson, H.	7.64
7th record ⟶	37634	Monroe, G.	5.29
8th record ⟶	38321	Price, S.	9.67
9th record ⟶	39435	Robbins, L.	8.50
10th record ⟶	39567	Williams, B.	7.20

Figure 10.4   A list of records

is considered as a separate list, which is stored in its own array. Using arrays, the correspondence between items for each individual employee is maintained by storing an employee's data in the same array position in each array.

The separation of the complete list into three individual arrays is unfortunate, because all of the items relating to a single employee constitute a natural organization of data into records, as illustrated in Figure 10.4.

Using a structure, the integrity of the data organization as a record can be maintained and reflected by the program. Under this approach, the lists illustrated in Figure 10.4 can be processed as a single array of ten structures.

Declaring an array of structures is the same as declaring an array of any other variable type. For example, if the structure type `PayRecord` is declared as

```
struct PayRecord {long idnum; char name[20]; float rate;};
```

then an array of ten such structures can be defined as

```
struct PayRecord employee[10];
```

This definition statement constructs an array of ten elements, each of which is a structure of the type `PayRecord`. Notice that the creation of an array of ten structures has the same form as the creation of any other array. For example, creating an array of ten integers named `employee` requires the declaration

```
int employee[10];
```

In this declaration the data type is integer, while in the former declaration for `employee` the data type is a structure of the `PayRecord` form.

Once an array of structures is declared, a particular data item is accessed by giving the position of the desired structure in the array followed by a period and the appropriate structure member. For example, the variable `employee[0].rate` accesses the `rate` member of the first structure in the `employee` array. Including structures as elements of

Programming Note

Using a `typedef` Statement

A commonly used programming technique when dealing with structure declarations is to use a `typedef` statement. This provides a simple method for creating a new and typically shorter name for an existing structure type (see Section 12.1 for a complete description of `typedef`). For example, assuming the following global structure declaration has been made

```
struct Date
{
   int month;
   int day;
   int year;
};
```

then the `typedef` statement

```
typedef struct Date DATE
```

makes the name DATE a synonym for the terms `struct Date`. Now, whenever a variable is to be declared as a `struct Date`, the term DATE can be used instead. Thus, for example, the declaration

```
struct Date a, b, c;
```

can be replaced by the statement

```
DATE a, b, c;
```

Similarly, if a record structure named `PayRecord` has been declared and the statement

```
typedef struct PayRecord PAYRECS
```

had been made, the declaration

```
PAYRECS employee[10];
```

could be used in place of the longer declaration

```
struct PayRecord employee[10];
```

By convention all `typedef` names are written in uppercase but this is not mandatory. The names used in a `typedef` statement can be any name that conforms to C's identifier naming rules.

an array permits a list of records to be processed using standard array programming techniques. Program 10.3 displays the first five employee records illustrated in Figure 10.4.

 Program 10.3

```c
#include <stdio.h>
struct PayRecord          /* construct a global structure type */
{
  long id;
  char name[20];
  float rate;
};
int main()
{
  int i;
  struct PayRecord employee[5] =
        {
          { 32479, "Abrams, B.", 6.72 },
          { 33623, "Bohm, P.", 7.54},
          { 34145, "Donaldson, S.", 5.56},
          { 35987, "Ernst, T.", 5.43 },
          { 36203, "Gwodz, K.", 8.72 }
        };

  for ( i = 0; i < 5; ++i)
    printf("%\nld %-20s %4.2f",employee[i].id,employee[i].name,employee[i].rate);

  return 0;
}
```

The output displayed by Program 10.3 is

```
32479 Abrams, B.          6.72
33623 Bohm, P.            7.54
34145 Donaldson, S.       5.56
35987 Ernst, T.           5.43
36203 Gwodz, K.           8.72
```

In reviewing Program 10.3, notice the initialization of the array of structures. Although the initializers for each structure have been enclosed in inner braces, these are not strictly necessary because all members have been initialized. As with all external and static variables, in the absence of explicit initializers, the numeric elements of both static and external arrays or structures are initialized to zero and their character elements are initialized to nulls. The %-20s format included in the printf() function call forces each name to be displayed left justified in a field of 20 spaces.

Exercises 10.2

1. Define arrays of 100 structures for each of the structures described in Exercise 1 of Section 10.1.

2. a. Using the following declaration

```
struct MonthDays
{
  char name[10];
  int days;
};
```

define an array of 12 structures of type MonthDays. Name the array convert[], and initialize the array with the names of the 12 months in a year and the number of days in each month.

   b. Include the array created in Exercise 2a in a program that displays the names and number of days in each month.

3. Using the structure defined in Exercise 2a, write a C program that accepts a month from a user in numeric form and displays the name of the month and the number of days in the month. Thus, in response to an input of 3, the program displays March has 31 days.

4. a. Declare a single structure type suitable for an employee record for the following data:

Number	Name	Rate	Hours
3462	Jones	4.62	40
6793	Robbins	5.83	38
6985	Smith	5.22	45
7834	Swain	6.89	40
8867	Timmins	6.43	35
9002	Williams	4.75	42

   b. Using the structure type declared in Exercise 4a, write a C program that interactively accepts the above data into an array of six structures. Once the data have been entered, the program should create a payroll report listing each employee's name, number, and gross pay. Include the total gross pay of all employees at the end of the report.

5. a. Declare a single structure type suitable for a car record for the following data:

Car Number	Miles Driven	Gallons Used
25	1,450	62
36	3,240	136
44	1,792	76
52	2,360	105
68	2,114	67

b. Using the structure type declared for Exercise 5a, write a C program that interactively accepts the above data into an array of five structures. Once the data have been entered, the program should create a report listing each car number and the miles per gallon achieved by the car. At the end of the report include the average miles per gallon achieved by the complete fleet of cars.

10.3 Passing and Returning Structures

Individual structure members may be passed to a function in the same manner as any scalar variable. For example, given the structure definition

```
struct
{
  int idNum;
  double payRate;
  double hours;
} emp;
```

the statement

```
display(emp.idNum);
```

passes a copy of the structure member `emp.idNum` to a function named `display()`. Similarly, the statement

```
calcPay(emp.payRate,emp.hours);
```

passes copies of the values stored in structure members `emp.payRate` and `emp.hours` to the function `calcPay()`. Both functions, `display()` and `calcPay()`, must declare the correct data types of their respective parameters.

On most compilers, complete copies of all members of a structure can also be passed to a function by including the name of the structure as an argument to the called function. For example, the function call

```
calcNet(emp);
```

passes a copy of the complete `emp` structure to `calcNet()`. Internal to `calcNet()`, an appropriate declaration must be made to receive the structure. Program 10.4 declares a global structure type for an employee record. This type is then used by both the `main()` and `calcNet()` functions to define specific structures with the names `emp` and `temp`, respectively.

Program 10.4

```
#include <stdio.h>

struct Employee      /* declare a global structure type */
{
  int idNum;
  double payRate;
  double hours;
};

double calcNet(struct Employee);  /* function prototype */

int main()
{
  struct Employee emp = {6782, 8.93, 40.5};
  double netPay;
  netPay = calcNet(emp);          /* pass copies of the values in emp */
  printf("The net pay of employee %d is $%6.2f",emp.idNum,netPay);

  return 0;
}

double calcNet(struct Employee temp)
                               /* temp is of data type struct Employee */
{
  return(temp.payRate * temp.hours);
}
```

The output produced by Program 10.4 is

```
The net pay for employee 6782 is $361.66
```

In reviewing Program 10.4, observe that both main() and calcNet() use the same global structure type to define their individual structures. The structure defined in main() and the structure defined in calcNet() are two completely different structures. Any changes made to the local temp structure in calcNet() are not reflected in the emp structure of main(). In fact, since both structures are local to their respective functions, the same structure name could have been used in both functions with no ambiguity.

When calcNet() is called by main(), copies of emp's structure values are passed to the temp structure. calcNet() then uses two of the passed member values to calculate a number, which is returned to main().

Although the structures in both `main()` and `calcNet()` use the same globally defined structure type, this is not strictly necessary. For example, the structure variable in `main()` could have been defined directly as:

```
struct
{
  int idNum;
  double payRate;
  double hours;
}  emp = {6782, 8.93, 40.5};
```

Similarly, the structure variable in `calcNet()` could have been defined as:

```
struct
{
  int idNum;
  double payRate;
  double hours;
} temp;
```

The global declaration of the `Employee` structure type provided in Program 10.4 is highly preferable to these latter two individual structure specifications because the global structure type centralizes the declaration of the structure's organization. Any change that must subsequently be made to the structure need only be made once to the global declaration. Making changes to individual structure definitions requires that all occurrences of the structure definition be located in every function defining the structure. For larger programs this usually results in an error when a change to one of the structure definitions is inadvertently omitted.

An alternative to passing a copy of a structure is to pass the address of the structure. This, of course, allows the called function to make changes directly to the original structure. For example, referring to Program 10.4, the call to `calcNet()` can be modified to

```
calcNet(&emp);
```

In this call, an address is passed. To correctly store this address `calcNet()` must declare its parameter as a pointer. A suitable function header line for `calcNet()` to accept this address is

```
double calcNet(struct Employee *pt)
```

Here, the declaration for `pt` declares this parameter as a pointer to a structure of type `employee`. The pointer variable, `pt`, receives the starting address of a structure whenever `calcNet()` is called. Within `calcNet()`, this pointer is used to directly access any member in the structure. For example, `(*pt).idNum` refers to the `idNum` member of the structure, `(*pt).payRate` refers to the `payRate` member of the structure, and

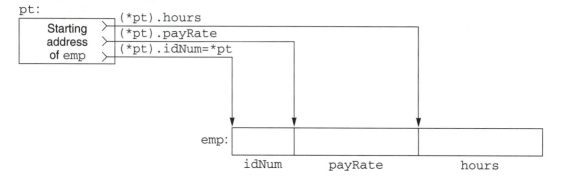

Figure 10.5 A pointer can be used to access structure members

(*pt).hours refers to the hours member of the structure. These relationships are illustrated in Figure 10.5.

The parentheses around the expression *pt in Figure 10.5 are necessary to initially access "the structure whose address is in pt." This is followed by an identifier to access the desired member within the structure. In the absence of the parentheses, the structure member operator . takes precedence over the indirection operator *. Thus, the expression *pt.hours is another way of writing *(pt.hours), which refers to *the variable whose address is in the* pt.hours *variable*. This last expression clearly makes no sense because there is no structure named pt, and hours does not contain an address.

As illustrated in Figure 10.5, the starting address of the emp structure is also the address of the first member of the structure. Thus, the expressions *pt and (*pt).idNum both refer to the idNum member of the emp structure.

The use of pointers is so common with structures that a special notation exists for them. The general expression (*pointer).member can always be replaced with the notation pointer->member, where the -> operator is constructed using a minus sign followed by a right-facing arrow (the greater-than symbol). Either expression can be used to locate the desired member. For example, the following expressions are equivalent:

    (*pt).idNum   can be replaced by pt->idNum
    (*pt).payRate can be replaced by pt->payRate
    (*pt).hours   can be replaced by pt->hours

Program 10.5 illustrates passing a structure's address and using a pointer with the new notation to access the structure directly.

The name of the pointer parameter declared in Program 10.5 is, of course, selected by the programmer. When calcNet() is called, emp's starting address is passed to the function. Using this address as a starting point, individual members of the structure are accessed by including their names with the pointer.

🖥️ **Program 10.5**

```
#include <stdio.h>

struct Employee      /* declare a global structure type */
{
  int idNum;
  double payRate;
  double hours;
};
double calcNet(struct Employee *);   /* function prototype */

int main()
{
  struct Employee emp = {6782, 8.93, 40.5};
  double netPay;

  netPay = calcNet(&emp);        /* pass an address*/
  printf("The net pay for employee %d is $%6.2f"\n,emp.idNum,netPay);

  return 0;
}

double calcNet(struct Employee *pt)  /* pt is a pointer to a */
{                                    /* structure of Employee type */
return(pt->payRate * pt->hours);
}
```

As with all C expressions that access a variable, the increment and decrement operators can also be applied to them. For example, the expression

```
++pt->hours
```

adds one to the hours member of the emp structure. Because the -> operator has a higher priority than the increment operator, the hours member is accessed first and then the increment is applied.

Alternatively, the expression (pt++)->hours uses the postfix increment operator to increment the address in pt after the hours member is accessed. Similarly, the expression (++pt)->hours uses the prefix increment operator to increment the address in pt before the hours member is accessed. In both of these cases, however, there must be sufficient defined structures to ensure that the incremented pointers actually point to legitimate structures.

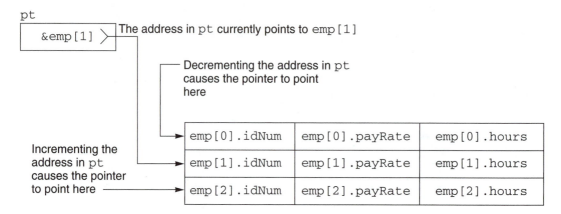

Figure 10.6 Changing pointer addresses

As an example, Figure 10.6 illustrates an array of three structures of type employee. Assuming that the address of emp[1] is stored in the pointer pt, the expression ++pt changes the address in pt to the starting address of emp[2], while the expression --pt changes the address to point to emp[0].

Returning Structures

In practice, most structure-handling functions receive direct access to a structure by passing the address of the structure to the function. Then any changes can be made directly by the function using pointer notation. If you want to have a function return a separate structure, however, and your compiler supports this option, you must follow the same procedures for returning complete structures as for returning scalar values. These include both declaring the function appropriately and alerting any calling function to the type of structure being returned. For example, the function getValues() in Program 10.6 returns a complete structure to main().

The following output is displayed when Program 10.6 is run:

```
The employee id number is 6789
The employee pay rate is $16.25
The employee hours are 38.00
```

Because the getValues() function returns a structure, the function header for getValues() must specify the type of structure being returned. As getValues() does not receive any arguments, the function header has no parameter declarations and consists of the line

```
struct Employee getValues()
```

Program 10.6

```c
#include <stdio.h>
struct Employee        /* declare a global structure type */
{
   int idNum;
   double payRate;
   double hours;
};

struct Employee getValues();   /* function prototype */

int main()
{
   struct Employee emp;

   emp = getValues();
   printf("\nThe employee id number is %d\n", emp.idNum);
   printf("The employee pay rate is $%5.2f\n", emp.payRate);
   printf("The employee hours are %5.2f\n", emp.hours);

   return 0;
}

struct Employee getValues()
{
   struct Employee newemp;

   newemp.idNum = 6789;
   newemp.payrate = 16.25;
   newemp.hours = 38.0;
   return(newemp);
}
```

Within `getValues()`, the variable `newemp` is defined as a structure of the type to be returned. After values have been assigned to the new structure, the structure values are returned by including the structure name within the parentheses of the return statement.

On the receiving side, `main()` must be alerted that the function `getValues()` will be returning a structure. This is handled by the function prototype for `getValues()`. Notice that these steps for returning a structure from a function are identical to the procedures for returning scalar data types previously described in Chapter 6.

Exercises 10.3

1. Write a C function named days() that determines the number of days from the date 1/1/1900 for any date passed as a structure. Use the Date structure

```
struct Date
{
  int month;
  int day;
  int year;
};
```

In writing the days() function, use the convention that all years have 360 days and each month consists of 30 days. The function should return the number of days for any date structure passed to it. Make sure to declare the returned variable a long integer to reserve sufficient room for dates such as 12/19/2002.

2. Write a C function named difDays() that calculates and returns the difference between two dates. Each date is passed to the function as a structure using the following global structure:

```
struct Date
{
  int month;
  int day;
  int year;
};
```

The difDays() function should make two calls to the days() function written for Exercise 1.

3. Rewrite the days() function written for Exercise 1 to receive a pointer to a date structure, rather than a copy of the complete structure.

4. a. Write a C function named larger() that returns the later date of any two dates passed to it. For example, if the dates 10/9/2001 and 11/3/2001 are passed to larger(), the second date would be returned.
   b. Include the larger() function that was written for Exercise 4a in a complete program. Store the date structure returned by larger() in a separate date structure and display the member values of the returned date.

5. a. Modify the function days() written for Exercise 1 to account for the actual number of days in each month. Assume, however, that each year contains 365 days (that is, do not account for leap years).
   b. Modify the function written for Exercise 5a to account for leap years.

10.4   Linked Lists

A classic data-handling problem is making additions or deletions to existing records that are maintained in a specific order. This is best illustrated by considering the alphabetical

Acme, Sam
(555) 898-2392

Dolan, Edith
(555) 682-3104

Lanfrank, John
(555) 718-4581

Mening, Stephanie
(555) 382-7070

Zemann, Harold
(555) 219-9912

Figure 10.7   A telephone list in alphabetical order

telephone list shown in Figure 10.7. Starting with this initial set of names and telephone numbers, we desire to add new records to the list in the proper alphabetical sequence and to delete existing records in such a way that the storage for deleted records is eliminated.

Although the insertion or deletion of ordered records can be accomplished using an array of structures, these arrays are not efficient representations for adding or deleting records internal to the array. Arrays are fixed and prespecified in size. Deleting a record from an array creates an empty slot that requires either special marking or shifting up all elements below the deleted record to close the empty slot. Similarly, adding a record to the body of an array of structures requires that all elements below the addition be shifted down to make room for the new entry, or the new element could be added to the end of the existing array and the array then resorted to restore the proper order of the records. Thus, either adding or deleting records to such a list generally requires restructuring and rewriting the list—a cumbersome, time-consuming, and inefficient practice.

A linked list provides a convenient method for maintaining a constantly changing list without the need to continually reorder and restructure the complete list. A *linked list* is simply a set of structures in which each structure contains at least one member whose value is the address of the next logically ordered structure in the list. Rather than requiring each record to be physically stored in the proper order, each new record is physically added either to the end of the existing list, or wherever the computer has free space in its storage area. The records are "linked" together by including the address of the next record in the record logically preceding it. From a programming standpoint, the current record being processed contains the address of the next record, no matter where the next record is actually stored.

The concept of a linked list is illustrated in Figure 10.8. Although the actual data for the Lanfrank structure illustrated in the figure may be physically stored anywhere in the computer, the additional member included at the end of the Dolan structure maintains the proper alphabetical order. This member provides the starting address of the location where the Lanfrank record is stored. As you might expect, this member is a pointer.

To see the usefulness of the pointer in the Dolan record, let us add a telephone number for June Hagar into the alphabetical list shown in Figure 10.7. The data for June Hagar are stored in a data structure using the same data structure as that used for the

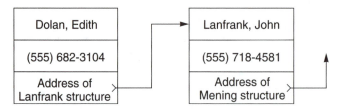

Figure 10.8 Using pointers to link structures

existing records. To ensure that the telephone number for Hagar is correctly displayed after the Dolan telephone number, the address in the Dolan record must be altered to point to the Hagar record, and the address in the Hagar record must be set to point to the Lanfrank record. This is illustrated in Figure 10.9. Notice that the pointer in each structure simply points to the location of the next ordered structure, even if that structure is not physically located in the correct order.

Removal of a structure from the ordered list is the reverse process of adding a record. The actual record is logically removed from the list simply by changing the address in the structure preceding the deleted record to point to the structure immediately following it.

Each structure in a linked list has the same format; however, it is clear that the last record cannot have a valid pointer value that points to another record since there is none. C provides a special pointer value called NULL that acts as a sentinel or flag to indicate when the last record has been processed. The NULL pointer value, like its end-of-string counterpart, has a numerical value of zero.

Besides an end-of-list sentinel value, a special pointer must also be provided for storing the address of the first structure in the list. Figure 10.10 illustrates the complete set of pointers and structures for a list consisting of three names.

The inclusion of a pointer in a structure should not seem surprising. As we discovered in Section 10.1, a structure can contain any C data type. For example, the structure declaration

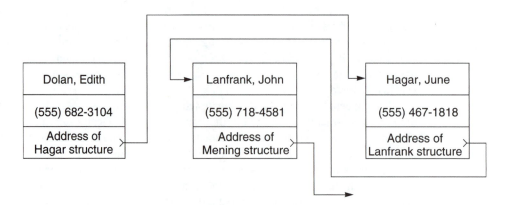

Figure 10.9 Adjusting addresses to point to appropriate records

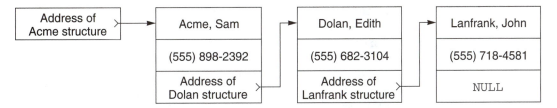

Figure 10.10   Use of the initial and final pointer values

```
struct Test
{
  int idNum;
  double *ptPay
};
```

declares a structure consisting of two members. The first member is an integer variable named idNum, and the second variable is a pointer named ptPay, which is a pointer to a double precision number. Program 10.7 illustrates that the pointer member of a structure is used like any other pointer variable.

🖥 Program 10.7

```
#include <stdio.h>
struct Test
{
  int idNum;
  double *ptPay;
};
int main()
{
  struct Test emp;
  double pay = 456.20;

  emp.idNum = 12345;
  emp.ptPay = &pay;

  printf("Employee number %d was paid $%6.2f",
         emp.idNum, *emp.ptPay);

  return 0;
}
```

The output produced by executing Program 10.7 is

```
Employee number 12345 was paid $456.20
```

Figure 10.11 illustrates the relationship between the members of the emp structure defined in Program 10.7 and the variable named pay. The value assigned to emp.idNum is 12345, and the value assigned to pay is 456.20. The address of the pay variable is assigned to the structure member emp.ptPay. Because this member has been defined as a pointer to a double precision number, placing the address of the double precision variable pay in it is a correct use of this member. Finally, because the member operator . has a higher precedence than the indirection operator *, the expression used in the printf() call in Program 10.7 is correct. The expression *emp.ptPay is equivalent to the expression *(emp.ptPay), which is translated as *the variable whose address is contained in the member* emp.ptPay.

Although the pointer defined in Program 10.7 has been used in a rather trivial fashion, the program does illustrate the concept of including a pointer in a structure. This concept can be easily extended to create a linked list of structures suitable for storing the names and telephone numbers previously listed in Figure 10.7. The following declaration creates such a structure:

```
struct TeleType
{
  char name[30];
  char phoneNum[15];
  struct TeleType *nextaddr;
};
```

The TeleType structure type consists of three members. The first member is an array of 30 characters, suitable for storing names with a maximum of 29 letters and an end-of-string marker. The next member is an array of 15 characters suitable for storing telephone numbers with their respective area codes. The last member is a pointer suitable for storing the address of a structure of the TeleType type.

Program 10.8 illustrates the use of the TeleType type by specifically defining three structures having this form. The three structures are named t1, t2, and t3, respectively, and the name and telephone members of each of these structures are initialized when the structures are defined, using the data listed in Figure 10.7.

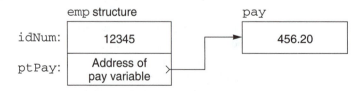

Figure 10.11   Storing an address in a structure member

Program 10.8

```c
#include <stdio.h>
struct TeleType
{
  char name[30];
  char phoneNum[15];
  struct TeleType *nextaddr;
};
int main()
{
  struct TeleType t1 = {"Acme, Sam","(555) 898-2392"};
  struct TeleType t2 = {"Dolan, Edith","(555) 682-3104"};
  struct Teletype t3 = {"Lanfrank, John","(555) 718-4581"};
  TeleType *first;     /* create a pointer to a structure */

  first = &t1;              /* store t1's address in first */
  t1.nextaddr = &t2;        /* store t2's address in t1.nextaddr */
  t2.nextaddr = &t3;        /* store t3's address in t2.nextaddr */
  t3.nextaddr = NULL;       /* store the NULL address in t3.nextaddr */

  printf("\n%s %s %s",first->name,t1.nextaddr->name,t2.nextadddr->name);

  return 0;
}
```

The output produced by Program 10.8 is

```
Acme, Sam
Dolan, Edith
Lanfrank, John
```

Program 10.8 demonstrates the use of pointers to access successive structure members. As illustrated in Figure 10.12, each structure contains the address of the next structure in the list.

The initialization of the names and telephone numbers for each of the structures defined in Program 10.8 is straightforward. Although each structure consists of three members, only the first two members of each structure are initialized. As both of these members are arrays of characters, they can be initialized with strings. The remaining member of each structure is a pointer. To create a linked list, each structure pointer must be assigned the address of the next structure in the list.

The four assignment statements in Program 10.8 perform the correct assignments. The expression `first = &t1` stores the address of the first structure in the list in the pointer variable named `first`. The expression `t1.nextaddr = &t2` stores the starting address of the t2 structure into the pointer member of the t1 structure. Similarly, the expression t2.nextaddr = &t3 stores the starting address of the t3 structure into the pointer member of the t2 structure. To end the list, the value of the NULL address, which is zero, is stored into the pointer member of the t3 structure.

Once values have been assigned to each structure member and correct addresses have been stored in the appropriate pointers, the addresses in the pointers are used to access each structure's name member. For example, the expression t1.nextaddr->name refers to the name member of the structure whose address is in the nextaddr member of the t1 structure. The precedence of the member operator . and the structure pointer operator -> are equal, and are evaluated from left to right. Thus, the expression t1.nextaddr->name is evaluated as (t1.nextadd)->name. Because t1.nextaddr contains the address of the t2 structure, the proper name is accessed.

The expression t1.nextaddr->name can, of course, be replaced by the equivalent expression (*t1.nextaddr).name, which uses the more conventional indirec-

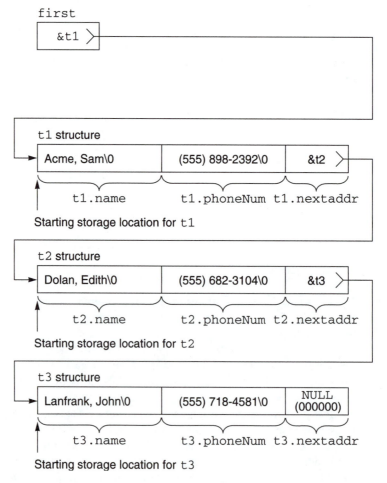

Figure 10.12   The relationship between structures in Program 10.8

tion operator. This expression also refers to *the* name *member of the variable whose address is in* t1.nextaddr.

The addresses in a linked list of structures can be used to loop through the complete list. As each structure is accessed it can be either examined to select a specific value or used to print out a complete list. For example, the display() function in Program 10.9 illustrates the use of a while loop, which uses the address in each structure's pointer member to cycle through the list and successively display data stored in each structure.

Program 10.9

```c
#include <stdio.h>
struct TeleType
{
  char name[30];
  char phoneNum[15];
  struct TeleType *nextaddr;
};

void display(struct TeleType *);        /* function prototype */

int main()
{
  struct TeleType t1 = {"Acme, Sam","(555) 898-2392"};
  struct Teletype t2 = {"Dolan, Edith","(555) 682-3104"};
  struct Teletype t3 = {"Lanfrank, John","(555) 718-4581"};
  struct Teletype *first;   /* create a pointer to a structure */

  first = &t1;          /* store t1's address in first */
  t1.nextaddr = &t2;    /* store t2;s address in t1.nextaddr */
  t2.nextaddr = &t3;    /* store t3's address in t2.nextaddr */
  t3.nextaddr = NULL;   /* store the NULL address in t3.nextaddr */

  display(first);       /* send the address of the first structure */

  return 0;
}

void display(struct TeleType *contents) /* contents is a pointer */
{                               /* to a structure of type TeleType */
  while (contents != NULL)    /* display till end of linked list */
  {
    printf("\n%30s %-20s",contents->name, contents->phoneNum);
    contents = contents->nextaddr;     /* get next address */
  }
  return;
}
```

The output produced by Program 10.9 is

```
Acme, Sam                  (555) 898-2392
Dolan, Edith               (555) 682-3104
Lanfrank, John             (555) 718-4581
```

The important concept illustrated by Program 10.9 is the use of the address in one structure to access members of the next structure in the list. When the display() function is called, it is passed the value stored in the variable named first. Because first is a pointer variable, the actual value passed is an address (the address of the t1 structure). display() accepts the passed value in the parameter named contents. To store the passed address correctly, contents is declared as a pointer to a structure of the TeleType type. Within display(), a while loop is used to cycle through the linked structures, starting with the structure whose address is in contents. The condition tested in the while statement compares the value in contents, which is an address, to the NULL value. For each valid address the name and phone number members of the addressed structure are displayed. The address in contents is then updated with the address in the pointer member of the current structure. The address in contents is then retested, and the process continues while the address in contents is not equal to the NULL value. display() "knows" nothing about the names of the structures declared in main() or even how many structures exist. It simply cycles through the linked list, structure by structure, until it encounters the end-of-list NULL address. Because the value of NULL is zero, the tested condition can be replaced by the equivalent expression !contents.

A disadvantage of Program 10.9 is that exactly three structures are defined in main() by name, and storage for them is reserved at compile time. Should a fourth structure be required, the additional structure has to be declared and the program recompiled. In the next section, we show how to have the program dynamically allocate and release storage for structures at run time, as storage is required. Only when a new structure is to be added to the list, and while the program is running, is storage for the new structure created. Similarly, when a structure is no longer needed and can be deleted from the list, the storage for the deleted record is relinquished and returned to the computer.

Exercises 10.4

1. Modify Program 10.4 to prompt the user for a name. Have the program search the existing list for the entered name. If the name is in the list, display the corresponding phone number; otherwise display the message, The name is not in the current phone directory.

2. Write a C program containing a linked list of five integer numbers. Have the program display the numbers in the list.

3. Using the linked list of structures illustrated in Figure 10.12, write the sequence of steps necessary to delete the record for Edith Dolan from the list.

4. Generalize the description obtained in Exercise 3 to describe the sequence of steps necessary to remove the *n*th structure from a list of linked structures. The *n*th structure is preceded by the

(n–1)st structure and followed by the (n+1)st structure. Make sure to store all pointer values correctly.

5. a. A doubly linked list is a list in which each structure contains a pointer to both the following and previous structures in the list. Define an appropriate structure for a doubly linked list of names and telephone numbers.

   b. Using the structure defined in Exercise 5a, modify Program 10.9 to list the names and phone numbers in reverse order.

10.5 Dynamic Memory Allocation

As each variable is defined in a program, sufficient storage for it is assigned from a pool of available computer memory. Once specific memory locations have been reserved for a variable, these locations are fixed for the life of that variable, whether they are used or not. For example, if a function requests storage for an array of 500 integers, the storage for the array is allocated and fixed from the point of the array's definition. If the application requires less than 500 integers, the unused allocated storage is not released back to the system until the array goes out of existence. If, on the other hand, the application requires more than 500 integers, the size of the integer array must be increased and the function defining the array recompiled.

An alternative to this fixed or static allocation of memory storage locations is *dynamic allocation of memory*. Under a dynamic memory allocation, the amount of storage allocated is determined and adjusted as a program is run, rather than being fixed at compile time.

Dynamic allocation of memory is extremely useful when dealing with lists, because it allows the list to expand as new items are added and contract as items are deleted. For example, in constructing a list of grades, the exact number of grades ultimately needed may not be known. Rather than creating a fixed array to store the grades, it is extremely useful to have a mechanism whereby the array can be enlarged and shrunk as necessary. Two C functions, `malloc()` and `free()`, which together provide a simple general-purpose memory allocation package, are described in Table 10.1.[2]

In requesting a new allocation of storage space using `malloc()`, the user must provide the function with an indication of the amount of storage needed. This may be done by either requesting a specific number of bytes or, more usually, by requesting enough space for a particular type of data. For example, the function call `malloc(10 * sizeof(char))` requests enough memory to store 10 characters, while the function call `malloc(sizeof(int))` requests enough storage to store an integer number.

In a similar manner and of more usefulness is the dynamic allocation of arrays and structures. For example, the expression

```
malloc(200 * sizeof(int))
```

---

[2] These functions require the `stdlib.h` header file.

Table 10.1 General-purpose memory allocation functions

Function Name	Description
malloc()	Reserves the number of bytes requested by the argument passed to the function. Returns the address of the first reserved location or NULL if sufficient memory is not available.
free()	Releases a block of bytes previously reserved. The address of the first reserved location is passed as an argument to the function.

reserves a sufficient number of bytes to store 200 integers. Although we have used the constant 200 in this example declaration, a variable, as we will shortly show, can also be used. The space allocated by malloc() comes from the computer's free storage area.[3]

In allocating storage dynamically, we have no advance indication as to where the computer system will physically reserve the requested number of bytes, and we have no explicit name to access the newly created storage locations. To provide access to these locations, malloc() returns the address of the first location that has been reserved. This address must, of course, be assigned to a pointer. The return of a pointer by malloc() is especially useful for creating either arrays or a set of data structures. Before illustrating the actual dynamic allocation of an array or data structure, we need to consider one logistic problem created by malloc().

The malloc() function always returns the address of the first byte of storage reserved, where the returned address is declared as a pointer to a void. Any function that calls malloc() must include the stdlib.h header file, which contains the correct malloc() function prototype.

Because the returned address is always a pointer to a void, regardless of the data type requested, the returned address must always be reinterpreted as pointing to the desired type. The mechanism for converting one data type into another is called a *cast*. In this case, then, we need to cast (or force) the returned pointer into a pointer to the desired data type. For example, if the variable grades is a pointer to an integer and key is a pointer to a void, the statement

```
grades = (int *) key
```

redefines the address stored in key as the address of an integer. The address is not changed physically, but any subsequent reference to the address in grades will now

---

[3] The free storage area of a computer is formally referred to as the *heap*. The heap consists of unallocated memory that can be allocated to a program, as requested, while the program is executing. All such allocated memory is returned to the heap, either explicitly using the free() function or automatically when the program requesting additional memory is finished executing.

In a similar fashion the compiler automatically provides the same type of dynamic allocation and deallocation of memory for all automatic variables and function arguments. In these cases, however, the allocation and deallocation is made from the *stack* storage area.

cause the correct number of bytes to be accessed for an integer value. Casts are more fully described in Chapter 12. For now, however, we will simply use cast expressions to convert the address returned by `malloc()` into the correct pointer types. For example, consider the following section of code, which can be used to create an array of integers whose size is determined by the user at runtime as an input value:

```
int *grades;          /* define a pointer to an integer */

printf("\nEnter the number of grades to be processed: ");
scanf("%d", &numgrades);

   /* here is where the request for memory is made */
grades = (int *) malloc(numgrades * sizeof(int));
```

In this sequence of instructions the actual size of the array that is created depends on the number input by the user. Because pointer and array names are related, each value in the newly created storage area can be accessed using standard array notation, such as `grades[i]`, rather than the equivalent pointer notation `*(grades + i)`. Program 10.10 illustrates this sequence of code in the context of a complete program.

Following is a sample run using Program 10.10:

```
Enter the number of grades to be processed: 4
    Enter a grade: 85
    Enter a grade: 96
    Enter a grade: 77
    Enter a grade: 92

An array was created for 4 integers
The values stored in the array are:
85
96
77
92
```

As seen by this output, dynamic memory allocation is used to successfully create storage for four integer values as the program is running.

Although the call to `malloc()` in Program 10.10 is rather simple, two important concepts related to the call should be noted. First, notice the code immediately after the call to `malloc()`, which is repeated below:

```
   /* here we check that the allocation was satisfied */
if (grades == (int *) NULL)
{
  printf("\nFailed to allocate grades array\n");
   exit(1);
}
```

Program 10.10

```c
#include <stdio.h>
#include <stdlib.h>

int main()
{
  int numgrades, i;
  int *grades;

  printf("\nEnter the number of grades to be processed: ");
  scanf("%d", &numgrades);

  grades = (int *) malloc(numgrades * sizeof(int));
  if (grades == (int *) NULL)
  {
    printf("\nFailed to allocate grades array\n");
    exit(1);
  }
  for(i = 0; i < numgrades; i++)
  {
    printf("  Enter a grade: ");
    scanf("%d", &grades[i]);
  }
  printf("\nAn array was created for %d integers", numgrades);
  printf("\nThe values stored in the array are:\n");
  for (i = 0; i < numgrades; i++)
    printf(" %d\n", grades[i]);

  free(grades);

  return 0;
}
```

This section of code tests `malloc()`'s return value to ensure that the memory request was successfully satisfied. If `malloc()` cannot obtain the desired memory space it returns a NULL, which in Program 10.10 would be cast into a pointer to an integer by the statement making the `malloc()` call. Thus `grades` must subsequently be compared to `(int *)` NULL in the `if` statement. In making requests for dynamic memory allocation it is extremely important to always check the return value—otherwise the program will crash when a subsequent access to nonexisting memory is made.

Next, notice that Program 10.10 uses the `free()` function to restore the allocated block of storage back to the operating system at the end of the program.[4] The only address required by `free()` is the starting address of the block of storage that was dynamically allocated. Thus, any address returned by `malloc()` can subsequently be used by `free()` to restore the reserved memory back to the computer. The `free()` function does not alter the address passed to it, but simply removes the storage that the address references.

In addition to requesting data space for arrays, as is done in Program 10.10, `malloc()` is more typically used for dynamically allocating memory for data structures. For example, consider that we have declared a data structure named `OfficeInfo`:

```
struct OfficeInfo
{
   any number of data members declared in here;
};
```

Regardless of the number and type of data members declared in `OfficeInfo`, the call `malloc(sizeof(struct OfficeInfo))` requests enough storage for one structure of the `OfficeInfo` type. To use the return pointer value provided by `malloc()` once again requires us to cast the return address into a pointer of the correct structure type. Typically this is done using a sequence of statements similar to the following:[5]

```
struct OfficeInfo *Off;  /* create a pointer to store the allocated address */

   /*  request space for one record */
Off = (struct OfficeInfo *) malloc(sizeof(struct OfficeInfo));

   /* check that space was allocated */
if (Off == (struct OfficeInfo *) NULL)
{
  printf("\nAllocation of OfficeInfo record failed\n");
  exit(1);
}
```

This type of dynamic allocation is extremely useful in a variety of advanced programming situations, three of which are now presented.

---

[4] The allocated storage would automatically be returned to the heap when the program has completed execution. It is, however, good practice to explicitly restore the allocated storage back to the heap using delete when the memory is no longer needed. This is especially true for larger programs that make numerous requests for additional storage areas.

[5] Again, for clarity, we have separated the request for memory allocation from the verification that the request was successfully satisfied. In actual practice these would typically be combined as:

```
if ((Off = (struct OfficeInfo *) malloc(sizeof(struct OfficeInfo))) == (struct OfficeInfo *)NULL)
{
  printf("\nAllocation of OfficeInfo record failed\n");
  exit(1);
}
```

Programming Note

Checking `malloc()`'s Return Value

It is important to check the return value when making a `malloc()` call. Doing so ensures that you know when the operating system has not satisfied an allocation request and permits you to gracefully terminate your program. Failure to do so almost always results in a program crash if the memory was not allocated and a subsequent program statement attempts to use the memory. There are two styles of coding for checking the return value.

The first style is the one coded in Program 10.10. It is used to clearly separate the request for memory from the return value check, and is repeated below for convenience:

```
   /* here is where the request for memory is made */
grades = (int *) malloc(numgrades * sizeof(int));
   /* here we check that the allocation was satisfied */
if (grades == (int *) NULL)
{
  printf("\nFailed to allocate grades array\n");
  exit(1);
}
```

However, the request and check are more typically combined within the `if` statement as:

```
if ( (grades = (int *) malloc(numgrades * sizeof(int))) == (int *) NULL)
{
  printf("\nFailed to allocate grades array\n");
  exit(1);
}
```

Use the style with which you are initially more comfortable. As you gain experience in programming, be prepared to adopt the second style. It is the one used almost universally by advanced programmers.

Dynamically Linked Lists

In the previous section we saw how to construct a fixed set of linked lists. We now extend this concept and see how to dynamically allocate and free records from such a list. For example, in constructing a list of names and phone numbers the exact number of structures ultimately needed may not be known. Nevertheless, we may want to maintain the list in

Start of list
pointer

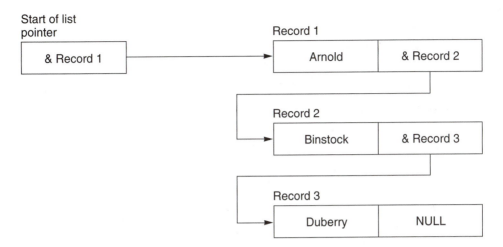

Figure 10.13   The initial linked list

alphabetical last name order regardless of how many names are added to or removed from the list. A dynamically allocated list that can expand and contract is ideally suited for this type of list maintenance. Constructing such a list means that we will have to provide the ability both to insert a new record into the list and to delete an existing record from the list.

The operation of adding a new record to a dynamically linked list is called an *insert*, and removing a record from such a list is called a *delete*. Let's see how these operations are implemented in practice.

Figure 10.13 illustrates a linked list consisting of three records. As shown, each record consists of a name member and a pointer member containing the address of the next record in the list. Several observations can be made for this list that apply to all dynamically maintained linked lists.

First, notice that each record shown in Figure 10.13 contains one pointer member, which is the address of the next record in the list. Also notice that the starting list pointer contains the address of the first record in the list and that the pointer member of the last record is a NULL address. This configuration is required of all dynamically linked lists regardless of any other data members present in each record.

Next notice that the records illustrated in Figure 10.13 are in alphabetical order. In general, every dynamically linked list is maintained based on the value of a particular field in each record. The field on which the list is ordered is referred to as the *key field,* and insertions and deletions are always made to preserve the ordering of this field.

Now assume that we want to insert the name "Carter" into the list. After dynamically allocating new memory space for the Carter record, the record addresses would have to be adjusted as shown in Figure 10.14 to maintain the proper alphabetical ordering.

The algorithm for performing an insertion into a linked list is as follows:

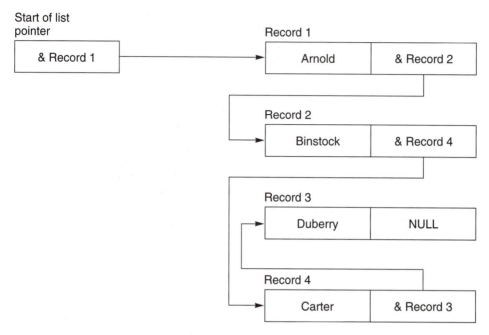

Figure 10.14   Adding a new name to the list

INSERT (add a new record into a linked list)
 Dynamically allocate space for a new record
 If no records exist in the list
   Set the address field of the new record to a NULL
   Set the address in the first record pointer to the address of the newly created record
 Else /* we are working with an existing list */
   Locate where this new record should be placed
   If this record should be the new first record in the list
     Copy the current contents of the first record pointer into
      the address field of the newly created record
     Set the address in the first record pointer to the address of
      the newly created record
   Else
     Copy the address in the prior record's address member into
      the address field of the newly created record
     Set the address field of the prior record's address member
      to the address of the newly created record
   EndIf
 EndIf

This algorithm provides the steps for correctly updating the pointer members of each record in a list such as shown in Figure 10.14, including the first record pointer when necessary. The algorithm does not, however, indicate how to locate the exact position in the list where the insertion should be made. The location of the insertion point can be made by a linear search of the existing list (see Section 7.7 for a discussion of searches). The pseudocode for a linear search to determine the correct insertion point is

> ***LINEAR LOCATION of a NEW RECORD***
>   ***If the key field of the new record is less than the first***
>   ***record's key field the new record should be the new first record***
>   ***Else***
>   ***While there are still more records in the list***
>   ***Compare the new record's key value to each record key***
>   ***Stop the comparison when the new record key either falls***
>   ***between two existing records or belongs at the end of***
>   ***the existing list***
>   ***EndWhile***
>   ***EndIf***

As a specific demonstration of insertions into a linked list, assume that the record type of data stored in the list is declared as:

```
#define MAXCHARS 30
struct NameRec
{
  char name[MAXCHARS];
  struct NameRec *nextAddr;
};
```

This is simply a record consisting of a name and pointer member of the type illustrated in Figures 10.13 and 10.14. The Insert and Linear Location algorithms are included within Program 10.11.

 Program 10.11

```
#include <stdio.h>
#include <stdlib.h>
#define MAXCHARS 30

/* here is the declaration of a linked list record */
struct NameRec
{
  char name[MAXCHARS];
  struct NameRec *nextAddr;
};
```

(Continued on next page)

(Continued from previous page)

```
/* here is the definition of the first record pointer */
struct nameRec *firstRec;

void readInsert();  /* function prototypes */
void display();
void insert(char []);

int main()
{
  firstRec = NULL;       /* initialize list pointer */
  readInsert();
  display();

  return 0;
}
/* get a name and insert it into the linked list */
void readInsert()
{

  char name[MAXCHARS];

  printf("\nEnter as many names as you wish, one per line");
  printf("\nTo stop entering names, enter a single x\n");
  while (1)
  {
    printf("Enter a name: ");
    gets(name);
    if (strcmp(name,"x") == 0)
      break;
    insert(name);
  return;
  }
}
void insert(char *name)
{
  struct NameRec *locate(char *);  /* function prototype */
  struct NameRec *newAddr, *here;  /* pointers to structure of type NameRec */

  newAddr = (struct NameRec *) malloc(sizeof(struct NameRec));
  if (newAddr == (struct NameRec *) NULL)  /* check the address */
  {
    printf("\nCould not allocate the requested space\n");
    exit(1);
  }
```

(Continued on next page)

(Continued from previous page)

```
    /* locate where the new record should be placed and */
    /* update all pointer members */
  if (firstRec == NULL)  /* no list currently exists */
  {
    newAddr->nextAddr = NULL:
    firstRec = newAddr; .
  }
  else if (strcmp(name, firstRec->name) < 0) /* a new first record */
  {
    newAddr->nextAddr = firstRec;
    firstRec = newAddr;
  }
  else  /* record is not the first record of the list */
  {
    here = locate(name);
    newAddr->nextAddr = here->nextAddr;
    here->nextAddr = newAddr;
  }
  strcpy(newAddr->name,name);   /* store the name */
  return;
}
/* locate the address of where a new record should be inserted */
/* within an existing list */
struct NameRec *locate(char *name)
{
  struct NameRec *one, *two;

  one = firstRec;
  two = one->nextAddr;

  if (two == NULL)
    return(one); /* new record goes after the existing single record */
  while(1)
  {
    if(strcmp(name,two->name) < 0)  /* we've located its position within the list */
    {
      break;
    }
    else if(two->nextAddr == NULL)  /* it goes after the last record */
    {
      one = two;
      break;
    }
    else  /* more records to search against */
```

(Continued on next page)

(Continued from previous page)

```
    {
      one = two;
      two = one->nextAddr;
    }
  }    /* the break takes us here */
  return(one);
}


/* display names from the linked list */
void display()
{
  struct NameRec *contents;
  contents = firstRec;
  printf("\nThe names currently on the list are:\n");
  while (contents != NULL)  /* display till end of list */
  {
    printf("%s\n",contents->name);
    contents = contents->nextAddr;
  }
  return;
}
```

To adequately test Program 0.11 requires entering names to a new list and then adding names that should be inserted before the first name, after the last name, and between two existing names. The following sample run performs these tests.

```
Enter as many names as you wish, one per line
To stop entering names, enter a single x
Enter a name: Binstock
Enter a name: Arnold
Enter name: Duberry
Enter a name: Carter
Enter a name: x

The names currently on the list are:
Arnold
Binstock
Carter
Duberry
```

Notice that the first name entered forces insert to construct the list, while the second name forces insert to place this new name at the beginning of the list. The third

Programming Note

Stacks, Queues, and Deques

A *stack* is a special type of linked list where data can only be added and removed from the same end of the list. This type of list, where the last item placed on the list is the first item removed, is also referred to as a *LIFO* (Last In, First Out) structure.

Stacks are used by operating systems for storing and removing return addresses in function calls. For example, if function A calls function B, which in turn calls function C, the return addresses are used in the reverse order of the call. Thus, the return from function C to function B is made first, followed by the return to function A.

Another special type of linked list is a *queue* (pronounced "cue"). In this type of list items are removed in the same order that they are placed on the list. As such, a queue is also referred to as a *FIFO* (First In, First Out) structure.

Queues are frequently used to store jobs that are ready to be printed. Each job placed on the queue is sent to the printer, in its proper turn, as the printer becomes available for another job.

Both stacks and queues are special cases of a more general data structure called a dequeue or deque (pronounced "deck"), which stands for a "double-ended queue."

name, "Duberry," forces `locate` to correctly determine that this name should be placed at the end of the list, while the last name, "Carter," forces `locate` to correctly position the name between two existing names.

Deleting a record in a linked list is essentially the reverse process of inserting a record. That is, a deletion requires determining where the selected record currently resides—at the beginning, at the end, or within the list—adjusting all pointer values accordingly, and then deallocating record space. We leave the detailed construction of the deletion algorithm as an exercise.

Exercises 10.5

1. Draw a diagram that illustrates how the linked list created by Program 10.11 looks as each name is inserted into the list. Make sure to include the first record pointer in your diagram.

2. a. Write the pseudocode for deleting an existing structure for the linked list of structures created by Program 10.11. The algorithm for deleting a linked structure should follow the sequence developed for deleting a structure developed in Exercise 4 in Section 10.4.
   b. Write C code for the algorithm developed in Exercise 2a.

3. Write a function named `modify()` that can be used to modify the name member of the structures created in Program 10.11. The argument passed to `modify()` should be the address of

the structure to be modified. The modify() function should first display the existing name and phone number in the selected structure and then request new data for these members.

4. Write a C program that initially presents a menu of choices for the user. The menu should consist of the following choices:

```
A. Create an initial linked list of names and phone numbers.
B. Insert a new structure into the linked list.
C. Modify an existing structure into the linked list.
D. Delete an existing structure from the list.
E. Exit from the program.
```

Upon the user's selection the program should execute the appropriate functions to satisfy the request.

10.6 Unions

A *union* is a data type that reserves the same area in memory for two or more variables, each of which can be a different data type. A variable that is declared as a union data type can be used to hold a character variable, an integer variable, a double precision variable, or any other valid C data type. Each of these types, but only one at a time, can actually be assigned to the union variable.

The declaration for a union is identical in form to a structure declaration, with the reserved word union used in place of the reserved word struct. For example, the declaration

```
union
{
    char key;
    int num;
    double price;
} val;
```

creates a union variable named val. If val were a structure it would consist of three individual members. As a union, however, val contains a single member that can be either a character variable named key, an integer variable named num, or a double precision variable named price. In effect, a union reserves sufficient memory locations to accommodate its largest member's data type. This same set of locations is then accessed by different variable names depending on the data type of the value currently residing in the reserved locations. Each value stored overwrites the previous value, using as many bytes of the reserved memory area as necessary.

Individual union members are accessed using the same notation as structure members. For example, if the val union is currently used to store a character, the correct variable name to access the stored character is val.key. Similarly, if the union is used to store an integer, the value is accessed by the name val.num, and a double precision value is accessed by the name val.price. With union members, it is the programmer's responsibility to ensure that the correct member name is used for the data type currently residing in the union.

Typically, a second variable keeps track of the current data type stored in the union. For example, the following code could be used to select the appropriate member of `val` for display. Here, the value in the variable `uType` determines the currently stored data type in the `val` union.

```
switch(uType)
{
   case 'c': printf("%c", val.key);
           break;
   case 'i': printf("%d", val.num);
           break;
   case 'd': printf("%f", val.price);
           break;
   default : printf("Invalid type in uType : %c", uType);
}
```

As they are in structures, a *type name* can be associated with a union to create templates. For example, the declaration

```
union DateTime
{
   long int days;
   double time;
};
```

provides a union type without actually reserving any storage locations. The type name can then be used to define any number of variables. For example, the definition

```
union DateTime first, second, *pt;
```

creates a union variable named `first`, a union variable named `second`, and a pointer that can be used to store the address of any union having the form of `DateTime`. Once a pointer to a union has been declared, the same notation used to access structure members can access union members. For example, if the assignment `pt = &first;` is made, then `pt->date` refers to the `date` member of the union named `first`.

Unions may themselves be members of structures and arrays, or structures, arrays, and pointers may be members of unions. In each case, the notation used to access a member must be consistent with the nesting employed. For example, in the structure defined by

```
struct
{
   char uType;
   union
```

(Continued on next page)

(Continued from previous page)

```
    {
        char *text;
        float rate;
    } uTax;
}  flag;
```

the variable `rate` is referenced as

```
flag.uTax.rate
```

Similarly, the first character of the string whose address is stored in the pointer `text` is accessed as

```
*flag.uTax.text
```

Exercises 10.6

1. Assume that the following definition has been made:

```
union
{
    float rate;
    double taxes;
    int num;
} flag;
```

For this union write appropriate `printf()` function calls to display the various members of the union.

2. Define a union variable named `car` that contains an integer named `year`, an array of ten characters named `name`, and an array of ten characters named `model`.

3. Define a union variable named `lang` that allows a floating point number to be accessed by both the variable names `interest` and `rate`.

4. Declare a union with the tag name `amt` that contains an integer variable named `intAmt`, a double precision variable named `dblAmt`, and a pointer to a character named `ptKey`.

5. a. What do you think will be displayed by the following section of code?

```
union
{
    char ch;
    float btype;
} alt;
alt.ch = 'y';
printf("%f", alt.btype);
```

   b. Include the code presented in Exercise 5a in a program and run the program to verify your answer to Exercise 5a.

10.7 Common Programming Errors

Three common errors are often made when using structures or unions.

1. Structures and unions, as complete entities, cannot be used in relational expressions. For example, even if `TeleType` and `PhoneType` are two structure of the same type, the expression `TeleType == Phonetype` is invalid. Individual members of a structure or union can, of course, be compared using any of C's relational operators.

2. This error is really an extension of a pointer error as it relates to structures and unions. Whenever a pointer is used to "point to" either of these data types, or whenever a pointer is itself a member of a structure or a union, take care to use the address in the pointer to access the appropriate data type. Should you be confused about just what is being pointed to, remember, "If in doubt print it out."

3. Because a union can store only one of its members at a time, you must be careful to keep track of the currently stored variable. Storing one data type in a union and accessing it by the wrong variable name can result in an error that is particularly troublesome to locate.

10.8 Chapter Summary

1. A structure allows individual variables to be grouped under a common variable name. Each variable in a structure is accessed by its structure name, followed by a period, followed by its individual variable name. Another term for a structure is a record. The general form for declaring a structure is

```
struct
{
   individual member declarations;
}  structureVariableName;
```

2. A structure type name can be used to create a generalized structure type describing the form and arrangement of elements in a structure. This declaration has the syntax:

```
struct StructureTypeName
{
   individual member declarations;
};
```

Individual structure variables may then be defined as this `StructureTypeName`. By convention, the first letter of a `StructureTypeName` is always capitalized.

3. Structures are particularly useful as elements of arrays. Used in this manner, each structure becomes one record in a list of records.

4. Individual members of a structure are passed to a function in the manner appropriate to the data type of the member being passed. Most ANSI C compilers allow complete structures to be passed, in which case the called function receives a copy of each element in the structure. The address of a structure may also be passed, which provides the called function with direct access to the structure.

5. Structure members can be any valid C data type, including structures, unions arrays, and pointers. When a pointer is included as a structure member a linked list can be created. Such a list uses the pointer in one structure to "point to" (contain the address of) the next logical structure in the list.

6. Unions are declared in the same manner as structures. The definition of a union creates a memory overlay area, with each union member using the same memory storage locations. Thus, only one member of a union may be active at a time.

Part **5**

Additional Topics

Data Files

The data for the programs we have seen so far have either been defined internally within the programs or entered interactively during program execution. This type of data creation and retention precludes sharing data between programs and is a disadvantage in larger systems consisting of many interconnecting programs. For these larger systems, the data used by one program typically must be made available to other programs, without being recreated or redefined.

Sharing data between programs requires that it be saved independently and separately from any single program. For example, consider the following data:

Code	Description	Price	Amount in Stock
QA134	Battery	35.89	10
QA136	Bulbs	3.22	123
CM104	Fuses	1.03	98
CM212	Degreaser	4.74	62
HT435	Cleaner	3.98	50

This data might be needed by both an inventory control program and a billing program. Therefore, the data would be stored by itself on a floppy diskette, hard disk, or magnetic tape in a data file.

A *data file* is any collection of data that is stored together under a common name on a storage medium other than the computer's main memory. This chapter describes the C statements needed to create data files and to read and write data to them.

11.1   Declaring, Opening, and Closing Files

A file is physically stored on an external medium such as a disk using a unique file name referred to as the *external file name.* This external name is the name of the file as it is known by the operating system. It is the external name that is displayed when you use the operating system to display the contents of a folder in Windows or a directory in UNIX or DOS using the cat and DIR commands, respectively.

Each computer operating system has its own specification as to the maximum number of characters permitted for an external file name. Table 11.1 lists these specifications for the more commonly used operating systems.

To ensure that the examples presented in this text are compatible with all of the operating systems listed in Table 11.1, we adhere to the more restrictive DOS and VMX specifications. If you are using one of the other operating systems, however, you should take advantage of the increased length specification to create descriptive file names within the context of manageable length (generally, 12 to 14 characters). Very long file names should be avoided. Although such names can be extremely descriptive, they take more time to type and are prone to typing errors.

Using the DOS convention then, the following are all valid computer data file names:

```
balances.dat      records       info.dat
report.bnd        prices.dat    math.mem
```

Table 11.1   Maximum allowable file name characters

Operating System	Maximum Length
DOS	8 characters plus an optional period and 3 character extension
VMX	8 characters plus an optional period and 3 character extension
Windows 3.1	8 characters plus an optional period and 3 character extension
Windows 95 and 98	255 characters
UNIX (Early Versions)	14 characters
(Current Versions)	255 characters

Computer file names (that is, external file names, as they are stored by the operating system) should be chosen to indicate both the type of data in the file and the application for which it is used. Frequently, the first eight characters are used to describe the data and an extension (the three characters after the decimal point) is used to describe the application. For example, the Lotus 123 spreadsheet program automatically applies an extension of wk3 to all spreadsheet files; Microsoft Word and WordPerfect use the extensions doc and wp*x* (where *x* refers to the version number), respectively, and most C++ compilers require a program file to have the extension cpp. When creating your own external file names you should adhere to this practice. For example, the name prices.bnd is appropriate in describing a file of prices used in a bond application.

Within a C program a file is always referenced by a variable name that must be declared within the program. For files, the variable is actually a pointer to a special file structure, and as such must be declared as a pointer to a file. Examples of such variable declarations are

```
FILE *inFile;
FILE *prices;
FILE *fp;
```

In each of these declarations, the pointer name is selected by the programmer. It is the name of the data file as it will be referenced by the program. This name need not be the same as the external name used by the computer to store the file.

The term FILE in each declaration is the type name of a special data structure used by C for storing information about the file, including whether the file is available for reading or writing, the next available character in the file, and where this character is stored. The actual declaration of a file structure and the equivalence of the structure to the symbolic name FILE is contained in the stdio.h standard header file, which must be included at the top of each program that uses a data file.

Opening a File

Opening a file is a "cookbook" procedure that accomplishes two purposes, only one of which is directly pertinent to the programmer. First, opening a file establishes a physical communication link between the program and the data file. Because the specific details of this link are handled by the computer's operating system and are transparent to the program, the programmer normally need not consider them.

From a programming perspective, the second purpose of opening a file is relevant. Besides establishing the actual physical connection between a program and a data file, the open statement also equates the file's external computer name to the pointer name used internally by the program.

Appropriately enough, the file open function is called fopen() and is available in the standard C library supplied with each C compiler. As the function prototype for fopen() is included within the header file stdio.h, this header file should be included by any program using fopen().

It now remains to actually call fopen() to connect the file's external name to its internal name. In using fopen(), two arguments are required. The first argument is the computer's name of the file. The second argument is the mode in which the file is to be used, which must be placed in double quotes. Permissible modes are r, w, or a, which represent reading, writing, or appending to a file.[1]

A file opened for writing creates a new file and makes the file available for output by the function opening the file. If a file exists with the same name as a file opened for writing, the old file is erased. For example, the statement

```
outFile = fopen("prices.bnd","w");
```

opens a file named `prices.bnd` that can now be written to. Once this file has been opened, the program accesses the file using the internal pointer name `outFile`, while the computer saves the file under the external name `prices.bnd`.

A file opened for appending makes an existing file available for data to be added to the end of the file. If the file opened for appending does not exist, a new file with the designated name is created and made available to receive output from the program. For example, the statement

```
outFile = fopen("prices.bnd","a");
```

opens a file named `prices.bnd` and makes it available for data to be appended to the end of the file.

The only difference between a file opened in write mode and one opened in append mode is where the data is physically placed in the file. In write mode, the data is written starting at the beginning of the file, while in append mode the data is written starting at the end of the file. For a new file, the two modes are identical.

For files opened in either write or append mode, the functions needed to write data to it are similar to the `printf()`, `puts()`, and `putchar()` functions used for displaying data on a terminal. These functions are described in the next section.

A file opened in read mode retrieves an existing file and makes its data available as input to the program. For example the open statement

```
inFile = fopen("prices.bnd","r");
```

opens the file named `prices.bnd` and makes the data in the file available for input. Within the function opening the file, the file is read using the pointer name `inFile`. The functions used to read data from a file are similar to the `scanf()`, `gets()`, and `getchar()` functions used for inputting data from the keyboard. These functions are also described in the next section.

If a file opened for reading does not exist, the `fopen()` function returns the NULL address value. This is the same NULL address previously described in Section 10.4. It can be used to test that an existing file has, in fact, been opened.

Notice that in all the open statements, both the external file name and the mode arguments passed to `fopen()` were strings contained between double quotes. If the external

---

[1] Additionally, the modes r+, w+, and a+ are available. The r+ mode opens an existing file for reading and writing existing records; the w+ mode erases an existing file and opens a blank file for reading and writing; and the a+ mode allows reading, writing, and appending to a file.

file name is first stored in either an array of characters or as a string, the array or string name, without quotes, can be used as the first argument to fopen().

Program 11.1 illustrates the statements required to open a file in read mode and the use of the returned value from fopen() to check for a successful opening of the file. The program prompts the user for the external file name and stores the name in the array fileName[13].

Program 11.1

```
#include <stdio.h>
int main()
{
  FILE *inFile;
  char fileName[13];

  printf("\nEnter a file name: ");
  gets(fileName);

  inFile = fopen(fileName,"r");        /* open the file */

  if (inFile == NULL)
  {
    printf("\nThe file cannot be opened.");
    printf("\nPlease check that the file currently exists.");
    exit(1);
  }
  printf("\nThe file has been successfully opened for reading:");

  return 0;
}
```

Program 11.1 requests that an external data file name be entered by the user. The entered name is stored in the character array fileName and the array name is then passed to the fopen() function. A sample run using Program 11.1 produced the output:

```
Enter a file name: prices.bnd
The file has been successfully opened for reading:
```

Although Program 11.1 can be used to open an existing file in read mode, it clearly lacks statements to read the data in the file and then close the file. These topics are discussed next. Before leaving Program 11.1, however, note that the opening of the file and assignment of the returned address can be included directly within the program's if statement. The single expression

Programming Note

Checking the Return Value

It is important to check the return value when making an `fopen()` call. This is because the call is really a request to the operating system to open a file. For a variety of reasons, the open can fail (chief among these reasons is a request to open an existing file for reading that the operating system cannot locate). If the operating system cannot satisfy the open request you need to know about it and gracefully terminate your program. Failure to do so almost always results in some abnormal program behavior or a program crash.

There are two styles of coding for checking the return value. The first style is the one coded in Program 11.1. It is used to clearly illustrate the request for the opening as distinct from the return value check, and is repeated below for convenience:

```
  /* here is the request to open the file */
inFile = fopen("test.dat","r");

  /* here we check that the file was successfully opened */
if (inFile == NULL)
{
  printf("\nFailed to open the data file.\n");
  exit(1);
}
```

Alternatively, the open request and check can be combined together within the `if` statement as:

```
    if ((inFile = fopen("test.dat","r")) == NULL)
    {
      printf("\nFailed to open the data file.\n");
      exit(1);
    }
```

Use the style with which you are initially more comfortable. As you gain experience in programming, however, be prepared to adopt the second style. It is the one used almost universally by advanced programmers.

```
if ( (inFile = fopen(name,"r")) == NULL )
```

can be used to replace the two lines

```
inFile = fopen(name,"r");
if (inFile == NULL)
```

The `exit()` function is a systems call that passes its integer argument directly to the operating system and then terminates program operation.

Closing a File

A file is closed using the `fclose()` function. This function breaks the link between the file's external and internal names, releasing the internal file pointer name, which can then be used for another file. For example, the statement

```
fclose(inFile);
```

closes the `inFile` file. The argument to `fclose()` always should be the pointer name used when the file was opened.

Because all computers have a limit on the maximum number of files that can be open at one time, closing files that are no longer needed makes good sense. Any open files existing at the end of normal program execution are also automatically closed by the operating system.

Exercises 11.1

1. Using the reference manuals provided with your computer's operating system, determine:
   a. the maximum number of characters that can be used to name a file for storage by the computer system
   b. the maximum number of data files that can be open at the same time

2. Would it be appropriate to refer to a saved C program as a file? Why or why not?

3. Write a suitable declaration statement for each of the following file pointers: `prices`, `fp`, `coupons`, `distance`, `inData`, `outData`.

4. Write individual open statements to link the following external data file names to their corresponding internal pointer names:

External Name	Pointer Name	Mode
coba.mem	memo	write
book.let	letter	write
coupons.bnd	coups	append
yield.bnd	ptYield	append
prices.dat	priFile	read
rates.dat	rates	read

5. Write individual `FILE` declarations for each of the files opened in Exercise 4.

6. Write close statements for each of the files opened in Exercise 4.

7. a. Program 11.1 prompts the user for a file name and uses the `gets()` function to return a string into the character array `fileName`. Replace the prompt and the `gets()` statements with the single function call statement `getFile(name);`. Then write the `getFile()` function to prompt the user for a file name, accept a file name, and test that a valid file name has been entered. If a valid name has not been entered, print an appropriate message and have the program terminate. If a valid name has been entered, have the program open the file and check that a successful opening has occurred. Consider a valid file name as consisting of at most eight characters, the first of which is a letter.

   b. Modify the `getFile()` function written for Exercise 7a to request a file name continuously until a valid name has been entered. (*Hint:* Include the prompt and the `gets()` function call in a `while` or `do-while` loop that terminates when a valid file name is detected.)

11.2 Reading and Writing Files

Reading or writing to an open file involves almost the identical standard library functions for reading input from a terminal and writing data to a display screen. For writing to a file, these functions are

Function	Description
`fputc(c, filename)`	Write a single character to the file.
`fputs(string, filename)`	Write a string to the file.
`fprintf(filename, "format", args)`	Write the values of the arguments to the file according to the format.

The function prototypes for these functions are contained in `stdio.h`. In each of these functions, the file name is the internal pointer name specified when the file was opened. For example, if `outFile` is the internal pointer name of a file opened in either the write or append modes, the following output statements are valid.

```
fputc('a',outfile);            /* write an a to the file */
fputs("Hello world!",outFile); /* write the string to the file */
fprintf(outFile,"%s %n",descrip,price);
```

Notice that the `fputc()`, `fputs()`, and `fprintf()` file functions are used in the same manner as the equivalent `putchar()`, `puts()`, and `printf()` functions, with the addition of a file name as an argument. The file name simply directs the output to a specific file instead of to the standard display device. Program 11.2 illustrates the use of the file write function `fprintf()` to write a list of descriptions and prices to a file.

Program 11.2

```c
#include <stdio.h>
int main()
{
  int i;
  FILE *outFile;                          /* FILE declaration */
  float price[] = {39.95,3.22,1.03};      /* a list of prices */
  char *descrip[] = { "Batteries",        /*    a list of     */
                      "Bulbs",            /*    descriptions  */
                      "Fuses"};

  outFile = fopen("prices.dat","w");      /*   open the file  */
  if (outFile == NULL)
  {
    printf("\nFailed to open the file.\n");
    exit(1);
  }
  for(i = 0; i < 3; ++i)
    fprintf(outFile,"%-9s %5.2f\n",descrip[i],price[i]);
  fclose(outFile);

  return 0;
}
```

When Program 11.2 is executed, a file named `prices.dat` is created and saved by the computer. The file is a sequential file consisting of the following three lines:

```
Batteries 39.95
Bulbs      3.22
Fuses      1.03
```

The prices in the file line up one after another because the control sequence `%-9s` in the `printf()` function call forces the descriptions to be left justified in a field of nine character positions. Similarly, the prices are right justified in a field of five characters, beginning one space away from the end of the description field.

The actual storage of characters in the file depends on the character codes used by the computer. Although only 45 characters appear to be stored in the file, corresponding to the descriptions, blanks, and prices written to the file, the file actually contains 49 characters. The extra characters consist of the newline escape sequence at the end of each line and a special end-of-file marker placed as the last item in the file when the file is closed.

```
42 61 74 74 65 72 69 65 73 20 33 39 2e 32 35 0a 42 75 6c 62 73
 B  a  t  t  e  r  i  e  s     3  9  .  2  5 \n  B  u  l  b  s
```

```
20 20 20 20 20 20 33 2e 32 32 0a 46 75 73 65 73 20 20 20 20 20
                   3  .  2  2 \n  F  u  s  e  s
```

```
20 31 2e 30 33 0a 26
    1  .  0  3 \n ^Z
```

Figure 11.1   The `prices.dat` file as stored by a typical computer

Assuming characters are stored using the ASCII code, the `prices.dat` file is physically stored as illustrated in Figure 11.1.[2] For convenience, the character corresponding to each hexadecimal code is listed below the code. A code of 20 represents the blank character. Although the actual code used for the end-of-file marker depends on the system you are using, the hexadecimal code 26, corresponding to Control-Z, is common.

Reading data from a file is almost identical to reading data from a standard keyboard, with the addition of the file name to indicate where the data is coming from. The file functions available for reading from a file are

Function	Description
`fgetc(`*filename*`)`	Read a character from the file.
`fgets(`*stringname,n,filename,*`)`	Read *n*–1 characters from the file and store the characters in the given string name.
`fscanf(`*filename*`,"`*format*`",&`*args*`)`	Read values for the listed arguments from the file, according to the format.

For example, if `inFile` is the internal pointer name of a file opened in read mode, the following statements could be used to read data from the file:

```
fgetc(inFile);              /* Read the next character in the file */
fgets(message,10,inFile);   /* Read the next 9 characters from */
                            /* the file into message          */
fscanf(inFile,"%f",&price); /* Read a floating point number */
```

The function prototypes for all of these input functions are contained in `stdio.h`. All the input functions correctly detect the end-of-file marker. The functions `fgetc()` and `fscanf()`, however, return the named constant EOF when the marker is detected. The

---

[2] For systems that generate a separate line feed and carriage return for each newline character, the file will contain 52 characters.

function fgets() returns a NULL(\0) when it detects the end of a file. Both of these named constants, EOF and NULL, are useful sentinels for detecting the end of a file being read, depending on the function used.

Reading data from a file requires that the programmer know how the data appears in the file. This is necessary for correct "stripping" of the data from the file into appropriate variables for storage. All files are read sequentially, so that once an item is read the next item in the file becomes available for reading.

Program 11.3 illustrates reading the prices.dat file that was created in Program 11.2. The program also illustrates using the EOF marker, which is returned by fscanf() when the end of the file is encountered.

 Program 11.3

```c
#include <stdio.h>
int main()
{
  char descrip[10];
  float price;
  FILE *inFile;

  inFile = fopen("prices.dat","r");
  if (inFile == NULL)
  {
    printf("\nFailed to open the file.\n");
    exit(1);
  }

  while (fscanf(inFile, "%s %f",descrip,&price) != EOF)
    printf("%-9s %5.2f\n",descrip,price);

  fclose(inFile);

  return 0;
}
```

Program 11.3 continues to read the file until the EOF marker has been detected. Each time the file is read, a string and a floating point number are input to the program. The display produced by Program 11.3 is

```
Batteries 39.95
Bulbs      3.22
Fuses      1.03
```

Programming Note

A Way to Clearly Identify a File's Name and Location

During program development data files are usually placed in the same directory as the program. Therefore, an expression such as `fopen("prices.dat","r")` causes no problems to the operating system. In production systems, however, it is not uncommon for data files to reside in one directory while program files reside in another. For this reason it is always a good idea to include the full path name of any file opened.

For example, if the `prices.dat` file resides in the directory `/test/files`, the `fopen()` statement should include the full path name, viz: `fopen("/test/files/prices.dat", "r")`. Then, no matter where the program is run from, the operating system will know where to locate the file.

Another important convention is to list all file names at the top of a program instead of embedding the names deep within the code. This can easily be accomplished by using a pointer to each file name. For example, if a declaration such as:

```
char *inFile = "\test\files\prices.dat";
```

is placed at the top of a program file, it clearly lists both the name of the desired file and its location. Then, if some other file is to be tested, all that is required is a simple, one-line change at the top of the program.

Using a pointer to the file's name is also useful for the return code check. For example, consider the following code:

```
if ((inPtr = fopen(inFile,"r")) == NULL)
{
  printf("\nFailed to open the data file named %s.\n", inFile);
  exit(1);
}
```

Here, if the file is not successfully opened, the name of the offending file is printed as part of the error message without explicitly rewriting the full path name a second time.

In place of the `fscanf()` function used in Program 11.3, an `fgets()` function call can be used. `fgets()` requires three arguments: an address where the first character read will be stored, the maximum number of characters to be read, and the name of the input file. For example, the function call

```
fgets(line,81,inFile);
```

causes a maximum of 80 characters (one less than the specified number) to be read from the file named inFile and stored starting at the address contained in the pointer named line. fgets() continues reading characters until 80 characters have been read or a newline character has been encountered. If a newline character is encountered it is included with the other entered characters before the string is terminated with the end-of-string marker, \0. fgets() also detects the end-of-file marker, but returns the NULL character when the end of the file is encountered. Program 11.4 illustrates the use of fgets() in a working program.

 Program 11.4

```
#include <stdio.h>
int main()
{
  char line[81],descrip[10];
  float price;
  FILE *inFile;

  inFile = fopen("prices.dat","r");
  if (inFile == NULL)
  {
    printf("\nFailed to open the file.\n");
    exit(1);
  }

  while (fgets(line,81,inFile) != NULL)
    printf("%s",line);

  fclose(inFile);

  return 0;
}
```

Program 11.4 is really a line-by-line text-copying program, reading a line of text from the file and then displaying it on the terminal. Thus, the output of Program 11.4 is identical to the output of Program 11.3. If it were necessary to obtain the description and price as individual variables, either Program 11.3 should be used or the string returned by fgets() in Program 11.4 must be processed further using the string scan function, sscanf(). For example, the statement

```
sscanf(line,"%s %f",descrip,&price)
```

could be used to extract the description and price from the string stored in the line character array (see Section 9.4 for a description of in-memory string formatting).

Standard Device Files

The data file pointers we have used have all been logical file pointers. A *logical file pointer* is one that references a file of related data that has been saved under a common name; that is, it "points to" a data file. In addition to logical file pointers, C also supports physical file pointers. A *physical file pointer* "points to" a hardware device, such as a keyboard, screen, or printer.

The actual physical device assigned to your program for data entry is formally called the *standard input file*. Usually this is a keyboard. When a scanf() function call is encountered in a C program, the computer automatically goes to this standard input file for the expected input. Similarly, when a printf() function call is encountered, the output is automatically displayed or "written to" a device that has been assigned as the *standard output file*. For most systems this is a CRT screen, although it can be a printer.

When a program is run, the keyboard used for entering data is automatically opened and assigned to the internal file pointer name stdin. Similarly, the output device used for display is assigned to the file pointer named stdout. These file pointers are always available for programmer use.

The similarities between printf() and fprintf(), scanf() and fscanf() are not accidental. printf() is a special case of fprintf() that defaults to the standard output file, and scanf() is a special case of fscanf() that defaults to the standard input file. Thus,

```
fprintf(stdout,"Hello World!");
```

causes the same display as the statement

```
printf("Hello World!");
```

and

```
fscanf(stdin,"%d",&num);
```

is equivalent to the statement

```
scanf("%d",&num);
```

In addition to the stdin and stdout file pointers, a third pointer named stderr is assigned to the output device used for system error messages. Although stderr and stdout frequently refer to the same device, the use of stderr provides a means of redirecting any error messages away from the file being used for normal program output, as described in Appendix C.

Just as scanf() and printf() are special cases of fscanf() and fprintf(), respectively, the functions getchar(), gets(), putchar(), and puts() are also special cases of the more general file functions listed in Table 11.2.

The character function pairs listed in Table 11.2 can be used as direct replacements for each other. This is not true for the string-handling functions. The differences between the string-handling functions are described below.

Table 11.2 Correspondence between selected I/O functions

Function	General Form
putchar(*character*)	fputc(*character*, stdout)
puts(*string*)	fputs(*string*, stdout)
getchar()	fgetc(stdin)
gets(*stringname*)	fgets(*stringname*, *n*, stdin)

At input, as previously noted the fgets() function reads data from a file until a newline escape sequence or a specified number of characters has been read. If fgets() encounters a newline escape sequence, as we saw in Program 11.4, it is stored with the other characters entered. The gets() function, however, does not store the newline escape sequence in the final string. Both functions terminate the entered characters with an end-of-string NULL character.

At output, both puts() and fputs() write all the characters in the string except for the terminating end-of-string NULL. puts(), however, automatically adds a newline escape sequence at the end of the transmitted characters while fputs() does not.

Other Devices

The keyboard, display, and error-reporting devices are automatically opened and assigned the internal file names stdin, stdout, and stderr, respectively, whenever a C program begins execution. Additionally, other devices can be used for input or output if the name assigned by the system is known. For example, most IBM or IBM-compatible personal computers assign the name prn to the printer connected to the computer. For these computers, the statement fprintf("prn", "Hello World!"); causes the string Hello World! to be printed directly at the printer. As with stdin, stdout, and stderr, prn is the name of a physical device. Unlike stdin, stdout, and stderr, prn is not a pointer constant but the actual name of the device; as such, it must be enclosed in double quotes when used in a statement.

Exercises 11.2

1. a. Using the gets() and fputs() functions, write a C program that accepts lines of text from the keyboard and writes each line to a file named text.dat until an empty line is entered. An empty line is a line with no text—just a new line caused by pressing the ENTER (or RETURN) key.

   b. Replace the gets() function in the program written for Exercise 1a with an equivalent call to fgets().

   c. Modify Program 11.4 to read and display the data stored in the text.dat file created in Exercise 1a.

2. Determine the operating system command or procedure provided by your computer to display the contents of a saved file. Compare its operation with the program developed for Exercise 1c. (*Hint:* Typically the operating system command is called LIST, TYPE, or CAT.)

3. a. Create a file named employ.dat containing the following data:

Anthony	A.J.	10031	7.82	12/18/62
Burrows	W.K.	10067	9.14	6/ 9/63
Fain	B.D.	10083	8.79	5/18/59
Janney	P.	10095	10.57	9/28/62
Smith	G.J.	10105	8.50	12/20/61

   b. Write a program called fcopy.c to read the employ.dat file created in Exercise 3a and produce a duplicate copy of the file named employ.bak.

   c. Modify the program written in Exercise 3b to accept the names of the original and duplicate files as user input.

   d. Since fcopy.c always copies data from an original file to a duplicate file, can you think of a better method of accepting the original and duplicate file names than prompting the user for them each time the program is executed?

4. a. Write a program that opens a file and displays the contents of the file with associated line numbers. That is, the program should print 1 before displaying the first line, 2 before displaying the second line, and so on for each line in the file.

   b. Modify the program written in Exercise 4a to list the contents of the file on the printer assigned to your computer.

5. a. Create a file containing the following data:

H.Baker	614 Freeman St.	Orange	NJ
D.Rosso	83 Chambers St.	Madison	NJ
K.Tims	891 Ridgewood Rd.	Millburn	NJ
B.Williams	24 Tremont Ave.	Brooklyn	NY

   b. Write a program to read and display the data file created in Exercise 5a using the following output format:

```
Name:
Address:
City, State:
```

6. a. Create a file containing the following names, Social Security numbers, hourly rate, and hours worked:

B.Caldwell	163-98-4182	7.32	37
D.Memcheck	189-53-2147	8.32	40
R.Potter	145-32-9826	6.54	40
W.Rosen	163-09-4263	9.80	35

   b. Write a C program that reads the data file created in Exercise 6a and computes and displays a payroll schedule. The output should list the Social Security number, name, and gross pay for each individual.

7. a. Create a file containing the following car numbers, number of miles driven, and number of gallons of gas used by each car:

Car No.	Miles Driven	Gallons Used
54	250	19
62	525	38
71	123	6
85	1,322	86
97	235	14

b. Write a C program that reads the data in the file created in Exercise 7a and displays the car number, miles driven, gallons used, and the miles per gallon for each car. The output should additionally contain the total miles driven, total gallons used, and average miles per gallon for all the cars. These totals should be displayed at the end of the output report.

8. a. Create a file with the following data containing the part number, opening balance, number of items sold, and minimum stock required:

Part Number	Initial Amount	Quantity Sold	Minimum Amount
QA310	95	47	50
CM145	320	162	200
MS514	34	20	25
EN212	163	150	160

b. Write a C program to create an inventory report based on the data in the file created in Exercise 8a. The display should consist of the part number, current balance, and amount that is necessary to bring the inventory to the minimum level.

9. a. Create a file containing the following data:

Name	Rate	Hours
Callaway, G.	6.00	40
Hanson, P.	5.00	48
Lasard, D.	6.50	35
Stillman, W.	8.00	50

b. Write a C program that uses the information contained in the file created in Exercise 9a to produce the following pay report for each employee:

Name   Rate   Hours   Regular Pay   Overtime Pay   Gross Pay

Any hours worked above 40 hours are paid at time and a half. At the end of the individual output for each employee, the program should display the totals of the regular, overtime, and gross pay columns.

10. a. Store the following data in a file:

5 96 87 78 93 21 4 92 82 85 87 6 72 69 85 75 81 73

b. Write a C program to calculate and display the average of each group of numbers in the file created in Exercise 10a. The data is arranged in the file so that each group of numbers is preceded by the number of data items in the group. Thus, the first number in the file, 5, indicates that the next five numbers should be grouped together. The number 4 indicates that the following four numbers are a group, and the 6 indicates that the last six numbers are a group. (*Hint:* Use a nested loop. The outer loop should terminate when the EOF marker is encountered.)

11.3   Random File Access

File organization refers to the way data is stored in a file. All the files we have used have *sequential organization*. This means that the characters in the file are stored sequentially, one after another. Additionally, we have read the file in a sequential manner. The way data from a file is accessed is called *file access*. The fact that the characters in the file are stored sequentially, however, does not force us to access the file sequentially.

The standard library functions rewind(), fseek(), and ftell() can be used to provide *random access* to a file. In random access any character in the file can be read immediately, without first having to read all the characters stored before it.

The rewind() function resets the current position to the start of the file. rewind() requires the pointer name used for the file as its only argument. For example, the statement

```
rewind(inFile):
```

resets the file so that the next character accessed will be the first character in the file. A rewind() is done automatically when a file is opened in read mode.

The fseek() function allows the programmer to move to any position in the file. In order to understand this function, you must first clearly understand how data is referenced in the file.

Each character in a data file is located by its position in the file. The first character in the file is located at position 0, the next character at position 1, and so on. A character's position is also referred to as its offset from the start of the file. Thus, the first character has a 0 offset, the second character has an offset of 1, and so on for each character in the file.

The fseek() function requires three arguments: the pointer name of the file; the offset, as a long integer; and the position from which the offset is to be calculated. The general form of fseek() is

```
fseek(fileName, offset, origin)
```

The values of the origin argument can be either 0, 1, or 2, which are defined stdio.h as the named constants SEEK_SET, SEEK_CUR, and SEEK_END respectively. An origin of SEEK_SET means the offset is relative to the start of the file. An origin of SEEK_CUR means that the offset is relative to the current position in the file, and an origin of SEEK_END means the offset is relative to the end of the file. A positive offset means move forward in the file and a negative offset means move backward. Examples of fseek() are

```
fseek(inFile,4L,SEEK_SET);    /* go to the fifth character in the file */
fseek(infile,4L,SEEK_CUR);    /* move ahead five characters */
fseek(inFile,-4L,SEEK_CUR);   /* move back five characters */
fseek(inFile,0L,SEEK_SET);    /* go to start of file-same as rewind() */
fseek(inFile,0L,SEEK_END);    /* go to end of file */
fseek(inFile,-10L,SEEK_END);  /* go to 10 characters before the file's end */
```

In these examples, inFile is the name of the file pointer used when the data file was opened. Notice that the offset passed to fseek() must be a long integer. The appended L tells the compiler to convert the number to a long integer.

The last function, ftell(), simply returns the offset value of the next character that will be read or written. For example, if ten characters have already been read from a file named inFile, the function call

```
ftell(inFile);
```

returns the long integer 10. This means that the next character to be read is offset 10 byte positions from the start of the file and is the eleventh character in the file.

Program 11.5 illustrates the use of fseek() and ftell() to read a file in reverse order, from last character to first. Each character is also displayed as it is read.

 Program 11.5

```c
#include <stdio.h>
int main()
{
  int ch, n;
  long int offset, last;
  FILE *inFile;

  inFile = fopen("text.dat","r");
  if (infile == NULL)
  {
    printf("\nFailed to open the test.dat file.\n");
    exit(1);
  }
  fseek(inFile,0L,SEEK_END);          /* move to the end of the file */
  last = ftell(inFile);               /* save the offset of the last character */
  for(offset = 0; offset <= last; ++offset)
  {
    fseek(inFile, -offset, SEEK_END);    /* move back to the next character */
    ch = getc(inFile);                   /* get the character */
    switch(ch)
    {
      case '\n': printf("LF : ");
                 break;
      case EOF : printf("EOF: ");
                 break;
      default  : printf("%c : ",ch);
                 break;
    }
  }
  fclose(inFile);

  return 0;
}
```

Assuming the file `test.dat` contains the following data,

```
Bulbs     3.12
```

the output of Program 11.5 is

```
EOF : 2 : 1 : . : 3 :   :   :   : s : b : l : u : B :
```

Program 11.5 initially goes to the last character in the file. The offset of this character, which is the end-of-file character, is saved in the variable `last`. Since `ftell()` returns a long integer, `last` has been declared as a long integer. The function prototype for `ftell()` is contained in `stdio.h`.

Starting from the end of the file, `fseek()` is used to position the next character to be read, referenced from the back of the file. As each character is read, the character is displayed and the offset adjusted in order to access the next character.

Exercises 11.3

1. Determine the value of the offset returned by `ftell()` in Program 11.5. Assume that the file `test.dat` contains the data

   ```
   Bulbs     3.12
   ```

2. Rewrite Program 11.5 so that the origin for the `fseek()` function used in the `for` loop is the start of the file rather than the end. The program should still print the file in reverse order.

3. The function `fseek()` returns 0 if the position specified has been reached, or 1 if the position specified was beyond the file's boundaries. Modify Program 11.5 to display an error message if `fseek()` returns 1.

4. Write a C program that will read and display every second character in a file named `test.dat`.

5. Using the `fseek()` and `ftell()` functions, write a C function named `totChars()` that returns the total number of characters in a file.

6. a. Write a C function named `readBytes(()` that reads and displays *n* characters starting from any position in a file. The function should accept three arguments: a file pointer, the offset of the first character to be read, and the number of characters to be read.

   b. Modify the `readBytes()` function written in Exercise 6a to store the characters read into a string or an array. The function should accept the address of the storage area as a fourth argument.

7. Assume that a data file consisting of a group of individual lines has been created. Write a C function named `printLine()` that will read and display any desired line of the file. For example, the function call `printLine(fileName,5);` should display the fifth line of the file name passed to it.

11.4 Passing and Returning File Names

Internal file names are passed to a function using the same procedures for passing all function arguments. For passing a file name this requires declaring the passed argument as a pointer to a FILE. For example, in Program 11.6 a file named outFile is opened in main() and the file name is passed to the function inOut(), which is then used to write five lines of user-entered text to the file.

 Program 11.6

```c
#include <stdio.h>
void inOut(FILE *);    /* function prototype */
int main()
{
  FILE *outFile;

  outFile = fopen("prices.dat","w");
  if (outFile == NULL)
  {
    printf("\nFailed to open the file.\n");
    exit(1);
  }
  inOut(outFile);
  fclose(outFile);

  return 0;
}
void inOut(FILE *fname) /* fname is a pointer to a FILE */
{
  int count;
  char line[81]; /* enough storage for one line of text */

  printf("Please enter five lines of text:\n");
  for (count = 0; count < 5; ++count)
  {
    gets(line);
    fprintf(fname,"%s\n",line);
  }
  return;
}
```

Within main() the file is known as outFile. The value in outFile, which is an address, is passed to the inOut() function. The function inOut() stores the address in the parameter named fname and correctly declares fname to be a pointer to a FILE. Notice that the function prototype for inOut() declares that the function expects to receive a pointer to a FILE.

Returning a file name from a function also requires following the same rules used to return any value from a function. This means including the data type of the returned value in the function header, making sure the correct variable type is actually returned from the function, and alerting the calling function to the returned data type. For example, assume that the function getOpen() is called with no arguments. The purpose of this function is to prompt a user for a file name, open the file for output, and pass the file name back to the calling function. Since getOpen() returns a file name that is actually a pointer to a FILE, the correct function declaration for getOpen() is

```
FILE *getOpen()
```

This declaration specifically declares that the function getOpen() expects no argument and will return a pointer to a FILE. It is consistent with the pointer declarations that have been made previously.

Once a function has been declared to return a pointer to a FILE, there must be at least one variable or parameter in the function consistent with this declaration that can be used for the actual returned value. Consider Program 11.7. In this program, getOpen() returns a file name to main().

Program 11.7 is simply a modified version of Program 11.6 that now allows the user to enter a file name from the standard input device. Although the function getOpen() is in "bare bones" form, it does illustrate the correct function declaration for returning a file name. The getOpen() function declaration defines the function as returning a pointer to a FILE. Within getOpen(), the returned variable, fname, is the correct data type. Finally, main() is alerted to the returned value by the function prototype for the getOpen() function.

getOpen() is a "bare bones" function in that it does no checking on the file being opened for output. If the name of an existing data file is entered, the file will be destroyed when it is opened in write mode. A useful "trick" to prevent this type of mishap is to open the entered file name in read mode. Then, if the file exists, the fopen() function returns a nonzero pointer value to indicate that the file is available for input. This can be used to alert the user that a file with the entered name currently exists in the system and to request confirmation that the data in the file can be destroyed and the file name used for the new output file. Before the file can be reopened in write mode, of course, it would have to be closed. The implementation of this algorithm is left as an exercise.

Program 11.7

```c
#include <stdio.h>
FILE *getOpen();          /* function prototype */
void inOut(FILE *);       /* function prototype */
int main()
{
  FILE *outFile;

  outFile = getOpen();
  inOut(outFile);
  fclose(outFile);

  return 0;
}

FILE *getOpen()     /* getOpen() returns a pointer to a FILE */
{
  FILE *fname;
  char name[13];

  printf("\nEnter a file name: ");
  gets(name);
  fname = fopen(name,"w");
  if (fname == NULL)
  {
    printf("\nFailed to open the file %s.\n", name);
    exit(1);
  }

  return(fname);
}

void inOut(FILE *fname)       /* fname is a pointer to a FILE */
{
  int count;
  char line[81];   /* enough storage for one line of text */

  printf("Please enter five lines of text:\n");
  for (count = 0; count < 5; ++count)
  {
    gets(line);
    fprintf(fname,"%s\n",line);
  }
}
```

Exercises 11.4

1. A function named pFile() is to receive a file name as an argument. What declarations are required to pass a file name to pFile()?

2. a. A function name getFile() is to return a file name. What declarations are required in the function header and internal to the file?
   b. What declaration statement is required for each function that calls getFile()? Under what conditions can this declaration be omitted?

3. Write a C function named fcheck() that checks whether a file exists. The function should be passed a file name. If the file exists, the function should return a value of 1; otherwise the function should return a value of zero.

4. Rewrite the function getOpen() used in Program 11.7 to incorporate the file-checking procedures described in the text. Specifically, if the entered file name exists, an appropriate message should be displayed. The user should then be presented with the option of entering a new file name or allowing the program to overwrite the existing file, append to it, or exit.

11.5   Common Programming Errors

Four programming errors are common when using files. The first and most common error is to use the file's external name in place of the internal file pointer variable when accessing the file. The only standard library function that uses the data file's external name is the fopen() function. All the other standard functions presented in this chapter require the pointer variable assigned to the file when it was initially opened.

The second error is to omit the file pointer name altogether. Programmers used to functions that access the standard input and output devices, where a specific file pointer is not required, sometimes forget to include a file pointer when accessing data files.

A third error occurs when using the EOF marker to detect the end of a file. Any variable used to accept the EOF must be declared as an integer variable, not a character variable. For example, if ch has been declared as a character variable the expression

```
while ((c = getc(inFile)) != EOF)
```

produces an infinite loop. This occurs because a character variable can never take on an EOF code. EOF is an integer value (usually −1) that has no character representation. This ensures that the EOF code can never be confused with any legitimate character encountered as normal data in the file. To terminate the above expression, the variable ch must be declared as an integer variable.

The fourth error concerns the offset argument sent to the function fseek(). This offset must be a long integer constant or variable. Any other value passed to fseek() can result in an unpredictable effect.

11.6   Chapter Summary

1. A *data file* is any collection of data stored together in an external storage medium under a common name.

2. A text data file is opened using the `fopen()` standard library function. This function connects a file's external name with an internal pointer name. After the file is opened, all subsequent accesses to the file require the internal pointer name.

3. A file can be opened for reading, writing, or appending. A file opened for writing creates a new file and erases any existing file having the same name as the opened file. A file opened for appending makes an existing file available for data to be added to the end of the file. If the file does not exist it is created. A file opened for reading makes an existing file's data available for input.

4. An internal file name must be declared as a pointer to a `FILE`. This means that a declaration similar to

   ```
   FILE *fileName;
   ```

   must be included with the declarations in which the file is opened. `fileName` can be replaced with any user-selected variable name.

5. In addition to any files opened within a function, the standard files `stdin`, `stdout`, and `stderr` are automatically opened when a program is run. `stdin` is the pointer name of the physical file used for data entry by `scanf()`, `stdout` is the pointer name of the physical file device used for data display by `printf()`, and `stderr` is the pointer name of the physical file device used for displaying system error messages.

6. Data files can be accessed randomly using the `rewind()`, `fseek()`, and `ftell()` functions.

7. Table 11.3 lists the standard file library functions.

11.7   Chapter Supplement: Control Codes

In addition to responding to the codes for letters, digits, and special punctuation symbols, which are collectively referred to as *printable characters,* physical device files such as printers and CRT screens can also respond to a small set of *control codes*. These codes, which convey control information to the physical device, have no equivalent characters that can be displayed and are called *nonprintable characters.*

Table 11.3 Standard file library functions

Function Name	Purpose
fopen()	Open or create a file
fclose()	Close a file
fgetc()	Character input
getchar()	Character input from stdin
fgets()	String input
gets()	String input from stdin
fscanf()	Formatted input
scanf()	Formatted input from stdin
fputc()	Character output
putchar()	Character output to stdout
fputs()	String output
puts()	String output to stdout
fprintf()	Formatted output
printf()	Formatted output to stdout
fseek()	File positioning
rewind()	File positioning
ftell()	Position reporting

Two of these codes, which are extremely useful in applications, are the *clear* and *bell control codes*. When the clear control code is sent to a printer, the printer ejects a page of paper and begins printing on the next sheet of paper. For dot matrix printers if you take care to align the printer to the top of a new page when printing begins, the clear control character can be used as a "top-of-page" command. For laser printers the clear code acts as a straight page-eject code. When the equivalent clear code is sent to a CRT display, the screen is cleared of all text and the cursor is positioned at the lefthand corner of the screen.

Sending control codes to an output device is done in a manner similar to sending a printable character to a file. Recall that sending a printable character to a file requires two pieces of information: the file name and the character being written to the file. For example, the statement fputc('a',outFile); causes the letter *a* to be written to the file named outfile. Instead of including the actual letter as an argument to fputc(), we can substitute the numerical code for the letter. For computers that use the ASCII code, this amounts to substituting the equivalent ASCII numerical value for the appropriate letter. Referring to Appendix B, we see that in the ASCII code the value for *a* is 97 as a decimal number, 61 as a hexadecimal number, and 141 as an octal number. Any one of these numerical values can be used in place of the letter *a* in the previous `fputc()` function call. Thus, the following four statements are all equivalent:

```
fputc('a',outFile);
fputc(97, outFile);
fputc(0x61, outFile);
fputc('\141',outFile);
```

Note that in each of these statements we have adhered to the notation used in C to identify decimal and hexadecimal numbers. A number with no leading zero is considered a decimal number and a number with a leading `0x` is considered a hexadecimal value. Octal character codes must, however, be preceded by a backslash and enclosed in single apostrophes. The backslash identifies the number as an octal value, allowing us to omit the normal leading zero associated with octal values. Because most control codes, by convention, are listed as octal values using three significant digits, we will retain this convention in all further examples.

The importance of substituting the numerical code for the letter is only realized when a control code rather than a character code must be sent. Because no equivalent character exists for control codes, the actual code for the command must be used. Although each computer can have its own code for clearing the CRT screen, the bell code and the code for clearing a printer are fairly universal. To activate the bell, the octal code 07 is used. The octal clear code for most printers is 014. Thus, if the file `outFile` has been opened as the printer in write mode, the statement

```
fputc('\014',outfile);
```

causes the printer to eject the current page. Similarly, if `scrn` has been opened as the CRT screen in write mode, the statement

```
fputc('\07',scrn);
```

causes the bell to be activated for a short "beep."

For personal computers, the CRT screen has its own clear code. For your computer, check the manual for the CRT screen to obtain the proper clear-screen control code. You must also check the name by which your computer "knows" the printer and CRT screen. For IBM personal computers the printer has the name `prn` and the CRT screen the name `con` (short for console). Program 11.8 illustrates the use of control codes to eject a page of paper from the printer and alert the user with a "beep" if the printer is not turned on. Using `#define` commands, the appropriate codes have been equated to more readable symbolic names.

Program 11.8

```c
#include <stdio.h>
#define BELL '\07'
#define TOP_OF_PAGE '\014' /* page eject code */
void check(FILE *);        /* function prototype */
int main()
{
  FILE *printer;

  printer = fopen("prn", "w");
  check(printer);

  return 0;
}
                    /* make sure printer is ready and eject a page */
void check(FILE *printer)
{

  if(printer == 0)          /* check that the file has been opened */
  {
    fputc(BELL,stdout);
    printf("The printer cannot be opened for output.");
    printf("\nPlease check the printer is on and ready for use.");
    exit(1);
  }
  else
    fputc(TOP_OF_PAGE,printer);
  return;
}
```

The statements in the function check() are used to ensure that the printer has been opened and is ready for output. The symbolic constants BELL and TOP_OF_PAGE can be used freely within the check() function because they have been defined globally at the top of the program. Each of these constants is sent using a fputc() function call. Because the CRT screen is the standard output device for the computer used to run Program 11.8, the CRT did not have to be opened as a new file. Instead, the file name stdout was used to send the BELL constant to the screen.

In addition to the BELL code, all CRT screens have control codes to position the cursor directly at different screen locations. This enables the programmer to place messages anywhere on the screen. Because these codes differ for various CRT models, you should check the manual for your computer to determine the proper codes. Additionally, many C compilers for personal computers include standard library functions that provide the same cursor-positioning capabilities.

Additional Capabilities

Previous chapters have presented C's basic capabilities, statements, and structure. The variations on each of these, which are almost endless, are a source of delight to many programmers, who continuously find new possibilities of expression using variations of the basic language building blocks. This chapter presents additional capabilities that you will find useful as you progress in your understanding and use of C. For completeness we also include one statement that is part of the C language but is almost never used by knowledgeable C programmers.

12.1 Additional Features

In this section five additional features are presented. Of these only the `typedef` declaration and casts are used extensively.

The `typedef` Declaration Statement

The `typedef` declaration statement permits constructing alternate names for an existing C data type name. For example, the statement

```
typedef float REAL;
```

makes the name REAL a synonym for float. The name REAL can now be used in place of the term float anywhere in the program after the synonym has been declared. For example, the definition

```
REAL val;
```

is equivalent to the definition

```
float val;
```

The typedef statement does not create a new data type; it creates a new name for an existing data type. Using uppercase names in typedef statements is not mandatory. It is done simply to alert the programmer to a user-specified name, similar to uppercase names in #define statements. In fact, the equivalence produced by a typedef statement can frequently be produced equally well by a #define statement. The difference between the two, however, is that typedef statements are processed directly by the compiler while #define statements are processed by the preprocessor. Compiler processing of typedef statements allows for text replacements that are not possible with the preprocessor. For example the statement

```
typedef float REAL;
```

actually specifies that REAL is a placeholder that will be replaced with another variable name. A subsequent declaration such as

```
REAL val;
```

has the effect of substituting the variable named val for the placeholder named REAL in the terms following the word typedef. Substituting val for REAL in the typedef statement and retaining all terms after the reserved word typedef results in the equivalent declaration float val;.

Once the mechanics of the replacement are understood, more useful equivalences can be constructed. Consider the statement

```
typedef int ARRAY[100];
```

Here, the name ARRAY is actually a placeholder for any subsequently defined variables. Thus, a statement such as ARRAY first, second; is equivalent to the two definitions int first[100]; and int second[100];. Each of these definitions is obtained by replacing the name ARRAY with the variable names first and second in the terms following the reserved word typedef.

As another example, consider the following statement:

```
typedef struct
{
  char name[20];
  int idNum;
} empRecord;
```

Here `empRecord` is a convenient placeholder for any subsequent variable. For example, the declaration `empRecord employee[75];` is equivalent to the declaration

```
struct
{
  char name[20];
  int idNum;
} employee[75];
```

This last declaration is obtained by directly substituting the term `employee[75]` in place of the word `EMP_REC` in the terms following the word `typedef` in the original `typedef` statement. More typically a `typedef` is used in place of a structure data type name using the method illustrated in the Programming Note on page 382.

The **enum** Specifier

The `enum` specifier creates an enumerated data type, which is simply a user-defined list of values that is given its own data type name. Such data types are identified by the reserved word `enum` followed by an optional, user-selected name for the data type and a listing of acceptable values for the data type. Consider the following user-specified data types:

```
enum flag {true, false};
enum time {am, pm};
enum day {mon, tue, wed, thr, fri, sat, sun};
enum color {red, green, yellow};
```

The first user-specified data type is a type named `flag`. Any variable subsequently declared to be of this type can take on only a value of `true` or `false`. The second statement creates a data type named `time`. Any variable subsequently declared to be of type `time` can take on only a value of am or pm. Similarly, the third and fourth statements create the data types `day` and `color`, respectively, and list the valid values for variables of these two types. For example, the statement

```
enum color a,b,c;
```

declares the variables a, b, and c to be of type `color`, and is consistent with the declaration of variables using standard C data types such as `char`, `int`, `float`, or `double`. Once variables have been declared as enumerated types, they may be assigned values or compared to variables or values appropriate to their type. This again is consistent with standard variable operations. For example, for the variables a, b, and c declared above, the following statements are valid:

```
a = red;
b = a;
if (c == yellow) printf("\nThe color is yellow");
```

Programming Note

Conditional Preprocessor Directives

In addition to the `#include` directive, the preprocessor provides a number of other valuable directives. Two of the more useful of these are the conditional directives, `#ifndef`, which means "if not defined," and `#ifdef`, which means "if defined." These directives work in almost the same manner as the if and else statements. For example, the syntax of the "#ifndef" statement is

```
#ifndef condition
  compile the statements placed here
#else
  compile the statements placed here
#end if
```

As with the if/else statement, the `#else` directive is optional.

Both the `#ifndef` and `#ifdef` directives permit *conditional compilation* in that the statements immediately following these directives, up to either the `#else` or `#endif` directives, are compiled only if the condition is true, whereas the statements following the `#else` are compiled only if the condition is false.

By far, `#ifndef` is the most frequently used conditional preprocessor directive. Its most common usage is in the form:

```
#ifndef header-file
  #include <header-file>
#endif
```

For example,

```
#ifndef iostream.h
  #include <stdio.h>
#endif
```

What this statement does is to check if the `stdio.h` header file has already been included. Only if it has not been previously defined is the `#include` directive executed. This prevents multiple inclusions of the `stdio.h` header file.

The `#ifdef` works in a manner similar to the `#ifndef`, except that the statements immediately following the `#ifdef`, up to either the `#else` or `#endif` directives are only executed if the tested condition has been defined.

The relationship between the `#ifdef` and `#ifndef` directives is that the expression `#ifndef condition` performs the same task as the expression `#ifdef !condition`, and these two expressions can be used interchangeably.

Internally, the acceptable values for each enumerated datatype are ordered and assigned sequential integer values beginning with 0. For the values of the user-defined type `color`, the correspondences created by the C compiler are that `red` is equivalent to 0, `green` is equivalent to 1, and `yellow` is equivalent to 2. The equivalent numbers are required when inputting values using `scanf()` or printing values using `printf()`.

Program 12.1 illustrates a user-defined data type.

  Program 12.1

```
#include <stdio.h>
int main()
{
  enum color {red,green,yellow};
  enum color crayon = red;    /* crayon is declared to be of type */
                              /* color and initialized to red     */
  printf("\nThe color is %d\n", crayon);
  printf("Enter in a value: ");
  scanf("%d", &crayon);
  if (crayon == red)
    printf("The crayon is red.\n");
  else if (crayon == green)
    printf("The crayon is green.\n");
  else if (crayon == yellow)
    printf("The crayon is yellow.\n");
  else
    printf("The color is not defined.\n");

  return 0;
}
```

A sample run of Program 12.1 produced the following:

```
The color is 0
Enter a value: 2
The crayon is yellow.
```

As illustrated in Program 12.1, expressions containing variables declared as user-defined data types must be consistent with the values specifically listed for the type. Although a `switch` statement would be more appropriate in Program 12.1, the expressions in the `if-else` statement better highlight the use of enumerated values. Program 12.1 also shows that the initialization of a user-specified data type variable is identical to the initialization of standard data type variables. For input and output purposes, however, the equivalent integer value assigned by the C compiler to each enumerated value must be used in place of the actual data type value. This is also seen in the program.

In order to assign equivalent integers to each user-specified value, the C compiler retains the order of the values as they are listed in the enumeration. A side effect of this ordering is that expressions can be constructed using relational and logical operators. Thus, for the data type `color` created in Program 12.1, expressions such as `crayon < yellow` and `red < green` are both valid.

The numerical value assigned by the compiler to enumerated values can be altered by direct assignment when a data type is created. For example, the definition

```
enum color (red,green = 7, yellow);
```

causes the compiler to associate the value `red` with the integer 0 and the value `green` with the integer 7. Altering the integer associated with the value `green` causes all subsequent integer assignments to be altered too; thus, the value `yellow` is associated with the integer 8. If any other values were listed after `yellow`, they would be associated with the integers 9, 10, 11, and so on, unless another alteration was made.

Naming a user-defined data type is similar to naming a template for structures. Just as a template name can be omitted when defining a structure by declaring the structure directly, the same can be done with user-defined data types. For example, the declaration `enum {red,green,yellow} crayon;` defines crayon to be a variable of an unnamed data type with the valid values of `red`, `green`, and `yellow`.

Scope rules applicable to the standard C data types also apply to enumerated data types. For example, placing the statement `enum color {red, green, yellow};` before the `main()` function in Program 12.1 would make the data type named `color` global and available for any other function in the file.

Finally, since there is a one-to-one correspondence between integers and user-defined data types, the `cast` operator can either coerce integers into a user-specified data value or coerce a user-specified value into its equivalent integers. Assuming that `val` is an integer variable with a value of 1, and `color` has been declared as in Program 12.1, the expression `(enum color) val` has a value of `green` and the expression `(int) yellow` has a value of 2. The compiler will not warn you, however, if a cast to a nonexistent value is attempted.

Casts

We have already seen the forced conversion of an operand's data type in mixed binary arithmetic expressions. Such expressions consist of a binary arithmetic operator (+, -, *, /, or %) connecting two operands of different data types. For example, if `val` is a double precision variable and `num` is an integer variable, `num`'s value is converted to double precision in the expression `val + num`.

The general rules for converting operands in mixed arithmetic expressions were presented in Chapter 2. A more complete set of conversion rules for arithmetic operators is listed in Table 12.1.

Forced conversions also take place across assignment operators. Here the value of the expression on the right side of the equal sign is converted to the data type of the variable

Table 12.1 Conversion rules for arithmetic operators (these rules are applied in sequence)

Rule 1.	All character and short integer operands are always converted to integer values. All floating point operands are converted to double precision values.
Rule 2.	If one operand is a double precision value, then the other operand is converted to a double precision value and the result of the expression is a double precision value.
Rule 3.	If one operand is a long integer value, then the other operand is converted to a long integer value and the resulting value of the expression is a long integer value.
Rule 4.	If one operand is an unsigned integer value, then the other operand is converted to an unsigned integer value and the resulting value of the expression is an unsigned value.
Rule 5.	If both operands are of type `int`, no conversions occur and the resulting value of the expression is an integer value.

to the left of the equal sign, which also becomes the value of the complete expression. For example, consider the evaluation of the expression

```
a = b * d - e % f
```

where `a` and `d` are integer variables, `e` is a short integer variable, `f` is a long integer variable, and `b` is a floating point variable. According to the order of operator precedence, the `*` and `%` operators will be evaluated first, followed by the subtraction and assignment operators. Thus, the priority of evaluation is

```
a = ( (b * d) - (e % f) )
```

Internally, the expression `b * d` consists of a floating point and integer operand. Referring to Rule 1 in Table 12.1, the value of `b` is converted to a double precision number. Because one of the operands is a double precision variable, Rule 2 provides that the second operand's value is converted to a double precision number and the resulting value of the expression `b * d` is a double precision number.

In the expression of `e % f`, since `f` is a long integer variable, the value of `e` is converted to a long integer (Rule 3) and the value of the expression is itself a long integer value.

The subtraction of `(e % f)` from `(b * d)` forces the conversion of `(e % f)` to a double precision number. This occurs because the operand `(b * d)` is a double precision value. Finally, since the left side of the assignment operator is an integer value, the double precision value of the expression `(b * d) - (e % f)` is forced to become an integer value.[1]

In addition to the forced conversions that are made automatically to operands in mixed arithmetic expressions, C also provides for user-specified type conversions. The

---

[1] Note: All stored values remain unchanged. Values are converted for purposes of evaluation only.

operator used to force the conversion of a value to another type is the *cast operator*. This is a unary operator having the symbol (*data type*), where *data type* is the desired data type of the operand following the cast. For example, the expression

```
(int)(a * b)
```

assures that the value of the expression a * b is converted to an integer value. The parentheses around the expression (a * b) are required because the cast operator has a higher precedence than the multiplication operator.

As a last example, consider the expression (int) a * b, where both a and b are double precision variables. Here, only a's value is cast into an integer before multiplication by b. The cast into an integer value causes the fractional part of a's value to be truncated for the computation (a's stored value is unchanged). Because b is a double precision operand, the value of the operand (int) a is converted back to a double precision number (Rule 2 in Table 12.1). The forced conversion back to a double precision number, however, does not restore the fractional part of a in the computation.

Conditional Expressions

In addition to expressions formed with the arithmetic, relational, logical, and bit operators, C provides a conditional expression. A conditional expression uses the conditional operator, ?: and provides an alternate way of expressing a simple if-else statement.

The general form of a conditional expression is

```
expression1 ? expression2 : expression3
```

If the value of *expression1* is nonzero (true), *expression2* is evaluated, otherwise *expression3* is evaluated. The value of the complete conditional expression is the value of either *expression2* or *expression3*, depending on which expression was evaluated. As always, the value of the expression may be assigned to a variable.

Conditional expressions are most useful in replacing simple if-else statements. For example, the if-else statement

```
if (hours > 40)
   rate = 0.045;
else
   rate = 0.02;
```

can be replaced with the one-line conditional statement

```
rate = (hours > 40) ? 0.045 : 0.02;
```

Here, the complete conditional expression

```
(hours > 40) ? 0.045 : 0.02
```

is evaluated before any assignment is made to rate, because the conditional operator, ?:, has a higher precedence than the assignment operator. Within the conditional expression, the expression hours > 40 is evaluated first. If this expression has a nonzero value, which is equivalent to a logical true value, the value of the complete conditional expression is set to 0.045. Otherwise the conditional expression has a value of 0.02. Finally, the value of the conditional expression, either 0.045 or 0.02, is assigned to the variable rate.

The conditional operator, ?:, is unique in C in that it is a *ternary* operator. This means that the operator connects three operands. The first operand is always evaluated first. It is usually a conditional expression that uses the logical operators.

The next two operands are any other valid expressions, which can be single constants, variables, or more general expressions. The complete conditional expression consists of all three operands connected by the condition operator symbols, ? and :.

Conditional expressions are only useful in replacing if-else statements when the expressions in the equivalent if-else statement are not long or complicated. For example, the statement

```
maxVal = a > b ? a : b;
```

is a one-line statement that assigns the maximum value of the variables a and b to max-Val. A longer, equivalent form of this statement is

```
if (a > b)
  maxVal = a;
else
  maxVal = b;
```

Because of the length of the expressions involved, a conditional expression would not be useful in replacing the following if-else statement:

```
if (amount > 20000)
  taxes = 0.025(amount - 20000) + 400;
else
  taxes = 0.02 * amount;
```

The goto Statement

The goto statement provides an unconditional transfer of control to some other statement in a program. The general form of a goto statement is

```
goto label;
```

where *label* is any unique name chosen according to the rules for creating variable names. The label name must appear, followed by a colon, in front of any other statement in the function that contains the goto statement. For example, the following section of code transfers control to the label named err if division by zero is attempted:

```
if (denom == 0.0)
   goto err;
else
   result = num /denom;
            .
            .

err: printf("Error - Attempted Division by Zero";
```

The astute reader will realize that in this case goto provides a cumbersome solution to the problem. It would require a second goto above the printf() statement to stop this statement from always being executed. Generally, it is much easier either to call an error routine for unusual conditions or to use a break statement if this is necessary.

Theoretically, a goto statement is never required because C's normal structures provide sufficient flexibility to handle all possible flow control requirements. Also, gotos tend to complicate programs. For example, consider the following code:

```
if (a == 100)
   goto first;
else
   x = 20;
   goto sec;
first: x = 50
  sec: y = 10;
```

Written without a goto this code is

```
if (a == 100)
   x = 50;
else
   x = 20;
y = 10;
```

Both sections of code produce the same result; however, the second version is clearly easier to read. It is worthwhile to convince yourself that the two sections of code do, in fact, produce the same result by running the code on your computer. This will let you experience the sense of frustration when working with goto-invaded code.

Using even one goto statement in a program is almost always a sign of bad programming structure. Possibly the only case that conceivably might use a goto is in a nested loop where some error condition requires escape from both the inner and outer loop structure (a break will only exit from the inner loop). If such an escape was ever used in developing a program, the code should ultimately be rewritten as a function where the escape is replaced by an exit from the function.

12.2   Bitwise Operations

C operates with complete data entities that are stored as one or more bytes, such as character, integer and double precision constants and variables. In addition, C provides for the manipulation of individual bits of character and integer constants and variables.

The operators that are used to perform bit manipulations are called *bit operators*. They are listed in Table 12.2.

All the operators listed in Table 12.2 are binary operators, requiring two operands. In using the bit operators each operand is treated as a binary number consisting of a series of individual 1s and 0s. The respective bits in each operand are then compared on a bit-by-bit basis, and the result is determined based on the selected operation.

The AND Operator

The AND operator causes a bit-by-bit AND comparison between its two operands. The result of each bit-by-bit comparison is a 1 only when both bits being compared are 1s, otherwise the result of the AND operation is a 0. For example, assume that the following two eight-bit numbers are to be ANDed:

```
1 0 1 1 0 0 1 1
1 1 0 1 0 1 0 1
```

To perform an AND operation, each bit in one operand is compared to the bit occupying the same position in the other operand. Figure 12.1 illustrates the correspondence between bits for these two operands. AND comparisons are determined by the following rule: *The result of an AND comparison is 1 when both bits being compared are 1s; otherwise the result is a 0.* The result of each comparison is, of course, independent of any other bit comparison.

Table 12.2   Bit Operators

Operator	Description
&	Bitwise AND
|	Bitwise inclusive OR
^	Bitwise exclusive OR
~	Bitwise one's complement
<<	Left shift
>>	Right shift

```
   1  0  1  1  0  0  1  1
&  1  1  0  1  0  1  0  1
```

```
   1  0  0  1  0  0  0  1
```

Figure 12.1   A sample AND operation

Program 12.2 illustrates the use of an AND operation. In this program, the variable op1 is initialized to the octal value 325, which is the octal equivalent of the binary number 11010101, and the variable op2 is initialized to the octal value 263, which is the octal representation of the binary number 10110011. These are the same two binary numbers illustrated in Figure 12.1.

🖳 Program 12.2

```c
#include <stdio.h>
int main()
{
   int op1 = 0325, op2 = 0263;

   printf("%o ANDed with %o is %o\n", op1, op2, op1 & op2);

   return 0;
}
```

Program 12.2 produces the following output:

```
325 ANDed with 263 is 221
```

The result of ANDing the octal numbers 325 and 263 is the octal number 221. The binary equivalent of 221 is the binary number 10010001, which is the result of the AND operation illustrated in Figure 12.1.

AND operations are extremely useful in *masking,* or eliminating, selected bits from an operand. This is a direct result of the fact that ANDing any bit (1 or 0) with a 0 forces the resulting bit to be a 0, while ANDing any bit (1 or 0) with a 1 leaves the original bit unchanged. For example, assume that the variable op1 has the arbitrary bit pattern xxxxxxxx, where each x can be either 1 or 0, independent of any other x in the number. The result of ANDing this binary number with the binary number 00001111 is

```
op1  =   x  x  x  x  x  x  x  x
op2  =   0  0  0  0  1  1  1  1
```

```
Result  =   0  0  0  0  x  x  x  x
```

As can be seen from this example, the zeros in op2 effectively mask, or eliminate, the respective bits in op1, while the ones in op2 *filter,* or pass, the respective bits in op1 through with no change in their values. In this example, the variable op2 is called a *mask.* By choosing the mask appropriately, any individual bit in an operand can be selected, or filtered, out of an operand for inspection. For example, ANDing the variable op1 with the mask 00000100 forces all the bits of the result to be 0, except for the third bit. The third bit of the result will be a copy of the third bit of op1. Thus, if the result of the AND is 0, the third bit of op1 must have been 0, and if the result of the AND is a nonzero number, the third bit must have been a 1.

The Inclusive OR Operator

The inclusive OR operator, |, performs a bit-by-bit comparison of its two operands in a fashion much like that of the bit-by-bit AND. Inclusive OR comparisons, however, are determined by the following rule: *The result of an inclusive OR comparison is 1 if either bit being compared is a 1; otherwise the result is a 0.* As with all bit operations, the result of each comparison is, of course, independent of any other comparison. Figure 12.2 illustrates an inclusive OR operation.

Program 12.3 illustrates an inclusive OR operation, using the octal values of the operands illustrated in Figure 12.2.

 Program 12.3

```
#include <stdio.h>
int main()
{
  int op1 = 0325, op2 = 0263;

  printf("%o ORed with %o is %o\n", op1, op2, op1 | op2);

  return 0;
}
```

Program 12.3 produces the following output:

```
325 ORed with 263 is 367
```

```
  1 0 1 1 0 0 1 1
| 1 1 0 1 0 1 0 1
  ---------------
  1 1 1 1 0 1 1 1
```

Figure 12.2   A sample OR operation

The result of inclusive ORing the octal numbers 325 and 263 is the octal number 367. The binary equivalent of 367 is 11110111, which is the result of the inclusive OR operation illustrated in Figure 12.2.

Inclusive OR operations are extremely useful in forcing selected bits to take on a 1 value or for passing through other bit values unchanged. This is a direct result of the fact that inclusive ORing any bit (1 or 0) with a 1 forces the resulting bit to be a 1, while inclusive ORing any bit (1 or 0) with a 0 leaves the original bit unchanged. For example, assume that the variable op1 has the arbitrary bit pattern xxxxxxxx, where each x can be either 1 or 0, independent of any other x in the number. The result of inclusive ORing this binary number with the binary number 11110000 is

```
op1 =   x x x x x x x x
op2 =   1 1 1 1 0 0 0 0
_____

Result =   1 1 1 1 x x x x
```

As can be seen from this example, the 1s in op2 force the resulting bits to 1, while the 0s in op2 filter, or pass, the respective bits in op1 through with no change in their values. Thus, inclusive OR and AND perform a similar masking operations, except that in OR operations the masked bits are set to 1s rather than cleared to 0s. Another way of looking at this is to say that inclusive ORing with a 0 has the same effect as ANDing with a 1.

The Exclusive OR Operator

The exclusive OR operator, ^, performs a bit-by-bit comparison of its two operands. The result of the comparison is determined by the following rule: *The result of an exclusive OR comparison is 1 if one and only one of the bits being compared is a 1; otherwise the result is 0.*

Figure 12.3 illustrates an exclusive OR operation. As shown in the figure, when both bits being compared are the same value (both 1 or both 0), the result is a 0. Only when both bits have different values (one bit a 1 and the other a 0) is the result a 1. Again, each pair or bit comparison is independent of any other bit comparison.

An exclusive OR operation can be used to create the opposite value, or complement, of any individual bit in a variable. This is a direct result of the fact that exclusive ORing any bit (1 or 0) with a 1 forces the resulting bit to be of the opposite value of its original state, while exclusive ORing any bit (1 or 0) with a 0 leaves the original bit unchanged. For example, assume that the variable op1 has the arbitrary bit pattern xxxxxxxx, where each x can be either 1 or 0, independent of any other x in the number. Using the

```
      1 0 1 1 0 0 1 1
^     1 1 0 1 0 1 0 1
    _____

      0 1 1 1 0 1 1 1
```

Figure 12.3   A sample exclusive OR operation

notation that $\bar{x}$ is the complement (opposite) value of x, the result of exclusive ORing this binary number with the binary number 01010101 is

```
op1 =  x x x x x x x x
op2 =  0 1 0 1 0 1 0 1
```
___

```
Result =  x x̄ x x̄ x x̄ x x̄
```

As can be seen from this example, the 1s in op2 force the resulting bits to be the complement of their original bit values, while the 0s in op2 filter, or pass, the respective bits in op1 through with no change in their values.

The Complement Operator

The complement operator, ~, is a unary operator that changes each 1 bit in its operand to 0 and each 0 bit to 1. For example, if the variable op1 contains the binary number 11001010, ~op1 replaces this binary number with the number 00110101. The complement operator is used to force any bit in an operand to zero, independent of the actual number of bits used to store the number. For example, the statement

```
op1 = op1 & ~07;
```

or its shorter form,

```
op1 &= ~07;
```

both set the last three bits of op1 to 0, regardless of how op1 is stored within the computer. Either of these two statements can, of course, be replaced by ANDing the last three bits of op1 with 0s, if the number of bits used to store op1 is known. In a computer that uses 16 bits to store integers, the appropriate AND operation is

```
op1 = op1 & 0177770;
```

For a computer that uses 32 bits to store integers, the above AND sets the leftmost or higher-order 16 bits to 0 also, which is an unintended result. The correct statement for 32 bits is

```
op1 = op1 & 027777777770;
```

Using the complement operator in this situation frees the programmer from having to determine the storage size of the operand and, more importantly, makes the program portable between machines using different integer storage sizes.

Different-Sized Data Items

When the bit operators &, | and ^ are used with operands of different sizes, the shorter operand is always increased in bit size to match the size of the larger operand. Figure 12.4 illustrates the extension of a 16-bit unsigned integer into a 32-bit number.

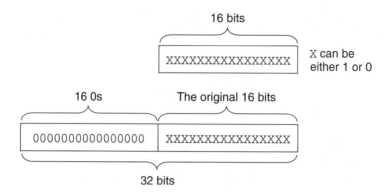

Figure 12.4 Extending 16-bit unsigned data to 32 bits

As the figure shows the additional bits are added to the left of the original number and filled with 0s. This is the equivalent of adding leading 0s to the number, which has no effect on the number's value.

When extending signed numbers, the original leftmost bit is reproduced in the additional bits that are added to the number. As illustrated in Figure 12.5, if the original leftmost bit is 0, corresponding to a positive number, 0 is placed in each of the additional bit positions. If the leftmost bit is 1, which corresponds to a negative number, 1 is placed in the additional bit positions. In either case, the resulting binary number has the same sign and magnitude of the original number.

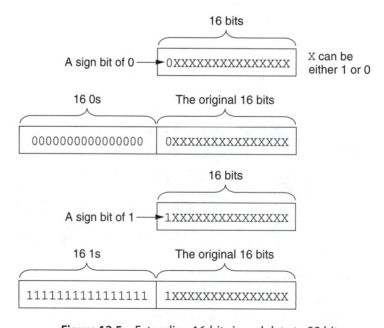

Figure 12.5 Extending 16-bit signed data to 32 bits

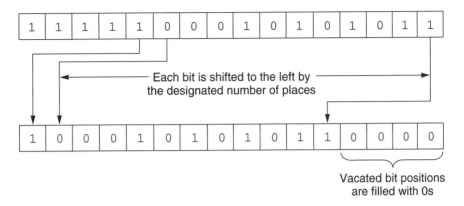

Figure 12.6   An example of a left shift

The Shift Operators

The left shift operator, <<, causes the bits in an operand to be shifted to the left by a given amount. For example, the statement

```
op1 = op1 << 4;
```

causes the bits in op1 to be shifted four bits to the left, filling any vacated bits with a 0. Figure 12.6 illustrates the effect of shifting the binary number 1111100010101011 to the left by four bit positions.

For unsigned integers, each left shift corresponds to multiplication by two. This is also true for signed numbers using two's complement representation, as long as the left-most bit does not switch values. Since a change in the leftmost bit of a two's complement number represents a change in both the sign and magnitude represented by the bit, such a shift does not represent a simple multiplication by two.

The right shift operator, >>, causes the bits in an operand to be shifted to the right by a given amount. For example, the statement

```
op1 = op1 >> 3;
```

causes the bits in op1 to be shifted to the right by three bit positions. Figure 12.7a illustrates the right shift of the unsigned binary number 1111100010101011 by three bit positions. As illustrated, the three rightmost bits are shifted "off the end" and are lost.

For unsigned numbers, the leftmost bit is not used as a sign bit. For this type of number, the vacated leftmost bits are always filled with 0s. This is the case that is illustrated in Figure 12.7a.

For signed numbers, what is filled in the vacated bits depends on the computer. Most computers reproduce the original sign bit of the number. Figure 12.7b illustrates the right shift of a negative binary number by four bit positions, where the sign bit is reproduced in the vacated bits. Figure 12.7c illustrates the equivalent right shift of a positive signed binary number.

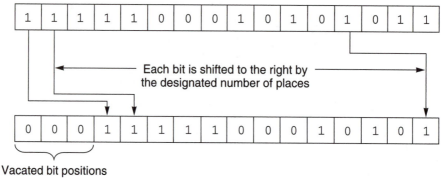

Figure 12.7a An unsigned arithmetic right shift

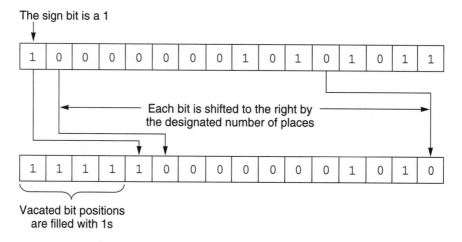

Figure 12.7b The right shift of a negative binary number

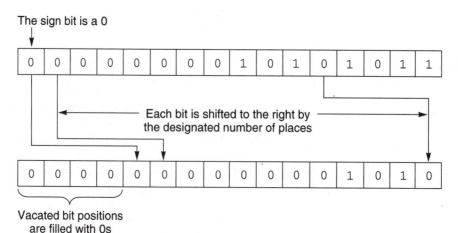

Figure 12.7c The right shift of a positive binary number

The type of fill illustrated in Figures 12.7b and 12.7c, where the sign bit is reproduced in vacated bit positions, is called an *arithmetic right shift*. In an arithmetic right shift, each single shift to the right corresponds to a division by two.

Instead of reproducing the sign bit in right-shifted signed numbers, some computers automatically fill the vacated bits with 0s. This type of shift is called a *logical shift*. For positive signed numbers, where the leftmost bit is 0, both arithmetic and logical right shifts produce the same result. The results of these two shifts are only different when negative numbers are involved.

12.3   Macros

In its simplest form, the #define preprocessor is used to equate constants and operators to symbolic names. For example, the statement

```
#define SALESTAX 0.05
```

equates the symbolic name SALESTAX to the number 0.05.When SALESTAX is used in any subsequent statement or expression the equivalent value of 0.05 is substituted for the symbolic name. The substitutions are made by the C preprocessor just prior to program compilation.

C places no restrictions on the equivalences that can be established with the #define statement. Thus, in addition to using #define preprocessor statements for simple equivalences, these statements can also be used to equate symbolic names to text, a partial or complete expression, and may even include arguments. When the equivalence consists of more than a single value, operator, or variable, the symbolic name is referred to as a *macro,* and the substitution of the text in place of the symbolic name is called a *macro expansion* or *macro substitution.* The word macro refers to the direct, in-line expansion of one word into many words. For example, the equivalence established by the statement

```
#define FORMAT "The answer is %f\n"
```

enables us to write the statement

```
printf(FORMAT, 15.2);
```

When this statement is encountered by the preprocessor, the symbolic name FORMAT is replaced by the equivalent text "The answer is %f\n". The compiler always receives the expanded version after the text has been inserted in place of the symbolic name by the preprocessor.

In addition to using #define statements for straight text substitutions, these statements can also be used to define equivalences that use arguments. For example, in the equivalence statement

```
#define SQUARE(x)  x * x
```

x is an argument. Here, SQUARE(x) is a true macro that is expanded into the expression x * x, where x is itself replaced by the variable or constant used when the macro is utilized. For example, the statement

```
y = SQUARE(num);
```

is expanded into the statement

```
y = num * num;
```

The advantage of using a macro such as SQUARE(x) is that since the data type of the argument is not specified, the macro can be used with any data type argument. If num, for example, is an integer variable, the expression num * num produces an integer value. Similarly, if num is a double precision variable, the SQUARE(x) macro produces a double precision value. This is a direct result of the text substitution procedure used in expanding the macro and is an advantage of making SQUARE(x) a macro rather than a function.

Care must be taken when defining macros with arguments. For example, in the definition of SQUARE(x), there must be no space between the symbolic name SQUARE and the left parenthesis used to enclose the argument. There can, however, be spaces within the parentheses if more than one argument is used.

Additionally, because the expression of a macro involves direct text substitution, unintended results may occur if you do not use macros carefully. For example, the assignment statement

```
val = SQUARE(num1 + num1);
```

does not assign the value of $(num1 + num2)^2$ to val. Rather, the expansion of SQUARE(num1 + num2) results in the equivalent statement

```
val = num1 + num2 * num1 + num2;
```

This statement results from the direct text substitution of the term num1 + num2 for the argument x in the expression x * x that is produced by the preprocessor.

To avoid unintended results, always place parentheses around all macro arguments wherever they appear in the macro. For example, the definition

```
#define SQUARE(x)    (x) * (x)
```

ensures that a correct result is produced whenever the macro is invoked. Now the statement

```
val = SQUARE(num1 + num2);
```

is expanded to produce the desired assignment

```
val = (num1 + num2) * (num1 + num2);
```

Macros are extremely useful when the calculations or expressions they contain are relatively simple and can be kept to one or at most two lines. Larger macro definitions tend to become cumbersome and confusing and are better written as functions. If necessary, a macro definition can be continued on a new line by typing a backslash character, \, before the ENTER key is pressed. The backslash acts as an escape character that causes the preprocessor to treat the ENTER literally and not include it in any subsequent text substitutions.

The advantage of using a macro instead of a function is an increase in execution speed. Because the macro is directly expanded and included in every expression or statement using it, there is no execution time loss due to the call and return procedures required by a function. The disadvantage is the increase in required program memory space when a macro is used repeatedly. Each time a macro is used the complete macro text is reproduced and stored as an integral part of the program. Thus, if the same macro is used in ten places, the final code includes ten copies of the expanded text version of the macro. A function, however, is stored in memory only once. No matter how many times the function is called, the same code is used. The memory space required for one copy of a function used extensively throughout a program can be considerably less than the memory required for storing multiple copies of the same code defined as a macro.

12.4   Command-Line Arguments

Arguments can be passed to any function in a program, including the `main()` function. In this section we describe the procedures for passing arguments to `main()` when a program is initially invoked and having `main()` correctly receive and store the arguments passed to it. Both the sending and receiving sides of the transaction must be considered. Fortunately, the interface for transmitting arguments to a `main()` function has been standardized in C, so both sending and receiving arguments can be done almost mechanically.

All the programs that have been run so far have been invoked by typing the name of the executable version of the program after the operating system prompt is displayed. The command line for these programs consists of a single word, which is the name of the program. For computers that use the UNIX operating system the prompt is usually the $ symbol and the executable name of the program is `a.out`. For these systems, the simple command line

```
$a.out
```

begins program execution of the last compiled source program currently residing in `a.out`.

If you are using a C compiler on an IBM PC, the equivalent operating system prompt is either C> or A>, and the name of the executable program is typically the same name as the source program with an `.exe` extension rather than a `.c` extension. Assuming that you are using an IBM PC with the C> operating system prompt, the complete command line for running an executable program named `showad.exe` is C> `showad`. As illustrated in

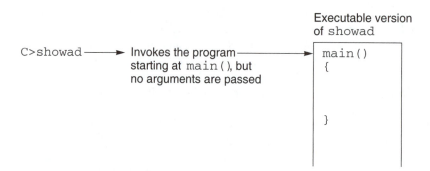

Figure 12.8   Invoking the showad program

Figure 12.8, this command line causes the showad program to begin execution with its main() function, but no arguments are passed to main().

Now assume that we want to pass the three separate string arguments three blind mice directly into showad's main() function. Sending arguments into a main() function is extremely easy. It is accomplished by including the arguments on the command line used to begin program execution. Because the arguments are typed on the command line, they are, naturally, called *command-line arguments*. To pass the arguments three blind mice directly into the main() function of the showad program, we only need to add the desired words after the program name on the command line:

    A showad three blind mice

Upon encountering the command line showad three blind mice, the operating system stores it as a sequence of four strings. Figure 12.9 illustrates the storage of this command line, assuming that each character uses one byte of storage. As shown in the figure, each string terminates with the standard C null character \0.

Sending command-line arguments to main() is always this simple. The arguments are typed on the command line, and the operating system nicely stores them as a sequence of separate strings. We must now handle the receiving side of the transaction and let main() know that arguments are being passed to it.

Arguments passed to main(), like all function arguments, must be declared as part of the function's definition. To standardize argument passing to a main() function, only two items are allowed: a number and an array. The number is an integer variable, which must be named argc (short for *argument counter*), and the array is a one-dimensional list, which must be named argv (short for *argument values*). Figure 12.10 illustrates these two arguments.

Figure 12.9   The command line stored in memory

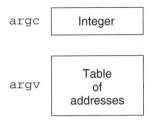

Figure 12.10 An integer and an array are passed to main()

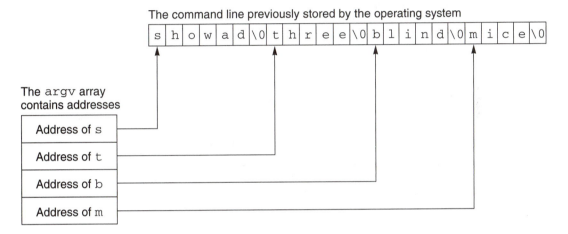

Figure 12.11 Addresses are stored in the argv array

The integer passed to main() is the total number of items on the command line. In our example, the value of argc passed to main() is four, which includes the name of the program plus the three command-line arguments. The one-dimensional list passed to main() is a list of pointers containing the starting storage address of each string typed on the command line, as illustrated in Figure 12.11.[2]

We can now write the complete function definition for main() to receive arguments by declaring their names and data types. For main()'s two arguments C requires that they be named argc and argv, respectively. Because argc is an integer, its declaration will be int argc. Because argv is the name of an array whose elements are addresses that point to where the actual command-line arguments are stored, its proper declaration is char *argv[]. This is nothing more than the declaration of an array of pointers. It is read "argv is an array whose elements are pointers to characters." Putting all this together, the full function header of a main() function that will receive command-line arguments is

```
int main(int argc, char *argv[]) /* complete main() header line */
```

[2] If the full path name of the program is stored, showad in Figure 12.11 should be replaced by its full path name.

No matter how many arguments are typed on the command line, `main()` only needs the two standard pieces of information provided by `argc` and `argv`: the number of items on the command line and the list of starting addresses indicating where each argument is actually stored.

Program 12.4 verifies our description by printing the data actually passed to `main()`. The variable `argv[i]` used in Program 12.4 contains an address. The notation `*argv[i]` refers to "the character pointed to" by the address in `argv[i]`.

 Program 12.4

```
#include <stdio.h>
int main(int argc, char *argv[])
{
  int i;

  printf("\nThe number of items on the command line is %d\n\n",argc);
  for (i = 0; i < argc; i++)
  {
    printf("The address stored in argv[%d] is %p\n", i, argv[i]);
    printf("The character pointed to is %c\n", *argv[i]);
}

  return 0;
}
```

Assuming that the executable version of Program 12.4 is named `showad.exe`, a sample output for the command line `showad three blind mice` is[3]

```
The number of items on the command line is 4

The address stored in argv[0] is 00780D39
The character pointed to is s
The address stored in argv[1] is 00780D40
The character pointed to is t
The address stored in argv[2] is 00780D46
The character pointed to is b
The address stored in argv[3] is 00780D4C
The character pointed to is m
```

The addresses displayed by Program 12.4 depend, of course, on the machine used to run the program. Figure 12.12 illustrates the storage of the command line as displayed by

---

[3] If the full path name of the program is stored, the first character displayed is the disk drive designation, which is usually C.

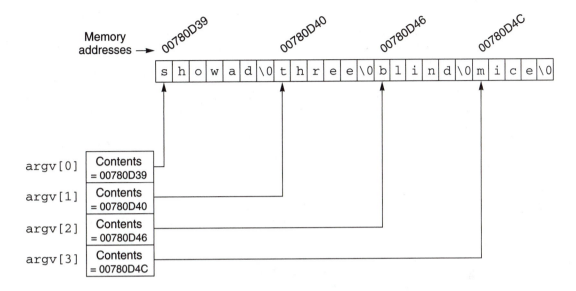

Figure 12.12 The command line stored in memory

the sample output. As anticipated, the addresses in the argv array "point" to the starting characters of each string typed on the command line.

Once command-line arguments are passed to a C program, they can be used like any other C strings. Program 12.5 causes its command-line arguments to be displayed from within main().

Program 12.5

```
/* A program that displays command line arguments */
#include <stdio.h>
int main(int argc, char *argv[])
{
  int i;

  printf("\nThe following arguments were passed to main(): ");
  for (i = 1; i < argc; i++)
    printf("%s ", argv[i]);
  printf("\n");

  return 0;
}
```

Assuming that the name of the executable version of Program 12.5 is a.out, the output of this program for the command line a.out three blind mice is

> The following arguments were passed to main(): three blind mice

Notice that when the addresses in `argv[]` are passed to the `printf()` function in Program 12.5, the strings pointed to by these addresses are displayed. When these same addresses were passed to the `printf()` function in Program 12.4, the actual values of the addresses were printed. The difference in displays is caused by the `printf()` function. When a `%s` control sequence is used in `printf()`, as it is in Program 12.5, it alerts the function that a string will be accessed. `printf()` then expects the address of the first character in the string; this is exactly what each element in `argv[]` supplies. Once `printf()` receives the address, the function performs the required indirection to locate the actual string that is displayed. The `%p` control sequence used in Program 12.4 displays the value of the address stored in `argv[i]`. As we have noted before, because pointers are a unique data type, C provides the specific control sequence, `%p`, of the output of the addresses stored in pointer variables.

One final comment about command-line arguments is in order. Any argument typed on a command line is considered to be a string. To pass numerical data to `main()`, you must convert the passed string into its numerical counterpart. This is seldom an issue, however, since most command-line arguments are used as flags to pass appropriate processing control signals to an invoked program.

Exercises

1. Rewrite each of the following `if-else` statements using a conditional expression:

   a. `if (a < b);`
   `    minVal = a;`
   `  else`
   `    minVal = b;`

   b. `if (num < 0)`
   `    sign = -1;`
   `  else`
   `    sign = 1;`

   c. `if (flag == 1)`
   `    val = num;`
   `  else`
   `    val = num & num;`

   d. `if (credit == plus)`
   `    rate = prime;`
   `  else`
   `    rate = prime + delta;`

   e. `if (!bond)`
   `    cou = .075;`
   `  else`
   `    cou = 1.1;`

2. Determine the results of the following operations:

   a.   `  11001010`
   `  & 10100101`
   _____

   b.   `  11001010`
   `  | 10100101`
   _____

   c.   `  11001010`
   `  ^ 10100101`
   _____

3. Write the octal representations of the binary numbers given in Exercise 2.

4. Determine the octal results of the following operations, assuming unsigned numbers:
   a. the octal number 0157 shifted left by one bit position
   b. the octal number 0701 shifted left by two bit positions
   c. the octal number 0673 shifted right by two bit positions
   d. the octal number 067 shifted right by three bit positions

5. Repeat Exercise 4 assuming that the numbers are treated as signed values.

6. a. Assume that the arbitrary bit pattern *xxxxxxxx*, where each *x* can represent either 1 or 0, is stored in the integer variable `flag`. Determine the octal value of a mask that can be ANDed with the bit pattern to reproduce the third and fourth bits of `flag` and set all other bits to 0. The rightmost bit in `flag` is considered bit 0.

   b. Determine the octal value of a mask that can be inclusively ORed with the bit pattern in `flag` to reproduce the third and fourth bits of `flag` and set all other bits to 1. Again, consider the rightmost bit in `flag` to be bit 0.

   c. Determine the octal value of a mask that can be used to complement the values of the third and fourth bits of `flag` and leave all other bits unchanged. Determine the bit operation that should be used with the mask value to produce the desired result.

7. a. Write the two's complement form of the decimal number −1, using eight bits. (*Hint:* Refer to Section 2.8 for a review of two's complement numbers.)

   b. Repeat Exercise 7a using 16 bits to represent the decimal number −1 and compare your answer to your previous answer. Could the 16-bit version have been obtained by sign-extending the 8-bit version?

8. Write a C program that displays the first eight bits of each character value input into a variable named `ch`. (*Hint:* Assuming each character is stored using eight bits, start by using the hexadecimal mask 80, which corresponds to the binary number 10000000. If the result of the masking operation is a 0, display a 0; else display a 1. Then shift the mask one place to the right to examine the next bit, and so on until all bits in the variable `ch` have been processed.)

9. Write a C program that reverses the bits in an integer variable named `okay` and stores the reversed bits in the variable named `revOkay`. For example, if the bit pattern 11100101, corresponding to the octal number 0345, is assigned to `okay`, the bit pattern 10100111, corresponding to the octal number 0247, should be produced and stored in `revOkay`.

10. a. Define a macro named `NEGATE(x)` that produces the negative of its argument.

   b. Include the `NEGATE(x)` macro defined in Exercise 10a in a complete C program and run the program to confirm proper operation of the macro for various cases.

11. a. Define a macro named `ABS_VAL(x)` that produces the absolute value of its argument.

   b. Include the `ABS_VAL(x)` macro defined in Exercise 11a in a complete C program and run the program to confirm proper operation of the macro for various cases.

12. a. Define a macro named `CIRCUM(r)` that determines the circumference of a circle of radius `r`. The circumference is determined from the relationship *circumference = 2.0 * PI * radius,* where PI = 3.1416.

   b. Include the `CIRCUM(r)` macro defined in Exercise 12a in a complete C program and run the program to confirm proper operation of the macro for various cases.

13. a. Define a macro named `MIN(x,y)` that determines the minimum value of its two arguments.

   b. Include the `MIN(x,y)` macro defined in Exercise 13a in a complete C program and run the program to confirm proper operation of the macro for various cases.

14. a. Define a macro named `MAX(x,y)` that determines the maximum value of its two arguments.

   b. Include the `MAX(x,y)` macro defined in Exercise 14a in a complete C program and run the program to confirm proper operation of the macro for various cases.

15. a. Write a program that accepts the name of a data file as a command-line argument. Have your program open the data file and display its contents, line by line, on the CRT screen.

   b. Would the program written for Exercise 15a work correctly for a program file?

16. a. Modify the program written for Exercise 15a so that each line displayed is preceded by a line number.

b. Modify the program written for Exercise 16a so that the command-line argument −p will cause the program to list the contents of the file on the printer attached to your system.

17. Write a program that accepts a command-line argument as the name of a data file. Given the name, your program should display the number of characters in the file. (*Hint:* Use the `fseek()` and `ftell()` library functions discussed in Section 11.3.)

18. Write a program that accepts two integer values as command-line arguments. The program should multiply the two values entered and display the result. (*Hint:* The command line must be accepted as string data and converted to numerical values before multiplication.)

12.5 Chapter Summary

1. A `typedef` statement creates synonym names for any C data type name. For example, the statement

```
typedef int WHOLENUM;
```

makes `WHOLENUM` a synonym for int.

2. An enumerated data type is a user-defined scalar data type. The user must select a name and list the acceptable values of the data type. For example, the enumeration

```
enum color {red, green, yellow}
```

creates a color data type. Any variable may be subsequently declared with this data type and may store one of the acceptable values listed. An enumerated data type may also be `typedef`ed.

3. A conditional expression provides an alternate way of expressing a simple if-else statement. The general form of a conditional expression is

```
expression1 ? expression2 : expression3
```

The equivalent if-else statement for this is

```
if (expression1)
   expression2;
else
   expression3;
```

4. C also provides a `goto` statement. In theory this statement need never be used. In practice it produces confusing and unstructured code, and should be used only in a very limited and controlled manner, if at all.

5. Individual bits of character and integer variables and constants can be manipulated using C's bit operators. These are the AND, inclusive OR, exclusive OR, complement, left shift, and right shift operators.

6. The AND and inclusive OR operators are useful in creating masks. These masks can be used to pass or eliminate individual bits from the selected operand. The exclusive OR operator is useful in complementing an operand's bits.

7. When the AND and OR operators are used with operands of different sizes, the shorter operand is always increased in bit size to match the size of the larger operand.

8. The shift operators produce different results depending on whether the operand is a signed or an unsigned value.

9. Using the #define command, complete expressions can be equated to symbolic names. When these expressions include arguments they are referred to as macros.

10. Arguments passed to main() are termed command-line arguments. C provides a standard argument-passing procedure in which main() can accept any number of arguments passed to it. Each argument passed to main() is considered a string and is stored using a pointer array named argv. The total number of arguments on the command line is stored in an integer variable named argc.

Part **6**

Introduction to C++

Introduction to C++

Besides being an improved version of C, the distinguishing characteristic of C++ is its support of object-oriented programming. Central to this object orientation is the concept of an *abstract* data type, which is a programmer-defined data type. In this chapter we explore the implications of permitting programmers to define their own data types and then present C++'s mechanism for constructing abstract data types. As we will see, the construction of a data type is based on both structures and functions; structures provide the means for creating new data configurations and functions provide the means for performing operations on these structures. What C++ provides is a unique way of combining structures and functions together in a self-contained, cohesive unit from which objects can be created.

13.1 Object-Based Programming and Abstract Data Types

The emergence of graphical screen and the subsequent interest in window applications has dramatically changed the programming environment since the mid-1990s. Programming

Programming Note

Procedural, Hybrid, and Pure Object-Oriented Languages

Most high-level programming languages can be categorized into one of three main categories: procedural, hybrid, or object-oriented. FORTRAN, which was the first commercially available high-level programming language, is procedural. This makes sense because FORTRAN was designed to perform mathematical calculations that used standard algebraic formulas. Formally, these formulas were described as algorithms, and then the algorithms were coded using function and subroutine procedures. Other procedural languages that followed FORTRAN included BASIC, COBOL, and Pascal.

Currently, there are only two pure object-oriented languages; Smalltalk and Eiffel. The first requirement of a pure object-oriented language is that it contain three specific features: classes, inheritance, and polymorphism (each of these features is described in this chapter). In addition to providing these features, however, a "pure" object-oriented language must always use classes. In a pure object-oriented language, this means that all data types are constructed as classes, all data values are objects, all operators can be overloaded (that is, the same function name can be used with different parameter lists), and every data operation can only be executed using a class member function. *It is impossible in a pure object-oriented language not to use object-oriented features throughout a program.* This is not the case in a hybrid language.

In a hybrid language, such as C++, *it is impossible not to use elements of a procedural program.* This is because the use of any built-in data type or operation effectively violates the pure object-oriented paradigm. Although a hybrid language must have the ability to define classes, the distinguishing feature of a hybrid language is that it is possible to write a complete program using only procedural code. Additionally, hybrid languages need not even provide inheritance and polymorphic features—but they must provide classes. Languages that use classes but do not provide inheritance and polymorphic features are referred to as *object-based* rather than *object-oriented* languages.

multiple and possibly overlapping windows on the same graphical screen is extremely difficult using standard procedural, input/output programming techniques. Similarly, providing a graphical user interface (GUI) where a user can easily move around in even a single window is a challenge in C.

Unlike a procedural approach, however, an object-oriented approach works well in a graphical windowed environment, where each window can be specified as a self-contained rectangular object that can be moved and resized in relation to other objects on the screen. Additionally, within each window, other graphical objects, such as check boxes, option buttons, labels, and text boxes, can easily be placed and moved.

To provide this object creation capability, extensions to the procedural language C were developed. These extensions became the new language named C++, which permits a programmer to both use and create new objects.

Central to the creation of objects is the concept of an abstract data type which is simply a user-defined data type, as opposed to the built-in data types provided by all languages (such as integer and floating point types). Permitting a programmer to define new data types, such as a rectangular type, out of which specific rectangular objects can be created and displayed on a screen, forms the basis of C++'s object orientation.

Abstract Data Types

To gain a clear understanding of an abstract data type, consider the following three built-in data types supplied in C: int, float, and char. In using these data types, we typically declare one or more variables of the desired type, use them in their accepted ways, and avoid using them in ways that are not specified. Thus, for example, we do not use the modulus operator on two floating point numbers. Because this operation makes no sense for floating point numbers, it is never defined, in any programming language, for such numbers. Thus, although we typically don't consider it, each data type consists of both a type of data, such as integer or float, *and* specific operational capabilities provided for each type.

In computer terminology, a *data type* is the combination of data and their associated operations. That is, a data type defines both the types of data and the types of operations that can be performed on the data. Seen in this light, the int data type, the float data type, and the char data type provided in C are all examples of built-in data types that are defined by a type of data and specific operational capabilities provided for initializing and manipulating the type. In a simplified form this relationship can be described as

$$\text{Data Type} = \text{Allowable Data} + \text{Operational Capabilities}$$

Although we don't normally associate the operations that we apply to C's built-in data types with the data type itself, these operations are an inherent part of each data type. Clearly the designers of C had to carefully consider, and then implement, specific operations for each type of data supplied by the language.

To understand the importance of the operational capabilities provided by a programming language, let's take a moment to list some of those supplied with C's built-in data types (integer, floating point, and character). The minimum set of the capabilities provided by C's built-in data types is listed in Table 13.1.

Now let's see how all of this relates to abstract data types (ADTs). By definition an abstract data type is simply a user-defined type that defines both a type of data and the operations that can be performed on it. Such user-defined data types are required when we wish to create objects that are more complex than simple integers and characters. If we are to create our own data types, we must be aware of both the type of data we are creating and the capabilities that we provide to initialize and manipulate the data.

A specific example, assume that we are programming an application that uses dates extensively. Clearly we can define a data structure named Date that consists of three data members as follows:

Table 13.1 Capabilities of built-in data types in C

Capability	Example
Define one or more variables of the data type	`int a, b;`
Initialize a variable at definition	`int a = 5;`
Assign a value to a variable	`a = 10;`
Assign one variable's value to another variable	`a = b;`
Perform mathematical operations	`a + b`
Convert from one data type to another	`a = (int) 7.2;`

```
struct Date
{
   int month;
   int day;
   int year;
};
```

Specifically, we have chosen to store a date using three integers, one for the month, day, and year, respectively. In addition, we will require that the year be stored as a four-digit number. Thus, for example, we will store the year 1999 as 1999 and not 99. Making sure to store all years with their correct century designation eliminates a number of problems that can crop up if only the last two digits, such as 99, are stored. For example, the number of years between 2003 and 1999 can quickly be calculated as 2003 − 1999 = 4 years, while this same answer is not so easily obtained if only the year values 03 and 99 are used. Additionally, we are sure of what the year 2003 refers to, whereas a two-digit value such as 03 could refer to either 1903 or 2003.

The data structure for storing a date, unfortunately, supplies only half of the answer. We must still supply a set of operations that can be used with dates. Clearly, such operations could include assigning values to a date, subtracting two dates to determine the number of days between them, comparing two dates to determine which is earlier and which is later, or displaying a date in a form such as 6/3/02. The combination of the `Date` data structure with a set of `Date` operations would then define an abstract `Date` data type. Although C does not provide a direct capability for constructing abstract data types (providing this capability was the impetus for developing C++), it is possible to simulate an abstract data type in C. This is done by using a data structure for defining a type of data and then defining a set of functions to specifically operate on the data structure. We now construct a set of suitable functions for our `Date` data structure. Specifically we will develop two functions for operating on dates, assignment and display, and leave the development of some of the remaining operations as an exercise. Following are the specifications that our two functions must meet:

Assignment:
Accept three integers as arguments
Assign the first number as the Date's month member
Assign the second number as the Date's day member
Assign the third number as the Date's year member
Return the Date

Display:
Accept a Date as a parameter
Display the values in the form month/day/year

Notice that the details of each function are of interest to us only as we develop each operation. Once developed, however, we need never be concerned with *how* the operations are performed. When we use an operation all we will need to know is what the operation does and how to invoke it, much as we use C's built-in operations. For example, we don't really care how the addition of two integers is performed but only that it is performed correctly.

The actual coding of our two specified functions is rather simple:

```
/* operation to assign values to a Date object */
struct Date setdate(int mm, int dd, int yyyy)
{
   struct Date temp;

   temp.month = mm;
   temp.day = dd;
   temp.year = yyyy;
   return(temp);
}

/* operation to display a Date object */
void showdate(struct Date a)
{
   printf("%02d/%02d/%02d", a.month, a.day, a.year%100);
}
```

The first function header line

```
struct Date setdate(int mm, int dd, int yyyy)
```

defines a function that will return a `Date` structure and uses three integer parameters, `mm`, `dd`, and `yyyy`. The body of this function assigns the data members `month`, `day`, and `year` with the values of these parameters and returns the assigned `Date` structure.

The last function header line defines a function named `showdate()`. This function has no parameters and returns no value. The body of this function, however, needs a little more explanation.

Although we have chosen to internally store all years as four-digit values that retain century information, users are accustomed to seeing dates with the year represented as a two-digit value, such as 12/15/99. To display the last two digits of the year value, the expression year % 100 is used in the printf() function. For example, the expression 1999 % 100 yields the value 99, and if the year is 2001, the expression 2001 % 100 yields the value 1. The %02d format forces each value to be displayed in a field width of 2 with a leading zero, if necessary. Doing this ensures that a date such as December 9, 2002 appears as 12/09/02 and not 12/9/2.

To see how our simulated Date abstract data type can be used within the context of a complete program, consider Program 13.1. To make the program easier to read it has been shaded in lighter and darker areas. The lighter area contains the data structure declaration and operation implementation sections that define the abstract data type. The darker area contains the header and main() function.

The declaration and implementation sections contained in the light-shaded region of Program 13.1 should look familiar—they contain the declaration and implementations that have already been discussed. Notice, however, that this region only declares a Date type, it does not create any Date variables. This is true of all data types, including built-in types such as integer and floating point. Just as a variable of an integer type must be defined, variables of a user-defined data type must also be defined. Variables defined to be of a user-declared data type are referred to as *objects*.

Using this new terminology, the first statement in Program 13.1's main() function, contained in the darker area, defines a single object, named a, to be of the type Date. The next statement in main(), a = setdate(6,3,2001), assigns the argument values 6, 3, and 2001 to a's data members, resulting in the assignment:

```
a.month = 6
a.day = 3
a.year = 2001
```

Finally, the next-to-last statement in main() calls the showdate() function to display the values of a Date object. As the following output of Program 13.1 illustrates, our two functions are operating correctly.

```
The value of the a object is: 06/03/01
```

It should be reemphasized that we have not created an abstract data type in Program 13.1 but only simulated two essential pieces of a user-created data type—that is, a type of data declared by a record structure and a very limited set of operations defined as straightforward C functions. In order to create a true user-created data type we will need to more closely "bundle" the data with its defined set of operations and include many more operations. The capability to create a true abstract data type is provided in C++. This is because C++ provides the ability to incorporate functions as well as data members within the declaration of a structure, whereas in C, structures can contain only data members.

In addition to providing the capability of constructing true abstract data types, C++ also provides a substantial set of improvements to traditional ANSI C. Most of these extend function capabilities and add new capabilities for handling input and output. As

Program 13.1

```c
#include <stdio.h>
/* declaration of the data structure */
struct Date
{
  int month;
  int day;
  int year;
};

/* implementation of associated functions */

/* operation to assign values to a Date object */
struct Date setdate(int mm, int dd, int yyyy)
{
  struct Date temp;

  temp.month = mm;
  temp.day = dd;
  temp.year = yyyy;
  return(temp);
}

/* operation to display a Date object */
void showdate (struct Date a)
{
  printf("%02d/%02d/%02d", a.month, a.day, a.year % 100);
}
int main()
{
  struct Date a;

  a = setdate(6,3,2001);
  printf("\nThe value of the a object is: ");
  showdate(a);
  printf("\n");

  return 0;
}
```

these enhancements are almost always incorporated in constructing abstract data type, we will need to consider them if we are to fully understand and create true C++ abstract data types.

We can, however, provide a preview of a C++ abstract data type that should make sense to you. Program 13.2 shows how Program 13.1 could be written in C++. The important part of Program 13.2 to notice and compare to Program 13.1 is the middle, lightly shaded area, which contains the `Date` structure declaration. Notice in Program 13.2 that the C++ `Date` structure includes declarations for both data and function members, whereas the C `Date` structure includes only data declarations. Also notice the use of the `private` and `public` keywords contained within the structure. These keywords permit restricted access to the data members through the member functions and are described more fully in Section 13.4. Finally, although we have included numerous `printf()` function calls within Program 13.2, each of these calls would be replaced by an equivalent C++ output statement. Exactly how C++'s input and output are performed are the topic of Section 13.2.

Comments in C++

In addition to the comments specified by C's `/*` and `*/` notation, C++ provides for line comments. A *line comment* begins with two slashes (`//`) and continues to the end of the line. For example,

```
// this is a comment
// this program prints out a message
// this program calculates a square root
```

are all line comments. The symbols `//`, with no white space between them, designate the start of a line comment. The end of the line on which the comment is written designates the end of the comment.

A line comment can be written either on a line by itself or at the end of a line containing a program statement. For example,

```
float average; // this is a declaration statement
```

contains a line comment on the same line as a declaration statement. If a comment is too long to be contained on one line, it can either be separated into two or more line comments with each separate comment preceded by the double slash symbol set, `//`, or be designated using C's comment notation. Thus, the multiline comment:

```
// this comment is used to illustrate a
// comment that extends across two lines
```

can also be written by placing the comment between the `/*` and `*/` symbols.

Program 13.2

```c
#include <stdio.h>
/* declaration of the data structure */
struct Date
{
  private:
    int month;
    int day;
    int year;
  public:
    void setdate(int, int, int);   /* notice the function    */
    void showdate();               /* declarations within the */
};                                 /* Date structure          */

/* implementation of associated functions */

/* operation to assign values to a Date object */
void Date :: setdate(int mm, int dd, int yyyy)
{
  month = mm;
  day = dd;
  year = yyyy;
  return;
}

/* operation to display a Date object */
void Date :: showdate()
{
  printf("%02d/%02d/%02d", month, day, year % 100);
}
int main()
{
  struct Date a;

  a.setdate(6,3,2001);
  printf("\nThe value of the a object is: ");
  a.showdate();
  printf("\n");

  return 0;
}
```

Exercises 13.1

1. Modify Program 13.1 by adding a function named `convert()`. The function should access the `month`, `year`, and `day` data members of a `Date` and then return a long integer that is the calculated as *year * 10000 + month * 100 + day*. For example, if the date is 4/1/2002, the returned value is 20020401 (dates in this form are useful when performing sorts, because placing the numbers in numerical order automatically places the corresponding dates in chronological order). Make sure to declare the return value as a long integer to accommodate larger integer values.

2. Modify Program 13.1 to contain a function that compares two `Date` objects and returns the larger of the two. The function should be written according to the following algorithm:

   Comparison function
      Accept two Date values as arguments
      Determine the later date using the following procedure:
         Convert each date into an integer value having the form
         yyyymmdd. This can be accomplished by using the algorithm
         described in Exercise 1. Compare the corresponding integers
         for each date. The larger integer corresponds to the later
         date.
      Return the later date

3. a. Add a member function named `leapyr()` to Program 13.1. The function should return a 1 when a `Date` object falls in a leap year and a 0 if it is does not. A leap year is any year that is evenly divisible by 4 but not evenly divisible by 100, with the exception that years evenly divisible by 400 are leap years. For example, the year 1996 was a leap year because it is evenly divisible by 4 and not evenly divisible by 100. The year 2000 is a leap year because it is evenly divisible by 400.

4. Write data structures appropriate for each of the following specifications. Also list appropriate operations for each data structure.
   a. A structure named `Time` that has integer data members named `secs`, `mins`, and `hours`.
   b. A structure named `Circle` that has integer data members named `xcenter` and `ycenter` and a floating point data member named `radius`.
   c. A structure named `Complex` that has floating point members named `real` and `imaginary`.
   d. A structure named `System` that has character data members named `computer`, `printer`, and `screen`, each capable of holding 30 characters (including the end-of-string NULL), and floating point data members named `compPrice`, `printPrice`, and `scrnPrice`.

5. a. Construct C functions for the function members you listed in Exercise 4a.
   b. Construct C functions for the function members you listed in Exercise 4b.
   c. Construct C functions for the function members you listed in Exercise 4c.
   d. Construct C functions for the function members you listed in Exercise 4d.

6. a. Include the declaration and function definitions for Exercises 4a and 5a in a complete working program.
   b. Include the declaration and function definitions for Exercises 4b and 5b in a complete working program.

c. Include the declaration and function definitions for Exercises 4c and 5c in a complete working program.

d. Include the declaration and function definitions for Exercises 4d and 5d in a complete working program.

13.2 Input and Output in C++

Although the `printf()` and `scanf()` functions are available in C++, the standard
method of C++'s input and output is *stream I/O*. In many situations stream I/O is much
simpler to use than the comparable C functions, and it avoids many of the mistakes programmers tend to make with `printf()` and `scanf()`.

Output in C++

An output display in C++ is constructed as a stream of characters using a C++-provided
object named `cout` (pronounced "see out"). This object, whose name was derived from
"Console OUTput," simply sends data given to it to the standard system display device.
For most systems this display device is a video screen. The `cout` object simply gathers
together all the data passed to it and sends it on for display. For example, if the data
`Hello there world!` is passed to `cout`, this data is printed (or displayed) on your
terminal by the `cout` object. The data `Hello there world!` is passed to the `cout`
object by simply putting the insertion ("put to") symbol, `<<`, before the message and after
the object's name.

```
cout << "Hello there world!";
```

Within a working C++ program this statement could appear as shown in Program 13.3.

 Program 13.3

```
#include <iostream.h>
int main()
{
  cout << "Hello there world!";

  return 0;
}
```

Notice the first line of the program:

```
#include <iosteam.h>
```

Programming Note

Input and Output Streams

In place of the `printf()` and `scanf()` functions used in C, C++ uses the `cout` and `cin` stream objects. More generally, you can think of a stream as a one-way transmission path between a source and a destination. What gets sent down this transmission path is a stream of bytes. A good analogy to this "stream of bytes" is a stream of water that provides a one-way transmission path of water from a source to a destination.

In C++ the `cout` object provides a transmission path from a program to terminal screen and replaces C's `printf()` function, while the `cin` object provides a transmission path from keyboard to program and replaces C's `scanf()` function (although in both cases, there is not a one-to-one correspondence). When the `iostream.h` header file is included in a program using the `#include <iostream.h>` directive, the `cin` and `cout` stream objects are automatically declared and opened by the C++ compiler for the compiled program. This is equivalent to opening `stdin` and `stdout` in a C program using the `<stdio.h>` header file.

This is a required preprocessor command when `cout` is being used and effectively replaces the equivalent `stdio.h` header file used in C. In particular, the `iostream.h` file provides two abstract date types, *istream* and *ostream,* that contain the actual data definitions and operations used for data input and output.[1]

In addition to displaying strings, the `cout` object also provides for the display of an expression's numerical value. For example, the statement

```
cout << (6 + 15);
```

yields the display 21. Strictly speaking, the parentheses surrounding the expression 6 + 15 are required to indicate that it is the value of the expression, which is 21, that is being placed on the output stream. In practice most compilers will accept and correctly process this statement without the parentheses.

Both strings and expressions may be included in the same `cout` statement. For example, the statement:

```
cout << "The total of 6 and 15 is " << (6 + 15) << '\n';
```

causes three pieces of data to be sent to `cout`: a string, a numerical value, and the newline constant. As illustrated by this statement, each piece of data is sent to `cout` preceded by its

---

[1] Formally, `cout` is an object of the class `ostream`.

own insertion symbol (<<). Here, the first data item sent to the stream is the string `"The total of 6 and 15 is "`, the second item is the value of the expression `6 + 15`, and the third item is the newline character. The display produced by this statement is

```
The total of 6 and 15 is 21
```

Notice that the space between the word `is` and the number `21` is caused by the space placed within the string passed to `cout`. As far as `cout` is concerned, its input is simply a set of characters that are then sent on to be displayed in the order they are received. Characters from the input are queued, one behind the other, and sent to an output stream for display. Placing a space in the input causes this space to be part of the output stream that is ultimately displayed. For example, the statement

```
cout << "The sum of 12.2 and 15.754 is " << (12.2 + 15.754) << '\n';
```

yields the display

```
The sum of 12.2 and 15.754 is 27.954
```

It should be mentioned that insertion of data into the output stream can be made over multiple lines and is terminated only by a semicolon. Thus, the prior display is also produced by the statement

```
cout << "The sum of 12.2 and 15.754 is "
     <<    (12.2 + 15.754)
     << '\n';
```

The requirements in using multiple lines are that a string contained within double quotes cannot be split across lines and that the terminating semicolon appear only on the last line. Within a line multiple insertion symbols can be used.

As the last display indicates, floating point numbers are displayed with sufficient decimal places to the right of the decimal place to accommodate the fractional part of the number. This is true if the number has six or fewer decimal digits. If the number has more than six decimal digits, the fractional part is rounded to six decimal digits, and if the number has no decimal digits, neither a decimal point nor any decimal digits are displayed.[2]

Formatted Output[3]

The format of numbers displayed by `cout` can be controlled by field-width manipulators included in each output stream. Table 13.2 lists the most commonly used manipulators available for this purpose.

---

[2] It should be noted that none of this output is defined as part of the C++ language. Rather, it is defined by a set of classes and routines provided with each C++ compiler.

[3] This topic may be omitted on first reading with no loss of subject continuity.

Table 13.2   Commonly used stream manipulators

Manipulator	Action
setw(n)	Set the field width to *n*. The setting remains in effect only for the next insertion.
setprecision(n)	Set the floating point precision to *n* places. If the display format is exponential or fixed, then the precision indicates the number of digits after the decimal point; otherwise, the precision indicates the total number of displayed digits. The setting remains in effect until the next change.
setiosflags(flags)	Set the format flags (see Table 13.4 for flag settings). The setting remains in effect until the next change.
setfill(n)	Set the fill character to be used as padding. The default is a space. The setting remains in effect until the next change.
dec	Set output for decimal display. The setting remains in effect until the next change.
hex	Set output for hexadecimal display. The setting remains in effect until the next change.
oct	Set output for octal display. The setting remains in effect until the next change.
endl	Insert a newline character and flush the stream.

For example, the statement

```
cout << "The sum of 6 and 15 is" << setw(3) << 21 << endl;
```

causes the printout

```
The sum of 6 and 15 is 21
```

The setw(3) field-width manipulator included in the stream of data passed to cout is used to set the displayed field width. The 3 in this manipulator sets the default field-width for the next number in the stream to be three spaces wide. This field-width setting causes the 21 to be printed in a field of three spaces, which includes one blank and the number 21. As illustrated, integers are right-justified within the specified field. The endl manipulator inserts a \n into the stream and flushes the stream buffer.

Field-width manipulators are useful in printing columns of numbers so that the numbers in each column align correctly, as illustrated in Program 13.4.

Program 13.4

```
#include <iostream.h>
#include <iomanip.h>
int main()
{
   cout << '\n' << setw(3) << 6
        << '\n' << setw(3) << 18
        << '\n' << setw(3) << 124
        << "\n---"
        << '\n' << setw(3) << (6+18+124)
        << endl;

   return 0;
}
```

The output of Program 13.4 is

```
  6
 18
124
___

148
```

Notice that the field-width manipulator must be included for each occurrence of a number inserted onto the data stream sent to cout and that the manipulator applies only to the insertion of data immediately following it. Also notice that if manipulators are to be included within an output display, the iomanip.h header field must be included as part of the program. This is accomplished by the preprocessor command #include <iomanip.h>.

Formatted floating point numbers require the use of two field-width manipulators. The first manipulator sets the total width of the display, including the decimal point; the second manipulator determines how many digits can be printed to the right of the decimal point. For example, the statement

```
cout << "|" << setw(10) << setiosflags(ios::fixed) << setprecision(3) << 25.67 << "|";
```

causes the printout

```
|    25.670|
```

The bar symbol, |, in the example is used to mark the beginning and end of the display field. The `setw` manipulator tells `cout` to display the number in a total field width of ten digits, while the `setprecision` manipulator tells `cout` to display a maximum of three digits to the right of the decimal point. The `setiosflags` manipulator using the `ios::fixed` flag ensures that the output is displayed in conventional decimal format; that is, as a fixed-point rather than an exponential number.

For all numbers (integer, floating point, and double precision), `cout` ignores the `setw` manipulator specification if the total specified field width is too small and allocates enough space for the integer part of the number to be printed. The fractional part of both floating point and double precision numbers is displayed up to the precision set with the `setprecision` manipulator (in the absence of a `setprecision` manipulator, the precision is set to the default of six decimal places). If the fractional part of the number to be displayed contains more digits than called for in the `setprecision` manipulator, the number is rounded to the indicated number of decimal places; if the fractional part contains fewer digits than specified, the number is displayed with the fewer digits. Table 13.3 illustrates the effect of various format manipulator combinations. Again, for clarity, the bar symbol, |, is used to clearly delineate the beginning and end of the output fields.

In addition to the `setw` and `setprecision` manipulators, a field justification manipulator is also available. As we have seen, numbers sent to `cout` are normally displayed right-justified in the display field, while strings are displayed left-justified. To alter the default justification for a stream of data, the `setiosflags` manipulator can be used. For example, the statement

```
cout << "|" << setw(10) << setiosflags(ios::left) << 142 << "|";
```

causes the following left-justified display

```
|142       |
```

As we have previously seen, since data passed to `cout` may be continued across multiple lines, the previous display would also be produced by the statement

```
cout << "|" << setw(10)
     << setiosflags(ios::left)
     << 142 << "|";
```

As always, the field-width manipulator is in effect only for the next single set of data passed to `cout`. Right-justification for strings in a stream is obtained by the manipulator `setiosflags(ios::right)`.

In addition to the left and right flags that can be used with the `setiosflags` manipulator, other flags may also be used to affect the output. The most commonly used flags for this manipulator are listed in Table 13.4.

Table 13.3 Effect of format manipulators*

Manipulator	Number	Display	Comment
`setw(2)`	3	`| 3|`	Number fits in field
`setw(2)`	43	`|43|`	Number fits in field
`setw(2)`	143	`|143|`	Field width ignored
`setw(2)`	2.3	`| 2.3|`	Field width ignored

`setw(5)`
`setiosflags(ios::fixed)`
`setprecision(2)`
	2.366	`| 2.37|`	Field width of 5 with 2 decimal digits

`setw(5)`
`setiosflags(ios::fixed)`
`setprecision(2)`
	42.3	`| 42.3|`	Number fits in field

`setw(5)`
`setiosflags(ios::fixed)`
`setprecision(2)`
	142.364	`|142.36|`	Field width ignored but precision specification used

`setw(5)`
`setiosflags(ios::fixed)`
`setprecision(2)`
	142.366	`|142.37|`	Field width ignored but precision specification used

`setw(5)`
`setiosflags(ios::fixed)`
`setprecision(2)`
	142	`|142|`	Field width used; precision irrelevant

* If either the manipulator flags `ios::fixed` or `ios::scientific` are not in effect, the `setprecision` value indicates the total number of significant digits displayed rather than the number of digits after the decimal point.

For example, the output stream

```
cout << setiosflag(ios::showpoint)
     << setiosflags(ios::fixed)
     << setprecision(4);
```

forces the next number sent to the output stream to be displayed with a decimal point and four decimal digits. If the number has less than four decimal digits it will be padded with trailing zeros.

In addition to outputting integers in decimal notation, the `ios::oct` and `ios:hex` flags permit conversions to octal and hexadecimal, respectively. Program 13.5 illustrates the use of these flags. Because decimal is the default display, the `dec` manipulator is not required in the first output stream.

Table 13.4 Format flags for use with `setiosflags`

Flag	Meaning
`ios::showpoint`	Always display a decimal point. In the absence of the `ios::fixed` flag, a numerical value with a decimal point is displayed with a default of 6 significant digits. If the integer part of the number requires more than 6 digits the display will be in exponential notation, unless the `ios::fixed` flag is in effect. For example, the value 1234567. is displayed as 1.23457e0 unless the `ios::fixed` flag is in effect. This flag has no effect on integer values.
`ios::showpos`	Display a leading + sign when the number is positive
`ios::fixed`	Display the number in conventional fixed-point decimal notation (that is, with an integer and fractional part separated by a decimal point), and not in exponential notation.
`ios::scientific`	Use exponential display on output
`ios::dec`	Display in decimal format
`ios::oct`	Display in octal format
`ios::hex`	Display in hexadecimal format
`ios::left`	Left-justify output
`ios::right`	Right-justify output

 Program 13.5

```cpp
#include <iostream.h>
#include <iomanip.h>
int main()  // a program to illustrate output conversions
{
  cout << "The decimal (base 10) value of 15 is " << 15
       << "\nThe octal (base 8) value of 15 is "
       << setiosflags(ios::oct) << 15
       << "\nThe hexadecimal (base 16) value of 15 is "
       << setiosflags(ios::hex) << 15
       << endl;

  return 0;
}
```

The output produced by Program 13.5 is

```
The decimal (base 10) value of 15 is 15
The octal (base 8) value of 15 is 17
The hexadecimal (base 16) value of 15 is f
```

In place of the conversion flags ios::dec,ios::oct, and ios::hex, three simpler manipulators, dec, oct, and hex are provided in <iostream.h>. These simpler manipulators, unlike their longer counterparts, leave the conversion base set for all subsequent output streams. Using these simpler manipulators, Program 13.5 can be rewritten as:

```
#include <iostream.h>
int main()   // a program to illustrate output conversions
{
  cout << "The decimal (base 10) value of 15 is " << 15
       << "\nThe octal (base 8) value of 15 is " << oct << 15
       << \nThe hexadecimal (base 16) value of 15 is " << hex << 15
       << end;
  return 0;
}
```

Input in C++

Just as the cout object displays a copy of the value stored inside a variable, the cin (pronounced "see in") object allows the user to enter a value at the terminal. Figure 13.1 illustrates the relationship between these two objects.

For example, a statement such as cin >> num1; is a command to accept data from the keyboard. When a data item is entered, the cin object stores the item into the variable listed after the extraction ("get from") operator, >>. The program then continues execution with the next statement after the call to cin. The use of cin is illustrated by Program 13.6.

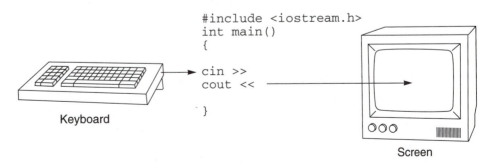

Figure 13.1   cin is used to enter data; cout is used to display data

Program 13.6

```
#include <iostream.h>
int main()
{
  float num1, num2, product;

  cout << "Please type in a number: ";
  cin >> num1;
  cout << "Please type in another number: ";
  cin >> num2;
  product = num1 * num2;
  cout << num1 << " times " << num2 << " is " << product << endl;

  return 0;
}
```

The following sample run was made using Program 13.6

```
Please type in a number: 30
Please type in another number: 0.05
30 times 0.05 is 1.5
```

In Program 13.6, each time `cin` is invoked it is used to store one value into a variable. The `cin` object, however, can be used to enter and store as many values as there are extraction symbols, `>>`, and variables to hold the entered data. For example, the statement

```
cin >> num1 >> num2;
```

results in two values being read from the terminal and assigned to the variables `num1` and `num2`. If the data entered at the terminal were

```
0.052 245.79
```

the variables `num1` and `num2` would contain the values `0.052` and `245.79`, respectively. Notice that when actually entering numbers such as `0.052` and `245.79`, there must be at least one space between the numbers. The space between the entered numbers clearly indicates where one number ends and the next begins. Inserting more than one space between numbers has no effect on `cin`.

The same spacing is also applicable to entering character data; that is, the extraction operator, `>>`, will skip blank spaces and store the next nonblank character in a character variable. For example, in response to the statements

```
char ch1, ch2, ch3;  // declare three character variables
cin >> ch1 >> ch2 >> ch3;  // accept three characters
```

the input

a   b c

causes the letter a to be stored in the variable ch1, the letter b to be stored in the variable ch2, and the letter c to be stored in the variable ch3. Because a character variable can only be used to store one character the input

abc

can also be used.

The cin extraction operation, like the cout insertion operation, is "clever" enough to make a few data type conversions. For example, if an integer is entered in place of a floating point or double precision number, the integer will be converted to the correct data type.[4] Similarly, if a floating point or double precision number is entered when an integer is expected, only the integer part of the number will be used. For example, assume the following numbers are typed in response to the statement cin >> num1 >> num2 >> num3;, where num1 and num3 have been declared as floating point variables and num2 is an integer variable:

56   22.879   33.923

The 56 will be converted to a floating point number, 56.0, and stored in the variable num1. The extraction operation continues extracting data from the input stream sent to it, expecting an integer value. As far as cin is concerned, the decimal point after the 22 in the number 22.879 indicates the end of an integer and the start of a decimal number. Thus, the number 22 is assigned to num2. Continuing to process its input stream, cin takes the .879 as the expected next floating point number and assigns it to num3. As far as cin is concerned, 33.923 is extra input and is ignored. If you do not initially type enough data, however, the cin object will continue to make the computer pause until sufficient data has been entered.

Exercises 12.3

1. Using cout, write and execute a C++ program that prints your name on one line, your street address on a second line, and your city, state, and zip code on the third line.

---

[4] Strictly speaking, what comes in from the keyboard is not of any data type, such as int or float, but is simply a sequence of characters. The extraction operation handles the conversion from the character sequence to a defined data type.

2. Write and execute a C++ program to print out the following verse:

```
Computers, computers everywhere
  as far as I can see
I really, really like these things,
  Oh joy, Oh joy for me!
```

3. Determine the output of the following two programs:

   a.
```
#include <iostream.h>

int main()   // a program illustrating integer truncation
{

  cout << "answer1 is the integer " <<  9/4
        << "\nanswer2 is the integer " <<  17/3 << '\n';

  return 0;

}
```
   b.
```
#include <iostream.h>

int main()   // a program illustrating the % operator
{

  cout << "The remainder of 9 divided by 4 is " <<  9 % 4
        << "\nThe remainder of 17 divided by 3 is " <<  17 % 3 << '\n';

  return 0;

}
```

4. Write a C++ program that displays the results of the expressions `3.0 * 5.0`, `7.1 * 8.3 - 2.2` and `3.2 / (6.1 * 5)`. Calculate the value of these expressions manually to verify that the displayed values are correct.

5. Determine the errors in each of the following statements:

   a. `cout << "\n << " 15)`
   b. `cout << "setw(4)" <<  33;`
   c. `cout << "setprecision(5)" <<  526.768;`
   d. `"Hello World!" >> cout;`
   e. `cout << 47 << setw(6);`
   f. `cout << set(10) << 526.768 << setprecision(2);`

6. Determine and write out the display produced by the following statements:

   a. `cout << "|" << 5 << "|";`
   b. `cout << "|" << setw(4) << 5 << "|";`
   c. `cout << "|" << setw(4) << 56829 << "|";`
   d. `cout << "|" << setw(5) << setprecision(2) << 5.26 << "|";`
   e. `cout << "|" << setw(5) << setprecision(2) << 5.267 << "|";`
   f. `cout << "|" << setw(5) << setprecision(2) << 53.264 << "|";`
   g. `cout << "|" << setw(5) << setprecision(2) << 534.264 << "|";`
   h. `cout << "|" << setw(5) << setprecision(2) << 534. << "|";`

7. For the following declaration statements, write a statement using the `cin` object that will cause the computer to pause while the appropriate data is typed by the user.

   a. `int firstnum;`
   b. `float grade;`
   c. `double secnum;`

d. `char keyval;`

e. `int month years;`
   `float average;`

f. `char ch;`
   `int num1,num2;`
   `double grade1,grade2;`

g. `float interest, principal, capital;`
   `double price,yield;`

h. `char ch,letter1,letter2;`
   `int num1,num2,num3;`

i. `float temp1,temp2,temp3;`
   `double volts1,volts2;`

8. Write a C++ program that displays the following prompts:

   ```
   Enter the length of the room:
   Enter the width of the room:
   ```

   After each prompt is displayed, your program should use a `cin` object call to accept data from the keyboard for the displayed prompt. After the width of the room is entered, your program should calculate and display the area of the room. The area displayed should be included in an appropriate message and calculated using the equation *area = length * width.*

9. Write a C++ program that displays the following prompts:

   ```
   Enter a number:
   Enter a second number;
   Enter a third number:
   Enter a fourth number:
   ```

   After each prompt is displayed, your program should use a `cin` object call to accept a number from the keyboard for the displayed prompt. After the fourth number has been entered, your program should calculate and display the average of the numbers. The average should be included in an appropriate message.

10. Write a C++ program that prompts the user to type in a number. Have your program accept the number as an integer and immediately display the integer using a `cout` object call. Run your program three times. The first time you run the program enter a valid integer number, the second time enter a floating point number, and the third time enter a character. Using the output display, see what number your program actually accepted from the data you entered.

11. Repeat Exercise 10 but have your program declare the variable used to store the number as a floating point variable. Run the program four times. The first time enter an integer, the second time enter a decimal number with less than six decimal places, the third time enter a number having more than six decimal places, and the fourth time enter a character. Using the output display, keep track of what number your program actually accepted from the data you typed in. What happened, if anything, and why?

12. Repeat Exercise 10 but have your program declare the variable used to store the number as a double precision variable. Run the program four times. The first time enter an integer, the second time enter a decimal number with less than six decimal places, the third time enter a number having more than six decimal places, and the fourth time enter a character. Using the output display, keep track of what number your program actually accepted from the data you typed in. What happened, if anything, and why?

13.3 Function Enhancements in C++

The driving force for the development of C++ was to extend C by providing it with an abstract data type (ADT) capability. An essential component in the construction of ADTs is the design and implementation of suitable operations for each new user defined data type. In C++ such operations are all constructed as functions. As such C++ includes four main extensions to C's standard function capabilities, three of which provide additional ways of using and processing function arguments. These modifications consist of providing default arguments, reference arguments, function overloading, and inline function compilation. This section describes these four enhanced function capabilities.

Default Arguments

A convenient feature of C++ is the ability to use default arguments in a function call. The default argument values are listed in the function prototype and are automatically transmitted to the called function when the corresponding arguments are omitted from the function call. For the example, the function prototype:

```
void example(int, int = 5, float = 6.78);
```

provides default values for the last two arguments. If any of these arguments are omitted when the function is actually called, the C++ compiler will supply these default values. Thus, all of the following function calls are valid:

```
example(7, 2, 9.3)   // no defaults used
example(7, 2)        // same as example(7, 2, 6.78)
example(7)           // same as example(7, 5, 6.78)
```

Four rules must be followed when using default parameters. The first is that default values can only be assigned in the function prototype. The second is that if any argument is given a default value in the function prototype, all arguments following it must also be supplied with default values. The third rule is that if one argument is omitted in the actual function call, then all arguments to its right must also be omitted. These latter two rules make it clear to the C++ compiler which arguments are being omitted and permits the compiler to supply correct default values for the missing arguments. The last rule specifies that the default value used in the function prototype may be an expression consisting of both constants and previously declared variables. If such an expression is used, it must pass the compiler's check for validly declared variables, even though the actual value of the expression is evaluated and assigned at run time.

Default arguments are extremely useful when extending an existing function to include more features that require additional arguments. Adding the new arguments to the right of the existing arguments and providing each new argument with a default value permits all existing function calls to remain as they are. Thus, the effect of the new changes are conveniently isolated from existing code in the program.

Reusing Function Names (Overloading)

In C each function requires its own unique name. While in theory this makes sense, in practice it can lead to a profusion of function names, even for functions that perform essentially the same operations. For example, consider determining and displaying the absolute value of a number. If the number passed into the function can be either an integer, a long integer, or a double precision value, three distinct functions must be written to correctly handle each case. In C, we would give each of these functions a unique name, such as `intabs()`, `longabs()`, and `dblabs()`, respectively, having the function prototypes:

```
void intabs(int);
void longabs(long);
void dblabs(double);
```

Clearly, each of these three functions performs essentially the same operation, differing only in data type. C++ provides the capability of using the same function name for more than one function, which is referred to as *function overloading*. The only requirement in creating more than one function with the same name is that the compiler must be able to determine which function to use based on the data types of the parameters (not the data type of the return value, if any). For example, consider the three following functions, all named `showabs()`.

```cpp
void showabs(int x)   // display the absolute value of an integer
{
  if ( x < 0 )
    x = -x;
  cout << "The absolute value of the integer is " << x << endl;
}

void showabs(long x)   // display the absolute value of a long integer
{
  if ( x < 0 )
    x = -x;
  cout << "The absolute value of the long integer is " << x << endl;
}

void showabs(double x)   // display the absolute value of a double
{
  if ( x < 0 )
    x = -x;
  cout << "The absolute value of the float is " << x << endl;
}
```

Which of the three functions named `showabs()` is actually called depends on the argument types supplied at the time of the call. Thus, the function call `showabs(10);`

would cause the compiler to use the function named `showabs` that expects an integer argument, and the function call `showabs(6.28);` would cause the compiler to use the function named `showabs` that expects a double valued argument.[5]

Notice that overloading a function's name simply means using the same name for more than one function. Each function that uses the name must still be written and exists as a separate entity. The use of the same function name does not require that the code within the functions be similar, although good programming practice dictates that functions with the same name should perform essentially the same operation. All that is formally required in using the same function name is that the compiler can distinguish which function to select based on the data types of the arguments when the function is called.

Overloaded functions are extremely useful for creating multiple constructor functions, a topic that is presented in Section 13.5. For other functions, such as our `showabs()` example, where all that is different about the overloaded functions is the parameter types, a better programming solution is to create a C++ function template.

Function Templates[6]

A *function template* is a single, complete function that serves as a model for a family of functions. Which function from the family that is actually created depends on subsequent function calls. To make this more concrete, consider a function template that computes and displays the absolute value of a passed argument. An appropriate function template is

```
template <class T>
void showabs(T number)
{
  if (number < 0)
    number = -number;
  cout << "The absolute value of the number "
       << " is " << number << endl;

  return
}
```

For the moment, ignore the first line `template <class T>`, and look at the second line, which consists of the function header `void showabs(T number)`. Notice that this header line has the same syntax that we have been using for all of our function definitions, except for the T in place of where a data type is usually placed. For example, if the header line were `void showabs(int number)`, you should recognize this as a function named `showabs` that expects one integer argument to be passed to it, and that

---

[5] This is accomplished by *name mangling*. This is a process whereby the function name generated by the C++ compiler differs from the function name used in the source code. The compiler appends information to the source code function name depending on the type of data being passed, and the resulting name is said to be a mangled version of the source code name.

[6] This topic may be omitted on first reading with no loss of subject continuity

returns no value. Similarly, if the header line were `void    showabs(float number)`, you should recognize it as a function that expects one floating point argument to be passed when the function is called.

The advantage in using the T within the function template header line is that it represents a general data type that is replaced by an actual data type, such as `int`, `float`, `double`, etc., when the compiler encounters an actual function call. For example, if a function call with an integer argument is encountered, the compiler will use the function template to construct the code for a function that expects an integer parameter. Similarly, if a call is made with a floating point argument, the compiler will construct a function that expects a floating point parameter. As a specific example of this, consider Program 13.7.

 Program 13.7

```
#include <iostream.h>

template <class T>
void showabs(T number)
{

  if (number < 0)
    number = -number;
  cout << "The absolute value of the number is "
       << number << endl;

  return;
}

int main()
{
  int num1 = -4;
  float num2 = -4.23;
  double num3 =-4.23456;

  showabs(num1);
  showabs(num2);
  showabs(num3);

  return 0;
}
```

First notice the three function calls made in the `main()` function shown in Program 13.7, which call the function `showabs()` with an integer, float, and double value, respectively. Now review the function template for `showabs()` and let us consider the first line, `template <class T>`. This line, which is called a *template prefix,* is used to inform the compiler that the function immediately following is a template that uses a data type named T. Within the function template, T is used in the same manner as any other data type, such as `int`, `float`, `double`, etc. Then, when the compiler encounters an actual function call for `showabs()`, the data type of the argument passed in the call is substituted for T throughout the function. In effect, the compiler creates a specific function, using the template, that expects the argument type in the call. Because Program 13.7 makes three calls to `showabs()`, each with a different argument data type, the compiler creates three separate `showabs()` functions. The compiler knows which function to use based on the arguments passed at the time of the call. The output displayed when Program 13.7 is executed is

```
The absolute value of the number is 4
The absolute value of the number is 4.23
The absolute value of the number is 4.23456
```

The letter T used in the template prefix `template <class T>` is simply a placeholder for a data type that is defined when the function is invoked. Any letter or nonkeyword identifier can be used instead. Thus, the `showabs()` function template could have been defined as:

```
template <class DTYPE>
void showabs(DTYPE number)
{

  if (number < 0)
    number = -number;
  cout << "The absolute value of the number is "
       << number << endl;

  return;
}
```

In this regard, it is sometimes simpler and clearer to read the word *class* in the template prefix as the words *data type.* Thus, the template prefix `template <class T>` can be read as "we are defining a function template that has a data type named T." Then, within both the header line and body of the defined function, the data type T (or any other letter or identifier defined in the prefix) is used in the same manner as any built-in data type, such as `int`, `float`, `double`, etc.

Now suppose we want to create a function template to include both a return type and an internally declared variable. For example, consider the following function template:

```
template <class T> // template prefix
T abs(T value)      // header line
{
  T absnum;  // variable declaration
```

```
    if (value < 0)
      absnum = -value;
    else
      absnum = value;

    return absnum;
  }
```

In this template definition, we have used the data type T to declare thee items: the return type of the function, the data type of a single function parameter named `value`, and one variable declared within the function. Program 13.8 illustrates how this function template could be used within the context of a complete program.

 Program 13.8

```
#include <iostream.h>

template <class T> // template prefix
T abs(T value       // header line
{
  T absnum;   // variable declaration

  if (value < 0)
    absnum = -value;
  else
    absnum = value;

  return absnum;
}
int main()
{
  int num1 = -4;
  float num2 = -4.23;
  double num3 = -4.23456;

  cout << "The absolute value of " << num1
       << " is " << abs(num1) << endl;
  cout << "The absolute value of " << num2
       << " is " << abs(num2) << endl;
  cout << "The absolute value of " << num3
       << " is " << abs(num3) << endl;

  return 0;
}
```

In the first call to `abs(0` made within `main()`, an integer value is passed as an argument. In this case, the compiler substitutes an `int` data type for the T data type in the function template and creates the following function:

```
int showabs(int value) // header line
{
  int absnum;  // variable declaration

  if (value < 0)
    absnum = -value;
  else
    absnum = value;

  return (absnum);
}
```

Similarly, in the second and third function calls, the compiler creates two more functions, one in which the data type T is replaced by the keyword `float`, and one in which the data type T is replaced by the keyword double. The output produced by Program 13.8 is

```
The absolute value of -4 is 4
The absolute value of -4.23 is 4.23
The absolute value of -4.23456 is 4.23456
```

The value of using the function template is that one function definition has been used to create three different functions, each of which uses the same logic and operations but operates on different data types.

Finally, although both Programs 13.7 and 13.8 define a function template that uses a single placeholder data type, function templates with more than one data type can be defined. For example the template prefix

```
template <class DTYPE1, class DTYPE2, class DTYPE3>
```

can be used to create a function template that requires three different data types. As before, within the header and body of the function template, the data types DTYPE1, DTYPE2, and DTYPE3 are used in the same manner as any built-in data type, such as an `int`, `float`, `double`, etc. Additionally, as noted previously, the names DTYPE1, DTYPE2, and DTYPE3 can be any nonkeyword identifier. Conventionally, the letter T followed by zero or more digits would be used, such as T, T1, T2, T3, etc.

Inline Functions[7]

Calling a function places a certain amount of overhead on a computer: this consists of placing argument values in a reserved memory region that the function has access to (this

---

[7] This topic may be omitted on first reading without loss of subject continuity.

memory region is called the *stack*), passing control to the function, providing a reserved memory location for any returned value (again, the stack region of memory is used for this purpose), and, finally, returning to the proper point in the calling program. Paying this overhead is well justified when a function is called many times, because it can significantly reduce the size of a program. Rather than repeating the same code each time it is needed, the code is written once, as a function, and called whenever it is needed.

For small functions that are not called many times, however, paying the overhead for passing and returning values may not be warranted. It still would be convenient, though, to group repeating lines of code together under a common function name and have the compiler place this code directly into the program wherever the function is called. This capability is provided by inline functions.

Telling the C+ compiler that a function is *inline* causes a copy of the function code to be placed in the program at the point the function is called. For example, consider the function tempvert() defined in Program 13.9. Since this is a relatively short function it is an ideal candidate to be an inline function. As shown in the program, making this or any other function inline simply requires placing the reserved word inline before the function name and defining the function before any calls are made to it.

Program 13.9

```cpp
#include <iostream.h>

inline double tempvert(double inTemp)  // an inline function
{
  return( (5.0/9.0) * (inTemp - 32.0) );
}

int main()
{
  int count;                 // start of declarations
  double fahren;

  for(count = 1; count <= 4; count++)
  {
    cout << "\nEnter a Fahrenheit temperature: ";
    cin >> fahren;
    cout << "The Celsius equivalent is " << tempvert(fahren)
         << endl;

  return 0;
}
```

Observe in Program 13.9 that the inline function is placed ahead of any calls to it. This is a requirement of all inline functions and obviates the need for a function prototype.

Because the function is now an inline one, its code is be expanded directly into the program wherever it is called.

The advantage of using an inline function is an increase in execution speed. Because the inline function is directly expanded and included in every expression or statement calling it, there is no loss of execution time due to the call and return overhead required by a noninline function. The disadvantage is the increase in program size when an inline function is called repeatedly. Each time an inline function is referenced, the complete function code is reproduced and stored as an integral part of the program. A noninline function, however, is stored in memory only once. No matter how many times the function is called, the same code is used. Therefore, inline functions should only be used for small functions that are not extensively called in a program.

Reference Parameters

The standard method of making a function call in C is to pass parameters by value. The same is true for function calls in C++. In both languages, when a call by reference is required, pointer parameters can be used. Such parameters, as we have seen, permit the called function to directly access the calling function's variables. In addition, C++ provides an alternative call-by-reference capability. This alternative method is accomplished by using a new type of parameter, called a *reference parameter,* that can be used in place of pointer arguments.

Essentially, a reference parameter is a pointer parameter with restricted capabilities that is simpler to use because it hides a lot of internal pointer manipulations from the programmer.[8] Before seeing how reference parameters are used, however, it will be helpful to first introduce the concept of a *reference variable.*

Reference variables provide a means of giving a previously declared variable an additional name. This is accomplished using a *reference declaration,* which has the form

```
data-type& new-name = existing-name;
```

For example, the reference declaration

```
float& sum = total;
```

equates the name `sum` to the name `total`—both now refer to the same variable, as illustrated in Figure 13.2.[9]

Once another name has been established for a variable using a reference declaration, the new name, which is referred to as an *alias,* can be used in place of the original name. For example, consider Program 13.10.

---

[8] Pointer arithmetic is not provided for reference parameters and variables. Thus, reference parameters and variables in C++ operate much like pointers in Pascal and Fortran 90.

[9] Knowledgeable C programmers should not confuse the use of the ampersand symbol, &, in a reference declaration with the address operator or with the use of a reference variable as an address. A reference variable simply equates two variable names.

Program 13.10

```
#include <iostream.h>
int main()
{
   float total = 20.5;     // declare and initialize total
   float& sum = total;     // declare another name for total

   cout << "sum = " << sum << endl;
   sum = 18.6;                  // this changes the value in total
   cout << "total = " << total << endl;

   return 0;
}
```

The following output is produced by Program 13.10

```
sum = 20.5
total = 18.6
```

Because the variable sum is simply another reference to the variable total, it is the value stored in total that is obtained by the first call to cout in Program 13.10. Changing the value in sum then changes the value in total, which is displayed by the second call to cout in Program 13.10.

In constructing references, two considerations must be kept in mind. First, the reference should be of the same data type as the variable to which it refers. For example, the sequence of declarations

```
int num = 5;
double& numref = num;
```

does not equate numref to num, because they are not of the same data type. Rather because the compiler cannot correctly associate the reference with a variable; it creates

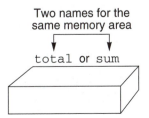

Figure 13.2   sum is an alternative name for total

an unnamed variable of the reference type first, and then references this unnamed variable with the reference variable. Such unnamed variables are called *anonymous variables*. For example, consider Program 13.11, which illustrates the effect of creating an anonymous variable.

 Program 13.11

```
#include <stream.h>
int main()
{
  int num = 10;
  float& numref = num;   // this does not equate numref to num
                         // instead, it equates numref to an
                         // anonymous floating point variable
  numref = 23.6;
  cout << "The value of num is " << num << endl
       << "The value of numref is " << numref << endl;

  return 0;
}
```

The output produced by Program 13.11 is

```
The value of num is 10
The value of numref is 23.6
```

Notice that the value of num is not affected by the value stored in numref. This is because numref could not be created as a reference for num; rather, it is another name for an unnamed (anonymous) floating point variable that can be reached only by using the reference name numref.

Just as declaring a reference to an incorrect data type produces an anonymous variable, so does equating a reference to a constant. For example, the declaration

```
int& val = 5;   // an anonymous variable is created
```

creates an anonymous variable with the number 5 stored in it. The only way to access this variable is by the reference name. Clearly, creating references to anonymous variables should be avoided. Once a reference name has been equated to either a legal or an anonymous variable, the reference cannot be changed to refer to another variable.

As with all declaration statements, multiple references may be declared in a single statement as long as each reference name is preceded by the ampersand symbol. Thus, the declaration

```
float& sum = total, & mean = average;
```

creates two reference variables named sum and average.[10]

Passing and Using References

The real usefulness of reference variables is in their ability to act as function parameters, because they provide a simplified means of providing a pass-by-reference capability. As always, in exchanging data between two functions we must be concerned with both the sending and receiving sides of the data exchanged. From the sending side, however, calling a function and passing a reference is exactly the same as calling a function and passing a value: the called function is summoned into action by giving its name and a list of arguments. For example, the statement calc(firstnum, secnum, thirdnum, sum, product); both calls the function named calc() and passes five arguments to it. Let us now write the calc() function so that it receives direct access to the last two variables, sum and produce, which we will assume to be floating point variables.

The parameter declarations float &total and float &product can be used to declare two reference parameters. Here total and product are declared as reference parameters to floating point variables. As always, the choice of the parameter names total and product is up to the programmer. Including these declarations within the parameter list for calc(), and assuming that the function returns no value (void), a valid function header for calc() becomes

```
void calc(float num1, float num2, float num3, float& total, float& product)
```

This function header includes five parameters, which include three floating point parameters and two reference parameters. As we will see in a moment, the two reference parameters can be employed for returning values much as pointer parameters are, but using a much simpler notation.

Assume that the purpose of the calc() function is to accept three values, compute the sum and product of these values, and return the computed results to the calling routine. The following function provides this capability.

```
void calc(float num1, float num2, float num3, float& total, float& product)
{
   total = num1 + num2 + num3;
   product = num1 * num2 * num3;
   return;
}
```

---

[10] Reference declarations may also be written in the form *data-type &new-name = existing-name;*, where a space is placed between the data type and ampersand symbol. This form, is not used much, however, because it does not clearly distinguish reference variable notation from that used in taking the address of a variable.

As we have seen, this function has five parameters, named num1, num2, num3, total, and product, of which only the last two are declared as references. Within the function only the last two parameters are altered. The value of the fourth parameter, total, is calculated as the sum of the first three parameters and the last parameter, product, is computed as the product of the parameters num1, num2, and num3. Program 13.12 includes this function in a complete program.

 Program 13.12

```cpp
#include <iostream.h>
int main()
{
  float firstnum, secnum, thirdnum, sum, product;
  void calc(float, float, float, float&, float&);   // prototype

  cout << "Enter three numbers: ";
  cin >> firstnum >> secnum >> thirdnum;

  calc(firstnum, secnum, thirdnum, sum, product);   // function call

  cout << "\nThe sum of the numbers is: " << sum;
  cout << "\nThe product of the numbers is: " << product << endl;

  return 0;
}

void calc(float num1, float num2, float num3, float& total, float& product)
{
  total = num1 + num2 + num3;
  product = num1 * num2 * num3;
  return;
}
```

Within main(), the function calc() is called using the five arguments first-num, secnum, thirdnum, sum, and product. As required, these arguments agree in number and data type with the parameters declared by calc(). Of the five arguments passed, only firstnum, secnum, and thirdnum have been assigned values when the call to calc() is made. The remaining two arguments have not been initialized and will be used to receive values back from calc(). Depending on the compiler used in compiling the program, these arguments initially contain either zeros or "garbage" values. Figure 13.3 illustrates the relationship between argument and parameter names and the values they contain after the return from calc().

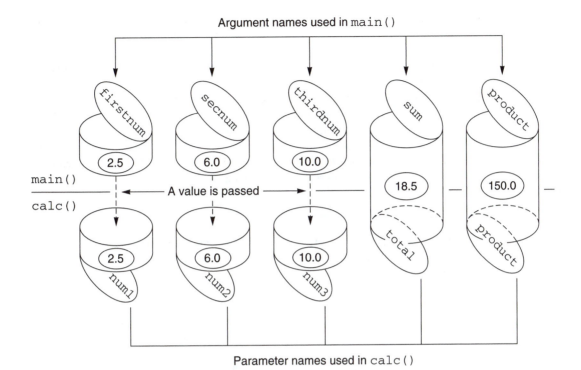

Figure 13.3   Relationship between arguments and parameters

In calling the `calc()` function in Program 13.12 it is important to understand the connection between the argument names, `sum` and `product`, used in the function call and the parameter names used in the function header. As shown in Figure 13.3, *both refer to the same data items*. The significance of this is that the values in the arguments (`sum` and `product`) can now be altered from within `calc()` by using the parameter names (`total` and `product`). This, of course, is the same correspondence provided by pointers, but with simpler notation.

Once `calc()` is called, it uses its first three parameters to calculate values for `total` and `product` and then returns control to `main()`. Because of the order of its calling arguments, `main()` knows the values calculated by `calc()` as sum and product, which are then displayed. Following is a sample run of Program 13.12.

```
Enter three numbers: 2.5 6.0 10.0

The sum of the entered numbers is: 18.5
The product of the entered numbers is: 150
```

In using reference parameters two cautions need to be mentioned. The first is that reference parameters *cannot* be used to change constants. For example, calling `calc()`

with five constants, such as in the call `calc(3.0, 4.0, 5.0, 6.0, 7.0)` passes five constants to the function. Although `calc()` may execute, it does not change the values of these constants.[11]

The second caution to note is that a function call itself gives no indication that the called function will be using reference parameters. The convention in C++ is to make passes by value rather than passes by reference, precisely to limit a called function's ability to alter variables in the called function. This convention should be adhered to whenever possible, which means that reference parameters should be used only in very restricted situations that actually require multiple return values. The `calc()` function included in Program 13.12, while useful for illustrative purposes, could also be written as two separate functions, each returning a single value.

References versus Pointers

At this point you might be wondering when to use a reference and when to use a pointer. To answer this question we first compare the two in a rather simple case. For example, consider the statements:

```
int b;       // b is an integer variable
int& a = b;  // a is a reference variable to b
a = 10;      // this changes b's value to 10
```

Here, a is declared as a reference variable. Because the compiler knows, from the declaration, that a is a reference variable, it automatically equates the address of b (rather than the contents of b) to the address of a in the declaration statement. Finally, in the statement a = 10; the compiler uses the reference variable to change the value stored in b to 10. The advantage of using the reference is that an automatic indirect access of b's value is performed without the need for explicitly using the indirection symbol, *. This type of access is referred to as an *automatic dereference.*

Implementing this same correspondence between a and b using pointers is done by the following sequence of instructions:

```
int b;        // b is an integer variable
int *a = &b;  // a is a pointer - store b's address in a
*a = 10;      // this changes b's value to 10
```

Here, a is defined as a pointer that is initialized to store the address of b. Thus, `*a`, which can be read as either "the variable whose address is in a" or "the variable pointed to by a", is b, and the expression `*a = 10` changes b's value to 10. Notice in the pointer case that the stored address can be altered to point to another variable; in the reference case the reference variable cannot be altered to refer to any variable except the one to which it is initialized. To use the address in a, an explicit dereference must be specified using the indirection operator. Notationally, then, the reference variable is simpler to use because it does not require the indirection operator for dereferencing.

---

[11] Most compilers will catch this error.

Thus, for simple cases, such as this example, the use of references over pointers is easier and clearly preferred. The same is true when a pass by reference is required—C++'s reference parameters provide a simpler notational interface and are easier to use than equivalent pointer parameters. For other situations, such as dynamically allocating memory or using alternatives to array notation where pointer arithmetic is needed, pointers are required.

Exercises 13.3

1. Write a function named check(), that has three parameters. The first parameter should accept an integer number, the second parameter a floating point number, and the third parameter a character. The default values for each passed argument should be 100, 22.4, and 'a', respectively. The function should simply display the values of its passed arguments.

   Check that your check function works properly by making four calls to it; the first call should be made with three values passed to the function, the second call with two values, the third call with one value, and the last call with no passed values.

2. Write a function named seconds() that determines the total number of seconds contained in the hours and minutes arguments passed to the function. Both arguments should be integer values with defaults of 0. Check that your function works correctly by making three calls to it; the first call should be made with both an hour and minute value, the second call with just an hour value, and the third call with no passed values.

3. Write parameter declarations for:
   a. a parameter named amount that will be a reference to a floating point value
   b. a parameter named price that will be a reference to a double precision number
   c. a parameter named minutes that will be a reference to an integer number
   d. a parameter named key that will be a reference to a character
   e. a parameter named yield that will be a reference to a double precision number

4. Three integer arguments are to be used in a call to a function named time(). Write a suitable function header for time(), assuming that time() accepts these integers as the reference parameters sec, min, and hours, respectively, and returns no value to its calling function.

5. Rewrite the findMax() function in Program 6.2 so that a reference to the variable maxnum, declared in main(), is accepted by findMax().

6. Write a function named change() that has a floating point parameter and four integer reference parameters named quarters, dimes, nickels, and pennies, respectively. The function is to consider the floating point passed value as a dollar amount and convert the value into an equivalent number of quarters, dimes, nickels, and pennies. Using the reference parameters the function should directly alter the respective arguments in the calling function.

7. Write a function named time() that has an integer parameter named seconds and three integer reference parameters named hours, min, and sec. The function is to convert the passed number of seconds into an equivalent number of hours, minutes, and seconds. Using the reference parameters the function should directly alter the respective arguments in the calling function.

13.4 Abstract Data Types in C++ (Classes)

In C++ an abstract data type is referred to as a *class*. Construction of a class is inherently easy, and we already have all the necessary tools in structures and functions. What C++ provides is a mechanism for packaging a structure and functions together in a self-contained unit. In this section we show how this is done.

Class Construction

Unlike a data structure, which we have used to define data, a class defines both data and functions.[12] This is usually accomplished by constructing a class in two parts, a declaration section and an implementation section. As illustrated in Figure 13.4, the declaration section declares both the data type and functions of the class. The implementation section is then used to define the function whose prototypes have been declared in the declaration section.[13]

Variables and functions listed in the class declaration section are referred to as both *data members* and *class members*. The data members, as illustrated in Figure 13.4, are also referred to as *instance variables*. The functions are referred to as *member functions*. A member function name may not be the same as a data member name.

```
// class declaration section
class ClassName
{
  Variable declarations    // instance variables
    and
  function prototypes
};

// class implementation section
function definitions
```

Figure 13.4 Format of a class definition

Consider the following definition of a class named Date.

---

[12] The structures presented in Chapter 10 can be expanded to include functions. In this text, however, we will only use classes for this purpose.

[13] This separation into two parts is not mandatory; the implementation can be included within the declaration section if inline functions are used.

```
//--- class declaration section
class Date
{
  private:          // notice the colon after the word private
    int month;      // a data member
    int day;        // a data member
    int year;       // a data member
  public:           // again; notice the colon here
    Date(int, int, int);     // a member function - the constructor
    void setdate(int = 7, int = 4, int = 2001  // a member function
    void showdate();                           // a member function
};
//--- class implementation section

Date::Date(int mm, int dd, int yyyy)
{
  month = mm;
  day = dd;
  year = yyyy;
}

void Date::setdate(int mm, int dd, int yyyy)
{
  month = mm;
  day = dd;
  year = yyyy;

  return;
}
void Date::showdate()
{
  cout << "The date is "
       << setfill('0')
       << setw(2) << month << '/'
       << setw(2) << day << '/'
       << setw(2) << year % 100
       << endl;

  return;
}
```

Because this definition may initially look overwhelming, first simply notice that it does consist of two sections—a declaration section and an implementation section. Now consider each of these sections individually.

A class *declaration section* consists of variable declarations and function prototypes. A commonly used form for this section is

```
class Name
{
  private:
    a list of variable declarations
  public:
    a list of function prototypes
};
```

Notice that this format is followed by our Date class, which for convenience we have listed below with no internal comments:

```
//--- class declaration section

class Date
{
  private:
    int month;
    int day;
    int year;
  public:
    Date(int = 7, int = 4, int = 2001);
    void setdate(int, int, int);
    void showdate();
};   // this is a declaration—don't forget the semicolon
```

The name of this class is Date. Although the initial capital letter is not required, it is conventionally used to designate a class. The body of the declaration section, which is enclosed within braces, consists of variable and function declarations. In this case, the variables month, day, and year are declared as integers and three functions named Date(), setdate(), and showdate() are declared via prototypes. The keywords private and public are *access specifiers* that define access rights. The private keyword specifies that the class members following, in this case the variables month, day, and year, *cannot* be accessed from outside of the class and may only be accessed by other class functions (or friend functions, as will be discussed in Section 14.2). Thus, for example, a statement made outside of the class, such as

```
birth.month = 7;
```

where birth is a variable of type Date, is illegal with private class members.[14] The purpose of the private designation is specifically to force all accesses to private data through the provided member functions.[15] Once a class category such as private is designated, it remains in force until a new category is listed.

---

[14] Such statements are clearly acceptable for the data structure members presented in Chapter 10. One of the purposes of a class is to prevent such global type accesses and force all changes to member variables to be made through member functions.

[15] It should be noted that the default membership category in a class is private, which means that this keyword can be omitted. In this text, we explicitly use the private designation to reinforce the idea of access restrictions inherent in class membership.

```
return-type ClassName::functionName(parameter list)
{
   function body
}
```

Figure 13.5   Format of a member function

As with the equivalent C functions (see Section 13.1) we have chosen to store a date using three integers, one for the month, day, and year, respectively. In addition, we will require that the year be stored as a four-digit number. Doing so ensures that we know what the year 2003, for example, refers to, whereas a two-digit value such as 03 could refer to either 1903 or 2003. Four-digit years also permit an easy determination of the difference between two years by simply subtracting the earlier from the latter year. This is not possible for two-digit years that reside in different centuries.

Following the private class data members, the function prototypes listed in the Date class have been declared as public. This means that these class functions *can* be called from outside of the class. In general, all class functions should be public; as such they furnish capabilities to manipulate the class variables from outside of the class. For our Date class, we have initially provided three functions, named Date(), setdate(), and showdate(). Notice that one of these member functions has the same name, Date, as the class name. This particular function is referred to as a *constructor* function, and it has a specially defined purpose; it can be used to initialize class data members with values. The default argument values that are used for this function are the numbers 7, 4, and 2001, which, as we will shortly see, are used as the default month, day, and year values, respectively. The one point to notice here is that the default year is correctly represented as a four-digit integer that retains the century designation. Also notice that the constructor function has no return type, which is a requirement for this special function. The two remaining functions declared in our declaration example are setdate() and showdate(), both of which have been declared as returning no value (void). In the implementation section of the class these three member functions will be written to permit initialization, assignment, and display capabilities, respectively.

The *implementation section* of a class is where the member functions declared in the declaration section are written.[16] Figure 13.5 illustrates the general form of functions included in the implementation section. This format is correct for all functions except the constructor, which, as we have stated, has no return type.

As shown in Figure 13.5, member functions have the same format as all user-written C++ functions, with the addition of the class name and scope resolution operator, ::, which is used to identify the function as a member of a particular class. Let us

---

[16] It is also possible to define these functions within the declaration section by declaring and writing them as inline functions. Examples of inline member functions are presented in Section 13.5.

now reconsider the implementation section of our `Date` class, which is repeated below for convenience:

```
//--- class implementation section

Date::Date(int mm, int dd, int yyyy)
{
  month = mm;
  day = dd;
  year = yyyy;
}

void Date::setdate(int mm, int dd, int yyyy)
{
  month = mm;
  day = dd;
  year = yyyy;

  return;
}
void Date::showdate()
{
  cout << "The date is "
       << setfill('0')
       << setw(2) << month << '/'
       << setw(2) << day << '/'
       << setw(2) << year % 100
       << endl;

  return;
}
```

Notice that the first function in this implementation section has the same name as the class, which makes it a constructor function. Hence, it has no return type. The `Date::` included at the beginning of the function header line identifies this function as a member of the `Date` class. The rest of the header line, `Date(int mm, int dd, int yyyy)`, defines the function as having three integer parameters. The body of this function simply assigns the data members `month`, `day`, and `year` with the values of the parameters `mm`, `dd`, and `yyyy`, respectively.

The next function header line

```
void Date::setdate(int mm, int dd, int yyyy)
```

defines this as the `setdate()` function belonging to `Date` class (`Date::`). This function returns no value (`void`) and uses three integer parameters, `mm`, `dd`, and `yyyy`. In a manner similar to the `Date()` function, the body of this function assigns the data members month, day, and year with the values of these parameters. In a moment we will see the difference between Date() and setdate().

Finally, the last function header line in the implementation section defines a function named showdate(). This function has no parameters, returns no value, and is a member of the Date class. The body of this function, however, needs a little more explanation.

Although we have chosen to internally store all years as four-digit values that retain century information, users are accustomed to seeing dates where the year is represented as a two-digit value, such as 12/15/99. To display the last two digits of the year value, the expression year % 100 can be used. For example, if the year is 1999, the expression 1999 % 100 yields the value 99, and if the year is 2001, the expression 2001 % 100 yields the value 1. Notice that if we had used an assignment such as year = year % 100; we would actually be altering the stored value of year to correspond to the last two digits of the year. Because we want to retain the year as a four-digit number, we must be careful to only manipulate the displayed value using the expression year % 100 within the cout stream. The setfill and setw manipulators are used to ensure that the displayed values correspond to conventionally accepted dates. For example, a date March 9, 2002, should appear as either 3/9/02 or 03/09/02. The setw manipulator forces each value to be displayed in a field width of 2. Because this manipulator only remains in effect for the next insertion, we have included it before the display of each date value. As the setfill manipulator, however, remains in effect until the fill character is changed, we only have to include it once.[17] We have used the setfill manipulator here to change the fill character from its default of a blank space to the character 0. Doing this ensures that a date such as December 9, 2002, will appear as 12/09/02 and not 12/ 9/ 2.

To see how our Date class can be used within the context of a complete program, consider Program 13.13. To make the program easier to read it has been shaded in lighter and darker areas. The lighter area contains the class declaration and implementation sections we have already considered. The darker area contains the header and main() function. For convenience, we retain this shading convention for all programs using classes.[18]

 Program 13.13

```
#include <<iostream.h>>
#include <iomanip.h>


// class declaration section
class Date
{
  private:
    int month;                                          (Continued on next page)
```

---

[17] This type of information is easily obtained using the on-line Help facility, as described in Section 2.8.

[18] This shading is not accidental. In practice, the lightly shaded region containing the class definition would be placed in a separate file. A single #include statement would then be used to include this class definition into the program. Thus, the final program would consist of the two darker-shaded regions illustrated in Program 13.13 with the addition of one more #include statement in the first region.

(Continued from previous page)

```cpp
    int day;
    int year;
  public:
    Date(int = 7, int = 4, int = 2001);  // constructor
    void setdate(int, int, int);         // member function to assign a date
    void showdate();                     // member function to display a date
};

// implementation section
Date::Date(int mm, int dd, int yyyy)
{
  month = mm;
  day = dd;
  year = yyyy;
}

void Date::setdate(int mm, int dd, int yyyy)
{
  month = mm;
  day = dd;
  year = yyyy;
}
void Date::showdate()
{
  cout << "The date is "
       << setfill('0')
       << setw(2) << month << '/'
       << setw(2) << day << '/'
       << setw(2) << year % 100
       << endl;
}
int main()
{
  Date a, b, c(4,1,1998);   // declare 3 objects - initializes 1 of them

  b.setdate(12,25,2002);    // assign values to b's data members
  a.showdate();             // display object a's values
  b.showdate();             // display object b's values
  c.showdate();             // display object c's values

  return 0;
}
```

The declaration and implementation sections contained in the lightly shaded region of Program 13.13 should look familiar, as they contain the class declaration and implementation sections we have already discussed. Notice, however, that this region only declares the class; it does not create any variables of this class type. This is true of all C++ types, including the built-in types such as integer and floating point. Just as a variable of an integer type must be defined, variables of a user-defined class must also be defined. Variables defined to be of user-defined class are referred to as *objects.*

Thus, the first statement in Program 13.13's `main()` function, contained in the darker area, defines three objects, named a, b, and c, to be of class type `Date`. In C++, whenever a new object is defined, memory is allocated for the object and its data members are automatically initialized. This is done by an automatic call to the class constructor function. For example, consider the definition `Date a, b, c(4,1,1998);` contained in `main()`. When the object named a is defined the constructor function `Date()` is automatically called. Because no arguments have been assigned to a, the default values of the constructor function are used, resulting in the initialization:

```
a.month = 7
a.day = 4
a.year = 2001
```

Notice the notation that we have used here. It consists of an object name and an attribute name separated by a period. This is the standard syntax for referring to an object's attribute, namely,

object-name.attribute-name

where *object-name* is the name of a specific object and *attribute-name* is the name of a data member defined for the object's class. This should be familiar to you because it is the same notation that is used in accessing structure members.

Thus, the notation `a.month = 7` refers to the fact that object a's month data member has been set to the value 7. Similarly, the notation `a.day = 4` and `a.year = 2001` refer to the fact that a's `day` and `year` data members have been set to the values 4 and 2001, respectively. In the same manner, when the object named b is defined, the same default arguments are used, resulting in the initialization of b's data members as:

```
b.month = 7
b.day = 4
b.year = 2001
```

The object named c, however, is defined with the arguments 4, 1, and 1998. These three arguments are passed into the constructor function when the object is defined, resulting in the initialization of c's data members as:

```
c.month = 4
c.day = 1
c.year = 1998
```

The next statement in main(), b.setdate(12,25,2002), calls b's setdate() function, which assigns the argument values 12, 25, 2002 to b's data members, resulting in the assignment:

```
b.month = 12
b.day = 25
b.year = 2002
```

Finally, the last three statements call a, b, and c's showdate() function. The first call results in the display of a's data values, the second call in the display of b's data value, and the third call in the display of c's data values. Thus, the output of Program 13.11 is

```
The date is 07/04/01
The date is 12/25/02
The date is 04/01/98
```

Notice that a statement such as cout << a; is invalid within main() because cout does not know how to handle an object of class Date. Thus, we have supplied our class with a function that can be used to access and display an object's internal values.

Terminology

There is sometimes confusion between the terms "classes," "objects," and other terminology associated with object-oriented programming. Let us take a moment to clarify and review the terminology.

A *class* is a programmer-defined abstract data type out of which objects can be created. *Objects* are created from classes; they have the same relationship to classes as variables do to C++'s built-in data types. For example, in the declaration

```
int a;
```

a is said to be a variable, while in Program 13.13's declaration

```
Date a;
```

a is said to be an object. If it helps you to initially think of an object as a variable, do so.

Objects are also referred to as *instances* of a class and the process of creating a new object is frequently referred to as an *instantiation* of the object. Each time a new object is instantiated (created), a new set of data members belonging to the object is created.[19] Individually, each data member represents an attribute of interest that is modeled by the class. The particular values contained in these data members for each object determine the object's *state*.

---

[19] It should be noted that only one set of class functions is created. These functions are shared between objects. The mechanism for using the same function on different objects' data members is presented in Section 14.2.

Seen in this way, a class can be thought of as a blueprint out of which particular instances (objects) can be created. Each instance (object) of a class will have its own set of particular values for the set of data members specified in the class declaration section.

In addition to the data types allowed for an object, a class also defines *behavior,* that is, the operations that are permitted to be performed on an object's data members. Users of the object need to know what these functions can do and how to activate them through function calls, but they do not need to know how the operation is done. The actual implementation details of an object's operations are contained in the class implementation, which can be hidden from the user. Other names for the operations defined in a class implementation section are *procedures, functions, services,* and *methods.* We will use these terms interchangeably throughout the remainder of the text.

Exercises 13.4

1. Define the following terms:
   a. class
   b. object
   c. declaration section
   d. implementation section
   e. instance variable
   f. member function
   g. data member
   h. constructor
   i. class instance
   j. services
   k. methods
   l. interface

2. Write a class declaration section for each of the following specifications. In each case include a prototype for a constructor and a member function named `showdata()` that can be used to display member values.
   a. A class named `Time` that has integer data members named `secs, mins,` and `hours.`
   b. A class named `Complex` that has floating point data members named `real` and `imaginary.`
   c. A class named `Circle` that has integer data members named `xcenter` and `ycenter` and a floating point data member named `radius.`
   d. A class named `System` that has character data members named `computer, printer,` and `screen,` each capable of holding 30 characters (including the end-of-string NULL), and floating point data members named `compPrice, printPrice,` and `scrnPrice.`

3. a. Construct a class implementation section for the constructor and `showdate()` function members corresponding to the class declaration created for Exercise 2a.
   b. Construct a class implementation section for the constructor and `showdate()` function members corresponding to the class declaration created for Exercise 2b.
   c. Construct a class implementation section for the constructor and `showdate()` function members corresponding to the class declaration created for Exercise 2c.
   d. Construct a class implementation section for the constructor and `showdate()` function members corresponding to the class declaration created for Exercise 2d.

4. a. Include the class declaration and implementation sections prepared for Exercises 2a and 3a in a complete working program.

    b. Include the class declaration and implementation sections prepared for Exercises 2b and 3b in a complete working program.

    c. Include the class declaration and implementation sections prepared for Exercises 2c and 3c in a complete working program.

    d. Include the class declaration and implementation sections prepared for Exercises 2d and 3d in a complete working program.

5. Determine the errors in the following class declaration section:

```
class Employee
{
  public:
    int empnum;
    char name[31];
  private:
    class(int = 0);
    void showemp(int, char *);
};
```

6. a. Add another member function named `convert()` to Program 13.11. The function should access the `month`, `year`, and `day` data members and display and then return a long integer that is calculated as *year * 10000 + month * 100 + day.* For example, if the date is 4/1/2002, the returned value is 20020401 (dates in this form are useful when performing sorts, as placing the numbers in numerical order automatically places the corresponding dates in chronological order).

    b. Include the modified `Date` class constructed for Exercise 6a in a complete C++ program.

7. a. Add an additional member function to Program 13.11's class definition named `leapyr()` that returns a 1 when the year is a leap year and a 0 if it is not. A leap year is any year that is evenly divisible by 4 but not evenly divisible by 100, with the exception that years evenly divisible by 400 are leap years. For example, the year 1996 is a leap year because it is evenly divisible by 4 and not evenly divisible by 100. The year 2000 is a leap year because it is evenly divisible by 400.

    b. Include the class definition constructed for Exercise 7a in a complete C++ program. The `main()` function should display the message `The year is a leap year` or `The year is not a leap year` depending on the `Date` object's year value.

8. a. Add a member function to Program 13.11's class definition named `dayOfWeek()` that determines the day of the week for any `Date` object. An algorithm for determining the day of the week, known as Zeller's algorithm, is the following:

       This algorithm assumes a date of the form `mm/dd/ccyy`, where `mm` is the month, `dd` is the day, `cc` is the century, and `yy` is the year in the century (for example, in the date `12/5/2000`, `mm` = 12, `dd` = 5, `cc` = 20, and `yy` = 0).

cc = int(ccyy/100)
yy = ccyy % 100
If the mm is less than 3,
   Set mm = mm + 12 and ccyy = ccyy - 1
EndIf
*Set the variable T = dd + int(26 * (mm + 1)/10) + yy + int(yy/4) + int(cc/4) - (2 * cc)*
dayOfWeek = T % 7

> *If dayOfWeek is less than 0*
>   *dayOfWeek = dayOfWeek + 7*
> *EndIf*

Using this algorithm, the variable `dayOfWeek` has a value of 0 if the date is a Saturday, 1 if a Sunday, etc.

b. Include the class definition constructed for Exercise 8a in a complete C++ program. The `main()` function should display the name of the day (Sun, Mon, Tue, etc.) for the `Date` object being tested.

13.5 Constructors and Destructors

A *constructor function* is any function that has the same name as its class. More than one constructor for each class can be defined. One constructor function is automatically called each time an object is created with the intended purpose of initializing the new object's data members. Constructor functions may also perform other tasks when they are called and can be written in a variety of ways. In this section we present the possible variations of constructor functions and introduce another function, the destructor, which is automatically called whenever an object goes out of existence.

Figure 13.6 illustrates the general format of a constructor. As shown in this figure, a constructor:

1. Must have the same name as the class to which it belongs
2. Must have no return type (not even `void`)

```
ClassName::ClassName(list)
{
   function body
}
```

Figure 13.6 Constructor format

If you do not include a constructor in your class definition, the compiler will supply one for you. The supplied constructor, however, is a do-nothing constructor. For example, consider the following class declaration:

```
class Date
{
  private:
    int month, day, year;
  public:
    void setdate(int, int, int);
    void showdate()
};
```

Programming Note

Constructors

A *constructor* is any function that has the same name as its class. The primary purpose of a constructor is to initialize an object's member variables when an object is created. Hence, a constructor is automatically called when an object is declared.

A class can have multiple constructors provided that each constructor is distinguishable by having a different parameter list. A compiler error results when unique identification of a constructor is not possible. If no constructor is provided the compiler supplies a do-nothing default constructor.

Every constructor function must be declared *with no return type* (not even void). Because they are functions, constructors may also be explicitly called in nondeclarative statements. When used in this manner, the function call requires parentheses following the constructor name, even if no parameters are used. However, when used in a declaration, parentheses *must not* be included for a zero parameter constructor. For example, the declaration Date a(); is incorrect. The correct declaration is Date a;. When parameters are used, however, they must be enclosed within parentheses in both declarative and nondeclarative statements. Default parameter values should be included within the constructor's prototype.

Since no user-defined constructor has been declared here, the compiler creates a default constructor. For our Date class this default constructor is equivalent to the implementation Date(void) {}, that is, the compiler-supplied default constructor expects no parameters and has an empty body. Clearly this default constructor is not very useful, but it does exist if no other constructor is declared.

The term *default constructor* is used quite frequently in C++. It refers to any constructor that does not require any arguments when it is called. This can be because no arguments are declared, which is the case for the compiler-supplied default, or because all arguments have been given default values. For example, the prototype Date(int = 7, int = 4, int = 2001); is also valid for a default constructor. Here, each argument has been given a default value, and, when the corresponding constructor is written, an object can be declared as type Date without supplying any further arguments. Using such a constructor, the declaration Date a; initializes the a object with the default values 7, 4, and 2001.

To verify that a constructor function is automatically called whenever a new object is created, consider Program 13.14. Notice that in the implementation section the constructor function uses cout to display the message Created a new object with data values. Thus, whenever the constructor is called this message is displayed. Since the main() function creates three objects, the constructor is called three times and the message is displayed three times.

📟 **Program 13.14**

```cpp
#include <iostream.h>

// class declaration section
class Date
{
  private:
    int month;
    int day;
    int year;
  public:
    Date(int = 4, int = 7, int = 2001);     // constructor
};

// implementation section
Date::Date(int mm, int dd, int yyyy)
{
    month = mm;
    day = dd;
    year = yyyy;
    cout << "Created a new data object with data values "
         << month << ", " << day << ", " << year << endl;
}

int main()
{
  Date a;              // declare an object
  Date b;              // declare an object
  Date c(4,1,2002);    // declare an object

  return 0;
}
```

The following output is produced when Program 13.14 is executed.

```
Created a new data object with data values 7, 4, 2001
Created a new data object with data values 7, 4, 2001
Created a new data object with data values 4, 1, 2002
```

Although any legitimate C++ statement can be used within a constructor function such as the cout statement used in Program 13.14, it is best to keep constructors simple and use them only for initializing purposes. One further point needs to be made with respect to the constructor function in Program 13.14. According to the rules of C++, object data members are initialized in the order they are declared in the class declaration section, *not* in the order they may appear in the function's definition within the implementation section. Usually, this is not an issue, unless one member is initialized using another data member's value.

Calling Constructors

As we have seen, constructors are called whenever an object is created. The actual declaration, however, can be made in a variety of ways.

For example, the declaration

```
Date c(4,1,2002);
```

used in Program 13.14 could also have been written as

```
Date c = Date(4,1,2002);
```

This second form declares c as being of type `Date` and then makes a direct call to the constructor function with the arguments 4, 1, and 2002. This second form can be simplified when only one argument is passed to the constructor. For example, if only the `month` data member of the c object needed to be initialized with the value 8 and the `day` and `year` members can use the default values, the object can be created using the declaration

```
Date c = 8;
```

Because it resembles declarations in C, this form and its more complete equation form above are said to be the *C style of initialization.* The nonequation form of declaration in Program 13.14 is called the C++ *style of initialization* and is the form we will use predominantly throughout the remainder of the text.

Regardless of which initialization form you use, in no case should an object be declared with empty parentheses. For example, the declaration `Date a();` is not the same as the declaration `Date a;`. The latter declaration uses the default constructor values while the former declaration results in no object being created.

Overloaded and Inline Constructors

The primary difference between a constructor and other user-written functions is how the constructor is called: constructors are called automatically each time an object is created, whereas other functions must be explicitly called by name.[20] As a function, however, a constructor must still follow all of the rules applicable to user-written functions. This means that constructors may have default argument values, as illustrated in Program 13.14, may be overloaded, and may be written as inline functions.

---

[20] This is true for all other functions except destructors, which are described later in this section. A destructor function is automatically called each time an object is destroyed.

Programming Note

Accessor Functions

An *accessor function* is any nonconstructor member function that accesses a class' private data members. For example, the function showdate() in the Date class is an accessor function. Such functions are extremely important because they provide a means of displaying private data member's stored values.

When you construct a class, make sure to provide a complete set of accessor functions. Each accessor function does not have to return a data member's exact value, but it should return a useful representation of the value. For example, assume that a date such as 12/25/2002 is stored as a long integer member variable in the form 20022512. Although an accessor function could display this value, a more useful representation would typically be either 12/25/02, or December 25, 2002.

Besides being used for output, accessor functions can also provide a means of data input. For example, the setdate() function in the Date class is an example of an input accessor function. Constructor functions, whose primary purpose is to initialize an object's member variables, are not considered as accessor functions.

Recall from Section 13.3 that function overloading permits the same function name to be used with different parameter lists. Based on the supplied argument types, the compiler determines which function to use when the call is encountered. Let's see how this can be applied to our Date class. For convenience, the appropriate class declaration is repeated below:

```
// class declaration section
class Date
{
  private:
    int month;
    int day;
    int year;
  public:
    Date(int = 7, int = 4, int = 2001);          // constructor
};
```

Here, the constructor prototype specifies three integer values that are used to initialize the month, day, and year data members.

An alternate method of specifying a date is to use a long integer in the form *year * 10000 + month * 100 + day*. For example, using this form the date 12/24/1999 is

19991224 and the date 2/5/2002 is 20020205.[21] A suitable prototype for a constructor that uses dates of this form is

```
Date(long);   // an overloaded constructor
```

Here, the constructor is declared as receiving one long integer value. The code for this new `Date` function must, of course, correctly convert its single argument value into a month, day, and year, and would be included within the class implementation section. The actual code for such a constructor is

```
Date::Date(long yyyymmdd)      // a second constructor
{
  year = (int) (yyyymmdd/10000.0);      // extract the year
  month = (int)( (yyyymmdd - year * 10000.0) / 100.00 ); // extract the month
  day = (int) (yyyymmdd - year * 10000.0 - month * 100.0); // extract the day
}
```

Do not be overly concerned with the conversion code within the function's body. The important point here is the concept of overloading the `Date()` function to provide two constructors. Program 13.15 contains the complete class definition within the context of a working program.

Program 13.15

```
#include <iostream.h>
#include <iomanip.h>

// class declaration
class Date
{
  private:
    int month;
    int day;
    int year;
  public:
    Date(int = 7, int = 4, int = 2001); // constructor
    Date(long);                          // another constructor
    void showdate();                     // member function to display a date
};

// implementation section
Date::Date(int mm, int dd, int yyyy)                    (Continued on next page)
```

---

[22] The reasons for specifying dates in this manner are that only one number needs to be used per date and that sorting the numbers automatically puts the corresponding dates into chronological order.

(Continued from previous page)

```
{
  month = mm;
  day = dd;
  year = yyyy;
}
Date::Date(long yyyymmdd)   // here is the overloaded constructor
{
  year = (int)(yyyymmdd/10000.0);    // extract the year
  month = (int)( (yyyymmdd - year*10000.0)/100.00 ); // extract the month
  day = (int)(yyyymmdd - year*10000.0 - month*100.0); // extract the day
}
void Date::showdate()
{
  cout << "The date is "
       << setfill('0')
       << setw(2) << month << '/'
       << setw(2) << day << '/'
       << setw(2) << year % 100
       << endl;

  return;
}
int main()
{
  Date a, b(4,1,1998), c(20020515L): // declare three objects

  a.showdate();    // display object a's values
  b.showdate();    // display object b's values
  c.showdate();    // display object c's values

  return 0;
}
```

The output provided by Program 13.15 is

```
The date is 07/04/01
The date is 04/01/98
The date is 05/15/02
```

Three objects are created in Program 13.15's main() function. The first object, a, is initialized with the default constructor using its default argument values. Object b is also initialized with the default constructor but uses the argument values 4, 1, and 1998. Finally, object c, which is initialized with a long integer, uses the second constructor in the class implementation section. The compiler knows to use this second constructor because the argument specified, 20020515L, is clearly designated as a long integer. It is worthwhile pointing out that a compiler error occurs if both `Date` constructors had default values. In such a case a declaration such as `Date d;` is ambiguous to the compiler, as it is not able to determine which constructor to use. Thus, in each implementation section, only one constructor can be written as the default.

Just as constructors may be overloaded, they may also be written as inline functions. Doing so simply means defining the function in the class declaration section. Making both the constructors in Program 13.15 inline is accomplished by the declaration section

```cpp
// class declaration
class Date
{
  private:
    int month;
    int day;
    int year;
  public:
    Date(int mm = 7, int dd = 4, int yyyy = 2001)
    {
      month = mm;
      day = dd;
      year = yyyy;
    }
    Date(long yyyymmdd)    // here is the overloaded constructor
    {
      year = (int)(yyyymmdd/10000.0);    // extract the year
      month = (int)( (yyyymmdd - year * 10000.0)/100.00 );  // extract the month
      day = (int)(yyyymmdd - year * 10000.0 - month * 100.0); // extract the day
    };
```

The keyword `inline` is not required in this declaration because member functions defined inside the class declaration are inline by default.

Generally, only functions that can be coded on one or two lines are good candidates for inline functions. This reinforces the convention that inline functions should be small. Thus, the first constructor is more conventionally written as

```cpp
Date(int mm = 7, int dd = 4, int yyyy = 2001)
  { month = mm; day = dd; year = yyyy; }
```

The second constructor, which extends over three lines, should not be written as an inline function.

Destructors

The counterpart to constructor functions is destructor functions. Destructors are functions having the same class name as constructors, but preceded with a tilde (~). Thus, for our

`Date` class, the destructor name is `~Date()`. Like constructors, a default do-nothing de-structor is provided by the C++ compiler in the absence of an explicit destructor. Unlike constructors, however, there can be only one destructor function per class. This is because destructors take no arguments and return no values.

Destructors are automatically called whenever an object goes out of existence and are meant to "clean up" any undesirable effects that might be left by the object. Generally, such effects only occur when an object contains a pointer member.

Arrays of Objects

The importance of default constructors becomes evident when arrays of objects are cre-ated. Because a constructor is called each time an object is created, the default constructor provides an elegant way of initializing all objects to the same state.

Declaring an array of objects is the same as declaring an array of any built-in type. For example, the declaration

```
Date thedate[5];
```

will create five objects named `thedate[0]` through `thedate[4]`, respectively. Mem-ber functions for each of these objects are called by listing the object name followed by a dot (`.`) and the desired function. An example using an array of objects is provided by Pro-gram 13.16, which also includes `cout` statements within both the constructor and de-structor. As illustrated by the output of this program, the constructor is called for each declared object, followed by five member function calls to `showdate()`, followed by five destructor calls. The destructor is called when the objects go out of scope. In this case, the destructor is called when the `main()` function terminates execution.[22]

 Program 13.16

```
#include <iostream.h>
#include <iomunip.h>

// class declaration
class Date
{
  private:
    int month;
    int day;
    int year;
```
(Continued on next page)

---

[22] A destructor for a local object is called when the smallest block containing the object's definition goes out of scope. The destructor for a global object is called when the program terminates.

(Continued from previous page)

```
  public:
    Date();    // constructor
    ~Date();   // destructor
    void showdate();
};

// implementation section
Date::Date()  // user-defined default constructor
{
  cout << "*** A Date object is being initialized ***\n";
  month = 1;
  day = 1;
  year = 2002
}

Date::~Date()  // user-defined destructor
{
  cout << "*** A Date object is going out of existence ***\n";
}

void Date::showdate()
{
  cout << "The date is "
       << setfill('0')
       << setw(2) << month << '/'
       << setw(2) << day << '/'
       << setw(2) << year % 100
       << endl;

  return;
}
int main()
{
  Date thedate[5];

  for(int i = 0; i < 5; i++)
    thedate[i],showdate();

  return 0;
}
```

The output produced by Program 13.16 is

```
*** A Date object is being initialized ***
*** A Date object is being initialized ***
*** A Date object is being initialized ***
*** A Date object is being initialized ***
*** A Date object is being initialized ***
            The date is 01/01/02
            The date is 01/01/02
            The date is 01/01/02
            The date is 01/01/02
            The date is 01/01/02
*** A Date object is going out of existence ***
*** A Date object is going out of existence ***
*** A Date object is going out of existence ***
*** A Date object is going out of existence ***
*** A Date object is going out of existence ***
```

Exercises 13.5

1. Determine whether the following statements are true or false:
   a. A constructor function must have the same name as its class.
   b. A class can have only one constructor function.
   c. A class can have only one default constructor function.
   d. A default constructor can only be supplied by the compiler.
   e. A default constructor can have no arguments or all arguments must have default values.
   f. A constructor must be declared for each class.
   g. A constructor must be declared with a return type.
   h. A constructor is automatically called each time an object is created.
   i. A class can have only one destructor function.
   j. A destructor must have the same name as its class, preceded by a tilde (~).
   k. A destructor can have default arguments.
   l. A destructor must be declared for each class.
   m. A destructor must be declared with a return type.
   n. A destructor is automatically called each time an object goes out of existence.
   o. Destructors are not useful when the class contains a pointer data member.

2. For Program 13.15, what date is initialized for object c if the declaration Date c(2002); is used in place of the declaration Date c(20020515L);?

3. Modify Program 13.15 so that the only data member of the class is a long integer named yyyymmdd. Do this by substituting the declaration

```
long yyyymmdd;
```

for the existing declarations

```
int month;
int day;
int year;
```

Then, rewrite the same constructor function prototypes currently declared in the class declaration section so that the Date(long) function becomes the default constructor and the Date(int, int, int) function converts a month, day, and year into the proper form for the class data member.

4. a. Construct a Time class containing integer data members seconds, minutes, and hours. Have the class contain two constructors: the first should be a default constructor having the prototype time(int, int, int), which uses default values of 0 for each data member. The second constructor should accept a long integer representing a total number of seconds and disassemble the long integer into hours, minutes, and seconds. The final function member should display the class data members.

   b. Include the class written for Exercise 4a within the context of a complete program.

5. a. Construct a class named Student consisting of an integer student identification number, an array of five floating point grades, and an integer representing the total number of grades entered. The constructor for this class should initialize all Student data members to 0. Included in the class should be member functions to

   1. Enter a student ID number
   2. Enter a single test grade and update the total number of grades entered
   3. Compute an average grade and display the student ID followed by the average grade.

   b. Include the class constructed in Exercise 5a within the context of a complete program. Your program should declare two objects of type Student and accept and display data for the two objects to verify operation of the member functions.

13.6 An Application

Now that you have an understanding of how classes are constructed and the terminology used in describing them, let us apply this knowledge to a particular application. In this application we simulate the operation of an elevator. We assume that the elevator can travel between the first and fifteenth floors of a building and that the location of the elevator must be known at all times.

For this application the location of the elevator corresponds to its current floor position and is represented by an integer variable ranging between 1 and 15. The value of this variable, which we name currentFloor, for current floor, effectively represents the current state of the elevator. The services that we provide for changing the state of the elevator are an initialization function to set the initial floor position when a new elevator is put in service and a request function to change the elevator's position (state) to a new floor. Putting an elevator in service is accomplished by declaring a single class instance (declaring an object of type Elevator). Requesting a new floor position is equivalent to pushing an elevator button. To accomplish this, a suitable class declaration is

```
                // class declaration section
                class Elevator
                {
                  private:
                    int currentFloor;
                  public:
                    Elevator(int);      // constructor
                    void request(int);
                };
```

Notice that we have declared one data member, currentFloor, and two class functions. The data member, currentFloor, is used to store the current floor position of the elevator. As a private member it can be accessed only through member functions. The two public member functions, Elevator() and request() define the external services provided by each Elevator object. The Elevator() function, which has the same name as its class, becomes a constructor function that is automatically called when an object of type Elevator is created. We use this function to initialize the starting floor position of the elevator. The request() function is used to alter its position. To accomplish these services, a suitable class implementation section is

```
// class implementation section

Elevator::Elevator(int cfloor)      // constructor
{
  currentFloor = cfloor;
}

void Elevator::request(int newfloor)  // access function
{
  if (newfloor < 1 || newfloor > MAXFLOOR || newfloor == currentFloor)
    ;  // do nothing
  else if ( newfloor > currentFloor)  // move elevator up
  {
    cout << "\nStarting at floor " << currentFloor << endl;
    while (newfloor > currentFloor)
    {
      currentFloor++;    // add one to current floor
      cout << "   Going Up - now at floor " << currentFloor << endl;
    }
    cout << "Stopping at floor " << currentFloor << endl;
  }
  else  // move elevator down
  {
    cout << "\nStarting at floor " << currentFloor << endl;
    while (newfloor < currentFloor)
```

(Continued on next page)

(Continued from previous page)

```
  {
    currentFloor--;    // subtract one from current floor
    cout << "   Going down - now at floor " << currentFloor << endl;
  }
  cout << "Stopping at floor " << currentFloor << endl;
  }
}
```

The constructor function is straightforward. When an `Elevator` object is declared, it is initialized to the floor specified; if no floor is explicitly given, a default value of 1, specified in the prototype, is used. For example, the declaration

```
Elevator a(7);
```

initializes the variable `a.currentFloor` to 7, while the declaration

```
Elevator a;
```

uses the default argument value and initializes the variable `a.currentFloor` to 1.

The `request()` function defined in the implementation section is more complicated and provides the class's primary service. Essentially this function consists of an `if-else` statement having three parts: if an incorrect service is requested no action is taken; if a floor above the current position is selected the elevator is moved up; and if a floor below the current position is selected the elevator is moved down. For movement up or down the function uses a `while` loop to increment the position one floor at a time and reports the elevator's movement using a `cout` stream. Program 13.17 includes this class in a working program.

 Program 13.17

```
#include <iostream.h>

const int MAXFLOOR = 15;

// class declaration section
class Elevator
{
  private:
    int currentFloor;
  public:
    Elevator(int = 1);    // constructor
    void request(int);
};

//implementation section
Elevator::Elevator(int cfloor)   // constructor
```

(Continued on next page)

(Continued from previous page)

```
{
  currentFloor = cfloor;
}

void Elevator::request(int newfloor)   // access function
{
  if (newfloor < 1 || newfloor > MAXFLOOR || newfloor == currentFloor)
    ;   // do nothing
  else if ( new floor > currentFloor)   // move elevator up
  {
    cout << "\nStarting at floor " << currentFloor << endl;
    while (newfloor > currentFloor)
    {
      currentFloor++;     // add one to current floor
      cout << "  Going up - now at floor " << currentFloor << endl;
    }
    cout << "Stopping at floor " << currentFloor << endl;
  }
    else  // move elevator down
    {
      cout << "\nStarting at floor " << currentFloor << endl;
      while (newfloor < currentFloor)
      {
        currentFloor--;   // subtract one from current floor
        cout << "  Going Down - now at floor " << currentFloor << endl;
      }
      cout << "Stopping at floor " << currentFloor << endl;
    }
  }
int main()
{
  Elevator a;     // declare 1 object of type Elevator

  a.request(6);
  a.request(3);

  return 0;
}
```

The lightly shaded portion of Program 13.17 contains the class construction that we have already described. To see how this class is used, concentrate on the darker-shaded section of the program. At the top of the program we have included the `iostream.h` header file and declared a named constant, `MAXFLOOR`, that corresponds to the highest floor that can be requested.

Within the `main()` function three statements are included. The first statement creates an object named a of type `Elevator`. Because no explicit floor has been given, this elevator will begin at floor 1, which is the default constructor argument. A request is then made to move the elevator to floor 6, which is followed by a request to move the elevator to floor 3. The output produced by Program 13.7 is

```
Starting at floor 1
   Going Up - now at floor 2
   Going Up - now at floor 3
   Going Up - now at floor 4
   Going Up - now at floor 5
   Going Up - now at floor 6
Stopping at floor 6

Starting at floor 6
   Going Down - now at floor 5
   Going Down - now at floor 4
   Going Down - now at floor 3
Stopping at floor 3
```

The basic requirements of object-oriented programming are evident in even so simple a program as Program 13.17. Before the `main()` function can be written a useful class must be constructed. This is typical of programs that use objects. For such programs the design process is front-loaded with the requirement that careful consideration of the class—its declaration and implementation—be given. Code contained in the implementation section effectively removes code that would otherwise be part of `main()`'s responsibility. Thus, any program that uses the object does not have to repeat the implementation details within its `main()` function. Rather, the `main()` function and any function called by `main()` is concerned only with sending messages to its objects to activate them appropriately. How the object responds to the messages and how the state of the object is retained is not `main()`'s concern; these details are hidden within the class construction.

Exercises 13.6

1. Enter Program 13.17 into your computer and execute it.

2. Modify the `main()` function in Program 13.17 to put a second elevator in service starting at the fifth floor. Have this second elevator move to the first floor and then to the twelfth floor.

3. Verify that the constructor function is called by adding a message within the constructor that is displayed each time a new object is created. Run your program to ensure its operation.

4. Modify the `main()` function in Program 13.17 to use a `while` loop that calls the elevator's `request()` function with a random number between 1 and 15. If the random number is the same as the elevator's current floor, generate another request. The `while` loop should terminate after 5 valid requests have been made and satisfied by movement of the elevator. (*Hint:*

Review Section 6.8 for the use of random numbers and add a movement return code ro the modified `request()` function.)

5. a. Construct a class definition that can be used to represent an employee of a company. Each employee is defined by an integer ID number, a name consisting of no more than 30 characters, a floating point pay rate, and the maximum number of hours the employee should work each week. The services provided by the class should be the ability to enter data for a new employee, the ability to change data for a new employee, and the ability to display the existing data for a new employee.

   b. Include the class definition created for Exercise 4a in a working C++ program that asks the user to enter data for three employees and displays the entered data.

6. a. Construct a class definition that can be used to represent types of food. A type of food is classified as basic or prepared. Basic foods are further classified as either dairy, meat, fruit, vegetable, or grain. The services provided by the class should be the ability to enter data for a new food, the ability to change data for a new food, and the ability to display the existing data for a new food.

   b. Include the class definition created for Exercise 5a in a working C++ program that asks the user to enter data for four food items and displays the entered data.

13.7   Common Programming Errors

The more common programming errors initially associated with the construction of classes are

1. Failing to terminate the class declaration section with a semicolon.
2. Including a return type with the constructor's prototype or failing to include a return type with the other functions' prototypes.
3. Using the same name for a data member as for a member function.
4. Defining more than one default constructor for a class.
5. Forgetting to include the class name and scope operator, `::`, in the header line of all member functions defined in the class implementation section.

All of these errors result in a compiler error message.

13.8   Chapter Summary

1. The lack of an easy-to-use high-resolution graphics capability is a serious difficulty when creating a graphical user interface that utilizes the full potential of a graphical monitor. This was one of the reasons for the development of object-oriented languages such as C++. In addition to providing the procedural aspects of C, the object-oriented C++ language provides the capability for creating user-defined data-types.

2. A central concept in object-oriented languages is that of an abstract data type (ADT), which is a programmer-defined data type that includes both a data type and operations that can be applied to the data.

3. The data types provided in all programming languages, such as integers, are examples of built-in data types. They contain the two required elements of an abstract data type, data and operations applicable to the data, but they are provided as an intrinsic part of the language.

4. Once an abstract data type has been created, objects of that abstract data type may be defined. Objects have the same relationship to an abstract data type as variables do to a language's built-in data types.

5. In C++ an abstract data type is referred to as a *class,* which is simply a programmer-defined abstract data type. *Objects* of a class may be declared and have the same relationship to their class as variables do to C++'s built-in data types.

6. A class definition consists of declaration and implementation sections. The most common form of a class definition is

```
// class declaration section
class Name
{
  private:
    a list of variable declarations;
  public:
    a list of function prototypes;
};

// class implementation section
class function definitions
```

The variables and functions declared in the class declaration section are collectively referred to as *class members.* The variables are individually referred to as *class data members* and the functions as *class member functions.* The terms `private` and `public` are *access specifiers.* Once an access specifier is listed it remains in force until another access specifier is given. The `private` keyword specifies that the class members following it are private to the class and can be accessed only by member functions. The `public` keyword specifies that the class members following may be accessed from outside the class. Generally all data members should be specified as `private` and all member functions as `public`.

7. Class functions listed in the declaration section may either be written inline or their definitions included in the class implementation section. Except for constructor and destructor functions, all class functions defined in the class implementation section have the header line:

```
return-type ClassName::functionName(parameter list);
```

Except for the addition of the class name and scope operator, : :, which are required to associate the function name with the class, this header line is identical to the header line used for any user-written function.

8. A *constructor function* is a special function that is automatically called each time an object is declared. It must have the same name as its class and cannot have any return type. Its purpose is to initialize each declared object.

9. If no constructor is declared for a class, the compiler supplies a *default constructor.* This is a do-nothing function having the form `ClassName(void) {}`.

10. The term *default constructor* refers to any constructor that does not require any arguments when it is called. This can be because no parameters are declared (as is the case for the compiler-supplied default constructor) or because all arguments have been given default values.

11. Each class may only have one default constructor. If a user-defined default constructor is defined the compiler will not create its default constructor.

12. are created using either a C++ or C style of declaration. The C++ style of declaration has the form:

```
ClassName list-of-object-names(list of initializers);
```

where the list of initializers is optional. An example of this style of declaration, including initializers, for a class named `Date` is

```
Date a,b,c(12,25,2002);
```

Here, the objects a and b are declared to be of type `Date` and are initialized using the default constructor values, while the object c is initialized with the values 12, 25, and 2002.

The equivalent C style of declaration, including the optional list of initializers, has the form:

```
ClassName objectName = ClassName(list of initializers);
```

An example of this style of declaration for a class named `Date` is

```
Date c = Date(12,25,2002)
```

Here the object c is created and initialized with the values 12, 25, and 2002.

13. Constructors maybe overloaded in the same manner as any other user-written C++ function.

14. If a constructor is defined for a class, a user-defined default constructor also should be written, as the compiler does not supply it.

15. A *destructor function* is called each time an object goes out of scope. Destructors must have the same name as their class, but preceded with a tilde (~). There can only be one destructor per class.

16. A destructor function takes no arguments and returns no value. If a user-defined destructor is not included in a class, the compiler provides a do-nothing destructor.

17. Arrays of objects are declared in the same manner as arrays of C++'s built-in data types. For example, if Date is a class name, the declaration

```
Date thedate[5];
```

creates five Date objects named thedate[0] through thedate[4]. Member functions for each of these objects are called by listing the object name, such as thedate[3], followed by a dot (.) and the desired member function name.

Chapter **14**

Additional Class Capabilities

14.1	Assignment	**14.5**	Class Inheritance
14.2	Additional Class Features	**14.6**	Common Programming Errors
14.3	Operator Functions	**14.7**	Chapter Summary
14.4	Data Type Conversions		

In the previous chapter the declaration, initialization, and display of objects were presented. In this chapter we continue our construction of classes and see how to provide class operator and conversion capabilities similar to those inherent in C++'s built-in types. With these additions, our user-defined types will have the functionality of built-in types.

This functionality is then extended by showing how a class designed by one programmer can be altered by another in a way that retains the integrity and design of the original class. This is accomplished using inheritance, a new feature central to object-oriented programming. Inheritance permits reusing and extending existing code in a way that ensures the new code does not adversely affect what has already been written.

14.1 Assignment

In Chapter 13, we saw how C++'s assignment operator, =, performs assignment between variables. In this section we see how assignment works when it is applied to objects and how to define our own assignment operator to override the default provided for user defined classes.

For a specific assignment example, consider the `main()` function of Program 14.1.

Program 14.1

```cpp
#include <iostream.h>
#include <iomanip.h>

// class declaration
class Date
{
  private:
    int month;
    int day;
    int year;
  public:
    Date(int = 7, int = 4, int = 2001);    // constructor
    void showdate();                        // member function to display a date
};
// implementation section
Date::Date(int mm, int dd, int yyyy)
{
  month = mm;
  day = dd;
  year = yyyy;
}
void Date::showdate()
{
  cout << setfill('0')
       << setw(2) << month << '/'
       << setw(2) << day << '/'
       << setw(2) << year % 100
       << endl;
  return;
}
int main()
{
  Date a(4,1,1999), b(12,18,2001); // declare two objects

  cout << "The date stored in a is originally ";
  a.showdate();  // display the original date
  a = b;          // assign b's value to a
  cout << "After assignment the date stored in a is ";
  a.showdate();  // display a's values

  return 0;
}
```

Notice that the implementation section of the `Date` class in Program 14.1 contains no assignment function. Nevertheless, we would expect the assignment statement a = b; in `main()` to assign b's data member values to their counterparts in a. This is, in fact, the case, and it is verified by the output produced when Program 14.1 is executed:

```
The date stored in a is originally 04/01/99
After assignment the date stored in a is 12/18/01
```

This type of assignment is called *memberwise assignment.* In the absence of any specific instructions to the contrary, the C++ compiler builds this type of default assignment operator for each class. If the class *does not contain any pointer data members* this default assignment operator is adequate and can be used without further consideration.[1]

Assignment operators, like all class members, can be declared in the class declaration section and defined in the class implementation section. For the declaration of operators, however, the keyword `operator` must be included in the declaration. Using this keyword, a simple assignment operator declaration has the form

```
void operator=(className&);
```

Here the keyword `void` indicates that the assignment returns no value, the `operator=` indicates that we are overloading the assignment operator with our own version, and the class name and ampersand within the parentheses indicates that the argument to the operator is a class reference. For example, to declare a simple assignment operator for our `Date` class, the declaration

```
void operator=(Date&);
```

can be used.

The actual implementation of the assignment operator is defined in the implementation section. For our declaration, a suitable implementation is

```
void Date::operator=(Date& newdate)
{
  day = newdate.day;       // assign the day
  month = newdate.month;   // assign the month
  year = newdate.year;     // assign the year
}
```

The use of the reference parameter in the definition of this operation is not accidental. In fact, one of the primary reasons of adding references to C++ was to facilitate the construction of overloaded operators and make the notation more natural. In this definition `newdate` is defined as a reference to a `Date` class. Within the body of the definition the `day` member of the object referenced by `newdate` is assigned to the `day` member of

---

[1] Memberwise assignment of a pointer means the address in the pointer is copied. What is usually required is that the contents being pointed to gets copied.

the current object, with the subsequent assignments for the month and year members. Assignments such as a.operator=(b); can then be used to call the overloaded assignment operator and assign b's member values to a. For convenience, the expression a.operator=(b) can be replaced with a = b;. Program 14.2 contains our new assignment operator within the context of a complete program.

 Program 14.2

```
#include <iostream.h>
#include <iomanip.h>

// class declaration
class Date
{
  private:
    int month;
    int day;
    int year;
  public:
    Date(int = 7, int = 4, int = 2001); // constructor
    void operator=(Date&);                // define assignment of a date
    void showdate();                      // member function to display a date
};

// implementation section
Date::Date(int mm, int dd, int yyyy)
{
  month = mm;
  day = dd;
  year = yyyy;
}
void Date::operator=(Date& newdate)
{
  day = newdate.day;        // assign the day
  month = newdate.month;    // assign the month
  year = newdate.year;      // assign the year

  return;
}
void Date::showdate()
{
  cout << setfill('0')
       << setw(2) << month << '/'
```

(Continued on next page)

(Continued from previous page)

```
        << setw(2) << day << '/'
        << setw(2) << year % 100
        << endl;

    return;
}
int main()
{
    Date a(4,1,1999), b(12,18,2001); // declare two objects

    cout << "The date stored in a is originally ";
    a.showdate();    // display the original date
    a = b;           // assign b's value to a
    cout << "After assignment the date stored in a is ";
    a.showdate();    // display a's values

    return 0;
}
```

Except for the addition of the overloaded assignment operator declaration and definition, Program 14.2 is identical to Program 14.1 and produces the same output. Its usefulness to us is that it illustrates how we can explicitly construct our own assignment definitions. Before moving on, however, one important modification to our assignment operator needs to be made.

The required modification concerns the operations' return value. As constructed, our simple assignment operator returns no value which precludes us from using it in multiple assignments such as a = b = c. The reason for this is that overloaded operators retain the same precedence and associativity as their equivalent built-in versions. Thus, an expression such as a = b = c is evaluated in the order a = (b = c). As we have defined assignment, unfortunately, the expression b = c returns no value, making subsequent assignment to a an error. To provide for multiple assignments, a more complete assignment operation would return a reference to its class type. Because the implementation of such an assignment requires a special class pointer, the presentation of this more complete assignment operator is deferred until the material presented in the next section is introduced. Until then, our simple assignment operator is more than adequate for our needs.

Copy Constructors

Although "assignment" seems similar to "initialization," it is worthwhile noting that they are two entirely different operations. In C++, an *initialization* occurs every time a new object is created. In an *assignment* no new object is created—the value of an existing object is simply changed. Figure 14.1 illustrates this difference.

```
                              c = a              ◀——— Assignment
        Type definition ——▶ Date c = a;  ◀——— Initialization
```

Figure 14.1 Initialization and assignment

One type of C++ initialization that closely resembles assignment is initialization of an object using another object of the same class. For example, in the declaration

```
Date b = a;
```

or its equivalent form

```
Date b(a);
```

the b object is initialized to a previously declared a object. The constructor that performs this type of initialization is called a *copy constructor.* If you do not declare one, the compiler constructs one for you. The compiler's default copy constructor performs much like the default assignment operator by doing a memberwise copy between objects. Thus, for the declaration Date b = a; the default copy constructor sets b's month, day, and year values to their respective counterparts in a. As with default assignment operators, default copy constructors work just fine unless the class contains pointer data members. Before considering the complications that can occur with pointer data members and how to handle them, it will be helpful to see how to construct our own copy constructors.

Copy constructors, like all class functions, can be declared in the class declaration section and defined in the class implementation section. The declaration of a copy constructor has the general form[2]

```
ClassName(ClassName&);
```

As with all constructors, the function name must be the class name. As further illustrated by the declaration, the parameter is a reference to the class, which is a characteristic of all copy constructors.[3] Applying this general form to our Date class, a copy constructor can be explicitly declared as

```
Date(Date&);
```

The actual implementation of this constructor, if it were to perform the same memberwise initialization as the default copy constructor, would take the form

---

[2] More formally, the function's parameter should be declared as const Date&. The const keyword ensures that the reference parameter cannot be modified from within the function.

[3] A copy constructor is frequently defined as a constructor whose first parameter is a reference to its class type, with any additional parameters being defaults.

```
Date:: Date(Date& olddate)
{
  month = olddate.month;
  day = olddate.day;
  year = olddate.year;
}
```

As with the assignment operator, the use of a reference parameter for the copy constructor is no accident: the reference parameter again facilitates a simple notation within the body of the function. Program 14.3 contains this copy constructor within the context of a complete program.

 Program 14.3

```
#include <iostream.h>
#include <iomanip.h>

// class declaration
class Date

  private:
    int month;
    int day;
    int year;
  public:
    Date(int = 7, int = 4, int = 2001);    // constructor
    Date(const Date&);                      // copy constructor
    void showdate();                        // member function to display a date
};

// implementation section
Date::Date(int mm, int dd, int yyyy)
{
  month = mm;
  day = dd;
  year = yyyy;
}
Date::Date(const Date& olddate)
{
  month = olddate.month;
  day = olddate.day;
  year = olddate.year;
}
void Date::showdate()
{
  cout << setfill('0')
```

(Continued on next page)

(Continued from previous page)

```
       << setw(2) << month << '/'
       << setw(2) << day << '/'
       << setw(2) << year % 100
       << endl;

  return;
}
int main()
{
   Date a(4,1,1999), b(12,18,2001); // use the constructor
   Date c(a);     // use the copy constructor
   Date d = b;    // use the copy constructor

   cout << "The date stored in a is ";
   a.showdate();
   cout << "The date stored in b is ";
   b.showdate();
   cout << "The date stored in c is ";
   c.showdate();
   cout << "The date stored in d is ";
   d.showdate();

   return 0;
}
```

The output produced by Program 14.3 is

```
The date stored in a is 04/01/99
The date stored in b is 12/18/01
The date stored in c is 04/01/99
The date stored in d is 12/18/01
```

As illustrated by this output, c's and d's data members have been initialized by the copy constructor to a's and b's values, respectively. Although the copy constructor defined in Program 14.3 adds nothing to the functionality provided by the compiler's default copy constructor, it does provide us with the fundamentals of defining copy constructors.

Base/Member Initialization[4]

Except for the reference names olddate and newdate, a comparison of Program 14.3's copy constructor to Program 14.2's assignment operator shows them to be essen-

---

[4] The material in this section is presented for completeness only and may be omitted without loss of subject continuity.

tially the same function. The difference in these functions is that the copy constructor first creates an object's data members before the body of the constructor uses assignment to specify member values. Thus, the copy constructor does not perform a true initialization, but rather a creation followed by assignment.

A true initialization would have no reliance on assignment whatsoever and is possible in C++ using a *base/member initialization list*. Such a list can only be applied to constructor functions and may be written in two ways.

The first way to construct a base/member initialization list is within a class's declaration section using the form

```
ClassName(parameter list) : list of data members(initializing values) {}
```

For example, using this form, a default constructor that performs true initialization is

```
// class declaration section
public:
  Date(int mo=4, int da=1, int yr=1999) : month(mo), day(da), year(yr) {}
```

The second way is to declare a prototype in the class's declaration section followed by the initialization list in the implementation section. For our `Date` constructor this takes the form

```
// class declaration section
public:
  Date(int=4, int=1, int=1999);   // prototype with defaults

// class implementation section
  Date::Date(int mo, int da, int yr):month(mo), day(da), year(yr) {}
```

Notice that in both forms the body of the constructor function is empty. This is not a requirement, and the body can include any subsequent operations that you want the constructor to perform. The interesting feature of this type of constructor is that it clearly differentiates between the initialization tasks performed in the member initialization list contained between the colon and the braces and any subsequent assignments that might be contained within the function's body. Although we will not be using this type of initialization subsequently, it is required whenever there is a `const` class instance variable.

Exercises 14.1

1. Describe the difference between assignment and initialization.

2. a. Construct a class named `Time` that contains three integer data members named `hrs`, `mins`, and `secs`, which will be used to store hours, minutes, and seconds. The function members should include a constructor that provides default values of 0 for each data member, a display function that prints an object's data values, and an assignment operator that performs a memberwise assignment between two `Time` objects.

    b.   Include the `Time` class developed in Exercise 2a in a working C++ program that creates and displays two `Time` objects, the second of which is assigned the values of the first object.

3. a.   Construct a class named `Complex` that contains two floating point data members named `real` and `imag`, which will be used to store the real and imaginary parts of a complex number. The function members should include a constructor that provides default values of 0 for each member function, a display function that prints an object's data values, and an assignment operator that performs a memberwise assignment between two `Complex` number objects.

    b.   Include the program written for Exercise 1a in a working C++ program that creates and displays the values of two `Complex` objects, the second of which is assigned the values of the first.

4. a.   Construct a class named `Car` that contains the following three data members: a floating point variable named `engineSize`, a character variable named `bodyStyle`, an integer variable named `colorCode`. The function members should include a constructor that provides default values of 0 for each numeric data member, 'X' for each character variable; a display function that prints the engine size, body style, and color code; and an assignment operator that performs a memberwise assignment between two `Car` objects for each instance variable.

    b.   Include the program written for Exercise 4a in a working C++ program that creates and displays two `Car` objects, the second of which is assigned the values of the first, except for the pointer data member.

5.   For a class that contains a pointer data member, such as the one described in Exercise 4, what problems can you anticipate for such a class when a memberwise assignment is performed between two class objects?

14.2   Additional Class Features[5]

This section presents several additional features pertaining to classes. These include the scope of a class, creating static class members, granting access privileges to nonmember functions, and a special class pointer named `this` that provides the link between member functions and member variables. Each of these topics may be read independently of the others.

Class Scope

We have already encountered local and global scope in Sections 6.4 and 6.5. As we saw, the scope of a variable defines the portion of a program where the variable can be accessed.

    For local variables, this scope is defined by any block contained within a brace pair, `{ }`. This includes both the complete function body and any internal subblocks. Additionally, all parameters of a function are considered as local function variables.

---

[5] Except for the material on the `this` pointer, which is required for the material in Section 14.3, the remaining topics in this section may be omitted on first reading with no loss of subject continuity.

Global variables are accessible from their point of declaration throughout the remaining portion of the file containing them, with three exceptions:

1. If a local variable has the same name as a global variable, the global variable can only be accessed within the scope of the local variable by using the scope resolution operator, `: :`.
2. The scope of a nonstatic global variable can be extended into another file by using the keyword `extern`.
3. The same global name can be reused in another file to define a separate and distinct variable by using the keyword `static`. Static global variables are unknown outside of their immediate file.

In addition to local and global scopes, each class also defines an associated *class scope*. That is, the names of the data and function members are local to the scope of their class. Thus, if a global variable name is reused within a class, the global variable is hidden by the class data member in the same manner as a local function variable hides a global variable of the same name. Similarly, member function names are local to the class they are declared in and can only be used by objects declared for the class. Additionally, local function variables also hide the names of class data members having the same name. Figure 14.2 illustrates the scope of the variables and functions for the following declarations:

```
float rate;    // global scope
// class declaration
class Test
{
  private:
```

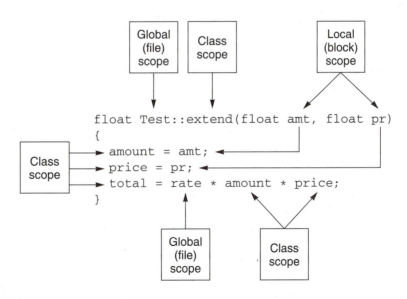

Figure 14.2   Examples of scopes

```
      float amount, price, total;   // class scope
   public:
      float extend(float, float);   // class scope
};
```

Static Class Members

As each class object is created it gets its own block of memory for its data members. In some cases, however, it is convenient for every instantiation of a class to share the same memory location for a specific variable. For example, consider a class consisting of employee records, where each employee is subject to the same state sales tax. Clearly we could make the sales tax a global variable, but this is not very safe. Such data could be modified anywhere in the program, could conflict with an identical variable name within a function, and certainly violates C++'s principle of data hiding.

This type of situation is handled in C++ by declaring a class variable to be static. Static data members share the same storage space for all objects of the class; as such, they act as global variables for the class and provide a means of communication between objects.

C++ requires that static variables be declared as such within the class's declaration section. Since a static data member requires only a single storage area, regardless of the number of class instantiations, it is defined in a single place outside of the class definition. This is typically done in the global part of the program where the class implementation section is provided. For example, assuming the class declaration

```
//class declaration
class Employee
{
  private:
    static float taxRate;
    int idNum;
  public:
    Employee(int);   //constructor
    void display();
}
```

the definition and initialization of the static variable taxRate is accomplished using a subsequent statement such as

```
float Employee::taxRate = 0.0025;
```

Here the scope resolution operator, ::, is used to identify taxRate as a member of the class Employee and the keyword static is not included. Program 14.4 uses this definition within the context of a complete program.

The output produced by Program 14.4 is

```
Employee number 11122 has a tax rate of 0.0025
Employee number 11133 has a tax rate of 0.0025
```

Program 14.4

```
include <iostream.h>

// class declaration
class Employee
{
  private:
    static float taxRate;
    int idNum;
  public:
    Employee(int);    // constructor
    void display();      // access function
};

// static member definition
float Employee::taxRate = 0.0025;

// class implementation
Employee::Employee(int num = 0)
{
  idNum = num;
}
void Employee::display()
{
  cout << "Employee number " << idNum
       << " has a tax rate of " << taxRate < endl;
}
int main()
{
  Employee emp1(11122), emp2(11133);

  emp1.display();
  emp2.display();

  return 0;
}
```

Although it might appear that the initialization of taxRate is global, it is not. Once the definition is made, any other definition will result in an error. Thus, the actual definition of a static member remains the responsibility of the class creator. The storage sharing produced by the static data member and the objects created in Program 14.4 are illustrated in Figure 14.3.

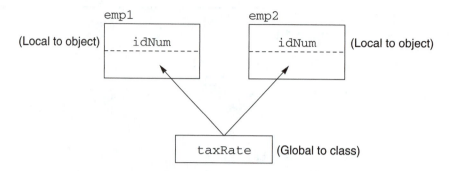

Figure 14.3 Sharing the static data member `taxRate`

In addition to static data members, static member functions can also be created. Such functions apply to a class as a whole rather than for individual class objects and can only access static data members and other static member functions of the class.[6] An example of such a function is provided by Program 14.5.

Program 14.5

```
#include <iostream.h>

// class declaration
class Employee
{
  private:
    static float taxRate;
    int idNum;
  public:
    Employee(int);       // constructor
    void display();         // access function
    static void disp();   // static function
};

// static member definition
float Employee::taxRate = 0.0025;

// class implementation
Employee::Employee(int num = 0)
{
```
(Continued on next page)

---

[6] The reason for this is that the `this` pointer, discussed next, is not passed to static member functions.

(Continued from previous page)

```cpp
   idNum = num;
}
void Employee::display()
{
   cout << "Employee number " << idNum
        << " has a tax rate of " << taxRate << endl;
}
void Employee::disp()
{
   cout << "The static tax rate is " << taxRate << endl;
}
int main()
{
   Employee::disp();    // call the static functions
   Employee emp1(11122), emp2(11133);

   emp1.display();
   emp2.display();

   return 0;
}
```

The output produced by Program 14.5 is

```
The static tax rate is 0.0025
Employee number 11122 has a tax rate of 0.0025
Employee number 11133 has a tax rate of 0.0025
```

In reviewing Program 14.5 notice that the keyword `static` is used only when static data and function members are declared: it is not included in the definition of these members. Also notice that the static member function is called using the resolution operator with the function's class name. Finally, since static functions access only static variables that are not contained within a specific object, static functions may be called before any instantiations are declared.

The `this` Pointer

Except for static data members, each class instance contains its own set of member variables, which are stored together in a separate data structure. This permits each object to have its own clearly defined state as determined by the values stored in its member variables.

For example, consider the `Date` class presented in Section 14.1, which is repeated here for convenience:

```
// class declaration
class Date
{
  private:
    int month;
    int day;
    int year;
  public:
    Date(int = 7, int = 4, int = 2001);  // constructor
    void showdate();                      // member function to display a Date
};

// class implementation
Date::Date(int mm, int dd, int yyyy)
{
  month = mm;
  day = dd;
  year = yyyy;
}
void Date::showdate()
{
  cout << setfill('0')
       << setw(2) << month << '/'
       << setw(2) << day << '/'
       << setw(2) << year % 100
       << endl;

  return;
}
```

Each time an object is created from this class, a separate structure in memory is set aside for its data members. For example, if two objects named a and b are created from this class, the memory storage for these objects would be as illustrated in Figure 14.4. Notice that each data structure has its own starting address in memory, which corresponds to the address of the first data member in the structure.

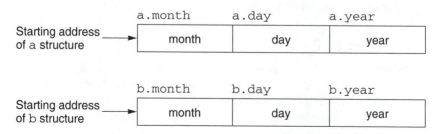

Figure 14.4   The storage of two Date objects in memory

This replication of data storage is not implemented for member functions. In fact, for each class *only one copy of the member functions is retained in memory,* and each object uses these same functions.

Sharing member functions requires providing a means of identifying which specific data structure a member function should be operating on. This is accomplished by providing address information to the function indicating where in memory the particular data structure, corresponding to a specific object, is located. This address is provided by the name of the object, which is in fact a reference name. For example, again using our `Date` class and assuming a is an object of this class, the statement `a.showdate()` passes the address of the a object into the `showdate()` member function.

An obvious question at this point is how this address is passed to `showdate()` and where it is stored. The answer is that the address is stored in a special pointer variable named `this`, which is automatically supplied as a hidden argument to each nonstatic member function when the function is called. For our `Date` class, which has two member functions, the parameter list of `Date()` is equivalent to

```
Date(Date *this, int mm, int dd, int yyyy)
```

and the parameter list of `showdate()` is equivalent to

```
showdate(Date *this)
```

That is, each member function actually receives an extra parameter that is the address of a data structure. Although it is usually not necessary to do so, this pointer data member can be explicitly used in member functions. For example, consider Program 14.6, which incorporates the `this` pointer in each of its member functions to access the appropriate instance variables.

 Program 14.6

```
#include <iostream.h>
#include <iomanip.h>

// class declaration
class Date
{
  private:
    int month;
    int day;
    int year;
  public:
    Date(int = 7, int = 4, int = 2001);    // constructor
    void showdate();                        // member function to display a date
};
```
(Continued on next page)

(Continued from previous page)

```
// class implementation
Date::Date(int mm, int dd, int yyyy)
{
  this->month = mm;
  this->day = dd;
  this->year = yyyy;
}
void Date::showdate(void)
{
  cout << setfill('0')
       << setw(2) << this->month << '/'
       << setw(2) << this->day << '/'
       << setw(2) << this->year % 100
       << endl;

  return;
}
int main()
{
  Date a(4,1,1999), b(12,18,2001); // declare two objects

  cout << "The date stored in a is originally ";
  a.showdate();  // display the original date
  a = b;            // assign b's value to a
  cout << "After assignment the date stored in a is ";
  a.showdate();  // display a's values

  return 0;
}
```

The output produced by Program 14.6 is

```
The date stored in a is originally 04/01/99
After assignment the date stored in a is 12/18/01
```

This is the same output produced by Program 14.1, which omits using the `this` pointer to access the data members. Clearly, using the `this` pointer in Program 14.6 is unnecessary and simply clutters the member function code. There are times, however, when an object must pass its address on to other functions. In these situations, one of which we will see in the next section, the address stored in the `this` pointer must be used explicitly.[7]

---

[7] The pointer notation used in Program 14.6 `this->` can be replaced by the equivalent notation `(*this)`..

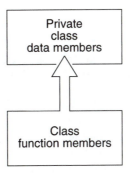

Figure 14.5   Direct access is provided to member functions

Friend Functions

The only method we currently have for accessing and manipulating private class data members is through the class's member functions. Conceptually, this arrangement can be viewed as illustrated in Figure 14.5. There are times, however, when it is useful to provide such access to selected nonmember functions.

Although the implementation and implications of using nonmember functions is beyond the scope of this text, the procedure for providing this external access is rather simple: The class maintains its own approved list of nonmember functions that are granted the same privileges as member functions. The nonmember functions on the list are called *friend functions,* and the list is referred to as a *friends list.*[8]

Figure 14.6 conceptually illustrates the use of such a list for nonmember access. Any function attempting access to an object's private data members is first checked against the friends list: if the function is on the list access is approved, otherwise access is denied.

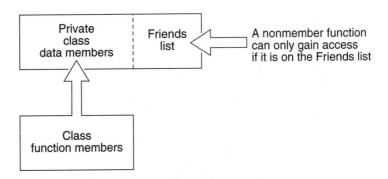

Figure 14.6   Access provided to nonmember functions

---

[8] For a complete discussion of friend functions refer to the author's *A First Book of C++,* also by Brooks/Cole Publishing Company.

Exercises 14.2

1. a. Rewrite Program 14.5 to include an integer static data member named numemps. This variable should act as a counter that is initialized to 0 and is incremented by the class constructor each time a new object is declared. Rewrite the static function disp() to display the value of this counter.

   b. Test the program written for Exercise 1a. Have the main() function call disp() after each Employee object is created.

2. a. Construct a class named Circle that contains two integer data members named xCenter and yCenter, and a floating point data member named radius. Additionally, the class should contain a static data member named scalefactor. Here the xCenter and yCenter values represent the center point of a circle, radius represents the circle's actual radius, and scalefactor represents a scale factor that will be used to scale the circle to fit on a variety of display devices.

   b. Include the class written for Exercise 2a in a working C++ program.

3. Rewrite the Date(), setdate(), and showdate() member functions in Program 13.11 to explicitly use the this pointer when referencing all data members. Run your program and verify that the same output as produced by Program 13.11 is achieved.

4. a. Construct a class named Coord that contains two floating point data members named xval and yval, which will be used to store the x and y values of a point in rectangular coordinates. The function members should include appropriate constructor and display functions and a member function named PolarToRect(). The PolarToRect() function should accept two floating point numbers that represent a point in polar coordinates and convert them into rectangular coordinates. For conversion from polar to rectangular coordinates use the formulas

$$x = r \cos \theta$$
$$y = r \sin \theta$$

   b. Include the program written for Exercise 7a in a working C++ program.

14.3 Operator Functions

A simple assignment operator was constructed in Section 14.1. In this section we extend this capability and show how to broaden C++'s built-in operators to class objects. As we will discover, class operators are themselves either member or friend functions.

The only symbols permitted for user-defined purposes are the subset of C++'s built-in symbols listed in Table 14.1. Each of these symbols may be adopted for class use with almost no limitation on its meaning.[9] This is done by making each operation a function that can be overloaded like any other function.

---

[9] The only limitation is that the syntax of the operator cannot be changed. Thus, a binary operator must remain binary and a unary operator must remain unary. Within this syntax restriction, an operator symbol can be used to produce any operation, whether or not the operation is consistent with the symbol's accepted usage. For example, we could redefine the addition symbol to provide multiplication. Clearly this violates the intent and spirit of making these symbols available to us. We shall be very careful to redefine each symbol in a manner consistent with its accepted usage.

Table 14.1   Operators available for class use

Operator	Description
() [] -> new delete	Function call Array element Structure member pointer reference Dynamically allocate memory Dynamically deallocate memory
++ -- - ! ~ *	Increment Decrement Unary minus Logical negation Bitwise complement Indirection
* / % + -	Multiplication Division Modulus (remainder) Addition Subtraction
<< >>	Left shift Right shift
< <= > >= == != && ||	Less than Less than or equal to Greater than Greater than or equal to Equal to Not equal to Logical AND Logical OR
& ^ |	Bitwise AND Bitwise exclusive OR Bitwise inclusive OR
= += -= *= /= %= &= ^= |= <<= >>=	Assignment Assignment Assignment Assignment Assignment
,	Comma

The operation of the symbols listed in Table 14.1 can be redefined as we see fit for our classes, subject to the following restrictions:

1. Symbols not in Table 14.1 cannot be redefined. For example, the `.`, `::`, and `?:` symbols cannot be redefined.

2. New operator symbols cannot be created. For example, since %% is not an operator in C++, it cannot be defined as a class operator.

3. Neither the precedence nor the associativity of C++'s operators can be modified. Thus, you cannot give the addition operator a higher precedence than the multiplication operator.

4. Operators cannot be redefined for C++'s built-in types.

5. A C++ operator that is unary cannot be changed to a binary operator, and a binary operator cannot be changed to a unary operator.

6. The operator must either be a member of a class or be defined to take at least one class member as an operand.

The first step in providing a class with operators from Table 14.1 is to decide which operations make sense for the class and how they should be defined. As a specific example, we continue to build on the `Date` class introduced previously. For this class, a small, meaningful set of class operations is defined.

Clearly, the addition of two dates is not meaningful. The addition of a date with an integer, however, does make sense if the integer is taken as the number of days to be added to the date. Likewise, the subtraction of an integer from a date makes sense. Also, the subtraction of two dates is meaningful if we define the difference to mean the number of days between the two dates. Similarly, it makes sense to compare two dates and determine if the dates are equal or one date occurs before or after another date. Let's now see how these operations can be implemented using C++'s operator symbols.

A user-defined operation is created as a function that redefines C++'s built-in operator symbols of class use. Functions that define operations on class objects and use C++'s built-in operator symbols are referred to as *operator functions.*

Operator functions are declared and implemented in the same manner as all member functions, with one exception: it is the function's name that connects the appropriate operator symbol to the operation defined by the function. An operator function's name is always of the form `operator <symbol>` where `<symbol>` is one of the operators listed in Table 14.1. For example, the function name `operator+` is the name of the addition function, while the function name `operator==` is the name of the "equal to" comparison function.

Once the appropriate function name is selected, the process of writing the function simply amounts to having it accept the desired input and produce the correct returned value.[10] For example, in comparing two `Date` objects for equality, we would select C++'s equality operator. Thus, the name of our function becomes `operator==`. We would want our comparison operation to accept two `Date` objects, internally compare them, and return an integer value indicating the result of the comparison (for example, 1 for equality and 0 for inequality). As a member function a suitable prototype that could be included in the class declaration section is

```
int operator==(Date&);
```

---

[10] As previously noted, this implies that the specified operator can be redefined to perform any operation. Good programming practice, however, dictates against such redefinitions.

This prototype indicates that the function is named `operator==`, that it returns an integer, and that it accepts a reference to a `Date` object.[11] Only one `Date` object is required here because the second `Date` object is the object that calls the function. Let's now write the function definition to be included in the class implementation section. Assuming our class is named `Date`, a suitable definition is

```
int Date::operator==(Date& date2)
{
  if( day == date2.day && month == date2.month && year == date2.year)
    return (1);
  else
    return(0);
}
```

Once this function has been defined, it may be called using the same syntax as for C++'s built-in types. For example, if a and b are objects of type `Date`, the expression `if (a == b)` is valid. Program 14.7 includes this `if` statement as well as the declaration and definition of this operator function within the context of a complete program.

The output produced by Program 14.7 is

```
Dates a and b are not the same.
Dates a and c are the same.
```

The first new feature illustrated in Program 14.7 is the declaration and implementation of the function named `operator==()`. Except for its name, this operator function is constructed in the same manner as any other member function: it is declared in the declaration section and defined in the implementation section. The second new feature is how the function is called. Operator functions may be called using their associated symbols rather than in the way other functions are called. Because operator functions are true functions, however, the traditional method of calling them can also be used—specifying their names and including appropriate arguments. Thus, in addition to being called by the expression a == b in Program 14.7, the call `a.operator==(b)` could also have been used.

Let's now create another operator for our `Date` class—an addition operator. As before, creating this operator requires that we specify three items:

1. The name of the operator function
2. The processing that the function is to perform
3. The data type, if any, that the function is to return

---

[11] The prototype `int operator==(Date)` also works. Passing a reference, however, is preferable to passing an object because it reduces the function call's overhead. This is because passing an object means that a copy of the object must be made for the called function, while passing a reference gives the function direct access to the object whose address is passed.

Program 14.7

```cpp
#include <iostream.h>

// class declaration
class Date
{
  private:
    int month;
    int day;
    int year;
  public:
    Date(int = 7, int = 4, int = 2001);  // constructor
    int operator==(Date &);              // declare the operator== function
};

// implementation section
Date::Date(int mm, int dd, int yyyy)
{
  month = mm;
  day = dd;
  year = yyyy;
}
int Date::operator==(Date& date2)
{
  if(day == date2.day && month == date2.month && year == date2.year)
    return (1);
  else
    return(0);
}
int main()
{
    Date a(4,1,1999), b(12,18,2001), c(4,1,1999); // declare 3 objects

    if (a == b)
      cout << "Dates a and b are the same." << endl;
    else
      cout << "Dates a and b are not the same." << endl;

    if (a == c)
      cout << "Dates a and c are the same." << endl;
    else
      cout << "Dates a and c are not the same." << endl;

    return 0;
}
```

For addition we will, of course, name the operator function `operator+`. Having selected the function's name, we must now determine what we want this function to do, as it specifically relates to `Date` objects. As noted previously, the sum of two dates makes no sense. Adding an integer to a date is meaningful, however, when the integer represents the number of days either before or after the given date. Here the sum of an integer to a `Date` object is simply another `Date` object, which should be returned by the addition operation. Thus, a suitable prototype of our addition function is

```
Date operator+(int);
```

This prototype is included in the class declaration section. It specifies that an integer is to be added to a class object and the operation returns a `Date` object. Thus, if a is a `Date` object, the function call `a.operator+(284)`, or its more commonly used alternative, `a + 284`, should cause the number `284` to be correctly added to a's date value. We must now construct the function to accomplish this.

Constructing the function requires that we first select a specific date convention. For simplicity we will adopt the special financial date convention that considers each month to consist of 30 days and each year to consist of 360 days. Using this convention our function will first add the integer number of days to the `Date` object's `day` value and then adjust the resulting `day` value to lie within the range 1 to 30 and the `month` value to lie within the range 1 to 12. A function that accomplishes this is

```
Date operator+(int days)
{
  Date temp;   // a temporary Date object to store the result

  temp.day = day + days;    // add the days
  temp.month = month;
  temp.year = year;
  while (temp.day > 30)     // now adjust the months
  {
    temp.month++;
    temp.day -= 30;
  }
  while (temp.month > 12)   // adjust the years
  {
    temp.year++;
    temp.month -= 12;
  }
  return temp;       // the values in temp are returned
}
```

The important feature to notice here is the use of the `temp` object. The purpose of this object is to ensure that none of the function's arguments, which become the operator's operands, are altered. To understand this consider a statement that uses this operator function, such as `b = a + 284;`, where a and b are `Date` objects. This statement should never modify a's value. Rather, the expression a + 284 should yield a Date value that is then assigned to b. The result of the expression is, of course, the Date object called temp that is returned by the operator+() function. Without using the temp object the 284 would have to be added to the a object directly, as in the following code:

```
Date operator+(int days)     // BAD CODE - Date OPERAND IS CHANGED
{
  day = day + days;     // add the days - this changes the Date operand
    while (day > 30)     // now adjust the months
  {
    month++;
    day -= 30;
  }
  while (month > 12)   // adjust the years
  {
    year++;
    month -= 12;
  }
  return *this;        // the values in calling object are returned
}
```

Although this function returns the correct value, it also alters the value of its Date operand, which is the object making the call. The correct version of this function is included in Program 14.8.

Program 14.8

```
#include <iostream.h>
#include <iomanip.h>

// class declaration
class Date
{
  private:
    int month;
    int day;
    int year;
  public:
    Date(int = 7, int = 4, int = 2001);    // constructor
    Date operator+(int);                   // overload the + operator
    void showdate();                       // member function to display a date
};

// implementation section
Date::Date(int mm, int dd, int yyyy)
{
```

(Continued on next page)

(Continued from previous page)

```cpp
  month = mm;
  day = dd;
  year = yyyy;
}
Date Date::operator+(int days)
{
  Date temp;  // a temporary date object to store the result

  temp.day = day + days;  // add the days
  temp.month = month;
  temp.year = year;
  while (temp.day  30)    // now adjust the months
  {
    temp.month++;
    temp.day -= 30;
  }
  while (temp.month  12)  // adjust the years
  {
    temp.year++;
    temp.month -= 12;
  }
  return temp;       // the values in temp are returned
}
void Date::showdate()
{
  cout << setfill('0')
       << setw(2) << month << '/'
       << setw(2) << day << '/'
       << setw(2) << year % 100
       << endl;

  return;
}
int main()
{
   Date a(4,1,1999), b; // declare two objects

   cout << "The initial date is ";
   a.showdate();
   b = a + 284;    // add in 284 days = 9 months and 14 days
   cout << "The new date is ";
   b.showdate();

   return 0;
}
```

The output produced by Program 14.8 is

```
The initial date is 04/01/99
The new date is 01/15/00
```

We can actually improve on the `operator+()` function contained in Program 14.8 by initializing the `temp` object with the value of its calling `Date` object. This is accomplished using either of the following declarations:

```
Date temp(*this);
Date temp = *this;
```

Both declarations initialize the `temp` object with the object pointed to by the `this` pointer, which is the calling `Date` object. If the initialization is done, the first assignment statement in the function can be altered to

```
temp.day += days;
```

The Assignment Operator Revisited

In Section 14.1 a simple assignment operator function was presented and is repeated here for convenience.

```
void Date::operator=(Date& newdate)
{
  day = newdate.day;        // assign the day
  month = newdate.month;    // assign the month
  year = newdate.year;      // assign the year
}
```

The drawback of this function is that it returns no value, making multiple assignments such as `a = b = c` impossible. Now that we have introduced operator functions with return types and have the `this` pointer at our disposal, we can fix our simple assignment operator function to provide an appropriate return type. In this case the return value should be a `Date`. Thus, an appropriate prototype of our operator is

```
Date operator=(Date&);
```

A suitable function for this prototype is

```
Date operator=(Date& newdate)
{

  day = newdate.day;        // assign the day
  month = newdate.month;    // assign the month
  year = newdate.year;      // assign the year
```

```
        return *this;
      }
```

In the case of an assignment such as b = c, or its equivalent form, b.operator=(c), the function first alters b's member values from within the function and then returns the value of this object, which may be used in a subsequent assignment. Thus, as illustrated in Program 14.9, a multiple assignment expression such as a = b = c is possible.

 Program 14.9

```
#include <iostream.h>
#include <iomanip.h>

// class declaration
class Date
{
  private:
    int month;
    int day;
    int year;
  public:
    Date(int = 7, int = 4, int = 2001);     // constructor
    Date operator=(const Date&);            // define assignment of a date
    void showdate();                        // member function to display a date
};

// implementation section
Date::Date(int mm, int dd, int yyyy)
{
  month = mm;
  day = dd;
  year = yyyy;
}
Date Date::operator=(const Date& newdate)
{

  day = newdate.day;       // assign the day
  month = newdate.month;   // assign the month
  year = newdate.year;     // assign the year

  return *this;
}
void Date::showdate()
{
```

(Continued on next page)

(Continued from previous page)

```
  cout << setfill('0')
       << setw(2) << month << '/'
       << setw(2) << day << '/'
       << setw(2) << year % 100
       << endl;

  return;
}
int main()
{
   Date a(4,1,1999), b(12,18,2001), c(1,2,2003); // declare three objects

   cout << "Before assignment a's date value is ";
   a.showdate();
   cout << "Before assignment b's date value is ";
   b.showdate();
   cout << "Before assignment c's date value is ";
   c.showdate();

   a = b = c;    // multiple assignment

   cout << "\nAfter assignment a's date value is ";
   a.showdate();
   cout << "After assignment b's date value is ";
   b.showdate();
   cout << "After assignment c's date value is ";
   c.showdate();

   return 0;
}
```

The output produced by Program 14.9 is

```
Before assignment a's date value is 04/01/99
Before assignment b's date value is 12/18/01
Before assignment c's date value is 01/02/03

After assignment a's date value is 01/02/03
After assignment b's date value is 01/02/03
After assignment c's date value is 01/02/03
```

The only restriction on the assignment operator function is that it can be overloaded only as a member function. It cannot be overloaded as a friend.

Exercises 14.3

1. a. Define a "greater than" relational operator function named `operator>()` that can be used with the `Date` class declared in Program 14.7.

   b. Define a "less than" operator function named `operator<()` that can be used with the `Date` class declared in Program 14.7.

   c. Include the operator functions written for Exercises 1a and 1b in a working C++ program.

2. a. Define a subtraction operator function named `operator-()` that can be used with the `Date` class defined in Program 14.7. The subtraction should accept a long integer argument that represents the number of days to be subtracted from an object's `Date` and return a `Date`. In doing the subtraction, use the special financial assumption that all months have 30 days and all years have 360 days. Additionally, an end-of-month adjustment should be made, if necessary, that converts any resulting day of 31 to a day of 30, except if the month is February. If the resulting month is February and the day is either 29, 30, or 31, it should be changed to 28.

   b. Define another subtraction operator function named `operator-()` that can be used with the `Date` class defined in Program 14.7. The subtraction should yield a long integer that represents the difference in days between two dates. In calculating the day difference use the financial day count basis that assumes all months have 30 days and all years have 360 days.

   c. Include the overloaded operators written for Exercises 2a and 2b in a working C++ program.

3. a. Determine if the following addition operator function provides the same result as the function used in Program 14.8.

```
Date Date::operator+(int days)    // return a Date object
{
  Date temp;

  temp.day = day + days;    // add the days in
  temp.month = month + int(day/30);       // determine total months
  temp.day = temp.day % 30;               // determine actual day
  temp.year = year + int(temp.month/12);  // determine total years
  temp.month = temp.month % 12;           // determine actual month

  return temp;
}
```

   b. Verify your answer to Exercise 3a by including the function in a working C++ program.

4. a. Rewrite the addition operator function in Program 14.7 to account for the actual days in a month, neglecting leap years.

   b. Verify the operation of the operator function written for Exercise 4a by including it within a working C++ program.

5. a. Construct an addition operator for the `Complex` class declared for Exercise 3a in Section 14.1. This should be a member function that adds two complex numbers and returns a complex number.

   b. Add a member multiplication operator function to the program written for Exercise 5a that multiplies two complex numbers and returns a complex number.

   c. Verify the operation of the operator functions written for Exercises 5a and 5b by including them within a working C++ program.

6. a. Create a class named `String` and include an addition operator function that concatenates two strings. The function should return a `String` object.

   b. Include the overloaded operator written for Exercise 6a within a working C++ program.

14.4 Data Type Conversions

The conversion from one built-in data type to another was previously described in Section 12.1. With the introduction of user-defined data types, the possibilities for conversion between data types expands to the following cases:

1. Conversion from built-in type to built-in type
2. Conversion from built-in type to user-defined (class) type
3. Conversion from user-defined (class) type to built-in type
4. Conversion from user-defined (class) type to user-defined (class) type

The first conversion is handled by either C++'s built-in implicit conversion rules or its explicit cast operator. The second conversion type is made using a *type conversion constructor*. The third and fourth conversion types are made using a *conversion operator function*. In this section the specific means of performing each of these conversions is presented.

Built-in to Built-in Conversion

The conversion from one built-in data type to another has already been presented in Section 12.1. To review this case briefly, this type of conversion is either implicit or explicit.

An implicit conversion occurs in the context of one of C++'s operations For example, when a floating point value is assigned to an integer variable only the integer portion of the value is stored. The conversion is implied by the operation and is performed automatically by the compiler.

An explicit conversion occurs whenever a cast is used. In C++ two cast notations exist. Using the older C notation, a cast has the form `(data-type) expression`, whereas the newer C++ notation has the functionlike form `data-type(expression)`. For example, both of the expressions `(int)24.32` and `int(24.32)` cause the floating point value `24.32` to be truncated to the integer value `24`.

Built-in to User-defined (Class) Conversion

User-defined casts of converting a built-in to a user-defined data type are created using constructor functions. A constructor whose first argument is not a member of its class and whose remaining arguments, if any, have default values is a *type conversion constructor*. If the first argument of a type conversion constructor is a built-in data type, the constructor can be used to cast the built-in data type to a class object. Clearly, one restriction of such functions is that, as constructors, they must be member functions.

Although this type of cast occurs when the constructor is invoked to initialize an object, it is actually a more general cast than might be evident at first glance. This is because a constructor function can be explicitly invoked after all objects have been declared, whether or not it was invoked previously as part of an object's declaration. Before exploring this further, let's first construct a type conversion constructor. We will then see how to use it as a cast independent of its initialization purpose.

The cast we construct converts a long integer into a `Date` object. Our `Date` object will consist of dates in the form *month/day/year* and use our by now familiar `Date` class. The long integer is used to represent dates in the form *year * 10000 + month * 100 + day*. For example, using this representation the date 12/31/2002 becomes the long integer 20021231. Dates represented in this fashion are very useful for two reasons: first, it permits a date to be stored as a single integer, and second, such dates are in numerically increasing date order, making sorting extremely easy. For example, the date 01/03/2002, which occurs after 12/31/2001, becomes the integer 20020103, which is larger than 20011231. Because the integers representing dates can exceed the size of a normal integer the integers are always declared as long integers.

A suitable constructor function for converting from a long integer date to a date stored as a month, day, and year is

```
// type conversion constructor from long to Date

Date::Date(long findate)
{
  year = int(findate/10000.0);
  month = int((findate - year * 10000.0)/100.0);
  day = int(findate - year * 10000.0 - month * 100.0);
}
```

Program 14.10 uses this type conversion constructor both as an initialization function at declaration time and as an explicit cast later on in the program.

📺 Program 14.10

```
#include <iostream.h>
#include <iomanip.h>

class Date
{
  private:
    int month, day, year;
  public:
    Date(int = 7, int = 4, int = 2001);   // constructor
    Date(long);                           // type conversion constructor
    void showdate();
};
// constructor
Date::Date(int mm, int dd, int yyyy)                          *(Continued on next page)*
```

(Continued from previous page)

```cpp
{
  month = mm;
  day = dd;
  year = yyyy;
}
// type conversion constructor from long to Date
Date::Date(long findate)
{
  year = int(findate/10000.0);
  month = int((findate - year * 10000.0)/100.0);
  day = int(findate - year * 10000.0 - month * 100.0);
}
// member function to display a date
void Date::showdate()
{
  cout << setfill('0')
       << setw(2) << month << '/'
       << setw(2) << day << '/'
       << setw(2) << year % 100;

  return;
}
int main()
{
  Date a, b(20011225L), c(4,1,1999); // declare 3 objects - initialize 2 of them

  cout << "Dates a, b, and c are ";
  a.showdate();
  cout << ", ";
  b.showdate();
  cout << ", and ";
  c.showdate();
  cout << ".\n";

  a = Date(20020103L);  // cast a long to a Date

  cout << "Date a is now ";
  a.showdate();
  cout << ".\n";

  return 0;
}
```

The output produced by Program 14.10 is

```
Dates a, b, and c are 07/04/01, 12/25/01, and 04/01/99.
Date a is now 01/03/02.
```

The change in a's date value illustrated by this output is produced by the assignment expression a = Date(20020103L), which uses a type conversion constructor to perform the cast from long to Date.

User-defined (Class) to Built-in Conversion

Conversion from a user-defined data type to a built-in data type is accomplished using a *conversion operator function,* which is a member operator function having the name of a built-in data type or class. When the operator function has a built-in data type name it is used to convert from a class to a built-in data type. For example, a conversion operator function for casting a class object to a long integer would have the name operator long(). Here, the name of the operator function indicates that conversion to a long integer will take place. If this function were part of a Date class, it would be used to cast a Date object into a long integer. This usage is illustrated by Program 14.11.

 Program 14.11

```
#include <iostream.h>
#include <iomanip.h>

// class declaration for Date
class Date
{
  private:
    int month, day, year;
  public:
    Date(int = 7, int = 4, int = 2001);     // constructor
    operator long();                        // conversion operator function
    void showdate();
};
// constructor
Date::Date(int mm, int dd, int yyyy)
{
  month = mm;
  day = dd;
  year = yyyy;
}
// conversion operator function converting from Date to long
Date::operator long()    // must return a long
```

(Continued on next page)

(Continued from previous page)

```
{
  long yyyymmdd;

  yyyymmdd = year * 10000.0 + month * 100.0 + day;
  return(yyyymmdd);
}
// member function to display a date
void Date::showdate()
{
  cout << setfill('0')
       << setw(2) << month << '/'
       << setw(2) << day << '/'
       << setw(2) << year % 100
       << endl;

  return;
}
int main()
{
  Date a(4,1,1999);   // declare and initialize one object of type Date
  long b;             // declare an object of type long

  b = a;              // a conversion takes place here

  cout << "a's date is ";
  a.showdate();
  cout << "This date, as a long integer, is " << b << endl;

  return 0;
}
```

The output produced by Program 14.11 is

```
a's date is 04/01/99
This date, as a long integer, is 19990401
```

The change in a's date value to a long integer illustrated by this output is produced by the assignment expression b = a. This assignment, which also could have been written as b = long(a), calls the conversion operator function long() to perform the cast from Date to long. In general, since explicit conversion more clearly documents what is happening, its use is preferred to implicit conversion.

Notice that the conversion operator function has no explicit parameter and has no explicit return type. This is true of all conversion operators: its implicit parameter is always an object of the class being cast from, and the return type is implied by the name of the function. Additionally, as previously indicated, a conversion operator function *must* be a member function.

User-defined (Class) to User-defined (Class) Conversion

Converting from a user-defined data type to a user-defined data type is performed in the same manner as a cast from a user-defined to built-in data type—using a member *conversion operator function.* In this case, however, the operator function uses the class name being converted to rather than a built-in data name. For example, if two classes named `Date` and `Intdate` exist, the operator function named `operator Intdate()` could be placed in the `Date` class to convert from a `Date` object to an `Intdate` object. Similarly, the operator function named `Date()` could be placed in the `Intdate` class to convert from an `Intdate` to a `Date`.

Notice that, as before, in converting from a user-defined data type to a built-in data type, *the operator function's name determines the result of the conversion;* the class containing the operator function determines the data type being converted from.

Before providing a specific example of a class-to-class conversion, one additional point must be noted. Converting between classes clearly implies that we have two classes, one of which is defined first and the other second. Having within the second class a conversion operator function with the name of the first class poses no problem because the compiler knows of the first class's existence. However, including a conversion operator function with the second class's name in the first class does pose a problem because the second class has not yet been defined. This is remedied by including a declaration for the second class prior to the first class's definition. This declaration, which is formally referred to as a *forward declaration,* is illustrated in Program 14.12, which also includes conversion operators between the two defined classes.

 Program 14.12

```
#include <iostream.h>
#include <iomanip.h>

// forward declaration of class Intdate
class Intdate;

// class declaration for Date
class Date
{
  private:
    int month, day, year;
  public:
    Date(int = 7, int = 4, int = 2001);    // constructor
    operator Intdate();                     // conversion operator Date to Intdate
    void showdate();
};
```

(Continued on next page)

(Continued from previous page)

```
// class declaration for Intdate
class Intdate
{
  private:
    long yyyymmdd;
  public:
    Intdate(long = 0);     // constructor
    operator Date();       // conversion operator Intdate to Date
    void showint();
};

// class implementation for Date
Date::Date(int mm, int dd, int yyyy)   // constructor
{
  month = mm;
  day = dd;
  year = yyyy;
}
// conversion operator function converting from Date to Intdate class
Date::operator Intdate()   // must return an Intdate object
{
  long temp;

  temp = year * 10000.0 + month * 100.0 + day;
  return(Intdate(temp));
}
// member function to display a Date object
void Date::showdate()
{
  cout << setfill('0')
       << setw(2) << month << '/'
       << setw(2) << day << '/'
       << setw(2) << year % 100;

  return;
}

// class implementation for Intdate
Intdate::Intdate(long ymd)   // constructor
{
  yyyymmdd = ymd;
}
// conversion operator function converting from Intdate to Date class
Intdate::operator Date()     // must return a Date object
```

(Continued on next page)

(Continued from previous page)

```
{
  int mo, day, yr;

  yr = int(yyyymmdd/10000.0);
  mo = int((yyyymmdd - yr * 10000.0)/100.0);
  da = int(yyyymmdd - yr * 10000.0 - mo * 100.0);
  return(Date(mo,da,yr));
}
// member function to display an Intdate object
void Intdate::showint()
{
  cout << yyyymmdd;
}
int main()
{
  Date a(4,1,1999), b;      // declare two Date objects
  Intdate c(20011215L), d;  // declare two Intdate Objects

  b = Date(c);       // cast c into a Date object
  d = Intdate(a);    // cast a into an Intdate object

  cout << " a's date is ";
  a.showdate();
  cout << "\n   as an Intdate object this date is ";
  d.showint();

  cout << "\n c's date is ";
  c.showint();
  cout << "\n   as a Date object this date is ";
  b.showdate();

  return 0;
}
```

The output produced by Program 14.12 is

```
a's date is 04/01/99
   as an Intdate object this date is 19990401
c's date is 20011215
   as a Date object this date is 12/15/01
```

As illustrated by Program 14.12, the cast from `Date` to `Intdate` is produced by the assignment `b = Date(c)` and the cast from `Intdate` to `Date` is produced by the assignment d = Intdate(a). Alternatively, the assignments b = c and d = a produce the same results. Notice also the forward declaration of the Intdate class prior to the Date class's declaration. This is required so that the Date class can reference Intdate in its operator conversion function.

Exercises 14.4

1. a. Define the four data type conversions available in C++ and the method of accomplishing each conversion.

b. Define the terms "type conversion constructor" and "conversion operator function" and describe how they are used in user-defined conversions.

2. Write a C++ program that declares a class named Time having integer data members named hours, minutes, and seconds. Include in the program a type conversion constructor that converts a long integer, representing the elapsed seconds from midnight, into an equivalent representation as *hours:minutes:seconds*. For example, the long integer 30336 should convert to the time 8:25:36. Use a military representation of time so that 2:30 P.M. is represented as 14:30:00. The relationship between time representations is

*elapsed seconds = hours * 3600 + minutes * 60 + seconds.*

3. A Julian date is a date represented as the number of days from a known base date. One algorithm for converting from a Gregorian date, in the form *month/day/year,* to a Julian date with a base date of 0/0/0 is given below. All of the calculations in this algorithm use integer arithmetic, which means that the fractional part of all divisions must be discarded. In this algorithm, M = month, D = day, and Y = 4-digit year.

If M is less than or equal to 2
 Set the variable MP = 0 and YP = Y – 1
Else
 *Set MP = int(0.4 * M + 2.3) and YP = Y*

T = int(YP/4) – int(YP/100) + int(YP/400)
*Julian date = 365 * Y + 31 * (M – 1) + D + T – MP*

Using this algorithm modify Program 14.11 to cast from a Gregorian date object to its corresponding Julian representation as a long integer. Test your program using the Gregorian dates 1/31/1985 and 3/16/1986, which correspond to the Julian dates 725037 and 725446, respectively.

4. Modify the program written for Exercise 2 to include a member conversion operator function that converts an object of type Time into a long integer representing the number of seconds from twelve o'clock midnight.

5. Write a C++ program that has a Date class and a Julian class. The Date class should be the same Date class as that used in Program 14.12, while the Julian class should represent a date as a long integer. For this program include a member conversion operator function within the Date class that converts a Date object to a Julian object, using the algorithm presented in Exercise 3. Test your program by converting the dates 1/31/1995 and 3/15/1996, which correspond to the Julian dates 728689 and 729099, respectively.

6. Write a C++ program that has a `Time` class and an `Ltime` class. The `Time` class should have integer data members named `hours`, `minutes`, and `seconds`, while the `Ltime` class should have a long data member named `elsecs`, which represents the number of elapsed seconds since midnight. For the `Time` class include a member conversion operator function named `Ltime()` that converts a `Time` object to an `Ltime` object. For the `Ltime` class include a member conversion operator function named `Time()` that converts an `Ltime` object to a `Time` object.

14.5   Class Inheritance

The ability to create new classes from existing ones is the underlying motivation and power behind class and object-oriented programming techniques. Creating new classes from existing ones facilitates reusing existing code in new ways without the need for retesting and revalidation. It permits the designers of a class to make it available to others for additions and extensions, without relinquishing control over the existing class features.

Constructing one class from another is accomplished using a capability called inheritance. Related to this capability is an equally important feature named polymorphism. Polymorphism provides the ability to redefine how member functions of related classes operate based on the class object being accessed. In fact, for a programming language to be classified as an object-oriented language it must provide the features of classes, inheritance, and polymorphism. In this section we describe the inheritance and polymorphism features provided in C++.

Inheritance

Inheritance is the capability of deriving one class from another class. The initial class used as the basis for the derived class is referred to as either the *base, parent,* or *superclass.* The derived class is referred to as either the *derived, child,* or *subclass.*

A derived class is a completely new class that incorporates all of the data and member functions of its base class. It can, and usually does, however, add its own additional new data and function members and can override any base class function.

As an example of inheritance, consider three geometric shapes consisting of a circle, cylinder, and sphere. All of these shapes share a common characteristic, and we can make the circle a base type for the other two shapes, as illustrated in Figure 14.7.[12] Reformulating these shapes as class types we would make the circle the base class and derive the cylinder and sphere classes from it.

The relationships illustrated in Figure 14.7 are examples of simple inheritance. In *simple inheritance,* each derived type has only one immediate base type. The complement to simple inheritance is multiple inheritance. In *multiple inheritance,* a derived type has two or more base types. Figure 14.8 illustrates an example of multiple inheritance. In this text, we will only consider simple inheritance.

---

[12] By convention, arrows always point from the derived class to the base class.

Programming Note

Object-Based versus Object-Oriented Languages

An *object-based* language is one in which data and operations can be incorporated together in a structure in such a way that data values can be isolated and accessed through the specified functions. C is not an object-based language because its structures only permit data members, and these data members can be accessed directly as individual data variables. The ability to bind the data members with operations in a single unit is referred to as *encapsulation*.

For a language to be classified as *object-oriented*, it must also provide inheritance and polymorphism. *Inheritance* is the capability to derive one abstract data type from another. A derived data type is a completely new data type that incorporates all of the data members and member functions of the original data type plus any new data and function members unique to itself. The data type used as the basis for the derived type is referred to as the *base* or *parent* type, and the derived data type is referred to as the *derived* or *child* type.

Polymorphism permits the same function name to invoke one operation in objects of a parent data type and a different operation in objects of a derived data type.

Since C does not provide encapsulation, it is neither an object-based nor object-oriented language. C++, which provides encapsulation, inheritance, and polymorphism, is an object-oriented language.

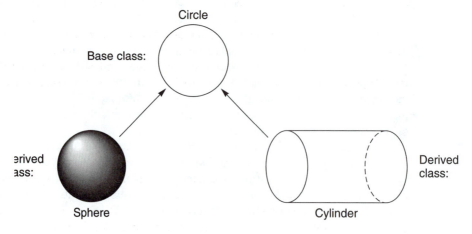

Figure 14.7   Relating object types

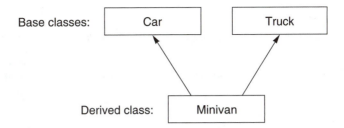

Figure 14.8   An example of multiple inheritance

The class derivations illustrated in both Figures 14.7 and 14.8 are formally referred to as *class hierarchies* because they illustrate the hierarchy, or order, in which one class is derived from another. Let's now see how to derive one class from another.

A derived class has the same form as any other class in that it consists of both a declaration and an implementation. The only difference is in the first line of the declaration section. For a derived class this line is extended to include an access specification and a base class name and has the form:

```
class derivedClassName : class-access BaseClassName
```

For example, if `Circle` is the name of an existing class, a new class named `Cylinder` can be derived as follows:

```
class cylinder : public Circle
{
    // add any additional data and
    // function members here
}; // end of Cylinder class declaration
```

Except for the class-access specifier after the colon and the base class name, there is nothing inherently new or complicated about the construction of the `Cylinder` class. Before providing a description of the `Circle` class and adding data and function members to the derived `Cylinder` class, we will need to reexamine access specifiers and how they relate to derived classes.

Access Specifications

Until now we have used only private and public access specifiers within a class. Giving all data members private status ensured that they could be accessed only by class member functions or friends. This restricted access prevents access by any nonclass functions (except friends), *which also precludes access by any derived class functions.* This is a sensible restriction; if it did not exist anyone could "jump around" the private restriction by simply deriving a class.

Table 14.2 Inherited access restrictions

Base Class Member	Derived Class Access	Derived Class Member
private ➤	: `private` ➤	inaccessible
protected ➤	: `private` ➤	private
public ➤	: `private` ➤	private
private ➤	: `public` ➤	inaccessible
protected ➤	: `public` ➤	protected
public ➤	: `public` ➤	public
private ➤	: `protected` ➤	inaccessible
protected ➤	: `protected` ➤	protected
public ➤	: `protected` ➤	protected

To retain a restricted type of access across derived classes, C++ provides a third access specification—protected. Protected access behaves identically to private access in that it permits only member or friend function access, but it permits this restriction to be inherited by any derived class. The derived class then defines the type of inheritance it is willing to take on, subject to the base class's access restrictions. This is done by the class-access specifier, which is listed after the colon at the start of its declaration section. Table 14.2 lists the resulting derived class member access based on the base class member specifications and the derived class-access specifier.

The shaded region of Table 14.2 shows that if a base class member has a protected access and the derived class specifier is public, then the derived class member is protected to its class. Similarly, if a base class has a public access and the derived class specifier is public, the derived class member is public. As this is the most commonly used type of specification for base class data and function members respectively, it is the one we will use. This means that for all classes intended for use as a base class we will use a protected data member access in place of a private designation.

An Example

To illustrate the process of deriving one class from another we will derive a Cylinder class from a base `Circle` class. The definition of the `Circle` class is

```
class Circle
{
  protected:
    double radius;
  public:
    Circle(double = 1.0);  // constructor
    double calcval();
};
```

```
// class implementation
Circle::Circle(double r)     // constructor
{
  radius = r;
}
double Circle::calcval()    // this calculates an area
{
  return(pi * radius * radius);
}
```

Except for the substitution of the access specifier `protected` in place of the usual `private` specifier for the data member, this is a standard class definition. The only variable not defined is `PI`, which is used in the `calcval()` function. We define this as

```
double PI = 2.0 * asin(1.0);
```

This is simply a "trick" that forces the computer to return the value of `PI` accurate to as many decimal places as allowed by your computer. This value is obtained by taking the arcsin of 1.0, which is $\pi/2$, and multiplying the result by 2.

Having defined our base class, we can now extend it to a derived class. The definition of the derived class is

```
class Cylinder : public Circle  // Cylinder is derived from Circle
{
  protected:
    double length;   // add one additional data member and
  public:            // two additional function members
    Cylinder(double r = 1.0, double 1 = 1.0) : Circle(r), length(1) {}
    double calcval();
};

// class implementation
double Cylinder::calcval()   // this calculates a volume
{
  return (length * Circle::calcval()); // note the base function call
}
```

This definition encompasses several important concepts relating to derived classes. First, as a derived class, `Cylinder` contains all of the data and function members of its base class, `Circle`, plus any additional members that it may add. In this particular case the `Cylinder` class consists of a `radius` data member, inherited from the `Circle` class, plus an additional length member. Thus, each `Cylinder` object contains *two* data members, as illustrated in Figure 14.9.

In addition to having two data members the `Cylinder` class also inherits `Circle`'s function members. This is illustrated in the `Cylinder` constructor, which uses a base

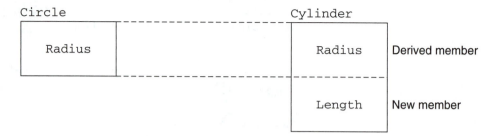

Figure 14.9 Relationship between `Circle` and `Cylinder` data members

member initialization list that specifically calls the `Circle` constructor. It is also illustrated in `Cylinder`'s `calcval()` function, which makes a call to `Circle::calcval()`.

In both classes, the same function name, `calcval()`, has been specifically used to illustrate the overriding of a base function by a derived function. When a `Cylinder` object calls `calcval()`, it is a request to use the `Cylinder` version of the function, while a `Circle` object call to `calcval()` is a request to use the `Circle` version. In this case the `Cylinder` class can access only the class version of `calcval()` using the scope resolution operator, as is done in the call `Circle::calcval()`. Program 14.13 uses these two classes within the context of a complete program.

Program 14.13

```
#include <iostream.h>
#include <math.h>

const double PI = 2.0 * asin(1.0);

class Circle
{
  protected:
    double radius;
  public:
    Circle(double = 1.0);   // constructor
    double calcval();
};

// class implementation
Circle::Circle(double r)    // constructor
{
  radius = r;
}
double Circle::calcval()    // this calculates an area
{
```

(Continued on next page)

(Continued from previous page)

```
   return(PI * radius * radius);
}

class Cylinder : public Circle   // Cylinder is derived from Circle
{
  protected:
    double length;   // add one additional data member and
  public:            // two additional function members
    Cylinder(double r = 1.0, double l = 1.0) : Circle(r), length(l) {}
    double calcval();
};

// class implementation
double Cylinder::calcval()    // this calculates a volume
{
  return (length * Circle::calcval()); // note the base function call
}
int main()
{
  Circle circle_1, circle_2(2);   // create two Circle objects
  Cylinder cylinder_1(3,4);       // create one Cylinder object

  cout << "The area of circle_1 is " << circle_1.calcval() << endl;
  cout << "The area of circle_2 is " << circle_2.calcval() << endl;
  cout << "The volume of cylinder_1 is " << cylinder_1.calcval() << endl;

  circle_1 = cylinder_1;   // assign a Cylinder to a Circle

  cout << "\nThe area of circle_1 is now " << circle_1.calcval() << endl;

  return 0;
}
```

The output produced by Program 14.13 is

```
The area of circle_1 is 3.141593
The area of circle_2 is 12.566371
The volume of cylinder_1 is 113.097336

The area of circle_1 is now 28.274334.
```

The first three output lines are all straightforward and are produced by the first three `cout` statements in the program. As the output shows, a call to `calcval()`

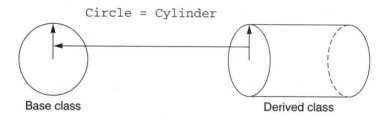

Circle = Cylinder

Base class   Derived class

Figure 14.10 Assignment from derived to base class

using a `Circle` object activates the `Circle` version of this function, while a call to `calcval()` using a `Cylinder` object activates the `Cylinder` version.

The assignment statement `circle_1 = cylinder_1;` introduces another important relationship between a base and derived class: *a derived class object can be assigned to a base class object.* This should not be surprising because both base and derived classes share a common set of data member types. In this type of assignment it is only this set of data members, which consist of all the base class data members, that is assigned. Thus, as illustrated in Figure 14.10, our `Cylinder`-to-`Circle` assignment results in the following memberwise assignment:

```
circle_1.radius = cylinder_1.radius;
```

The `length` member of the `Cylinder` object is not used in the assignment because it has no equivalent variable in the `Circle` class. The reverse cast, from base to derived class, is not as simple and requires a constructor to correctly initialize the additional derived class members not in the base class.

Before leaving Program 14.13 one additional point should be made. Although the `Circle` constructor was explicitly called using a base/member initialization list of the `Cylinder` constructor, an implicit call could also have been made. In the absence of an explicitly derived class constructor the compiler automatically calls the default base class constructor first, before the derived class constructor is called. This works because the derived class contains all of the base class data members. In a similar fashion, the destructor functions are called in the reverse order: first derived class and then base class.

Polymorphism

The overriding of a base member function using an overloaded derived member function, as illustrated by the `calcval()` function in Program 14.13, is an example of polymorphism. *Polymorphism* permits the same function name to invoke one response in objects of a base class and another response in objects of a derived class. In some cases, however, this method of overriding does not work as one might desire. To understand why this is so, consider Program 14.14.

Program 14.14

```cpp
#include <iostream.h>
#include <math.h>

class one                   // the base class
{
  protected:
    float a;
  public:
    one(float = 2);    // constructor
    float f1(float);     // a member function
    float f2(float);     // another member function
};

// class implementation
one::one(float val)    // constructor
{
  a = val;
}
float one::f1(float num)  // a member function
{
  return(num/2);
}
float one::f2(float num)  // another member function
{
  return( pow(f1(num),2) );  // square the result of f1()
}


class two : public one  // the derived class
{
  public:
    float f1(float);       // this overrides class one's f1()
};

// class implementation
float two::f1(float num)
{
  return(num/3);
}
int main()
{
  one object_1;  // object_1 is an object of the base class
```

(Continued on next page)

(Continued from previous page)

```
two object_2;   // object_2 is an object of the derived class

    // call f2() using a base class object call
cout << "The computed value using a base class object call is "
     << object_1.f2(12) << endl;

    // call f2() using a derived class object call
cout << "The computed value using a derived class object call is "
     << object_2.f2(12) << endl;

return 0;
}
```

The output produced by this program is

```
The computed value using a base class object call is 36
The computed value using a derived class object call is 36
```

As this output shows, the same result is obtained no matter which object type calls the f2() function. This result is produced because the derived class does not have an override to the base class f2() function. Thus, both calls to f2() result in the base class f2() function being called.

Once invoked, the base class f2() function always calls the base class version of f1() rather than the derived class override version. The reason for this is because of a process called *function binding*. In normal function calls static binding is used. In *static binding,* the determination of which function should be called is made at compile time. Thus, when the compiler first encounters the f1() function in the base class, it makes the determination that whenever f2() is called, either from a base or derived class object, it will subsequently call the base class f1() function.

In place of static binding we want a binding method that is capable of determining which function should be invoked at run time based on the object type making the call. This type of binding is referred to as *dynamic binding.* To achieve dynamic binding C++ provides virtual functions.

A *virtual function* specification tells the compiler to create a pointer to a function, but not fill in the value of the pointer until the function is actually called. Then, at run time, *and based on the object making the call,* the appropriate function address is used. Creating a virtual function is extremely easy—all that is required is that the keyword virtual be placed before the function's return type in the declaration section. For example, consider Program 14.15, which is identical to Program 14.14 except for the virtual declaration of the f1() function.

Program 14.15

```cpp
#include <iostream.h>
#include <math.h>

class One              // the base class
{
  protected:
    float a;
  public:
    One(float = 2);    // constructor
    virtual float f1(float);   // a member function
    float f2(float);   // another member function
};

// class implementation
One::One(float val)  // constructor
{
  a = val;
}
float One::f1(float num)  // a member function
{
  return(num/2);
}
float One::f2(float num)  // another member function
{
  return( pow(f1(num),2) );  // square the result of f1()
}


class Two : public One  // the derived class
{
  public:
    virtual float f1(float);    // this overrides class One's f1()
};

// class implementation
float Two::f1(float num)
{
  return(num/3);
}
int main()
{
```

(Continued on next page)

(Continued from previous page)

```
One object_1;   // object_1 is an object of the base class
Two object_2;   // object_2 is an object of the derived class

   // call f2() using a base class object call
cout << "The computed value using a base class object call is "
     << object_1.f2(12) << endl;

   // call f2() using a derived class object call
cout << "The computed value using a derived class object call is "
     << object_2.f2(12) << endl;

return 0;
}
```

The output produced by Program 14.15 is

```
The computed value using a base class object call is 36
The computed value using a derived class object call is 16
```

As illustrated by this output the f2() function now calls different versions of the overloaded f1() function based on the object type making the call. This selection, based on the object making the call, is the classic definition of polymorphic function behavior and is caused by the dynamic binding imposed on f1() by virtue of its being a virtual function. Once a function is declared as virtual *it remains virtual for the next derived class with or without a virtual declaration in the derived class.* Thus, the second virtual declaration in the derived class is not strictly needed but should be included both for clarity and to ensure that any subsequently derived classes correctly inherit the function. To understand why, consider the inheritance diagram in Figure 14.11, where class C is derived from class B and class B is derived from class A.[13] In this situation, if function f1() is virtual in class A, but is not declared in class B, it will not be virtual in class C. The only other requirement is that once a function has been declared as virtual the return type and parameter list of all subsequent derived class override versions *must* be the same.

Exercises 14.5

1. Define the following terms:
   - a. inheritance
   - b. base class
   - c. derived class
   - d. simple inheritance
   - e. multiple inheritance
   - f. class hierarchy

---

[13] By convention, as previously noted, arrows point from the derived class to the base class.

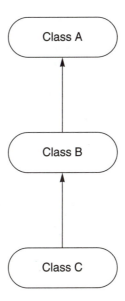

Figure 14.11   Inheritance diagram

g. polymorphism

h. static binding

i. dynamic binding

j. virtual function

2. Describe the two methods C++ provides for implementing polymorphism.

3. What three features must a programming language provide for it to be classified as an object-oriented language?

4. Describe the difference between a private and a protected class member.

5. a. Modify Program 14.13 to include a derived class named `Sphere` from the base `Circle` class. The only additional class members of `Sphere` should be a constructor and a `calcval()` function that returns the volume of the sphere. (*Note: Volume = 4/3 π radius³*)

b. Include the class constructed for Exercise 5a in a working C++ program. Have your program call all of the member functions in the `Sphere` class.

6. a. Create a base class named `Point` that consists of an x and y coordinate. From this class derive a class named `Circle` having an additional data member named `radius`. From this derived class the x and y data members represent the center coordinates of a circle. The function members of the first class should consist of a constructor, an area function named `area()` that returns 0, and a `distance()` function that returns the distance between two points, where

$$distance = \sqrt{(x2 - x1)^2 + (y2 - y1)^2}$$

Additionally, the derived class should have a constructor and an override function named `area()` that returns the area of a circle.

b. Include the classes constructed for Exercise 6a in a working C++ program. Have your program call all of the member functions in each class. In addition call the base class `distance()` function with two `Circle` objects and explain the result returned by the function.

7. a. Using the classes constructed for Exercise 6a, derive a class named `Cylinder` from the derived `Circle` class. The `Cylinder` class should have a constructor and a member function named `area()` that determines the surface area of the cylinder. For this function use the algorithm *surface area = 2 π r (l + r)*, where *r* is the radius of the cylinder and *l* is the length.

   b. Include the classes constructed for Exercise 7a in a working C++ program. Have your program call all of the member functions in the `Cylinder` class.

   c. What do you think might be the result if the base class `distance()` function was called with two `Cylinder` objects?

8. a. Create a base class named `Rectangle`, that contains `length` and `width` data members. From this class derive a class named `Box` having an additional data member named `depth`. The function members of the base `Rectangle` class should consist of a constructor and an `area()` function. The derived `Box` class should have a constructor, an override function named `area()` that returns the surface area of the box, and a `volume()` function.

   b. Include the classes constructed for Exercise 8a in a working C++ program. Have your program call all of the member functions in each class and explain the result when the distance function is called using two `Circle` objects.

14.6 Common Programming Errors

1. Using the default assignment operators and the default copy constructor with classes containing pointer members. Because these default functions do a memberwise copy, the address in the source pointer is copied to the destination pointer. Typically this is not what is wanted because both pointers end up pointing to the same memory area.

2. Using a user-defined assignment operator in a multiple-assignment expression when the operator has not been defined to return an object.

3. Using the keyword `static` when defining either a static data or function member. The `static` keyword should be used only within the class declaration section.

4. Failing to instantiate `static` data members before creating class objects that must access these data members.

5. Forgetting that `this` is a pointer that must be dereferenced using either `(*this).` or `this->`.

6. Attempting to redefine an operator's meaning as it applies to C++'s built-in data types.

7. Redefining an overloaded operator to perform a function not indicated by its conventional meaning. Although this works it is an example of extremely bad programming practice.

8. Forgetting that a conversion operator function can only be a member function (not a friend).

9. Attempting to specify a return type for a member conversion operator function.

10. Attempting to override a virtual function without using the same type and number of arguments as the original function.

11. Using the keyword `virtual` in the class implementation section. Functions are only declared as virtual in the class declaration section.

14.7 Chapter Summary

1. An *assignment operator* may be declared for a class with the function prototype

   ```
   void operator=(ClassName&);
   ```

   Here, the argument is a reference to the class name. The return type of `void` precludes using this operator in multiple-assignment expressions such as a = b = c.

2. A type of initialization that closely resembles assignment occurs in C++ when one object is initialized using another object of the same class. The constructor that performs this type of initialization is called a *copy constructor* and has the function prototype:

   ```
   ClassName(ClassName&);
   ```

   This is frequently represented using the notation `X(X&)`.

3. The default copy constructor and default assignment operators are typically not useful with classes containing pointer members. This is because these default functions do a memberwise copy in which the address in the source pointer is copied to the destination pointer, resulting in both pointers "pointing to" the same memory area. For these situations you must define your own copy constructor and assignment operator.

4. Each class has an associated class scope, which is defined by the brace pair, { }, containing the class declaration. Data and function members are local to the scope of their class and can be used only by objects declared for the class. If a global variable name is reused within a class, the global variable is hidden by the class variable. Within the scope of the class variable the global variable may be accessed using the scope resolution operator, ::.

5. For each class object a separate set of memory locations is reserved for all data members, except those declared as `static`. A `static` data member is shared by all class objects and provides a means of communication between objects. Static data members must be declared as such within the class declaration section and are defined outside of the declaration section.

6. Static function members apply to the class as a whole rather than to individual objects. Hence, a `static` function member can access only static data members and other `static` function members. All `static` function members must be declared as such within the class declaration section and are defined outside of the declaration section.

7. For each class, only one copy of the member functions is retained in memory, and each object uses the same function. The address of the object's data members is provided to the member function by passing a hidden parameter, corresponding

to the memory address of the selected object, to the member function. The address is passed in a special pointer parameter named `this`. The `this` pointer may be used explicitly by a member function to access a data member.

8. User-defined operators can be constructed for classes using member operator functions. An operator function has the form `operator <symbol>`, where `<symbol>` is one of the following:

```
()   []   ->   new   delete   ++   --   !   ~   *   /   %   +   -
<<   >>   <   <=   >   >=   ++   !=   &&   ||   &   ^   |   =   +=
-=   *=   /=   %=   &=   ^=   |=   <<=   >>=   ,
```

For example, the function prototype `Date operator+(int);` declares that the addition operator is defined to accept an integer and return a `Date` object.

9. User-defined operators may be called in either of two ways: as a conventional function with arguments, or as an operator expression. For example, for an operator having the header line

```
Date Date::operator+(int)
```

if `dte` is an object of type `Date`, the following two calls produce the same effect:

```
dte.operator+(284)
dte + 284
```

10. There are four categories of data type conversions. They are conversions from

1. Built-in type to built-in type
2. Built-in type to user-defined (class) type
3. User-defined (class) type to built-in type
4. User-defined (class) type to user-defined (class) type

Built-in to built-in type conversions are done using C++'s implicit conversion rules or explicitly using casts. Built-in to user-defined type conversions are done using type conversion constructors. Conversions from user-defined types to either built-in or other user-defined types are done using conversion operator functions.

11. A *type conversion constructor* is a constructor whose first parameter is not a member of its class and whose remaining arguments, if any, have default values.

12. A conversion operator function is a member function having the name of a built-in data type or class. It has no explicit arguments or return type; rather, the return type is the name of the function.

13. *Inheritance* is the capability of deriving one class from another class. The initial class used as the basis for the derived class is referred to as the base, parent, or superclass. The derived class is referred to as the derived, child, or subclass.

14. Base member functions can be overridden by derived member functions with the same name. The override function is simply an overloaded version of the base member function defined in the derived class.

15. *Polymorphism* is the capability of having the same function name invoke different responses based on the object making the function call. It can be accomplished using overloaded and virtual functions.

16. In *static binding*, the determination of which function actually is invoked is made at compile time. In *dynamic binding*, the determination is made at run time.

17. A *virtual function* specification designates that dynamic binding should take place. The specification is made in the function's prototype by placing the keyword `virtual` before the function's return type. Once a function has been declared as virtual it remains so for all derived classes as long as there is a continuous trail of function declarations through the derived chain of classes.

Appendices

Operator Precedence Table

Table A.1 presents the symbols, precedence, descriptions, and associativity of C's operators. Operators toward the top of the table have a higher precedence than those toward the bottom. Operators within each box have the same precedence and associativity.

Table A.1   Summary of C operators

Operator	Description	Associativity
( )	Function call	Left to right
[ ]	Array element	
->	Structure member pointer reference	
.	Structure member reference	
++	Increment	Right to left
--	Decrement	
-	Unary minus	
!	Logical negation	
~	One's complement	
(type)	Type conversion (cast)	
sizeof	Storage size	
&	Address of	
*	Indirection	
*	Multiplication	Left to right
/	Division	
%	Modulus (remainder)	
+	Addition	Left to right
-	Subtraction	

(Continued on next page)

Table A.1   Summary of C operators *(continued)*

Operator	Description	Associativity
<< >>	Left shift Right shift	Left to right
< <= > >=	Less than Less than or equal to Greater than Greater than or equal to	Left to right
== !=	Equal to Not equal to	Left to right
&	Bitwise AND	Left to right
^	Bitwise exclusive OR	Left to right
|	Bitwise inclusive OR	Left to right
&&	Logical AND	Left to right
||	Logical OR	Left ro right
? :	Conditional expression	Right to left
= += -= *= /= %= &= ^= |= <<= >>=	Assignment Assignment Assignment Assignment Assignment	Right to left
,	Comma	Left to right

ASCII Character Codes

Key(s)	Dec	Oct	Hex	Key	Dec	Oct	Hex	Key	Dec	Oct	Hex
Ctrl 1	0	0	0	Ctrl Q	17	21	11	"	34	42	22
Ctrl A	1	1	1	Ctrl R	18	22	12	#	35	43	23
Ctrl B	2	2	2	Ctrl S	19	23	13	$	36	44	24
Ctrl C	3	3	3	Ctrl T	20	24	14	%	37	45	25
Ctrl D	4	4	4	Ctrl U	21	25	15	&	38	46	26
Ctrl E	5	5	5	Ctrl V	22	26	16	'	39	47	27
Ctrl F	6	6	6	Ctrl W	23	27	17	(	40	50	28
Ctrl G	7	7	7	Ctrl X	24	30	18	)	41	51	29
Ctrl H	8	10	8	Ctrl Y	25	31	19	*	42	52	2A
Ctrl I	9	11	9	Ctrl Z	26	32	1A	+	43	53	2B
Ctrl J (\n)	10	12	A	Esc	27	33	1B	,	44	54	2C
Ctrl K	11	13	B	Ctrl <	28	34	1C	-	45	55	2D
Ctrl L	12	14	C	Ctrl /	29	35	1D	.	46	56	2E
RETURN	13	15	D	Ctrl =	30	36	1E	/	47	57	2F
Ctrl N	14	16	E	Ctrl -	31	37	1F	0	48	60	30
Ctrl O	15	17	F	Space	32	40	20	1	49	61	31
Ctrl P	16	20	10	!	33	41	21	2	50	62	32

(Continued on next page)

Key(s)	Dec	Oct	Hex	Key	Dec	Oct	Hex	Key	Dec	Oct	Hex
3	51	63	33	M	77	115	4D	g	103	147	67
4	52	64	34	N	78	116	4E	h	104	150	68
5	53	65	35	O	79	117	4F	i	105	151	69
6	54	66	36	P	80	120	50	j	106	152	6A
7	55	67	37	Q	81	121	51	k	107	153	6B
8	56	70	38	R	82	122	52	l	108	154	6C
9	57	71	39	S	83	123	53	m	109	155	6D
:	58	72	3A	T	84	124	54	n	110	156	6E
;	59	73	3B	U	85	125	55	o	111	157	6F
<	60	74	3C	V	86	126	56	p	112	160	70
=	61	75	3D	W	87	127	57	q	113	161	71
>	62	76	3E	X	88	130	58	r	114	162	72
?	63	77	3F	Y	89	131	59	s	115	163	73
@	64	100	40	Z	90	132	5A	t	116	164	74
A	65	101	41	[	91	133	5B	u	117	165	75
B	66	102	42	\	92	134	5C	v	118	166	76
C	67	103	43	]	93	135	5D	w	119	167	77
D	68	104	44	^	94	136	5E	x	120	170	78
E	69	105	45	_	95	137	5F	y	121	171	79
F	70	106	46	`	96	140	60	z	122	172	7A
G	71	107	47	a	97	141	61	{	123	173	7B
H	72	110	48	b	98	142	62	/	124	174	7C
I	73	111	49	c	99	143	63	}	125	175	7D
J	74	112	4A	d	100	144	64	~	126	176	7E
K	75	113	4B	e	101	145	65	del	127	177	7F
L	76	114	4C	f	102	146	66				

Input, Output, and Standard Error Redirection

The display produced by the `printf()` function is normally sent to the terminal where you are working. This terminal is called the *standard output device* because it is where the display is automatically directed, in a standard fashion, by the interface between your C program and your computer's operating system.

On most systems it is possible to redirect the output produced by `printf()` to some other device, or to a file, using the output redirection symbol, >, at the time the program is invoked. In addition to this symbol, you must specify where you want the displayed results to be sent.

For purposes of illustration, assume that the command to execute a compiled program named `salestax`, without redirection, is

```
salestax
```

This command is entered after your computer's system prompt is displayed on your terminal. When the salestax program is run, any `printf()` function calls within it automatically cause the appropriate display to be sent to your terminal. Suppose we would like to have the display produced by the program sent to a file named `results`. To do this requires the command

```
salestax > results
```

The redirection symbol, >, tells the operating system to send any display produced by `printf()` directly to a file named `results` rather than to the standard output device used by the system. The display sent to `results` can then be examined by using either an editor program or issuing another operating system command. For example, under the UNIX operating system the command

```
cat results
```

causes the contents of the file `results` to be displayed on your terminal. The equivalent command under the IBM PC disk operating system (DOS) is

```
type results
```

In redirecting an output display to a file, the following rules apply:

1. If the file does not exist, it will be created.
2. If the file exists, it will be overwritten with the new display.

In addition to the output redirection symbol, the output append symbol, >>, can also be used. The append symbol is used in the same manner as the redirection symbol, but causes any new output to be added to the end of a file. For example, the command

```
salestax >> results
```

causes any output produced by `salestax` to be added to the end of the `results` file. If the `results` file does not exist, it will be created.

Besides having the display produced by `printf()` redirected to a file, using either the > or >> symbols, the display can also be sent to a physical device connected to your computer, such as a printer. You must, however, know the name used by your computer for accessing the desired device. For example, on an IBM PC or compatible computer, the name of the printer connected to the terminal is designated as `prn` and on a UNIX system it is typically `lpr`. Thus, if you are working on an IBM or compatible machine, the command

```
salestax > prn
```

causes the display produced in the salestax program to be sent directly to the printer connected to the terminal. In addition to `printf()`, output redirection also affects the placement of displays produced by the `puts()` and `putchar()` functions and any other function that uses the standard output device for display.

Corresponding to output redirection, it is also possible to redesignate the standard input device for an individual program run using the input redirection symbol, <. Again, the new source for input must be specified immediately after the input redirection symbol.

Input redirection works much like output redirection but affects the source of input for the `scanf()`, `gets()`, and `getchar()` functions. For example, the command

```
salestax < dataIn
```

causes any input functions within `salestax` that normally receive their input from the keyboard to receive it from the `dataIn` file instead. This input redirection, like its output counterpart, is only in effect for the current execution of the program. As you might expect, the same run can have both an input and output redirection. For example, the command

```
salestax < dataIn > results
```

causes an input redirection from the file `dataIn` and an output redirection to the file `results`.

In addition to standard input and output redirection, the device to which all error messages are sent can also be redirected. On many systems this file is given an operating system designation as device file 2. Thus, the redirection

```
2> err
```

causes any error messages that would normally be displayed on the standard error device, which is usually your terminal, to be redirected to a file named `err`. As with standard input and output redirection, standard error redirection can be included on the same command line used to invoke a program. For example, the command

```
salestax < dataIn > show 2> err
```

causes the compiled program named `salestax` to receive its standard input from a file named `dataIn`, write its results to a file named `show`, and send any error messages to a file named `err`.

As the redirection of input, output, and error messages is generally a feature of the operating system used by your computer and not typically part of your C compiler, you must check the manuals for your particular operating system to ensure that these features are available.

The Standard C Library

The standard C library is defined by the ANSI C standard and is composed of the functions, definitions, and macros that are declared in fifteen header files. These header files and the types of routines that they provide are listed in Table D.1:

Table D.1 Standard C library header files

Name	Type of Routines
`<assert.h>`	Diagnostic
`<ctype.h>`	Single-character testing
`<errno.h>`	Error detection
`<float.h>`	System-defined floating point limits
`<limits.h>`	System-defined integer limits
`<locale.h>`	Country definitions
`<math.h>`	Mathematical
`<stjump.h>`	Nonlocal function calls
`<signal.h>`	Exception handling and interrupt signals
`<stdarg.h>`	Variable-length argument processing
`<stddef.h>`	System constants
`<stdio.h>`	Input/output
`<stdlib.h>`	Miscellaneous utilities
`<string.h>`	String manipulation
`<time.h>`	Time and date functions

Of these fifteen header files, the most commonly used file is `<stdio.h>`, which contains approximately one-third of all standard library functions and macros. The next most commonly used headers consist of `<ctype.h>`, `<math.h>`, `<stdlib.h>`, and `<string.h>`. The most commonly used routines contained in each of these five header files are presented in this appendix.

`<stdio.h>`

The functions, macros, and data types defined in `<stdio.h>` are concerned with input and output. The most commonly used of these follow:

Prototype	Description
`int fclose(FILE *)`	Close a file
`int fflush(FILE *)`	Causes any buffered but unwritten output data to be written on output; undefined for input
`int fgetc(FILE *)`	Return the next character from the file (converted to an int) or EOF if end of file is encountered
`char fgets(char *s, int n, FILE *)`	Read at most n-1 characters into the s array; stops at a newline, which is included in the array. The array is automatically terminated with a \0
`FILE *fopen(char *fname, char *mode)`	Open the file named fname in the designated mode, which can be "r" open a file for reading "w" open a file for writing; old contents discarded if file exists "a" open a file for writing at the end of the file; a new file is created if one does not exist "r+" open a text file for reading and writing "w+" create a text file for update; old contents discarded if file exists "a+" open a text file for writing at the end of the file; a new file is created if one does not exist
`int fprintf(FILE *, char *format, args)`	Write the args to the file under control of the format string
`int fputc(int c, FILE *)`	Write c, converted to an unsigned char, to the file
`int fputs(char *s, FILE *)`	Write string s to the file

Prototype	Description
`int fscanf(FILE *, char *format, &args)`	Read from the file under control of the format string
`int fseek(FILE *, long offset, int origin)`	Set the file position; the position is set to offset characters from the origin; the origin may be `SEEK_SET`, `SEEK_CUR`, or `SEEK_END`, which is the beginning, current position, or end of the file, respectively
`long ftell(file *)`	Return the current file position of a `-1L` if an error
`int getc(FILE *)`	`fgetc()` written as a macro
`int getchar(void)`	Same as `getc(stdin)`
`char *gets(char *s)`	Read the next input line into `s` array, replacing the newline with `\0`
`void perror(char *s)`	Print the string `s` and a compiler-defined error message corresponding to the last error number (`errno`) reported
`int printf(char *format, args)`	Write output to standard output under control of the format string. Equivalent to `fprintf(stdout, char *format, args)`
`int putc(int c, FILE *)`	`fputc()` written as a macro
`int putchar(int c)`	Same as `putc(c, stdout)`
`int puts(char *s)`	Write the string `s`, followed by a newline character to `stdout`
`rewind(FILE *)` `int scanf(char *format, &args)`	Read from standard input under control of the format string; equivalent to `fscanf(stdin, char *format, args)`
`int sscanf(char *s, char *format, &args)`	Equivalent to `scanf()` except that input is taken from the `s` string
`sprintf(char *s, char *format, args)`	Equivalent to `printf()` except that output is written to the `s` string; the string is terminated with a `\0` and must be large enough to hold the data
`int ungetc(int c, FILE *)`	Push `c` (converted to an unsigned char) back onto the file

`<ctype.h>`

Each function declared in `<ctype.h>` returns a nonzero (true) integer if the argument satisfies the condition or a zero (false) value if it does not. The argument must have a value representable as an unsigned char.

Prototype	Description
`int isalnum(int c)`	Is c alphanumeric (isalpha || isdigit)
`int isalpha(int c)`	Is c alphabetic
`int iscntrl(int c)`	Is c a control character
`int isdigit(int c)`	Is c a digit
`int isgraph(int c)`	Is c printable (excluding space)
`int islower(int c)`	Is c lowercase
`int isprint(int c)`	Is c printable (including space)
`int ispunct(int c)`	Is c printable except a space, letter, or digit
`int isspace(int c)`	Is c a space, formfeed, newline, carriage return, or tab
`int isupper(int c)`	Is c uppercase
`int isxdigit(int c)`	Is c a hexadecimal digit
`int tolower(int c)`	Convert to lowercase
`int toupper(int c)`	Convert to uppercase

`<math.h>`

This header file contains mathematical functions and macros.

Prototype	Description
`double acos(double x)`	Arc cosine of x
`double asin(double x)`	Arc sine of x
`double atan(double x)`	Arc tangent of x
`double ceil(double x)`	Smallest integer not less than x
`double cos(double x)`	Cosine of x
`double cosh(double x)`	Hyperbolic cosine of x
`double exp(double x)`	e^x
`double fabs(double x)`	Absolute value of x
`double floor(double x)`	Largest integer not greater than x

Prototype	Description
`double fmod(double x, double y)`	Remainder of x/y, with the sign of x
`double ldexp(x,n)`	$x . 2^n$
`double log(double x)`	$\ln(x)$
`double log10(double x)`	$\log10(x)$
`double mod(double x, double *ip)`	Fraction part of x, with the sign of x. Integer part of x, with the sign of x, is pointed to by `ip`
`double pow(x,y)`	x^y
`double sin(double x)`	Sine of x
`double sinh(double x)`	Hyperbolic sine of x
`double sqrt(double x)`	Square root of x
`double tan(double x)`	Tangent of x
`double tanh(double x)`	Hyperbolic tangent of x

`<stdlib.h>`

This header declares number conversion and storage allocation functions.

Prototype	Description
`int abs(int n)`	Absolute value of integer
`long labs(long n)`	Absolute value of long integer
`double atof(char *s)`	Convert `s` to double
`int atoi(char *s)`	Convert `s` to int
`int atol(char *s)`	Convert `s` to long
`int rand(void)`	Pseudo-random integer
`void srand(unsigned int seed)`	Seed for pseudo-random integers
`void *calloc(size_n, size_n)`	Allocate space for an array of n objects, each of size n. Initialize all allocated bytes to zero.
`void *malloc(size_t n)`	Allocate space for an object of size n.
`void *realloc(void *p, size_n)`	Reallocate space to size n, contents remains the same for old contents up to the new size.
`void free(void *p)`	Deallocate space pointed to
`void exit(int status)`	Normal program termination

`<string.h>`

This header contains string handling functions. All functions starting with the letters `str` assume NULL terminated strings as arguments and return a NULL-terminated string. The functions starting with the letters `mem` do not assume a NULL-terminated string and process data in memory.

Prototype	Description
`char *strcat(char *d, char*s)`	Concatenate string s to string d
`char *strncat(char *d, char *s, int n)`	Concatenate at most n characters of string s to string d
`char *strcpy(char *d, char *s)`	Copy string s to string d
`char *strncpy(char *d, char *s, int n)`	Copy at most n characters of string s to string d; pad with \0's if s has fewer than n characters
`char *strcmp(char *d, char *s)`	Compare string d to string s; return <0 if d < s, 0 if d == s, and > 0 if d > s
`char *strncmp(char *d, char *s, int n)`	Compare at most n characters of string d to string s; return < 0 if d < s, 0 if d == s, and > 0 if d > s
`char *strchr(char *d, char c)`	Return a pointer to the first occurrence of c in string d or a NULL if c is not found
`char *strrchr(char *d, char c)`	Return a pointer to the last occurrence of c in string d or a NULL if c is not found
`char *strstr(char *d, char *s)`	Return a pointer to the first occurrence of string s in string d or a NULL if s is not found
`int strlen(char *d)`	Return the length of string d, not including the terminating NULL
`void *memcpy(void *d, void *s, int n)`	Copy n characters from s to d
`void *memmove(void *d, void *s, int n)`	Same as memcpy but works even if d overlaps s
`void *memcmp(void *d, void *s, int n)`	Compare the first n characters of d to s; same return as strcmp
`void *memchr(void *d, char c, int n)`	Return a pointer to the first occurrence of c in the n characters pointed to by d or a NULL if c is not found
`void *memset(void *d, char c, int n)`	Fill d with n occurrences of c

The Standard Template Library (C++)[1]

A driving force behind object-oriented programming was the desire to create easily reusable source code. For example, recreating source code each time an array or queue is needed wastes both time and programming effort, which is added to by the additional time required for fully testing and verifying code that may be only minimally modified. Suppose, for example, that a single program needs to use three arrays: an array of characters, an array of integers, and an array of double precision numbers. Rather than coding three different arrays, it makes more sense to implement each array from a single, fully tested generic array class that comes complete with methods and algorithms for processing the array, such as sorting, inserting, finding maximum and minimum values, locating values, randomly shuffling values, copying arrays, comparing arrays, and dynamically expanding and contracting the array, as needed. This generic type of data structure, which is referred to as a container, forms the basis of the Standard Template Library (STL). In addition to providing seven types of generic data structures, one of which is the array container class (which is formally referred to as the vector container class), the STL provides methods and algorithms for appropriately operating on each of its generic data structures.

This generic programming approach for the STL was initially provided by Hewlett-Packard Corporation in 1994 and has subsequently been incorporated as part of the ANSI/ISO C++ Standard Library.[2] In addition to the STL, the Standard Library provides two other majors sections, which are

- **Input/Output headers:** These provide support for conversions between text and encoded data, and input and output to external files. More specifically these headers consist of `<fstream>`, `<iomanip>`, `<ios>`, `<iosfwd>`, `<iostream>`, `<istream>`, `<ostream>`, `<stream>`, `<streambuf>`, and `<strstream>`.

---

[1] This is a C++ topic that requires understanding of the material in Chapter 13.

[2] The initial Hewlett-Packard STL developers were Alexander Stepanov and Meng Lee, with major contributions made by David Musser.

- **Other Standard C++ headers:** These include language support for common type definitions, such as `<limits>`; diagnostic components for reporting exceptional conditions, such as `<stdexcept>`; string components of string classes, which is provided by `<string>`; and the 18 additional Standard C Library headers.

The Standard Template Library, which is the third major section of the standard library, is divided into the following three categories:

- *Containers,* which are the template classes from which individual data structures can be constructed. By definition a *container* is an STL template class that manages a sequence of elements. There are currently seven container classes that are used to construct vector, list, deque, stack, queue, set, and map data structures.
- *Algorithms,* which are template functions (see Section 6.1) that provide useful search, sort, location, and other numeric functions that can be applied to the various data structures created from the container classes.
- *Iterators,* which can be considered as generalized pointers for keeping track of the beginning, ending, and other positions within a data structure. Specifically, iterators are used to keep track of the first and last positions in a data structure and for establishing the boundaries of sequences of elements to which an algorithm is applied.

Table E.1 lists the 13 headers provided by the Standard Template Library. As seen, seven of the headers are container types, which are used to create data structures; three of the headers are concerned with providing algorithmic capabilities; and three of the headers are concerned with providing iterator capabilities.

In its most general usage, one or more container classes are first used to construct the desired data structures. Once these desired data structures have been created, class methods and algorithms, both of which are always constructed as functions, can be applied to them. Iterators, which act like generalized pointers, are used as arguments by all of the algorithms to determine and keep track of which elements in the data structure are to be operated upon.

To make this more tangible and provide a meaningful introduction to using the STL, we will use the vector container class to create two vectors: one for holding integers and one for holding characters. A vector is similar to a C++ array, except that it can automatically expand and contract as needed. We will then use two vector methods and two algorithms to operate on the instantiated vectors. Specifically, one method is used to change an existing element value and another to insert an element within each vector. The first algorithm is then used to sort the elements in each vector, while the second algorithm is used to randomly reshuffle each vector's elements. After each method and algorithm is applied a cout object is employed to display the results. To see how this is accomplished, consider Program E.1.

Table E.1 Standard template headers

Name	Type	Description
`<algorithm>`	algorithm	defines numerous function templates that implement algorithms
`<functional>`	algorithm	defines templates required by <algorithm> and <numeric>
`<numeric>`	algorithm	defines several function templates that implement numeric functions
`<deque>`	container	defines a template class that implements a deque container
`<list>`	container	defines a template class for implementing a list container
`<map>`	container	defines template classes for implementing associative containers
`<queue>`	container	defines a template class for implementing a queue container
`<set>`	container	defines template classes for implementing associative containers having unique elements
`<stack>`	container	defines a template class for implementing a stack container
`<vector>`	container	defines a template class for implementing a vector container
`<iterators>`	iterator	defines templates for defining and manipulating iterators
`<memory>`	iterator	defines templates for allocating and freeing container class memory storage
`<utility>`	iterator	defines several general utility templates

Program E.1

```
#include <iostream>
#include <vector>
#include <algorithm>
using namespace std;

int main()
{
  const int NUMELS = 5;
  int a[NUMELS] = {1,2,3,4,5};
  char b[NUMELS] = {'a', 'b', 'c', 'd', 'e'};
  int i;
```

(Continued on next page)

(Continued from previous page)

```
   // instantiate an integer and character vector
   // using a constructor to set the size of each vector
   // and initialize each vector with values
vector<int> x(a, a + NUMELS);
vector<char> y(b, b + NUMELS);

cout << "\nThe vector x initially contains the elements: " << endl;
for (i = 0; i < NUMELS; i++)
   cout << x[i] << "   ";
cout << "\nThe vector y initially contains the elements: " << endl;
for (i = 0; i < NUMELS; i++)
   cout << y[i] << "   ";

   // instantiate two ostream objects
ostream_iterator<int> outint(cout, "   ");
ostream_iterator<char> outchar(cout, "   ");

   // modify elements in the existing list
x.at(3) = 6;     //set element at position 3 to a 6
y.at(3) = 'f'; // set element at position 3 to an 'e'
   // add elements to the end of the list
x.insert(x.begin() + 2,7);   // insert a 7 at position 2
y.insert(y.begin() + 2,'g'); // insert an f at position 2

cout << "\n\nThe vector x now contains the elements: "  << endl;
copy(x.begin(), x.end(), outint);
cout << "\nThe vector y now contains the elements: " << endl;
copy(y.begin(), y.end(), outchar);

   //sort both vectors
sort(x.begin(), x.end());
sort(y.begin(), y.end());

cout << "\n\nAfter sorting, vector x's elements are: "  << endl;
copy(x.begin(), x.end(), outint);
cout << "\nAfter sorting, vector y's elements are:" << endl;
copy(y.begin(), y.end(), outchar);

   // random shuffle the existing elements
random_shuffle(x.begin(), x.end());
random_shuffle(y.begin(), y.end());

cout << "\n\nAfter random shuffling, vector x's elements are:"  << endl;
copy(x.begin(), x.end(), outint);
```
(Continued on next page)

(Continued from previous page)

```
cout << "\nAfter random shuffling, vector y's elements are:" << endl;
copy(y.begin(), y.end(), outchar);

cout << endl;
return 0;
}
```

In reviewing Program E.1, notice the inclusion of the three header files `<iostream>`, `<vector>`, and `<algorithm>` with the `using namespace std;` statement.[3] Here we need the `<iostream>` header to create and use the `cout` stream; the `<vector>` to create one or more vector objects; and the `<algorithm>` header for the two algorithms we will be using, named `sort()` and `random_shuffle()`.

The two statements in Program E.1 that are used to create and initialize each vector are

```
vector<int> x(a, a + NUMELS);
vector<char> y(b, b + NUMELS);
```

Here, the vector x is declared as a vector of type `int` and is initialized with elements from array a starting with the first element of the array, located at address a, which contains the element a[0], and ending with the element at location a + NUMELS, which contains the element a[NUMELS - 1]. Thus, the vector x now has a size sufficient for five integers and has been initialized with the values 1, 2, 3, 4, and 5. Similarly, vector y now has an exact size for five characters and has been initialized with the values a, b, c, d, and e. The next set of statements in Program E.1 displays the initial values in each vector, using standard subscripted vector notation that is identical to the notation used for accessing array elements. Displaying the vector values in this manner, however, requires knowing how many elements each vector contains. As we insert and remove elements we would like the vector class itself to keep track of where the first and last elements are; this capability is, in fact, automatically provided by two iterators methods furnished for each vector, named `begin()` and `end()`. Before using these two functions we will construct two iterator dependent output objects for making the output display of elements rather simple, using the statements:

```
ostream_iterator<int> outint(cout, "  ");
ostream_iterator<char> outchar(cout, "  ");
```

As we will see momentarily, the `outint` and `outchar` objects (the two names are programmer selected) can be used to display all vector values contained between two iterators with two spaces provided between each value, before the value is placed on the `cout` stream.

---

[3] The rationale for this statement, which is required, can be found in the author's *A First Book of C++*.

The next major set of statements

```
// modify elements in the existing list
x.at(3) = 6;     //set element at position 3 to a 6
y.at(3) = 'f'; // set element at position 3 to an 'e'
   // add elements to the end of the list
x.insert(x.begin() + 2,7);   // insert a 7 at position 2
y.insert(y.begin() + 2,'g'); // insert an f at position 2
```

is used to both modify existing vector values and insert a new value into each vector. Specifically, the at() method requires an integer value for its argument, while the insert() method requires an iterator and the value to be inserted, as arguments. Specifically, the at() argument of 3 indicates that the 4th element in each vector will be changed (remember that vectors, like arrays, begin at index position 0). This means that the value 4, which is in the 4th position in the integer array, will be changed to a 6, and the value 'd' in the character array will be changed to an 'f'. The insert() method is then used to insert values of 7 and 'g' in the third position for both vectors. Notice that, like pointers, iterator arithmetic is allowed. Because the begin() method returns the iterator value corresponding to the start of the vector, adding 2 to it points to the third position in the array. It is at this position the new value is inserted with all subsequent values moved up by one position in the vector. The vector automatically expands to accept the inserted value. At this point in the program, the vector x now contains the elements

```
1  2  7  3  6  5
```

and the vector y now contains the elements

```
a  b  g  c  f  e
```

For vector x, this arrangement was obtained by replacing the original value of 4 with a 6 and then inserting a 7 in the third position, which moved all subsequent elements up by one position and increased the total vector size to accommodate 6 integers. A similar process resulted in the arrangement shown for vector y's elements. To have the program display these elements the statements

```
cout << "\n\nThe vector x now contains the elements: "  << endl;
copy(x.begin(), x.end(), outint);
cout << "\nThe vector y now contains the elements: " << endl;
copy(y.begin(), y.end(), outchar);
```

were used. The copy() algorithm uses two iterators, which are the values returned by the begin() and end() methods to delimit the beginning and ending positions to copy. In this case a copy of each complete vector is made to the outint and outchar objects, respectively. As these objects are standard output objects, the values placed on them are displayed on the screen, suitably interspaced with two spaces between each element.

Finally, the last section of code used in Program E.1 uses the `sort()` and `random_shuffle()` algorithms to first sort the elements in each vector and then randomly shuffle them. Notice that both of these algorithms use iterator values to determine the sequence of elements to be operated upon. After each algorithm is applied, the `copy()` algorithm is once again used to force an output display. Following is the complete output produced by Program E.1:

```
The vector x initially contains the elements:
1   2   3   4   5
The vector y initially contains the elements:
a   b   c   d   e

The vector x now contains the elements:
1   2   7   3   6   5
The vector y now contains the elements:
a   b   g   c   f   e

After sorting, vector x's elements are:
1   2   3   5   6   7
After sorting, vector y's elements are:
a   b   c   e   f   g

After random shuffling, vector x's elements are:
6   5   1   3   7   2
After random shuffling, vector y's elements are:
e   a   f   c   g   b
```

Program Entry, Compilation, and Execution

In this appendix, we first examine the steps to take to enter, compile, and execute a C program. The specific instructions required by the DOS, UNIX, and VAX-VMS operating systems are then provided.

General Introduction

As illustrated in Figure F.1, a computer can be thought of as a self-contained world that is entered by a special set of steps called a *log-in procedure*. For IBM, Apple, and other desktop computers, the log-in procedure is usually as simple as turning the computer's power switch on. Larger, multiuser systems, such as DEC VAX computers, typically require a log-in procedure consisting of turning a terminal on and supplying an account number and password.

Once you have successfully logged in to your computer system, you are automatically placed under the control of a computer program called the operating system (unless the computer is programmed to switch into a specific application program). The operating system is the program that controls the computer. It is used to access the services provided by the computer, which include the programs needed to enter, compile, and execute a C program.

Communicating with the operating system is always accomplished using a specific set of commands that the operating system recognizes. Although each computer system has its own set of operating system commands, all operating systems provide commands that allow you to log in to the system, exit the system, create your own programs, and quickly list, delete, copy, or rename your programs.

The specific operating system commands and any additional steps used for exiting a computer, such as turning the power off, are collectively referred to as the *log-out procedure*.

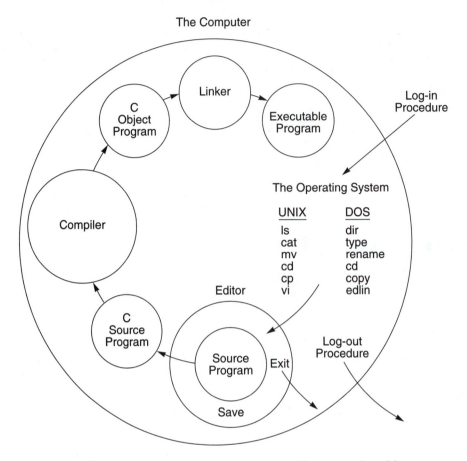

Figure F.1 Viewing a computer as a self-contained world

Make sure you know the log-out procedure for your computer at the time you log-in to ensure that you can effectively "escape" when you are ready to leave the system. Because the log-in and log-out procedures for each computer are system-dependent, determine these procedures for the system you will be using and list them below:

Log-in Procedure: _____

_____

Log-out Procedure:_____

_____

Specific Operating Systems

Each operating system provides a basic set of commands that allow you to list the names of the programs in the system, type the contents of a program, copy programs, rename

Table F.1   Operating system commands

Task	DOS	UNIX	VAX	Your System
Obtain a directory of programs	dir	ls	dir	
Change to a new directory	cd	cd	cd	
List current directory name	cd	pwd	cd	
List a program	type	cat	cat	
Copy a program	copy	cp	cp	
Delete a program	delete, del, erase	rm	rm	
Rename a program	rename	mv	rn	

programs, and delete programs. Table F.1 lists the operating system commands provided by the DOS, UNIX and VAX-VMS operating systems to perform these and other functions. Space has also been left in the table to list the specific operating system command names used by your system to perform these tasks.

The commands listed in Table F.1 to list, copy, delete, or rename programs are all concerned with manipulating existing programs. Let us now turn our attention to creating, compiling, and executing a new C program. The procedures for doing these tasks are illustrated in Figure F.2. As shown in this figure, the procedure for creating an executable C program consists of three distinct operations: editing (creating or modifying the source code), compiling, and linking. Although every operating system provides an editor program that can be used to create C programs, not all operating systems provide a C compiler. Fortunately, UNIX and VAX operating systems all have a C compiler that is typically installed along with the operating system. For IBM and IBM-compatible PC computers, a separate compiler must be purchased and installed to provide the capability of compiling C programs (see appendixes G and H).

Editing

Both the creation of a new C program and the modification of an existing C program require the use of an editor program. The function of the editor is to allow a user to type statements at a keyboard and save the typed statements together under a common name, called a *source program file name.*

As previously illustrated in Figure F.1, an editor program is contained within the environment controlled by the operating system. Like all services provided by the operating system, this means that the editor program can only be accessed using an operating system command. Table F.2 lists operating system commands required by the UNIX, DOS, and VAX-VMS operating systems to enter their respective editors. Because the UNIX operating system supplies two editor programs, a screen editor named vi and a line editor named ed, two separate commands are provided in UNIX for accessing the desired editor.

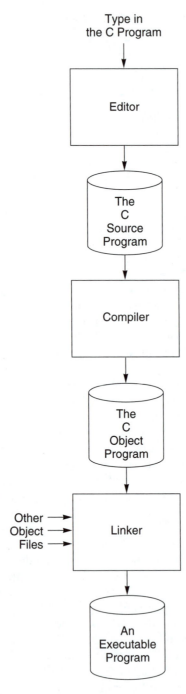

Figure F.2   Creating an executable C program

Table F.2 Operating system editor commands

Operating System	Command to Enter the Editor	Command to Save and Exit	Command to Exit without Saving
DOS	EDLIN	E	q
UNIX (screen editor)	vi	:wq or ZZ	:q!
UNIX (line editor)	e	w and then q or ctrl Z	q
VAX-VMS	E	ctrl E	ctrl Q

Once the editor program has been requested, the operating system relinquishes control to it. Again, as illustrated in Figure F.1, this means that you temporarily leave the world controlled by the operating system and its commands and enter the world controlled by the editor. The editor, like the operating system, has its own set of services and commands. The services provided by the editor include entering C statements, modifying and deleting existing statements in a program, listing a program, naming a program, saving a program, and exiting from the editor back into the operating system with or without saving the program.

In using an editor, you must carefully distinguish between entering a C statement and entering an editor command. Some editors make this distinction by using special keys to alert the editor that what is being typed is a command to the editor rather than the line of a program (for example, in BASIC, the line number informs the editor that the entered line is a program statement, and the absence of a line number informs the editor that the entered line is an editor command). Other editors, including those listed in Table F.2, contain two modes: a *text mode* for entering and modifying program statements, and a *command mode* for entering editor commands. Table F.3 lists the commands provided by the UNIX, DOS, and VAX-VMS editors for alerting the editor as to whether the text being typed is a command or a program statement.

In command mode, each editor permits you to perform the tasks listed in Table F.4. Once you have determined the editor you will be using, fill in Table F.4 (for some of these tasks, the required commands can be found in Tables F.2 and F.3).

Table F.3 Switching between command and text modes

Editor	Commands to Enter Text Mode from Command Mode	Commands to Enter Command Mode from Text Mode
DOS–EDLIN	i or type at line no.	Ctrl and C keys
UNIX–vi	a, i, o, c, s	Esc key
UNIX–ed	a, i, o, c, s	.(period)
VAX–EDT	c	Ctrl Z

Table F.4   Editor commands worksheet

Task	Command	Example
Save the program and exit the editor		
Save the program without exiting the editor		
Exit the editor without saving the program		
Switch to text mode (if applicable)		
Switch to command mode (if applicable)		
List the complete program from within the editor		
List a set of lines from within the editor		
List a single line from within the editor		
Delete the complete program from within the editor		
Delete a set of lines from within the editor		
Delete a single line from within the editor		
Name a program from within the editor		

Compiling and Linking

Translating a C source program into a form that can be executed by the computer is accomplished using a *compiler* program. The output produced by the compiler is called an *object* program. An object program is simply a translated version of the source program that can be executed by the computer system with one more processing step. Let us see why this is so.

Most C programs contain statements that use preprogrammed routines, called library functions, for finding such quantities as square roots, logarithms, trigonometric values, absolute values, or other commonly encountered mathematical calculations. Additionally, a large C program may be stored in two or more separate program files. However, multiple files must ultimately be combined to form a single program before the program can be

Table F.5 Specific operating system compile and link commands

Operating System	Compile and Link Command	Compile-Only Command	Link Command
UNIX	cc filename(s)	cc filename(s) -c	ld objectname(s) -lc
VAX-VMS	—	cc filename	lin filename
Your System			

Note: For each operating system listed in Table F.5, every source filename being compiled must end in a .c, and every object filename being linked must end in a .o. The output of a compile-only command automatically produces an equivalent .o object file if the compilation is successful.

executed. In both of these cases it is the task of the *linker* to combine all of the intrinsic functions and individual object files into a single program ready for execution. This final program is called an executable program.

Both the compiler and the linker programs can be accessed using individual operating system commands. For ease of operation, however, all operating systems that provide a C compiler also provide a single command that both compiles a C program and links it correctly with any other required object programs using one command. Table F.5 lists the commands required by the UNIX and VAX-VMS operating systems to either compile only, link only, or compile and link a C program to produce an executable program. (DOS does not provide a C compiler, so no entry is included in Table F.5 for this operating system.) Space has been left in the table to enter the command used by your computer or performing these operations.

Finally, once the C source program has been compiled and linked, it must be run. For the VAX-VMS operating system execution of the executable program is begun by simply typing the name of the program in response to the operating system prompt. In the UNIX operating system the executable program produced by the linker is named a.out. Thus, for the UNIX operating system, the execution of the last compiled and linked C program is initiated by typing a.out in response to the operating system prompt. Determine and then list the command used by your computer for performing this operation:

Operating system command to
execute a compiled and linked program: _____

Using Visual C++ Version 6.0

All of the C programs presented in the text can be created as console application project types using Visual C++ Version 6.0. These types of applications hide all of the visual components that can be created using Visual C++ and permit concentration on the basic syntax of C++ programming. The steps necessary to create console applications in Visual C++ Version 6.0 are presented in this appendix.

To successfully create C programs using Visual C++, you must first understand the development environment provided by a product known as Developer Studio. Developer Studio is the coordinating program under which many programming languages, such as Visual C++ and Java™, are developed, compiled, and executed.[1] When you start Visual C++ the screen shown in Figure G.1 is presented. This initial screen is referred to as the integrated development environment (IDE—pronounced as both the individual letters I-D-E and as the single word IDEE, which rhymes with the name Heide). The IDE provides a single, centralized screen from which all program development tools, from editing source code to compilation and production of an executable program, are accessible.[2]

As seen in Figure G.1, the IDE consists of a standard Microsoft window, where the conventional window components, such as the Title Bar, Menu Bar, and various toolbars, have been labeled around the window's outside border. Table G.1 lists the purpose of each of these components.

The complete process, from providing an editor for creating a source code file to building an executable program from one or more object files, can be controlled from Developer Studio's Integrated Development Environment. Keeping track of when the executable program is out of date because one or more of the source files have been modified, maintaining all graphical components used by a program, and handling other details

---

[1] Developer Studio currently supports the following development products: Visual C++, Visual J++®, Visual InterDev®, Visual SourceSafe™, and Microsoft Development Library (MSDN®). Visual Basic has its own development system.

[2] Historically, the concept of an IDE was introduced with Borland's Turbo Pascal product.

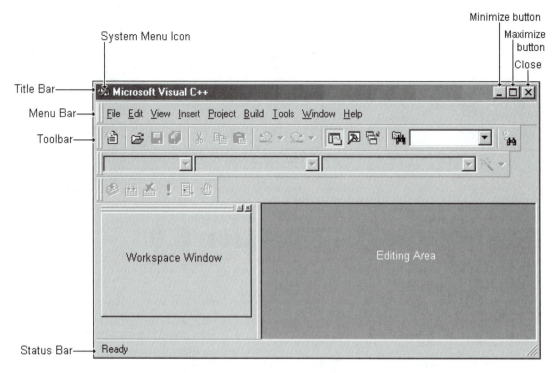

Figure G.1 The Developer Studio's Integrated Development Environment (IDE)

required in the building of an executable file are accomplished by Developer Studio using a number of internal files that it also automatically maintains. The complete set of files needed to build a Visual C++ program, including all user-entered source code files and all graphical resources, is referred to as a *project.*

Another term used in relation to all Windows operating systems is *application.* This term is frequently used in preference to the word program for two reasons. First, it is the term selected by Microsoft to designate any program that can be run under a Windows operating system. Second it can be used to avoid confusion with older procedural programs that had no graphical capabilities. In common practice, the terms program and application are frequently used interchangeably. Formally, however, it is more correct to say that each Visual C++ application is developed and stored as a project.

For each Visual C++ application that you create, Developer Studio uses a project workspace to store all of the files needed for a project, where a *project workspace,* or *workspace* for short, is simply a folder under which files related to a specific project are stored.[3] With the understanding that a project consists of a number of files, one of which must be a source code file if an executable application is to be created and all of which are typically stored under the same workspace folder,[4] we now proceed to use Developer Studio to select a project type.

---

[3] The files need not all reside in the same workspace folder, although for convenience they typically do.

[4] There are also a number of subfolders contained within the main project folder.

Table G.1 IDE window components

Component	Description
Title Bar	The colored bar at the top edge of a window that contains the window's name.
Menu Bar	Contains the names of the menus that can be used with the currently active window. The Menu Bar can be modified but cannot be deleted from the window.
Toolbars	The IDE contain ten toolbars, all of which can be visible at the same time. A toolbar contains icons, also referred to as buttons, that provide quick access to commonly used Menu Bar commands. Clicking a Toolbar button initiates the designated action represented by the button.
Status Bar	The Status Bar consists of individual "panes" that provide indicators about the window and its current status.
System Menu Icon	Clicking on this icon causes a pop-up menu to appear. The pop-up menu contains options to set the window's size and position or to close the window.
Minimize Box	Clicking on this icon causes the Windows operating system to reduce the window to the size of an icon.
Resize Box	Clicking on this icon causes the Windows operating system to reduce the size of the window and replaces the Resize Box with a Maximize Box.
Maximize Box	Clicking on this icon causes the Windows operating system to enlarge the window to the size of the screen and replaces the Maximize Box with a Resize Box.
Close Box	Clicking on this icon causes the Windows operating system to close the window.

The first step in creating a new C++ console application is to choose the File item from the Menu Bar, which brings up the File submenu illustrated in Figure G.2. The File submenu provides a number of file options, which we will use for creating a new application, as well as saving and recalling existing applications. For now, select the New option from within this submenu, which brings up the New dialog box shown in Figure G.3.

As shown in Figure G.3, Visual C++ provides a choice of project types, which are listed in Table G.2.[5] To create C++ programs for this text always select a Win32 Console Application project type from the New dialog box shown in Figure G.3

---

[5] The number of project types displayed depends on the number of installed Developer Studio products. For example, if you have also installed Visual J++ (Microsoft's JAVA product), the options appropriate to this language will also appear.

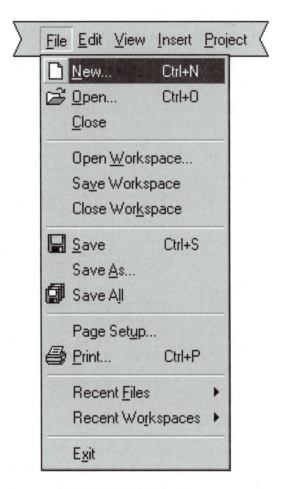

Figure G.2   The File submenu

(if you inadvertently select another project type, press the Cancel button on the next screen that appears).

As shown in Figure G.3, when starting a new project, first make sure that the Projects tab is active. From within the Projects tab, you must actively designate three items. The first item is to select the project type. The second item that must be provided is the name of the project. This project name must be entered in the Project name Text box shown in Figure G.3. In this text, each individual application is constructed in its own project workspace, using project names such as pgm1_1. Specifically, what this does for new projects is to create a new folder, which in this case is named pgm1_1. As shown in Figure G.3, the location of this folder is within the path listed in the Location drop-down list box, which is the third item that must be provided. Typically, the initial path for all project workspaces (again, this means folders) that you create is a default selectable from within the Options submenu of Developer Studio's Tools menu.

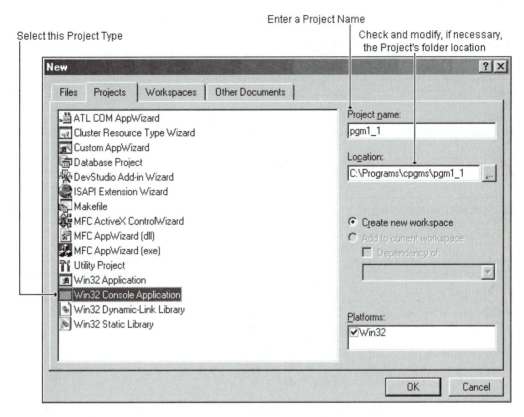

Figure G.3   The New Dialog Box

Once you have provided the information required by the dialog shown in Figure G.3 and selected the OK Command button, the dialog shown in Figure G.4 appears. From this dialog, select the first radio button option labeled `An empty project`. This selection brings up the information dialog shown in Figure G.5.

Pressing the OK button on the dialog box shown in Figure G.5 causes two things to happen. The first is that a number of files are automatically created and placed in the workspace folder for the new project. A list of the file types that are created is provided in Table G.3. Next, Developer Studio's IDE appears as shown in Figure G.6. In this figure, pay particular attention to the Workspace window. This window, which is also referred to as the Project Workspace window, displays a hierarchical list of projects in the current workspace and shows all of the items contained within each project.

Although only one workspace can be open at one time, a single workspace can contain multiple projects. Also notice that two additional tabs have been added to the Workspace window: the ClassView and FileView tabs. As files are now added or removed from a project, Visual C++ reflects all of these changes within the displayed hierarchical tree.

Table G.2 The professional edition's available project types

Project Type	Description
ATL COM AppWizard	Use an applications wizard to develop a COM object.
Custom AppWizard	Use an applications wizard to develop a complete customized application.
ISAPI Extension Wizard	Use an applications wizard to create modules that extend Internet Web servers.
Makefile	Create your own makefile that automatically compiles source code and creates an executable application.
MFC ActiveX Control Wizard	Use an applications wizard to create an ActiveX control.
MFC AppWizard (dll)	Use an applications wizard to create a dynamic link library MFC based module.
MFC AppWizard (exe)	Use an applications wizard to create an executable MFC based application.
Win32 Console Application	Create an empty project file with options correctly set to build a character-mode application.
Win32 Application	Create a Windows-based application that does not have to use the Microsoft Foundation Classes (the MFC can also be used in these applications).
Win32 Dynamic-Link Library	Create an empty project file with options correctly set to build a DLL.
Win32 Static Library	Create a static library file.
Cluster Resource Type Wizard	This wizard generates two projects for implementing a Microsoft Cluster Server (MSCS) resource type.
Custom AppWizard	Permits construction of a customized wizard that is useful for generating programs with a common functionality.
Database Project	(Enteprise edition only) Permits construction of a database project that can be used to directly test a SQL stored procedure.
Utility Project	Creates a project with no files. Used to generate a project that can be used as a container for files you can build without a link step:

The hierarchical tree used in both the ClassView and FileView tabs is a standard window's folder tree structure, which means that you can expand and contract tree sections by clicking on plus (+) and minus (−) symbols, respectively. As always, sections of the tree that are hidden from view due to the size of the window can be displayed using the attached scroll bars.

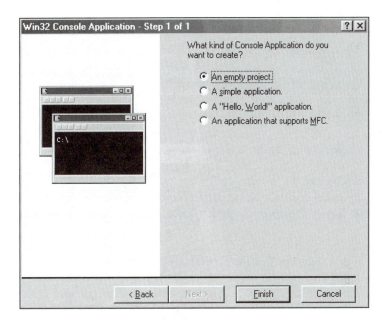

Figure G.4   Selecting the type of console application

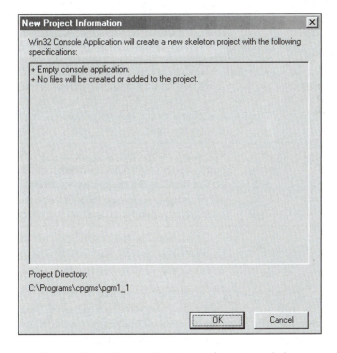

Figure G.5   The application's information dialog

Programming Note

Creating a Console Application

To create a console application:

1. Select the File menu and select New (or use the accelerator key sequence Ctrl+N), which brings up a New dialog box.
2. Click on the Projects tab.
3. Select Win32ConsoleApplication as the project type.
4. Enter a Project name, which becomes the name of the workspace folder for the project.
5. Modify, if necessary, the workspace folder's path.
6. Click the OK Command button.

Table G.3 File types provided within a workspace folder

File Extension	Description
.dsw	A project workspace file used to store information at the workspace level, such as the number of projects stored in the workspace. Clicking on this file will bring up the complete project.
.dsp	A project file that contains information about how the executable version of a single project is to be built. This is equivalent to the makefile used in earlier versions of Visual C++ that had the extension .mak.
.opt	The workspace options file, which is used to store project workspace settings. This file contains local settings, such as the appearance of the project workspace using your hardware configuration. A new options file is created automatically whenever a workspace is opened and no workspace options file is found.

The procedure for creating a C++ source code file is almost identical to the one used in creating a new project. To create the source code file, select the New option from within the Menu Bar's File menu. This brings up the New dialog, which we previously used in creating a new project (see Figure G.3). In this case, however, activate the Files tab, as illustrated in Figure G.7. Within this dialog, you see that the check box to add a file to the existing project has been checked, and the active project workspace name has been inserted within the first drop-down List box. Additionally, the drive and path for this

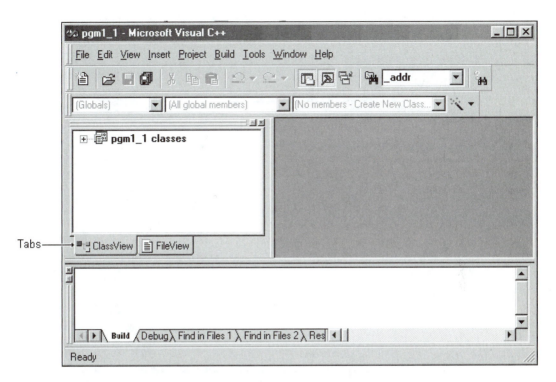

Figure G.6   The IDE containing an active workspace

current project workspace folder are automatically provided in the file Location text box. Your responsibility is now to select a file type and provide the file with a name.

From the list of file types provided in the New dialog shown in Figure G.7, select the C++ Source File choice and then provide a name for the file. As shown in Figure G.7, the name we have given to the source file is pgm1_1. Upon providing this information and pressing the dialog's OK Command button, Developer Studio creates a file named pgm1_1.cpp within the pgm1_1 folder. Notice that the cpp extension to the file name is automatically appended by Developer Studio because Visual C++ requires that all source code files have this extension. After this is done, the IDE appears as shown in Figure G.8.

In reviewing Figure G.8 pay particular attention to the Workspace window. Note that the ClassView tab is active. Activating the FileView tab and then expanding the tree, as shown in Figure G.9, reveals that a file named pgm1_1.cpp has been added to the hierarchy tree. The arrow that is displayed within the icon indicates that this file is an active part of the project (for example, it is not part of some other project that is being stored in the current workspace folder) and will be used when an executable file is ultimately built. At this stage, the Visual C++ text editor has been loaded and you can now enter C source code in the Editing area. The entered source code can now be saved as the file pgm1_1.cpp.

Select this File Type

Enter a File Name - <u>Does Not</u> have to be the same name as the Project Name

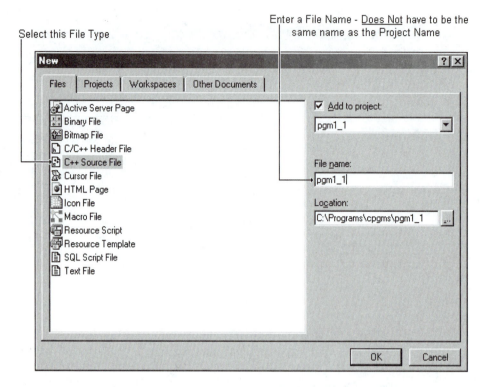

Figure G.7 Creating a C++ source code file

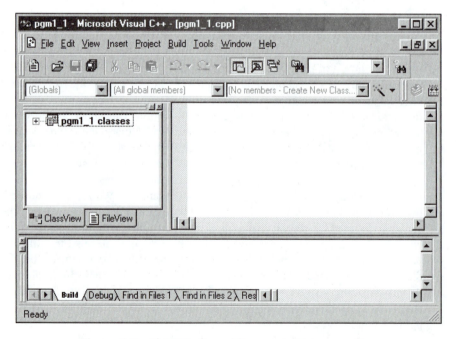

Figure G.8 The IDE after adding an empty source file

Programming Note

Adding a Source Code File to a Project

To add a new source code file to a currently active project:

1. Select the File menu and select New (or use the accelerator key sequence Ctrl+N), which will bring up a New dialog box
2. Click on the Files tab
3. Select C++ Source File as the file type
4. Enter a File name
5. Modify, if necessary, the file's folder path
6. Click the OK Command button
7. Enter the desired source code in the now active Editing Area

An alternative to creating a new source file, as illustrated in Figure G.7, is to select either of the middle two options previously shown in Figure G.4. Both of these choices automatically create a source code file and display the editor window shown in Figure G.9, with a number of code lines already added. Because all of the provided code is not needed, you can delete it and type in the desired code starting with the line `#include <iostream.h>`.

An alternative to entering source code manually is to insert an existing source code file into the current project. For example, if you wanted to run one of the programs contained in this text, you could insert the desired source code directly from the student disk supplied with the text. To do this, you first select the File As Text option from the Insert menu, as shown in Figure G.10, and then provide the correct path and file name in the next displayed dialog.

Once your source code has been entered, select the Build menu's Execute to compile and run your program. Alternatively, you can press the Control and F5 function keys together to activate the accelerator keys for compiling and running an application.

Saving and Recalling a Project

To save a project, first select the File menu and then select either the Save Workspace or the Save All option from the File menu previously shown in Figure G.2. Doing so saves all of the files in the current workspace.

To retrieve a project, either select the Open Workspace option from the File submenu or select the Recent Workspaces option from this same submenu (see Figure G.2). If you select the Open Workspace option, you are presented with a standard Window's Open dialog, which requires that you select a disk, folder, and file name. By using the Recent Workspace option, you are presented with a number of recently used workspaces from

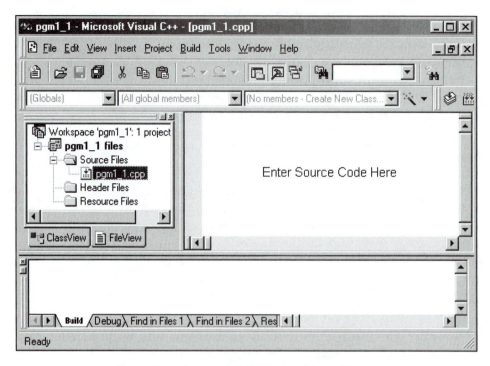

Figure G.9　An expanded FileView hierarchy tree

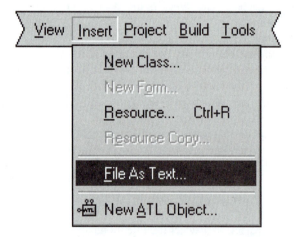

Figure G.10　Inserting a source code file

which you can select the desired workspace (the maximum number of recently used workspaces that is displayed can be set using the Workspace tab under the Options selection of the Tools submenu).

Using the Toolbar

Once you have become comfortable with the Menu Bar items and understand how they operate and interconnect, you should take a closer look at the standard Toolbar. For the most commonly used features of Visual C++, a click on the appropriate Toolbar icon performs the desired operation. To make sure the standard Toolbar is visible, right-click the mouse on the Menu Bar and make sure that a check mark (✔) appears to the left of the Standard item. For your immediate use, the most useful standard Toolbar button is the Save All icon, which is the fourth icon from the left. It is the icon that appears as a stacked set of three diskettes.

Using C++ Builder

All of the C programs presented in this text can be created as console applications in C++ Builder. These types of applications hide all of the visual components that can be created using C++ Builder and permit concentration on the basic syntax of C programming. The steps necessary to create console applications in C++ Builder are presented in this appendix.

When you start C++ Builder, the screen shown in Figure H.1 is presented. This initial screen is referred to as the integrated development environment (IDE—pronounced as both the individual letters I-D-E and as the single word IDEE, which rhymes with the name Heide). The IDE provides a single centralized screen from which all program development tools, from editing source code to compilation and production of an executable program, are accessible.

The first step in creating a new C++ console application is to choose the File item from the Menu Bar, which brings up the File submenu illustrated in Figure H.2. The File submenu provides a number of file options, which we will use for creating a new program, as well as saving and recalling existing programs. For now, select the New option from within this submenu, which brings up the New dialog box shown in Figure H.3.

As shown in Figure H.3, the Professional Edition of C++ Builder provides a choice of ten new item types. To create C++ console programs for this text always select the `Console App` icon, contained within the New tab shown in Figure H.3. This brings up the editor window shown in Figure H.4, which includes a number of code lines already added. Because all of these lines are not needed, you can delete them all and type in the desired code, starting with the line `#include <stdio.h>`, or just delete those lines that are not required by your program.[1] To compile and run your program, you can either click the Toolbar's arrowhead icon (the one shown in Figure H.1, directly under the Main menu's Project option) or use the Main menu's Run option. Similarly, a program can be saved and recalled the File option's Save and Open suboptions, as previously shown in Figure H.1.

---

[1] Notice that `main()`'s header line provides for the input of command line arguments, which are presented in Section 12.4. You can either use this expanded header line or replace it with `int main()`.

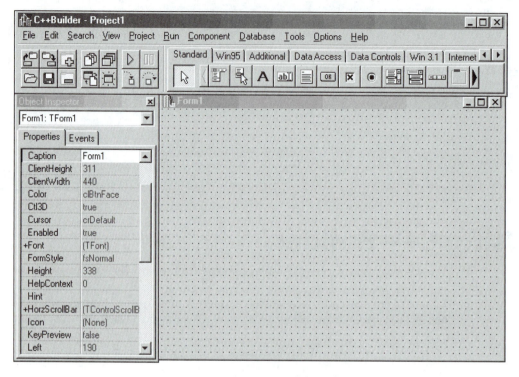

Figure H.1   The C++ Builder's IDE

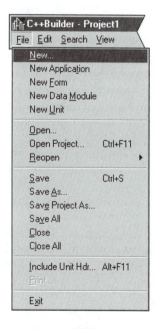

Figure H.2   The File submenu

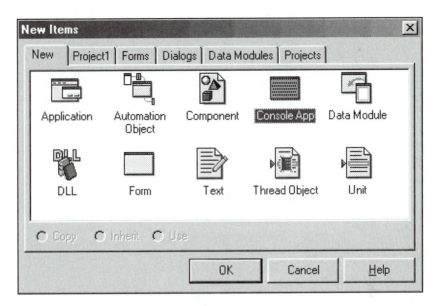

Figure H.3   The new items dialog box

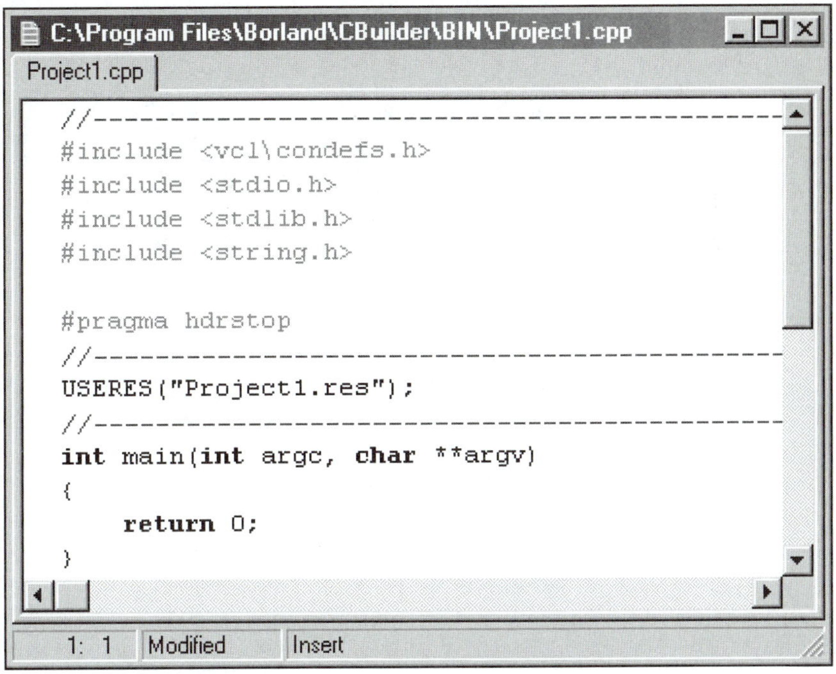

```
//------------------------------------------------
#include <vcl\condefs.h>
#include <stdio.h>
#include <stdlib.h>
#include <string.h>

#pragma hdrstop
//------------------------------------------------
USERES("Project1.res");
//------------------------------------------------
int main(int argc, char **argv)
{
    return 0;
}
```

Figure H.4   The initial editor window

A Potential Problem

One annoying problem that is typically encountered when executing a C++ Builder console application under a Windows operating system is the immediate closure of the DOS window under which the program is run. To keep this DOS window from immediately closing, you can use code similar to the following:

```
int i;                 /* place this after the opening brace { */
scanf("%d", &i);    /* place this before the return statement */
```

This code will hold the window open, waiting for the user to input a value. Pressing any digit key will then cause the program to terminate.

Appendix I

Solutions

Section 1.1

1. a. A computer program is a sequence of instructions used to operate a computer to produce a specific result.
   b. Programming is the process of writing instructions in a programming language to produce a computer program.
   c. A programming language is the set of instructions that can be used to construct a program.
   d. An algorithm is a step-by-step sequence of instructions that describes how to perform a computation; more generally, it details how data is to be processed to produce the desired result.
   e. Pseudocode is a means of describing an algorithm using simple English phrases.
   f. A flowchart uses specifically defined graphical shapes to pictorially describe an algorithm.
   g. A source program consists of the program statements comprising a C or other programming language program.
   h. An object program is a machine language version of a source program.
   i. A compiler is a program that is used to translate a high-level source program as a complete unit before any one statement is actually executed.
   j. An interpreter is a program that translates individual source program statements, one at a time, into executable statements. Each statement is executed immediately after translation.

3. Step 1: Pour the contents of the first cup into the third cup
   Step 2: Rinse out the first cup
   Step 3: Pour the contents of the second cup into the first cup
   Step 4: Rinse out the second cup
   Step 5: Pour the contents of the third cup into the second cup

5. Step 1: Compare the first number with the second number and use the smallest of these numbers for the next step.

   Step 2: Compare the smallest number found in step 1 with the third number. The smallest of these two numbers is the smallest of all three numbers.

7. a. Step 1: Compare the first name in the list with the name "Jones." If the names match, stop the search; else go to step 2.

Step 2: Compare the next name in the list with the name "Jones." If the names match, stop the search; else repeat this step.

Section 1.2

1.

m1234()	Valid. Not a mnemonic.
newBal()	Valid. A mnemonic.
abcd()	Valid. Not a mnemonic.
A12345()	Valid. Not a mnemonic.
1A2345()	Invalid. Violates rule 1; starts with a number.
power()	Valid. A mnemonic.
absVal()	Valid. A mnemonic.
invoices()	Valid. A mnemonic.
do()	Invalid. Violates Rule 3; is a reserved word.
while()	Invalid. Violates Rule 3; is a reserved word.
add5()	Valid. Could be a mnemonic.
taxes()	Valid. A mnemonic.
netPay()	Valid. A mnemonic.
12345()	Invalid. Violates Rule 1; starts with a number.
int()	Invalid. Violates rule 3; is a reserved word.
newBalance()	Valid. A mnemonic.
a2b3c4d5()	Valid. Not a mnemonic.
salestax()	Valid. A mnemonic.
amount()	Valid. A mnemonic.
$taxes()	Invalid. Violates Rule 1; starts with a special character.

3. a.
```
int main()
{
    input();       /* input the items purchased */
    salestax();    /* compute required salestax */
    balance();     /* determine balance owed */
    calcbill();    /* determine and output bill */

    return 0;
}
```

b. These functions might be used to determine the billing for an order for goods purchased. The purpose of each function, as indicated by its name, is given in the comment statements (/* . . . */) for each function call.

Note for Exercises 5 through 9

Many solutions are possible for these exercises. The following are possible answers.

5. Determine the guest list
   Determine the time and place of the party
   Invite people on the guest list
   Order a cake
   Determine the type of other refreshments needed
   Determine the party favors needed
   Order the refreshments and party favors
   Designate someone to bring the birthday person

7. Determine which vegetables to grow
   Determine how much land each vegetable will require
   Buy the seeds and plants
   Prepare the soil for each vegetable
   Find out when last major frost is expected to determine the right time to plant each seed or plant
   Properly plant each type of seed or plant

Section 1.3

1. a.
```
#include <stdio.h>
int main()
{
   printf("Joe Smith");
   printf("\n99 Somewhere Street");
   printf("\nNonesuch, N.J., 07030");

   return 0;
}
```

3. a. Five `printf()` statements would be used.
   b. One would work by including newline escape sequences between each two items displayed. Using one line is undesirable since it would make column alignment difficult and the program code hard to debug.
   c.
```
#include <stdio.h>
int main()
{
   printf("PART No.          PRICE\n\n");
   printf("T1267             $6.34\n");
   printf("T1300             $8.92\n");
   printf("T2401             $65.40\n");
   printf("T4482             $36.99\n");

   return 0;
}
```

Section 1.4

1. a. Yes.
   b. It is not in standard form. To make programs more readable and easier to debug, the standard form presented in Section 1.4 of the textbook should be used.

3. a. Two backslashes in a row results in one backslash being displayed.
   b. `printf("\\ is a backslash.\n");`

Section 1.5

1. a. One output: the total dollar amount
   b. Five inputs: the number of half-dollars, quarters, dimes, nickels, and pennies.
   c. 5 * half-dollars + .25 * quarters + .10 * dimes + 0.5 * nickels + .01 * pennies

3. a. One output: the value of Ergies
   b. Two inputs: the number of Fergies and the number of Lergies
   c. Use the given formula

5. a. One output: the distance traveled
   b. Three inputs: the values of s, t, and d
   c. Use the given formula

7. a. Two outputs: the weekly gross and net pay of each individual
   b. Eight inputs: the hourly rate, hours worked, income tax rate, and medical benefits rate for each individual (Note, if you consider the tax and benefits rates as fixed, then there are four inputs)
   c. Gross pay = Hourly rate * Hours worked
       The general formula for calculating Net pay is

   Net pay = Gross pay – Tax rate * Gross pay – Medical benefits rate * Gross pay
   = Gross pay * (1 – Tax rate – Medical benefits rate)

   If the tax and benefits rates are considered as fixed numbers that will not change, this formula can be written as:

   Net Pay = Gross pay (1 – 0.2 – 0.02) = 0.78 * Gross pay

9. a. One output: the value of y
   b. One input, the value of x
   c. Use the given formula

Section 2.1

1. a. float or double   d. integer
   b. integer   e. float or double
   c. float or double

3. $1.26e^2$ $6.5623e^2$ $3.42695e^3$ $4.8932e^3$ $3.21e^{-1}$ $1.23e^{-2}$ $6.789e^{-3}$

5.

S	W	A	N	S	O	N
01010011	01010111	01000001	01001110	01010011	01001111	01001110

9. a. $8 * 1{,}048{,}576 = 8{,}388{,}608$ bytes
   b. $16 * 1{,}048{,}576 = 16{,}777{,}216$ bytes
   c. $32 * 1{,}048{,}576 = 33{,}554{,}432$ bytes
   d. $128 * 1{,}048{,}576 = 134{,}217{,}728$ bytes
   e. $8 * 1{,}048{,}576 = 8{,}388{,}608$ words x 2bytes/word $= 16{,}777{,}216$ bytes
   f. $16 * 1{,}048{,}576 = 16{,}777{,}216$ words x 4bytes/word $= 67{,}108{,}864$ bytes
   g. $1.44 * 1{,}048{,}576 = 1{,}509{,}949$ bytes

Section 2.2

1. a. $2 * 3 + 4 * 5$
   b. $(6 + 18) / 2$
   c. $4.5 / (12.2 - 3.1)$
   d. $4.6 * (3.0 + 14.9)$
   e. $(12.1 + 18.9) * (15.3 - 3.8)$

3. As all operands are floating point numbers, the result of each valid expression is a floating point number.

a.	5.	g.	–50.
b.	10.	h.	–2.5
c.	24.0	i.	invalid expression
d.	0.2	j.	10.
e.	3.6	k.	53.
f.	invalid expression		

5. a. 27.0   e.   22.67
   b. 8.0   f. 19.78
   c. 1.0   g. 6.0
   d. 22.0   h. 2.0

7. a. $\text{'m'} - 5 = \text{'h'}$ e. $\text{'b'} - \text{'a'} = 1$
   b. $\text{'m'} + 5 = \text{'r'}$ f. $\text{'g'} - \text{'a'} + 1 = 6 + 1 = 7$
   c. $\text{'G'} + 6 = \text{'M'}$ g. $\text{'G'} - \text{'A'} + 1 = 6 + 1 = 7$
   d. $\text{'G'} - 6 = \text{'A'}$

Section 2.3

1. answer1 is the integer 5
   answer2 is the integer 2

5. a. The comma is within the control string and the statement is not terminated with a semi-colon. This statement will generate a compiler error, even if the semicolon is appended to the statement.

b. The statement uses a floating point control sequence with an integer argument. The statement will compile and print an unpredictable result.

c. The statement uses an integer control sequence with a floating point constant. The statement will compile and print an unpredictable result.

d. The statement has no control sequences for the numerical arguments. The statement will compile and print the letters a b c. The numerical values are ignored.

e. The statement uses a floating point control sequence with an integer argument. The statement will compile and print an unpredictable result.

f. The f conversion character has been omitted from the control string. The statement will compile and print %3.6. The second numerical value has no effect.

g. The formatting string must come before the arguments. The statement will compile and produce no output.

9. The value of 14 in octal is 16
The value of 14 in hexadecimal is E.
The value of 0xA in decimal is 10.
The value of 0xA in octal is 12.

Section 2.4

1. The following are not valid:

12345	does not begin with either a letter or underscore
while	reserved word
$total	does not begin with either a letter or underscore
new bal	cannot contain a space
9ab6	does not begin with either a letter or underscore
sum.of	contains a special character

3. a. `int count;`
   b. `float grade;`
   c. `double yield;`
   d. `char initial;`

5. a. `int firstnum, secnum;`
   b. `float price, yield, coupon;`
   c. `double maturity;`

7. a.

```
#include <stdio.h>
int main()
{
  int num1;       /* declare the integer variable num1  */
  int num2;       /* declare the integer variable num2  */
  int total;      /* declare the integer variable total */
```

```
num1 = 25;               /* assign the integer 25 to num1         */
num2 = 30;               /* assign the integer 30 to num2         */
total = num1 + num2;     /* assign the sum of num1 and num2 to total   */
printf("The total of %d and %d is %d.\n",num1,num2,total");
 /*          prints:  The total of 25 and 30 is 55. */

return 0;
}
```

9.
```
#include <stdio.h>
int main()
{
   int length, width, perim;

   length = 16;
   width = 18;
   perim = 2 * (length + width);
   printf("The perimeter is %d.",perim);

   return 0;
}
```

13. Every variable has type (e.g., `int`, `float`, etc.), a value, and an address in memory where it is stored.

15. a.

Addresses:	159	160	161	162	163	164	165	166
					W	O	W	!
	rate				ch1	ch2	ch3	ch4

Addresses:	167	168	169	170	171	172	173	174
	taxes							

Addresses:	175	175	177	178	179	180	181	182
			0	0				
	num		count					

The empty addresses are usually filled with "garbage" values, meaning their contents are whatever happened to be placed there by the computer or by the previously run program.

Section 2.5

1. a. For an IBM PC or compatible computer using an Intel Pentium chip, the storage size of a character is one byte and of an integer four bytes.

   b. On an IBM PC or compatible computer using an Intel Pentium chip, two bytes are reserved for short integers, four bytes for unsigned integers, and four bytes for long integers.

3. Only a definition statement is necessary to set aside the right amount of storage space for a variable.

Section 3.1

1. a.
```
include <stdio.h>
int main()
{
```
   ← missing declaration for all variables
```
    width = 15 ← missing semicolon
    area = length * width; ← no value assigned to length
    printf("The area is %d",area ← missing ");

    return 0;
}
```
The corrected program is
```
#include <stdio.h>
int main()
{
    int length, width, area;

    width = 15;
    length = 20;    /* must be assigned some value */
    area = length * width;
    printf("The area is %d", area);

    return 0;
}
```
   b.
```
#include <stdio.h>
int main()
{
    int length, width, area;

    area = length * width; ← this should come after the assignment of values to
                                              length and width
    length = 20;
    width = 15;
    printf("The area is %d", area);

    return 0;
}
```

The corrected program is

```c
#include <stdio.h>
int main()
{
    int length, width, area;

    length = 20;
    width = 15;
    area = length * width;
    printf("The area is %d", area);

    return 0;
}
```

c.
```c
#include <stdio.h>
int main()
{
    int length, width, area;

    length = 20;
    width = 15;
    length * width = area;  ← incorrect assignment statement
    printf("The area is %d", area);

    return 0;
}
```

The corrected program is

```c
#include <stdio.h>
int main()
{
    int length, width, area;

    length = 20;
    width = 15;
    area = length * width;
    printf("The area is %d", area);

    return 0;
}
```

3. a.
```c
#include <stdio.h>
int main()
{
    float radius, circum;

    radius = 3.3; /* could have been done in the declaration */
    circum = 2 * 3.1416 * radius;
    printf("The circumference is %f inches",circum);

    return 0;
}
```

5. a.
```
#include <stdio.h>
int main()
{
    float length, width, depth, volume;

    length= 25.0;
    width = 10.0;
    depth = 6.0;
    volume = length * width * depth;
    printf("The volume of the pool is %f",volume);

    return 0;
}
```

7. a.
```
#include <stdio.h>
int main()
{
    float  total;

    total = 12*.50 + 20*.25 + 32*.10 + 45*.05 + 27*.01;
    printf("The total amount is $%5.2f\n", total);

    return 0;
}
```

9. c.
```
#include <stdio.h>
int main()
{
    float speed = 58.0, dist = 183.67, time;

    time = dist/speed;
    printf("The elapsed time for the trip is %f hours",time);

    return 0;
}
```

11. The second expression is correct because the assignment of 25 to b is done before the subtraction. Without the parentheses the subtraction has the higher precedence, and the expression a – b is calculated, yielding a value, say 10. The subsequent attempt to assign the value of 25 to this value is incorrect and is equivalent to the expression 10 = 25. Values can only be assigned to variables.

Section 3.2

1. `&average` means "the address of the variable named average."

3. a.
```
#include <stdio.h>
int main()
{
   char key, choice;
   int num, count;
   long date;
   float yield;
   double price;

   printf("The address of the variable key is %p\n",&key);
   printf("The address of the variable choice is %p\n",&choice);
   printf("The address of the variable num is %p\n",&num);
   printf("The address of the variable count is %p\n"&count);
   printf("The address of the variable date is %p\n"&date);
   printf("The address of the variable yield is %p\n",&yield);
   printf("The address of the variable price is %p\n",&price);

   return 0;
}
```

5. a. `*xAddr`
  b. `*yAddr`
  c. `*ptYld`
  d. `*ptMiles`
  e. `*mptr`
  f. `*pdate`
  g. `*distPtr`
  h. `*tabPt`
  i. `*hoursPt`

7. a. Each of these variables is a pointer. This means that addresses will be stored in each of these variables.
  b. They are not very descriptive names and do not give an indication that they are pointers.

9. All pointer variable declarations must have an asterisk. Therefore, c, e, g, and i are pointer declarations.

11.

Variable: ptNum	Variable: amtAddr
Address: 500	Address: 564
8096	16256

Variable: zAddr	Variable: numAddr
Address: 8024	Address: 10132
20492	18938

Variable: ptDay	Variable: ptYr
Address: 14862	Address: 15010
20492	694

Variable: years	Variable: m
Address: 694	Address: 8096
1987	

Variable: amt	Variable: firstnum
Address: 16256	Address: 18938
154	154

Variable: balance	Variable: k
Address: 20492	Address: 24608
25	154

Section 3.3

1. a. `scanf("%d", &firstnum);`

b. `scanf("%f", &grade);`

c. `scanf("%lf", &secnum);  /* note - the lf is required */`

d. `scanf("%c", &keyval);`

e. `scanf("%d %d %f", &month, &years, &average);`

f. `scanf("%c %d %d %lf %lf",&ch, &num1, &num2, &grade1, &grade2);`

g. `scanf("%f %f %f %lf %lf",&interest, &principal, &capital,`
   `                                &price, &yield);`

h. scanf("%c %c %c %d %d %d",&ch, &letter1, &letter2, &num1,
&num2, &num3);

i. scanf("%f %f %f %lf %lf %lf",&temp1, &temp2, &temp3,
&volts1, &volts2);

3. a. Missing & operator in front of num1. The correct form is

scanf("%d", &num1);

b. Missing & operator in front of firstnum and wrong control sequence for price. The correct form is

scanf("%d %f %lf", &num1, &firstnum, &price);

c. The wrong control sequence for num1 and secnum. The correct form is

scanf("%d %f %lf", &num1, &secnum, &price);

d. Missing & operators in front of all the variables. The correct form is

scanf("%d %d %lf", &num1, &num2, &yield);

e. Missing control string entirely. The correct form is

scanf("%d %d", &num1, &num2);

f. Reversed address and control string. The correct form is

scanf("%d", &num1);

5. a.
```
#include <stdio.h>
int main()
{
  float fahr, cel;

  printf("Enter the temperature in degrees Fahrenheit: ");
  scanf("%f", &fahr);
  cel = (5.0/9.0) * (fahr - 32.0);
  printf("\n%f degrees Fahrenheit is %f degrees Celsius", fahr, cel);

  return 0;
}
```

7. a.
```
#include <stdio.h>
int main()
{
  float miles, gallons;

  printf("Enter the miles driven: ");
  scanf("%f",&miles);
  printf("Enter the gallons of gas used: ");
  scanf("%f",&gallons);
  printf("The miles/gallon is %5.2f",miles/gallons);

  return 0;
}
```

9. a.
```c
#include <stdio.h>
int main()
{
    float num1, num2, num3, num4, avg;

    printf("Enter a number: ");
    scanf("%f", &num1);
    printf("\nEnter a second number: ");
    scanf("%f", &num2);
    printf("\nEnter a third number: ");
    scanf("%f", &num3);
    printf("\nEnter a fourth number: ");
    scanf("%f", &num4);
    avg = (num1 + num2 + num3 + num4) / 4.0;
    printf("\nThe average of the four numbers is %f", avg);

    return 0;
}
```

13. a. It is easy for a user to enter incorrect data. If wrong or unexpected data is given by the user, either incorrect results will be obtained or the program will "crash." A *crash* is an unexpected and premature program termination.

b. In a data type check the input is checked to ensure that the values entered are of the correct type for the declared variables. This includes checking that integer values are entered for integer variables, and so on. A data reasonableness check, on the other hand, determines that the value entered is reasonable for the particular program. Such a check would determine that a large number was entered when a very small number was expected, or a small number was entered when a large number was expected, or that a zero or a negative number was entered when a positive number was expected (which, for example, could cause problems if the number was the denominator in a division), and so on.

c. Data type checks would ensure that the month, day, and year were all entered as integers. Some simple reasonableness checks would ensure that a month was between 1 and 12, a day between 1 and 31, and a year between reasonable limits for the application. More complex reasonableness checks might check that a day in months 1, 3, 5, 7, 8, 10, and 12 were between 1 and 31, those in months 4, 6, 9, and 11 between 1 and 30, and those in month 2 between 1 and 28, except if the year is a leap year, in which case the day must be between 1 and 29 in month 2.

15.
```c
#include <stdio.h>
int main()
{
    float num1, num2, temp;

    printf("Please type in a number: ");
    scanf("%f", &num1);
    printf("Please type in another number: ");
    scanf("%f", &num2);
    printf("\nBefore the swap num1 is %f and num2 is %f", num1, num2);
    temp = num1;    /* store num1 in temp */
    num1 = num2;    /* copy num2 to num1  */
    num2 = temp;    /* copy temp to num2  */
```

```
      printf("\nAfter the swap num1 is %f and num2 is %f", num1, num2);

      return 0;
   }
```

Section 3.5

1.
```
   #include <stdio.h>
   #define PI 3.1416
   int main()
   {
      float radius,cirucum;

      printf("\nEnter a radius; ");
      scanf("%f", &radius);
      circum = 2.0 * PI * radius;
      printf("\nThe circumference of the circle is %f", circum);

      return 0;
   }
```

3.
```
   #include <stdio.h>
   #define CONVERT (5.0/9.0)
   #define FREEZING 32.0
   int main()
   {
      float fahren,celsius;

      printf("\nEnter a temperature in degrees Fahrenheit: ");
      scanf("%f", &fahren);
      celsius = CONVERT * (fahren - FREEZING);
      printf("\nThe equivalent Celsius temperature is %f", celsius);

      return 0;
   }
```

Section 4.1

1. a. The relational expression is true. Therefore, its value is 1.
 b. The relational expression is true. Therefore, its value is 1.
 c. The final relational expression is true. Therefore, its value is 1.
 d. The final relational expression is true. Therefore, its value is 1.
 e. The final relational expression is true. Therefore, its value is 1.
 f. The arithmetic expression has a value of 10.
 g. The arithmetic expression has a value of 4.
 h. The arithmetic expression has a value of 0.
 i. The arithmetic expression has a value of 10.

3. a. `age == 30`   f.   `age == 30 && ht > 6.00`
   b. `temp > 98.6`   g. `day == 15 && month == 1`
   c. `ht < 6.00`   h. `age > || employ >= 5`
   d. `month == 12`   i. `id < 500 && age > 55`
   e. `letter == 'm'`   j. `len > 2.00 && len < 3.00`

Section 4.2

1. a. `if (angle == 90)`
          `printf("The angle is a right angle");`
       `else`
          `printf("The angle is not a right angle");`
   b. `if (temperature > 100)`
          `printf("above the boiling point of water");`
       `else`
          `printf("below the boiling point of water");`
   c. `if (number > 0)`
          `positiveSum = number + positiveSum;`
       `else`
          `negativeSum = number + negativeSum;`
   d. `if (slope < .5)`
          `flag = 0;`
       `else`
          `flag = 1;`
   e. `if ((num1 - num2) < .001)`
          `approx = 0;`
       `else`
          `approx = (num1 - num2)/2.0;`
   f. `if ((temp1 - temp2) > 2.3)`
          `error = (temp1 - temp2) * factor;`
   g. `if ((x > y) && (z < 20))`
          `scanf("%d", &p);`
   h. `if ((distance > 20) && (distance < 35))`
          `scanf("%ld", &time);`

3. a.
```
#include <stdio.h>
int main()
{
  float grade;

  printf("Enter a grade: ");
  scanf("%f", &grade);
  if (grade >= 70)
    printf("A passing grade \n");
  else
    printf("A failing grade\n");

  return 0;
}
```

b. Three runs should be made using input values of 70, a value higher than 70, and a value lower than 70.

5. a.
```c
#include <stdio.h>
#define SENIORPAY 400.00
#define JUNIORPAY 275.00

int main()
{
  char status;

  printf("Enter the status code (Ex. s):");
  scanf("%c", &status);
  if (status == 's' || status == 'S')
    printf("The pay is $%5.2f\n", SENIORPAY);
  else
    printf("The pay is $%5.2f\n", JUNIORPAY);

  return 0;
}
```

7. a.
```c
#include <stdio.h>
int main()
{
  int month, day;

  printf("Enter a month (use a 1 for Jan, 2 for Feb, etc.): ");
  scanf("%d", &month);
  printf("Enter a day of the month: ");
  scanf("%d", &day);

  if (month > 12 || month < 1)
    printf("\nAn incorrect month was entered.");

  if (day < 1 || day > 31)
  printf("\nAn incorrect day was entered.");

  return 0;
}
```

b. If the user enters a floating point number, the `scanf` format string will assign the integer part of the number to the integer month variable, so that the month will be correct. It will then attempt to use the remaining fractional value for the day input, resulting in an incorrect value assigned to the day variable.

A possible solution is to accept the month variable as a floating point number, and then reassign it to an integer variable to correctly truncate it. No harm is done then if an integer is entered for the month (`scanf()` will first convert it to a floating point number) or if a floating point number is entered. More correctly, a cast should be used.

9.

```c
#include <stdio.h>
int main()
{
  char inKey;
  int position;

  printf("Enter a lowercase letter: ");
  scanf("%c", &inKey);
  if (inKey >= 'a' && inKey <= 'z')
  {
    position = inKey - 'a' + 1;
    printf("The character's position is %d", position);
  }
  else
    printf("The character just entered is not a lowercase letter");

  return 0;
}
```

11.

```c
#include <stdio.h>
int main()
{
  char inKey;
  int position;

  printf("Enter a letter: ");
  scanf("%c", &inKey);
  if (inKey >= 'A' && inKey <= 'Z')
  {
    position = inKey - 'A' + 1;
    printf("The character just entered is an uppercase letter\n");
    printf("Its position in the alphabet is %d\n", position);
  }
  else
    printf("The character just entered is not an uppercase letter\n");

  return 0;
}
```

13. The error is that the intended relational expression `letter == 'm'` has been written as the assignment expression `letter = 'm'`. When the expression is evaluated the character m is assigned to the variable letter and the value of the expression itself is the value of `'m'`. Since this is a nonzero value, it is taken as true and the message is displayed.

Another way of looking at this is to realize that the `if` statement, as written in the program, is equivalent to the following two statements:

```c
letter = 'm';
if(letter) printf("Hello there!");
```

A correct version of the program is

```
#include <stdio.h>
int main()
{
  char letter;

  printf("Enter a letter: ");
  scanf("%c", &letter);
  if (letter == 'm') printf("Hello there!");

  return 0;
}
```

Section 4.3

1.
```
#include <stdio.h>
int main()
{
  float grade;
  char letter;

  printf("Enter the student's numerical grade: ");
  scanf("%f", &grade);
  if (grade >= 90.0) letter = 'A';
  else if (grade >= 80.0) letter = 'B';
  else if (grade >= 70.0) letter = 'C';
  else if (grade >= 60.0) letter = 'D';
  else letter = 'F';
  printf("\nThe student receives a grade of %c", letter);

  return 0;
}
```

Note that an `else-if` chain is used. If simple `if` statements were used, a grade entered as `75.5`, for example, would be assigned to a `"C"` because it was greater than `70.0`. But, the grade would then be reassigned to `"D"` because it is also greater than `60.0`.

3.
```
#include <stdio.h>
int main()
{
  float fahr,cels,inTemp;
  char letter;

  printf("Enter a temperature followed by");
  printf(" one space and the temperature's type\n");
  printf(" (an f designates a fahrenheit temperature\n");
  printf(" and a c designates a celsius temperature): ");
```

```
scanf("%f %c", &inTemp, &letter);
if (letter == 'f' || letter == 'F')
{
  cels = (5.0/9.0) * (inTemp - 32.0);
  printf("\n%6.2f deg Fahrenheit = %6.2f deg Celsius", inTemp, cels);
}
else if (letter == 'c' || letter = 'C')
{
  fahr = (9.0/5.0) * inTemp + 32.0;
  printf("\n%6.2f deg Celsius = %6.2f deg Fahrenheit", inTemp, fahr);
}
else printf("\nThe data entered is invalid.");

return 0;
}
```

5. a. This program will run. It will not, however, produce the correct result.

   b. and c. This program evaluates correct incomes for mon_sales less than 20000.00 only.
   If 20000.00 or more were entered, the first else if statement would be executed and
   all others would be ignored. That is, for 20000.00 or more, the income for >= 1000.00
   would be calculated and displayed.

   Had if statements been used in place of the else if statements, the program would
   have worked correctly, but inefficiently (see comments for Exercise 4b.).

Section 4.4

1.
```
switch (letterGrade)
{
  case 'A':
    printf("The numerical grade is between 90 and 100");
    break;
  case 'B':
    printf("The numerical grade is between 80 and 89.9");
    break;
  case 'C':
    printf("The numerical grade is between 70 and 79.9");
    break;
  case 'D':
    printf("How are you going to explain this one");
    break;
  default:
    printf("Of course I had nothing to do with the grade.");
    printf('\nThe professor was really off the wall.");
}
```

3.
```
#include <stdio.h>
int main()
{
```

```
    int code;

    printf("Enter a code (1,2,3 or 4): ");
    scanf("%d", &code);
    switch (code)
    {
      case 1:
        printf("3M Corporation\n");
        break;
      case 2:
        printf("Maxell Corporation\n");
        break;
      case 3:
        printf("Sony Corporation\n");
        break;
      case 4:
        printf("Verbatim Corporation\n");
        break;
      default:
        printf("An invalid code was entered\n");
    }

    return 0;
}
```

Section 5.1

1.
```
#include <stdio.h>
int main()
{
  int count = 2;

  while (count <= 10)
  {
    printf("%d  ",count);
    count += 2;

  }

  return 0;
}
```

3. a. 21 items are displayed, which are the integers from 1 to 21.
   c. 21 items are still displayed, but they would be the integers from 0 to 20 because the `printf` now occurs before the increment.

Section 5.2

3. a.
```c
#include <stdio.h>
int main()
{
   float cels, fahr, incr;
   int num;

   printf("Enter the starting temperature ");
   printf("in degrees Celsius: ");
   scanf("%f", &cels);
   printf("\n\nEnter the number of conversions to be made: ");
   scanf("%d", &num);
   printf("\n\nNow enter the increment between conversions ");
   printf("in degrees Celsius: ");
   scanf("%f", &incr);
   printf("\n\n\nCelsius      Fahrenheit\n");
   printf("--------------------\n");
   while (count <= num)
   {
      fahr = (9.0/5.0) * cels + 32.0;
      printf("%7.2f%15.2f\n", cels, fahr);
      cels = cels + incr
   }

   return 0;
}
```

7. This program will still calculate the correct values, but the average is now calculated four times. It is only the final average that is desired, so it is better to calculate the average once, outside of the `while` loop.

9. a.
```c
#include <stdio.h>
int main()
{
   int id, inven, income, outgo, bal, count;

   count = 1;
   while (count <= 3)
   {
      printf("\nEnter book ID: ");
      scanf("%d", &id);
      printf("\nEnter inventory at the beginning of the month: ");
      scanf("%d", &inven);
      printf("\nEnter the number of copies received during the month: ");
      scanf("%d", &income);
      printf("\nNow enter the number of copies sold during the month: ");
      scanf("%d", &outgo);
      bal = inven + income - outgo;
```

```
        printf("\n\nBook #%d new balance is %d", id, bal);
        ++count;
    }

    return 0;
}
```

Section 5.3

1. 20 16 12 8 4 0

5.
```
#include <stdio.h>
int main()
{

    int conv, count;
    float f, c;

    printf("Enter the number of temperature conversions");
    printf("\nfrom Fahrenheit to Celsius to be performed: ");
    scanf("%f", &conv);
    printf("\nFahrenheit    Celsius\n");
    printf("----------    -------\n");
    for (f = 20.0, count = 1; count <= conv; ++count)
    {
       c = (f - 32.0) * (5.0/9.0);
       printf("%4.1f       %5.2f\n", f, c);
       f += 4.0;
    }

    return 0;
}
```

7.
```
#include <stdio.h>
int main()
{
   int count;
   float fahren, celsius;

   for(count = 1 ; count <= 6; ++count)
   {
     printf("\nEnter a fahrenheit temperature: ");
     scanf("%f", &fahren);
     celsius = (5.0/9.0) * (fahren - 32.0);
     printf(" The corresponding celsius temperature is %5.2f\n",celsius);
   }

   return 0;
}
```

13.
```
#include <stdio.h>
int main()
{
  int yr;
  double sales, profit, totSales=0.0, totProfit=0.0;

  printf("SALES AND PROFIT PROJECTION\n");
  printf("--------------------------\n\n");
  printf("YEAR            EXPECTED SALES        PROJECTED PROFIT\n");
  printf("----            --------------        ----------------\n");
  for (yr = 1, sales = 10000000.00; yr <= 10; ++yr)
  {
    profit = 0.10*sales;
    printf("%3d             $%11.2f               $%10.2f\n",
            yr, sales, profit);
    totSales = totSales + sales;
    totProfit = totProfit + profit;
    sales = 0.96*sales;
  }
  printf("-----------------------------------------------------------");
  printf("\nTotals:          $%10.2f               $%9.2f\n",
          totSales, totProfit);

  return 0;
}
```

15.
```
#include <stdio.h>
int main()
{
int i, j, results;
float total, avg, data;

for (i = 1; i <= 4; ++i)
{
  printf("Enter the number of results for experiment #%d: ",i);
  scanf("%d",&results);
  printf("Enter %d results for experiment #%d: ",results,i);
  for (j = 1, total = 0.0; j <= results; ++j)
  {
    scanf("%f", &data);
    total += data;
  {
  avg = total/results;
  printf("   The average for experiment #%d is %.2f\n\n", i, avg);
  }

  return 0;
}
```

Section 5.4

1. a.
```c
#include <stdio.h>
int main()
{
    float grade;

    do
    {
        printf("Enter a grade: ");
        scanf("%f", &grade);
    } while (grade < 0 || grade > 100);
    printf("\nThe grade entered is %f\n", grade);

    return 0;
}
```

   b.
```c
#include <stdio.h>
int main()
{
    float grade;

    do
    {
        printf("Enter a grade: ");
        scanf("%f", &grade);
        if (grade < 0 || grade > 100)
          printf("Invalid grade - please retype it.\n");
    } while (grade < 0 || grade > 100);
    printf("\nThe grade entered is  %f\n", grade);

    return 0;
}
```

   c.
```c
#include <stdio.h>
int main()
{
    float grade;

    do
    {
        printf("Enter a grade: ");
        scanf("%f", &grade);
        if (grade == 999)
          return 0;
        else if (grade < 0 || grade > 100)
          printf("Invalid grade - please retype it.\n");
```

```
          } while (grade < 0 || grade > 100);
          printf("\nThe grade entered is  %f\n", grade);

          return 0;
        }
   d. #include <stdio.h>
      int main()
      {
        float grade, badGrade = 0.0;

        do
        {
          printf("Enter a grade: ");
          scanf("%f", &grade);
          if (grade < 0 || grade > 100)
          {
            ++badGrade;
            if (badGrade == 5)
              return 0;
            else
              printf("Invalid grade - please retype it.\n");
          }
        } while (grade < 0 || grade > 100);
        printf("\nThe grade entered is %f\n", grade);

        return 0;
      }
3. a. #include <stdio.h>
      int main()
      {
        int num, digit;

        printf("Enter an integer: ");
        scanf("%d", &num);
        printf("\nThe number reversed is: ");
        do
        {
          digit = num % 10;
          num ✓ = 10;
          printf("%d", digit);
        } while (num > 0);

        return 0;
      }
```

Section 6.1

1. a. `factorial()` expects to receive one integer value.
   b. `price()` expects to receive one integer and two double precision values, in that order.
   c. An int and two double precision values, in that order, must be passed to `yield()`.
   d. A character and two floating point values, in that order, must be passed to `interest()`.
   e. Two floating point values, in that order, must be passed to `total()`.
   f. Two integers, two characters, and two floating point values, in that order, are expected by `roi()`.
   g. Two integers and two character values, in that order, are expected by `getVal()`.
   h. The `tolower()` function expects to receive one character.
   i. `sin()` expects to receive one double precision value.

3. a. `int factorial(int);`
   b. `double price(int, double, double);`
   c. `double yield(int, double, double);`
   d. `char interest(char, float, float);`
   e. `int total(float, float);`
   f. `float roi(int, int, char, char, float, float);`
   g. `void getVal(int, int, char);`

5. a. The `findAbs()` function is included within the larger program written for Exercise 5b.
   b.
```
#include <stdio.h>
void findAbs(double);   /* function prototype */
int main()
{
  double dnum;
  printf("\nEnter a number: ");
  scanf("%lf", &dnum);        /* the %lf is required for doubles */
  findAbs(dnum);
}

void findAbs(double num)
{
  double absValue;   /* a double precision variable */

  if (num < 0) absValue = -num
    else absValue = num;
  printf("The absolute value of %f is %f",num, absValue);

  return 0;
}
```

7. a. The `sqrIt()` function is included within the larger program written for Exercise 7b.
   b.
```
#include <stdio.h>
void sqrIt(double);   /* function prototype */
int main()
```

```
{
  double first;

  printf("Please enter a number: ");
  scanf("%lf",&first);      /* the %lf must be used for a double */
  sqrIt(first);

  return 0;
}

void sqrIt(double num)
{
  printf("The square of %f is %f", num, num*num);
}
```

9. a. The function for producing the required table is included within the larger program written
       for Exercise 9b.

   b.
```
#include <stdio.h>
void table();   /* function prototype */
int main()
{

  table();       /* call the table() function */
}

void table()
{
  int num;

  printf("NUMBER    SQUARE    CUBE\n");
  printf("- ----    ------    ----\n");

  for (num = 1; num <= 10; ++num)
    printf("%3d      %3d      %4d\n", num, num&num, num*num*num);

  return 0;
}
```

Section 6.2

1.
```
#include <stdio.h>
#include <math.h>
int main()
{
  double x = 0.0;

  while(x != 999)
```

```
            {
                printf("Enter a number to take the square root of ");
                printf("\n or 999 to quit: ");
                scanf("%lf", &x);
                printf("\nThe square root of %lf is %lf\n\n", x, sqrt(x));
            }

            return 0;
        }
```

3.
```
#include <stdio.h>
#include <math.h>
#include <math.h>
int main()
{
  double base, expon;
  int i;

  for(i = 1; i <= 4; ++i)
  {
    printf("\nEnter the number to be raised, a space, and the exponent: ");
    scanf("%lf %lf", &base, &expon);
    printf("\n\n%lf raised to %lf is %lf\n", base, expon, pow(base, expon));
  }

  return 0;
}
```

5.
```
#include <stdio.h>
#include <ctype.h>
int main()
{
  char ch;

  ch = toupper(getchar());
  while(ch != 'F')
  {
    putchar(ch);
    ch = toupper(getchar());
  }

  return 0;
}
```

Section 6.3

1. a.

Variable name	Data type	Scope
price	integer	global to `main()`, `roi()`, and `step()`
years	long integer	global to `main()`, `roi()`, and `step()`
yield	double precision	global to `main()`, `roi()`, and `step()`
bondtype	integer	local to `main()` only
interest	double precision	local to `main()` only
coupon	double precision	local to `main()` only
count	integer	local to `roi()` only
effectiveInt	double precision	local to `roi()` only
numofyrs	integer	local to `step()` only
fracpart	float	local to `step()` only

Note that although arguments of each function assume a value that is dependent on the calling function, these arguments can change values within their respective functions. This makes them behave as if they were local variables within the called function.

Section 6.4

1. a. Local variables may be automatic, static, or register. It is important to realize, however, that not all variables declared inside functions are necessarily local. An example of this is an external variable.

b. Global variables may be static or external.

3. The first function declares `yrs` to be a static variable and assigns a value of 1 to it only once, when the function is compiled. Thereafter, each time the function is called the value in `yrs` is increased by 2. The second function also declares `yrs` to be static, but assigns it the value 1 every time it is called, and the value of `yrs` after the function is finished will always be 3. By resetting the value of `yrs` to 1 each time it is called, the second function defeats the purpose of declaring the variable to be static.

5. The scope of a variable means where in the program the variable is recognized and can be used within an expression. If, for example, the variable `years` is declared inside a function, it is local and its scope is inside that function only. If the variable is declared outside of any function, it is global and its scope is anywhere below the declaration but within that file, unless another file of the same program declares that same variable to be external.

Section 6.5

1. a. `double *price;`
   b. `int *minutes;`
   c. `char *key;`
   d. `double *yield;`

3.
```c
#include <stdio.h>
void findMax(int, int, int *);   /* function prototype */
int main()
{

  int firstnum, secnum, max;

  printf("Enter a number: ");
  scanf("%d", &firstnum);
  printf("\nGreat! Please enter a second number: ");
  scanf("%d", &secnum);
  findMax(firstnum, secnum, &max);
  printf("\n\nThe maximum of the two numbers is %d.", max);
}

void findMax(int x, int y, int *maxAddr)
{
  if (x >= y)
    *maxAddr = x;
  else
    *maxAddr = y;
  return;
}
```

Notice that findMax does not return any value directly; rather, there is a return through the parameter list. This is done by altering the contents of a memory location whose address is known to both main() and findMax().

9. In main() the variables min and hour refer to integer quantities, while in time() the variables min and hours are pointers to integers. Thus, there are four distinct variables in all, two of which are known in main() and two of which are known in time(). The computer (actually, the compiler) keeps track of each variable with no confusion. The effect on a programmer, however, may be quite different.

When used in main() the programmer must remember to use the names min and hour as integer variables. When in time() the programmer must "switch" viewpoints and use the same names as pointer variables. Debugging such a program can be quite frustrating because the same names are used in two different contexts. It is, therefore, more advisable to avoid this type of situation by adopting different names for pointers than those used for other variables. A useful trick is to either prepend each pointer name with a ptr notation or append each pointer name with Addr.

Section 7.1

1. a. `double interest[60];`
   b. `float temp[30];`
   c. `char code[25];`
   d. `int year[100];`
   e. `double coupon[26];`
   f. `float dist[100];`
   g. `int code[20];`

3. a. `scanf("%d %d %d", &grades[0], &grades[2], &grades[6]);`
   b. `scanf("%f %f %f", &prices[0], &prices[2], &prices[6]);`
   c. `scanf("%f %f %f", &amps[0], &amps[2], &amps[6]);`
   d. `scanf("%lf %lf %lf", &dist[0], &dist[2], &dist[6]);`
   e. `scanf("%lf %lf %lf", &velocity[0], &velocity[2], &velocity[6]);`
   f. `scanf("%lf %lf %lf", &time[0], &time[2], &time[6]);`

5. a. `a[1]  a[2]  a[3]  a[4]  a[5]`
   b. `a[1]  a[3]  a[5]`
   c. `b[3]  b[4]  b[5]  b[6]  b[7]  b[8]  b[9]  b[10]`
   d. `b[3]  b[6]  b[9]  b[12]`
   e. `c[2]  c[4]  c[6]  c[8]  c[10]`

7. a.
```
#include <stdio.h>
int main()
{
  int temp[15], total = 0, count;
  float avg;

  for(count = 0; count <= 14; ++count)
  {
    printf("Enter element #%d: ", count + 1);
    scanf("%d", &temp[count]);
    total += temp[count];
  }
            avg = total/15.0;
  for(count = 0; count <= 14; ++count)
    printf("\nElement #%d = %d", count, temp[count]);
  printf("\n   The average is %f\n\n", avg);

  return 0;
}
```

c.
```
#include <stdio.h>
int main()
{
  int temp[15], total = 0, count, inex, max = 0;
  float avg;

  for(count = 0; count <= 14; ++count)
  {
    printf("\nEnter element #%d: ", count + 1);
    scanf("%d", &temp[count]);
    if(temp[count]   max)
    {
      max = temp[count];
      index = count;
    }
  }
  for(count = 0; count <= 14; ++count)
    printf("\nElement #%d = d", count, temp[count]);
```

```
            printf("\n\nThe maximum value is: %d", max);
            printf("\nThis is element %d in the list of numbers\n\n", index);

            return 0;
        }
```

9.
```
#include <stdio.h>
int main()
{
  int i,quantity[10];
  float price[10], amount[10];

  for(i = 0; i <= 9; ++i)
  {
    printf("Enter price for item #%d: ", i + 1);
    scanf("%f", &price[i]);
    printf("Enter the quantity for item #%d: ", i + 1);
    scanf("%d", &quantity[i]);
    amount[i] = price[i]*quantity[i];
  }
  printf("\n\nQuantity         Price         Amount");
  printf("\n--------         -----         ------");
  for(i = 0; i <= 9; ++i)
    printf("\n%5d %17.2f %15.2f", quantity[i], price[i], amount[i]);

  return 0;
}
```

Section 7.2

1. a. int grades[10] = {89, 75, 82, 93, 78, 95, 81, 88, 77, 82};
  b. double amount[5] = {10.62, 13.98, 18.45, 12.68, 14.76};
  c. double rates[100] = {6.29, 6.95, 7.25, 7.35, 7.40, 7.42};
  d. float temp[64] = {78.2, 69.6, 68.5, 83.9, 55.4, 67.0, 49.8,
                       58.3, 62.5, 71.6};
  e. char code[15] = {'f', 'j', 'm', 'q', 't', 'w', 'z'};

3. a. The four declarations are contained within the program written for Exercise 3b.
  b.
```
     int main()
     {
        char messag1[] = "Input the following data";
        char messag2[] = "------------------------";
        char messag3[] = "Enter the date:";
        char messag4[] = "Enter the Account Number:";

        printf("\n%s",messag1);
        printf("\n%s",messag2);
        printf("\n%s",messag3);
        printf("\n%s",messag4);
```

```
              return 0;
          }
  5. a.  int main()
          {
              int i;
              float prices[8] = {16.24, 18.98, 23.75, 16.29,
                                  19.54, 14.22, 11.13, 15.39};

              printf("\nThe values stored in the array are:");
              for(i = 0; i < 7; ++i)
                printf("\n  %5.2f", prices[i]);

              return 0;
          }
     b.  float prices[8] = {16.24, 18.98, 23.75, 16.29,
                            19.54, 14.22, 11.13, 15.39};
          int main()
          {
              int i;

              printf("\nThe values stored in the global array are:");
              for(i = 0; i < 7; ++i)
                printf("\n  %5.2f", prices[i]);

              return 0;
          }
  7.
#include <stdio.h>
double prices[5] = {9.92, 6.32, 12.63, 5.95, 10.29};
int main()
{
  int i;
  double units[5], amounts[5], total= 0;

  for(i = 0; i <= 4; ++i)
  {
    printf("\nEnter units[%d]: ", i);
    scanf("%lf", &units[i]);
    amounts[i] = units[i] *prices[i];
    total += amounts[i];
  }
  printf("\n\nPrice            Units            Amount");
  printf("\n-----            -----            ------");
  for(i = 0; i <= 4; ++i)
    printf("\n%5.2lf$%15.2lf%16.2lf", prices[i], units[i], amounts[i]);
  printf("\n                                   ------");
  printf("\nTotal: %29.2f", total);

  return 0;
}
```

Section 7.3

1.
```
void sortArray(double inArray[500])
or void sortArray(double inArray[])
```

5.
```c
#include <stdio.h>
void show(float[]);
int main()
{
  float rates[9] = {6.5, 7.2, 7.5, 8.3, 8.6,
                     9.4, 9.6, 9.8, 10.0};

  show(rates);
}

void show(float rates[])
{
  int i;

  printf("The elements stored in the array are:");
  for(i = 0; i <= 8; ++i)
    printf("\n %4.1f", rates[i]);

  return 0;
}
```

7.
```c
#include <stdio.h>
void extend(double [], double[], double []);
int main()

  double price[10] = {10.62, 14.89, 13.21, 16.55, 18.62,
                       9.47, 6.58, 18.32, 12.15, 3.98};
  double quantity[10] = {4.0, 8.5, 6.0, 7.35, 9.0,
                       15.3, 3.0, 5.4, 2.9, 4.8};
  double amount[10];   /* Automatically assigns zeros */
                       /* to each element */
  int i;

  extend(price, quantity, amount);
  printf("The elements in the amount array are:");
  for(i = 0; i <= 9; ++i)
    printf("\n %7.3lf", amount[i]);
}

void extend(double prc[], double qnty[], double amt[])
{
  int i;

  for(i = 0; i <= 9; ++i)
    amt[i] = prc[i]*qnty[i];
}
```

Section 7.4

1. a. `int array[6][10];`   d.   `char letter[15][7];`
   b. `int codes[2][5];`   e. `double vals[10][25];`
   c. `char keys[7][12];`   f. `double test[16][8];`

3. ```
   double addEles(double array[][5])
   {
       int i, j;
       double total = 0;

       for(i = 0; i <= 3; ++i)
        for(j = 0; j <= 4; ++j)
         total += array[i][j];
       return(total);
   }
   ```

5. a. ```
   void findMax(int val[10][20])
   {
       int i, j, max;
       for (i = 0; i < 10; ++i)
         for (j = 0; j < 20; ++j)
           if (val[i][j] > max)
             max = val[i][j];
       printf("\nThe maximum array value is %d\n", max);

       return;

   }
   ```
   c. Yes, any function receiving a multidimensional array can be generalized to handle any number of elements by passing either the number of elements in each dimension or the total number of array elements.

## Section 8.1

1. a. `*(prices + 5)`     f.     `*(temp + 20)`
   b. `*(grades + 2)`            g. `*(celsius + 16)`
   c. `*(yield + 10)`           h. `*(num + 50)`
   d. `*(dist + 9)`             i. `*(time + 12)`
   e. `*mile`

3. a. The declaration `double prices [5];` causes storage space for five double precision numbers, creates a pointer constant named `prices`, and equates the pointer constant to the address of the first element (`&prices[0]`).
   b. Each element in prices contains four bytes, and there are five elements for a total of 20 bytes.

c.

prices

&prices[0]

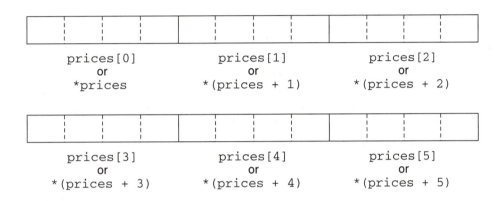

prices[0]
or
\*prices

prices[1]
or
\* (prices + 1)

prices[2]
or
\* (prices + 2)

prices[3]
or
\* (prices + 3)

prices[4]
or
\* (prices + 4)

prices[5]
or
\* (prices + 5)

d. The byte offset for this element, from the beginning of the array, is 3 \* 4 = 12 bytes.

**5.**
```
#include <stdio.h>
int main()
{
  float rates[] = {12.9, 18.6, 11.4, 13.7, 9.5, 15.2, 17.6};
  int i;

  printf("The elements of the array are:\n");
  for(i = 0; i <= 6; ++i)
    printf("\n%5.2f", *(rates + i)); /* The variable pointed to by */
                                     /* rates offset by i   */

  return 0;
}
```

Section 8.2

3. a.
```
#include <stdio.h>
int main()
{
    char strng[] = "Hooray for all of us";
    char *messPtr;

    messPtr = &strng[0];    /* messPtr = strng; is equivalent */
```

```
        printf("The elements in the array are: ");
        for(  ; *messPtr != '\0'; ++messPtr)
          printf("%c", *messPtr);

        return 0;
      }
    b.
    #include <stdio.h>
    int main()
    {
      char strng[] = "Hooray for all of us";
      char *messPtr;

      messPtr = &strng[0];    /* messPtr = strng; is equivalent */
      printf("The elements in the array are: ");
      while.(*messPtr != '\0')   /* search for the null character */
        printf("%c", *messPtr++);

      return 0;
    }
```

Section 8.3

1. `void sortArray(double inArray[500])`

`void sortArray(double inArray[])`

`void sortArray(double *inArray)`

5. The problem with this method of finding the maximum value lies in the line

`if(max < *vals++)   max = *vals;`

This statement compares the correct value to max, but then increments the address in the pointer before any assignment is made. The element assigned to max by the expression max = *vals is one element beyond the element pointed to within the parentheses.

7. a.
```
#include <stdio.h>
void display(char []);   /* function prototype */
int main()
{
  char message[] = "Vacation is near";

  display(message);

  return 0;
}

void display(char strng[])
{
  int i = 0;
```

```
        while (*(strng + i) != '\0')
        {
          printf("%c", *(strng + i));
          ++i;   /* point to next character */
        }
        printf("\n");
        return;
    }
```

9. a. The following output is obtained:

```
33
16
99
34
```

This is why:

```
*(*val)       = *(val[0])   = val[0][0]   = 33;
*(*val + 1)   = *(val[1])   = val[1][0]   = 16;
*(*(val + 1) + 2) = *(*(val[1]) + 2) = *(val[1][2]) = 99;
*(*val) + 1   = *(val[0]) + 1 = val[0][0] + 1 = 33 + 1 = 34.
```

In other words, for any two-dimensional array, `arr[x][y]`, what we really have is two levels of pointers. What's meant by `*(arr+x)` is that there are x number of pointers, each successively pointing to `arr[1][0], arr[2][0], arr[3][0], ..., arr[x][0]`. So an expression such as `*(*(arr + x) + y)` translates to `arr[x][y]`.

Section 9.1

1. b.

```
#include <stdio.h>
void vowels(char []);   /* function prototype */
int main()
{
  char line[81];

  printf("Enter a string.\n");
  gets(line);
  vowels(line);

  return 0;
}
void vowels(char strng[])
{
  int i = 0, v = 0;   /* Array element number = i; vowel counter = v */
  char c;
  while((c = strng[i++]) != '\0')
  switch(c)
  {
    case 'a':
    case 'e':
    case 'i';
```

```
      case 'o';
      case 'u':
        putchar(c);
        ++v;
    }
    putchar('\n');
    printf("There were %d vowels.", v);

    return;
}
```

3. a. The function is included in the program written for Exercise 3b.
b.

```
#include <stdio.h>
void countChar(char[]);   /* function prototype */
int main()
{
  char strng[81];

  printf("Enter a line of text\n");
  gets(strng);
  countChar(strng);

  return 0;
}


countChar(char message[])
{
  int i;

  for(i = 0; message[i] != '\n'; ++i);   /* The semicolon at the end  */
                                         /* of this statement is the  */
                                         /* null statement            */
  printf("\nThe number of total characters, including blanks, in");
  printf(" the line just entered is %d.", i);

  return;
}
```

7.

```
#include <stdio.h>
void delChar(char[], int, int);   /* function prototype */
int main
{
  char word[81];

  printf("Enter a string\n");
  gets(word);
  printf("\n%s\n",word);
  delChar(word, 13, 5); /* string, how many to delete, starting position */
  puts(word);           /* display the edited string */
}
```

```
delChar(char strng[], int x, int pos)
{
   int i, j;
   i = pos-1;    /* first element to be deleted (actually, overwritten) */
   j = i + x;    /* first element beyond delete range */
   while (strng[j] != '\0')
     strng[i++] = strng[j++];   /* copy over an element */
   strng[i] = '\0';    /* close off the edited string */
   return 0;
}
```

This program assumes the number of characters to be deleted actually exists. Otherwise the `while` loop would not terminate (unless it just happened to encounter another null character somewhere in memory beyond the original string).

9. a. The `toUpper()` function is included in the program written for Exercise 9c.

c.

```
#include <stdio.h>
char toUpper(char);   /* function prototype*/
int main()
{
  char strng[81];
  int i = 0;

  printf("Enter a line of text\n");
  gets(strng);
  while (strng[i] != '\n')   /* get the character */
  {
    strng[i] = toUpper(strng[i]); /* send it to the function */
    ++i;                          /* move to next character */
  }
  printf("The string, with all lowercase letters converted, is:\n");
  puts(strng);

  return 0;
}
char toUpper(char ch)
{

  if ( ch >= 'a' && ch <= 'z')    /* test it */
    return(ch - 'a' + 'A');       /* change it, if necessary */
  else
    return(ch);
}
```

11.
```
#include <stdio.h>
int main()
{
  char strng[81];
  int i = 0, count = 1;

  printf("Enter a line of text\n");
```

```
gets(strng);
if(strng[i] == ' ' || strng[i] == '\0')
  --count;
while(strng[i] != '\0')
{
  if(strng[i] == ' ' && (strng[i = 1] != ' ' && strng[i + 1] != '\n0'))
    ++count;        /* encountered a new word */
  ++i;              /* move to the next character */
}
printf("\nThe number of words in the line just entered is %d", count);

return 0;
}
```

The program increases the word count whenever a transition from a blank to a nonblank character occurs. Even if words are separated by more than one space the word count will be incremented correctly. Initially the program assumes the text starts with a word (count = 1). If the first character is either a blank or an end-of-string Null, this assumption is incorrect and the count is decremented to zero.

Section 9.2

1. a. *text = 'n'
       *(text + 3) = ' '
       *(text + 10) = ' '
   b. *text = 'r'
       *(text + 3) = 'k'
       *(text + 10) = 'o'
   c. *text = 'H'
       *(text + 3) = 'p'
       *(text + 10) = 'd'
   d. *text = 'T'
       *(text + 3) = ' '
       *(text + 10) = 'h'

3.
```
          #include <stdio.h>
void vowels(char *);  /* function prototype */
int main()
{
  char line[81];

  printf("Enter a string.\n");
  gets(line);
  vowels(line);

  return 0;
}
```

```
                        /* strng can be treated as a pointer variable */
vowels(char *strng)
{
  int v = 0;    /* v = vowel counter */
  char c;

  while((c = *strng++) != '\0')   /* an address is incremented */
  switch(c)
  {
    case 'a':
    case 'e':
    case 'i'
    case 'o':
    case 'u':
      putchar(c);
      ++v;
  }
  putchar('\n');
  printf("There were %d vowels.", v);

  return;
}
```

5.

```
#include <stdio.h>
void countChar(char *);  /* function prototype */
int main()
{
  char strng[81];

  printf("Enter a line of text\n");
  gets(strng);
  countChar(strng);

  return 0;
}
                          /* message can be used as a pointer variable */
void countChar(char *message)
{
  int count;

  for(count = 0; *message++ != '\0'; ++count) ; /* The semicolon at the  */
                                      /* end of this statement */
                                      /* is the null statement */
  printf("\nThe number of total characters, including blanks, in");
  printf(" the line just entered is %d.", count);

  return;
}
```

```
  7. #include <stdio.h>
     void reverse(char *,char *);   /* function prototype */
     int main()
     {
       char forward[81], rever[81];

       printf("Enter a line of text:\n");
       gets(forward);
       reverse(forward,rever);
       printf("\n\nThe text: %s \n",forward);
       printf("spelled backwards is: %s \n",rever);

       return 0;
     }

     void reverse(char *forw, char *rev)
     {
       int i = 0;

       while(*(forw + i) != '\0')        /* count the elements */
          ++i;                           /* in the string      */
       for(--i; i >= 0; --i)
          *rev++ = *(forw + i);
       *rev ='\0';                       /* close off reverse string */
       return;
     }
```

  9. The function is included within a complete program.

```
#include <stdio.h>
void appendC(char, char*);   /* function prototype */
int main()
{
  char ch, line[81];

  printf("Enter a line of text: ");
  gets(line);
  printf("Enter a single character: ");
  ch = getchar();
  appendC(ch, line);
  printf("The new line of text with the appended last character is:\n");
  puts(line);

  return 0;
}

void appendC(char c, char *strng)
{

  while(*strng++ != '\0')    /* this advances the pointer */
     ;                       /* one character beyond '\0 '*/
  --strng;                   /* point to the '\0') */
```

```
  *strng+ = c;              /* replace it with the new char */
  *strng = '\0';            /* close the new string        */
  return;
}
```

13.
```
void trimrear(char *strng)
{

   while(*strng != '\0') ++strng;   /* move to end of string     */
   --strng;                         /* move to char before '\0' */
   while(*strng == ' ') --strng;    /* skip over blank characters */
   *(++strng) = '\0';               /* close off string */
   return;

}
```

Section 9.3

1. `char *text = "Hooray!";`

`char test[] = {'H', 'o', 'o', 'r', 'a', 'y', '\0'};`

3. message is a pointer constant. Therefore, the statement ++message, which attempts to alter its address, is invalid. A correct statement is

`putchar(*(message + i));`

Here the address in message is unaltered and the character pointed to is the character offset i bytes from the address corresponding to message.

Section 9.4

1. a. `!four score and ten!   /* field width specifier is ignored */`

   b. `!           Home!!`

   c. `!Home!          !`

   d. `!Ho             !`

   e. `!           Ho!`

3.
```
#include <stdio.h>
void separate(char *, float *, float *, float *);   /* prototype */
int main()
{
  char strng[30];
  float num1, num2, num3;

  printf("Enter three numbers on the same line,");
  printf("\n separating the numbers with one or more spaces: ");
  gets(strn);     /* read the numbers in as a string */
```

```
    separate(strn, &num1, &num2, &num3);
    printf("The three numbers are %f %f %f",num1, num2, num3);

    return 0;
}

void separate(char *stAddr, float *n1Addr, float *n2Addr, float *n3Addr)
{
    sscanf(stAddr,"%f %f %f",n1Addr, n2Addr, n3Addr);
    return;
}
```

Functions like `separate()` are useful when reading data from a file. Rather than read individual items sequentially, a complete line of the file is read in as a string and then dissembled internally within the program. This isolates any line that does not have the required number and types of data items.

5.

```
#include <stdio.h>
void combine(char *, char *, int, int); /* function prototype */
int main()
{
    char strng1[80], strng2[100];
    int num1, num2;

    printf("Enter a string: ");
    gets(strng1);
    printf("Enter an integer number: ");
    scanf("%d",&num1);
    printf("Enter a second integer number: ");
    scanf("%d",&num2);
    combine(strng1, strng2, num1, num2);
    printf("A string containing all inputs is: ");
    puts(strng2);

    return 0;
}

void combine(chr *source, char *dest, int n1, int n2)
{
    sprintf(dest,"%s %d %d",source, n1, n2); /* write the string */
    return;
}
```

Functions like `combine()` are useful in assembling separate data items into a single line for output to a file. The file will then contain identically formatted lines, each line containing the same number and types of data items. Additionally, the file will be in ASCII, which can easily be read by any word processing program, for easy inspection external to the program that created it.

Section 10.1

1. a.
```
struct Stemp
{
  int idNum;
  int credits;
  float avg;
};
```
  b.
```
struct Stemp
{
  char name[40];
  int month;
  int day;
  int year;
  int credits;
  float avg;
};
```
  c.
```
struct Stemp
{
  char name[40];
  char street[80];
  char city[40];
  char state[2];
  char zip[10];
};
```
  d.
```
struct Stemp
{
  char name[40];
  float price;
  char date[10];   /* Assumes a date in the form mm/dd/yyyy */
};
```
  e.
```
struct Stemp
{
  int partNum;
  char desc[100];
  int quant;
  int reorder;
};
```
3. a.
```
        #include <stdio.h>
int main()
{
  struct
  {
    int month;
    int day;
    int year;
  } date;        /* define a structure variable named date */
```

```
        printf("Enter the current month: ");
        scanf("%d", &date.month);
        printf("Enter the current day: ");
        scanf("%d", &date.day);
        printf("Enter the current year: ");
        scanf("%d", &date.year);
        printf("\n\nThe date entered is %d/%d/%d.",
                date.month, date.day, date.year);

        return 0;
    }
```

b.
```
#include <stdio.h>
int main()
{
    struct Clock
    {
        int hours;
        int minutes;
        int seconds;
    } time;              /* define a structure variable named time */

    printf("Enter the current hour: ");
    scanf("%d", &time.hours);
    printf("Enter the current minute: ");
    scanf("%d", &time. minutes);
    printf("Enter the current second: ");
    scanf("%d", &time.seconds);
    printf("\n\nThe time entered is %02d:%02d:%02d", time.hours,
            time.minutes, time.seconds);

    return 0;
}
```

Note the use of the conversion sequence %02d. The 0 forces the field of 2 to be filled with leading zeros.

5.
```
#include <stdio.h>
int main()
{
    struct
    {
        int hours;
        int minutes;
    } time;

    printf("Enter the current hour: ");
    scanf("%d", &time.hours);
    printf("Enter the current minute: ");
    scanf("%d", &time.minutes);
    if(time.minutes != 59)
```

```
          time.minutes += 1;
      else
      {
        time.minutes = 0;
        if(time.hours != 12)
          time.hours += 1;
        else
          time.hours = 1;
      }
      printf("\nThe time in one minute will be %02d:%02d",
             time.hours, time.minutes);

      return 0;
}
```

Note the use of the conversion sequence %02d. The 0 forces the field of 2 to be filled with leading zeros.

Section 10.2

1. a.
```
struct Stemp
{
  int idNum;
  int credits;
  float avg;
};

#include <stdio.h>
int main()
{
  struct Stemp student[100];
```
   b.
```
struct Stemp
{
  char name[40];
  int month;
  int day;
  int year;
  int credits;
  float avg;
};

#include <stdio.h>
int main()
{
  struct Stemp student[100];
```
   c.
```
struct Stemp
{
  char name[40];
```

```
                 char street[80];
                 char city[40];
                 char state[2];
                 char zip[10];
             };

             #include <stdio.h>
             int main()
             {
                 struct Stemp Address[100];
         d.
       struct Stemp
       {
         char name[40];
         float price;
         char date[10];      /* Assumes a date in the form mm/dd/yyyy  */
       };
       #include <stdio.h>
       int main()
       {
         struct Stemp stock[100];
             e. struct Stemp
                {
                    int partNum;
                    char desc[100];
                    int quant;
                    int reorder;
                };
                #include <stdio.h>
                int main()
                {
                    struct Stemp inven[100];
```

3.

```
struct MonthDays
{
 char name[10];
 int days;
};

#include <stdio.h>
int main()
{
  struct MonthDays convert[12] =
                    { "January", 31, "February", 28,
                      "March", 31, "April", 30,
                      "May", 31, "June", 30,
                      "July", 31, "August", 31,
                      "September", 30, "October", 31,
                      "November", 30, "December", 31
                    };

  int i;
```

```
    printf("\nEnter the number of a month: ");
    scanf("%d", &i);
    printf("\n%s has %d days.", convert[i-1].name, convert[i-1].days);

    return 0;
}
```

Section 10.3

1.
```
struct Date
{
   int month;
   int day;
   int year;
};

#include <stdio.h>
int main()
{
   struct Date present;
   long num, days(struct Date);

   printf("Enter the month: ");
   scanf("%d", &present.month);
   printf("Enter the day: ");
   scanf("%d", &present.day);
   printf("Enter the year: ");
   scanf("%d", &present.year);
   num = days(present);
   printf("\nThe number of days since the turn of the century is %ld", num);
}

long days(struct Date temp)
{
   return(tempday + 30*(temp.month - 1) + 360*temp.year);
}
```

Note: The pointer version of the function `long days()` is written for Exercise 3.

3.
```
struct Date
{
   int month;
   int day;
   int year;
};

#include <stdio.h>
long days(struct Date*)   /* function prototype */
```

```
            int main()
            {
              struct Date present;
              long num;

              printf("Enter the month: ");
              scanf("%d", &present.month);
              printf("Enter the day: ");
              scanf("%d", &present.day);
              printf("Enter the year: ");
              scanf("%d", &present.year);
              num = days(&present);
              printf("\n\nThe number of days from 1/1/1900 is %ld", num);
            }

            long days(struct date *temp)
            {
              return(temp-> + 30*(temp->month - 1) + 360*(temp->year - 1900);
            }
```

5.

```
struct Date
{
  int month;
  int day;
  int year;
};

#include <stdio.h>
long days(struct Date); /* function prototype */
int main()
{
  struct Date present;
  long num;

  printf("Enter the date as mm/dd/yyyy: ");
  scanf("%d/%d/%d", &present.month, &present.day, &present.year);
2 num = days(present);
  printf("\nThe number of days from 1/1/1900 is %ld", num);
}

long days(struct Date temp)
{
  long actDays;
  int daycount[12] = { 0, 31, 59, 90, 20, 151,
                       180, 211, 241, 271, 302, 333};
  actDays = temp.day + daycount[temp.month - 1] + 364*(temp.year - 1900);
  return(actDays);
}
```

Section 10.4

1.
```c
#include <stdio.h>
struct TeleType
{
  char name[30];
  char phoneNum[15];
  strut TeleType *nextaddr;
};
void search(struct TeleType *, char *); /* function prototype */
int main()
{
  struct TeleType t1 = {"Acme, Sam", "(555) 898-2392"};
  struct TeleType t2 = {"Dolan, Edith", "(555) 682-3104"};
  struct TeleType t3 = {"Lanfrank, John", "(555) 718-4518"};
  struct TeleType *first;
  char strng[30];

  first = &t1;
  t1.nextaddr = &t2;
  t2.nextaddr = &t3;
  t3.nextaddr = NULL;
  printf("Enter a name: ");
  gets(strng);
  search(first, strng);

  return 0;
}

void search(struct TeleType *contents, char *strng)
{

  printf("\n%s",strng);
  while(contents != NULL)
  {
    if(strcmp(contents->name,strng) == 0)
    {
      printf("\nFound. The number is %s.", contents->phoneNum);
      return;
    }
    else
    {
      contents = contents->nextaddr;
    }
  }
  printf("\nThe name is not in the current phone directory.");
}
```

3. To delete the second record, the pointer in the first record must be changed to point to the third record.

5. a. ```
struct PhoneBk
{
   char name[30];
   char phoneNum[15];
   struct PhoneBk *previous;
   struct PhoneBk *next;
};
```

**3.** The modify() function is included below in a complete program used to verify that modify() works correctly. The driver function creates a single structure, populates it, and then calls modify(). modify() itself calls the function repop(). An interesting extension is to write repop() such that an ENTER key response retains the original structure member value.

```
#include <stdio.h>
#include <stdlib.h>
struct TeleType
{
   char name[25];
   char phoneNum[15];
   struct TeleType *nextaddr;
};
void modify(struct Teletype *);   /* function prototypes */
void populate(struct TeleType *);
void repop(struct TeleType *);
void display(struct TeleType *);
int main()
{
   int i;
   struct TeleType *list;

   list = (struct TeleType *) malloc(sizeof(struct TeleType));
   populate(list); /* populate the first structure */
   list->nextaddr = NULL;
   modify(list);   /* modify the structure members */

   return 0;
}

void modify(struct TeleType *addr)
{

   printf("\nThe current structure members are: ");
   display(addr);
   repop(addr);
   printf("\nThe structure members are now: ");
   display(addr);
   return 0;
}

void populate(struct TeleType *record)
```
```

```
{
  printf("\nEnter a name: ");
  gets(record->name);
  printf("Enter the phone number: ");
  gets(record->phoneNum);
  return 0;
}
repop(struct TeleType *record)
{
  printf("\n\nEnter a new name: ");
  gets(record->name);
  printf("Enter a new phone number: ");
  gets(record->phoneNum);
  return;
}

display(struct TeleType *contents)
{
  while(contents != NULL)
  {
    printf("\n%-30s %-20s", contents->name, contents->phoneNum);
    contents = contents->nextaddr;
  }
  return;
}
```

Section 10.6

1. `printf()` function calls, with the correct control sequences, are contained within the following program.

```
union
{
  float rate;
  double taxes;
  int num;
} flag;
#include <stdio.h>
int main()
{
  flag.rate = 22.5;
  printf("\nThe rate is %f",flag.rate);
  flag.taxes = 44.7;
  printf("\ntaxes are %f",flag.taxes);
  flag.num = 6;
  printf("\nnum is %d",flag.num);

  return 0;
}
```

5. Since a value has not been assigned to `alt.btype`, the display produced is unpredictable (the code for `'y'` resides in the storage locations overlapped by the variables `alt.ch` and `alt.btype`). Thus, either a garbage value will be displayed or the program could even crash.

Section 11.1

1. a. On an IBM or IBM-compatible personal computer (PC, XT, or AT), a file name may have up to eight characters, and optionally a decimal point followed by three more characters. If a string is used to hold the file name, an extra character should be provided for the NULL, for a total of 13 characters.

3.
```
FILE *prices;
FILE *fp;
FILE *coupons;
FILE *distance;
FILE *inData;
FILE *outData;
```

   Note: If all of these file pointers were used in the same program, the single declaration

```
FILE *prices, *fp, *coupons, *distance, *inData, *outData;
```

   could be used.

5.
```
FILE *memo;
FILE *letter;
FILE *coups;
FILE *ptYield;
FILE *priFile;
FILE *rates;
```

Section 11.2

1. a.
```
#include <stdio.h>
int main()
{
  FILE *out;
  char strng[81];

  out = fopen("text.dat", "w");
  if(out == NULL)
  {
    printf("\nFailed to open the file.\n");
    exit(1);
  }
  printf("Enter lines of text to be stored in the file.\n");
  printf("Enter a carriage return only to terminate input.\n\n");
  gets(strng);
```

```
    while(*strng != '\0')
    {
      fputs(strng, out);   /* fputs() does not add the '\n' */
      putc('\n', out);     /* write a newline escape sequence */
      gets(strng);
    }
    fclose(out);
    printf("End of data input.");
    printf("\nThe file has been written.");

    return 0;
}
```

Notes:

i. Recall that the gets() function does not return the newline escape sequence that terminates each input line, but appends a '\0' in its place. Therefore, when a single RETURN is entered a single '\0' is generated; it is this single character that is used to terminate the while loop.

ii. Since the gets() function does not store the newline escape sequence on input, a separate '\n' must be appended to each line on output. This is done using the putc() function.

iii. Since the gets() returns a NULL ('\0') value when an end-of-file (EOF) is encountered, the while statement could have been written as:

```
while (gets(strng) != NULL)
```

If this form is used, however, an EOF must be generated at the keyboard. For many systems this keyboard EOF is created when the Control-Z keys are pushed, followed by a RETURN to actually enter the EOF.

  b.
```
#include <stdio.h>
int main()
{
  FILE *out;
  char strng[81];

  out = fopen("text.dat", "w");
  if(out == NULL)
  {
    printf("\nFailed to open the file.\n");
    exit(1);
  }
  printf("Enter lines of text to be stored in the file.\n");
  printf("Enter a carriage return only to terminate input.\n\n");
  fgets(strng,81,stdin);
  while(*strng != '\n')
  {
    fputs(strng, out);   /* fputs() does not add the '\n' */
    fgets(strng,81,stdin);
  }
  fclose(out);
  printf("End of data input.");
  printf("\nThe file has been written.");
```

```
        return 0;
    }
```

Notes:

i. Recall that the `fgets()` function does return the newline escape sequence that terminates each input line. Therefore, when a single RETURN is entered a single `'\n'` is generated; it is this single character that is used to terminate the `while` loop.

ii. Unlike the `gets(0` function used in Exercise 1a, the `fgets()` function does transmit the carriage return typed at the end of each line input. Therefore, it is not necessary to add a newline escape sequence on output as was done in Exercise 1a.

iii. Since the `fgets()` returns a NULL (`'\0'`) value when an end-of-file (EOF) is encountered, the `while` statement could have been written as:

```
while (fgets(strng,81,stdin) != NULL)
```

If this form is used, however, an EOF must be generated at the keyboard. For many systems this keyboard EOF is created when the Control-Z keys are pushed, followed by a RETURN to actually enter the EOF.

c.

```
#include <stdio.h>
int main()

{
   FILE *inFile;
   char line[81];

   inFile = fopen("text.dat","r");
   if(inFile == NULL)
   {
      printf("The text.dat file does not exist.\n");
      printf("Please create this file before running this program.");
      exit(1);
   }
   while( fgets(line, 81, inFile) != NULL)
      puts(line);
   fclose(inFile);

   return 0;
}
```

Notes:

i. The `fgets()` function returns a NULL (`'\0'`) when it encounters the end-of-file (EOF) marker. Therefore, it is the NULL that is checked for to determine when to stop reading the file.

ii. Because the `fgets()` function retains the newline escape sequence at the end of each line in the file, and the `puts()` function adds a newline when it displays a line, the file is displayed on the screen in double spacing. To avoid this, either the `fputs()` function can be used or character-by-character input and output can be used.

iii. The `exit()` function terminates the running program and closes all files.

3. a. The data may be entered in a variety of ways. One possibility is to enter the data, line by line, and write each line to a file as was done in Exercise 1a. A second method is to use a text editor to write the data to a file. A third possibility is to enter the data as individual items of each line, assemble the items into a complete string, formatted as desired, and then write the string out. A fourth possibility is to enter the data as individual items and write the file as individual items. The following program uses the third approach, which illustrates the construction of an in-memory string.

```
#include <stdio.h>
int main()
{
  FILE *out;
  char name[30], date[30], strng[81];
  int i, id;
  float rate;

  out = fopen("employ.dat", "w");
  if(out == NULL)
  {
    printf("\nFailed to open the file.\n");
    exit(1);
  }
  for (i = 1; i <= 5; ++i)    /* get and write 5 records */
  {
    printf("\nEnter the name: ");
    gets(name);
    printf("Enter the ID No: ");
    scanf("%d", &id);
    printf("Enter the rate: ");
    scanf("%f",&rate);
    printf("Enter the date (ex. 12/6/65): ");
    scanf("%s",date);
    /* now the line to be written is assembled in memory */
    sprintf(strng, "%-18.15s %5d %6.2f %18.8s",name,id,rate,date);
    fputs(strng,out);       /* write the string out */
    putc('\n',out);         /* append a newline character */
    getchar();              /* clear out the input buffer */
  }
  fclose(out);
  printf("\nEnd of data input.");
  printf("\nThe file has been written.");

  return 0;
}
```

   b.
```
#include <stdio.h>
int main()
{
  FILE *inFile, *outFile;
  char line[81];
```

```
      inFile = fopen("employ.dat","r");
      if(inFile == NULL)
      {
        printf("\nFailed to open the employ.dat file for input.\n");
        exit(1);
      }
      outfile = fopen("employ.bak","w");
      if(outFile == NULL)
      {
        printf("\nFailed to open the employ.bak file for output.\n");
        exit(2);
      }
      while( fgets(line, inFile) != NULL)
          fputs(line, outFile);
      printf("\nFile copy completed.");
      fclose(inFile);
      fclose(outFile);
    }
      c.
  #include <stdio.h>
  #include <string.h>
  int main()
  {
    FILE *inFile, *outFile;
    char fName[15], sName[15], line[81];

    printf("Enter the name of the file to be copied: ");
    gets(fName);
    printf("Enter the name of the new file: ");
    gets(sName);
    if(strcmp(fName,sName) == NULL)
    {
      printf("\nYou have specified the same name for both files.");
      printf("\nPlease rerun using different names.");
      exit();
    }
    inFile = fopen(fName,"r");
    if(inFile == NULL)
    {
      printf("\nFailed to open the %s file for input.\n", fName);
      exit(1);
    }
    outFile = fopen(sName,"w");
    if(outFile == NULL)
    {
      printf("\nFailed to open the %s file for output.\n", sName);
      exit(2);
    }
    while( fgets(line, 81,inFile) != NULL)
        fputs(line, outFile);
```

```
    printf("\nFile copy completed.");
    fclose(inFile);
    fclose(outFile);
}
```

> *Note:* The strcmp() function checks that the same file name is not attempted to be used for both input and output. Use of this function requires inclusion of the string.h header file. The exit() function terminates program execution.
> d. A better way would be to enter the source and destination file names on the line used to invoke the executable program. Data entered in this manner are called *command-line arguments*. Command-line arguments are the topics of Section 12.4.

Section 11.3

1. The fseek() function call moves the character pointer to the last character in the file, which is the EOF character at offset position 12. The ftell() function reports the offset of the character currently pointed to. This is the EOF character. Thus, a 12 is returned by ftell().

5. The totChars() function is included within the working program listed below.

```
#include <stdio.h>
void totChars(FILE *);   /* function prototype */
int main()
{
  FILE *in;
  char fName[13];

  printf("\nEnter a file name: ");
  scanf("%s", fName);
  in = fopen(fName, "r");
  if(in == NULL)
  {
    printf("\nFailed to open the %s file for input.\n", fName);
    exit(1);
  }
  totChars(in);
  fclose(in);

  return 0;
}

void totChars(FILE *fname)     /* a pointer to a FILE is passed */
{
  long ftell();

  fseek(fname, 0L,SEEK_END);   /* move to the end of the file */
  printf("There are %ld characters in the file.\n",ftell(fname));
  return;
}
```

Section 11.4

1. The file referred to in the exercise is an internal pointer name. The definition of pFile() is

```
pfile(fname)
FILE *fname;
```

3. The fcheck() function is included below with a driver function used to test it:

```
#include <stdio.h>
int fcheck(char *);   /* function prototype */
int main()      /* driver function to test fcheck() */
{
  char name[13];

  printf("Enter a file name: ");
  scanf("%s", name);
  if(fcheck(name) == 1)
   printf("The file exists and can be opened.");
  else
   printf("The file cannot be opened - check that it exists.");
}

int fcheck(char *fname)
{
  FILE *fopen();

  if(fopen(fname, "r") == 0)
    return(0);
  else
    return(1);
}
```

Note: The fcheck() function performs essentially the same check as fopen(), except fopen() returns a non-zero pointer instead of an integer value.

Chapter 12

1. a. minVal = (a < b) ? a : b;
   b. sign = (num < 0) ? -1 : 1;
   c. val = (flag == 1) ? num: num*num;
   d. rate = (credit == plus) ? prime : prime + delta;
   e. cou = (!bond) ? .75 : 1.1;

3. a. 0200
   b. 0357
   c. 0157

5. a. `0336`

 b. `0701`

 c. If the octal number was valid in the exercise, the right shift would replicate the sign bit rather than fill it with zeros, as it does in a logical right shift.

 d. See the note for part c.

7. a. By either using an 8-bit value box, as described in Section 2.8, or using the more conventional one's complement plus one algorithm, the 8-bit two's complement representation of the decimal number –1 is `1111 1111`.

 b. By either using a 16-bit value box, as described in Section 2.8, or using the more conventional one's complement plus one algorithm, the 16-bit two's complement representation of the decimal number –1 is `1111 1111 1111 1111`. This representation could also have been obtained by sign-extending the 8-bit version.

9. The algorithm for this exercise is as follows:

> *For all bits in the variable okay:*
> *Mask the LSB of the variable okay*
> *Shift the bits of the variable revOkay to the left*
> *Add the masked bit to the variable revOkay*
> *Shift the bits of the variable okay one bit to the right*
> *End For*

A program to do this is

```
#include <stdio.h>
int main()
{
    int i, temp, okay, revOkay = 0;
    int mask = 001;   /* bit mask to isolate LSB */

    printf("Enter an octal number: ");
    scanf("%o",&okay);
    for (i = 1; i <= 8; ++i)
    {
        temp = okay & mask/         /* strip off LSB */
        revOkay = revOkay <<1;      /* shift left one position */
        revOkay += temp;            /* add LSB to revOkay */
        okay = okay >> 1;           /* shift next bit to LSB */
    }
    printf("\nThe reversed pattern, in octal, is %o",revOkay);
}
```

11. a. `#define ABS_VAL(x)-(x)`

 b. `#define ABS_VAL(x)-(x)`
```
    #include <stdio.h>
    int main()
    {
        float num, fudge;

        printf("Enter a number: ");
        scanf("%f", &num);
        fudge = -2.0 * num;
```

```
    printf("\nThe absolute value of -2 times %f is %f.",
           num, ABS_VAL(fudge));

    return 0;
}
```

13. a. `#defineMIN(x,y) ( (y)<= (x) ) ? (y) : (x)`
   b.
```
#define MIN(x,y) ( (y) <= (x) ) ? (y) : (x)
#include <stdio.h>
int main()
{
    float num1, num2;

    printf("Enter two numbers, separated by at least a space: ");
    scanf("%f %f", &num1, &num2);
    printf("\nThe smallest number entered is %f", MIN(num1,num2));

    return;
}
```

15. a. The following program opens the file, reads each character, and displays it. For a line-by-line input/output approach to reading and displaying a file see the solution to Exercise 1c of Section 11.2.

```
#include <stdio.h>
main(int argc, char *argv[])    /* standard argument declarations */
                                /* for command line arguments      */
{
    FILE *fopen(), *inFile;
    char cc;

    infile = fopen(argv[1],"r");
    while( (cc = getc(inFile)) != EOF)
        putchar(cc);
    fclose(inFile);
}
```

Note: Instead of reading each character until the end-of-file is reached, the `fgets()` function could have been used to read in a line at a time. `fgets()` returns a NULL when it encounters the end-of-file sentinel, so the appropriate statement would be

```
while (fgets(line, 81, inFile) != NULL);
```

If this statement is used, line would have to be declared as

```
char line[81];
```

To output a line at a time either the `puts()` or `fputs()` functions can be used. The `puts()` function adds its own newline escape sequence at the end of each line; the `fputs()` function does not.

   b. The program will open and display the contents of any file. The file can, therefore, be either a data or a program file.

Section 13.1

1. The `convert()` function is included within a complete program below:

```c
#include <stdio.h>

/* declaration of the data structure */
struct Date
{
  int month;
  int day;
  int year;
};

/* implementation of associated functions */

/* operation to assign values to a Date object */
struct Date setdate(int mm, int dd, int yyyy)
{
  struct Date temp;

  temp.month = mm;
  temp.day = dd;
  temp.year = yyyy;
  return(temp);
}

/* operation to display a Date object */
void showdate(struct Date a)
{
  Printf("%02d/%02d/%02d", a.month, a.day, a.year % 100);
}

/* operation to convert a date to a long integer */
long convert(struct Date a)
{
  return (a.year * 10000L + a.month * 100L + a.day);
}

int main()
{
  struct Date a;
  long b;

  a = setdate(6,3,2001);
  printf("\nThe value of the a object is: ");
  showdate(a);
  printf("\n");
```

```
            b = convert(a);
            printf("This date, as a long integer is: %ld\n",b);

            return 0;
        }
```

3. The `leapyr()` function is included within a complete function below. Note that to use this function the year must be given as a four-digit number such as 1996, rather than a two-digit number, such as 96. Thus, the `showdate()` function used in Program 13-1 has also been modified to display the year using four digits.

```c
#include <stdio.h>

/* declaration of the data structure */
struct Date
{
  int month;
  int day;
  int year;
};

/* implementation of associated functions */
/* operation to assign values to a Date object */
struct Date setdate(int mm, int dd, int yyyy)
{
  struct Date temp;

  temp.month = mm;
  temp.day = dd;
  temp.year = yyyy;
  return(temp);
}

/* operation to display a Date object */
void showdate(struct Date a)
{
  printf("%02d/%02d/%04d", a.month, a.day, a.year % 100);
}

int leapyr(struct Date a)
{
  if( (a.year % 4 == 0 && a.year % 100 != 0) || (a.year % 400 == 0) )
    return 1;    // is a leap year
  else
    return 0;    // is not a leap year
}

int main()
{
  struct Date a;
  int b;

  a = setdate(6,3,2001);
```

```
  printf("\nThe value of the a object is: ");
  showdate(a);
  b = leapyr(a);
  if (b == 1)
    printf("\nThis was a leap year\n");
  else
    printf("\nThis was not a leap year\n");

  return 0;
}
```

    5. a.
```
/* function to assign values to a Time object */
struct Time settime(int hh, int mm, int ss)
{
    struct Time temp;

    temp.hours = hh;
    temp.mins = mm;
    temp.secs = ss;
    return(temp);
}

/* function to display a Time object */
void showtime(struct Time a)
{
    printf("%02d:%02d:%02d", a.hours, a.mins, a.secs);
}
```

    b.
```
/* function to assign values to a Circle object */
struct Circle setvals(int xx, int yy, float rr)
{
  struct circle temp;

  temp.xcenter = xx;
  temp.ycenter = yy;
  temp.radius = rr;
  return (temp);
}

/* function to display a Circle object */
void showdata(struct Circle a)
{
  printf("\nThe center of the circle is at (%d,%d)", a.xcenter, a.ycenter);
  printf("\n  and the radius is %f\n", a.radius);
}
```

    c.
```
/* function to assign values to a Complex object */
struct Complex setvals(float re, float im)
{
  struct Complex temp;

  temp.real = re;
```

```
  temp.imaginary = im;
  return (temp);
}

/* function to display a Complex object */
void showdata(struct Complex a)
{
  float c;
  char sign = '+';

  c = a.imaginary;
  if (c < 0)
  {
    sign = '-';
    a.imaginary = -a.imaginary;
  }
  printf("\nThe complex number is %f %c %f\n", a.real, sign, a.imaginary);
}
```

Section 13.2

1. a.
```
   #include <iostream.h>
   int main()
   {
       cout << "Joe Smith";
       cout << "\n99 Somewhere Street";
       cout << "\nNonesuch, N.J., 07030";

       return 0;
   }
```

3. answer1 is the integer 2
   answer2 is the integer 5

5. a. The double quote after the second insertion symbol should come before the symbol, and the parentheses at the end of the statement should be a semicolon.
   b. The setw(4) manipulator should not be enclosed in double quotes.
   c. The setprecision(5) manipulator should not be enclosed in double quotes.
   d. The statement should be cout << "Hello World!";
   e. The setw(6) manipulator should appear before the insertion of the number 47.
   f. The setprecision(2) manipulator should appear before the insertion of the number 526.768.

7. a. cin >> firstnum;
   b. cin >> grade;
   c. cin >> secnum;
   d. cin >> keyval;
   e. cin >> month >> years >> average;
   f. cin >> num1 >> num2 >> grade1 >> grade2

g. `cin >> interest >> principal >> capital >> price >> yield;`

h. `cin >> ch >> letter1 >> letter2 >> num1 >> num2 >> num3;`

i. `cin >> temp1 >> temp2 >> temp3 >> volts1 >> volts2;`

9. a.
```cpp
#include <iostream.h>
int main()
{
    float num1, num2, num3, num4, avg;

    cout << "Enter a number: ";
    cin >> num1;
    cout << "\nEnter a second number: ";
    cin >> num2;
    cout << "\nEnter a third number: ";
    cin >> num3;
    cout << "\nEnter a fourth number: ";
    cin >> num4;
    avg = (num1 + num2 + num3 + num4) / 4.0;
    cout << "\nThe average of the four numbers is "
         << avg << '\n';

    return 0;
}
```

c.
```cpp
#include <iostream.h>
int main()
{
    float number, avg, sum = 0;

    cout << "Enter a number: ";
    cin >> number;
    sum = sum + number;
    cout << "\nEnter a second number: ";
    cin >> number;
    sum = sum + number;
    cout << "\nEnter a third number: ";
    cin >> number;
    sum = sum + number;
    cout << "\nEnter a fourth number: ";
    cin >> number;
    sum = sum + number;
    avg = sum / 4.0;
    cout << "\nThe average of the four numbers is "
         << avg << '\n';

    return 0;
}
```

Section 13.3

1. a. The check() function is included within the larger program written for Exercise 1b.

b.
```cpp
#include <iostream.h>
void check(int, float, double); // function prototype
int main()
{
   int first;
   float second;
   double third;

   cout << "Enter an integer: ";
   cin >> first;
   cout << "\nEnter a floating point number: ";
   cin >> second;
   cout << "\nEnter a double precision number: ";
   cin >> third;
   check(first, second, third);

   return 0;
}
void check(int num1, float num2, double num3)
{
   cout << "\n\nThe integer is " << num1;
   cout << "\nThe floating point number is " << num2;
   cout << "\nThe double precision number is " << num3;
}
```

3. a. float &amount;
   b. double &price
   c. int &minutes;
   d. char &key;
   e. double &yield;

5.
```cpp
#include <iostream.h>
void findMax(int, int, int &); // function prototype
int main()
{
   int firstnum, secnum, max;

   cout << "Enter a number: ";
   cin >> firstnum;
   cout << "\nGreat! Please enter a second number: ";
   cin >> secnum;

   findMax(firstnum, secnum, max); // call the function

   cout << "\nThe maximum of the two numbers is " << max << '\n';

   return 0;
```

```
}
void findMax(int x, int y, int &maxval)
{
  if (x >= y)
      maxval = x;
  else
    maxval = y;

  return;
}
```

7.
```
void time(int totSec, int &hrs, int &mins, int &secs)
{
  hrs = totSec/3600;   // 3600 seconds = 1 hour
                       // Integer division yields the whole
                       // number of times 3600 goes into
                       // totSec
  totSec -= hrs * 3600;
  mins = totSec/60;
  totSec -= mins * 60;
  secs = totSec;
  return;
}
```

Section 13.4

1. a. A *class* is a programmer-defined data type. The class specifies both the types of data and the types of operations that may be performed on the data.
   b. An *object* is a specific instance of a class.
   c. The *declaration section* declares both the data types and function prototypes of a class.
   d. The *implementation section* defines the class's functions.
   e. An *instance variable* is another name for a class data member.
   f. A *member function* is a function declared in the class declaration section.
   g. A *data member* is a variable declared in the class declaration section.
   h. A member function is a function that has the same name as the class and is used to initialize an object's data members.
   i. *Class instance* is synonymous with an object.
   j. *Services* are synonyms for the functions defined in a class implementation section.
   k. *Methods* are synonyms for the functions defined in a class implementation section.

3. a.
```
// implementation section
Time::Time(int hh = 0, int mm = 0, int ss = 0)
{
   hours = hh;
   mins = mm;
   secs = ss;
}
void Time::settime(int hh, int mm, int ss)
{
```

```
          hours = hh;
          mins = mm;
          secs = ss;
       }
       void Time::showdata(void)
       {
          cout << "The time is "
               << setw(2) << setfill('0') << hours << ':'
               << setw(2) << setfill('0') << mins << ':'
               << setw(2) << setfill('0') << secs << '\n';
       }
```

b.
```
   // implementation section
   Complex::Complex(float re = 0, float im = 0)
   {
      real = re;
      imaginary = im;
   }
   void Complex::setvals(float re, float im)
   {
      real = re;
      imaginary = im;
   }
   void Complex::showdata(void)
   {
      float c;
      char sign = '+';

      c = imaginary;
      if (c < 0)
      {
         sign = '-';
         c = -c;
      }
      cout << "The complex number is "
           << setiosflags(ios::fixed)
           << real << ' ' << sign << ' ' << c << "i\n";

   }
```

c.
```
   // implementation section
   Circle::Circle(int xx = 1, int yy = 1, float rr = 1.0)
   {
      xcenter = xx;
      ycenter = yy;
      radius = rr;
   }
   void Circle::setvals(int xx, int yy, float rr)
   {
      xcenter = xx;
      ycenter = yy;
      radius = rr;
```

```
            }
            void Circle::showdata(void)
            {
               cout << "The center of the circle is a "
                    << '(' << setfill('0') << xcenter << ','
                    << setfill('0') << ycenter << ')'
                    << " and the radius is " << radius << '\n';
            }
```

5. The class name should begin with a capital letter (for example, `Employee`). The data members should be declared as private and the function members should be declared as public. The declaration for the constructor prototype should be `class(int, char *)`.

7.

```
#include <iostream.h>
#include <iomanip.h>
// class declaration
class Date
{
  private:
    int month;
    int day;
    int year;
  public:
    Date(int = 7, int = 4, int = 2001); // constructor
    void setdate(int, int, int);        // member function to assign a date
    void showdate();                    // member function to display a date
    int leapyr();                       // the additional member function
};

// implementation section
Date::Date(int mm, int dd, int yyyy)
{
  month = mm;
  day = dd;
  year = yyyy;
}
void Date::setdate(int mm, int dd, int yy)
{
  month = mm;
  day = dd;
  year = yy;
}
void Date::showdate()
{
  cout << "The date is "
       << setfill('0')
       << setw(2) << month << '/'
       << setw(2) << day << '/'
       << setw(2) << year % 100
       << endl;
```

```
    return;
}
int Date::leapyr()
{
    int fullyr;

    fullyr = year + 1900;
    if( (fullyr % 4 == 0 && fullyr % 100 != 0) || (fullyr % 400 == 0) )
        return 1;    // is a leap year
    else
        return 0;    // is not a leap year
}

int main()
{
    Date a, b, c(4,1,1998);   // declare 3 objects

    b.setdate(12,25,2002);   // assign values to b's data members
    a.showdate();
    cout << "  The leap year indicator is " << a.leapyr() << '\n';
    b.showdate();
    cout << "  The leap year indicator is " << b.leapyr() << '\n';
    c.showdate();
    cout << "  The leap year indicator is " << c.leapyr() << '\n';

    return 0;
}
```

Section 13.5

1. a. true   i.   true

      b. false   j. true

      c. true   k. false

      d. false   l. false

      e. true   m. false

      f. false   n. true

      g. false   o. false

      h. true

3.

```
#include <iostream.h>
#include <iomanip.h>
// class declaration
class Date
{
    private:
        long yyyymmdd;
    public:
```

```
      Date(int, int, int);      // constructor
      Date(long = 20010704L);  // default constructor
      void showdate();          // member function to display a Date
};

// implementation section
Date::Date(int mm, int dd, int yyyy)
{
  yyyymmdd = yyyy * 10000L + mm * 100L + dd;
}
Date::Date(long ymd)
{
  yyyymmdd = ymd;
}
void Date::showdate()
{
  int year, month, day;

  year = (int)(yyyymmdd/10000.0);      // extract the year
  month = (int)( (yyyymmdd - year * 10000.0)/100.00 ); // extract the month
  day = (int)(yyyymmdd - year * 10000.0 - month * 100.0); // extract the day
  cout << "The date is "
       << setfill('0')
       << setw(2) << month << '/'
       << setw(2) << day << '/'
       << setw(2) << year % 100
       << endl;

  return;
}

int main()
{
  Date a, b(4,1,1998), c(20020515L); // declare three objects

  a.showdate();       // display object a's values
  b.showdate();       // display object b's values
  c.showdate();       // display object c's values

  return 0;
}
```

Section 14.1

1. *Assignment* stores a value into an existing variable or object; that is, it occurs after the variable or object has been created by a definition statement. *Initialization* occurs at the time a new variable or object is created and is part of the creation process.

    3. a. The required class is contained within the program solution to Exercise 3b.

       b.

```cpp
#include <iostream.h>
#include <iomanip.h>
// declaration section
class Complex
{
  private:
    float real;
    float imaginary;
  public:
    Complex(float, float);      // constructor
    void operator=(Complex &); // overloaded assignment operator function
    void showdata();            // display member function
};

// implementation section
Complex::Complex(float re = 0, float im = 0)
{
  real = re;
  imaginary = im;
}
void Complex::operator=(Complex &oldnum)
{
  real = oldnum.real;
  imaginary = oldnum.imaginary;
}
void Complex::showdata()
{
  float c;
  char sign = '+';

  c = imaginary;
  if (c < 0)
  {
    sign = '-';
    c = -c;
  }
  cout << "The complex number is "
       << setiosflags(ios::fixed)
       << real << ' ' << sign << ' ' << c << "i\n";

}

int main()
{
  Complex a(4.2, 3.6), b;  // declare 2 objects

  a.showdata();       // display object a's values
  b.showdata();       // display object b's values
```

```
    b = a;                  // assign a to b
    b.showdata();           // display object b's values

    return 0;
}
```

5. A copy of the pointer from object one to object two results in the loss of the address initially stored in object two. The memory space originally pointed to will, however, still contain data. An additional problem results when a destructor is called for object one. The destruction of object one causes the memory space pointed to by object one to be released. Object two points to the same memory area; this results in object two's pointer member having the address of unallocated memory.

Section 14.2

1. a.
```
#include <iostream.h>
// class declaration
class Employee
{
  private:
    static float taxRate;
    static int numemps;
    int idNum;
  public:
    Employee(int);      // constructor
    void display();     // access function
};

// static member definition
float Employee::taxRate = 0.0025;
int Employee::numemps = 0;
// class implementation
Employee::Employee(int num = 0)
{
  idNum = num;
  numemps++;
}
void Employee::display()
{
  cout << "Employee number " << idNum
       << " has a tax rate of " << taxRate << endl;
  cout << "There are currently " << numemps
       << " Employee objects" << endl;
}

int main()
{
  Employee emp1(11122);
```

```
            emp1.display();

            Employee emp2(11133);   // create a second object

            emp2.display();

            return 0;
        }
```

3. `// implementation section`

```cpp
   Date::Date(int mm, int dd, int yyyy)
   {
     this->month = mm;
     this->day = dd;
     this->year = yyyy;
   }
   void Date::setdate(int mm, int dd, int yyyy)
   {
     this->month == mm;
     this->day = dd;
     this->year = yyyy;
   }
   void Date::showdate()
   {
     cout << "The date is "
          << setfill('0')
          << setw(2) << this->month << '/'
          << setw(2) << this->day << '/'
          << setw(2) << this->year % 100
          << endl;

     return;
   }
```

Section 14.3

1. a. The required function is included within the following working program:

```cpp
#include <iostram.h>
// class declaration
class Date
{
  private:
    int month;
    int day;
    int year;
  public:
    Date(int = 7, int = 4, int = 2001);   // constructor
    int operator>(Date &);                // declare the operator > function
};
```

```cpp
// implementation section
Date::Date(int mm, int dd, int yyyy)
{
  month = mm;
  day = dd;
  year = yyyy;
}
int Date::operator>(Date &date2)
{
  long dt1, dt2;

  dt1 = year*10000L: + month*100 + day;
  dt2 = date2.year*10000L + date2.month*100 + date2.day;
  if (dt1 > dt2)
    return (1);
  else
    return (0);
}

int main()
{
  Date a(4,1,1999), b(12,18,2001), c(4,1,1999); // declare 3 objects

  if (a > b)
    cout << "Date a greater than b \n";
  else
    cout << "Date a less than or equal to b \n";

  if (a > c)
    cout << "Date a greater than c \n";
  else
    cout << "Date a less than or equal to c \n";

  return 0;
}
```

3. a. This operator function provides the same result as the `operator()` function used in Program 13.2.

5. a. The required function is incorporated within the complete program written for Exercise 5b.
   b.

```cpp
#include <iostream.h>
#include <math.h>
// class declaration
class Complex
{
  private:
    float real;
    float imag;
  public:
    Complex(float, float);  // constructor
    Complex operator+(Complex &); // declare the operator+ function
```

```
    void display();
};
// class implementation
Complex::complex(float rl = 0, float im = 0)
{
  real = rl;
  imag = im;
}
void Complex::display()
{
  char sign = '+';

  if(imag < 0) sign = '-';
  cout << real << sign << fabs(imag) << 'i';
}

Complex Complex::operator+(Complex &newnum)
{
  Complex temp;

  temp.real = real + newnum.real;
  temp.imag = imag + newnum.imag;

  return temp;    // return a complex number
}

int main()
{
  Complex a(3.2, 5.6), b(1.1, -8.4), c;
  float re, im;

  cout << "\nThe first complex number is ";
  a.display();
  cout << "\nThe second complex number is ";
  b.display();
  c = a + b;  // can be written as a = a.operator+(b);
  cout << "\n\nThe sum of these two numbers is ";
  c.display();

  return 0;
}
```

Section 14.4

1. a. Conversion from a built-in type to a built-in type is accomplished by C++'s implicit conversion rules or by explicit casting.

Conversion from a built-in type to a user-defined type is accomplished by a type conversion constructor.

Conversion from a user-defined type to a built-in type is accomplished by a conversion operator function.

Conversion from a user-defined type to a built-in type is accomplished by a conversion operator function.

b. A *type conversion constructor* is a constructor whose first argument is not a member of its class and whose remaining arguments, if any, have default values.

A *conversion operator function* is a class member operator function having the name of a built-in data type or class.

3.

```cpp
#include <iostream.h>
#include <iomanip.h>
// class declaration for Date
class Date
{
  private:
    int month, day, year;
  public:
    Date(int = 7, int = 4, int = 2001);   // constructor
    operator long();                       // conversion operator function
    void showdate();
};
// constructor
Date::Date(int mm, int dd, int yyyy)
{
  month = mm;
  day = dd;
  year = yyyy;
}
// conversion operator function converting from Date to long
Date::operator long()    // must return a long
{
  int mp, yp, t;
  long julian;

  if (month <= 2)
  {
    mp = 0;
    yp = year - 1;
  }
  else
  {
    mp = int(0.4 * month + 2.3);
    yp = year;
```

```
      }
      t = int(yp/4) - int(yp/100) + int(yp/400);
      julian = 365L * year + 31L * (month - 1) + day + t - mp;
      return (julian);
    }
    // member function to display a Date
    void Date::showdate()
    {
      cout << setfill('0')
           << setw(2) << month << '/'
           << setw(2) << day << '/'
           << setw(2) << year % 100;

      return;
    }

    int main()
    {
      Date a(1,31,2001);   // declare and initialize 1 object of type Date
      long b;              // declare an object of type long

      b = a;               // a conversion takes place here

      cout << "a''s date is ";
      a.showdate();
      cout << "\nThis Date, as a long integer, is " << b << endl;

      return 0;
    }
```

5.

```
#include <iostream.h>
#include <iomanip.h>
// forward declaration of class Julian
class Julian;

// class declaration for Date
class Date
{
  private:
    int month, day, year;
  public:
    Date(int = 7, int = 4, int = 2001);     // constructor
    operator Julian();                       // conversion operator to Julian
    void showdate();
};

// class declaration for Julian
class Julian
{
  private:
```

```cpp
    long yymmdd;
  public:
    Julian(long);    // constructor
    void showjulian();
};

// class implementation for Date
Date::Date(int mm, int dd, int yyyy)  // constructor
{
  month = mm;
  day = dd;
  year = yyyy;
}
// conversion operator function converting from Date to Julian class
Date::operator Julian()    // must return a Julian object
{
  int mp, yp, t;
  long temp;

  if (month <= 2)
  {
    mp = 0;
    yp = year - 1;
  }
  else
  {
    mp = int(0.4 * month + 2.3);
    yp = year;
  }
  t = int(yp/4) - int(yp/100) + int(yp/400);
  temp = 365L * year + 31L *s (month - 1) + day + t - mp;
  return (temp);
}
// member function to display a Date
void Date::showdate()
{
  cout << setfill('0')
       << setw(2) << month << '/'
       << setw(2) << day << '/'
       << setw(2) << year % 100;

  return;
}

// class implementation for Julian
Julian::Julian(long ymd = 0)  // constructor
{
  yyyymmdd = ymd;
}
```

```
// member function to display a Julian
void Julian::showjulian()
{
  cout << yyyymmdd;
}

int main()
{
  Date a(1,31,1995), b(3,16,1986);   // declare 2 Date objects
  Julian c, d;                       // declare 2 Julian objects

  c = Julian(a);     // cast a into a Julian object
  d = Julian(b);     // cast b into a Julian object
  cout << " a's date is ";
  a.showdate();
  cout << "\n   as a Julian object this date is ";
  c.showjulian();

  cout << "\n b's date is ";
  b.showdate();
  cout << "\n  as a Julian object this date is ";
  d.showjulian();

  return 0;
}
```

> *Note:* There is no conversion operator from Julian to Date. In general the Julian objects are extremely useful for determining actual day count differences between two dates and for sorting dates. In practice, the Julian date would be incorporated as a data member of the Date class. Also note that the forward reference to the Julian class could be omitted in this program if the Julian class were declared prior to the Date class.

Section 14.5

1. a. *Inheritance* is the capability of deriving one class from another class.
    b. A *base class* is the class that is used as the basis for deriving subsequent classes.
    c. A *derived class* is the class that inherits the characteristics of a base class,
    d. *Simple inheritance* is inheritance in which the parent of each derived class is a single base class.
    e. *Multiple inheritance* is inheritance in which a derived class has two or more parent base classes.
    f. *Class hierarchies* are the order in which classes are derived.
    g. *Polymorphism* is the ability of a function or operator to have multiple forms. The particular form that will be invoked is determined at run time and depends on the object being used.
    h. In *static binding* that determination of which function will be called is made at compile time.
    i. In *dynamic binding* the determination of which function will be called is made at run time.
    j. A *virtual function* is a function that is called by a pointer whose value is determined at run time depending on the object making the call.

3. The three features that must be provided for a programming language to be classified as object-oriented are classes, inheritance, and polymorphism. Object-based languages are languages that support objects but do not provide inheritance features.

5.

```cpp
#include <iostream.h>
#include <math.h>

const double PI = 2.0 * asin(1.0);

class Circle
{
  protected:
    double radius;
  public:
    Circle(double = 1.0);   // constructor
    double calcval();
};

// class implementation
Circle::Circle(double)  // constructor
{
  radius = r;
}
double Circle::calcval()  // this calculates an area
{
  return(PI * radius * radius);
}

class Cylinder : public Circle  // Cylinder is derived from Circle
{
  protected:
    double length;  // add one additional data member and
  public:           // two additional function members
    Cylinder(double r = 1.0, double l = 1.0) : Circle(r), length(l) ()
    double calcval();
};

class Sphere : public Circle  // Sphere is derived from Circle
{
  public:           // two additional function members
    Sphere(double r = 1.0) : Circle(r) () // base member initialization
    double calcval();
};
// class implementation
double Cylinder::calcval(void)  // this calculates a volume for a cylinder
{
  return (length * Circle::calcval()); // note the base function call
}

double Sphere::calcval(void)    // this calculates a volume for a sphere
```

```
{
  return (4.0/3.0 * radius * Circle::calcval()); // note the base function call
}
main()
{
  Circle circle_1, circle_2(2);   // create two Circle objects
  Cylinder cylinder_1(3,4);       // create one Cylinder object
  Sphere sphere_1(4);             // create one Sphere object

  cout << "The area of circle_1 is " << circle_1.calcval() << endl;
  cout << "The area of circle2 is " << circle_2.calcval() << endl;
  cout << "The volume of cylinder_1 is " << cylinder_1.calcval() << endl;
  cout << "The volume of sphere_1 is " << sphere_1.calcval() << endl;
  circle_1 = sphere_1;   // assign a Sphere to a Circle

  cout << "\nThe area of circle_1 is now " << circle_1.calcval() << endl;
}
```

Index